D0165006

The Minority Report

An Introduction to Racial, Ethnic, and Gender Relations

Third Edition

The Minority Report

An Introduction to Racial, Ethnic, and Gender Relations

Third Edition

Anthony Gary Dworkin
University of Houston

Rosalind J. Dworkin
Spring Branch Independent School District

Harcourt Brace College Publishers

Fort Worth Philadelphia San Diego New York Orlando Austin San Antonio
Toronto Montreal London Sydney Tokyo

Publisher	Earl McPeek
Acquisitions Editor	Brenda Weeks
Marketing Strategist	Kathleen Sharp
Project Editor	Lisa A. Cooper
Art Director	David A. Day
Production Manager	Andrea A. Johnson

ISBN: 0-03-047534-1
Library of Congress Catalog Card Number: 98-87890

Address for Domestic Orders
Harcourt Brace College Publishers, 6277 Sea Harbor Drive, Orlando, FL 32887-6777
800-782-4479

Address for International Orders
International Customer Service
Harcourt Brace & Company, 6277 Sea Harbor Drive, Orlando, FL 32887-6777
407-345-3800
(fax) 407-345-4060
(e-mail) hbintl@harcourtbrace.com

Address for Editorial Correspondence
Harcourt Brace College Publishers, 301 Commerce Street, Suite 3700, Fort Worth, TX 76102

Web Site Address
http://www.hbcollege.com

Printed in the Unites States of America

8 9 0 1 2 3 4 5 6 7 066 9 8 7 6 5 4 3 2 1

Harcourt Brace College Publishers

Preface to the Third Edition

After more than fifteen years, we have produced a new edition to *The Minority Report.* Since the production of the second edition in 1982, our society has experienced numerous dynamic changes in the domains of race, ethnic, and gender relations. We saw significant retrenchment during the Reagan years, driven in part by economic difficulties of the early 1980s, a conservative wave against government programs, fears about immigration, and suspicions about minority gains. Many of these issues continue into the 1990s and bear all indications of being salient issues in the new century and millennium. One ongoing legacy of the period has been a continued assault on affirmative action. While minority groups have made enormous gains since the 1960s, there remains a growing racial and ethnic underclass of people who are increasingly being left behind. There is some evidence that, while overall levels of racial and ethnic intolerance have declined, there remain virulent strains of hatred in our country, exemplified by attacks on black churches, atrocities committed against minority citizens, significant failures of the urban public schools, gang violence, and attacks on gays. The challenge to affirmative action issues, in part, from widespread misperceptions that the injustices of the past have been redressed and that residual inequality is a result of weaknesses on the part of the disadvantaged. Further, many middle-class members of minority communities have expressed concerns about the perception that, because of affirmative action, they may have attained unearned opportunities. Many feel that their personal efforts and abilities are being devalued and they do not actually merit their statuses. We may be a society in which *An American Dilemma,* the gap between the tenet that all men are created equal and the belief in the inferiority of some minority groups described by Gunnar Myrdal in 1944, is less obvious. There seems to be less wholesale intolerance against groups within the population, but there also seems to be less civility toward individuals within the society. In 1997, President Clinton established an advisory board to oversee and implement by 1998 "One America in the 21st Century: The President's Initiative on Race." A year dialogue, debate, and reports followed, with the goal being to reduce racial tensions and to recognize the need for greater tolerance of diversity. The decade of the 1990s has also seen "A Million Man March" organized by African Americans to take charge of their own destinies, families, and neighborhoods. The next year saw the organization of the "Million Woman March" intended to declare solidarity with the men's march. The marches were not part of a Civil Rights Movement that calls for societal changes on the part of the government and the majority group; rather, they were indicators of African American awareness that the government and society as a whole cannot solve the problems of a community.

The second edition of this book was written in light of the *Bakke* and *Weber* decisions by the United States Supreme Court and the emerging enforcement of affirmative action. It was also during the era of the Cold War in which the United States military, an institution that afforded minorities and women numerous career opportunities, had heightened salience. Since that time some conditions have changed in American ethnic and gender relations. While we currently are experiencing continued economic prosperity, there is concern among many that the population dynamics of immigration will eventually erode that prosperity. Thus, the 1980s and 1990s have been a time of much concern over immigration, especially from Latin America, as well as from the Caribbean and Asia.

This third edition is also set in the context of a troubled system of public education, the principal institution in our society for the mobility and opportunity of disadvantaged groups. Throughout the 1970s and 1980s, public confidence in public education waned. The year 1983 marked the publication of *A Nation at Risk* by the National Commission on Excellence in Education, which observed that the United States was at risk because the public schools were failing to adequately educate its students. The result would be a labor force in the twenty-first century that would make the United States unable to compete with other developed nations. The report called for wholesale school restructuring; some 300 other reports that followed it issued the same call (LeCompte and Dworkin, 1991; Dworkin, 1997). Some investigators have argued that the attack on our nation's public schools reflects an overall conservative agenda to divert tax dollars to private schools (see *The Manufactured Crisis* by Berliner and Biddle, 1996). The apparent intransigence of poverty and low student achievement in the inner city has led social conservatives, including Herrnstein and Murray, in their widely debated book *The Bell Curve* (1994), to attack government programs for the poor. Their book reissues the historic and racially charged contention that there is a known genetic link between intelligence and the class structure. Whole groups of people are characterized with this broad-sweeping claim. This age-old contention has been used to advance benefits for those already privileged and to champion theories of racial superiority.

This third edition of *The Minority Report* varies significantly from the previous two, and yet, follows the common theoretical perspectives of the previous editions. Like the previous editions, the third edition is divided into two distinct sections. The first presents the theoretical orientation of the book and explores the minority group experience from three sociological dimensions of analysis: the distributive, the organizational, and the social psychological. The second section, the reports involving sociologists who are members of the minority groups they discuss, recognizes that social reality is always filtered through experience—experience that is affected by racial, ethnic, and gender statuses. Where the present edition varies from its predecessors is the special statuses of many of the contributing authors to the reports section. Wherever possible, the contributors are former American Sociological Association Minority Fellows. The Minority Fellowship Program funded portions of the graduate education of highly talented minority students. The Minority Fellowship Program is a contracted beneficiary of a significant portion of the royalties from this third edition, thereby permitting the contributors also to contribute to the education of another generation of minority scholars. However, it must be understood that the contributors themselves are established sociologists, not graduate students, with extensive expertise in the area of minority group relations about which they write.

In the previous edition of *The Minority Report,* we noted that our definition could account for the emergence of new minority groups. The new edition reflects the changes in the constituency of the minority population by presenting chapters on newer groups that have attained minority status. Specifically, we have added chapters on immigrants and refugees from Central America; Southeast Asian groups, including the Vietnamese, Cambodians, and Laotians; and a chapter on gay and lesbian minorities. As had been the format from the two previous editions, the authors of these chapters are sociologists who are either members of the groups they study or have devoted an extensive portion of their careers conducting research on the minority populations.

The new edition also adapts our definition of minority groups to provide a model for the *process* by which groups are defined as minorities. The salience of institutions such as the public educational system and the health and mental health care systems have led us to incorporate more information on the impact of these areas on minority group individuals. Finally, of course, the new edition updates demographic and statistical information on each group and on minority-majority relations in American society. While much information is taken from the 1990 census, statistical analyses are augmented by information from the end of the decade. This is especially relevant because numerous changes have occurred over those years.

The Minority Report is divided into two distinct sections. Part 1, which provides students with the theoretical groundwork for addressing Part 2, contains a summary of current information about the condition of minorities in the United States, presented in a fashion oriented toward advanced undergraduates. It has been our experience that the theory section is actually useful for graduate students, too.

Chapter 1 introduces the sociological orientations used throughout the book, while Chapter 2 addresses the concept of a minority, offering a definition that is free from the restraints of typical "trait" definitions. Drawing from a sociological tradition dating from the beginning of the twentieth century, the chapter offers four necessary conditions for minority group status: identifiability, differential power, differential and pejorative treatment occasioned by the power differential, and group awareness facilitated by the differential treatment. Groups are seen as varying, relative to one another on each of these conditions. The extent to which these conditions exist will determine the group's chances of overcoming its minority status. Biological, legal, psychological, and sociological components of minority group status will also be explored relative to these four dimensions. Finally, the four components are synthesized into a model of minority group process, with hypothesized outcomes.

The next three chapters examine minority group status in terms of three distinct sociological levels of analysis: the distributive, the organizational, and the social psychological. Discussion in these chapters includes the development of a general theory of minority group stratification, theories of prejudice and discrimination, and a presentation of models of prejudice reduction. The previous edition discussed the ramifications of the *Bakke* and *Weber* decisions on affirmative action and future minority gains. In light of the years that have passed since that prior edition, the increasingly complex nature of the affirmative action debate is discussed, including its ramifications for higher education and the labor market.

Chapter 6 focuses upon theories that have been advanced to predict or explain the resolution of minority group status. After all, as illustrated by two reports presented in *The Minority Report,* some groups that were minorities at the beginning of the twentieth century are now firmly integrated and established within the dominant society. Two major forms are discussed—assimilation and separatism—and several models are presented. The chapter offers a discussion of still other outcomes. The theories, some of which were intensely debated at the beginning of our century as immigration swelled our numbers, are again being debated under the aegis of immigration law, restrictions of welfare for immigrants, bilingual education in the public schools, and the extent to which a society should be responsible for the children of immigrants and refugees.

Chapter 7 examines the emerging directions of minority-majority relations. The changing intersection of race/ethnicity and social class are explored, as they have occupied the sociological debate since the works of Gordon in the 1960s and Wilson in the 1980s. Multiple minority status and the rediscovery of ethnicity discussed in the previous edition are even more relevant today. In fact, one debate centering around the census for the year 2000 addresses what to do with people of mixed racial heritage who want to acknowledge their diversity.

Part 2, which has generally been written by members of the minority groups themselves, provides the substantive material to which the theoretical models can be fitted. We have selected groups that reflect the diversity of minority experiences with the result that each author provides a somewhat different twist to the report of the minority condition. When taken collectively, the different perspectives present with greater clarity the totality of minority group relations and the minority experience in America. This diversity and synthesis enrich *The Minority Report.*

The Minority Report in its first edition emerged from the suggestions of two people: the late Dr. Noel P. Gist of the Department of Sociology at the University of Missouri and Jim Bergin, then editor of Praeger Publishers, the house that produced that edition. We wish to thank the contributors, past and present, for their insights into minority group experiences. We wish to thank our colleagues and coauthors in sociology, mental health, social welfare, and public education over the past two decades since the first edition emerged; they too have contributed ideas and interpretations that have enriched the current work. Our first two editions were dedicated to our son, Jason Peter Dworkin. We dedicate this third edition to Jason and Karin Dworkin, two very special people.

Houston, Texas A.G.D.
R.J.D.

References

Berliner, David C., and Biddle, Bruce J. *The Manufactured Crisis: Myths, Fraud, and the Attack on America's Public Schools.* Reading, MA: Addison-Wesley, 1996.

Dworkin, Anthony Gary. "Coping with reform: The Intermix of Teacher Morale, Teacher Burnout, and Teacher Accountability," in B. J. Biddle, T. Good, and I. Goodson, eds. *International Handbook of Teachers and Teaching.* Amsterdam: Kluwer, 1997, pp. 509–52.

Herrnstein, Richard, and Charles Murray. *The Bell Curve: Intelligence and Class Structure in American Life.* New York: The Free Press, 1994.

LeCompte, Margaret D. and Anthony Gary Dworkin. *Giving Up on School: Student Dropouts and Teacher Burnouts.* Newbury Park, CA: Corwin/Sage, 1991.

Myrdal, Gunnar. *An American Dilemma.* New York: Harper, 1944.

National Commission on Excellence in Education. *A Nation at Risk: The Imperative for Educational Reform.* Washington, D.C.: U.S. Government Printing Office, 1983.

The Contributors

Anthony Gary Dworkin, coeditor of *The Minority Report* and coauthor of the theory section of the text, is Professor of Sociology and Director of the Sociology of Education Research Group for the Public Schools. He is the author of numerous books and articles in the areas of race, ethnic, and gender relations and the sociology of education. He is editor of the *New Inequalities* series at SUNY Press. He received his Ph.D. degree from Northwestern University.

Rosalind J. Dworkin, coeditor of *The Minority Report* and coauthor of the theory section of the text, is Facilitator for Research and Evaluation at the Spring Branch Independent School District. She is the author of a book on researching the mentally ill and has published extensively in the areas of race and ethnic relations, gender roles, the sociology of mental health and illness, and the sociology of education. She received her Ph.D. degree from Northwestern University.

Shelley J. Correll is a doctoral student in Sociology at Stanford University and author of the chapter on gay and lesbian Americans.

Dana Dunn is Associate Professor of Sociology at the University of Texas, Arlington and author of the chapter on women. She received her doctorate from the University of North Texas.

Yen Le Espiritu is Professor of Ethnic Studies at the University of California, San Diego and author of the chapter on Southeast Asian Americans. She received her doctorate from the University of California, Los Angeles, where she was an American Sociological Association Minority Fellow.

Lynn H. Fujiwara is a doctoral student and **Dana Y. Takagi** is Associate Professor of Sociology at the University of California, Santa Cruz. They are coauthors of the chapter on Japanese Americans. Professor Takagi received her doctorate from the University of California, Berkeley and was an American Sociological Association Minority Fellow.

Donald E. Green is departmental chair and Associate Professor of Sociology at the University of Wisconsin, Milwaukee. He is the author of the chapter on Native Americans. He received his doctorate from the University of Minnesota, where he was an American Sociological Association Minority Fellow.

Cedric Herring is Professor of Sociology and is affiliated with the Institute for Government and Public Affairs at the University of Illinois, Chicago. He is the author of the chapter on African Americans. He received his doctorate from the University of Michigan, where he was an American Sociological Association Minority Fellow.

Robert E. Kennedy is Professor Emeritus of Sociology at the University of Minnesota. His is the author of the chapter on Irish Catholic Americans. He received his doctorate from the University of California, Berkeley. He contributed to the two prior editions of *The Minority Report.*

Jan Lin is Associate Professor of Sociology at Occidental College in Los Angeles. He is the author of the chapter on Chinese Americans. He received his doctorate from the New School for Social Research in New York.

Nestor P. Rodriguez is Associate Professor of Sociology and Co-Director of the Center for Immigration Research at the University of Houston. He received his doctorate from the University of Texas, Austin and was an American Sociological Association Minority Fellow. **Jacqueline Hagan** is Associate Professor of Sociology and Co-Director of the Center for Immigration Research at the University of Houston. She received her doctorate from the University of Texas, Austin. Professors Rodriguez and Hagan are coauthors of the chapter on Central American immigrants and refugees.

Rogelio Saenz is Professor of Sociology at Texas A&M University. He is the author of the chapter on Mexican Americans. He received his doctorate from Iowa State University, where he was an American Sociological Association Minority Fellow.

Eugen Schoenfeld is Professor Emeritus of Sociology at Georgia State University, Atlanta. He is the author of the chapter on Jewish Americans. He received his doctorate from Southern Illinois University, Edwardsville. He contributed to the two prior editions of *The Minority Report.*

Ramon S. Torrecilha is Assistant Professor of Sociology at the University of California, Irvine and Program Director at the Social Science Research Council. He is a former American Sociological Association Minority Fellow and was Assistant Executive Director for Minority Affairs of the American Sociological Association. Professor Torrecilha was assisted in the writing of the chapter on Puerto Rican Americans by two doctoral students, **Lionel Cantú** and **Quan Nguyen.**

Contents

PART 1

Theoretical Perspectives

CHAPTER 1

INTRODUCTION

The world in which we live is radically and constantly changing. Our conventional understandings about the realities of social life, including the institutions, organizations, groups, and beliefs, have been challenged dramatically. One domain in which change has been most significant has been in the form and content of minority-majority relations. The past quarter century has seen a burgeoning of minority demands and the eventual entry of minorities into a diversity of careers, roles, and institutions previously denied to them. Today's greater participation by racial, ethnic, and gender minorities has forced scholars to rethink traditional models of minority-majority relations. Knowing an individual's race, ethnicity, or gender tells us less about his or her life experiences than it did even twenty years ago. Additionally, majority-group attitudes and explanations offered to account for minority disadvantage have changed in subtle but profound ways. The racist rhetoric of a genetic basis of advantage has been supplanted by motivational explanations. Nevertheless, the consequence has been to attack national policies that seek to redress a history of discrimination and to advance a denial that white privilege remains in our society.

The changing dynamic of intergroup relations has altered even the study of inter-group relations. Thus, although there are canons of scientific inquiry and proof, science, like all systems of knowledge, contains a subjective perception of reality. This perception is defined by the culture in which the scientist lives. Individuals from different cultures or subcultures may see "reality" in a different fashion. The difference may be great or small, depending upon the similarities between the cultures from which the scientists come. Among scientists whose data are remote from cultures and personalities, in such areas as physics, chemistry, geology, or even biology, culture-bound differentials in perception may be very slight, if observable at all. However, in the social sciences, where the data are the cultures and societies themselves, the differences in perception may be immense. Even within American society we may extract examples. A black male sociologist and a white female sociologist, each armed with the same body of data, may interpret those data differently. If the data involve interaction sequences among individuals of different races and genders, each sociologist might attribute different motivations to the actors involved. The first sociologist might emphasize the presence of racism in the interaction, the second might stress the presence of sexism. Both may be observing accurately, but each has a less complete view than the composite of the two.

Members of diverse heritages working together can provide a better understanding of the complexities of inter-group relations than can a single individual of a single heritage. The diversity between the observations of Freud[1] and Friedan[2] on women's motives, or Moynihan[3] and Billingsley[4] on black families, and of Heller[5] or Madsen[6] and Romano[7] or Vaca[8] on Hispanic cultures, or even Wilson[9] and Willie[10] on the significance of race illustrates the necessity that social science come from more than a single racial, ethnic, or gender group. We may demonstrate this further with the following metaphor. There is a parallax noticeable when we stare at a point of light with first the left eye and then the right eye closed. We discern two slightly different images. When both eyes are open our view has greater depth and is enlightened by the contribution of the viewpoint of each eye. In the same way each social scientist brings to the study of intergroup relations the uniqueness of his or her own people's perspective on the portrait of American minority group relations, and the composite thus is enhanced with greater precision and clarity.

This book seeks to maximize the contributions of minority-group social scientists, while simultaneously attempting to converge these contributions into a general sociological orientation to the data of minority relations. The title of our collective enterprise reflects the diversity we seek to encapsulate. *The Minority Report* has a double meaning. It is first a report by minority-group members about their own people, bringing to their presentations the uniqueness of their race, ethnicity, or gender, and is thus a report *by* minorities. But in a historical and legal sense, a minority report is also a dissenting report. It represents a divergence of opinion and view from those of the dominant society and the dominant makeup of the sociological profession. It is thus a critical perspective, filled with different and sometimes uncomplimentary interpretations of the functions and consequences of American institutions and their impact upon people other than the dominant population.

In the past many sociologists writing about minority groups have claimed to assume the vantage point of what was once regarded as value-neutral of value-free social science. Citing an interpretation of Max Weber's "Science as a Vocation,"[11] these authors argued that unbiased objectivity was possible and imperative for the study of any social issue. Other writers allowed sociologists to be human but required them to be schizophrenic. For them, when the social researcher was performing as a scientist, he or she was required to have no values except those deemed by the canons of science and logic—to explore the social issue to its fullest, ruthlessly and without concern for the people involved. However, after working hours, he or she could protest, assume value positions, and behave as a concerned citizen. Robert Lynd[12] and Alvin Gouldner,[13] among several others, have cogently argued that both positions are limiting, untenable, and unreal. The very decision to select a given social issue for study is a value commitment. After all, of the myriad of social issues, of the innumerable areas of human interaction, why have we elected to investigate the conditions of minorities if not because we have more than a dispassionate interest in it? Howard S. Becker[14] suggested that the issue is not whether we espouse values in our research, but "whose side we are on." In fact, Littrell[15] goes as far as to suggest that the sociological researcher should adopt an "adversarial methodology," especially in researching bureaucracies and their agents. That is, organizations and individuals, especially those in positions of power, whether they be the public schools or the police, welfare organizations and even civil rights organizations, do not always want to be studied. The sociological researcher, who usually is ideologically prone to support the disadvantaged groups and individuals, should be prepared to encounter obstructions to data collecting imposed by those in power. At a minimum, the adversarial method makes the researcher aware that organizations and their agents may have something to hide.

Many of the past generation of social scientists who endorsed a value-free position for research, or who argued that values could only be espoused when one was performing the citizen role, negated their contentions in a collective attempt to influence the United States Supreme Court. In 1952 a group of distinguished social researchers, long convinced of the evils of segregation, met to lend scientific credibility to Briggs and Davis Brown's argument that separate education is inherently unequal.[16] These researchers did not attempt to end segregation as individual citizens; rather, in their capacity as social scientists, where their impact would carry more influence, they attacked discrimination. In so doing they chose sides, thereby abandoning a value-neutral orientation.

The contributors to *The Minority Report* likewise cannot remain dispassionately associated with the study of the status of minority peoples. After all, they are themselves members of the very minority populations about which they write. The future of inter-group relations in America affects the life chances of the contributors. Each contributor thus has expressed a commitment to the study of inter-group relations for personal as well as intellectual reasons—if these two components can actually be separated. Several contributors have published extensively on minority-majority relations or on their own minority group.

Each contributor was required to maintain both a degree of objectivity and a degree of involvement. The balance of the two dimensions created *The Minority Report*. Good social science requires that one seek accuracy and truth as goals, but these goals must be pursued with a social conscience—a concern for the human costs to those subjected to investigation. If the data do not support the researcher's political stance, the reaction of the present contributors and other good social scientists is to attempt to understand the data more fully and to alter their political stance. It is never, as in the case with many polemicists, to alter the data to coincide with the political stance.

The contributors to *The Minority Report* also differ from those who shield themselves behind the myth of value-free social science. Many of the contributors, armed with both experiential and research-based knowledge, have engaged in informed social action to correct and attack the fallacies of the myths of racial, ethnic, or gender superiority, to debunk stereotypes, and to improve the quality of the society for all. Each realizes that the oppression and dehumanization of any group ultimately results in the dehumanization of us all.

Despite the fact that each of the contributors to this report brings to the study of minority groups a unique contribution tempered by his or her distinct cultural heritage, there is nonetheless a commonality among them: They are all sociologists. As such, they bring to the study of minority groups an orientation toward the data of social life, which includes a commitment to the canons of science and theory construction, and a methodological rigor, including a concern for the logic of proof. Two crucial components of the sociological orientation are synthesis and generalization. Sociologists seek to discern similarities as well as unique components among the experiences of people of different times, places, and backgrounds. Thus, out of the apparent diversity of such groups as the Burghers of Sri Lanka and the Chicanos of the United States, the sociologist attempts to construct a theory or model of interpersonal and intergroup dynamics and relations that will assist us in understanding past and present contacts among peoples, and to predict the consequences of future contacts. The ability to take from the mundane and the esoteric of social life and to ascertain the trends and patterns of human society depicts the distinctiveness of the social sciences.

THE SOCIOLOGICAL ORIENTATION

There have been numerous attempts over the past century to portray American minority groups. Sociologists have not been the only ones to observe the complexity of the American minority scene. Other social scientists, journalists, writers, dramatists, historians, and various political actors and strategists have commented on this complex mosaic. Obviously, each of these perspectives has been different, and not all have attempted to avoid polemical stances.

In sociology, too, there have been divergent stances, especially if we examine the sociological perspective historically. E. B. Reuter[17] once noted that the sociology of race relations went through three distinct stages. Early writings assumed an ethnocentric frame of reference steeped in social Darwinism and emphasizing the biological bases of racial differences (and assumed racial superiorities). A shift then occurred to the cultural orientation, which stressed the diversity not of biology but of heritage, language, and custom. This second stage was followed by the present concern over the interrelations and dynamics of interactions between groups.

Today, despite the distinctions between types of sociological theory, relatively few sociologists would dispute that a study of American minorities would involve three distinct levels of analysis. However, few of them might write or operate on all three levels. The levels widely accepted are the distributive, the organizational, and the attitudinal.

Distributive, Demographic, and Stratificational Analysis

A distributive analysis of minority groups is concerned with the manner in which minority-group members are arranged along the various dimensions of the social structure. The emphasis is upon difference. How do groups differ in their life chances? How do groups differ on such important dimensions as income, education, occupation, and political power? What are the bases and functions of minority stratification systems? The distributive level is usually the easiest to measure; it often involves the simple counting of people in different categories, as is done decennially by the U.S. Census Bureau. However, the distributive also involves the beginning element in a model of social change. Frequently (Marx would argue always) the root cause of social change is distributive, or material. That is, before people can have a felt dissatisfaction about their objective condition, and effect a new sociopolitical order, there needs to be a distributive condition to which they can point with outrage. In minority-group relations, it must be realized, especially in the United States, that distributive differences are most often matters of degree. That is, although there are many objectively very poor people in this nation, the difference in the distribution of resources is one of relative deprivation of one group compared to another group. One group has, relative to another, more or less income, more or less education, a better or worse job, more or less power, and so on. In *The Minority Report* we shall see groups who are more or less advantaged or disadvantaged, relative to other minority groups and relative to the dominant society. The degree of advantage or disadvantage relative to other groups may or may not provoke a collective social action bent on reform, change, or revolution. In our discussion of the manner in which people are distributed in the social structure we shall explore some prevailing theories of minority stratification, and develop a model of our own.

Organizational Analysis

The organizational dimension refers to the patterned relations and the character of the organizations and associations formed by groups as a consequence of the manner in which they are distributed within the society. Religious life, education systems, and voluntary associations comprise aspects of the organization analysis. A discussion of minority organizations must encompass their goals (whether assimilationist or separatist) and their strategies (accommodationism, legalism, nonviolence, or violent protest). Essential to the study of minority group relations would be an investigation of the interaction between the minorities and the organization of the dominant society, including corporations, the school system, the police, and the government bureaucracy. But the analysis should not stop there, for the organizational element must also include an analysis of the manner in which ethnic, racial, or gender-based organizations deal with their members and with members of other minorities.

Attitudinal or Social Psychological Analysis

The social psychological level deals with the imposition of the social structure and its organizations upon the individual and the manner in which he or she thinks, acts, and interacts. Here we study attitudes, beliefs, and behaviors. Our emphasis will focus on attempts to account for prejudice and to explain, using our knowledge of interpersonal dynamics, how these attitudes develop, change, and become translated into intergroup action. There is considerable controversy at this level of analysis. Some argue that we cannot measure attitudes adequately because we cannot comprehend the individual motivations expressed in the attitudes. Others point to the fact that attitudes and behaviors are not always conjoined, not always consistent. Some even contend that the attitudinal dimension is irrelevant because people are only puppets of the mass society and behave as they are told to behave. Each of these arguments must be examined and an assessment made of the impact of the social psychological dimension.

At each level of analysis the dimension of minority culture, including subcultural norms, plays a role. We do not wish to imply that there is a single minority culture. However, we must realize that a culture unique to the particular group studied provides the general context in which we can comprehend the consequences of the distributive, organizational, and social psychological dimensions. That is, a cultural setting of one type may produce a different set of reactions to the distribution of resources, a different set of organizations and relationships, and a different set of attitudes than another cultural setting.

Social scientists have long argued the respective merits of a functional and a cultural relativist frame of reference in the study of societies.[18] The former concentrates on the forms of society, the systematic consistencies and the functions each performs for the survival of that society across groups, while minimizing a concern for differences in content between groups. The cultural relativist approach emphasizes the unique content of societies, and sometimes ignores the similarities between groups. *The Minority Report* will remain eclectic. We shall note the similarites between the American Indians and the Chicanos and among the Jews, the Irish, the Japanese, and Chinese. But we shall also explore the impact of their unique belief systems, language, art, and artifacts which interpret their world for them in slightly or very different manners. We shall often assume that dissimilarities in content override similarities of structures among the minority communites. However, because each of these groups is also part of the larger American society, each shares a commonality even in content.

NOTES

1. Sigmund Freud, "Some Psychical Consequences of the Anatomical Distinction between the Sexes," in *The Collected Papers of Sigmund Freud,* Ernest Jones, ed. (New York: Basic Books, 1959), pp. 186–97.
2. Betty Friedan, *The Feminine Mystique* (New York: Norton, 1963).
3. Daniel P. Moynihan, *The Negro Family: The Case for National Action* (Washington, D.C.: Office of Policy Planning and Research, United States Department of Labor, 1965).
4. Andrew Billingsley, *Black Families in White America* (Englewood Cliffs, NJ Prentice-Hall, 1968).
5. Celia S. Heller, *Mexican-American Youth: Forgotten Youth at the Crossroads* (New York: Random House, 1966).
6. William Madsen, *The Mexican Americans of South Texas* (New York: Holt, 1964).
7. Octavio I. Romano V., "The Anthropology and Sociology of Mexican Americans," *El Grito* 2 (1968), pp. 13–26.
8. Nick C. Vaca, "The Mexican-American in the Social Sciences," *El Grito* 3 (1970), pp. 3–24, 17–51.
9. William J. Wilson, *The Declining Significance of Race: Blacks and Changing American Institutions,* 2nd ed. (Chicago: University of Chicago Press, 1980) and *The Truly Disadvantaged: The Inner City, the Underclass, and Public Policy.* (Chicago: University of Chicago Press, 1987).
10. Charles V. Willie, *The Caste and Class Controversy* (Bayside, NY: General Hall, 1979).
11. Weber was concerned with the politicization of the university by partisan faculty members. He feared that the state would take action and close down the universities. Some have generalized this remark to endorse a rejection of all value orientations in social sciences. See H. H. Gerth and C. W. Mills, eds., *From Max Weber: Essays in Sociology* (New York: Oxford University Press, 1958), pp. 129–56 ("Science as a Vocation").

12. Robert S. Lynd, *Knowledge for What?* (Princeton, N.J.: Princeton University Press, 1939).
13. Alvin Gouldner, "Anti-Minotaur: The Myth of a Value-Free Sociology," *Social Problems* 9 (1962), pp. 199–213.
14. Howard S. Becker, "Whose Side Are We On?" *Social Problems* 14 (1967), pp. 239–47.
15. Boyd Littrell, "Bureaucratic Secrets and Adversarial Methods of Research" in *A Critique of Contemporary American Sociology,* Ted R.Vaughan, Gideon Sjoberg, and Larry T. Reynolds, eds. (Dix Hills, NY: General Hall, 1993), pp. 207–31
16. "The Effects of Segregation and the Consequences of Desegregation: A Social Science Statement," Appendix to Appellants' Brief, September 22, 1952, in the Supreme Court of the United States, October Term 1952.
17. E. B. Reuter, "Racial Theory," *American Journal of Sociology* 50 (1945), pp. 452–61.
18. See, for example, Jonathan H. Turner and Royce Singleton, Jr., "A Theory of Ethnic Oppression: Toward a Reintegration of Cultural and Structural Concepts in Ethnic Relations Theory," *Social Forces* 56 (1978), pp. 1001–18.

SUGGESTED READINGS

Becker, Howard S. "Whose Side Are We On?" *Social Problems* 14 (1967), pp. 239–47.

Gouldner, Alvin W. "Anti-Minotaur: The Myth of a Value-Free Sociology." *Social Problems* 9 (1962), pp. 199–213.

———. *The Coming Crisis of Western Sociology.* New York: Basic Books, 1970.

Lee, Alfred McClung. *Sociology for Whom?* New York: Oxford University Press, 1978.

Lundberg, George. *Can Science Save Us?* New York: Longmans, 1947.

Lynd, Robert S. *Knowledge for What?* Princeton, NJ: Princeton University Press, 1939.

Myrdal, Gunnar. *Value in Social Theory.* Paul Streeten, ed. London: Routledge, 1958.

Vaughan, Ted R., Sjoberg, Gideon, and Reynolds, Larry T., eds. *A Critique of Contemporary American Sociology*. Dix Hills, NY: General Hall, 1993.

CHAPTER 2

What Is a Minority?

The Varieties of Definitions

If you turned to the want-ads section of most daily newspapers, you would find several advertisements for employment proclaiming, "We are an equal-opportunity employer; women and minorities encouraged to apply." Most of us know what the advertisers mean—women are females of the species and minorities are people who are black or brown. But what about Puerto Ricans, Native Americans, or Asian Americans? Are they included as minorities? Not too many years ago Jews would have been included in a popular definition of minorities. In 1880 employers who wished to discriminate in hiring might have advertised, "Jobs available; Negroes, Irish, and Criminals need not apply."

A few years ago a Puerto Rican was refused service at a bar in New Jersey. The man appealed to the courts on the grounds that his rights under the 1968 Civil Rights Act had been violated. The judge ruled that Puerto Ricans were white and therefore not protected under the Civil Rights Act. A similar example arose in a federal district court in Pittsburgh in January 1980. A Mexican American police officer contended that he was being excluded from promotion under the city's preferential promotion guidelines for sexual and racial minorities. The court ruled that Hispanics were not a racial minority and thus ineligible for consideration in antidiscrimination plans. Thus, although women were now considered a disadvantaged minority eligible for affirmative action, in Pittsburgh Hispanics were not.[1] However, in two Texas U.S. Circuit Court of Appeals rulings (*Cisneros et al.* v. *Corpus Christi Independent School District,* 1972, and *U.S.* v. *Texas Education Agency,* 1972)

Mexican Americans were defined as a separate race and thus could not be paired with black pupils in order to attain black-white school desegregation.

Many state colleges and universities in the 1990s operate under affirmative action guidelines to increase the admission of minority students and to direct scholarship aid to them. However, the definition of who belongs to a minority group, often identified as an "underserved population," can vary by state. In Texas and California, prior to that state's elimination of affirmative action practices in higher education, Asian Americans were not considered to be protected minorities because of the comparative overrepresentation of Asian American students in universities. Native Americans are not a minority or underserved population in Texas because a history of nineteenth-century genocide so reduced their numbers that they are rarely considered, except in the production of federal reports on student enrollments.

It appears that the popular definition of minority is highly variable over time and geographic space. Even African Americans are not always considered part of the minority. The authors know of a black man who was seeking a teaching position. He visited two areas, one in the Midwest and one in northern New England, along the Canadian border. When he inquired about housing in the midwestern community, the real estate agent showed him a series of all-black neighborhoods. Making the same inquiries in the New England community, the black teacher was shown a wealthy suburban white neighborhood. He asked the real estate agent if he could see some less expensive housing. The agent replied, "I could take you to that part of town over there, but you won't want to live there. Over there are French Canadians, but they don't keep up their property, and they're lazy, dirty, and sloppy." The black teacher later related that this was the first time he had ever been considered part of the majority, in a position to discriminate against others.

Popular definitions of minority do not control for variations over time and space. They merely reflect the current thinking in a relatively narrow environment. This produces problems in consistency. Individuals using a word such as *minority* may be referring to different concepts and may make statements which are absurd in the context of another definition.

Minority could be defined as a racial group different from the numerically dominant one. Or minority could mean a racial group different from the politically dominant group. Or minority could mean a cultural group different from the one that is currently dominant. Each of these definitions would compel us to designate different groups as minority in any particular social setting.

Consider the example of South Africa or even some areas of our Deep South. Most of the people in each of these areas are black. Using the first definition suggested above, whites would therefore be the minority group and blacks the majority, or dominant group. According to the second definition, whites would become the dominant group and blacks the minority because power, not numerical advantage, is salient. If we were to utilize the third definition, the designation of minority-majority would not be along racial lines but along lines of social class. Middle- and upper-class blacks and whites would both be considered dominant because these groups exercise the power. Lower-class blacks and lower-class whites would be grouped together as minority on the basis of their cultural similarities and relative powerlessness.

Thus we must go beyond the popular definitions of minority groups, because these are too often mere enumerations of classifications that are subject to temporal and regional differences.

The Varieties of Sociological Definitions

Social science seeks to maintain an adequate complement of objectivity, of which we spoke in the introduction, and a degree of methodological and conceptual rigor and precision. To provide for such rigor and precision there must be adequate agreement on the meanings—denotative and connotative—of the variables studied. Definitions of concepts cannot be conceived of in one fashion for one study and then differently for another study. Results would never be comparable, and findings could never be combined into a body of knowledge. The social scientific ideal is to create what Herbert Blumer[2] has called *generic variables*. That is, variables are needed about which there is sufficient agreement as to definition and operationalization (the activities, questionnaire items, measures used to represent the variable or concept) so that one social scientist can take the study conducted by another and replicate it, or look at another aspect of the variables and then compare the findings. Without attempts at consistency in definitions we shall forever be comparing apples and oranges and never build on our knowledge.

A sociological definition of minority must have six qualities. A definition must meet the canons of logic to the extent that it is a category that is *mutually exclusive* to its reciprocal, and to the extent that it is *exhaustive*. It is mutually exclusive in that only minority groups will possess the characteristics denoted in the definition, and exhaustive in that all groups considered to be minorities will fit the definition. Majorities will thus not possess the characteristics of our definition of minority, and no group considered to be a minority will be defined out of the category. Our definition must *reflect the social reality* it is intended to describe. It must extract the common denominators from various lay, legal, and other sociological definitions. Further, the definition must be *heuristic* in that it generates explanations for attitudes and behaviors of diverse groups and suggests similarities between groups that possess minority qualities. The heuristic definition should also demonstrate new lines of theoretical development. Thus by showing how groups not usually considered a minority possess the characteristics of a minority, insights into that group's behavior as well as insights into the theory of minorities will be gained. The definition must be *universal* so that it can be applied across societies and regions, rather than being bounded by specific cultures or locales. Finally, the definition must be *dynamic* in that it is not time-bounded and can be applied to emerging and assimilating groups as well as current and commonly recognized minorities.

There are at least two scientific ways in which we can approach the definition of minorities. The first is inductively; the second, deductively. In the first we look at the multitude of groups considered to be minorities and attempt to determine what they have in common. In the second we postulate a set of factors and then determine empirically whether or not minorities possess these qualities. Neither is the perfect solution, and each is used by social scientists. Therefore, in order to construct a sociological definition of minority we ought to turn first to definitions previously adopted by social scientists. Should these definitions be inadequate, we may be able to construct our own definition from salvageable aspects of several of them.

The earliest term used by social scientists to denote the groups we shall be studying was *race*. Although the term actually refers to groups that have common phenotypical and genotypical (physical and genetic) characteristics, it was also applied to groups that possessed distinctive cultural and other learned characteristics. Thus ethnic groups, language groups, and national groups were aggregated with biological groups under the rubric "race." In the 1920s social scientists like Bogardus studied attitudes toward such ethnic "races" as the French race, the English race, the American race, the Jewish race, and the Turkish race, as well as such biological groups as the Negro race and the Oriental race. Racists, from DeGobineau and Chamberlain in the nineteenth century to Hitler in the twentieth century, spoke of the Nordic race and the Aryan race, and attributed their preferred cultural and linguistic characteristics to biological superiorities. This usage so diluted the concept of race as to make the term almost meaningless.

In the United States, every twenty years or so another attempt to link race, intelligence, poverty, and public policy surfaces. In the 1970s it was the work of Arthur Jensen that tied that linkage, while in the 1990s it was the work of Herrnstein and Murray.

For that reason Donald Young[3] proposed an alternative. Young chose the term "minority," which would permit one to include racial as well as ethnic groups in a common term, which would not have the biological implication. He observed:

There is, unfortunately, no word in the English language which can with philological propriety be applied to all . . . groups which are distinguished by biological features, alien national cultures, or a combination of both. For this reason, the phrases, "minorities of racial or national origin," "American minorities," or "minority peoples" are here used as synonyms for the popular usage of the word *race*.[4]

Since Young's usage sociologists have removed the statistical connotation from the meaning of the term minority. Thus, although minorities generally are less than 50 percent of the population, the variable of size is of itself not crucial. The past five hundred years have seen countless examples of a relatively small number of western Europeans dominating and colonizing a vast number of indigenous peoples throughout the world. The numerical disadvantage of the westerners was more than compensated for by their technological and military advantages. Thus, they held the power and privilege in the region. In these cases the numerically underrepresented whites were the majority, not the minority.

Young does not give us an explicit definition of minority, but in his usage he defines minorities in terms of the groups' "traits." At best Young's definition is subjective, suggesting that minorities are whatever people label as minorities. Thus it is based upon the visibility of the minority group—the extent to which others can identify the group as a minority. Trait definitions such as Young's frequently prove inadequate, because they are based upon current minority groups in a particular society. They are both time- and location-bounded, which is the same criticism we lodged for lay definitions. The definition we seek must be more dynamic and universal. It must include groups that are emerging as minorities, and must be applicable in diverse locations and time periods.

A more universalistic and objective definition has been provided by Louis Wirth:

> We may define a minority as a group of people who, because of their physical or cultural characteristics, are singled out from others in the society in which they live for differential and unequal treatment and who therefore regard themselves as objects of collective discrimination.[5]

Wirth's definition possesses three components: the group must be visible to others, it must experience differential and pejorative treatment, and its members must be aware of themselves as members of a group that is considered a minority. Many social scientists have adopted Wirth's definition. It meets most of our needs for a definition. However, it does not indicate the power relationships between the minority and the majority groups, which may be more crucial than differential treatment.

Necessary to Wirth's definition is the subjective realization by the minority group. Wirth gives us no clue as to whether all members of the group, only the leaders, some significant number, or some unspecified percentage must possess such a realization of minority status. This has been a recurrent problem among those employing subjective definitions of group awareness or subjective definitions of social problems or social issues.[6]

Another widely adopted definition of minority has been advanced by Wagley and Harris:

> (1) Minorities are subordinate segments of complex state societies; (2) minorities have special physical or cultural traits which are held in low esteem by the dominant segments of the society; (3) minorities are self-conscious

> units bound together by the special traits which their members share and by the special disabilities which these bring; (4) membership in a minority is transmitted by a rule of descent which is capable of affiliating succeeding generations even in the absence of readily apparent special cultural or physical traits; (5) minority peoples, by choice or necessity, tend to marry within the group.[7]

It should be noted that the first three characteristics advanced by Wagley and Harris are in agreement with the definition provided by Wirth. Wagley and Harris elaborate by including two additional elements: ascriptive membership and a norm for endogamous marriage. People do not choose to be minority-group members and do not work to attain minority status (achievement is not the route to the status), but rather membership in a minority group is ascribed at birth through the society's rules of descent. Consequently, one is minority-group member because one's parent(s) is a minority-group member, and one cannot easily escape the minority label without drastic familial and personal consequences. Rules of endogamy are group norms or societal regulations that specify marriage within one's social group. Thus minorities are usually prohibited by the majority (and often prohibit themselves) from marrying outside of the minority group. This has beneficial consequences for the majority and may also be beneficial for the minority. It ensures for the majority that only they retain the resources needed to continue domination, social control, social power, and wealth. For the minority it ensures group solidarity, protects against extinction, and provides for physical and cultural homogeneity.

These last two criteria advanced by Wagley and Harris have been empirically correct and appropriate for groups with long-established histories. Many such groups are commonly included in older trait models advanced for minorities. Today, however, we are experiencing the emergence of groups claiming minority status who do not meet one or both of Wagley and Harris's new criteria. For example, the Gay Liberation Movement's claims of minority-group status for homosexuals calls into question the empirical relevance of the rule of descent as a defining criterion. One is not a homosexual because of his (her) parents' membership in that group; it is a status later achieved. Similarly, the case of women challenges the criterion of endogamy. As R. Dworkin[8] noted, there is much empirical evidence to support the contention that women constitute a minority group. However, we can plainly see that the rule of endogamy does not hold for them on the individual level. Women may not marry women. It would appear that endogamy is not a necessary component of minority status.

Both the endogamy and rule-of-descent criteria may be relevant for most racial and ethnic minorities.[9] However, they have less applicability for some of the new, emerging minorities in complex societies. Hence Wagley and Harris have not produced a definition of minority that is entirely universal (something social scientists since Young have sought) or empirically sound.

Several social scientists have argued that the essential quality of minority-majority relations is differential power, and that what makes a minority is the group's lack of the resources and power to determine its own destiny. The power dimension has been central in the models advanced by Blalock,[10] Lieberson,[11] and van den Berghe,[12] among others. In the next chapter we shall assess the role of power in determining minority-group stratification. However, Gelfand and Lee[13] have carried the power dimension to an extreme by positing it as the sole characteristic of groups we label as minorities. These authors argue that if we do not intend the term *minority* to imply numbers, then we ought to substitute the terms *subordination* and *domination,* and to ignore the concept minority.

We must conclude that although power is a necessary condition for minority status, it is not the only defining characteristic. As we have seen, Wirth, Young, Wagley and Harris, and others have pointed to the importance of identifiability, differential treatment, and group awareness as important defining criteria. By combining these with differential power, we may be able to develop a definition that is universal, dynamic, empirically based, and heuristic.

Minority Group Defined

How then shall we define *minority group?* Extracting from previous sociological efforts and satisfying the prerequisites for a good sociological definition, we propose that a minority group is a group characterized by four qualities: identifiability, differential power, differential and pejorative treatment, and group awareness. Minorities are actual groups of people who interact with one another and with the majority group in terms of their group membership. Minority groups are not simply statistical categories, such as all people who wear size nine shoes, or people who wear glasses. Such aggregates are not minorities or even groups; they lack social organization, social relationships between members, and consciousness of kind.[14] It is conceivable that a statistical category can move in the direction of group, and ultimately minority-group, formation. The statistical category of left-handed people is in the process of becoming a group, and perhaps a minority group, having formed organizations to pressure manufacturers to make equipment they can use, and interacting with one another to discuss their common problems. Similarly, women represent a statistical category that has progressed to the stage of being a minority group. It must be realized that because some groups are emerging and others are assimilating into the majority, any given minority group may possess more or less of each of the specified qualities. Further, these are group characteristics, and individual group members may possess each of them to a greater or lesser degree. These characteristics will vary over time and geographical region such that there will be variations in the specific operationalization of identifiability, nature and usage of power, form of treatment, and content of self-awareness. Citing relevant examples, let us examine each of these dimensions.

Identifiability

Football players of opposing teams wear uniforms of different colors to assist fans in distinguishing between the teams and to help each player to identify his teammates. In the area of minority-group relations, salient groups must be readily identifiable in order to ensure that an individual recognizes members of his own group and members of the others, and treats them accordingly. Without identifiability, group solidarity and differential treatment become difficult, if not impossible.

Selection of the relevant characteristics upon which identifiability is based is neither fixed nor self-evident. Rather, it is variable and socially defined and interpreted. There is nothing intrinsic in the sex, skin color, eye structure, language, or religion of a group that makes it inferior or undesirable. The definitions of such characteristics make them likely foci of identifiability, prejudice, and discrimination. What is often overlooked in minority-group relations is that there are more similarities than dissimilarities between peoples within the same society. Rather then emphasizing that all have human skin, eyes, and the facility for symbolic communication, people emphasize differences in skin color, eye shape and color, specific language, and even accent.[15] People in different societies selectively perceive and define as salient diverse physical and cultural variations.

In America skin color is the central element of identifiability, and black Americans (the most different from the white majority) are the prime outgroup. Until recently a popular maxim had been, "If you're white, you're right. If you're brown, hang around. If you're black, get back." Today, many companies hire a dark-complexioned token black and keep him or her in a visible location as proof of their compliance with civil rights legislation.

Americans have been so sensitized to shades of color that even within minority communities lighter-skinned individuals have greater esteem than darker persons. When a minority group develops a strong group awareness, a pride in the identifiable trait follows, accompanied by slogans such as "Black is beautiful."

Other salient criteria for distinguishing between groups, including religion, dress, speech style, and other cultural factors, tend to be more transitory than biological variables. It is possible to change status merely by adopting the customs and culture of the majority group, thus becoming less identifiable. This is essentially what has occurred with the Irish, Germans, and Italians. Within a few generations, European immigrant minorities became Americanized and blended into the majority population. When biological factors are involved, however, this is not so simple a task, and patterns of minority-group relations are retained as long as these biological factors are considered relevant.

In societies that are physically homogenous, culture factors become more critical and both informal social norms and formal legal procedures are instituted to ensure that identifiable distinctions remain.

Where identifiability is lacking, artificial visibility is sometimes created. In Nazi Germany, Jews looked like everyone else, so it became Nazi policy to force Jews to wear yellow arm bands to produce this element of identifiability and make differential treatment possible.

Differential Power

Power is the actual use of resources to influence and control others.[16] Power is the actual rather than the potential. In his model of racial discrimination, Blalock enters into the equation of power the combination of total resources ("money, property, prestige, authority, and natural and supernatural resources") plus the mobilization of resources (the amount of resources actually used).

Differential power implies relatively greater use of resources by one group compared to another. Hence, we are speaking not of a powerful group versus a powerless group, but of a relatively more powerful group versus a relatively less powerful group.

We must distinguish between a power group (independent of size) and a numerical majority (dependent only upon size). In terms of domination, it is the power rather than the number that matters. In fact, Blalock argues that numbers are not a resource and may actually drain away a group's strength as they pose coordination and resource distribution problems for the group. Usually the power group is also numerically larger, but one need only look historically and cross-culturally to find examples of the power group being numerically smaller. Parts of the American South during the 1950s and South Africa today illustrate the contention that a numerically small group can control a numerically large but relatively powerless group. Similarly, with only a handful of soldiers but with more resources and superior mobilization, Cortez conquered the more numerous Aztec people in two short years. In these cases the minority group is actually the numerically larger one.

Numbers can have some effect, however. As the numbers in the (power) minority increase, the resources mobilized by the (power) majority must also increase. Large numbers in the minority group require the power majority to remain on guard. In the early 1970s all white Rhodesians (now Zimbabwe) served in a militia, locked themselves in at night, and continually inspected native compounds. However, in this case and in most other minority-majority situations the power group has so many resources at its disposal that it is not easy to overwhelm it with sheer numbers.

When the power majority controls resources, it also controls the life chances of the minority: their access to resources, jobs, education, wealth, even food and health care. So doing guarantees that the minority[17] will remain dependent upon the majority in a colonial-type relationship. The analogy is not accidental. Many (including Blauner,[18] Memmi,[19] J. Moore,[20] and Carmichael and Hamilton[21]) have spoken of "internal colonialism" as typifying the relationships of whites with blacks, browns, and Indians in American society.

Differential and Pejorative Treatment

The differentials in power permit the dominant majority to exercise control over the minority group through differential and pejorative treatment or discrimination. Discrimination is the behavioral component of prejudicial attitudes of the majority toward the minority. According to Lieberson's[22] model of ethnic stratification, the dominant majority and the minority each seek to maintain their own social order. However, given limitations on resources and given the perception of mutually exclusive goals, the dominant group needs to enforce the subjugation of the minority group through various strategies. Allport itemized these processes and strategies as antilocution (stereotyping), avoidance, discrimination, physical attack, and extermination.[23] Each strategy has been implemented in various societies, including the United States.

Groups that are not economically beneficial to the majority or are identifiably quite different are often subjected to the more extreme strategies. For example, blacks provided a convenient labor pool enabling whites to maintain a high level of culture and comfort, whereas native Americans were perceived only as an obstacle to white expansion. Thus the treatment of blacks differed significantly from the treatment of native Americans: Blacks were enslaved while native Americans were threatened with extermination.

Differential treatment, or discrimination, is what group members actually experience as a consequence of their minority status. It is this differential treatment that most directly affects the life chances and lifestyle of the individual minority-group member and becomes the focus of minority protest and movements.

Group Awareness

As identifiable groups who are disadvantaged in power receive differential and pejorative treatment, they come to identify themselves as a group. Initially, only a few may be aware of the common bond among them that differentiates their group from the majority. In American society, with its stress upon individual achievement and self-blame for failure, there is a tendency for people not to blame the social system or discrimination.[24] Minority-group status is a process in which increasingly more group members perceive the similarities of their social position and the commonality of their fate. Hence, a minority may exist prior to general group awareness. However, if no individuals in the minority see themselves as a minority and subjected to differential treatment, then minority status cannot be said to exist. Group awareness does not refer to the ability to identify group membership (that is, identifiability). Rather, group awareness refers to the perception of common goals that can be achieved only through cooperation, rather than competition,[25] and the realization that differential treatment does not accrue from qualities intrinsic in the minority, but from definitions, evaluations, and actions of the majority.

Development of group awareness is a point of theoretical interest to social scientists, including the contributors to *The Minority Report*. It is heuristic to compare awareness as experienced by different minority groups over time. Such insights, when collected and compared, will enable us to expand upon a theory of minority-group process. A model for such a process will be elaborated in Chapter 3 of this report.

The relationships among the four characteristics of minorities are processual. Further, there are processual changes in the amount of each characteristic possessed by a group at different times in its history. Groups at different times may be more or less identifiable, have more or less power relative to others, be treated more or less differentially, and have more or less group awareness. A frequent pattern is that a group will first be identifiable, then, because of its differential power relative to a majority, receive differential and pejorative treatment, and then over time evolve a group awareness. In some instances differential power and differential treatment may tend to limit opportunities for endogamy, or may impose a given stage of poverty, such that identifiability follows later. Nonetheless, we must consider that, depending upon the vagaries of historical situations, the four components occur as a process.

Figure 2-1 displays the possible process for minority group status formation. Here, identifiability, conjoined with differential power, facilitates

FIGURE 2-1
The Process of Minority Group Formation

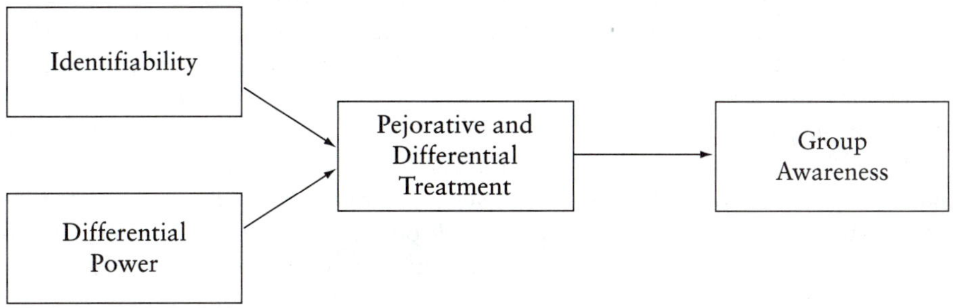

discrimination (pejorative and differential treatment), which sensitizes group members to their common plight (group awareness). It is most likely that the first three elements of minority group status are necessary prerequisites for group awareness. In fact, Chafetz and Dworkin[26] proposed that a necessary precondition for consciousness raising, minority group awareness, and the formation of a movement to change conditions was a process in which women compared their status with that of men and found themselves to be disadvantaged.

Specific Minorities and Minority-Group Members

Minority status is shared by numerous groups, not all of which are racial, ethnic, or gender groups. Although we shall focus upon racial, ethnic, and gender groups in *The Minority Report,* political groups, religious groups, deviant groups, social classes, national groups, and so on can constitute minorities if they possess the four characteristics we have delineated. For example, the Amish of Pennsylvania and the Mormons of nineteenth-century Utah constituted minorities. Catholics in Northern Ireland are clearly minority-group members. Communists (especially during the McCarthy era of the 1960s), Ku Klux Klanners, homosexuals, and prison inmates represent other groups that could be covered by a definition of minorities. Each of these groups, while constituting a minority, exemplifies minority status in slightly different ways (although there is sufficient overlap to generalize the definition), and each member of each of the groups possesses more or less of each of the qualities. That is, minority status is variable both across minorities and across individuals labeled as minority-group members.

The relative nature of minority-group status has been of particular concern to two writers, van den Berghe[27] and Kinloch.[28] Both investigators have suggested that the nature of intergroup relations, the characteristics of minority-group members that make them identifiable, and even the course of the resolution of minority-majority conflict are influenced by societal values, economics, history, and level of sociopolitical development. In fact, Kinloch suggests that the kinds of minority groups present represents an "index of societal development."[29]

Once we have determined that a group is a minority, it may still be difficult to place specific individuals into that group. For example, we could agree that black Americans are a minority group, but who is black? Agreement on this issue cannot be assumed.[30]

Georgia in 1927 defined as a person of color anyone who was not white who had Negro, African, or Asiatic Indian ancestry. A white was anyone who had no ascertainable trace of either Negro, African, West Indian, Asiatic Indian, Mongolian Japanese, or Chinese blood in his veins. Louisiana defined color as a person having an appreciable mixture of Negro blood. Texas declares that if a person has had no Negro ancestors for three generations he is white, while Arkansas says that one Negro ancestor anywhere makes one always Negro. Let us imagine the hypothetical case of J. Jones who lives in Texarkana, a community divided by the Texas-Arkansas state line. Suppose that Mr. Jones's great-great-grandfather was black, but that all parents since have been white. On the Texas side he would be white, but on the Arkansas side he would be black. Looking for a home prior to the 1968 Civil Rights Act (or since, with the real estate agents willing to violate the law), Mr. Jones would be shown houses in the black neighborhood on the Arkansas side and white neighborhoods on the Texas side. In fact, prior to the 1954 and 1957 Supreme Court rulings on interstate carriers, he would have had to shift from the front to the back of the bus if he were to take the cross town shuttle.

The legal definition of the Native American presents another aspect of the problem. The Bureau of Indian Affairs, the U.S. Census, and Indian organizations themselves use different definitions of what constitutes an Indian. Indians can be people who are defined by others as Indians, who define themselves as Indians, who can claim some special proportion of Indian blood, or some combination of these criteria. Brewton Berry, in a book about American mestizos,[31] refers to groups of people, mixtures of black, white, and Indian ancestry, who claim recognition as Indians. The Lumbees, the Brass Ankles, and many other such groups along the East Coast have been so recognized by some government agencies but not by others. The confusion of their ancestry, magnified by the confusion of legal definitions, has profound effects upon the future of these groups, as well as on the daily lives of group members.

It is thus true that labels such as minority, majority, or racial and ethnic group memberships are ultimately social definitions. The assignment of people to groups are sometimes made by the dominant-group member and sometimes made by the minority-group member. In some instances self-assignment may be made to serve some economic end, as in the case of light-complexioned minority-group members who pass as members of the dominant society in order to obtain better jobs. Likewise, with the advent of Affirmative Action programs in the 1960s, some individuals have attempted to pass as minority-group members for similar reasons.

In 1971 and 1972 the Bureau of the Census[32] conducted a survey of nearly seventy thousand Americans to determine the stability of self-reported racial and ethnic identities. In the total sample only 64.7 percent of the respondents who checked a box on the questionnaire identifying themselves as members of given racial or ethnic group in 1971 checked the same box on the 1972 questionnaire. There was, however, considerable variation across groups in the reliability with which individuals checked the boxes. Thus, 96.5 percent of Puerto Ricans, 94.2 percent of the black Americans, and 88.3 percent of the Mexican Americans reported the same race or ethnicity both years. However, only 57.1 percent of the Irish, 55.1 percent of the English, Scottish, and Welsh reported the same ethnicity both years. For individuals from Central and South America only 47.3 percent checked that category both times What these percentages also indicate is that groups that are more easily identifiable by members of the dominant society are less likely to be inconsistent in their self-reports. Aside from matters of minority-group pride, the assertion of one's ethnic identification is subject to the acceptance of that claim by others.

The fluidity of ethnic identity, and hence the assertion of minority group status, has been noted by numerous authors since the 1970s, including Richard Alba,[33] Herbert Gans,[34] and Stanley Lieberson and Mary Waters.[35] Recently, Karl Eschbach,[36] a colleague at the University of Houston, reported on the apparent burgeoning in the Native Americans between the 1970 and 1980 and 1990 Censuses. The number of Native Americans grew from 827,000 in 1970 to 1.42 million in 1980 to 1.96 million in 1990, much of which was due not to a natural increase in the population (the excess of birth rates over death rates), but to changes in identification among multiracial individuals. Eschbach and his co-authors discovered that a significant portion of the switching of identification was done by better-educated individuals living in urban areas. What the investigators were observing in the Census data was the phenomenon of "ethnogenesis," whereby groups attempt to reclaim ethnic heritages that had long been abandoned in the process of assimilation. It was fashionable to be an "ethnic" during the 1970s and beyond, as long as one's ethnicity was not tied to too many negative stereotypes.

SUMMARY

The term *race* has become a vague, broad word, which can no longer be used with precision for social science research. The term *minority* or *minority group* is more appropriate today. However, there are disagreements concerning the best definition of "minority group." Some definitions are lists of traits or lists of actual groups; these are time- and location-bounded and not particularly heuristic. Other definitions stress identifiability, discriminatory treatment, and awareness. Others have emphasized rules of descent and endogamy. Still others have used differential power as the sole defining characteristic.

In an attempt to develop a definition that is objective, universal, heuristic, and not bounded by time or place, the authors have proposed the following. A minority group is a group characterized by four qualities: identifiability, differential power, differential and pejorative treatment, and group awareness. The definition is processual, in that groups can become minorities and cease to be minorities. It allows for the observation that individual group members may display more or less of these characteristics. Finally, once a specific group has been defined as a minority it can be problematic as to which specific individuals are members of that group because of conflicting lay definitions.

NOTES

1. *Houston Chronicle,* January 3, 1980.
2. Herbert Blumer, "Sociological Analysis and the 'Variable,'" *American Sociological Review* 21 (1956), pp. 683–90.
3. Donald Young, *American Minority Peoples* (New York: Harper, 1932).
4. Ibid., p. xiii.
5. Louis Wirth, "The Problem of Minority Groups," in *The Science of Man in the World Crisis,* ed. Ralph Linton (New York: Columbia University Press, 1945), p. 347.
6. See the definitions of social problems advanced by Richard Fuller and Richard R. Myers, "Some Aspects of a Theory of Social Problems," *American Sociological Review* 6 (1941), pp. 24–32, and John Kituse and Malcolm Spector, "Toward a Sociology of Social Problems," *Social Problems* 20 (1973), pp. 407–18.
7. Charles Wagley and Marvin Harris, *Minorities in the New World* (New York: Columbia University Press, 1958), p. 10.
8. See Rosalind J. Dworkin, "A Woman's Report," in A.G. Dworkin and R. J. Dworkin, *The Minority Report,* 2nd ed. New York: Holt, Rinehart, and Winston, 1982, pp. 375–400.
9. An exception here are the mixed race minorities such as the Anglo-Indian, who exist because individuals marry outside their own group.
10. H. M. Blalock, Jr., "A Power Analysis of Racial Discrimination," *Social Forces* 39 (1960), pp. 53–59.
11. Stanley Lieberson, "A Societal Theory of Race and Ethnic Relations," *American Sociological Review* 26 (1961), pp. 902–10.
12. Pierre L. van den Berghe, *Race and Racism* (New York: Wiley, 1967).
13. Donald E. Gelfand and Russell D. Lee, *Ethnic Conflicts and Power: A Cross-National Perspective* (New York: Wiley, 1973).
14. Robert Bierstedt, "The Sociology of Majorities," *American Sociological Review* 13 (1948), pp. 700–10.
15. Racists, even in this century, have attempted to skirt the issue of the commonality between groups by defining particularly hated minorities out of the human species.
16. H. M. Blalock, Jr., ("A Power Analysis"; idem, *Toward a Theory of Minority Group Relations* [New York: Wiley, 1967]), has maintained that power must be used for it to exist. This is distinguished from conceptualizations by Max Weber (*The Theory of Social and Economic Organization,* ed. Talcott Parsons [New York: Free Press, 1964]), who saw power as a potential. The American involvement in Vietnam presents a good case for the preferability of Blalock's position. Although the United States had the potential to destroy all of North and South Vietnam through nuclear annihilation, the costs in exercising such potential were too great, thereby rendering the United States powerless to control the Vietcong and the North Vietnamese.

17. Hereafter *minority* and/or *majority* will be used to refer to a power minority and power majority, respectively. There is no connotation of relative size of population implied.
18. Robert Blauner, "Internal Colonialism and Ghetto Revolt," *Social Problems* 16 (1969), pp. 393–408.
19. Albert Memmi, *The Colonizer and the Colonized* (Boston: Beacon, 1967).
20. Jean W. Moore, "Colonialism: The Case of the Mexican Americans," *Social Problems* 17 (1970), pp. 463–71.
21. Stokely Carmichael and Charles Hamilton, *Black Power* (New York: Random House, 1967).
22. Lieberson, "A Societal Theory."
23. Gordon W. Allport, *The Nature of Prejudice* (Reading, MA: Addison-Wesley, 1954).
24. Robert K. Merton, *Social Theory and Social Structure* (New York: Free Press, 1957).
25. We can see that the process of minority-group awareness is similar to that of class consciousness first proposed by Karl Marx.
26. Janet S. Chafetz and Anthony Gary Dworkin, *Female Revolt: Women's Movements in World and Historical Perspective* (Totowa, NJ: Rowman and Allanheld, 1986), pp. 63–104.
27. Pierre van den Berghe, *Race and Racism* (New York: Wiley, 1967).
28. Graham C. Kinloch, *The Sociology of Minority Group Relations,* (Englewood Cliffs, NJ: Prentice-Hall, 1979).
29. Ibid.
30. John Hope Franklin and Isidore Starr, eds., *The Negro in the Twentieth Century* (New York: Vintage, 1967).
31. Brewton Berry, *Almost White* (New York: Macmillan, 1963).
32. U.S. Bureau of the Census, "Consistency of Reporting of Ethnic Origin in the Current Population Survey," Technical Paper No. 31 (Washington, D.C.: Government Printing Office, 1974).
33. Richard Alba, *Ethnic Identity: The Transformation of White America* (New Haven, CT: Yale University Press, 1990).
34. Herbert Gans, "Symbolic Ethnicity: The Future of Ethnic Groups and Culture in America," *Ethnic and Racial Studies* 2 (1979), pp.1–20.
35. Stanley Lieberson and Mary Waters, *From Many Strands: Ethnic and Racial Groups in Contemporary America* (New York: Russell Sage Foundations, 1988).
36. Karl Eschbach, Khalil Supple, and Matthew Snipp, "Changes in Racial Identification and the Educational Attainment of American Indians: 1970–1990," *Demography* 35 (1998), pp. 1–9.

Suggested Readings

Blalock, H. M., Jr. *Toward a Theory of Minority-Group Relations.* New York: Wiley, 1967.

Blumer, Herbert. "Sociological Analysis and the 'Variable,'" *American Sociological Review* 21 (1956), pp. 683–90.

Gordon, Milton M. *Human Nature, Class, and Ethnicity.* New York: Oxford University Press, 1978.

Gossett, Thomas F. *Race: The History of an Idea in America.* Dallas: Southern Methodist University Press, 1963.

Kinloch, Graham C. *The Sociology of Minority Group Relations.* Englewood Cliffs, NJ: Prentice-Hall, 1979.

Merton, Robert K. *Social Theory and Social Structure.* New York: Free Press, 1968.

Simpson, George Eaton, and J. Milton Yinger. *Racial and Cultural Minorities: An Analysis of Prejudice and Discrimination,* 4th ed. New York: Harper, 1972.

Wagley, Charles, and Marvin Harris. *Minorities in the New World.* New York: Columbia University Press, 1958.

CHAPTER 3

THE DISTRIBUTIVE DIMENSION

Many are the resources that people need in order to live within a social community. Generally, these resources are ones of property, social prestige, and power, which are unevenly distributed to various groups in the society. Some groups consistently, generation after generation, get more than other groups. In essence this inequality of distribution is a phenomenon of social stratification. When we consider minority and majority relations, we find that the majority group consistently is allocated more resources than the minority groups, and that there is uneven distribution among the minority groups themselves. This chapter will investigate the uneven distribution of resources.

PROPERTY

The Bureau of the Census of the United States is the official counter of people in America. This vast social bookkeeping contains information on the distribution of property (economic and economic-related resources). Not only does the census tell us how many members are within the various minority groups, it also gives us a report on the state of their welfare. It indicates their income level, the nature and types of their employment, the quality of their housing, the availability of their health care, and so on.

Although the census provides us with the best estimates of the distribution of groups of people in the United States, it is not free from errors or difficulties. The census is selective in the types of data it collects for its social bookkeeping. For example, it does not provide breakdowns for all minority groups of interest to us. Ethnic or cultural minorities are often not separated from one another. In fact, for many indices information is provided only for whites, blacks, Hispanics and Asian and Pacific Islanders, and is cross-classified by gender. Some census breakdowns only distinguished among blacks, whites, and others, while the censuses of 1970 and earlier either did not identify Hispanics or referred to the group as "persons of Spanish surname" or "Spanish origin." Some earlier censuses pooled different groups with African Americans as "non-whites" or even as "Negroes and other races."

Since 1950, the census has provided breakdowns of persons of "Spanish surname." This enumeration is not without its own difficulties. First, grouped under this rubric are such varied groups as Mexican Americans, Puerto Ricans, Cubans, persons from a variety of Latin American and Caribbean nations and the Philippines. Only since the current 1980 Census and a few of the special reports released earlier had there been an attempt to differentiate between the various Spanish-surname populations. Furthermore, in earlier censuses name changes due to marriage hindered the accurate counting of women of Spanish-surname backgrounds.

Second, until 1980, the category of persons of Spanish surname was not mutually exclusive from the categories of black and white. Some Puerto Ricans and others of Caribbean descent were likely to be categorized as both black and Spanish surname. In addition, because the census relies upon self-report, race is always a subjective measure. The 1990 Census recognized that Hispanics could be of any race, but differentiated between whites and non-Hispanic whites. The census of 2000 incorporates mixed ethnicity options in the self-identification of ethnicity.

In addition, the Census is notorious for its underestimation of African Americans and other minorities. Because the census samples residences, it tends to miss individuals who are hanging out on the street. Estimates from the 1970 through the 1990 censuses are that as many as one-fifth of all African American males between the ages of twenty-five and twenty-nine were missed. Since these individuals may be more likely to be unemployed or underemployed, the income levels for blacks and other minorities may be overestimated, making the differentials between the majority and minorities even greater. For a detailed understanding of the distributive aspect of minority relations, sources other than the census must often be used.

However, the census can give some overall views about the distribution of resources and rewards among groups. For this discussion we will compare those groups represented clearly in the census. For information about other groups, the reader is referred to the reports on individual groups in Part Two of the book.

Of the more than 265 million persons in the country (based on 1996 Bureau of the census estimates), slightly more than half (51.1 percent) are female. Again, based on 1996 estimates, some 82.8 percent of the total population are categorized as white. (This includes the majority white population, plus various "white minorities" such as Jews, Irish, some Puerto Ricans and some Mexican Americans, and, of course, white females.) Of the remaining

17 percent, most are African American (12.6 percent), with relatively small proportions of Native Americans (0.8 percent), and people of Asian and Pacific Island origin (3.7 percent), including Japanese, Chinese, and Southeast Asian. Persons of Hispanic origin account for 10.7 percent of the population. Hispanic origin individuals may be of any race and hence their percentage cannot be directly added together to make 100 percent.[1]

Property resources are not evenly allocated among these groups. For example, whites have higher incomes. In 1995, the median family income of whites was $42,646, while that of African Americans was $25,970 (or 60.9 percent of the white median), and that of persons of Hispanic origin was $24,570 (or 57.6 percent of the white median). By contrast, Asian and Pacific Islanders had a median family income of $46,356, or 108.7 percent of the white median. Even when corrections are made to compare only individuals of the same age, education, number of hours worked, minority-group members still may be expected to have lower incomes. Differences between males and females are also apparent on this level, with males earning significantly more in each of the minority groups as well as in the majority group.[2]

Another way to compare the property differentials associated with race is to look at net worth (all assets minus all debt). Oliver and Shapiro[3] have observed that while African Americans earn about 62 percent of what white Americans earn, their net worth is only one-twelfth that of whites ($43,800 for whites and $3,700 for African Americans). What the figures are controlled for family size, educational attainment, region of the country, work experience, and occupation, African Americans still have a net worth that is one half that of whites.

Differentials in income become more meaningful when percent of families at or below the poverty level is considered. Some 8.5 percent of all white families fell below the poverty level in 1995. However, 26.4 percent of African American families and 27.0 of Hispanic origin families fell below the poverty level during the same time period.[4] Native American poverty rates were over 30 percent and while Asian American rates were only slightly higher than white rates, there was significant diversity in the experience of poverty among the Asian American population. Japanese Americans and Asian Indians had poverty rates that were less than whites, but Southeast Asian groups had poverty rates that were at or above the levels of African Americans, Hispanics, and native Americans.[5]

Poverty hits highest among female-headed families, where, by the mid-1990s, 36.5 percent of such families lived in poverty. While one-quarter of white female-headed families lived in poverty, about one-half of African American and Hispanic female-headed families live in poverty, while nearly two-thirds of Puerto Rican female-headed families lived in poverty.[6] Female-headed households are more likely to experience low incomes that are more likely to be accompanied by dilapidated housing and welfare assistance. Researchers began to comment on the growing "feminization of poverty" in the

1980 census. Divorced women with children often experienced a 73 percent drop in standard of living following their divorce, compared with a 42 percent increase in the standard of living of their ex-husbands.[7]

Furthermore, unemployment rates are consistently higher for minority groups. While 4.7 percent of white workers were unemployed in 1996, 10.5 percent of African American workers and 8.9 percent of Hispanic workers were unemployed. Unemployment rates also vary considerably by age, with the younger people being affected most by unemployment. Among young adults between the ages of twenty and twenty-four, 7.8 percent of whites, 18.8 percent of African Americans, and 11.8 percent of Hispanic workers were unemployed in 1996. For the youngest group of workers (ages 16 to 19 years), whites experienced an unemployment rate of 14.2 percent, while African Americans and Hispanics had unemployment rates of 33.6 percent and 23.6 percent, respectively.[8]

Translated into personal costs, lower income means more minority group members living in dilapidated housing, receiving inferior health care, being subjected to more life-threatening violence, and having lower life expectancies. An African American baby boy born in 1990 is expected to live 8.4 fewer years than a white baby boy (to age 64.9 compared with 73.3 years), while an African American baby girl is likely to live 5.7 fewer years than a white baby girl (to age 73.9 compared with 79.6 years), and the quality of that life is diminished.[9]

The conditions of minority groups are compounded by the growing bifurcation by social class of the minority populations themselves. Many of the benefactors of the Civil Rights Movement, the Chicano Movement, and related social movements were members of the middle class within the minority groups. Their children now of college age or in the labor force have economic and occupational opportunities that are fairly commensurate with those of the majority of the same age and education level. Many of the middle-class minority group members have moved out to suburbs to escape the blight of the central cities. The result is that there remains a growing underclass in the cities without hope of improved life chances. William J. Wilson in his seminal work *The Truly Disadvantaged,* notes that this underclass (especially African Americans), as a consequence of past discriminatory practices, were concentrated into the central cities while possessing few skills that are needed by employers.[10] They now experience unemployment and underemployment as the economy shifted from labor-intensive work to skill-intensive work. The abundance of social ills found in the central city, including drug abuse, teen pregnancy, gang activity, hopelessness, and crime can be traced to the abandonment of the inner city by the middle class and their institutions and by the disappearance of jobs. Wilson expands his argument in *When Work Disappears* to demonstrate the continuation of the underclass was not a result of failed welfare policies, but due to the out-migration of employment opportunities.[11] The concentration of enduring poverty in the central cities as a demographic phenomenon has been noted by Douglas Massey and Nancy Denton[12] in their work *American Apartheid.*

Social Prestige

Social prestige is the respect with which an individual or group is held. It is the status honor given to members of any society. Prestige is intertwined with property in an elaborate cycle. Having property resources enables one to command the respect and deference of others. In our society a wealthy person is held in higher esteem than one whose income is below the poverty level. It may be unfortunate, but true, that "money makes the man." With property resources one can purchase prerequisites for high social esteem, including an extensive education at a "good" university. This education will qualify one for a "good" occupation, which is another source of social prestige and also a means of obtaining economic resources.

Usually these three components of social class—income, education, and occupation—are on approximately the same level for any one individual. Thus one with high educational attainment would also have a high income and a prestigious occupation, and conversely, one with low education would have a low income and a less prestigious occupation. These are examples of a consistent pattern, but it sometimes happens (and frequently to minority-group members) that the pattern is inconsistent.[13] A typical example is that of a well-educated man who has been underemployed in a low-income low-prestige job. He has the prerequisites for high status, but it is denied to him. Some sociologists[14] documented that the vanguard of minority reform movements of the 1960s and 1970s was composed of status-inconsistent persons. It would appear that inconsistency may be a necessary condition to activism, but it certainly is not a sufficient one, since many inconsistent persons never become active reformers. Unfortunately, research on the effects of status inconsistency has yielded contradictory results, and no firm conclusion can be drawn.[15]

Social prestige can be considered on two levels: the individual and the group. American society is characterized by the absence of titles of nobility, so questions of who you are can be answered most easily in terms of what you do. Furthermore, what you do almost invariably refers to what kind of work you do or the nature of your occupation. On the individual level, education is often perceived as the key to unlock the doors to better occupations and middle-class standing for minority persons. However, education has not been equally experienced by all groups in our society. The National Center for Education Statistics[16] reported that the dropout rate for students in 1993 was 7.9 percent of individuals between the ages of sixteen and twenty-four. However, the dropout rate for African Americans between those ages was 13.6 percent and for Hispanics it was 27.5 percent. LeCompte and Dworkin[17] demonstrated that since the 1960s high school dropouts have increasingly been more likely than high school graduates to be unemployed, as well as underemployed. The rate of unemployment among dropouts is currently more than twice that of graduates. With the completion of high school as a prerequisite for college admission and in turn good jobs, higher minority dropout rates mean lower access to both higher education and quality employment for minority youth. Further, minority public elementary, middle, and high schools often have fewer educational resources, rely on more out-of-date books, and have a smaller percentage of teachers who specialized in the areas they teach. In an age of information technology, minority schools, especially those in the inner city are less likely to offer access to computers, and if they have computers, are more likely to have older equipment and antiquated software. In fact, many school occupied by low-income minority students are characterized by what Jonathan Kozol has called "savage inequality."[18]

In the 1960s the federal government initiated numerous programs (as part of the "War on Poverty") to improve the educational opportunities of minority-group members. The frequent assumption of both the government and the minority groups was that education is the only attainment needed to narrow the gap between minorities and the majority. Jencks[19] has argued that, despite programs to equilibrate educational opportunities, minority gains in occupations and income levels have not met expectations. Some minorities have even experienced a widening of the gap. Thus education has not been the panacea for all.

Individuals with the proper educational credentials still experience discrimination in the job market, receiving low-prestige and low-income jobs. Furthermore, success in business often depends upon informal networks formed by "knowing the right people." A qualified individual outside of these networks may often experience great difficulties entering into many occupations. Receiving a bank loan, joining a union, becoming an apprentice, or being a professor's protégé are often denied to minority-group members who "don't know the right people." In other instances, in industries under a full range of affirmative action guidelines minority-group membership may actually serve to facilitate access to the necessary networks, but this remains an experience for only a small percentage of minority-group individuals. In the past several years a number of social scientists have questioned whether upward mobility accrues from educational attainment.[20]

In fact, Christopher Jencks[21] in his analysis of national data on race, class, and education, John S. Butler[22] in his study of mobility in the military, and A. G. Dworkin[23] in his analysis of class origins of public school teachers have each argued the greater significance of luck than skill in mobility. Furthermore, Dworkin[24] found that among minority teachers and those teachers of lower social class origins (the social class of their parents), extreme dissatisfaction with a job was not associated with quitting behavior because such individuals had no other network of influential friends upon whom they could rely to aid them in entering a new career ladder. This creates an additional burden on the public schools and the quality of the education of children in poverty. Teachers willing to make extra efforts for their students are needed to raise student achievement and reduce the chances of dropout behavior. However, if large numbers of burned out and uncommitted teachers in inner-city schools do not quit, then educational reform intended to raise student achievement is often doomed.[25]

The census reflects the uneven allocation of persons into occupations. Table 3-1 presents the percentages of experienced persons in the labor force (excluding the military) for the year 1990. Each of the groups tabulated is broken down by sex. The table will enable us to make comparisons across groups and between sexes.

The first observation that can be made from the table is that whites and people of Asian and Pacific Island heritage (as groups) have a larger percentage of their labor force participants located in the highest status occupational category (managers, professionals, and officials) than do African Americans and Hispanic Origin populations. In fact, more than one-half of white and Asian and Pacific Island males and females are in white-collar occupations.

TABLE 3-1
Occupations of Experienced Civilian Labor Force by Race and Sex: 1990

	WHITE, NOT HISPANIC ORIGIN		BLACK		HISPANIC ORIGIN		ASIAN, PACIFIC ISLANDERS	
	Male	Female	Male	Female	Male	Female	Male	Female
Mgr.-Prof.-Official	**31.01**	**31.73**	**15.51**	**22.21**	**12.25**	**17.01**	**32.74**	**28.29**
Managers-Officials	16.13	13.18	7.77	8.54	6.70	7.69	13.71	11.38
Professionals	14.88	18.38	7.74	13.65	5.53	9.32	19.03	16.91
Tech.-Sales-Support	**24.73**	**46.23**	**20.36**	**40.72**	**17.25**	**39.39**	**27.71**	**40.39**
Technical	4.19	3.85	2.94	3.90	2.40	2.63	6.97	5.26
Sales	13.51	13.39	6.43	9.38	7.58	11.37	11.37	12.43
Administrative Support (clerical, secretarial)	7.03	28.99	10.98	27.45	7.32	25.34	9.37	22.57
Service	**8.99**	**14.16**	**19.66**	**24.65**	**16.68**	**23.35**	**13.54**	**16.12**
Private Household	0.03	0.53	0.11	2.01	0.10	3.16	0.06	0.79
Other Service	8.96	13.63	19.55	22.64	15.58	20.19	13.48	15.33
Farming, Mining, Forestry	**0.14**	**0.36**	**1.86**	**0.22**	**5.51**	**1.26**	**1.43**	**0.39**
Craft, Skilled	**17.67**	**1.91**	**14.09**	**2.20**	**19.90**	**3.57**	**11.43**	**4.08**
Operatives-Laborers	**16.17**	**5.61**	**28.67**	**9.99**	**28.40**	**15.43**	**13.09**	**10.79**
Operatives	11.48	4.29	19.72	8.15	19.00	12.54	9.06	9.28
Laborers	4.69	1.32	8.95	1.85	9.40	2.89	3.49	1.51

Source: U.S. Bureau of the Census, *Census of Population: 1990* (Washington, D.C.: Government Printing Office, 1993), 1990 CP-2–1, Table 81, pp. 1–86.

*Raw frequencies have been converted to percentages. Percentages do not total to exactly 100 percent down columns because of rounding error.

Managerial, professional, and official occupations carry more prestige, offer greater incomes, and require more education attainment than do the other occupations. Conversely, African American and Hispanic Origin groups have greater proportions of their numbers in the service and blue-collar jobs. These are the groups who do the heavy, dirty work for more minimal pay and minimal prestige. The exception is that about one-quarter of women of all racial and ethnic groups have jobs in the technical and sales support category, holding down relatively low paying pink-collar, clerical, and secretarial jobs.

Next we can compare males and females and make some additional observations. There are higher percentages of female professionals than male professionals across all groups except for Asian and Pacific Islanders. However, as shall be expanded upon later, within the professional category women are concentrated in the so-called semiprofessions such as public school teaching and nursing. These occupations are lower in pay and prestige, and practitioners have less autonomy than do those in other professions.

Women are also well represented in sales, in the broad category of clerical workers, and in the service occupations. Finally, a larger proportion of women (black women especially) than men are private household workers. Housecleaning, maid service, and babysitting for a salary can be viewed as an extension of the traditional female gender roles.

It is pertinent to note that African American and Hispanic women are more likely to be managers and officials than their male counterparts; the reverse is true of whites and Asian and Pacific Islanders. Nevertheless, minority women are most likely to serve in such jobs in small firms that pay relatively low wages and have few job benefits and little job security. Women, furthermore, are not represented well in the extremes of the blue-collar occupations. They are neither skilled craftsmen nor unskilled laborers. Thus females receive different treatment vis-à-vis occupations. Sometimes this treatment is pejorative; sometimes it is termed "protective."

Table 3-1 may be misleading in that it paints a more optimistic picture for some minorities than is the reality. First, there are many occupations represented in a given category (e.g., professional/technical includes such diverse occupations as brain surgeons, corporation lawyers, public school teachers, clergymen, and registered nurses), and minority-group members tend to be concentrated in the lower-paying and lower-status end of the scale. Second, when minorities are employed in the same occupation as majority-group members, they tend to be paid less because they do not have seniority, and they tend to be concentrated in positions with "unsteady employment, and in low-wage firms even in the same industry."[26] José Hernandez and Joe Henderson may both be skilled machinists of the same age, but José works for Smalltown Flange Company, earns less than $16,000 per year because his company cannot pay him more, has not had many years on the job, and is subject to frequent layoffs (minorities are the last hired and the first fired). Joe Henderson, on the other hand, works for World-Wide Flange Company, is protected by his union, has experienced few if any layoffs, and is paid more than $30,000 per year by a large company with considerable control over the economic market.

In a subsequent chapter we shall explore the relationship between economic competition and intergroup conflict. However, it is sufficient for the present to recognize that the experiences of minorities in occupations have followed a split labor market model.[27] In this model high-priced labor and low-priced labor compete for jobs, with high-priced labor exerting a greater control over industry, government, and public opinion because of its better organization (including unionization). Thus high-priced labor, which often is majority labor, has the ability to exclude low-priced labor, or minority labor, from an industry, or to create labor castes in which "better" jobs are allocated to high-priced labor and poorer jobs to low-priced labor. As minority groups gain a foothold in an occupation, the prestige of the occupation may decline, the pay may decrease, and the percentage of majority-group members in the occupation is lowered. Many whole occupational categories have historically shifted from one group to another, with an accompanying change in prestige and income. Prior to the 1920s public school teaching was primarily a man's job, and prior to the 1950s and 1960s it was primarily a white's job. With the entry of women and then racial and ethnic minorities into teaching, the prestige of public school teacher declined and the salary of teachers decreased relative to other occupations requiring college training. At the turn of the century, secretaries, and telephone-telegraph operators were males. As more women entered these jobs, men left, and the salary and prestige relative to other white-collar jobs declined.

When we speak of the prestige of groups, the achievement of individuals plays a relatively less significant role. Some individuals within a minority group may have achieved high status, but the group of which they are members will still be ranked very low. Individual mobility is distinct from collective mobility, and sociologically a group is different than the sum of its individual parts. There have been minority-group members who have achieved wealth, fame, and the respect of the majority community. Thurgood Marshall was an associate justice of the United States Supreme Court and a black man, while Clarence Thomas, also an African American, now fills that position. Tiger Woods, of African American and Asian American heritage, has become a superstar in professional golf. Retired Army General Colin Powell (African American), former Housing and Urban Development Secretary Henry Cisneros (Mexican American), and civil rights leader Jesse Jackson were each considered as viable candidates for the U.S. presidency. Part Native American Will Rogers was the most loved humorist and political satirist in the late 1920s and 1930s. Congresswoman Geraldine Ferraro was the 1984 Democratic candidate for vice president of the United States, and Sandra Day O'Connor and Ruth Bader Ginsburg are associate justices of the U.S. Supreme Court. There are numerous other examples, but these few are enough to indicate that individuals can be mobile while the group of which each is a member remains of low prestige. In Chapter 6 we shall discuss theories of acceptance of minority groups, but suffice it to note that structural assimilation necessitates the widespread acceptance of a group into the clubs and cliques of the majority, not simply the acceptance of a few notables.

Social distance measures have often been used as indicators of the relative ranking of minority groups. These scales are assessments of the extent to which people are willing to enter into close, personal, and intimate relations with members of the minority group qua group. The most widely known of such indicators is the Bogardus Social Distance Scale, first devised in 1926 by Emory Bogardus, and used periodically[28] by him and systematically by dozens of other researchers. The scale asks individuals to indicate whether they would interact with members of specified minority groups in the following seven situations: marriage partner, close friend, office co-worker, neighbor, casual acquaintance, prefer out of neighborhood, and prefer out of country. The items in the scale are arranged in decreasing degrees of intimacy and increasing amounts of social distance. Groups with which the respondents are willing to have more intimate interactions are thus considered to be of higher status or prestige. Presented in Table 3-2 are the relative rankings of a selection of minority groups studied by Bogardus over a forty-year period. Although Bogardus died in 1973, others have continued his work. Included in the table are the results of a follow-up study. The scale asks individuals to rate thirty groups and the rankings presented in the table are the relative ranks of the selected groups from among the thirty. The higher the score assigned to the group, the greater the social distance and hence the less the minority-group prestige.

Social distance is not identical to minority-group prestige, but it represents one of the less compromised measures of prestige. Assessments of social distance more sophisticated than the Bogardus scale tend to differentiate between classes and subgroups within the minority community. In that sense they are better indicators of individual preference for interaction with individual members of minority groups, but they move further from an indication of group prestige. In the construction of his measure of status consistency, Lenski[29] used minority-group prestige as one of four measures of status, along with income, education, and occupation. His measure was even cruder than the use of the Bogardus measure. Lenski simply asked a group of students to rank the groups. Sinha and Sinha[30] measured minority prestige of castes in India in a similar manner by having individuals rank the castes in order of general importance. The task of the latter researchers was aided by the fact that India is a much more rigidly stratified society, with an institutionalized and governmentally ranked hierarchy of groups.

Lieberson argues that in light of the difficulties in measuring minority-group rankings, hierarchies ought to be measured in terms of a twofold dimension of stratification: "discrimination against a group in terms of economic

TABLE 3–2
*Relative Bogardus Social Distance Rankings of Minority Groups**

	1926 SAMPLE N = 1,725		1946 SAMPLE N = 1,950		1956 SAMPLE N = 2,053		1966 SAMPLE N = 2,605		1977 SAMPLE N = 1,488	
Group	SDS†	Rank	SDS	Rank	SDS	Rank	SDS	Rank	SDS	Rank
White Americans	1.10	2	1.04	1	1.08	1	1.07	1	1.25	1
Irish	1.30	5	1.24	5	1.56	5	1.40	5	1.69	7
American Indians	2.38	18	2.45	20	2.35	20	2.12	18	1.84	10
Jews	2.39	19	2.32	19	2.15	16	1.97	15	2.01	15
Mexican Americans	(not ranked)		2.52	22	2.51	22	2.37	23	2.17	19
Japanese Americans	(not ranked)		2.90	26	2.34	19	2.14	19	2.18	20
Negroes	3.28	26	3.60	29	2.74	27	2.56	29	2.03	17
Chinese	3.36	28	2.50	21	2.68	25	2.34	22	2.29	23

Sources: Adapted from E. Bogardus, "Comparing Racial Distance in Ethiopia, South Africa, and the United States," *Sociology and Social Research* 52 (1968): 152. The 1977 data are from C. A. Owen, H. C. Eisner, and T. R. McFaul, "A Half-Century of Social Distance Research: National Replication of the Borgardus' Studies," *Sociology and Social Research* 66 (1981), pp. 95–96.

*The range of possible scores is from 1.00 (highest prestige and lowest social distance) to 7.00 (lowest prestige and highest social distance).

†Social Distance Score

opportunity or political power, or both."[31] He contends that because minority groups have the potential of forming their own nation-state (or at least being separatists within the society—a possibility not available to purely social classes), and because minority stratificational systems in a society will affect other stratificational systems (including class solidarity and solidarity across class lines but within minority-group lines), one may not be able to use stratificational models in dealing with minority stratification. However, if one defines minority hierarchies in terms of economic opportunities and political power (two of our dimensions of stratification), one eliminates the prestige dimensions altogether, or creates a logical error in defining a concept in terms of two other concepts in the typology. Lieberson would have omitted the prestige dimension, but to do so would ignore the fact that some groups may have prestige without power and property, while others might have power and property without prestige. The Italians and Irish were identified with big-city corruption and with organized crime in the 1930s. Many subgroups of these minorities possessed considerable power and property but were not held in respect. Similarly, Table 3-2 reveals that in 1977 Native Americans had relatively high prestige (ranked tenth among all groups, ahead of Jews and relatively close to the Irish) but possessed little power or property.

As we note from Table 3-2, racial minorities tend generally to be ranked lower than ethnic minorities. Many factors, including historical events, may account for changes in the ranking of groups. Thus during and immediately after World War II Japanese Americans experienced a marked decline in prestige in the eyes of the majority. Three forms of determinants can generally be proposed to account for the ranking of groups: (1) the power of the minority groups relative to one another and to the majority; (2) the extent to which the minority resembles the majority, and hence the probability that the minority may soon assimilate to the majority; and (3) the extent to which the minority is seen as making a substantial contribution to the society in which it lives. These three dimensions are highly interrelated. There are also some instances, though relatively rare, in which achievements by "race men" make it possible for others of their minority group to attain mobility, but the ranking of the group as a whole is usually not altered.[32]

The Irish gained political power through control of ward politics and political machines. They were identifiably very similar to the white Anglo-Saxon Protestant majority (both racially and culturally) and have been identified with much of American history. Thus their status is high. Blacks have, until recently, enjoyed little political control (even of the ghettos). They are dissimilar from the majority in appearance, and their contributions have been ignored in much of the writing of American history. They thus occupy a low status among minorities. However, blacks have attempted through several means (to be discussed in the next section) to gain political power, and they have demanded the correction of history books to include the manifold contributions of blacks to American society. Similar efforts have been made by

Asian Americans, Mexican Americans, Native Americans, and women, as well as by gay and lesbian groups.

Although research on the Bogardus Social Distance Scale *per se* is much rarer today than it was during Bogardus' lifetime, some of the relevant items from the scale regularly appear in national surveys. The National Opinion Research Center (NORC)[33] of the University of Chicago periodically conducts a General Social Survey of a random and representative sample of Americans. Social distance attitudes about intergroup marriages, neighborhood desegregation, intergroup invitations to one's house for dinner, and school desegregation have been asked in surveys between 1972 and 1996. Generally, white Americans feel less social distance between themselves and Jewish Americans (who are also white) than between themselves and Asian Americans and Hispanic Americans. They feel the most social distance between themselves and African Americans. This pattern resembles that found by Bogardus over a forty-year period. Chapter 5 will present these data from the General Social Survey.

POWER

Earlier we noted that power was the actual use of resources to influence and control others. The variables of power are total number of resources and their mobilization. Power is interconnected with property and prestige in that property represents material resources to be mobilized, and prestige represents influence to induce others to mobilize resources or to induce others, out of respect, to comply with one's wishes. Power, when achieved, can be utilized to increment one's prestige and property. In essence, minorities seek to gain power so as to increase their property and prestige. Because they lack property and prestige, poor people are usually unable to run for political office and hence increase their power. The cycle may be vicious: Without property and prestige one cannot gain power, but without power one may not be able to influence others so as to gain property and prestige.

There have been many taxonomies of power, but it may be helpful in discussing minorities to distinguish between two general types: legal and extralegal. Legal power, or authority, is power obeyed because of its legitimacy. As Hopkins, commenting upon Max Weber's use of the term "authority," notes: "People obey when they feel a moral obligation to do so, because specifically, they and everyone else define the statuses they occupy as allowing or requiring them to do so."[34] Thus, compliance with and exercise of such power is not a function of coercion or force, but rather of willingness and obligation. Political incumbents do not leave office and surrender power when they lose an election because they fear punishment should they refuse, but because they accept as morally correct and legitimate the rules of political succession. Office holding, legal petitions before the courts, and voting activities represent some forms of legal power available to minorities.

Extralegal power is that power which is not mutually acceptable to the parties involved. In some instances use of such power may involve coercion and force, and is met with the exercise of power by the opposing group. Revolts, riots, protests, sit-ins, marches, boycotts, and similar activities represent some forms of extralegal power available to minorities.

Legal Power

Legal power can be exercised within the formal structure of government. Some European immigrant minorities have assimilated to the extent of acquiring great political power in the highest levels of government. The Irish Kennedy family is such an example. Jews also have achieved national prominence and power. Although not yet gaining the presidency, there have been powerful Jewish Americans in Congress, in the Cabinet, and on the Supreme Court.

Other minority groups have not fared as well. African Americans and, to a lesser extent, Hispanics have gained elective seats in Congress with some regularity over the past several years, but other groups have been elected only sporadically to Capitol Hill. Table 3-3 shows the distribution of minority-group members in Congress in 1985 and 1995. The U.S. Senate remains overwhelmingly white and male. The U.S. House of Representatives, too, is predominantly white and male, although women, African Americans, and Hispanics have doubled their membership between 1985 and 1995. Key positions in Congress, especially committee chairships are still the domain of white males.

TABLE 3–3
Makeup Congress: 1985* and 1995

	Senate		House of Representatives	
Group	1985	1995	1985	1995
Male	98	92	412	388
Female	2	8	22	47
White	98	97	401	374
African American	0	1	20	40
Hispanic	0	0	10	17
Asian American	2	2	3	4

Source: U.S. Department of Commerce, Bureau of the Census, *Statistical Abstracts of the United States: 1997,* 117th ed. (Washington, D.C.: Government Printing Office, 1997), Table 448, p. 281.
*Excludes vacant seats in the House of Representatives.

The National Opinion Research Center's General Social Survey has tapped public opinion regarding the election of blacks and women to the office of president of the United States. Since the first survey in 1972, a large majority of Americans have supported the women and African Americans as hypothetical candidates for the presidency. Within a few percentage points, men and women equally found women as acceptable presidential candidates and the percentages agreeing with the statement have been rising. However, while the majority of whites and African Americans both found African American candidates as acceptable, African American respondents have been more supportive than whites of a Black candidate by as many as ten to fifteen percentage points. Table 3-4 displays the acceptability of women and blacks as presidential candidates for the years from 1972 to 1996.

Before one concludes that the election of a black American or a female American for president is imminent, one should realize that the NORC questions were worded in such a way that they may have increased the likelihood of a liberal response. Specifically, the questions asked respondents if they would vote for a woman (or black) if the candidate was *nominated by their party* and was qualified. R. Dworkin[35] pointed out that the question is really asking whether a person would vote for women or blacks *if* they were truly qualified and *if* the respondent's party nominated the individual. The respondent's answer might actually be a challenge: "I dare you to find me one who is qualified and can get nominated. If you find me one, then I'll vote for the person." The same could be true of Martians. If you find a Martian who is qualified to be president as defined by the respondent and who gets the nomination of the respondent's political party, then the respondent will vote for him/her/it.

Minorities tend to exert more political power on the local levels of government, and this power is increasing. According to the Statistical Abstracts of the United States, Black elected officials in county, city, law enforcement, and education districts in the United States have increased almost eight-fold between 1970 and 1992 (from 1,472 in 1970 to 11,542 in 1992).[36] However, there were approximately one-half million elected officials in the United States in 1979 and in 1992, and African Americans represented about 2.3 percent of that total in 1992. The number of women who held elective offices at the local level increased from nearly 12,000 in 1979 to more than 100,000 in 1992, that is, from 2.4 percent in 1979 to 20 percent in 1992.[37]

Over recent years some minority groups have achieved a measure of political power—and in some instances even great power. What mechanisms have minority groups used to gain such power?

Ironically, segregation and ghettoization of minorities, though unfortunate for a variety of reasons, are actually functional for the acquisition of political office in this nation. Where members of a minority group have been residentially isolated, they may be able to obtain voting majorities in congressional districts, school districts, and even entire municipalities. Municipal control is enhanced by the majority flight to the suburbs. This isolation has

TABLE 3–4

Percentage Support for Women and African Americans as Presidential Candidates

Would Vote for a Woman for President

Year	1972	1974	1975	1977	1978	1982	1983	1985	1986	1988	1989	1990	1991	1993	1994	1996
Male	73.6	80.5	82.2	82.1	83.3	85.9	86.2	85.0	89.0	89.7	84.5	90.3	90.0	90.2	91.5	91.7
Female	73.7	80.1	78.7	77.0	80.3	86.3	86.7	80.1	84.4	86.4	87.9	88.8	91.0	91.1	92.3	94.1

Would Vote for an African American for President

Year	1972	1974	1975	1977	1978	1982	1983	1985	1986	1988	1989	1990	1991	1993	1994	1996
White	73.8	81.2	81.7	77.8	83.2	86.2	84.6	83.4	86.0	79.4	81.0	86.6	88.3	87.4	89.5	91.8
African American	NA	96.4	NA	NA	95.5	98.4	95.0	98.6	97.2	98.4	96.0	91.1	98.5	99.1	99.2	97.8
Other	NA	NA	NA	NA	NA	92.3	NA	81.8	86.5	84.4	85.7	83.3	96.2	92.2	90.4	98.2

Source: *General Social Surveys, 1972–1996: Cumulative Codebook* (Chicago: National Opinion Research Center, 1997).

been a recent source of power for African Americans and for Mexican Americans; the lack of such isolation has sometimes been a handicap for women.

Historically, the Irish and other European immigrant groups were able to achieve much political power and ultimately assimilation through manipulation of the urban political machine.[38] The relationship between the precinct captain and the new immigrant was reciprocal. In return for votes, the petty politicians helped their constituency obtain employment and facilitated adaptation to the new social environment. Thus the new immigrant was able to wield considerable political power in a relatively short time.

Legal power can be exercised not only by gaining elective office but by using legitimate tactics to influence those who are in office. Lobbying, lawsuits, court appeals, and other such strategies used by reform movements are exercises of power. The most famous of these include the 1954 *Brown* v. *Board of Education of Topeka, Kansas,* decision of the Supreme Court, which ruled school segregation unconstitutional.

Often members of minority groups differ in their approval of methods of exercising what power they possess. Within the population of native Americans there is controversy about the utility of lawsuits over such displays of power as the taking of Wounded Knee. Within the black communities of the 1960s there was much debate about the legalism of the NAACP as against the tactics of sit-ins, demonstrations, and protests. The latter tactics can all be categorized as extralegal forms of power.

Extralegal Power

When legal forms of power are denied, it sometimes becomes necessary to develop extralegal power. The power might be used to call attention to abuses by the majority, to shame the majority into granting concessions to the minority, to gain independence from domination by the majority, or to gain control over one's own destiny. The use of extralegal power to change the social system, alter the societal definition of the minority by the majority, and in turn ensure greater resources and prestige for the minority is thus reform-oriented. Techniques of civil disobedience ranging from sit-ins to riots represent uses of reform-oriented extralegal power.

When minorities have few resources to mobilize in order to affect the majority, they may resort to the one resource all have: their bodies. By blocking the activities of the majority (as in a sit-in), attacking the symbols of the majority (the police and fire departments), or destroying some of the majority's property (as well as the minority's) in a riot or violent protest, the minority can achieve an influence over the behavior of the majority. The boycotts, marches, and sit-ins of the black civil rights movement forced the South to abandon many of the Jim Crow practices that had been prevalent for nearly a century. The riots and violent protests that swept the nation in the 1960s forced the white majority to recognize the existence of a serious problem and to induce federal funding to attempt to ameliorate the plight of the urban black.[39] Many researchers have commented on the tokenism of such efforts and the extent to which these token efforts helped to consolidate black group awareness.[40]

It has been the experience of minority relations in America that as the reform-oriented means to power have become successful, they begin to acquire legitimacy, and their effectiveness and impact are diminished. Then the majority begins to adopt similar tactics as counterdisplays of power. Initial marches were met by hoses, dogs, and mass arrests; later marches were sanctioned with police protection and legislative support. Protest activities became routinized to the extent that rules for their conduct were established and enforced. For example, parade permits and adherence to a predetermined route of march became necessary.

The 1970s had seen majority counter demonstrations protesting busing and forced school desegregation, while the 1990s have seen increases in hate crimes against minority gains. The visibility and violence of white supremacist groups, the wave of burning of black churches in the 1990s and the rise of militia groups that oppose the federal government, the immigration of non-white groups to the United States, affirmative action, and the political and economic gains of minorities represent marginal populations who wish to return the country to a time when being white along guaranteed an individual great privilege. Nevertheless, there still remains a significant amount of white privilege in American society.

Some writers have felt that the riot behavior of the 1960s was merely an aggressive response to total frustration, in which the hopeless minority "explodes" in anger.[41] But others have shown that protesters of all kinds tend to be those who have feelings of personal control over their destinies and convictions of political efficacy.[42] According to these writers, extralegal power strategies are attempted exactly because the individuals in the minority feel that they have a high probability of attaining resources through such exercise of their power. The riots in Miami in the 1980s reflected the frustrations of African Americans who saw jobs disappear into Hispanic hands. The riots in Los Angeles in 1992, after a first trial led to the acquittal of the Los Angeles police officers who beat Rodney King, an African American, involved many ethnic groups and reflected a form of class warfare, as economically disadvantaged groups revolted against what they perceived to be an unjust system that advantages those with wealth. In 1995, the nation was transfixed by the televised murder trial in Los Angeles of O.J. Simpson, who was simultaneously black, wealthy, and famous. His acquittal was received by different racial groups in distinct ways. Many whites concluded that he was guilty but that he "got away with it" because of his wealth and fame, while many African Americans who believed him to be innocent concluded that minorities can obtain a fair trial and justice only if they are wealthy and famous enough to buy it.

MAJORITY RESPONSES

The majority, by definition, has relatively greater power than the minority. Thus it has the capacity to retard or defeat minority exercises of power. Generally, minorities are effective only to the extent that the majority is unwilling to mobilize its full resources to halt the minority. The vast changes in intergroup relations in the first half of the present century have occurred in part because the majority was no longer willing to oppose the minority maximally and in part because the changes were incremental and accompanied by attitude shifts. Further, in hundreds of overt and covert ways the majority has ensured its control while granting token benefits to minorities. We may itemize at least six techniques used by majorities to maintain dominance over minorities.

Tokenism

By minimally meeting some of the demands of minorities, majorities can give the impression of granting resources without actually doing so. By permitting a few minority-group members in an overwhelmingly majority school, majorities have attempted to meet school desegregation orders without changing the balance of power in the schools. Coleman and his associates[43] and Mack and his associates[44] have documented the manner in which southern schools first attempted to bypass desegregation orders by providing better physical facilities for black schools while keeping the schools segregated and unequal. White employers have hired one or two minority-group members, given them executive titles, but provided them with few options to exercise decision making while appearing to be an equal opportunity employer. Often an individual who represents two minority groups (such as a black woman) is hired. Thus the employer gets "two for the price of one."

The sociologist Rosabeth Moss Kanter[45] examined the way in which tokenism in major corporate offices defined the roles that women executives could play and how those definitions affected their performances and commitments. Tokens serve as representatives of their group such that their personal failures on the job do not represent personal failure per se, but the failure of their whole group (a kind of aggregation error). The fact of being a token adversely affected the level of work satisfaction of the women. Research on gender tokens in public school teaching extended these findings.[46] When members of societally dominant groups (e.g., white males) are in positions of being tokens their sense of work satisfaction increases, as they can take advantage of the dominant group gender stereotypes applied to men. However, when women and racial or ethnic minorities are in token positions they are doubly disadvantaged. They suffer from the aggregation errors that generalize personal failures to their group and from stereotypic expectations in the first place that lead to expectations of failure.

Coercion

The most common use of majority power has been to force the minorities to comply with their demands. The threat of violence, imprisonment, and even death have accompanied these demands. From Ku Klux Klan night rides to mass arrests or loss of job security, the majority has controlled the minorities.

Co-optation

Here minority groups, minority organizations, or minority-group members are incorporated into the majority to avert threats to the control of the majority. Particularly dynamic and active members of the minority may be appointed to majority-controlled organizations and then given tasks which minimize their effectiveness in leading the minority. In fact, the individual may soon find that his task is to "keep down" or control the activities of other members of his group.

Gerrymandering Districts

Minority political power, although heightened by residential segregation, may be diluted if the majority redistributes voting districts so that minorities do not have a plurality in their district. Congressional redistricting in 1981 and urban annexation plans were challenged by minority groups using the power of the 1965 Voting Rights Act. Minorities have charged that the dominant population redrew boundaries to dilute minority voting power. In the 1990s redrawn congressional boundaries that enhanced the election of minorities have been challenged by conservatives and white groups who feel that minorities have made too many gains. In 1993 and 1995 the U.S. Supreme Court called for the redrawing of some district boundaries in North Carolina and Texas with the effect of diluting minority voting power. The court has challenged the use of racial criteria for the drawing of congressional district boundaries. The issue, however, like that of affirmative action, is far from resolved.

Divide and Conquer

In this technique majority-group members pit minorities against one another, especially by promoting economic competition between groups.[47] Dr. Martin Luther King, Jr., recognized this strategy and attempted before his assassination to expand his campaign from a black civil rights movement to a poor people's movement, involving all the disinherited of the country.

Socialization and "Anglo Conformity"

The majority may attempt to educate the young of the minority group to believe in the legitimacy of the majority's control. If these individuals are taught to desire the language, beliefs, values, and customs of the majority, they may be less likely to question the resources owned by the majority. They will identify less with the minority and more with the majority. Thus a minority individual's desire for mobility will be personal and individualistic, and not group-oriented. He will achieve not to help "his people" but to help himself.

Another aspect of socialization is the teaching of minorities that only the majority has made significant achievements. Omission of minority contributions from history books has the effect of minimizing minority-group pride and self-awareness and maximizing desires to emulate and identify with the majority. Adults and children alike can be socialized through the mass media, including newspapers, literature, radio, and television. The appearance of minorities and minority-life situations on television programs reflects the initial influence of minority power (especially economic power in terms of buying advertised products) on the identity process. Much of the programming, however, retains the majority group's stereotyped definition of life in the minority communities.

A System Model for Minority Access to Resources

Figure 3-1 represents a model created by J. Chafetz, A. G. Dworkin, and R. J. Dworkin[48] in an attempt to account for the manner in which minority groups may gain property and prestige through entry into the labor force of the majority. The full ramifications of the model cannot be developed in this text. However, the essential components include conditions of the society (A) in which the minority and majority live (population size, level of technology, state of economy, and natural resources), which affect the demand for labor (B). Should the traditional labor force (majority-group members) be scarce (C), other sources of labor will be sought (D). These other sources should include minority-group members, provided that subcultural and societal definitions of minority capabilities (E_1) and definitions of the nature of the tasks involved (E_2) are comparable. The competing demands of minority groups, representing low-priced labor, through their social movements (F) and traditional labor force organizations (G), representing high-priced labor affect the definitions and determine whether nontraditional labor is utilized (G_1). This in turn influences future role allocations (G_2) and definitions of minority capabilities (H), thereby making it easier for minorities to be incorporated into the labor pool in the future. Obviously minority-group members do perform work and are part of a labor force, even when these mechanisms are not activated. The tasks they perform, however, are usually low-paying and low in

FIGURE 3-1
A System Model for Minority Access to Resources

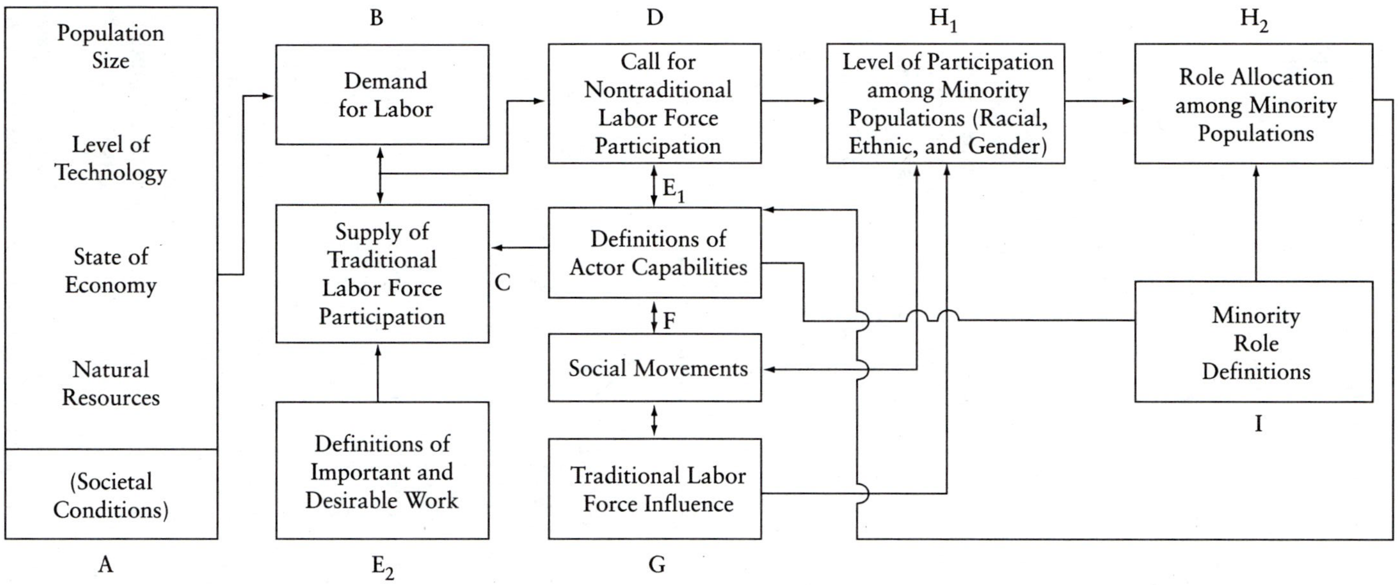

Source: Adapted from J. S. Chafetz, A. G. Dworkin, and R. J. Dworkin, "New Migrants to the Rat Race: A Systems Model for changes in Work Force Allocation and Role Expectations, by Gender, Race, and Ethnicity," mimeographed (University of Houston, 1975).

prestige. The current model attempts to account for changes in allocation of jobs (particularly higher-paying and higher-prestige jobs) to minorities. The model, modified to include different reference groups that affect perceptions of relative deprivation, system blame, and system illegitimacy, was used by Chafetz and Dworkin to account for the emergence of social protest movements by women.[49]

Because we have posed a system model, it can be seen that role allocations and definitions are reversible. As the demand for labor diminishes, minorities may become barred from these higher-paying and higher-prestige occupations. A classic example of the process accounted for by the model is the position of women in the labor force.

Prior to World War II most women were housewives or in traditionally female occupations (schoolteacher, nurse, salesclerk, typist). The war depleted the masculine labor force and simultaneously created a need for a manufacturing labor force that was literate, skilled, and immediately available. Women could be easily trained to perform the tasks of skilled craftsmen and had a willingness to perform the tasks. They were thus incorporated into this labor pool, and "Rosie the Riveter" became a folk heroine. With the end of the war the diminished demand for labor could be satisfied by returning veterans. The female nontraditional labor force was no longer required. Role definitions reversed themselves and women were again relegated to the home. However, the experience of the 1940s was not forgotten, and became a precedent for a new feminist movement of the late 1960s.[50]

Class and Caste: Open and Closed Models of Minority Stratification

American society has been variously characterized as having either an open *class* system for mobility in terms of power, prestige, and property, or a rigid, closed, color *caste* system of immobility in terms of these indicators.

In societies founded upon a caste system, such as traditional India, a vast amount of a person's status characteristics are ascribed. That is, people are born into a set of status and role relationships and expectations, as well as other important dimensions of their[51] lives. There is no mobility out of one's subcaste. Marriage across caste lines is forbidden, and since caste determines occupational possibilities, career mobility is rigid. Although caste guarantees that no group will monopolize another's occupational group and steal away jobs, it also prohibits individuals from attaining careers not deemed suitable for their subcaste. The entire social order is maintained, indeed sanctified, by the religious system. To violate the rules of caste is to violate the religion and to incur considerable sanction.

Class systems are much more open. In the ideal they guarantee that even within a family across generations all members have an opportunity to move up (or down) in the social order. In reality, of course, class system operates somewhat more rigidly than the ideal, but much less rigidly than caste systems. Elites tend to beget elites, and stratificational systems tend to be self-perpetuating. But there remains the potential, through self-improvement and education, for considerable mobility from parent to child. Assignment of roles and statuses ideally is based upon achievement—what you have done and how hard you have attempted to gain it. We know, however, that it is many times easier for a rich man's son to become a rich man than it is for a poor man's son. Aside from marriage to the rich man's son, or through inheritance, the task is somewhat more difficult for a rich man's daughter to become a rich woman.

Some writers have likened American minority-group relations to a caste system of stratification; Warner,[52] Dollard,[53] and Davis, Gardner, and Gardner[54] have characterized black-white relations in America as caste-like. In the 1930s and 1940s, when these works were written, there was little black mobility to the status dimensions occupied by whites. Further, most whites could boast that no matter how low they got as individuals, there were always many blacks below them in a lower caste. Changes in the balance of power, prestige, and property occasioned by the civil rights movement have moved the caste barrier from a near-horizontal line, demarcating the white population on the top from the African American population on the bottom, to a more nearly vertical line with parallel stratificational systems (social-class-based within each caste). There is still little exogamy, but there are many more middle-and upper-class African Americans than in the earlier model. Whites no longer assume that most African Americans are below them in status regardless of their own low position. In fact, the transition from a caste-based to a class-based race relations system has been the hallmark of black-white relations in the post World War II and post Civil Rights Movement era and has led some scholars such as William Julius Wilson to argue that the role of race has declined in significance.[55]

Similar caste models based upon intermarriage have been advanced in the 1940s to account for religious groups. Kennedy[56] argued that there was a triple melting pot, Catholic, Protestant, and Jew, and that intermarriage among these groups was infrequent. Herberg[57] found a similar triple melting pot in the 1950s. But the current generation is not so bounded by pressures against interfaith marriages, and the caste system based on religious groupings is rapidly becoming a phenomenon of the past. Hacker[58] and Andreas[59] have posited a caste system vis-à-vis sex categories.

The caste model has been seriously challenged by many writers. Cox[60] argued nearly thirty years ago that the metaphor of caste adapted from India was being stretched too much to be applicable to the United States. Cox called for some alternative concept to denote the black-white situation. Perhaps what Blauner[61] and Carmichael and Hamilton[62] have termed "internal colonialism" (to be discussed in the next section) may be the preferable metaphor for the black-white relationship. Simpson and Yinger[63] argued that a caste model is inexorably tied to the religious system of India, and cannot be transported to the United States without suffering irreparable damage. Some, however, have argued that there is a quasi-religious basis for a color caste in the United States—white racism.

Class models have been prolific in American sociology. Some writers have viewed classes as discrete categories with clear-cut boundaries separating upper, middle, and lower groups.[64] Others have contended that classes are continuous categories without clear-cut boundaries.[65] When applied to minority-group relations, the models proposed have tended to deal with blacks and whites, and hence twofold parallel class (one for blacks and one for whites) structure models have been advanced, including those by Hunter in Atlanta, Drake and Cayton in Chicago, and Burgess in North Carolina.[66]

Perhaps the most viable model has been that proposed by Milton Gordon.[67] The model, termed "ethclass," is based on the cross-classification of ethnic groups and social class categories. A grid is constructed (Figure 3-2) in which each column represents a group, and each row the social classes (upper, middle, and lower, or some more delineated breakdown). Minority groups are

FIGURE 3-2
Display of Gordon's Ethclass Model

		GROUPS							
		WASP	Irish	Jews	American Indians	Japanese American	Chinese American	Mexican American	Blacks
Social Classes (Ranked)	Upper-Upper								
	Lower-Upper								
	Upper-Middle								
	Lower-Middle								
	Upper-Lower								
	Lower-Lower								

Groups are ranked according to data presented in Table 3-2.

then compared both across columns and rows for given social classes. Gordon had proposed that groups of the same social class, regardless of ethnicity, might have more values, beliefs, and aspirations in common, and hence have a greater common ground on which to develop inter-group harmony, than would different classes within a given ethnic group.

Recently social scientists writing from a Marxian perspective[68] have suggested that social class, measured in terms of one's relationship to the means of production, explains minority experiences better than do race, gender, or social status. In a classic piece, Wright and Perrone[69] demonstrated that in terms of returns on educational investments, there are no significant differences *within* social classes (workers, managers, and owners) between racial or gender groups. There have been only significant differences *between* social classes. That is, knowing whether people are workers or managers tells us more about their ability to convert their educational attainment into higher salaries than knowing whether they are male or female, black or white. Before one dispenses with race and gender as factors in minority status, however, it is essential that one realize that returns on education represent only a single dimension of the minority experience. In the ensuing chapters we shall examine the organizational and social psychological aspect of the minority situation.

Class models, because they assume a greater degree of mobility and permit greater exogamy than do caste models, tend to view the ultimate outcome of minority-group relations as one of assimilation, whereby the minority becomes part of the majority in terms of identifiability, power, prestige, and property. Caste models, on the other hand, maintain minority nationalism or continued minority separatism as a plausible outcome. It appears from the experiences of minority groups, and is the contention of the contributors to *The Minority Report,* that neither model may be applied without caution. Class systems and assimilation models depict the outcomes and goals of ethnic minorities. Caste systems, separatism, and/or a degree of nationalism better depict the conditions of racial minorities. Certainly in terms of power, prestige, and property, there may be viability to the class models for racial groups, but these minorities are often unwilling to surrender their identity and intermarry with the majority. Likewise, the majority is unwilling to admit the minority into intermarriage in any significant numbers.

INTERNAL COLONIALISM

Several authors[70] writing principally about the African American and Hispanic experiences have suggested that, rather than a color caste or class model, a colonial model is more appropriate. To any extent it appears that minority status in general fits the colonial analogy. In such a model the relationship between majority and minority is similar to that between colonizer and native. The colony (or ghetto) supplies the "mother country" with raw materials and buys back the finished product at exorbitant rates. In the internal colonial analogy the raw materials are simply cheap labor, and the finished product is purchased at the inflated prices charged for products in the minority communities. Moore[71] has argued that the analogy is better for Chicanos than for blacks, inasmuch as the Chicanos did originally own the land occupied and literally colonized by the Anglos.

We have noted that there is a dependency relationship between colony and mother country. The colonizer needs the supply of raw materials (cheap labor) and needs the colonized people as a captive market to buy the finished products. But there will be pressures of several sorts to mitigate the stability of the relationship. First, as technology advances, the tasks requiring cheap labor will diminish, reducing the need of the colonial power for the raw materials. Wilhelm[72] has suggested that, under such conditions, drives may arise to exterminate the minority when it is no longer needed. Second, there will be pressure within the minority community or colony to manufacture its own goods and buy only within its boundaries. There have been some attempts at such actions, but the mother country generally owns the necessary supply of capital to limit this possibility.

Third, as is inherent in all capitalist enterprises, there is a contradiction. Capitalists seek to minimize their costs, especially labor costs, and so they pay low wages. But if they pay too little, their customers, who collectively are the employees of all capitalists, will be unable to afford the merchandise. The solution generally is to turn to imperialism: to seek colonies that will supply a cheap source of labor in order to lower prices and to find markets abroad to sell their goods. But when the colony is internal to the mother country, the relationship becomes tenuous. If the mother country has no need for cheap labor (because of technology) and the colony lacks the ability to buy the commodities, the internal colony becomes a burden.

Perhaps Wilhelm's prediction may be accurate. It is true that the majority still turns to the minority to buy its commodities. Even when the minority is seeking to attain self-identity, the majority plays a role that enables it to profit. Fortunes have been made off women and other minorities by selling them cigarettes or other products that play on the new feminism, or the new minority self-awareness. Numerous artifacts of group identity are made by the majority and sold to the minority for a profit. Even in the revolt, the majority gains. Further, as the majority finds its commodities obsolete, it often turns to the minority to buy them. The dumping ground for gas-guzzling, oversized, inefficient automobiles of the 1960s and 1970s was the minority communities of the 1980s. The equivalence for the twenty-first century is that the dumping ground for outmoded computer technology has often been minority schools, where any computer is welcome. However, the good jobs require training on more advanced computers with more advanced software. Children in inner-city schools are thus trained for jobs that require skills they cannot get.

SUMMARY

The distributive dimension includes resources of property, social prestige, and power. In each of these areas minorities are differentially and pejoratively treated.

According to the U.S. census, minority groups have lower income levels and larger percentages below the poverty level than do the white majority. Unemployment rates are higher, and housing and health standards are lower. These are differentials in property.

Intertwined with property is social prestige. Minority individuals have less education and hold more lower-status occupations than do majority individuals. This inhibits opportunities to secure property. On the group level, entire minorities are differentially ranked, with racial minorities ranked lower than ethnic minorities. There is no comparable data available for gender groups.

There are two general types of power: legal and extralegal. Although minority groups have been gaining power in the past several years, they are still underrepresented in elective government. Ghettoization has become a source of legal power.

Extralegal power, both violent and nonviolent, has been used to change the social system and ensure greater resources for minorities. Many of these extralegal strategies have acquired legitimacy.

The majority has reacted to the power of minorities in several ways: tokenism; coercion; co-optation; gerrymandering; divide and conquer; and socialization. To redress wrongs committed against minorities, the federal government has developed strategies of affirmative action. The late 1970s witnessed the beginning of a white reaction to the preferential treatment of minority members.

A system model of minority access to resources indicates the ways in which societal conditions affect demands for additional labor forces that can be satisfied by minority groups. This allows minorities (temporarily) to enter nontraditional occupations and to influence definitions of minority capabilities and future role allocations.

The system of stratification of minorities in this society has been sometimes described as a caste system. This conceptualization has been challenged, and perhaps it should be replaced by the metaphor of internal colonialism.

Parallel class structures have also been posited. The model of "ethclass" is a heuristic conceptualization of minority class structure.

Class models tend to assume an outcome of assimilation, whereas caste models generate a minority nationalism as an outcome. The former may be more descriptive of ethnic minorities, and the latter may be more appropriate for racial minorities. Finally, internal colonialism as a model has gained much currency as a heuristic and empirical formulation.

NOTES

1. These and all following statistics, unless otherwise noted, are from U.S. Department of Commerce, Bureau of the Census, *Statistical Abstracts of the United States: 1997,* 117th ed. (Washington, D.C.: Government Printing Office, 1997).
2. Ibid.
3. Melvin L Oliver and Thomas M. Shapiro, *Black Wealth/White Wealth: A New Perspective on Racial Inequality* (New York: Routledge, 1995), pp. 88 and 204.
4. *Statistical Abstracts.*
5. Mary C. Waters and Karl Eschbach, "Immigration and Racial Inequality in the United States," *Annual Review of Sociology* 21 (1995), pp. 419–46.
6. *Statistical Abstracts.*
7. Diana Pierce, "Women in Poverty," in *The American Promise: Equal Justice and Economic Opportunity,* A.I. Blaustein, ed. (New Brunswick, NJ: Transaction Books, 1982), pp. 7–32, and Lenore Weitzman, *The Divorce Revolution* (New York: The Free Press, 1985).
8. *Statistical Abstracts.*
9. *Statistical Abstracts.*
10. William Julius Wilson, *The Truly Disadvantaged: The Inner City, the Underclass, and Public Policy* (Chicago: The University of Chicago Press, 1987).
11. William Julius Wilson, *When Work Disappears: The World of the New Urban Poor* (New York: Alfred A. Knopf, 1996).
12. Douglas S. Massey and Nancy A. Denton, *American Apartheid: Segregation and the Making of the Underclass* (Cambridge, MA: Harvard University Press, 1993).
13. Everett C. Hughes, "Dilemmas and Contradictions of Status," *American Journal of Sociology* 50 (1945), pp. 353–59.
14. See Marvin E. Olsen, "Social and Political Participation of Blacks," *American Sociological Review* 35 (1970), pp. 682–97; Jeffrey Paige, "Political Orientation and Riot Participation," *American Sociological Review* 36 (1971), pp. 810–20; and Donald T. Warren, "Status Modality and Riot Behavior," *Sociological Quarterly* 12 (1971), pp. 350–68.
15. Two major problems in status consistency research have been: (1) lack of generic variables (i.e., consistency and inconsistency have been variously defined and operationalized); and (2) status inconsistency not necessarily being perceived by the individual. Without the experiential component and the resultant social psychological awareness, it is doubtful that the initial inconsistency would affect behavior. For a more detailed exposition see Leonard Broom, "Social Differentiation and Stratification," in *Sociology Today,* ed. Robert K. Merton, Leonard Broom, and Leonard S. Cottrell, Jr. (New York: Basic Books, 1959), pp. 429–41, and Kaare Svalastoga "Social Differentiation," in *Handbook of Modern Sociology,* ed. Robert E. L. Faris (Chicago: Rand McNally, 1964), pp. 530–75.
16. National Center for Education Statistics, *The Condition of Education 1995* (Washington, D.C., U.S. Department of Education, Office of Educational Research and Improvement, NCES #5–273).

17. M.D. LeCompte and A. G. Dworkin, *Giving Up on School: Student Dropouts and Teacher Burnouts* (Newbury Park, CA: Corwin/Sage, 1991).
18. Jonathan Kozol, *Savage Inequalities: Children in America's Schools* (New York: Crown, 1991).
19. Christopher Jencks et al., *Inequality* (New York: Basic Books, 1972).
20. The view held by Peter M. Blau and Otis Dudley Duncan in *The American Occupational Structure* (New York: Wiley, 1967) that one's position in the social structure is more a function of one's own educational achievements than one's parents' position in the social structure has received considerable challenge. See, for example, C. Hurn, *The Limits and Possibilities of Schooling* (Boston: Allyn and Bacon, 1993) and J. Matras, "Comparative Social Mobility," *Annual Review of Sociology* 6 (1980), pp. 401–431.
21. Jencks, et al., *Inequality.*
22. John S. Butler, "Inequality in the Military: An Examination of Promotion Time for Black and White Enlisted Men," *American Sociological Review* 41 (1976), pp. 807–18.
23. A. G. Dworkin, "The Changing Demography of Public School Teachers: Some Implications for Faculty Turnover in Urban Areas," *Sociology of Education* 53 (1980), pp. 65–73.
24. Ibid.
25. A.G. Dworkin, *Teacher Burnout in the Public Schools: Structural Causes and Consequences for Children* (Albany, NY: State University of New York Press, 1987).
26. Leo Grebler, Joan W. Moore, and Ralph C. Guzman, *The Mexican-American People* (New York: Free Press, 1970), p. 214.
27. Edna Bonacich, "A Theory of Ethnic Antagonism: The Split Labor Market," *American Sociological Review* 37 (1972), pp. 547–59.
28. For a summary of his results see Emory Bogardus, "Comparing Racial Distance in Ethiopia, South Africa, and the United States," *Sociology and Social Research* 52 (1968), pp. 149–56.
29. Gerhard E. Lenski, "Status Crystallization: A Non-Vertical Dimension of Social Status," *American Sociological Review* 19 (1954), pp. 405–13.
30. Gopal Sharan Sinha and Ramesh Chandra Sinha, "Exploration in Caste Stereotypes," *Social Forces* 46 (1967), pp. 42–47.
31. Stanley Lieberson, "Stratification and Ethnic Groups" *Sociological Inquiry* 40 (1970), pp. 172–81.
32. "Race men" are individuals of their race (or gender) who excel in an area (occupation) previously barred to members of their group. By their excellence they make it possible for others like them to gain entry into these areas. Jackie Robinson was such an individual. He broke the color bar against blacks in major league baseball.
33. National Opinion Research Center, *General Social Surveys, 1972–1996: Cumulative Codebook* (Chicago: National Opinion Research Center, University of Chicago, 1997).

34. Terence K. Hopkins, "Bureaucratic Authority: The Convergence of Weber and Barnard," in *Complex Organizations,* ed. Amitai Etzioni (New York: Holt, 1964), p. 87.
35. Rosalind J. Dworkin, "A Woman's Report," *The Minority Report,* 2nd ed., (New York: Holt, Rinehart, and Winston, 1982), pp. 375–400.
36. *Statistical Abstracts.*
37. Ibid.
38. Robert K. Merton, *Social Theory and Social Structure* (New York: Free Press, 1968).
39. Jerome Jerome H. Skolnick, *The Politics of Protest* (New York: Simon and Schuster, 1969).
40. J. Kenneth Benson, "Militant Ideologies and Organizational Contexts," in Ibid. Dworkin, ed., *Symposium on Violent Confrontation,* pp. 328–39.
41. See H. Edward Ransford, "Isolation, Powerlessness, and Violence: A Study of Attitudes and Participation in the Watts Riot," *American Journal of Sociology* 73 (1968), pp. 581–91, and Robert A. Wilson, "Anomia and Militancy Among Urban Negroes," in Dworkin, ed., *Symposium on Violent Confrontation,* pp. 369–86.
42. See Paige, "Political Orientation"; Warren, "Status Modality"; P. Gore and J. Rotter, "A Personality Correlate of Social Action," *Journal of Personality* 31 (1963): 58–64; J. Forward and J. Williams, "Internal-External Control and Black Militancy," *Journal of Social Issues* 26 (1970), pp. 75–92. Robert Blauner, *Racial Oppression in America* (New York: Harper, 1972), and others have shown that ghetto revolt or riot behavior are in fact revolutions against colonialism.
43. James S. Coleman et al., *Equality of Educational Opportunity* (Washington, D.C.: Government Printing Office, 1966).
44. Raymond W. Mack, ed., *Our Children's Burden* (New York: Random House, 1968).
45. Rosabeth Moss Kanter, *Men and Women of the Corporation* (New York: Basic Books, 1977).
46. A. G. Dworkin, J. S. Chafetz, and R. J. Dworkin, "The Effects of Tokenism on Work Alienation among Urban Public School Teachers," *Work and Occupations* 13 (1986), pp. 399–420.
47. Edna Bonacich, "A Theory of Ethnic Antagonism: The Split Labor Market," *American Sociological Review* 37 (1972), pp. 547–559.
48. Janet S. Chafetz, Anthony Gary Dworkin, and Rosalind J. Dworkin, "New Migrants to the Rat Race: A Systems Model for Changes in Work Force Allocation and Role Expectations, by Gender, Race and Ethnicity," mimeographed (University of Houston, 1975).
49. Janet S. Chafetz and Anthony Gary Dworkin, *Female Revolt: Women's Movements in World and Historical Perspective* (Totowa, NJ: Rowman and Allanheld, 1986).
50. W. Lloyd Warner, "American Caste and Class," *American Journal of Sociology* 42 (1936), pp. 234–37.

51. John Dollard, *Caste and Class in a Southern Town* (New York: Harper, 1949).
52. W. A. Davis, B. B. Gardner, and M. R. Gardner, *Deep South: A Social Anthropological Study* (Chicago: University of Chicago Press, 1941).
53. William Julius Wilson, *The Declining Significance of Race: Blacks and Changing American Institutions* (Chicago: University of Chicago Press, 1978).
54. Ruby Jo Reeves Kennedy, "Single or Triple Melting Pot? Intermarriage Trends in New Haven, 1870–1940," *American Journal of Sociology* 49 (1944), pp. 331–39; idem, "Single or Triple Melting Pot? Intermarriage in New Haven, 1870–1950," *American Journal of Sociology* 58 (1953), pp. 56–59.
55. Will Herberg, *Protestant-Catholic-Jew* (Garden City, NY: Doubleday, 1955).
56. Helen Mayer Hacker, "Women as a Minority Group," *Social Forces* 30 (1951), pp. 60–69.
57. Carole Andreas, *Sex and Caste in America* (Englewood Cliffs, NJ: Prentice-Hall, 1971).
58. Oliver C. Cox, *Caste, Class, and Race: A Study in Social Dynamics* (Garden City, NY: Doubleday, 1948).
59. Robert Blauner, "Internal Colonialism and Ghetto Revolt" *Social Problems* 16 (1969), pp. 393–408; idem, *Racial Oppression in America.*
60. Stokely Carmichael and Charles Hamilton, *Black Power* (New York: Random House, 1967).
61. George Eaton Simpson and J. Milton Yinger, *Racial and Cultural Minorities,* 3rd ed. (New York: Harper, 1958).
62. W. Lloyd Warner, Marcia Meeker, and Kenneth Eells, *Social Class in America* (New York: Harper, 1960 [1949]), and August B. Hollingshead, *Elmtown's Youth* (New York: Wiley, 1949).
63. Gunnar Myrdal, *An American Dilemma* (New York: Harper, 1944); Cox, *Caste, Class, and Race;* and John F. Cuber and William F. Kenkel, *Social Stratification in the United States* (New York: Appleton, 1954).
64. Floyd Hunter, *Community Power Structure* (Chapel Hill, N.C.: University of North Carolina Press, 1953); St. Clair Drake and Horace R. Cayton, *Black Metropolis* (New York: Harcourt, 1945); and M. Elaine Burgess, *Negro Leadership in a Southern City* (Chapel Hill, NC: University of North Carolina Press, 1962).
65. Milton M. Gordon, *Assimilation in American Life: The Role of Race, Religion, and National Origins* (New York: Oxford University Press, 1964).
66. See Erik Olin Wright and Luca Perrone, "Marxist Class Categories and Income Inequality," *American Sociological Review* 42 (1977), pp. 32–55, and John D. Stephens, "Class Formation and Class Consciousness: A Theoretical and Empirical Analysis with Reference to Britain and Sweden," *British Journal of Sociology* 30 (1979), pp. 389–414.
67. Wright and Perrone, ibid.
68. See Blauner, "Internal Colonialism"; idem, *Racial Oppression in America:* Carmichael and Hamilton, *Black Power;* Jean W. Moore, "Colonialism: The Case of the Mexican Americans," *Social Problems* 17 (1970), pp. 463–71; Albert

Memmi, *The Colonizer and the Colonized* (Boston: Beacon, 1967); and Harold Cruse, *Rebellion or Revolution* (New York: Morrow, 1968).

69. Moore, "Colonialism."

70. Sidney M. Wilhelm, *Who Needs the Negro?* (Cambridge, Mass.: Schenkman, 1970).

Suggested Readings

Blauner, Robert. *Racial Oppression in America.* New York: Harper, 1972.

Blauner, Robert. *Black Lives, White Lives: Three Decades of Race Relations in America.* Berkeley, Calif.: University of California Press, 1989.

Carmichael, Stokely, and Charles Hamilton. *Black Power.* New York: Random House, 1967.

Chafetz, Janet S., and Anthony Gary Dworkin. *Female Revolt: Women's Movements in World and Historical Perspective.* Totowa, NJ: Rowman and Allanheld, 1986.

Oliver, Melvin L., and Thomas M. Shapiro. *Black Wealth/White Wealth: A New Perspective on Racial Inequality.* New York: Routledge, 1995.

Massey, Douglas S., and Nancy A. Denton. *American Apartheid: Segregation and the Making of the Underclass.* Cambridge, MA: Harvard University Press, 1993.

Reskin, Barbara and Melvin M. Tumin. *Social Stratification.* Englewood Cliffs, N.J.: Prentice-Hall, 1967.

Waters, Mary C., and Karl Eschbach. "Immigration and Racial Inequality in the United States," *Annual Review of Sociology* 21(1995), pp. 419–46.

Wilson, William Julius. *The Declining Significance of Race: Blacks and Changing American Institutions.* Chicago: University of Chicago Press, 1978.

Wilson, William Julius. *The Truly Disadvantaged: The Inner City, the Underclass, and Public Policy.* Chicago: The University of Chicago Press, 1987.

Wilson, William Julius. *When Work Disappears: The World of the New Urban Poor.* New York: Alfred A. Knopf, 1996.

CHAPTER 4

THE ORGANIZATIONAL DIMENSION

In a complex society such as ours, people are surrounded by organizations. We act in them; we react to them; and they react upon us. Members of minority groups are actors in organizations, not only as individuals, but also in their capacity as members of minority groups. The organizational dimension has two global elements: those formal and informal groupings created by the dominant society and those formal and informal groupings created by minorities to react to or to seek protection from the majority.

Organizations are social units (or human groupings) deliberately constructed and reconstructed to seek specific goals. . . . Organizations are characterized by (1) divisions of labor, power, and communications responsibilities . . . (2) the presence of one or more power centers which control the concerted efforts of the organization and direct them towards its goals . . . (3) the substitution of personnel, i.e., unsatisfactory persons can be removed and others assigned their tasks.[1]

Examples of some of the organizations with which minorities are concerned include the police, the school system, the health care system, welfare agencies, the military, corporations and other bureaucracies, churches, civil rights groups such as the National Association for the Advancement of Colored People, the Congress of Racial Equality, the Anti-Defamation League of B'nai B'rith, the National Organization of Women (NOW), the Black Panther party, the Black Muslims, the United Farm Workers of America, La Raza Unita Party, the League of United Latin American Citizens, the Japanese American Citizens League, the Consolidated Chinese Benevolent Association, the Arab

American Anti-Discrimination Committee, Native American tribal councils, the Lambda Legal Defense Fund, ACT UP, Aspira, and a multitude of others.

MINORITY EXPERIENCES WITH MAJORITY ORGANIZATIONS

Over the years the senior author has asked Hispanic and African American students in his classes to identify the white organizations that cause the most problems for them. While as students they were most likely to comment that it was "the university," as minority group members it was not uncommon for individuals to respond with "all of them." The majority of individuals, however, enumerated such organizations as the public school system, the police, public welfare agencies, banks, realty agencies, retail establishments, health care institutions, and organizations where they were employed. If you were to ask a member of any other minority to specify which organizations cause problems, a similar list would probably be encountered. The following organizations have been selected because of the typical problems they present.

The Schools

The public schools perform two basic functions in society. First, by their instruction they socialize individuals to desire to perform the myriad tasks necessary in a complex society, and transmit to individuals the culture of the majority, including its values and assumptions. Second, the schools create a trained labor pool and, through their system of testing and counseling, allocate individuals to positions within the social structure, thereby maintaining traditional role definitions within the labor force. This latter function has been central to what conflict theory perspective defines as "Reproduction Theory" in the sociology of education.[2] Schools are seen as serving to reproduce the existing class structure of society by preserving privilege for the children of higher socieoeconomic groups and disadvantage for lower socioeconomic groups.

In the past three to four decades schools have also been asked to eradicate and ameliorate quality of performance gaps between the minorities and the majority. The charge that schools should provide equality of educational opportunity raises the ironic fact that schools also tend to perpetuate inequality of opportunity. The educational system is geared toward middle-class white Anglo-Saxon Protestant children. In the 1960s, Poverty Program projects designed to bridge the gap between the minorities (generally those minority-group members who are poor) and the majority were funded to school systems that had originally created the labels and stigmas and helped to perpetuate the gap itself. Federal programs since the 1970s have had as a goal the narrowing and elimination of the achievement gap between minority and low-income children and that of the majority. The gap in achievement is not due to differentials in aspirations among groups. One of the conclusions of the Coleman and Campbell report[3] was that although most minority children had goals as high as those of majority children, they never were taught how to attain them. For example, school counselors and teachers advise minority students less often than they do members of the majority on how to apply for and get into college.

Colin Greer observed:

> The great myth on which our traditional faith in schools is based has been that mobility and social improvement were its goals. Instead, immobility and stratification have been reflected and reinforced by schools and their measures of intelligence.[4]

Samuel Bowles and Herbert Gintis[5] have argued persuasively that the educational system replicates the class structure and corporate system of capitalist societies. That is, schools prepare a labor force to assume the tasks demanded by the corporations. Some schools, dominated by low income and minority youth, teach the skills of punctuality needed to maintain the assembly line. Other schools, populated by majority and high-income youth, teach the skills of independent thought and personnel management necessary for higher levels of the corporation. Thus the school system operates as an arm of the stratification system, ensuring that some get the opportunity to do important work and attain property, prestige, and power while relegating others to menial tasks and relative deprivations. This relegation is based not on individual merits but on group membership. Cicourel and Kitsuse[6] discovered that school personnel counseled students into college preparatory or trade-technical courses on the basis of students' social class and assumptions of their parents' ability to pay for their education. In a study conducted for the state of Texas, Schulman and his colleagues[7] indicated that teachers interpreted high aspirations of Mexican American students as fantasies and similar aspirations of Anglo students as realistic, and counseled their students accordingly. Maldonado and Byrne[8] reported this same teacher proclivity in their study of Mexican American education in Utah.

Differential counseling represents only one form of adverse treatment experienced by minorities in the school system. In the classroom, majority teachers have been shown to define minority children as less competent, to praise them less often, to assign lower grades to them and seldom to encourage minority students to be full, active participants in the classroom. The Civil Rights Commission[9] has reported that minority-group teachers sometimes tend to adopt the majority interpretation of minority children's abilities and motives. Minority teachers often pay less attention to the minority-group children than to the majority-group children in their classrooms. This is particularly disheartening because one of the expectations regarding the desegregation of public school faculty was that minority teachers would provide minority students with positive role models to be emulated.

Federal redress of school segregation has been categorical. That is, the federal government has established guidelines and mandates that shift whole categories of children and teachers from school to school in an attempt to effect desegregation. Beginning in the 1970s, the federal courts supported metropolitan desegregation. The metropolitan plans involve the busing of children between school districts. Typically involved are large, predominantly minority urban schools and a series of smaller, predominantly majority suburban schools. Court rulings justify the practice in situations where there have been *de jure* (by law) housing patterns that have excluded minorities and where the education of the children will not be substantially disrupted. However, the success of metropolitan desegregation remains in doubt because of the probability of white flight to private schools and the growing opposition to busing by the federal government, especially during the Reagan and Bush administrations. Today, because of the extent of white flight to the suburbs, most urban school districts are predominantly minority with a large percentage of the students on free or reduced lunch status. The census of 1990 and estimates for the census of 2000 have also indicated that low-income students are moving to the suburbs, too.

The quality of education for many low-income students in urban schools, the majority of whom come from minority groups, is inferior to that offered to higher income students in the suburbs, most of whom come from the majority group. As Jonathan Kozol documented in *Savage Inequalities,*[10] many inner-city schools are characterized by inadequate and dated textbooks, limited school supplies, few computers, and as Dworkin noted, burned-out teachers.[11] The National Center for Education Statistics reported that low-income minority students in inner-city schools are more likely to be taught science and mathematics by a teacher who is not certified in those subject areas and did not major or minor in those subject areas in college than a majority-group student in the middle-class suburbs.[12] Inner-city schools are also less likely to offer advanced science and math courses to their students than suburban schools, in part because there is a shortage of teachers able to offer the courses, in part because the students have not been given the necessary prerequisite skills to succeed in those courses, and in part because the courses would not make minimum enrollment criteria if they were offered. The lack of advanced courses, especially in science and math, handicaps college success and access the high-paying technical jobs.

Compounding the picture of inner-city minority schools is the level of hopelessness among the students. Significant research findings have pointed to the cultural myth endorsed by some African American students in poverty-ridden schools. One version of the myth discussed by Ogbu and Fordham is that passing one's courses means "acting white."[13] Another suggests that while education may be the route toward upward mobility for most people, it does not work for African Americans and Hispanics.[14] The National Center for Education Statistics decried the differentials in school dropout rates by ethnic groups: 7.9 percent for whites, 13.6 for African Americans, and 27.5 for Hispanics.[15] Further, high school dropouts are more than twice as likely to be unemployed or underemployed than high school graduates.

There is some evidence that private and parochial schools produce higher academic achievement than do the public schools, and that such schools are less likely to be segregated by social class and race than public schools.[16] Such schools do not tolerate disruptive students, mandate considerable parental involvement in their children's education, have strict and fair discipline as seen by the students, require more homework, and mandate more difficult courses for their students. Many of the highest achievers in the study were from the parochial schools, schools that also benefit from having what has been termed a "functional community," in which the administration, teachers, parents, and students share a common set of values about education and discipline. However, private and parochial schools, by their very nature, are selective and possess the ability to remove disruptive students permanently. They do not provide a good test case for solving the problems of inner-city schools.

Some conservative groups has proposed voucher plans, whereby children in low-performing, high poverty schools may be sent by their parents to a higher-performing private or public schools, with the state and local tax dollars following that child to the selected schools. However, the potential receiving school is not obligated to accept the child if the school has reached enrollment capacity, or if the child is too low-performing. The high-performing private and public schools, often being in high demand, are unlikely to be able or willing to accept many of the inner-city students. Further, the population of inner-city schools that would most likely take advantage of the voucher plan are among the highest test scorers at those schools. They also have parents who are most likely to be active in the life of the inner-city campus. Their departure would further weaken the public schools. Dworkin and his colleagues have recently found that children in poverty who attend suburban schools are likely to do worse on standardized tests than their counterparts in the urban schools. This is because (1) the suburban teachers often do not know how to teach a student who comes from poverty and (2) several suburban school districts have a mandate from the majority of the parents and local voters to address the needs of middle-class students, not the special needs of low-income students who do not bring to school an abundance of economic and educational resources.[17] The conservative agenda for vouchers is not principally intended to aid minority and low-income student; it is also to assist middle- and upper-class families already in private schools by enabling their students to be subsidized by the public sector funds. That is, they too would want to receive a voucher to continue to attend the private school of their choice.

Other areas of debate in education that affect minority groups include the issues of bilingual education and the extent to which public education should be offered to the children of undocumented workers, especially from Mexico and Central America. Bilingual education involves the initial instruction of non-English-speaking students in their native tongue until some time at which they can make the transition into English instruction. Groups that oppose bilingual education argue that it retards learning development, although they often mean that it retards assimilation into the dominant culture. Bilingual education programs vary widely, and evidence of their success in teaching reading is mixed, often dependent upon how well they are implemented. Children who hear their native language spoken at home and in their neighborhoods are more likely to learn to read effectively if they are also taught in that same language. California voters have recently outlawed bilingual education effective in the 1998–99 academic year. Other states are considering the issue, too. To a considerable extent the public sentiment against bilingual education is guided in part by fear of people who are different. In other words, sometimes prejudice and xenophobia enter into the argument.

In 1994, California voters passed Proposition 187, which makes it illegal for the state to spend public money on the education of illegal immigrant children and requires to schools to report to federal authorities children who are thought to be in the country illegally. The voter-passed initiative is currently being held in abeyance until federal court rulings determine its constitutionality. Many majority-group voters are fearful that the state has become predominantly minority and feel that they must fight to retain their dominance. Issues of the undocumented and their education are covered in detail in Chapter 12 by Rodriguez and Hagan.

Because of the differential treatment of their children in the schools, minorities have focused their discontents on the following issues.

1. Local versus districtwide control of school policy and educational content.
2. The use of standardized achievement tests to determine promotion and graduation.
3. Hiring practices.
4. Appropriateness of bilingual education.
5. Minority studies programs.
6. Desegregation guidelines and busing (the latter being an issue of considerable confrontation with majority parents).
7. Career counseling.
8. Intelligence testing.
9. Styles of discipline.
10. Truancy and dropouts.
11. Choice of textbooks and teaching materials.
12. Teacher competency and teacher commitment to inner-city children.
13. Control of gangs and drugs in the schools.

The Police

In order for society to exist there need to be norms and rules of conduct to regulate the interaction among individuals. In simple societies the regulation may be accomplished informally by every member of the system. But as a society becomes more complex, the process of social control becomes more specialized. Norms become codified into laws, the enforcement of which becomes the task of an agency with the legitimate authority to use coercion and violence. This agency is the police.

Police officers tend to be recruited from lower-class and working-class populations.[18] Such populations are usually identified as being more prejudiced toward minority groups. Furthermore, the role of police officer necessitates that the incumbent expect the worst in people and react immediately to that expectation.

Reported crime tends to be significantly higher in minority business and majority residential areas, so the police are likely to be concentrated in minority areas. Furthermore, the police generally initiate interaction with minorities, whereas majorities more frequently initiate their interaction with the police. Majorities tend to call the police; the police tend to call on minorities. Therefore, minority-group members see more police violence, of which they are most likely to be the targets. When minorities are residentially segregated, as in the case of African Americans, observation and receipt of police-initiated violence tends to be uniform across social classes.[19] Because middle- and lower-class African Americans live together in the same ghettos and are subject to homogeneous experiences with the police, their perceptions of the police are inclined to be more consistent than those of whites of varying social classes.

Recently, Klinger has raised a significant issue in the assessment of police arrest behaviors. He has noted that during the 1960s through the 1980s social researchers have focused upon extra-legal issues (such as demeanor) in determining whether there was an arrest, but that whether there was evidence of a crime was not controlled for in police arrest model building. By introducing data on the severity of the crime, Klinger [20] has been able to show predominant reliance on prejudice is not adequate in explaining much arrest behavior of the police. Other factors enter into the arrest equation. Smith, Visher, and Davidson[21] analyzed arrest records of police officers. They found support for selectivity in arrest by the police with more African Americans being arrested proportionately than other groups, especially when there are no complainants. However, they note that the higher arrest rate for African Americans is partly due to the fact that the police spend more time patrolling in low-income neighborhoods than in higher income neighborhoods and that such low income neighborhoods have higher percentages of African American residents. They do note that where there is a complainant an arrest is more likely to occur if the complainant is white and the accused is African American.

There still remains, however, both a belief on the part of minorities, supported by such experience, and data on differential enforcement, that minority group members are more likely to have unpleasant experiences with the police than majority group members. This belief is supported by the findings of Feagin and Sikes,[22] who documented that the African American middle class is more likely than the white middle class to experience slurs, slights, and suspicions. They also have to spend more time, energy, and other resources to obtain redress from such racist practices.

The police, as Galliher[23] observes, are not the creators of social policy; they only perform the tasks assigned them by dominant classes who make the laws. Minorities are perceptive in their recognition that the police are symbols of the social order that relegates them to less property, prestige, and power. Majorities make laws partly to ensure the continuity of their way of life and the stratification system that maintains them as majorities. Stanley Lieberson[24] posited in his theory of majority-minority relations that in the battle to maintain a social order compatible with one's culture, majorities and minorities conflict over institutions. The institution of policing is the focus of numerous battles. These include:

1. Citizen's review boards of police activities.
2. Recruitment practices of the police (more minority recruitment).
3. Police procedures for dealing with minority-group members accused of a crime, including both physical brutality and verbal abuse.
4. Differential enforcement of laws (minorities more often arrested for acts for which the majority is not arrested).
5. As a corollary of differential enforcement of the law, differential adjudication of offenses by the courts (minorities go to prison, whereas a member of the majority may only get a suspended sentence, a fine, or an acquittal).

The friction between police and minorities has been intense. So intense that police-minority misunderstandings, overlapped upon economic frustrations, have been the precipitating events in many of the urban riots, including the 1980 Miami riot. The riots in Los Angeles in 1995 following the acquittal of the police officers who beat Rodney King, an African American, represent a clear example of the response of groups to perceived police violence and the failure of the justice system to serve minorities and the poor.

Health Care

There are clear and dramatic differences between minority and majority groups in their access to the health care system and its consequences. Among those under retirement age, access to health care is dependent primarily upon private health insurance. While low-income individuals may qualify for Medicaid (state health insurance for the poor), the extent of coverage for others is largely a function of employer benefits. The unemployed and the part-time and seasonally employed characteristically do not qualify for benefits, nor can these individuals usually afford to purchase their own insurance coverage. In 1995, while over 73.8 percent of white (non-Hispanics) had private health insurance, only 50.5 percent of African Americans in the United States had private health insurance, and merely 42.9 percent of Hispanics had such coverage. If state Medicaid insurance that is available to those in poverty is added in, then 85.8 percent of whites had private or public health insurance, while 79.0 percent of African Americans and 66.7 percent of Hispanics had health coverage.[25] Minority differences remain, even after subtracting the effects of income.[26] Access to health care also means children's access to immunizations against childhood diseases. Here too, race makes a difference. In 1994, a total of 90.6 percent of white children between 19 and 35 months of age had received immunizations against diphtheria, tetanus, and pertussis, while 84.4 percent of African American and 87.9 percent of all other groups (primarily Hispanics, who are much underimmunized and Asian Americans, who are immunized at about the white rate) had been immunized.[27]

With differences in resources for health care, the nature of care received varies. Whites have a greater number of patient visits per year than do African Americans, for all age categories and gender groupings.[28] Furthermore, while whites tend more often to be treated during office visits or telephone consultations, African Americans utilize emergency room services at twice the rate of whites, and often for nonemergency type care.

Limited access to the health care system, as well as poor nutrition among the economically disadvantaged, and greater crime victimization are among the factors resulting in differential death rates and life expectancies. Whereas a white male born in 1994 may expect to live 73.2 years, non-white males may expect to live only 67.5 years, and African American males only to age 64.9 years. Although females have longer life expectancies than males across all ethnic/racial groups, there remain differences here as well. White females born in 1994 have a life expectancy of 79.6 years, while nonwhite females have an expectancy of 75.8 years, and African American females only to age 74.1 years.[29]

Nowhere in medicine has there been a greater history of the interjection of racist and sexist-inspired beliefs into diagnosis and treatment of patients than in psychiatry. In the past, the identification of symptoms relied upon observance of behavior and unstructured diagnostic interviews, encouraged the intrusion of prejudices into the arena of mental health/illness. Labels such as "drapetomania" that assigned a psychiatric diagnosis to runaway slaves in the nineteenth century is perhaps the most dramatic, but by no means, the only example of this. The overprescription of tranquilizers to discontented housewives and the limiting of the insight-oriented "talking therapies" to white, affluent, educated patients are also historic examples of how the subjectivity of clinical practice resulted in unequal and often injurious treatment of individuals suffering from a range of emotional and mental disorders. Nevertheless, patients from different cultural groups do tend to present with different symptoms for a given problem. For example, individuals raised in traditional Chinese culture tend to somatosize depression and anxiety more than do others, perhaps because of the great stigma attached to mental illness.[30]

Technologies are emerging that are encouraging the use of more objective measurement of mental illness. Newer theories of brain dysfunction have led to the search for objective, organically based diagnostic techniques, such as Positron Emission Tomography (PET) scans. More immediately accessible are a variety of structured and systematic diagnostic interview protocols developed over the last twenty years.[31] Using one such instrument, the National Institutes of Mental Health sponsored a large survey, The Epidemiological Catchment Area Project, to establish the prevalence of mental disorder in the United States. Across three sites of the study, there were no appreciable differences found among racial groups in the life time rates of diagnosable mental illness.[32] However, major differences have been found between males and females in the incidence of some disorders, including major depression, panic disorder, and drug and alcohol dependence.

Minority discontent with the health care system has focused upon:

1. Differentials in access to treatment and quality of treatment.
2. Differentials in access to health insurance, especially for disorders where the resultant behavior does not pose a physical threat to others.
3. Medical research inattention to diseases that have a higher or exclusive incidence in minority populations (e.g., sickle cell anemia and, earlier, AIDS in the gay and African American communities).

Governmental Welfare Agencies

For sixty years the U.S. government had maintained a program of Aid to Families with Dependent Children (AFDC). The intent was to provide a minimum safety net under low income children to reduce the most ravaging effects of poverty. A frequent complaint about the welfare system was that it encouraged dependency on continued welfare and disrupted families. However, the welfare reform push led to a major revamping of the system of welfare by Congress in 1996. This change in the welfare system was in response to concerns about intergenerational welfare dependency, public stereotypes of the welfare Cadillac (welfare recipients who were affluent enough to own an expensive car), and concern over the federal deficit. In 1994, the Republicans offered a "Contract with America," which called for less government and less government spending. In the 1994 general election, Republicans captured both houses of Congress and began to implement welfare reform, among other things. Thus, this section examines the welfare system before and after the 1996 changes.

Welfare before the 1996 Law. The poverty resulting from differential and pejorative treatment implies dilapidated and deteriorated housing, inadequate health care, and substandard employment and education. These conditions are pervasive across slums of different hues, whether they be "Soulside," "Chinatown," Spanish Harlem," "*colonias*" or "*barrios,*" or a reservation. Accompanying poverty and the poor were a multitude of governmental agencies whose official function was to ameliorate, rehabilitate, direct, correct, consult, refer, or help one to adapt and cope with the exigencies of minority status. The agencies, however, brought to the poor a double-edged sword. In attempting to end poverty they frequently perpetuated it. The massiveness of the federal, state, and large urban programs invited great bureaucratic structures that were impersonal and dehumanized the clientele they were created to serve.

By placing a ceiling on supplemental personal income, agencies discouraged many welfare recipients from surrendering their welfare checks to accept a low-paying job in industry. Not only would employment in a low-paying job (often too low to support one's family) be economically unwise, but the implications to self-esteem could be as disastrous as welfare itself. In American society one is measured by what one does and how much one gets for doing it. Low pay tells the world two things: that the person's employer thinks so little about him or her as to offer minuscule wages for the person's labor, and the worker thinks so little about himself or herself as to accept the employer's definition.[33] Furthermore, there were restrictions on the use of welfare payments and food stamps such that the individual, in accepting governmental support, surrendered autonomy as a consumer. Perhaps consumer education could have been a viable solution, rather than restrictions that foster dependency and treated adults as children.

Welfare agencies also made the assumption that a mother's place was at home with her children. Thus they discouraged women from seeking employment by refusing to facilitate day care. Since a large portion of a woman's salary might have to be spent on private day care for her children, she often found it economically impossible to accept employment.

Aid to families with dependent children (AFDC) required that the recipient mother not have a spouse living with her. Since her spouse may have been unable to find work (especially during recessions), or to find work that paid enough to support his family, he was permanently or sporadically driven from the home. This produced unusual and sometimes unstable family relations, and a hectic family life at best.[34]

Many social service projects have actually been pilot projects based on short-term grants and minimal funds. Agencies, in order to demonstrate high success rates or favorable cost/benefit rations and thus gain continuation funds, sought out individuals who were likely to be successes, leaving the "hard-core" unemployed or poor to subsist on their own. Other programs, because of their short-term funding, could not render full service to their clientele. A dramatic illustration of this sort occurred in a large city in the Southwest. According to a city official, a dental program for the elderly was instituted. Dental checkups were given, largely to minority-group members who were indigent; where excessive tooth decay was found, all of their teeth were extracted. Before the individuals could be issued dentures, funds for the program dried up, and dozens of elderly people were left worse off than before the social service program attempted to serve them.

Implementation of federal revenue sharing,[35] rather than facilitating local government in providing social services, actually hampered it. In some instances programs provided by the cities that were previously funded directly by other federal sources (libraries, zoos, sewers, streets) were placed in a common pool with local social welfare projects, and thus all competed for these funds. Given the tendency for voters of the majority group to be hostile toward welfare programs and welfare recipients, politicians were pressured into diverting these funds toward services desired by the middle and upper classes and away from the poor.

Welfare Beginning with the 1996 Law. Congress passed and the president signed the Personal Responsibility and Work Opportunity Reconciliation Act (PRWORA) in 1996. The act included a Temporary Assistance to Needy Families (TANF) provision that supplanted Aid to Families with Dependent Children. As Thomas Corbett of the University of Wisconsin's Institute for Research on Poverty noted:

> Key provisions of the act convert public assistance to poor families with children from an open, individual entitlement, in which the fiscal cost of providing cash support is shared by the federal and state governments, to an entitlement to states, in which future assistance is time-limited and the federal contribution is a fixed or capped amount ("block grant").[36]

States are permitted to determine the criteria for assistance, and large numbers of the needy have been deleted from the welfare rolls. Under the new law the temporary assistance has a limit of two years and a lifetime benefit of five years. The act requires heads of households to obtain work within two years (longer if no child care is available for their preschool children). Further, unmarried teen mothers are required to live with an adult and remain in school. The act permits states to limit Medicaid benefits and welfare payments to low income immigrants, and can even deny benefits to legal immigrants who have not become citizens.

While the program is expected to save the federal government billions of dollars, primarily through the reduction of the number of people eligible for food stamps, and is supposed to end welfare dependency by fostering educational attainment and employment for the poor, there are many people who will fall between the cracks. The welfare system is not without its critics. As William Julius Wilson has observed in *The Truly Disadvantaged* and *When*

Work Disappears,[37] changes in the labor market structure have caused jobs to vanish in the inner city, heightening poverty levels. Many of the low-skill jobs have migrated to the Third World. It is doubtful that the job training programs will raise the skills of enough poor people high enough to make them competitive in an increasingly "credentialist," high-technology society. If the employment gained by mothers with young children pays too poorly to permit them to afford day care, their plight and that of their children will be worse. Too few companies offer childcare for their employees, and even fewer offer such care for their lowest paid employees. Thus, while many poor may have reluctantly chosen welfare over work because the work was impossible to obtain or too costly in terms of child care under the old system, as Christopher Jencks noted, the current system may lead to nonexistent jobs and no welfare benefits. The psychological result of the loss of job opportunities has been described by Cornell West in *Race Matters* as *nihilism,* or ". . . the profound sense of psychological depression, personal worthlessness, and social despair so widespread in black America."[38]

In response to the conditions of the welfare agencies as perceived by the minority groups, issues of conflict have focused upon:

1. Neighborhood or localized control of welfare strategies and programs.
2. Location of welfare facilities.
3. Debureaucratization of welfare agencies.
4. Collection and immoderate use of confidential, personal information by welfare agencies.
5. Recruitment and training of social workers and social agency employees.
6. Public financing of voluntary abortions.
7. Child care options for the poor.
8. The vanishing labor market in central cities.

We would be belaboring the issue if we enumerated other examples of minority experiences with majority organizations. Minorities have had similar experiences with credit organizations in trying to secure consumer and business loans, with the realty industry in obtaining housing, with unions, with the military, and elsewhere. In each of these organizations the complaints have been similar. Minorities demand that they be treated as equals, that they not be subjected to dehumanizing bureaucratization, that they gain a share of control over the agencies which regulate and rule their lives, and that they be granted equal opportunities in being hired and recruited into the organizations.

Minority Organizations

Minority-group members, especially those with long histories of experience with social service agencies and other majority institutions, have developed techniques for coping with those agencies. In fact, many have learned how to work the system extremely well. This puts some minorities at a relative advantage over majority members who might occasionally find themselves in need of welfare. A medical sociologist[39] tells about a welfare mother in Florida who came upon a technique for gaining immediate service in public health clinics. She borrows neighborhood children—all of them toddlers—to bring with her. The sight of a dozen climbing, crawling, crying children in a waiting room usually compels the nurses to arrange that she be seen by the doctors without delay.

Another coping mechanism is extended familism. The presence of several generations of kinsmen or of many families of kinsmen living either in the same household or in adjoining households provides a functional alternative to social security and unemployment insurance. Not only will the old be cared for, but they can also provide babysitting services, counsel, and social support for the other family members. Further, the mutual interdependence of several nuclear families or several households increases the probability that at any one time there will be at least one wage earner present. When one member loses a job, there are other kinsmen to help. When a group cannot afford insurance premiums, extended familism and close kinship provides a viable and sensible alternative. Burma,[40] Sexton,[41] and Lewis[42] have each reported such mechanisms in the Puerto Rican and Chicano barrios.

Minority groups have also devised less individualistic, more organized techniques for coping with differential and pejorative treatment—for meeting majority power with minority power. We shall enumerate three forms of these organized techniques. The first are culture-maintaining organizations, which function to ensure cultural survival and provide emotional support. The second technique creates specifically issue- or problem-oriented organizations, including such areas as economics, self-help, and self-defense. The third involves more generalized civil rights and liberation organizations. The first two may be patterned after majority organizational counterparts and may exist because majorities have excluded minorities from those specific organizations. Groups of the third type are designed to change the majority institutions, beliefs, and behaviors while providing identities for minorities. All are inexorably connected with minority survival and minority success.

Culture-Maintaining Organizations

This category includes numerous organizations whose main purposes are to sustain the culture—the way of life—of a minority group embedded in a somewhat alien majority environment. These organizations also provide escape temporarily from the ill treatment outside. Many immigrant minorities, even those most nearly assimilated, still maintain this type of organization. The Sons of Italy, B'nai B'rith, and the Japanese-American Citizen's League are only three out of scores of examples.

Organized religion also performs culture-maintaining functions. The Roman Catholic church, the Jewish synagogue, the Buddhist temple, and the storefront Baptist church each help their respective groups to sustain at least the religious aspects of their culture. They also provide a large measure of emotional support for their members.

Many have accused religions not only of sustaining minority culture, but also of supporting the majority's status quo. By lifting the eyes to the rewards of the "next world," religious organizations have discouraged members from focusing on the injustices of the present. Indeed, religion has resembled the "opiate of the masses" which Karl Marx accused it of being. However, organized religion has produced leaders (such as Rev. Dr. Martin Luther King, Jr. or the Rev. Jesse Jackson) who use the structure of the church to initiate reform movements that challenge the status quo.

Economic Coping Organizations

When the majority group is unwilling to support minority-group members in their attempt to gain economic independence, minorities may need to seek within their own community for assistance. The white majority is "implicated in the ghetto" not only in terms of its creation, but also in the ownership of businesses located there. Thus minority individuals and the minority communities as a whole may reap few benefits from sales in the ghetto. The Black Muslims' insistence that African Americans buy only from Muslim stores and buy only African American–made commodities is designed in part to break white domination of African Americans. Other black groups have made the same demand.[43] Carey McWilliams[44] documented how the Japanese were reproached by whites for attempting to save their earnings and establish Japanese-owned truck farms in California. One cannot help but suspect that the motivation behind the "yellow peril" claims of whites at the turn of the century and the action taken against the Japanese Americans on the West Coast was in part sparked by this anger.[45]

For many years Ivan Light[46] has offered an analysis of a mechanism in the Chinese and Japanese communities that provides economic resources in lieu of majority support. The institution is that of revolving credit associations, which are systems organized among kinsmen and friends. When no formal organization, such as a bank, will grant credit, an individual can rely upon relatives and friends. Each member of the association contributes to a central fund; when one needs money he bids an interest rate, and the highest bidder in the association gets the supply of funds to build his business. Credit rotates among members over time. The structure had been brought from Asia by immigrating families of Japanese and Chinese. Thus, when white-owned banks refuse to support their business ventures, the rotating credit associations are ready to step in.

There were similar associations in parts of Africa. Among the Yoruba (from whom many African Americans were taken as slaves) the concept was named *esusu*. Light[47] has proposed that slavery so destroyed the traditional family, so broke tribes, and so decimated the traditional culture of the enslaved that *esusu* was lost. Thus African Americans in this society have been slower in developing businesses and economic investments than have the Japanese and Chinese. The concept of the rotating credit association, however, has been viable in immigrant populations coming from the Caribbean.[48]

Other types of organizations that have helped groups cope with the economic realities of minority status have frequently been parallels to majority organizations, and were created because of exclusionary practices. Minority labor unions (e.g., United Farm Workers of America, Brotherhood of Sleeping Car Porters) have provided protection for minorities when there was no general union for this purpose. These organizations have sometimes broadened their goals and, rather than helping individual members cope with society, have sought to reform and change the system itself.

Ghetto life, poverty, crime, and other aspects of minority status often compel minority-group members to band together for their survival. Like the economic organizations, these associations frequently expand their scope. In the 1970s the Black Panther party grew from a local organization protecting African Americans against police harassment to a multichapter organization encompassing food distribution programs, legal defense programs, and the liberation and control of the African American community by African Americans as Third World peoples.[49] The party was originally known as the Black Panther Party for Self-Defense, but as Foner observes, it dropped the "Self-Defense" part of its title in 1967 as a realization that it had to take the offensive against racism and for black liberation.[50] It thus ceased to be purely a coping organization.

Marshall Sklare[51] discussed how Jewish organizations, originally local and designed to provide philanthropic aid to Jews, combined together and became national and even international in scope. Some, such as the Anti-Defamation League of B'nai B'rith, are concerned with elimination of prejudice, while others, such as the United Jewish Appeal, have provided refugee relief and aid to Israel.

Throughout the Chinatowns of the United States *tongs,* or benevolent associations, emerged during the era of exclusion of the Chinese, as noted by Jan Lin in Chapter 14. Whenever new immigrants arrived, the various associations serve as caravansaries, credit and loan societies, and employment agencies. Each ethnic organization follows the generalization offered by Aldrich and Waldinger that "ethnic groups adapt to the resources made available by their environments, which vary substantially across societies and over time."[52]

Civil Rights and Liberation Organizations

Outsiders tend to look at a minority group and perceive a sea of identical faces espousing identical beliefs and desires. This is far from an accurate observation. Just as there is diversity between groups, there is also diversity within groups. And nowhere is the range of heterogeneity within any one minority group more apparent than in intragroup disagreements over the course of social reform.

Although several of the other minority organizations have developed expanded foci, civil rights and liberation organizations *began* with an emphasis on changing the society rather than changing the minority individuals or helping them cope with the existing society. Generally these organizations held one of two basic orientations: *separatist* or *integrationist.* The former argued that the majority was too intransigent, and minorities would gain their freedom only through physical, cultural, and social separation. Integrationist groups argued that ultimately the day would come when the majority would accept the minority as a full member of society. Although each minority group has some elements of each orientation within its ranks, the African American minority has had the most varied and developed forms.

In addition, there were divergent strategies employed by the civil rights and liberation groups. Some deferred their goals through accommodationism, or the temporary adjustment and cessation of hostilities between groups. Thus the minority endures until it is "ready." Others engaged in legal protest, working through the courts and within the legal structure of the society. Still others engaged in extralegal practices, including civil disobedience, nonviolent protest, and even open, violent confrontation.

A sociologist studying the various civil rights and liberation organizations of minority groups presented in this text is struck by two factors: the diversity of goals and strategies within specific groups, and the similarities to be found across groups. Among Puerto Ricans there are political movements orientated toward independence and nationhood (separatists), and others oriented toward statehood (which implies political equalization and assimilation). There have been African American organizations that preached accommodationism, including Booker T. Washington's "Atlanta Compromise"; others have used lawsuits and legislation (NAACP); some have utilized civil disobedience, sit-ins, marches, and boycotts (CORE, Southern Christian Leadership Conference or SCLC); still others have suggested or entertained violent responses to majority provocations (Black Panther party, Black Muslims). Today, more than 40 years after the Montgomery bus boycott, there is still debate among African Americans about the effectiveness and utility of these diverse strategies.

Among Chicanos, some have used legalism, some have fought with passive resistance, and others have advocated and attempted the violent expulsion of majority persons from land previously belonging to people of Mexican heritage (e.g., Reies Tijerina's *La Alianza Federal de Mercedes*). The feminist movement and the American Indian Movement (AIM) exhibit similar diversity among their members. Historically, the Irish, the Jews, and other minorities also experienced such differences.

There are also striking similarities across groups. The Japanese American Citizen's League and the National Women's Political Caucus support political candidates in ways similar to the Mexican American Political Association and the League of United Latin American Citizens (LULAC). The National Congress of American Indians (NCAI) and NOW bear striking resemblances to NAACP in terms of their legalistic approaches. Within AIM are elements similar to the Black Panthers: each organization was originally created to protect members from police harassment. Finally, the Jewish Defense League (JDL) of today advocates violent responses in defense of Israel against Arab nations in the same manner that, a century before, the Fenian Brotherhood advocated violence in defense of Ireland.

Institutional Racism

Racism, sexism, and homophobia are total ideologies that pervade American society. They represent holistic and encapsulating belief systems and world views that are intertwined throughout the fabric of our society and may be found within each of our institutions and organizations. Although prejudice may be compatible with institutional racism, it is distinct. Prejudice is an individual, personal phenomenon; institutional racism is a societal phenomenon. Institutional racism is the ideology of racism operating within the organizations and institutions of the society. Racism and sexism are world views that define groups of people a priori as inferior or superior and mark as "rational," "sensible," and even "reasonable" organizational and societal behavior that maintains these definitions. There emerges a unity of intent, which mitigates efforts at societal changes. Because racism is present in all aspects of the society, it is not easy for individuals and groups to divorce themselves from the ideology unless they divorce themselves from the culture, the language, the everyday assumptions. No group holds a monopoly on the ideological tenets of racism and sexism. Minorities, if they accept their condition, deal with other minorities, and even when they rebel against the majority, reaffirm the ideology.

Racism and sexism are not new phenomena. They have persisted throughout our cultural heritage. Gossett[53] noted the presence of salient racial distinctions in India more than five thousand years ago, as well as among the early Egyptians, the classical Greeks and Romans, and the early Hebrews. Racism has served to maintain one group over another. It fit well with early capitalism, with its need for colonialism and imperialism. If Western Europeans were superior and destined to rule the world, as the ideology preached, then it was only "manifest destiny" that Western Europeans should colonize the New World, Africa, and the Far East; it was likewise only part of the divine nature of things that the native populations were to be subjugated. Van den Berghe noted:

> The egalitarian and libertarian ideas of the Enlightenment spread by the American and French Revolutions conflicted, of course, with racism, but they also paradoxically contributed to its development. Faced with the blatant contradiction between the treatment of slaves and colonial peoples and the official rhetoric of freedom and equality, Europeans and white North Americans began to dichotomize humanity between men and submen (or the "civilized" and the "savages").[54]

In fact, if minorities were less than human, as the enlightened colonizer thought, it would be inhumane to treat them as equals and demand from them the responsibilities of peers and adults. To treat them as children unable to decide for themselves became a humane gesture. How fortunate for the colonizers that they could be humane and get goods and services for almost nothing!

Racism, sexism, and homophobia are manifested in many small, everyday ways. The assumption that a flesh-colored Band-Aid is pink is racist. The belief that girls are natural-born mothers with maternal instincts while boys have no paternal instincts is sexist. The public outcry over the hiring of a gay or lesbian teacher for fear that he or she might "recruit" the student body into a gay lifestyle reflects prejudice and homophobia. Racism, sexism, and homophobia are also manifested in more dramatic ways. The fear of homosexuality has led the military to end the careers of effective officers. Even the policy of "don't ask, don't tell" has had a chilling effect on recruitment. The assumption that white males are more academically talented and educable produces a self-fulfilling prophecy whereby all others are given inferior education. Inferior education in turn leads to poorer jobs. Poorer jobs mean that the individual is less able to purchase for himself and his family a better standard of living. At each step we are aware of the assumptions of the inferiority of one group and the superiority of the other. Not only in the school, but in the job market and in the consumer market, these assumptions of superiority and inferiority heighten one group's chances of success and the other's chances of failure. We define as inferior, we treat as inferior, and the product appears to be inferior. Further, by the limitations placed upon the parents we ensure that the children will have disadvantages, and the process thus repeats itself.

Events of the 1990s, ranging from the Rodney King beating and the O.J. Simpson trial in Los Angeles, with its reliance on the "race card" by the defense, the passage of anti-immigrant initiatives in California, the dragging death of an African American in Texas, the burning of African American churches in various states, and the concerted attack on affirmative action suggest that the issue of race is not dead in America as it enters a new millenium. The contributors to the reports section of *The Minority Report,* as well as Feagin and Vera's *White Racism*[55] chronicle evidence that racism is still virulent throughout America society.

We have explored minority experiences with organizations and have seen common treatments, definitions, and complaints. We have looked at alternative organizations established by minorities and found many to be patterned after those that they have sought to challenge or that have excluded them. This interconnection of organizations with racist beliefs, goals, and intents confronts the minority-group member. Individual prejudice can be changed because it is an individual problem subject to individual solutions. But the ideologies of institutional racism and sexism, which are mutually comparable and rather similar, are not so easily corrected.

The social science of the 1930s through the 1950s viewed minority-majority relations as solely a problem of prejudice—of misinformed or sick individuals. Techniques were devised to change individuals. The civil rights movement, observes Skolnick, likewise was built upon the assumption that

> racism [prejudice in reality] was a localized [to the South] malignancy within a relative healthy political and social order; it was a move to force American morality and American institutions to root out the last vestiges of the disease.[56]

Because the belief system of racism (sexism, and homophobia) was so ingrained, the civil rights activists failed to see its pervasiveness. They tended to assume that moral persuasion would correct the evil. But each side saw their cause in moral terms, and so the pervasive ideology blinded both.

The recognition of institutionalized racism, like the organizations it describes, is a double-edged instrument. By contending that the ideology blinds one to the consequences of one's acts, by contending that the causes of the differential treatment of minorities are so ingrained in the very fabric of the society as to be covert and unconscious, is to argue that: (1) only total societal change is effective in dealing with the problem—a point that has validity; but also (2) individuals cannot be held culpable for their discriminatory behavior and prejudicial attitudes—which is not correct. To contend that racism is principally a societal problem is to excuse the actions of prejudiced individuals who are seen merely as victims of the society's system of socialization.

In the next chapter we shall look at the manifold causes of prejudice, and suggest some ways in which such prejudice can be reduced. Even if racism is a societal problem (and in part it is), individuals separately and in groups must be responsible for changing that society. We are not contending that an institutionalized racism perspective is invalid. Rather, we are suggesting that it is one of several viable explanations, and that the error lies in insisting on its predominance and abandoning social psychological models of prejudice and discrimination.

Summary

Organizational analysis provides many insights into minority-group relations. Minorities generally have had similar experiences with majority organizations. The schools are geared to the majority child and tend to reinforce the traditional role definitions of minority groups, while under pressure from both specific minorities and the federal government to relieve minority problems. Similarly, the police have been a source of friction and discontent in most minority communities. The police have, for many, become symbols of that social order that relegates them to an inferior position. Government welfare agencies, ostensibly charged with relieving the problems of the poor and the minority person, often accomplish the opposite. Through top-heavy bureaucracies, impersonal and laden with often contradictory rules, welfare agencies often either discourage needy individuals from using their services or encourage dependency and career welfare recipients. The welfare reform legislation of 1996 changed the nature of welfare by demanding that recipients find work within two years. However, the exodus of jobs from the central city has made meeting the requirement very difficult. Access to quality health care is also problematic for minority-group members. Differentials still remain in access to treatment. Medical insurance remains an important arbitrator of who gets treatment, especially for disorders where the resultant behavior does not pose a physical threat to others.

Minority groups have generated several different types of organizations to react to and serve as a buffer against the treatment of the majority. Most minorities have evolved some types of culture-maintaining organizations; economic organizations, as well as self-defense leagues, as coping mechanisms; and a range of civil rights and liberation organizations. The last have had two basic orientations, either separatist or integrationist. Strategies also vary from accommodationism to legal, violent, and nonviolent protests.

Noteworthy in the study of minority-group organization is the divergence of opinions within any one minority group, and the similarity in structures and experiences across groups.

Much of the organizational behaviors can be understood in terms of institutional racism and sexism. Racism and sexism are total ideologies that pervade our society. These ideologies have become the rationalizers for minority subjugation, and they are so embedded in our culture—so much a part of our organizations, institutions, and expectations—that they operate in very subtle, nearly unnoticeable ways to maintain the power relationships between groups.

Notes

1. Amitai Etzioni, *Modern Organizations* (Englewood Cliffs, NJ: Prentice-Hall, 1964), p. 3.
2. See especially, M. Carnoy, *Schooling in a Corporate Society: The Political Economy of Education in America* (New York: McKay, 1972); C. H. Persell, *Education and Inequality: the Roots and Results of Stratification in America's Schools*

(New York: The Free Press, 1977); P. Bourdieu and J. Passeron, *Reproduction in Education: Society and Culture* (London: Sage, 1977).

3. James S. Coleman et al., *Equality of Educational Opportunity* (Washington, D.C.: Government Printing Office, 1966).
4. Colin Greer, "A Review of Christopher Jencks's *Inequality*," *Society* 11 (1974), p. 92.
5. Samuel Bowles and Herbert Gintis, *Schooling in Capitalist America* (New York: BasicBooks, 1976).
6. Aaron V. Cicourel and John I. Kitsuse, *The Educational Decision-Makers* (Indianapolis: Bobbs-Merrill, 1963).
7. Sam Schulman et al., *Mexican American Youth and Vocational Education in Texas* (Houston: Center for Human Resources, University of Houston, 1973).
8. Lionel A. Maldonado and David R. Byrne, *The Social Ecology of Chicanos in Utah* (Iowa City: The University of Iowa Press, 1978).
9. U.S. Commission on Civil Rights, *Teachers and Students: Differences in Teacher Interaction with Mexican American and Anglo Students* (Washington, D.C.: Government Printing Office, 1973).
10. Jonathan Kozol, *Savage Inequalities*.
11. Anthony Gary Dworkin, *Teacher Burnout in the Public Schools: Structural Causes and Consequences for Children,* (Albany, NY: SUNY Press, 1987), and Margaret D. LeCompte and Anthony Gary Dworkin, *Giving Up on School: Student Dropouts and Teacher Burnouts.* (Newbury Park: CA: Corwin/Sage, 1991).
12. U.S. Department of Education, National Center for Education Statistics, *The Condition of Education, 1995.* (Washington, D.C.: 1995).
13. John U. Ogbu, *Minority Education and Caste* (New York: Academic Press, 1978) and S. Fordham and John U. Ogbu, "Black Students' School Success: Coping with the Burden of 'Acting White,'" *Urban Review* 18 (1986), pp. 176–206.
14. Roslyn A. Mickelson, "The Attitude-Achievement Paradox among Black Adolescents," *Sociology of Education* 63 (1990), pp. 44–61.
15. U.S. Department of Education, National Center for Education Statistics, op. cit.
16. James S. Coleman, Thomas Hoffer, and Sally Kilgore, *High School Achievement: Public, Catholic, and Private High Schools Compared* (New York: Basic Books, 1982), and James S. Coleman and Thomas Hoffer, *Public and Private Schools: The Impact of Communities* (New York: Basic Books, 1987).
17. Anthony Gary Dworkin, Laurence A. Toenjes, Margaret A. Purser, and Ayman Sheikh-Hussin, "Modeling of the Effects of Changing Demography on Student Learning: Applications Designed to Change School District Practices," in *Urban Education: Challenges for the Sociology of Education,* Theodore Mitchell and Carlos Alberto Torres (eds.) (Greenwich, CT: JAI Press, forthcoming).
18. Jack J. Preiss and Howard J. Ehrlich, *An Examination of Role Theory* (Lincoln: University of Nebraska Press, 1966).
19. Kenneth B. Clark, *Dark Ghetto* (New York: Harper, 1965).

20. David A. Klinger, "Bringing Crime Back In: Toward a Better Understanding of Police Arrest Decisions," *Journal of Research in Crime and Delinquency* 33 (1996), pp. 333–36.

21. Douglas A. Smith, Christy A. Visher, and Laura A. Davidson, "Equity and Discretionary Justice: The Influence of Race on Arrest Decisions," *The Journal of Criminal Law and Criminology* 75 (1984), pp. 234–249.

22. Joe R. Feagin and Melvin P. Sikes, *Living with Racism: The Black Middle-Class Experience* (Boston, MA: Beacon, 1994).

23. John F. Galliher, "Explanations of Police Behavior: A Critical Review and Analysis," in *Symposium on Violent Confrontation,* ed. Anthony Gary Dworkin, *Sociological Quarterly* 12 (1971), pp. 308–18.

24. Stanley Lieberson, "A Societal Theory of Race and Ethnic Relations," *American Sociological Review* 26 (1961), pp. 902–10.

25. *Statistical Abstracts of the United States,* p. 120.

26. Karen Davis and Diane Rowland, "Uninsured and Underserved: Inequities in Health Care in the United States," in *The Sociology of Health and Illness: Critical Perspective,* Peter Conrad and Rochelle Kern, eds. (New York: St. Martin's Press, 1990).

27. *Statistical Abstracts of the United States,* p. 210.

28. William Cockerham, *Medical Sociology,* 4th ed. (Englewood Cliffs, NJ: Prentice Hall, 1989).

29. *Statistical Abstracts of the United States,* p. 88.

30. Philip Rack, *Race, Culture, and Mental Disorder* (London: Tavistock Publications, 1982).

31. Rosalind J. Dworkin, *Researching Persons with Mental Illness* (Newbury Park, CA: Sage, 1992).

32. Lee N. Robins, John E. Helzer, Myrna M. Weissman, Helen Orvaschel, Ernest Gruenberg, Jack D. Burke, and Darrel A. Regier, "Lifetime Prevalence of specific Psychiatric Disorders in the Three Sites," *Archives of General Psychiatry* (1984), pp. 949–58.

33. Elliot Liebow, *Tally's Corner* (Boston: Little, Brown, 1967), chap. 2.

34. See Andrew Billingsley, *Black Families in White America* (Englewood Cliffs, NJ: Prentice-Hall, 1968), chap. 7, and Frances Fox Piven and Richard A. Cloward, *Regulating the Poor* (New York: Random House, 1971).

35. One especially disastrous consequence of the switch to reliance upon revenue-sharing funds was seen in the early 1980s. In order to reduce the federal budget to curb inflation, revenue sharing was cut back, leaving many programs in limbo. Without alternative sources for funding social welfare agencies, the plight of the poor and of minorities will only be exacerbated.

36. Thomas Corbett, "The Next Generation of Welfare Reforms: The Challenge to Evaluation," *Focus* 18 (University of Wisconsin-Madison Institute for Research on Poverty), p.5.

37. William Julius Wilson, *The Truly Disadvantaged,* op. cit., and Willaim Julius Wilson, *When Work Disappears,* op. cit.
38. Cornell West, *Race Matters* (New York: Vintage Books, 1993), p. 20.
39. Our thanks to Allen Haney, who told us this anecdote.
40. John H. Burma, *Spanish-Speaking Groups in the United States* (Durham, NC: Duke University Press, 1954).
41. Patricia Cayo Sexton, *Spanish Harlem* (New York: Harper, 1965).
42. Oscar Lewis, *La Vida* (New York: Random House, 1966).
43. Floyd B. McKissick, "Black Business Development with Social Commitment to Black Communities," in *Black Nationalism in America,* John H. Bracey, Jr., August Meier, and Elliott Rudwick, eds. (Indianapolis: Bobbs-Merrill, 1970).
44. Carey McWilliams, *Brothers under the Skin* (Boston: Little, Brown, 1964).
45. See Fujiwara and Takagi on Japanese Americans and Lin on Chinese Americans in chapters 12 and 13, respectively.
46. Ivan H. Light, *Ethnic Enterprise in America: Business and Welfare among Chinese, Japanese, and Blacks* (Berkeley and Los Angeles: University of California Press, 1972). K. Ikeda has suggested that unique historical factors have been ignored in the application of Light's model to the Japanese Americans. See Kiyoshi Ikeda, "A Different 'Dilemma,'" *Social Forces* 51 (1973), pp. 497–99.
47. Ibid.
48. Aubrey W. Bonnett, *Institutions Adaptation of West Indian Immigrants to America: An Analysis of Rotating Credit Associations.* (Washington, D.C.: University Press of America, 1981).
49. Philip S. Foner, ed., *The Black Panthers Speak* (Philadelphia: Lippincott, 1970).
50. Ibid., p. xix.
51. Marshall Sklare, *America's Jews* (New York: Random House, 1971), chap. 4; see also Schoenfeld on Jewish Americans in Chapter 16 of this book.
52. Howard E. Waldrich and Roger Waldinger, "Ethnicity and Entrepreneurship," *Annual Review of Sociology* 16 (1990), pp. 111–35.
53. Thomas F. Gossett, *Race: The History of an Idea in America* (Dallas: Southern Methodist University Press, 1963).
54. Pierre L. van den Berghe, *Race and Racism* (New York: Wiley, 1967), pp. 17–18.
55. Joe R. Feagin and Hernan Vera, *White Racism: The Basics* (New York: Routledge, 1995).
56. Jerome H. Skolnick, *The Politics of Protest* (New York: Simon and Schuster, 1969).

Suggested Readings

Bowles, Samuel, and Herbert Gintis. *Schooling in Capitalist America.* New York: Basic Books, 1976.

Coleman, James S., et al. *Equality of Educational Opportunity.* Washington, D.C.: Government Printing Office, 1966.

Coleman, James S., Thomas Hoffer, and Sally Kilgore. *High School Achievement: Public, Catholic, and Private Schools Compared.* New York: Basic Books, 1982.

Feagin, Joe R. and Hernan Vera. *White Racism.* New York: Routledge, 1995.

Hall, Richard H. *Organizations: Structures and Processes.* Englewood Cliffs, NJ: Prentice-Hall, 1977.

Jencks, Christopher, et al. *Inequality: A Reassessment of the Effects of Family and Schooling in America.* New York: Basic Books, 1972.

Jencks, Christopher. *Rethinking Social Policy: Race, Poverty, and the Underclass* Cambridge, MA: Harvard University Press, 1992.

Levine, Donald M., and Mary Jo Bane. *The "Inequality" Controversy: Schooling and Distributive Justice.* New York: Basic Books, 1975.

Percell, Carolyn Hodges. *Education and Inequality.* New York: Free Press, 1977.

Perrow, Charles. *Complex Organizations: A Critical Essay.* Glenview, IL: Scott, Foresman, 1979.

Piven, Frances Fox, and Richard A. Cloward. *Regulating the Poor.* New York: Random House, 1971.

Ryan, William. *Blaming the Victim.* New York: Random House, 1976.

West, Cornell. *Race Matters,* New York: Vintage Books, 1993.

Wilson, William Julius. *The Truly Disadvantaged: The Inner City, The Underclass, and Public Policy.* Chicago: University of Chicago Press, 1987.

Wilson, William Julius. *When Work Disappears: The World of the New Urban Poor.* New York: Alfred Knopf, 1996.

CHAPTER 5

The Social Psychological Dimension

Up to now we have been concerned with minority-group relations on a societal or institutional level. We have focused upon the minority and the majority as groups. The social psychological level, on the other hand, emphasizes the individual; the unit of analysis is the person. The concern is with the impact of the larger social structure and institutions upon the individual and upon relationships between individuals.

The essential components of the social psychological dimension in minority-group relations are the elements of *attitudes* and *behaviors*. There have been numerous definitions of attitudes, but in general they have emphasized that attitudes are interrelated sets of propositions about classes of ideas, groups, and objects, which tend to predispose individuals to behave in ways that are relatively consistent with those attitudes. Attitudes have cognitive (thoughts) and affective (feelings and emotions) components, and through their predisposing tendency imply conations (behaviors). Behaviors are observable acts committed by individuals. Attitudes are not directly observable, but must be inferred from the behavior. Thus when an individual expresses opinions or makes statements about an idea, group, or object, he or she is engaging in written or oral behavior. However, we infer something about this individual's mental images (attitudes) on the basis of these behaviors and then use these inferences to predict future behaviors. Social scientists usually measure attitudes in terms of responses on questionnaires and direct interviews, often through the use of standard scales (e.g., the Bogardus Social

Distance Scale mentioned in Chapter 3). In minority-group relations we are concerned with the attitude of *prejudice* and the behavior of *discrimination,* and their impact on the *self.*

PREJUDICE

Dimensions

Prejudice represents one of the concepts in the social sciences about which there is little agreement. Clearly prejudice is not a generic variable. The multitude of definitions have some things in common, and perhaps the best single definition has been advanced by Secord and Backman: "Prejudice is an attitude that predisposes a person to think, feel, and act in favorable or unfavorable ways toward a group or its individual members." [1] Prejudice is a prejudgment; the attitude is formed either in the absence of contact with the target group, or with limited contact with that group. In fact, Horowitz[2] and Bass[3] have each observed that individuals learn their prejudiced attitudes about minority groups, not through contact with the minorities but through contact with others who have prejudiced attitudes toward the minority group. Likewise, researchers[4] have enumerated several analytic dimensions of prejudice. Among the more important of these are direction, salience (or generalizability), intensity, commitment, and centrality. Direction is the valence (whether favorable, neutral, or unfavorable) of the attitude. Salience (or generalizability) is the extent to which the attitude can be applied to all, most, some, or a few in the class of such objects, groups, or ideas. Intensity is how strongly a person feels about his attitude. Commitment is the extent to which a person is willing to make sacrifices to hold to his attitude. Centrality is the degree to which the attitude is an integral part of the person's personality and self-conception.

As an illustration of the dimensions of prejudice, imagine a conversation between two friends. The first says, "I really dislike politicians *(direction)* very much *(intensity)*. They are all *(salience)* a bunch of crooks. I'd rather vote for my mother-in-law than a career politician *(commitment)*. I have become *(centrality)* a thorough politician hater."

The second replies, "I don't let it get to me so much *(centrality)*. Some of them *(salience)* seem to be all right *(direction)*. Not great, just all right *(intensity)*. I won't let political scandals stop me from voting for politicians *(commitment)*."

Not all statements of prejudice are necessarily detailed enough to display all the dimensions as clearly as illustrated above. Sometimes particular dimensions are implicit; sometimes they can be extracted through detailed, probing interviews. Though they are subtle, social scientists must nevertheless be cognizant of these dimensions.

Functions

The social psychologist Daniel Katz[5] proposed that prejudice serves four functions. First, prejudice provides a preknowledge of what to expect in a given situation (knowledge function). In a complex world where one meets and interacts with hundreds of different individuals, it becomes impossible to learn personally and make separate judgments about each one. Prejudices relieve one of that burden. It provides a kind of cognitive economy whereby, in applying bits of knowledge to whole categories of persons (such as African Americans, Japanese Americans, or women), one does not have to learn about a distinct individual but can react to the person according to a prejudgment of the category to which he or she belongs. Often this knowledge is accurate, or becomes so through the mechanisms of the self-fulfilling prophecy. But often the knowledge is wholly or partly inaccurate. Nevertheless, one is guided by it and it still serves a knowledge function.

Second, prejudice helps to protect the ego or self-esteem of the individual who holds prejudicial attitudes (ego-defensive function). The prejudiced individual, by holding pejorative attitudes about a group, is able to rationalize his or her failures and their successes. Thus the anti-Semite who fails in a competition for admission to a university might say, "The professors were all Jews and they helped their own kind first." The person never has to admit that his grades, letters of recommendation, or entrance examination scores were not good enough to earn him admission. If the target of prejudice is of low minority status, the prejudiced individual can also take comfort in believing that no matter how many failures he or she experiences, the prejudiced person is still better off than people in the disliked minority group.

A third function of prejudice is instrumental (instrumental function). Prejudice here serves to maintain patterns of superordination and subordination for economic, political, or social gain. The prejudice is instrumental in helping its user adapt to his environment and thus maximize gains and rewards. Prejudice may aid a merchant to keep low the wages of minority employees, thereby maximizing the merchant's profits. The merchant may assume that members of that group are "lazy" and "stupid." If they are lazy, they won't be doing a full day's work, so they should not be paid a full day's wages. If they are stupid, they won't know that they are being paid less. The merchant's prejudice helps keep his or her business overhead down, and thus aids the person in dealing successfully with competitors.

The fourth and final function of prejudice Katz calls the value-expressive function. Prejudice becomes rewarding for the individual when it permits him to voice his central personal values. As a corollary, prejudice may also permit the individual to express central societal values. We have seen that racism (the societal level ideology) is an integral part of the American ethic. Frank Westie[6] has argued that individual prejudice is normative in our society. There may be two norms with regard to prejudice in our society today: "Thou shall be prejudiced," and (since the civil rights movement) "Thou shall not be caught at it." Prejudice may become such a central part of the individual's personality that he or she may come to think of himself or herself as a champion of white supremacy or racial purity. To take away this prejudice without giving him or her a new cause (such as nonprejudice) may be sufficient to destroy the individual as a personality, as Adorno[7] has observed.

Prejudice may serve certain functions for minority-group members as well as for majorities.[8] The mutual prejudice of minorities and majorities reduces competition between groups for some resources such as jobs and housing. Thus, minorities do not need to compete with majorities in certain kinds of activities, provided that each group remains in its relatively segregated world. This restricted competition has sometimes worked to the relative advantage for minority individuals in service-related jobs and professions. For example, the African American physician is guaranteed a supply of African American patients with minimal fear of competition with white doctors. Likewise, prejudice helps to maintain in-group solidarity among minorities, which can ultimately be translated into political power. Their common plight may bring minorities together to fight a common enemy. Coupled with segregation, minorities build an electoral power base to make some demands upon the dominant society. Finally, prejudice can reduce the level of uncertainty for minorities. Dominant society prejudice makes predictable the manner in which minorities expect to be treated. Likewise, prejudiced images held by minority-group members provide them with ready-made strategies for interaction with majority individuals. Several writers have also noted that expectations about the dominant society and its members also allow minorities to rely upon system-blame definitions to explain personal failure.[9]

Underlying prejudice is a factor called *ethnocentrism,* or the tendency to use one's own group (racial, ethnic, or even gender) as a standard of reference upon which to evaluate other groups. When people are ethnocentric, they will see other groups as inferior to theirs. To the extent that another group is identifiably different in terms of physical features or cultural practices, they will be evaluated negatively. They may even be stereotyped as a homogeneous class. A related phenomenon of the social psychology of groups is the concept of *xenophobia,* or fear of those who are different. Perhaps because people seek predictability and regularity in their world, they tend to prefer the familiar and shun the different. Individuals who are viewed positively are ascribed values similar to their own, and individuals who are disliked are said to endorse dissimilar values.[10] Milton Rokeach[11] suggested that the basis of prejudice is not race or ethnicity, but assumed dissimilarity of values and beliefs. That is, minorities are not hated by members of the majority because they have a different skin color or speech style, but because they are presumed to hold different and sometimes antithetical values. Downs[12] argues that it is not the fact of an African American person's race that leads white property owners to fear residential desegregation, but fear that African Americans are not interested in property improvements, real estate values, and providing a middle-class environment for their children.

Manifestations

Prejudice is a phenomenon of many faces. It may take the form of beliefs resulting in simple avoidance reactions or in policies which advocate physical extermination of groups. In general, however, there are two principal manifestations of prejudice: *stereotypes* and *social distance*. Stereotypes are the language of prejudice, and social distance is the behavioral intent of prejudice.

About seventy-five years ago, journalist Walter Lippman[13] proposed the concept of the stereotype. For him, stereotypes were "accepted types" or "pictures we carry in our heads." Stereotypes—the language of prejudice—provide their users with a vocabulary of motives or a body of rhetoric to rationalize minority-majority relationships. They may be used to justify the status quo, or they may be developed to justify changing the social order. Minorities may attempt to supplant majority stereotypes with counter-images designed to change minority-majority relations. "Black is beautiful" is just such an image.

Stereotypes, like other attitudes, serve the four basic functions of attitudes: instrumental, ego-defensive, knowledge, and value-expressive. In addition, stereotypes provide a symbolic identification function.[14] By using stereotypes about a given group, an individual tells others whose side he or she is on. In fact, it is conceivable that if a person wanted to manage his or her presentation of self to infiltrate an organization like the Klan, he might choose to incorporate negative, anti-minority stereotypes in his or her conversations, thereby telling others he or she endorses that position.

In times of conflict stereotyping can reinforce group solidarity among the majority. During World War I the endorsement of stereotypes of Germans (also referred to as the "Hun") told others that even if you were German Americans, you were American first. Similarly, stereotypes of Germans and especially the Japanese (referred to as "Japs") became rampant during World War II. During the 1991 Gulf War, A. G. Dworkin and some of his graduate students (who were Arab American) conducted a study of the experiences of Arab Americans in the Houston area. The media had reported attacks on Arab American business around the country. Numerous Arab Americans, many of whom were native born to the United States, reported being viewed with fear and suspicion by other Americans. One was asked if he was a terrorist and another was referred to in his presence by the offensive ethnophaulism (derogatory ethnic term) as a "sand nigger," indicating both prejudice against Arab Americans and African Americans.[15]

Likewise, in other times of fear the use of stereotypes about an out-group will be used to separate oneself from that group. The AIDS epidemic, although certainly not limited to the gay community, has fostered fear of gays, attacks by the right wing on the prospect of gay marriages, and even a threatened boycott of Disney Productions in part because of the company's stance on extending health care coverage to same-sex partners of Disney employees. In the United States, homosexuality has been traditionally seen as contrary to Christianity. For that reason conservative religious groups also defined AIDS as God's punishment for homosexuality. In a sense, the fact of AIDS justified the negative stereotypes of gays for these groups. Shelley Correll examines this further in Chapter 19.

The best definition advanced for stereotypes comes from Gordon Allport, who proposed that "a stereotype is an exaggerated belief associated with a category. It functions to justify (rationalize) our conduct toward that category"[16] Stereotypes can be favorable and neutral, as well as unfavorable (direction); they are applied to images describing all as well as only some members of a group, thereby allowing for a range of saliency. Allport also notes the rationalizing function of stereotypes, and his definition does not preclude the other functions of attitudes.

Numerous writers have debated whether stereotypes are true or false, whether they are fixed or volatile, and whether they are conservative or liberal. Those who have maintained that stereotypes are false by definition (Bogardus[17] and Klapp[18]) have proposed an alternative term, "sociotypes," to describe images that are true. Some writers[19] insist there is a kernel of truth in every stereotype. The preference among investigators today is that some stereotypes are true while others are false, but what makes them true or false is the extent to which they are applied universally to a category. It is one thing to argue that all Tasmanians are ambitious, and quite another to contend that there is somewhere at least one ambitious Tasmanian. Many stereotypes are somewhat like astrological forecasts or predictions in fortune cookies. They are so general that they can be applied to at least some portion of any population.[20]

Some writers contend that stereotypes never change, or at least are relatively inflexible. If there have not been changes in the nature of the target group, the stereotyper, or the relationship between the two, one would not expect change.[21] When conditions do change, the stereotypes tend to follow suit. Likewise when the relationship between groups changes, their mutual stereotypes correspondingly change. In some instances the actual words used to describe a group change; in other instances the meanings or connotations of the words change. In their review of stereotypes used by Mexican Americans during the 1960s and 1970s, Dworkin and Eckberg[22] showed how a word such as "emotional" underwent changes in meaning. "Emotional" first meant "irrational," but during the era of the Chicano Movement it came to mean "having soul."

In other instances the social characteristics of the people who use the stereotypes change. The latter point may be illustrated by the changes in observers' images of the Japanese around the period of World War II. The Japanese were seen as "industrious" and "good gardeners" in the prewar period, as "cruel" during the war period, and again as "industrious" after the war. In reality all three images existed throughout the time periods, but before and after the war only a few endorsed "cruel" and most others endorsed the positive images; during wartime most endorsed "cruel," and those using positive stereotypes were considered traitors.[23]

There are some instances when stereotypes persist even in the face of contradictory information or when the groups themselves have undergone change. Richter[24] suggests that stereotypes operate both as stipulative definitions and empirical generalizations. The former specify the necessary and sufficient conditions for labeling objects; the latter are based upon actual observations and hypothesis testing. Thus when a stereotyper encounters an individual from the target group behaving in a fashion consistent with the stereotype, the behavior is used to support the stereotype. However, when a person is encountered who does not conform with the stereotype, rather than reject the image the stereotyper defines the person out of the category, saying "he's not a typical ____________."

A few writers[25] have debated whether stereotypes are basically conservative or liberal. Stereotypes are both conservative and liberal. They may be used to support a status quo or employed to change the status quo. Further, they may be used by both conservatives and liberals. No political orientation is identified with total refusal to use stereotypes, although the nature of the stereotypes may vary. Liberal individuals may endorse few negative statements about minorities. But as Mackie[26] noted, liberals often stereotype "establishment" types. Thus, although no liberal would assume that African Americans are lazy or stupid, many would agree that corporate capitalists are greedy and endowed with ulterior clandestine motives.

Exploration of the behavior and characteristics that stereotypes describe demonstrates two distinct processes. The first has been called "in-group virtues and out-group vices" by Merton.[27] In this process identical behavior by minority-group members and majority-group members is attributed to different and antithetical motivations. Merton makes the comparisons between Abe Lincoln and Abe Cohen. Abe Lincoln labored long hours far into the night, proving he was industrious and hard working. Abe Cohen labors far into the night, proving he is ruthless and will go to any lengths to undercut the competition. Lincoln saved his money and thus was thrifty; Cohen does the same, but he is a miser. The authors once encountered a woman who complained that her gardener, who was African American and in his late sixties, was no longer carrying out the heavy trash cans to the curb for garbage collection as he had done twenty years earlier. She contended that the reason he no longer did this chore was because she thought he had become a black militant. When asked if her husband, who was the same age as the gardener, carried out the trashcans, she replied, "Of course not. He's gotten too old to do that kind of heavy work."

A second process in stereotyping has been identified as the "Thomas theorem" after sociologist W. I. Thomas,[28] and is sometimes referred to as "the self-fulfilling prophecy." According to the theorem, if men define situations as real, they will be real in their consequences. Thus by defining a group in terms of a set of stereotypes, one tends to act toward the group in terms of these stereotypes, and in time the group's behavior conforms to the stereotypes. Liebow[29] reports that many white employers expect African Americans to steal on the job, so they are paid less than those who are not expected to steal. Because the wages are so low, the African American individual is faced with either stealing, and thereby reinforcing the stereotype held by the white, or taking home too little pay to support his family.

Thomas Pettigrew[30] has characterized stereotypes as the ultimate attribution error. Attribution theory in social psychology attempts to explain how individuals summon up cause and meaning for the behaviors of others. Under certain circumstances such explanations of motive are inaccurate or biased. In Pettigrew's model, ethnic stereotypes are seen as obeying the following rules:

1. When the act of an out-group member is antisocial or undesirable as defined by the user of stereotypes, the act will be attributed to innate character traits of the individual or his group (dispositions).
2. When the behavior of an out-group member is desirable as defined by the stereotyper, the act will be attributed to contextual or situational factors, to particular motivational (noninnate) qualities of the individual, or to exceptional qualities that set that particular individual apart from the group to which he or she belongs.

Causes of the ultimate attribution errors are of three types in Pettigrew's model. The first cause is *availability,* or the extent to which the individual can easily identify behavior patterns of the group members. The attribution error is easily made when the target group is seen in only limited contexts, such as when they collect garbage, change diapers, or clean floors. The second cause is *representativeness,* or the extent to which the attributor of motives has access to a limited number of individuals of the target groups from which to draw generalizations. For example, stereotyping is more negative and prevalent in relatively segregated public schools where majority-group members interact with a few minority students.[31] Likewise, Kanter[32] observed that women in token managerial positions in corporations experience the attribution of stereotypes about women applied to them. The result is that they are not judged as individuals, but as members of a category, and if they make mistakes their errors are attributed to all members of the category. The final cause is *adjustment and anchoring,* or the stereotyper's need to select some starting point in the explanation of behavior, prior to attempted clarification and modification. In this instance, stereotypes are not the end product of prejudicial thinking, but rather a beginning of either a logical process leading to the rejection of the stereotype, or merely a convention of speech.

Between 1988 and 1991, the National Opinion Research Center of the University of Chicago asked random samples of Americans about their images of members of different racial and ethnic groups.[33] Among the questions asked were whether the groups were seen by the respondents as "intelligent or unintelligent," "prone to violence or not prone to violence," "hard-working or lazy," and "patriotic or unpatriotic." Responses were on a scale from one to seven, with the higher the score, the more negative the stereotype (e.g., unintelligent, violent, lazy, and unpatriotic). Presented in Table 5-1 is a distribution of responses describing by white and African American respondents describing Blacks, Hispanics, Hispanics, Asians, and Jews as target groups. The table displays the percentage of respondents endorsing answers that represented the negative stereotypes.

It is clear that many African American and white respondents endorsed negative stereotypes about the target groups. One-fourth of the whites felt that blacks were "unintelligent" and nearly one-third thought that Hispanics were "unintelligent," while almost one-half thought that blacks were "lazy" and over one-third thought that Hispanics were "lazy." More than one-half of white respondents thought that blacks were "prone to violence," and nearly one-quarter thought that Hispanics were "unpatriotic." As might be expected, a much smaller percentage of the African American respondents endorsed the stereotypes describing blacks that there held by whites, although a large number did feel that blacks were "prone to violence."

Comparable percentages of African American and white respondents agreed that Hispanics were "prone to violence," "lazy," and "unpatriotic," and that Asians were "unintelligent," "lazy," and "unpatriotic." More African American than white respondents felt that whites were "unintelligent," "prone to violence, " "lazy," and "unpatriotic." More African Americans than whites had negative images of Jews, and more African Americans than whites had images of Asians being "prone to violence." Differences in the images of Jews reflect the fact that some of the white respondents were also Jewish and because African Americans and Jews have had a long-standing "bittersweet encounter,"[34] as Jewish merchants have had a history of participation in the inner-city black neighborhoods. Some of the dynamics of African American and Jewish interactions are discussed in Chapter 16 by Eugen Schoenfeld. The more negative images of Asians by African Americans compared to whites also reflect a degree of economic competition between African Americans and Asians in the inner city. A later section of this chapter will discuss the issue of mutual stereotypes and stereotypes of third parties.

Despite the retention of negative stereotypes found in the NORC data, it is also true that levels of negative stereotyping have declined over the past two decades. The implication is that racial prejudice has either declined or changed in format. Comparison of NORC data from the 1970s reveals significant in-

TABLE 5–1
Stereotypes about Selected Racial and Ethnic Groups Held by Whites and African Americans between 1988 and 1991 (Percent Endorsing the Negative Stereotype Moderately to Strongly)

Stereotype	Respondent Group	
Target Group	Whites	African Americans
"Intelligent vs. Unintelligent" (Percent Responding "Unintelligent")		
Blacks	25.8	11.4
Hispanics	32.3	23.7
Asians	14.9	15.9
Whites	8.6	14.0
Jews	7.7	13.1
"Prone to Violence vs. Not Prone to Violence" (Percent Responding "Prone to Violence")		
Blacks	53.7	42.8
Hispanics	42.5	46.0
Asians	19.6	31.5
Whites	16.6	34.3
Jews	11.2	16.5
"Hardworking vs. Lazy" (Percent Responding "Lazy")		
Blacks	44.5	17.5
Hispanics	36.5	33.4
Asians	15.6	11.5
Whites	8.0	16.5
Jews	5.1	6.5
"Patriotic vs. Unpatriotic" (Percent Responding "Unpatriotic")		
Blacks	18.1	15.2
Hispanics	26.4	26.4
Asians	21.6	24.2
Whites	2.9	5.8
Jews	8.8	18.0

Source: *General Social Surveys,* 1972–1996: *Cumulative Codebook* (Chicago: National Opinion Research Center, 1997).

creases in the percentage of people who disagree that "white people have a right to keep blacks out of their neighborhood if they want to" and that "blacks shouldn't push themselves where they're not wanted," while fewer whites oppose school busing to achieve racial integration or oppose interracial marriage. The patterns resemble those found in the next section on decreasing social distance. Nevertheless, as Massey and Denton reported in *American Apartheid,*[35] black and white families still live in separate neighborhoods with little change in the level of housing segregation since 1980. Likewise, Squires[36] notes that there remains considerable redlining of neighborhoods and steering of black families away from white housing by realtors. Other minority groups, however, have encountered less resistance and experience less residential segregation than in the past. Further, although the rate of interracial marriage remains low, it is now several times higher than it was in the 1970s.[37] Some researchers such as Mary Jackman and her colleagues[38] have argued that changes in prejudice and stereotyping have been "superficial." She distinguishes between endorsement liberal principles and the endorsement of real changes that would eliminate differentials in the status of majorities and minorities. Part of the superficial nature of the attitudes lies in the belief by whites that much of the inequalities in the society have vanished.

Social Distance

In Chapter 3 we noted that social distance scales could be used to approximate a measure of minority-group prestige. Social distance was first defined by Robert E. Park[39] in 1924 and first measured by Emory Bogardus[40] a year later. These researchers conceptualized social distance as the degree of "empathic understanding" between members of one group and some target population. An alternative definition suggests that social distance is the extent to which one prefers to be aloof and formal rather than to interact in a close relationship with members of another group. Generally, less social distance implies a perception of greater equality between the groups. Groups that are held at a distance are often segregated physically by ghettoization and/or socially through norms of etiquette. Thus, in the urban North, African Americans have been residentially segregated to demonstrate that there is a social *distance* between whites and African Americans. In the South until recently African Americans lived in geographical proximity to whites. However, racial etiquette, including patterns of deference and demeanor, were more rigidly enforced. Geographical proximity in the North implied equality; not so in the South, which had mechanisms to deny the equality that might be inferred from proximity.

Scales measuring social distance generally contain three elements. They specify a target group, a subject (i.e., one who is answering the questions), and an interaction situation between the two. The target group tends to be presented categorically; the subject is asked to accept or reject an entire category rather than specific individuals within the category. The most widely used social distance scale is the Bogardus measure.[41]

The scale is composed of seven items ranging from most intimate to most distant. The subject is asked if he or she would be willing to engage in each of the following interactions with the target group:

1. Would marry.
2. Would have as a regular friend.
3. Would work beside in an office.

4. Would have several families in my neighborhood.
5. Would have merely as speaking acquaintances.
6. Would have live outside my neighborhood.
7. Would have live outside my country.

Social distance is measured on many target groups to determine the relative rankings of the groups by the individual. The more groups from which a subject desires to maintain high social distance, the more that individual is perceived to be prejudiced. The scale has also been administered to subjects from various ethnic, racial, and gender groups.

Although this scale was widely used, and some of the components remain in national surveys today, it is not without its faults. Some have challenged its appropriateness outside the United States. Others have suggested that the weighting of items has changed over time, so that having minority-group members in one's neighborhood implies greater intimacy and equality than either the co-worker or the friendship items.[42] Rather than the workplace, the neighborhood has become a battleground for majority-minority conflicts. Furthermore, one may have minority-group friends without being necessarily subjected to the sanctions of neighbors.

A more advanced measure of social distance has been developed by Frank Westie.[43] His measure presents several sets of interaction situations like the Bogardus scale, but it permits variations within a specific target group. Thus if a person feels greater social distance from an African American who is of a low social class than from one of a high social class, the scale could be sensitive to that distinction.

There is some evidence[44] that white Americans would often prefer to have minority-group members in their neighborhood who are of the same social class as themselves, or higher, rather than other whites who are of a lower social class than themselves. In other areas of interaction, especially involving marriage and dating practices, the race of the target individual is more important than the social class.

Schuman and his colleagues[45] have analyzed trends in racial attitudes in America using national surveys conducted by the Gallup Organization, the National Opinion Research Center at the University of Chicago, and the Institute for Social Research at the University of Michigan. These surveys have examined several salient social distance issues over time, including white attitudes about school composition (objections to sending one's child to a school with different proportions of African American children), residential integration (African Americans moving into one's block or even next door), and social interaction (bringing a black friend home to dinner). During the era of the Civil Rights Movement in the late 1950s and 1960s, 30 to 50 percent of whites objected to sending their children to schools where one-half of the pupils were black; by the 1990s, the percent objecting was only 10 percent. In the 1950s and 1960s, slightly over half would not object to having a single black neighbor next door, while by 1990 about 95 percent would not object. Finally, in the 1950s and 1960s, about half would not mind having a black friend come home to dinner with them, compared to about 80 percent when the question was last asked in 1985.[46]

Since the 1970s the surveys have enumerated the attitudes of African Americans, too. There have been few changes over time in the African American attitudes about their children attending a school where half of the children were white. Over 90 percent have been willing to do so. The desegregated school experience involving African Americans attending schools where half of the students are white is more of an empirical reality for African American parents than the reverse is for white parents. Thus, the response is much less hypothetical for African Americans. About 95 percent of African Americans enumerated do not object to having a white neighbor and more than 95 percent do not object to having a white friend over as a dinner guest.[47]

Discrimination

Discrimination is a behavior. It is the application of differential and pejorative treatment to individuals on the basis of a person's membership in a particular category rather than on his or her individual characteristics and qualifications. In Chapter 3 we discussed discrimination on the aggregate level, which is a reflection of institutional racism. However, discrimination also is a personal and individualistic phenomenon. Individuals discriminate and individuals are the objects of discrimination.

Because discrimination is a behavior and is observable, it has often been measured by a technique called *participant observation.* Typical studies have involved placing observers incognito in a natural situation where discrimination is likely to occur, and then having them record behaviors. A classic study assessing discrimination was conducted by LaPiere[48] in the 1930s. LaPiere and a Chinese couple traveled widely across the United States, stopping at 250 restaurants and hotels. In only one instance were they subjected to discrimination and refused service. The fascinating part of the study was that some time later LaPiere sent a letter to each of the restaurants and hotels they had visited, asking whether they would "take members of the Chinese race as guests at your establishment." Over 90 percent of the restaurants and hotels replied that they would not. LaPiere concluded that attitudes as measured by a questionnaire (the letter) were not identical to behaviors as measured by actual practice. Campbell[49] has suggested that the contrasting situations—the letter and the actual presence of the couple—were dissimilar enough to prohibit comparisons. He contends that it is more difficult to refuse service to someone in front of you than to answer an impersonal letter. On the other hand, national television news magazines such *as 60 Minutes, Prime Time Live, 48 Hours,* and others have on occasion constructed situations in which reporters posed as potential customers, home buyers, or apartment renters to see if women or minorities are treated differently than white males. In those instances, the female and minority reporters were more likely to be subjected to discrimination than white male reporters.

It is generally assumed that a prejudiced person will discriminate and that a nonprejudiced person will not discriminate. Often this assumption is valid. However, the LaPiere study suggests that there are other possibilities. His findings suggest that individuals may verbalize prejudicial attitudes but not actively discriminate. It is indeed true, as Campbell suggests, that it is easier to be a verbal bigot than to behave like one, especially when the weight of the law or public opinion encourages equal treatment and condemns discrimination. In other circumstances, however, the reverse of the LaPiere phenomenon could occur. That is, people may discriminate against others without holding prejudicial attitudes toward them. Such individuals may be constrained to act in discriminatory ways because of economic or peer pressures. An Anglo boy may participate in throwing rocks at a lone Chicano, not because he has learned prejudicial attitudes but because his friends are there, cheering him on.

Adults can feel similar pressures to discriminate despite their personal attitudes. Kohn and Williams[50] report an observational study in which a African American couple entered a working-class white tavern and were confronted by the bartender. White observers were located at strategic points in the tavern to record the interactions. At the proprietor's insistence, the bartender approached the African American man and stated:

> Now, mind you, I don't have anything against you people. I went to school with you folks and I've got a lot of friends among you. But some of my customers don't like to see you in here. Five or six of them have already complained to me and left. Now I can't have that. I hope you'll understand if I ask you to leave.[51]

Whether or not we accept the sincerity of the bartender's comments, we must note that he was under a constraint by his boss and that his verbally expressed attitude (that he had nothing "against" African Americans) was not supportive of his behavior (to ask the African Americans to leave). It is not uncommon that individuals come to find that the exigencies of economic life do not permit them to implement their beliefs in action. The authors of this text once interviewed an African American woman who was suing her friend, the president of a local civil rights organization, because he had refused to rent an apartment to her in his complex. He confessed to her that he believed all of his white tenants would leave and he would be bankrupt if she moved in.

Merton[52] used these four possibilities (of the connection between prejudice and discrimination) to construct a paradigm of the following types. The nonprejudiced nondiscriminator, who under no circumstances will discriminate, is called the all-weather liberal. The nonprejudiced discriminator who will discriminate only when he is pressured by circumstances is the fair-weather liberal. The fair-weather illiberal is the prejudiced nondiscriminator—he would discriminate but circumstances prevent him from doing so. Finally there is the all-weather illiberal; he is the prejudiced discriminator who will discriminate regardless of the circumstances. It is estimated that most Americans are fair-weather types subject to some kind of pressure. Thus one cannot assume the direct connection between prejudiced attitudes and discriminatory behaviors.

There is another faulty assumption: that an individual who discriminates in one situation will discriminate in others. Quite the contrary is correct, as illustrated by another classic study. Lohman and Reitzes[53] studied a group of industrial workers and discovered that they supported with equal vigor desegregation of their workplace and segregation of their neighborhood. Killian[54] further supports this observation in his study of southern "hillbillies" in Chicago. Although these individuals had opposed working with African Americans on the same job in the South and approved of the southern practice of segregation, very few objected to working with African Americans on the same job in the urban North. Most had accommodated to the northern practices despite their previous behavior in the South.

Some social psychologists have begun looking for instances of reverse discrimination on the individual level that would be a counterpart to affirmative action on the organizational level. Dutton[55] reported a series of studies in which members of the majority treated persons of their own group more negatively than they treated members of minority groups. For example, restaurant maitre d's were more willing to seat African Americans who were inappropriately dressed than they were willing to seat whites in the same condition. This differential treatment occurred most frequently when the discrimination implied racial liberalism to chance observers.

Discrimination, then, is situation-specific. Since most Americans are fair-weather types, their willingness to discriminate will depend upon the specific social circumstances in which they find themselves: the kind of pressures they are under, and from whom. Switching the context of the situation from less to more intimate (as in the Lohman and Reitzes study) or switching from one region to another (as in Killian's study) can be sufficient to change the behavior. Merton's fourfold typology was developed into a theory by Yinger[56] and tested by Warner and DeFleur.[57] Four different structural situations were selected: a liberal university neighborhood, a northern city, a southern city, and the rural South. Yinger had predicted that in the liberal situation even the all-weather illiberal might not discriminate. In the rural South (most conservative) the all-weather liberal might discriminate. However, in the two intermediate situations (northern and southern cities) the fair-weather types would behave according to the norms of the area, and the all-weather types would behave according to their attitudes. Although there was general support for the Yinger model, Warner and DeFleur found a considerable zone of imprecision in predictability.

Where discrimination and prejudice do not accompany one another, it is generally possible to point to three possible explanations. First, the individual may not have sufficient *commitment* to his or her prejudicial attitude to back it up with discriminatory behavior. That is, the strength of beliefs about the inferiority of a group is not so great that he or she is willing to endure the consequences of acting in accordance with those beliefs. Second, the individual may not have the *volition* or control over the situation to do what he or she really wants to do. Constraints may be imposed by family, friends, employers, or even the law. Third, the attitude measured may not be equivalent to the behavior predicted. Imagine a subject who would not want to marry a member of a minority group but then signs a petition supporting the candidacy of a minority-group member as mayor of the city (behavior). The two are not equivalent in level of intimacy, and ought not be expected to be equivalent in level of performance.

Several writers[58] have attempted to construct theoretical models to relate attitudes and behaviors (prejudice and discrimination) to situation-bound relationships. Although there are variations in the models, their general form is as shown in Figure 5-1. This chart denotes that the commitment and volitional variables cited above determine the strength of attitudes, and these same commitment and volitional variables enter again to create the behavior. Once the behavior is executed, the individual has increased commitment to remaining consistent and hence reinforces the attitude.

FIGURE 5-1
Constraints on Attitude-Behavior Relationships

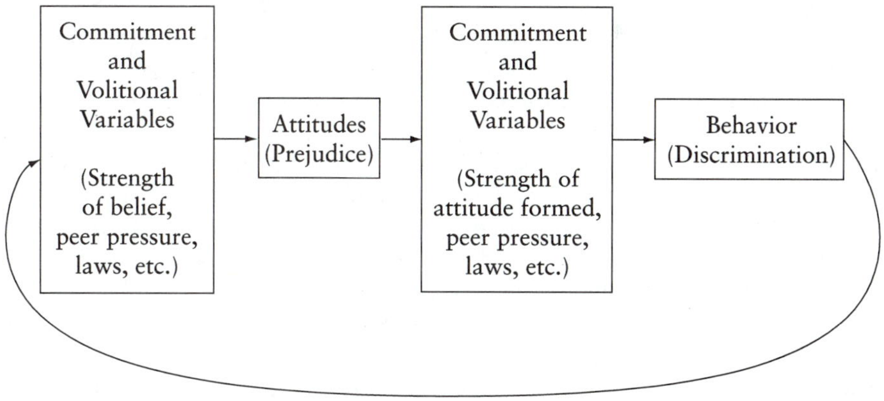

Prejudice, Discrimination, and the Self

Prejudice and discrimination are directed toward groups of individuals, and so they have consequences for both the target-group member and the prejudiced person. The functions that prejudices perform for the individual have already been discussed: preknowledge, ego defense, instrumentalism, and value expression. There are also dysfunctions for the prejudiced person, who relies upon stereotypes and other attitudes that may be incorrect, guiding him or her to behave inappropriately. Furthermore, when a society changes, prejudiced individuals locked into rigid thought processes do not change along with it, and soon find themselves out of step with the world. Prejudice is a limiting process; it constricts creativity and rationality—costs that are individual as well as societal. Prejudiced persons may live in fear of those groups about whom they feel negatively. They may sell their houses at the first hint of desegregation, moving still farther from the workplace. They may send their children to private schools, adding to their financial burdens. Their beliefs may alienate their children. They may quit jobs or lose interest in their workplace because of the presence of minority-group members.

There are costs to being prejudiced, but the costs to the target of prejudice are many times greater. Being a target of prejudice essentially means being a victim of rejection. Rejection in turn, if it is seen as legitimate, leads to lowered self-esteem and hatred of oneself and one's own group. It is an insidious fact of prejudice and discrimination that target-group members can become so well socialized through majority organizations and institutions such as the schools and the mass media that they may come to believe the derogatory statements made about them.

The socialization process taught women that they ought not to pursue careers in the sciences and in technological fields. It told women that they should seek challenging careers, but then confronts them with guilt feelings because of these ambitions. They fear that their desire to be economically independent means that they are axiomatically "bad spouses" or "bad mothers." This guilt drives many to seek counseling and even psychiatric help. Frequently, the psychiatrists they consult accept the societal definitions and only reinforce their guilt feelings, directing them not to question the societal values, but to look for and deal with internal inadequacies.[59] Chafetz and Dworkin posited and tested a model of the factors that affected the emergence of feminist movements across different societies. They argued that a sense of relative deprivation and system blame were necessary conditions for women to consider participating in feminist movements. The relative deprivation arose when women compared their status and rewards with that of men doing the same work and found that they were rewarded less than the men. The sense of system blame over self-blame arose when they recognized that the men had no more skill or merit than they, but only receive more status, honor, and reward because of systemic definitions of what it is to be male. However, relative deprivation would arise only if women used men as a comparison group and system blame would arise only if they sought interpretation of their relative disadvantage from women, rather than men. Men were more likely to justify their own higher status and rewards and women's disadvantage by referring to their own skill or experience.[60]

The society places a premium upon whiteness and blondness. Dark-complexioned minorities, especially some African Americans, have in the past been driven to buying skin-lightening creams, hair straighteners, and other devices to make them look more white. Grier and Cobbs, two black psychiatrists, observed:

> Caution must be exercised in distinguishing feelings of inferiority from emulation of the majority by a minority concerned with survival. But even taking this into account, there remains an increment of feelings which says emphatically: "White is right."
>
> For an African American man to straighten his hair chemically, to have what is known as a "process," is a painful, dangerous procedure. The result is a slick pompadour which in no way save one resembles a white man's hair. Only in that it is straight and nonkinky does it appear less black and more white. African Americans historically have referred to straight hair as good—and kinky hair as bad.[61]

Other groups have tried equally drastic alternations of their bodies. Some Japanese have had plastic surgery to give their eyes a more Caucasian appearance. In most instances minority individuals have accepted majority aesthetic judgments, and merely want to look "pretty." But in some instances the motive was to permit economic passing (in which the individual plays the role of a majority member in order to secure better employment opportunities, but emotionally continues to identify with the minority); others sought varying degrees of social passing (in which the individual breaks off all contact with his own group and tries to blend into the majority). The individual who passes socially must be on constant guard against being detected, and lives in fear and suspicion.

Attempts at social passing also incur the wrath of the individual's own minority community. Anger, jealousy, and withdrawal of respect by one's own family and friends may be more damaging to the individual than rejection by the majority. Each minority has a derogatory term to describe individuals of its own group who have become too Anglicized, too much like the majority group in thought and behavior. African Americans refer to such individuals as *Oreos* or *Uncle Toms;* Chicanos use the term *Tío Tacos* or *Tío Tomas;* Native Americans call such individuals of their group *Apples* (red on the outside, white on the inside); the Chinese and Japanese refer to them as *Bananas* (yellow on the outside, white on the inside); the Irish referred to their "traitors" as *Lace-Curtain Irish*. One Hispanic individual recounted to the authors that his own family refused to let him return to their home after he had changed his surname in order to become successful in his law practice. He commented "My own mother told me that she had no son; that he had died; and that she didn't want to have 'ghosts' in her house."

There have been a plethora of studies conducted by social scientists on minority children (usually African American) to discover at how early an age minorities learn to emulate whites and prefer to be like them. One classic study was conducted by Kenneth and Mamie Clark.[62] These social psychologists asked African American children, some in segregated southern schools and some in desegregated northern schools, to choose between an African American doll and a white doll. The children were asked which doll looked like them, which doll looked nice, which doll looked bad, and which doll had a nice color. African American children, especially in the segregated schools, preferred and more favorably evaluated the white doll over the black doll. Similar findings have been reported by other writers, including Miller,[63] who determined color preferences by white, Chicano, and African American children and reported the general acceptance of "the rightness of whiteness hypothesis"—the preference for white over brown or black.

The Clark study is not without some critical flaws. The research was done long before African American dolls were commercially available, so the African American doll was really a white doll with African American enamel paint all over its face. Thus it cannot be determined that the children were really evaluating skin color preference, or merely choosing a doll which looked less damaged or soiled and more like their own at home. This procedure required the children to make two cognitive leaps. They first had to see the racial nature of the dolls, and then had to translate their feelings toward that symbolic object into their feelings toward real groups. With two stages of cognitions required, there is twice the probability of miscuing. There is double the chance that the individuals will be unable to make the cognitive leaps. Not only is it problematic that children may accomplish the task, but the experience of those who run consciousness-raising groups suggests that adults also need help in making such leaps. In fact, those studies that have asked minority children to indicate with whom they wanted to play have generally shown that minorities tend to choose members of their own group. This observation was noted by Linda Teplin.[64] She compared what she called the "projectively based technique," in which children are to project onto inanimate objects (such as dolls or animals of different skin color) cognitions about self-acceptance or rejection, with the "reality-based technique," in which children choose sociometrically an individual with whom they would want to play and be photographed. Teplin noted that children's choices of friends were nearly unrelated to their preferences for inaminate objects. That is, a minority child may choose a toy that shares the color of a majority-group member, but tends to choose other minority-group members as friends. Teplin argues that we should place greater credence on the reality-based measures than the projective measures.

Exploration of early studies of minority-held stereotypes about the majority and about their own group suggests another area of the psychological cost of prejudice. Minority-group members have tended to evaluate the majority more favorably than they evaluate themselves. Bayton[65] in the 1940s found that African American college students stereotyped African Americans nearly as negatively as white college students stereotyped African Americans, and stereotyped whites as positively as whites stereotyped themselves. Simmons[66] noted comparable findings for Mexican Americans in south Texas in the 1950s. A. G. Dworkin[67] compared foreign-born Mexican Americans, who had just arrived in the United States from Mexico and were consequently not socialized to the majority ideology, with native-born Mexican Americans, who had lived in the barrio in East Los Angeles, California, all of their lives and had been socialized by the Anglo schools and media. The foreign born had favorable images of themselves and of the Anglos, while the native born had unfavorable images of themselves and also somewhat unfavorable images of the Anglos. A second study indicated that in a relatively short time (about six months) even the foreign-born Mexican Americans acquired the negative self-imagery pervasive in the barrio.[68]

Attributions of superiority to men and inferiority to women is another element of the socialization of minority groups that tends to have social and psychological consequences for minority-group members. Goldberg[69] found that, because of this socialization, women were more prejudiced against themselves than they were against men. In fact, women downgraded the accomplishments of female professionals in all fields, even in the traditionally female fields, while upgrading the evaluation of males in all fields.

Social scientists have debated whether minority-held stereotypes generally reflect mirror imagery (they are identical to the majority stereotypes, evolving from them and indicating acceptance of majority-based definitions) or whether they reflect reciprocal prejudice (counters to majority-held stereotypes, reflecting rejection of the majority and attacks upon the majority). Maykovich[70] advanced the thesis of general support for the latter form. Research by A. G. Dworkin and Eckberg[71] has illustrated that both processes are at work within the same individual. Minority-group members may accept the majority stereotypes of other minorities, but they reject majority stereotypes of themselves and hold reciprocal prejudiced images of the majority. These authors found that each minority group in their study (Jews, Chicanos, African Americans, and Japanese Americans) accepted between 50 and 60 percent of the images white Protestants held of other minority groups, but less than 30 percent of the images white Protestants held about themselves or about the minority's own group. The NORC data presented in Table 5-1 reinforce this point. While African Americans generally were less likely than whites to endorse the stereotypes whites held about them, they were often as likely to endorse the same stereotypes as did whites about Hispanics and Asians.

Social movements generally tend to have a positive psychological impact upon minority-group members. Movements for civil rights, African American, Chicano, and women's liberation, each of which stresses system blame for social ills rather than personal blame, tend to aid minority-group members in dealing with majority stereotypes. The movements not only affect the images the majority holds of the minority but also provide minority-group members with a vocabulary of motives to shape new self-identities and to account for majority-held images. The senior author has monitored the stereotypes held by Mexican Americans in the periods of 1963 (pre-Chicano movement), 1967–1968 (during the inception of the movement), and 1971–1972 (a period of movement gains).[72] During the ten-year period of these studies, Chicano images of themselves and of Anglos traded positions. In 1963 Chicanos saw Anglos as their superiors; in 1967–1968 they saw Anglos as their equals; and in 1971–1972 they saw Anglos as their inferiors.

The civil rights movement and the African American liberation movement similarly have increasingly insulated African Americans from possible ego threats induced by white prejudice. These movements have taught African Americans to view as illegitimate and motivated by racism the preponderance of white stereotypy. Researchers have found that African Americans and whites now report equally high estimates of self-esteem.[73] The basis for such self-esteem among African Americans is within the African American community through African American and not white evaluations,[74] and most usually through evaluations by one's friends and neighbors.[75]

When members of a minority group are relatively isolated from others of their group, as in the case of token minority students in a majority public school, self-esteem levels may be lower. This could be because the majority group provides the standard for self-comparison. Drury[76] has found that African American children in racially segregated schools had higher levels of self-esteem than did those children in racially balanced schools (near equal numbers of African Americans and whites) or those children in predominantly white schools. These differences remained even when Drury compared children of similar levels of academic achievement and social classes. It is possible that within the classroom, or within the campus, segregation practices, differentials in teacher praise and attention, and the attitudes of the white students may have combined to produce lowered self-esteem even in the balanced setting. That is, the balanced setting may actually not convey the message of equality to minority students. The impact of desegregation on self-esteem, however, remains inconclusive to date.[77] On the other hand, academic gains in desegregated settings are higher, provided that there are not great differentials in the social class between African American and white students.[78] Likewise, when African American and white children of similar class origins and abilities are placed together, interracial friendships are more common.[79] The adverse impact on achievement of desegregation into high social class settings may be due to the relative lack of attention teachers may given to the lower class students. Thus, the dynamics of classroom interaction again play a role.

The movements provide for a transition from psychological marginality to the development of marginal culture. Park[80] and Stonequist[81] advanced the concept of marginality, and numerous authors have improved upon it.[82] According to the theory, when an individual is part of two societies or subcultures and is accepted in neither, or finds that the subordinate subculture in which he or she is accepted is unsatisfactory but the superordinate one is unavailable, the person will manifest a series of social and psychological conditions. Stonequist itemizes some of the symptoms as a double consciousness, ambivalent feelings, moodiness, temperamentalness, hypersensitivity, and hyperactivity.

If, however, there are sufficient other individuals in his or her condition so that a social group with a strong sense of identity can evolve, they may be able to develop an alternative society based upon their common marginality. Social movements are useful in focusing the individual consciousness and in-group self-awareness into a viable entity. The new marginal culture is then capable of providing psychic and social rewards for its members, and the condition of psychological marginality terminates.[83]

Recent writings by Porter and Washington[84] have criticized much thought regarding minority self-esteem. The authors argue that while there is little doubt that African American, Hispanic, and Asian American peoples have each experienced considerable racism, prejudice, and discrimination, too many social science models have assumed homogeneity in the groups' perceptions of their ethnic status. The concepts Asian American and Hispanic are aggregations of diverse peoples who make finer distinctions than do either the dominant population or the U.S. census. The personal responses to discrimination reflect a plethora of group adaptations, but always include a component of ethnic awareness (e.g., the awareness of being Puerto Rican, rather than Mexican American, or being Chinese, rather than Thai). The African American response to discrimination is characterized as even more homogeneous because slavery shattered many ethnic distinctions. However, Afrocentrism and its challenge to the Eurocentric hegemony over definitions also present a challenge to white interpretations of minority experiences. Likewise, multicultural models, such as those presented in the next chapter, pose different conceptualizations of identity. It is for that reason alone that *The Minority Report* has individual chapters authored by members of the different groups experiencing American society.

The Causes of Prejudice

Prejudice and discrimination manifest themselves in numerous ways, and so there are numerous explanations for them. No one theory of prejudice is adequate to explain all of its manifestations, and prejudice itself is probably not a unitary phenomenon. That is, we might do well to consider that there are many kinds of prejudice and that each kind may be caused by combinations of a multitude of factors. Earliest theories of prejudice focused upon instinctive and biological factors, including instinctive fear of difference and instinctive hatreds. Some of these theories have been around since shortly after the French Revolution.[85] It is generally true that we can detect more plausible social, psychological, or cultural factors behind these manifestations of prejudice and discrimination than if we had to rely upon purely organismic explanations. Basically, we can discern three classes of theories of prejudice and discrimination: psychological theories, social structural theories, and normative and cultural theories.

Psychological Theories

Frustration-Aggression and Scapegoating Theory. Dollard[86] and his colleagues at the Yale Institute of Human Relations developed the hypothesis which maintains that aggressive impulses arise whenever one is frustrated. Prejudice is considered a type of aggression and is said to be a universal response to frustration. When people's needs are unsatisfied or their activities are interrupted, they respond with aggression. But often aggression cannot be directed toward the frustrating object, because that object is too powerful. Thus the aggression is directed toward members of the minority groups, who serve as a "scapegoat." For example, a "poor white," who cannot vent his aggression upon his landlord (because of custom and power structure pressures), displaces his aggression onto a convenient, easily identified object—the African American.

Hughes[87] gives the example of French Canadian farmers unable to strike back at the dominant English-speaking Canadian urbanites, who were attempting to do away with the rural way of life. The French Canadians, being too weak to affect the decisions of the English-speaking group, vented their aggressions upon the Jewish minority.

There are weaknesses in the frustration-aggression-scapegoating theory. While the above-mentioned cases seem to support the theory, the theory does not explain satisfactorily why aggression may be directed against one minority and not against another. Furthermore, although the theory explains a *possible* force behind prejudice in general, it fails to account for the fact that prejudice against minorities is not the only response to frustration. Berkowitz and Green[88] and Geen[89] have demonstrated that frustration does not necessarily lead to aggression but tends to require symbols of violence or aggression as intervening variables. That is, unless frustration occurs in the presence of or immediately before exposure to aggressive cues, aggression will not occur. The widespread displays of violence and symbols of violence in the mass media, especially on television, may provide the necessary connective link between frustration and aggression.

The Authoritarian Personality. In the 1930s, German philosopher and social scientist Max Horkheimer[90] first proposed that prejudice could be accounted for by a general personality type. In 1950 Adorno and his associates[91] published their massive study on the psychology of prejudice, The Authoritarian Personality. Studying over 2,000 Americans, the research concluded that about 10 percent of the population were authoritarian and an additional 30 percent had "the seeds of authoritarianism in them." The authoritarian personality is one that has been shaped by fear of authority, as in the relationship between the child and his strict patriarchal father who makes binding and arbitrary decisions and punishes for lack of respect. The child who has such a relationship responds to all authority as he did to his father, submissively, and as an adult becomes authoritarian in turn. Deeper studies demonstrate that obeying arbitrary authority in childhood results in bottled-up fear and resentment. The child who successfully weathers the discipline develops into an adult frightened by and morally indignant about people whose behavior is different from his own conduct. His fears and repressed wish to retaliate can easily be mobilized whenever the proper rationalization is supplied. Generally, the authoritarian is a person who has the following characteristics:[92]

1. He is a supreme conformist who irrationally and unquestioningly succumbs to the commands of a leader.
2. He views the world as menacing and unfriendly, agreeing that the "world is a jungle."
3. He is mechanical and rigid, showing little imagination.
4. He is quite ethnocentric and xenophobic. Because the world is menacing, he can find security only with those who are like him and hence predictable.
5. He is a phony conservative, waving the flag but hating the values of freedom and democracy.
6. He is a moral purist, who has come to reject all emotionality and sensuality.

The Authoritarian Personality has been immensely heuristic, generating volumes of research. Much of the research has brought into question the accuracy of the portrayal of a single personality factor to account for prejudice. The famous F-Scale, which emerged from the study and which was designed to measure authoritarianism, has also been the subject of much methodological criticism. Without the study, work in the analysis of prejudice and its causes would have been slower to develop. Nonetheless, we now know that psychological causes of prejudice cannot explain all or even most of the phenomenon.

Social Structure Theories

Unlike the psychological theories, which posit the cause of prejudice as located within the individual and his or her personality development, social structural theories locate the cause of prejudice within the context of relationships between people in the society. There are numerous structural theories, but those with which we shall deal concern economic competition, economic exploitation, and situational and mass society theories.

Economic Competition and Economic Exploitation. These two economic theories of prejudice are basically rather similar. The economic competition theory sees prejudice arising from groups that are in direct competition for scarce resources. The economic exploitation theory adds that if one group possesses far greater power than the other, the competition is turned into the exploitation of the weaker group by the more powerful. A leading exponent of the economic models in minority-group relations was Oliver C. Cox,[93] who viewed prejudice as a tool employed by the ruling class to suppress the minority class.

In support of the competition theory, McWilliams[94] noted that there was little prejudice against the Japanese in California until Japanese immigrants began to enter types of work which competed with Anglo occupations. Similarly, medieval anti-Semitism in Europe increased greatly when banking and finance, previously left to the Jews, grew to be profitable for the Gentiles. The economic exploitation of Mexican Americans, which kept them in stoop labor jobs at less than minimum wages, rewarded Anglo prejudice with low fruit and vegetable prices. However, when Mexican American field workers tried to unionize in 1931, growers got the police to arrest the workers and to place them into "concentration camps." Those who resisted were deported (repatriated—even though many were American born). Similar attacks on Cesar Chavez and members of the United Farm Workers can be explained by the same theory.

Slavery in the United States also conforms to the economic exploitation hypothesis. Until the invention of the cotton gin in the 1790s slavery was moving toward extinction. With this innovation, slavery was rapidly extended and cemented into the social structure with the rise of racist attitudes of prejudice. Whereas slavery had formerly existed as a weak institution, an economic incentive made it strong and apparently provided the stimulus for the introduction of race prejudice.

Wilhelm[95] has suggested in his theory of economic exclusion that African Americans were tolerated only so long as they could provide a pool of cheap labor that could not be technologically displaced. Now machines can do many tasks with minimal expense, especially those normally relegated to unskilled labor. Further, as William Julius Wilson[96] notes, the movement of jobs out from the inner city and to the Third World has resulted in massively high rates of unemployment in the central cities of the United States, leading to substantial deprivation for African Americans and other urban groups. Such labor market relocations have also resulted in the nihilism addressed by Cornell West.[97]

Split Labor Market Theory. Another social structural theory attempts to combine both economic competition and economic exploitation into a single framework. Bonacich[98] has proposed a "split labor market theory of ethnic antagonisms." The theory does not posit prejudice as an outcome per se, only discrimination. According to her theory two groups, with different levels of skill resources and expertise, are pitted against one another in the labor market. Employers seek to minimize labor costs and hence displace higher-paid labor with lower-paid labor. However, this increases the antagonisms between the labor groups, which often are minority and majority groups. The majority group of laborers, having greater power, engages in two discriminatory practices; exclusion movements, whereby the minority may be deported, and labor caste systems, whereby the minority is relegated to lower-status, less well-paying jobs, and the majority to higher-status, better-paying jobs. Thus prejudices become the rationalization for economic behaviors—both competitive and exploitive. Discrimination becomes the tool for securing and/or maintaining economic advantage. Simultaneously, contact between hostile groups in economic competition tends to validate and reinforce previously held prejudices.

Jonathan Turner and Royce Singleton[99] have amended the Bonacich model to incorporate cultural variables. These authors have noted that the purely structural and economic approach of split labor theory ignores the dynamic interplay of what they call "dominant beliefs" (held by the majority) and "progressive beliefs" (held by some majority elites not economically threatened by minorities and the minorities themselves). In societies that advocate norms of equality, the threat by low-priced labor is countered by oppressive and discriminatory practices (e.g., exclusion and labor castes), which must be rationalized and legitimated by beliefs that point to the inferiority of the threatening group. Groups that are not threatened by low-price labor come to see the contradiction between the general societal values and the specific oppressive practices and legitimating beliefs. They ideologically codify more progressive beliefs to challenge the beliefs that support oppression. As the size and power of the nonthreatened groups grow, they will be able to supplant the dominant beliefs with progressive beliefs. However, as the caste position of low-priced labor changes due to the progressive beliefs, some previously nonthreatened groups may become threatened. Such changes may lead to modified ideologies to rationalize different oppressive systems, which in turn will be challenged by new progressive beliefs. The theory thus links economic conditions, the society's value system, the roles of high- and low-priced labor, and the forces that change intergroup relations into a dynamic model.

Situational and Mass Society Theories. These theories[100] combine two observations about prejudice and discrimination in complex societies. The first is that prejudice and discrimination are situation specific. Individuals may express prejudicial beliefs and engage in discriminatory practices in one situation, and do and say antithetical things in another situation (recall several studies[101] reported earlier in this chapter). Second, people participate in many organizations, some of which may have contradictory goals. These organizations, sometimes massive in scale, are impersonal and unresponsive to individual inputs, so the actor exerts much less control over the organization than the organization exerts over the individual. Communications, typified by the mass media, tend to be one-way, in which the individual receives but does not send messages. Participation in these organizations (e.g., labor unions, churches, neighborhood associations) does not involve the total self, but only segments of specific roles performed. During participation in a specific organization, one's attitudes, goals, and behaviors must conform to the prescriptions of that organization. Because of the lowered commitment and the segmented participation in these mass organizations, individuals can tolerate a high degree of apparently contradictory behavior and attitudes within themselves.[102] Thus, under pressures to conform to the demands of multiple organizations and a large variation of peers, behavior toward minority groups may vary with the specific situation. Seen in this way, prejudice and discrimination are less individualistic and more organizational in origin. The individual bigot is merely an extension of institutional racism.

The general trend of the mass media and of large organizations has been to diminish prejudice and discrimination. The content of television programs, implementation of governmental policy, and other large organizational policies have been aimed toward more equality among citizens. Thus we might not expect the model depicted by the situational and mass society theory to lead to greater prejudice and discrimination. Nonetheless, there are significant differences in the amount and kind of exposure to organizations that different individuals encounter. Further, the messages from these organizations are not always consistent. A variety of studies of voting behavior has suggested that only individuals caught between conflicting pressure groups are likely to follow the mass media's suggestions. Social structural theories of prejudice and discrimination have proven to be viable explanations. They do not, however, explain the totality of attitudes and behaviors. For one thing, social structural models are embedded within a given culture. They assume the existence of cultural theories in order to operate. We now turn to the normative and cultural explanations of prejudice.

Normative and Cultural Theories

In Chapter 4 we spoke of institutional racism as an ideology of American society. Supported by this ideology is the norm for prejudice. That is, people are prejudiced because society teaches them to be prejudiced, rewards them for prejudice, and demands prejudicial beliefs and discriminatory behavior as forms of compliance to the norm.[103] Part of most people's socialization has included being discouraged by their parents from playing with "inappropriate playmates." No individual is born with prejudices, but through early socialization he or she quickly learns whom to hate. Many writers have noted that people rarely learn their prejudice from direct contact with minority-group members, but from members of their own group who are already prejudiced.

One must be cautious of a static view of the normative theory of prejudice. To accept the explanation of prejudice as static is to assume that ideas are passed from generation to generation without modification. We know, however, that there have been changes in the amount and level of prejudice observable in our society over the past three decades. A dynamic normative theory can account for this, because it would suggest that as norms concerning prejudice change, the level of prejudice should change. One should also be cautious not to assume that a normative theory can explain all prejudice. The previously discussed structural and personality theories do account for some of the presence of prejudice.

Prejudice as a Symbol. In some instances prejudice may persist even after it ceases to perform psychological, economic, structural, and other societal functions. In such instances the strength of the prejudice might be less intense. Some researchers have argued that these lingering prejudices stem from historical events in which the minority group was involved and for which it now serves as a symbol. Some aspects of anti-Semitism may be due to the historical view of Jews as "Christ-killers" or as symbols of the city, with its strange cosmopolitan atmosphere that frightened many rural peoples.[104] Some prejudice against African Americans may be a residual symbol of the South's defeat in the Civil War and Reconstruction.[105] It is quite possible that some of the prejudice encountered by Vietnamese refugees may have resulted from their role as a symbol of America's frustrations in Vietnam, and of the economic and political consequences of the defeat to American foreign policy in the 1970s.

The Linguistic Theory. A final theory of prejudice that operates on the cultural or macrosystem (as opposed to the social structural or interpersonal) level is the linguistic theory of prejudice.

Most linguistic theories of prejudice are based upon an interpretation of the Sapir-Whorf hypothesis,[106] which holds that the characteristics of a language determine how its speakers view their world. That is, "language is not 'merely' a vehicle of communication by which man talks about some objective reality 'out there' that exists previous to and independent of his language, but rather that language itself represents an objective reality by means of which man structures and organizes the 'out there' in certain characteristic ways."[107]

Much of human interaction involves manipulation of symbols. Without symbols, especially language, individuals would be able neither to think nor to possess a social self and social identity.[108] The culture—which specifies the appropriate modes of behavior, thinking, and dealing with others—is transmitted through the language. Thus some theorists have looked to the content of language for the roots and causes of prejudice and discrimination.

In Western societies and, as Allport notes, in many non-Western societies,[109] the term "black" has sinister connotations—witches are black, funerals and death are depicted as black, harmful or evil magic is "black magic," and "blacklisting" and "blackballing" refer to rejection. On the other hand, the term "white" has connotations of cleanliness and purity—angels are white, bridal gowns are white, Ivory Soap commercials once noted that the soap was white and 99 and 44/100 percent pure. Similarly, Orientals have yellowish skin, and since the color "yellow" connotes cowardly, stale, and untrustworthy, according to the theory, these negative characteristics are ascribed to Orientals. Thus the theory holds that because of the cultural connotations attached to them, people with skin resembling one of these three colors are attributed with the characteristics the colors connote.

Similarly, the English language has structured within it several assumptions about sex roles and the nature of males and females. Although gender designations of nouns and pronouns are more conspicuous in other languages (such as Spanish, Italian, and French), it is difficult to compose English paragraphs that do not demand gender designations of pronouns (e.g., his, her) even when gender is irrelevant to the meaning being communicated. In such instances the correct pronoun is considered to be the masculine, because of the assumed importance of the masculine in the entire culture. When various feminist groups rebel against the suffix "man" in words like "policeman," "chairman," and "postman," and insist on the substitution of "person," they are expressing an awareness of the sensitizing and symbolic function of language as a determinant of behavior.

Prejudice and Discrimination Reduction

The previous section began with the observation that there are many causes of prejudice and discrimination, and in fact, there probably are many kinds of prejudice. Hence it is unlikely that a cure-all procedure can be devised to eradicate prejudice and discrimination. The most effective technique would be to prevent a person from becoming prejudiced in the first place. Hence, child-raising practices that permit children to experience, meet, and learn about people of diverse identities and heritages are superior to any technique that seeks to rid an adult of his prejudices. Public television programs and other forms of the mass media are available to provide children with the lesson that all people, regardless of skin color, cultural background, or gender are human beings with equal rights to a productive life on our planet. But it is a reality of social life that people differentiate between groups, that people do evaluate others in terms of their race, ethnicity, and gender. Given that there is prejudice in the world and that children tend to learn that prejudice, the task then becomes one of reducing it.

Early in this chapter four functions of prejudice were enumerated: preknowledge, ego defense, instrumental, and value expressive. It was further noted that unless changes occurred in the nature of the target of prejudice, the nature of the prejudiced individual, or the relationship between the two, prejudice itself would not change. There have been programs to change minority-group members, including techniques that "Americanized" them. There have been programs oriented toward the prejudiced individual, providing aids such as psychiatric help, counseling, or correcting misinformation about the minority groups. And there have been programs that have attempted to instill better relations between the minorities and the majority. It has been the general experience of many programs geared toward the prejudiced individual or toward tightening bonds between majorities and minorities that the only individuals who attended the sessions were those already committed to nonprejudice, who came only to reinforce their beliefs. The really "hard-core" bigot never came to the various "human relations sessions."

Information Campaigns

One of the more dismal failures in prejudice reduction has been public information campaigns geared at debunking stereotypes. Most of the people who come to such sessions do not subscribe to the stereotype in the first place, and those that do believe the stereotype either supplant the debunked image with a new, equally negative one, or define the experience as proving nothing. A student in a class taught by the junior author complained after several myths about sex roles had been attacked, "You're just trying to confuse me with facts."

Education

There is some evidence that educational programs within the schools, particularly in the universities, can be effective. However, it is the *nature* of the programs that are essential, not simply their presence. In some instances, simply offering African American history courses in the public schools may have little or no effect, or may even heighten barriers. This is especially true if the material is presented by a teacher who is hostile to the concepts, or if the issues are freighted with political ramifications in the community which filter into the classroom. Although an integrated education potentially can benefit majority and minority participants, two things tend also to be true. First, much of what is called integrated education is simply desegregated in a token fashion, either with a few minority students in a majority classroom or desegregation at the school level but not at the classroom level.[110] A school in the latter situation may have many minority children, but all of them may be assigned to a "special educational program," separated from the majority children. Second, the potential benefits that could accrue to both minority- and majority-group members tend to be mitigated when community-wide hostilities arise over issues of busing and school-community politics. Students see the agitation created by their parents and are prepared to expect the worst from the educational situation. Considering that events defined negatively tend to be self-fulfilling, it is little wonder that results have been disappointing.

In college and university studies there is evidence that education, especially desegregated education, can reduce prejudice. The early Bennington studies demonstrated the liberalism fostered by a college environment.[111] The work of Perlmutter[112] and A. G. Dworkin[113] has illustrated that the liberal arts education tends to reduce reliance upon stereotypes. Dworkin found that although college students held a variety of stereotypes about minority groups, the stereotypes were not used to rationalize social distance feelings or discriminatory behavior. The stereotypes lingered as conventions of speech, not as the language of prejudice.

Ehrlich[114] makes two observations about the role of education in attitude change. The first is that education may produce decreased prejudice in instances in which the individual becomes educationally very mobile in relation to his or her family. He or she may lose the values and social support of the family, and will likely hold to disparate and more egalitarian values. Ehrlich's second observation is that it is vastly easier to change attitudes than to maintain the stability of those changed attitudes. The college experience may reduce prejudice, provided that the college which the student attends supports liberal values, because of social support (peer support) for the liberalism. However, once the student graduates and enters a world that is not so liberal, his or her attitudes may change back to conservatism. The situation-specific nature of prejudice is again apparent.

Jackman and her associates[115] are less sanguine about the influence of education in reducing discrimination. She notes that the apparent diminution in prejudice by college-educated individuals and liberal attitudes about race are superficial and not likely to be conjoined by action when their own group interests are at stake. Kluegel [116] has found that whites believe that African Americans have as equal a chance or even a greater chance of getting ahead in America today than do whites. It leads whites to resist endorsing affirmative action programs to improve the conditions of African Americans. Whites, however, are less likely to account for black-white differentials in terms of biological or genetic differences and more often to use motivational explanations for inequalities. Armed with a belief that African American economic disadvantages are due to lower levels of motivation to get ahead, many whites feel that government programs to end inequality are unjustified. However, other whites do see structural barriers to African American equality and are likely to endorse government intervention. Nevertheless, Kluegel concludes that as a society, "...we seem to have reached an era of stable, comfortable acceptance by whites of the black-white economic gap."[117]

Contact and Prejudice Reduction

If prejudice is formed in the absence of intergroup contact, reasoned many thinkers, it could be eliminated in the presence of intergroup contact. This was hoped because intergroup contact was more easily implemented than other techniques, such as those requiring massive resocialization of the populace.[118] But early in the attempts to reduce prejudice it was discovered that not all contact is the same. Contact that maintains social distance and is based upon the subordination of one group by another does not breed reductions in prejudice, discrimination, and hostility. It is now known that contact has to be equal status in nature. That is, individuals interacting with one another have to view each other as coequals. Early research by Deutsch and Collins[119] and Wilner, Walkley, and Cook[120] has shown that in desegregated public housing projects equal status contacts will reduce prejudice on the part of whites. Other studies have shown less conclusive results.[121]

Ford[122] discovered that the equal status between African Americans and whites actually tended to decrease white prejudice toward African Americans while not reducing African American prejudice toward whites. The explanation for the disparity in findings can be found in the nature of the equal status contacts. Whites frequently projected unconscious cues that told the African Americans that the situation was not really equal status; they behaved in ways that implied that the African Americans were really subordinate. What is clearly needed is a program that will alert majorities to the myriad ways in which they unconsciously announce their majority status. Otherwise majorities will not understand why their attempts at prejudice reduction are met with minority resistance. Faced with such rebuff, majority-group members may become even more hardened in their prejudice, and minority-group members will similarly have their prejudice reinforced. In instances where interracial contact is seen as equal status contact, conforming to group norms, where goals are shared across groups, and where the negative stereotypes are contradicted by the behavior of the members of each group, contact can lead to decreased levels of prejudice for both the minority and majority groups.[123]

Value Consensus and Superordinate Goals

Vastly more success has been afforded programs which involve the active participation of individuals in reducing prejudice.[124] Two distinct techniques should be noted here. The first is based upon value consensus and has been proposed by Allport[125] and Pettigrew.[126] In the value consensus design, individuals of different groups that are currently conflicting (e.g., African Americans and whites) are brought together to explore their common goals, ambitions, beliefs, and so on. Provided that these groups have much in common, they tend to discover additional avenues of dialogue and common understandings, which in turn further reduce hostility. The procedure works well if the individuals share many things in common and are not competing for scarce or mutually exclusive resources. For example, upper-class African Americans and whites could serve as tests of the value consensus approach. Economic competition is minimal, and they hold many values in common according to the class principle.

The senior author once worked on a study involving African American and white parents in a predominantly white neighborhood. The African American parents were concerned about the schools, as were the white parents. The African Americans feared that their children might be attacked by white children on the way to school; that the teachers would dilute the curriculum because of the presence of African Americans, thereby reducing their children's chances of getting into a prestigious college; and that whites would flee the neighborhood and lower property values. The white parents voiced the identical fears. Once the two groups realized they had so many values in common, most racial tensions in the neighborhood ceased.

If, however, the groups do not have common goals and values, value consensus is unlikely, and so is prejudice reduction. Muzafer Sherif[127] has offered an alternative procedure. Sherif demonstrated the principle of superordinate goals in a study of a boys' summer camp. Through a series of contrivances, Sherif created two hostile and conflicting groups within the camp. Then, by establishing a major goal that neither could attain without the cooperation of the other (hence a superordinate goal), Sherif was able to get the groups to coexist peacefully and to abandon their prejudices against one another.

It is essential that the superordinate goal be one that: (1) is of major importance to both groups; (2) can be attained only through the mutual cooperation of the groups; and (3) is actually attained after the cooperation. Should the third condition not be satisfied, each group may blame the other for failure and prejudice and hostilities may be heightened. McClendon and Eitzen[128] have shown that prejudice levels among college basketball teams diminish in those teams that are interracial and have successful win-lose records. The teams want to win, they can only win interracially, and they have been winners. All three of Sherif's conditions have been met. In another study, several researchers[129] have worked with the Houston Council on Human Relations in the testing and evaluation of an interracial simulation game that creates interdependence between racial groups. The simulation had been effective in reducing prejudice levels among the participants, who were students in the Houston public schools. However, the most dramatic reductions in prejudice occurred in those schools that were "balanced"—that is, having nearly equal numbers of African American, brown, and white students. In such schools the entire school situation provides an extension of the simulation and is in itself a superordinate goal. No school activity, whether it be a sports activity, a class play, or student government, can be executed without the cooperation of members of each group.

Superordinate goal situations tend to merge into value consensus situations. By working for a common goal, groups explore other areas of common cooperation, and in turn prejudice is reduced. The era of détente in the 1970s and again in the late 1980s between the United States and the former Soviet Union represented a set of superordinate goals: preventing a thermonuclear war, cooperating in space and technology, and coping with the world's food and energy crises. Likewise, the coalition during the Gulf War in 1991 involved a superordinate goal. Some Arab nations joined the coalition against Iraq not because of a love of American foreign policy, but because of a greater dislike of the policies of Saddam Hussein. It is apparent that models applicable to individuals can be applied under some conditions to groups, and even to nation-states.

SUMMARY

The social psychological level of analysis emphasizes the impact of the social structure upon the individual. The unit of analysis is the individual and the relationships between individuals. The essential aspects of such a level of analysis in minority-group relations are attitudes, behaviors, and the self. The attitude is prejudice and the behavior is discrimination.

Prejudice is multidimensional including the elements of direction, salience, intensity, commitment, and centrality. Prejudice serves its users with four functions. It provides knowledge to give meanings to interactions and to reduce the need to interact; it provides the prejudiced individual with ego-defense; it is instrumental in providing rewards to the prejudiced person, including maintenance of the pattern of superordination and subordination; and it is value-expressive, permitting the individual to express his key values, or the key values of his culture. Ethnocentrism supports prejudice and stereotypes provide prejudice with a language and a rhetoric. Changing stereotypes, like reducing prejudice, requires alterations in the nature of the target group, the nature of the stereotyper, and/or the relationship between the two. Nonetheless, there are conceptual mechanisms that may permit stereotypes to persist beyond their immediate functionality. Another manifestation of prejudice is social distance, or the degree to which a person is unwilling to have intimate contact with the minority. Several measures have been devised to assess social distance, including the Bogardus Social Distance Scale.

The relationship between discrimination and prejudice is not mutually contingent. Prejudiced people do not always discriminate, and discriminators are not always prejudiced. An individual's social situation plays an integral role. Commitment to one's beliefs and one's volition (the amount of control one can exercise over the situation) determine whether or not prejudice and discrimination will be conjoined. A theoretical model was advanced to show the manner in which peer and other influences could determine the relationship between prejudicial attitudes and discriminatory behaviors.

The costs of prejudice and discrimination to the prejudiced individual and to the target of prejudice were explored. An analysis of the concept of minority-group self-hatred was advanced. It is indeterminate whether the concept per se exists, or whether it is a symptom of emulation of the majority. Minority-based social movements tend to reduce the emulation and to heighten a group's self-pride. Evidence for this was demonstrated in material on stereotype change.

Prejudice is caused by many factors, and it is likely that there are many forms of prejudice, each caused by different sets of variables. Basic theories of prejudice can be subsumed under psychological, social structural, and cultural and normative theories. The psychological theories include, but are not limited to, frustration-aggression and scapegoating models and the theory of the authoritarian personality. Social structural theories include economic exploitation and economic competition, economic exclusion, and situational and mass society theories. Normative and cultural theories include ideology theories, symbolic theories, and linguistic theories.

Numerous attempts have been made to reduce prejudice and discrimination. Education and diversity of experience may be effective in preventing prejudice from emerging, but once it is present, information campaigns and other "passive" techniques tend to be ineffective. The techniques of value consensus and superordinate goals tend to be more effective in reducing prejudice, with the latter preferable if the groups initially have little in common. Even these attempts are sometimes problematic, since contact, which is a necessary condition for the two techniques to operate, may not be perceived as equal status contact by all. In such cases prejudice levels might be unaffected or even increased. A disturbing belief in white American society is that inequality has been eliminated, and that the only gaps that remain are those due to the lack of motivation on the part of minorities. This affects attitudes toward government intervention and leads to opposition to programs such as affirmative action.

Notes

1. Paul F. Secord and Carl W. Backman, *Social Psychology* (New York: McGraw-Hill, 1974), p. 165.
2. Eugene L. Horowitz, "Development of Attitudes Toward Negroes," Archives for *Psychology* 28, no. 194 (1936).
3. Joseph O. Bass, "Attitudes Toward Negroes of Selected Occupational Categories in Bangkok, Thailand" (Master's thesis, University of Missouri, 1969).
4. See Gordon W. Allport, *The Nature of Prejudice* (Cambridge, Mass: Addison-Wesley, 1954), and Howard J. Ehrlich, *The Social Psychology of Prejudice* (New York: Wiley-Interscience, 1973).
5. See Daniel Katz, "The Functional Approach to the Study of Attitudes," *Public Opinion Quarterly* 24 (1960), pp. 163–204, and Daniel Katz and E. Stotland

"A Preliminary Statement to Theory of Attitude Structure and Change," in *Psychology: A Study of Science,* ed. Sigmund Koch (New York: McGraw-Hill, 1959), pp. 423–75.

6. Frank R. Westie, "The American Dilemma: An Empirical Test," *American Sociological Review* 30 (1965), pp. 527–38.
7. T. W. Adorno et al., *The Authoritarian Personality* (New York: Harper, 1950).
8. Jack Levin, *The Functions of Prejudice* (New York: Harper, 1975).
9. Ibid.; Charles E. Sliberman, *Crisis in Black and White* (New York: Random House, 1964); and Richard A. Cloward and Lloyd E. Ohlin, *Delinquency and Opportunity* (New York: Free Press, 1960).
10. See Donn Byrne, "Interpersonal Attraction and Attitude Similarity," *Journal of Abnormal and Social Psychology* 62 (1961), pp. 713–15, and Donn Byrne and Terry J. Wong, "Racial Prejudice, Interpersonal Attraction, and Assumed Dissimilarity of Attitudes," *Journal of Abnormal and Social Psychology* 63 (1962), pp. 246–53.
11. Milton Rokeach, Patricia Smith, and Richard I. Evans, "Two Kinds of Prejudice or One?" in Milton Rokeach, *The Open and Closed Mind* (New York: Basic Books, 1960), pp. 132–68.
12. Anthony Downs, "Alternative Futures for the American Ghetto" *Daedalus* 97 (1968), pp. 1331–78.
13. Walter Lippmann, *Public Opinion* (New York: Macmillan, 1922), p. 95.
14. F. LaViolette and K. H. Silvert, "A Theory of Stereotypes," *Social Forces* 29 (1951), pp. 257–62.
15. Anthony Gary Dworkin, Chaoiki Moussa, and Hoda Badr, "Casualties in the Storm: The Social Marginality of Arabs and Arab Americans in the U.S." Unpublished paper presented at the American Sociological Association meetings, Pittsburgh, PA, 1992.
16. Allport, *Nature of Prejudice,* p. 191.
17. Emory S. Bogardus, "Stereotypes and Sociotypes," *Sociology and Social Research* 34 (1950), pp. 286–91.
18. Orrin E. Klapp, *Heroes, Villains, and Fools* (Englewood Cliffs, NJ: Prentice-Hall, 1962).
19. E. T. Prothro and L. Mellikian, "Studies in Stereotypes," *Journal of Social Psychology* 41 (1955), pp. 21–30; W. Buchanan, "Stereotypes and Tensions as Revealed by the UNESCO International Poll" *International Social Science Bulletin* 3 (1951), pp. 515–28; and W. Vinacki, "Stereotyping Among National-Racial Groups in Hawaii," *Journal of Social Psychology* 30 (1949), pp. 265–91.
20. Muzafer Sherif and Carolyn W. Sherif, *Social Psychology* (New York: Harper, 1969).
21. See Joshua Fishman, "An Examination of the Process and Functioning of Social Stereotyping" *Journal of Social Psychology* 43 (1956), pp. 27–64, and Hubertus C. J. Duijker and N. H. Frijda, *National Character and National Stereotypes* (Amsterdam: North-Holland, 1960).

22. Anthony Gary Dworkin and Douglas L. Eckberg, "Consciousness and Reality: the Chicano Movement and Chicano Anglo Mutual Stereotypes," *International Journal of Sociology and Social Policy* 6 (1986), pp. 61–75.

23. See Daniel Katz and Kenneth W. Braly, "Racial Stereotypes of 100 College Students," *Journal of Abnormal and Social Psychology* 28 (1933), pp. 280–90; Marvin Karlins, Thomas L. Coffman, and Gary Walters, "On the Fading of Social Stereotypes: Studies in Three Generations of College Students," *Journal of Personality and Social Psychology* 13 (1969), pp. 4–5; and Ehrlich, *Social Psychology.*

24. Maurice N. Richter, Jr., "The Conceptual Mechanism of Stereotyping," *American Sociological Review* 21 (1956), pp. 568–71.

25. Fishman, "Examination of the Process."

26. M. Mackie, "Arriving at 'Truth' by Definition: The Case of Stereotype Inaccuracy," *Social Problems* 21 (1973), pp. 431–47.

27. Robert K. Merton, *Social Theory and Social Structure* (New York: Free Press 1957), chap. 11.

28. W. I. Thomas and F. Znaniecki, *The Polish Peasant in Europe and America,* 2 vols. (1918; reprint, New York: Knopf, 1927).

29. Elliot Liebow, *Talley's Corner* (Boston: Little, Brown, 1967).

30. Thomas Fraser Pettigrew, "Three Issues in Ethnicity: Boundaries, Deprivations, and Perceptions," in J. Milton Yinger and Stephen J. Cutler, eds. *Major Social Issues: A Multidisciplinary View* (New York: Free Press, 1978).

31. Ibid.

32. Rosabeth Moss Kanter, *Men and Women of the Corporation.* (New York: Basic Books, 1977).

33. National Opinion Research Center, *General Social Surveys, 1972-1996: Cumulative Codebook* (Chicago: NORC, 1997).

34. Robert G. Weisbord and Arthur Steip, *Bitter-Sweet Encounter.* New York: Schockern Books, 1972.

35. Douglas S. Massey and Nancy A. Denton, *American Apartheid: Segregation and the Making of the Underclass.* (Cambridge, MA: Harvard University Press, 1993).

36. Gregory D. Squires, *Capital and Communities in Black and White: The Intersections of Race, Class, and Uneven Development* (Albany, NY: SUNY Press, 1994).

37. Howard Schuman, Charlotte Steeh, Lawrence Bobo, and Maria Krysan, *Racial Attitudes in America: Trends and Interpretations,* rev. ed. (Cambridge, MA: Harvard University Press, 1997).

38. Mary R. Jackman, *The Velvet Glove: Paternalism and Conflict in Gender, Class, and Race.* (Berkeley, CA: University of California Press, 1994), and Mary R. Jackman and Michael J. Muha, "Education and Intergroup Attitudes: Moral Enlightenment, Superficial Democratic Commitment, or Ideological Refinement?" *American Sociological Review* 49 (1984), pp. 751–769.

39. Robert E. Park, "The Concept of Social Distance," *Journal of Applied Sociology* 8 (1924), pp. 339–44.
40. Emory S. Bogardus, "Measuring Social Distance," *Journal of Applied Sociology* 9 (1925), pp. 299–308.
41. Emory S. Bogardus, "A Social Distance Scale," *Sociology and Social Research* 17 (1933), pp. 265–71.
42. Anthony Gary Dworkin, "Prejudice, Social Distance and Intergroup Perceptions: Explanatory Research in the Correlates of Stereotypy" (Ph.D. diss., Northwestern University, 1970), and Michael Banton, *Race Relations* (New York: Basic Books, 1967).
43. Frank Westie, "A Technique for the Measurement of Race Attitudes," *American Sociological Review* 18 (1953), pp. 73–78.
44. Anthony Gary Dworkin, Janet S. Chafetz, Everett Dyer, Helen Rose Ebaugh, Mark Matre, and Rosalind J. Dworkin, "Hell No! We Won't Go!: A Study of an Upper Middle Class White Neighborhood," paper presented at the Southwestern Sociological Association Meetings, Dallas, Texas, 1976.
45. Schuman, et al., *Racial Attitudes in America.*
46. Ibid., pp. 139–53.
47. Ibid., pp. 254–57
48. R. T. LaPiere "Attitudes Versus Actions," *Social Forces* 13 (1934), pp. 230–37.
49. Donald T. Campbell, "Social Attitudes and Other Acquired Behavioral Dispositions," in *Psychology: A Study of a Science,* ed. Sigmund Koch, vol. 6 (New York: McGraw-Hill, 1963), pp. 94–172.
50. Melvin L. Kohn and Robin M. Williams, Jr., "Situational Patterning in Intergroup Relations," in *Race, Class, and Power,* ed. Raymond W. Mack (New York: American Book, 1963).
51. Ibid., p. 130.
52. Robert K. Merton, "Discrimination and the American Creed," in *Discrimination and National Welfare,* ed. Robert M. MacIver (New York: Institute for Religious and Social Studies, 1949), pp. 99–126.
53. Joseph D. Lohman and Dietrich C. Reitzes, "Deliberately Organized Groups and Racial Behavior," *American Sociological Review 19* (1954), pp. 342–44.
54. L. M. Killian, "The Effects of Southern White Workers on Race Relations in Northern Plants," *American Sociological Review* 17 (1952), pp. 327–31.
55. Donald Dutton, "Tokenism, Reverse Discrimination, and Egalitarianism in Interracial Behavior," *Journal of Social Issues* 32 (1976), pp. 93–107.
56. J. Milton Yinger, *Toward a Field Theory of Behavior* (New York: McGraw-Hill, 1965).
57. Lyle G. Warner and Melvin L. DeFleur, "Attitude as an Interactional Concept: Social Constraint and Social Distance as Intervening Variables Between Attitudes and Action," *American Sociological Review* 34 (1969), pp. 153–69.

58. See Lawrence S. Linn, "Verbal Attitudes and Overt Behavior: A Study of Racial Discrimination," *Social Forces* 43 (1965), pp. 353–64; Gordon H. DeFriese and W. Scott Ford, Jr., "Open Occupancy—What Whites Say, What They Do," *Transaction* 5 (1968), pp. 53–56; and Irwin Deutscher, *What We Say/What We Do: Sentiments and Acts* (Glenview, IL: Scott, Foresman, 1973).
59. Phyllis Chesler, "Patient and Patriarch: Women in the Psychotherapeutic Relationship," in *Woman in Sexist Society,* ed. Vivian Gornick and Barbara K. Moran (New York: Basic Books, 1971), pp. 251–75.
60. Janet S. Chafetz and Anthony Gary Dworkin, *Female Revolt: Women's Movements in World and Historical* Perspective. (Totowa, NJ: Rowman and Allanheld, 1986), especially chap. 3.
61. William H. Grier and Price M. Cobbs, *Black* Rage (New York: Basic Books, 1968), p. 191.
62. See Kenneth B. and Mamie P. Clark, "Skin Color as a Factor in Racial Identifications of Negro Pre-School Children," *Journal of Social Psychology* 11 (1940), pp. 159–69, and idem, "Racial Identification and Preference in Negro Children," in *Readings in Social Psychology,* ed. T. M. Newcomb and E. L. Hartley (New York: Holt, 1947), pp. 169–78.
63. James Miller, Jr., "Rightness of Whiteness Value-Syndrome Among Pre-School Age Children, I, II, and III," mimeographed (University of California, Los Angeles, 1972).
64. Linda A. Teplin, "Racial Preference as Artifact? A Multitrait-Multimethod Analysis," *Social Science Quarterly* 57 (1977), pp. 834–48, and Linda A. Teplin, "Preference versus Prejudice: A Multimethod Analysis of Children's Discrepant Racial Choices," *Social Science Quarterly* 58 (1977), pp. 390–406.
65. J. A. Bayton, "The Racial Stereotypes of Negro College Students," *Journal of Abnormal and Social Psychology* 36 (1941), pp. 97–102.
66. Ozzie G. Simmons, "The Mutual Images and Expectations of Anglo Americans and Mexican Americans," *Daedalus* 90 (1961), pp. 286–99.
67. Anthony Gary Dworkin, "Stereotypes and Self-Images Held by Native-Born and Foreign-Born Mexican Americans," *Sociology and Social Research* 49 (1965), pp. 214–24.
68. Anthony Gary Dworkin, "National Origin and Ghetto Experience as Variables in Mexican American Stereotypy," in *Chicanos: Social and Psychological Perspectives,* ed. Nathaniel N. Wagner and Marsha J. Haug (St. Louis: Mosby, 1971), pp. 80–84.
69. Philip Goldberg, "Are Women Prejudiced Against Women?" *Trans-action* 5 (1968), pp. 28–30.
70. Minako Kurokawa Maykovich, "Reciprocity in Racial Stereotypes: White, Black and Yellow," *American Journal of Sociology* 77 (1972), pp. 876–97.
71. Dworkin and Eckberg, "Consciousness and Reality," op. cit.
72. Charles P. Loomis and Anthony Gary Dworkin, "The Mexican American Community," in *Social Systems: The Study of Sociology,* Charles P. Loomis and Everett D. Dyer, eds., (Cambridge, MA: Schenkman, 1976), pp. 344–408.

73. John D. McCarthy and William L. Yancey, "Uncle Tom and Mr. Charlie: Metaphysical Pathos in the Study of Racism and Personal Disorganization," *American Journal of Sociology* 76 (1971), pp. 648–72; William L. Yancey, Leo Rigsby, and John D. McCarthy, "Social Position and Self-Evaluation: The Relative Importance of Race," *American Journal of Sociology* 78 (1972), pp. 338–59; and Darrel W. Drury, "Black Self-Esteem and Desegregated Schools," *Sociology of Education* 53 (1980), pp. 88–103.
74. Jerold Heiss and Susan Owens, "Self-Evaluations of Blacks and Whites," *American Journal of Sociology* 78 (1972), pp. 360–70.
75. Donald I. Warren, "Neighborhood Status Modality and Riot Behavior: An Analysis of the Detroit Disorders of 1967," in *Symposium on Violent Confrontation,* ed. Anthony Gary Dworkin, *Sociological Quarterly* 12 (1971), pp. 350–68.
76. Drury, "Black Self-Esteem."
77. Nancy St. John, *School Desegregation: Outcomes for Children.* New York: Wiley, 1975.
78. Martin Patchen, Gerhard Hoffman, and William R. Brown, "Academic Performance of Black High School Students under Different Conditions of Contact with White Peers," *Sociology of Education* 53 (1980), pp. 33–51.
79. Drury, "Black Self-Esteem."
80. Robert E. Park, "Human Migration and the Marginal Man," *American Journal of Sociology* 33 (1928), pp. 881–93.
81. Everett V. Stonequist, *The Marginal Man: A Study in Personality and Culture Conflict* (New York: Scribner's, 1937).
82. For a discussion of these writers and for a paradigm on marginality, see Noel P. Gist and Anthony Gary Dworkin, eds., *The Blending of Races, Marginality and Identity in World Perspective* (New York: Wiley, 1972), chap. 1.
83. Ibid.
84. J. R. Porter and R. E. Washington, "Minority Identity and Self-Esteem," *Annual Review of Sociology* 19 (1993), pp. 139–161.
85. M. P. Huber, *The Natural History of Ants* (London, Longmans, 1810). At one point Huber makes the analogy between the crowding of ants into a too-small nest and the crowding of people into Paris slums; both, he thought, triggered instinctive hatred.
86. See John Dollard et al., *Frustration and Aggression* (New Haven: Yale University Press, 1939).
87. Everett Cherington Hughes, *French Canada in Transition* (Chicago: University of Chicago Press, 1943).
88. Leonard Berkowitz and Russell G. Geen, "Film Violence and the Cue Properties of Available Targets," *Journal of Personality and Social Psychology* 3 (1966), pp. 525–30, and idem, "Stimulus Qualities of the Target of Aggression: A Further Study," *Journal of Personality and Social Psychology* 5 (1967), pp. 364–68. See also Leonard Berkowitz, *Aggression* (New York: McGraw-Hill, 1962).

89. Russell G. Geen, "Some Implications of Experimental Social Psychology for the Study of Urban Disorders," in *Symposium on Violent Confrontation,* ed. Dworkin, pp. 340–49.
90. See Max Horkheimer, "Sociological Background of the Psychoanalytic Approach," in *Anti-Semitism: A Social Disease,* ed. Ernst Simmel (New York: International Universities Press, 1946), pp. 1–10.
91. Adorno et al., *Authoritarian Personality.*
92. Samuel H. Flowerman, "Portrait of the Authoritarian Man," *New York Times Magazine,* April 23, 1950.
93. Oliver C. Cox, *Caste, Class, and Race: A Study in Social Dynamics* (Garden City, NY: Doubleday, 1948).
94. Carey McWilliams, *Brothers Under the Skin* (Boston: Little, Brown, 1964).
95. Sidney M. Withelm, *Who Needs the Negro?* (Cambridge, MA: Schenkman, 1970).
96. William Julius Wilson, *The Truly Disadvantaged,* op. cit.
97. Cornell West, *Race Matters* (New York: Vintage Books, 1993).
98. See Edna Bonacich, "A Theory of Ethnic Antagonism: The Split-Labor Market," *American Sociological Review* 37 (1972), pp. 547–49; Edna Bonacich, "Abolition, the Extension of Slavery, and the Position of Free Blacks: A Study of Split-Labor Markets in the United States, 1830–1863," *American Journal of Sociology* 81 (1975), pp. 601–28; and Edna Bonacich, "Advanced Capitalism and Black/White Relations in the United States: A Split-Labor Market Interpretation," *American Sociological Review* 41 (1976), pp. 34–51.
99. Jonathan H. Turner and Royce Singleton, "A Theory of Ethnic Oppression: Toward a Reintegration of Cultural and Structural Concepts in Ethnic Relations Theory," *Social Forces* 56 (1978), pp. 1001–18.
100. Among those identified with various aspects of the mass society hypothesis and the situational theories of prejudice are Karl Mannheim, *Man and Society in an Age of Reconstruction* (New York: Harcourt, 1940); C. Wright Mills, *The Power Elite* (New York: Oxford University Press, 1959); Edward A. Shils, "Mass Society and Its Culture," in *Culture for the Millions?* ed. N. Jacobs (Princeton, NJ: Van Nostrand, 1961), pp. 1–27; Philip Olson, *America as a Mass Society* (New York: Free Press, 1963); and Frank Westie, "Race and Ethnic Relations," in *Handbook of Modern Sociology,* ed. Robert E. L. Faris (Chicago: Rand McNally, 1964), pp. 576–618.
101. Lohman and Reitzes, "Deliberately Organized Groups"; Kohn and Williams, "Situational Patterning"; and Killian, "Effects of Southern White Workers."
102. Frank Westie, "The American Dilemma: An Empirical Test," *American Sociological Review* 30 (1965), pp. 527–38.
103. Ibid.
104. Allport, *Nature of Prejudice.*
105. Ibid.

106. See, for example, Edward Sapir, "Language and Environment" *American Anthropologist* 14 (1912), pp. 226–42; idem, *Language* (New York: Harcourt, Brace & World, 1921); Benjamin Lee Whorf, "Science and Linguistics," *Technology Review* 44 (1940), pp. 229–31, 247, 248; idem, "The Relation of Habitual Thought and Behavior to Language," in *Language, Culture, and Personality,* ed. L. Spier (Menasa, Wis.: Sapir Memorial Publication Fund, 1941), pp. 75–93.

107. Joshua A. Fishman, "A Systematization of the Whorfian Hypothesis," *Behavioral Science* 5 (1960), pp. 82. More recently the Sapir-Whorf hypothesis has been subjected to a serious challenge. Max Black has argued that those who rely upon the language of a society to explain cultural behavior have often focused only upon supportive aspects of the language and ignored unsupportive ones. Further, some languages have been the vehicle for diverse philosophical orientations, suggesting a much "softer" determinism between language and thought. For more on this issue, see Max Black, *The Labyrinth of Language* (New York: Praeger, 1968), ch. 4.

108. There is a branch of sociological social psychology, known as symbolic interactionism, which looks at the role of language and other symbols in the development of the self. In contrast to psychological behaviorism, symbolic interactionism stresses the shared meanings attached to objects, events, and people. These meanings are communicated through gestures and language. The orientation developed in the works of William James, John Dewey, Charles Horton Cooley, George Herbert Mead, and others. The reader is referred to Herbert Blumer, *Symbolic Interactionism: Perspective and Method* (Englewood Cliffs, NJ: Prentice-Hall, 1969).

109. Allport, *Nature of Prejudice.*

110. James S. Coleman et al., *Equality of Educational Opportunity* (Washington, D.C.: Government Printing Office, 1966).

111. Theodore Newcomb, *Personality and Social Change* (New York: Dryden, 1943).

112. Howard V. Perlmutter, "Relations Between the Self-Image, the Image of the Foreigner, and the Desire to Live Abroad," *Journal of Psychology* 38 (1954), pp. 131–37.

113. Dworkin, "Prejudice."

114. Ehrlich, *Social Psychology.*

115. Jackman and Muha, op. cit.

116. Kluegel, op. cit.

117. Ibid. p. 524.

118. Wessley I. Robinson, "Interracial Contact and Desegregation: An Analysis of Tri-Ethnic Race Relations in the Houston Independent School District" (Master's thesis, University of Houston, 1975).

119. Morton Deutsch and Mary E. Collins, *Interracial Housing* (Minneapolis: University of Minnesota Press, 1951).

120. Daniel Wilner, Rosabelle P. Walkley, and Stuart W. Cook, *Human Relations in Interracial Housing—A Study of the Contact Hypothesis* (Minneapolis: University of Minnesota Press, 1955).

121. Ernest Q. Campbell, "Some Social Psychological Correlates of Direction in Attitude Change," *Social Forces* 36 (1958), pp. 335–40; Paul H. Mussen, "Some Personality and Social Factors Related to Change in Children's Attitudes Towards Negroes," *Journal of Abnormal and Social Psychology* 45 (1950), pp. 423–41; and Irwin Silverman and Marvin E. Shaw, "Effects of Sudden Mass School Desegregation on Interracial Interaction and Attitudes in One Southern City," *Journal of Social Issues* 29 (1973), pp. 133–42.
122. W. Scott Ford, "Interracial Public Housing in a Border City: Another Look at the Contact Hypothesis," *American Journal of Sociology* 78 (1973), pp. 1426–47. Nancy St. John, in *School Desegregation,* also concluded that the desegregation of the public schools decreased white prejudice, but increased black prejudice.
123. See, for example, Robin M. Williams, Jr., "Race and Ethnic Relations," *Annual Review of Sociology* 1 (1975), pp. 319–49; Yehuda Amir, "The Contact Hypothesis in Ethnic Relations," *Psychological Bulletin* 71 (1969), pp. 319–49; James D. Preston and Jerry W. Robinson, Jr., "On Modification of Interracial Interaction," *American Sociological Review* 39 (1974), pp. 283–85; and Jerry W. Robinson, Jr., and James D. Preston, "Equal-Status Contact and Modification of Racial Prejudice: A Reexamination of the Contact Hypothesis," *Social Forces* 54 (1976), pp. 911–24.
124. Kurt Lewin, "Group Decision and Social Change," in *Readings in Social Change,* 3rd ed. ed. E. Maccoby, T. M. Newcomb, and E. L. Hartley (New York: Holt, Rinehart and Winston, 1958), pp. 197–211.
125. Allport, *Nature of Prejudice.*
126. Thomas F. Pettigrew, *Racially Separate or Together?* (New York: McGraw-Hill, 1971).
127. Muzafer Sherif, "Superordinate Goals and the Reduction of Intergroup Conflict," *American Journal of Sociology* 63 (1958), pp. 349–56, and Muzafer Sherif et al., *Intergroup Conflict and Cooperation: The Robbers Cave Experiment* (Norman: University of Oklahoma Book Exchange, 1961).
128. McKee J. McClendon and D. Stanley Eitzen, "Interracial Contact on Collegiate Basketball Teams: A Test of Sherif's Theory of Superordinate Goals," *Social Science Quarterly* 55 (1975), pp. 926–38.
129. Anothony Gary Dworkin, Ronald G. Frankiewicz, Helen Copitka, and Wesley I. Robinson, *Intergroup Action Project Report* ("Balance on the Bayou: The Impact of Racial Isolation and Interaction on Stereotypy in the Houston Independent School District" and "Assessment of Attitudes Towards GROB as a Unit of Study") (Houston, Texas: Houston Council on Human Relations, 1974).

Suggested Readings

Adorno, T. W., et al. *The Authoritarian Personality.* New York: Harper, 1950.

Allport, Gordon W. *The Nature of Prejudice.* Cambridge, MA: Addison-Wesley, 1954.

Blumer, Herbert. *Symbolic Interactionism: Perspective and Method.* Englewood Cliffs, NJ: Prentice-Hall, 1969.

Deutscher, Irwin. *What We Say/What We Do: Sentiments and Acts.* Glenview, IL: Scott, Foresman, 1973.

Duneier, Mitchell. *Slim's Table: Race, Respectability, and Masculinity.* Chicago: University of Chicago Press, 1992.

Ehrlich, Howard J. *The Social Psychology of Prejudice.* New York: Wiley-Interscience, 1973.

Gist, Noel P., and Anthony Gary Dworkin. *The Blending of Races: Marginality and Identity in World Perspective.* New York: Wiley-Interscience, 1972.

Herman, Nancy J. and Larry T. Reynolds. Symbolic Interaction. Dix Hills, NY: General Hall, 1994.

Massey, Douglas S. and Nancy S. Denton. *American Apartheid: Segregation and the Making of the Underclass.* Cambridge, MA: Harvard University Press, 1993.

Pettigrew, Thomas F. *Racially Separate or Together?* New York: McGraw-Hill, 1971.

Schuman, Howard, Charlotte Steeh, Lawrence Bobo, and Maria Krysan. *Racial Attitudes in America: Trends and Interpretations,* rev. ed. Cambridge, MA: Harvard University Press, 1997.

Secord, Paul F., and Carl W. Backman. *Social Psychology.* New York: McGraw-Hill, 1974.

Sherif, Muzafer, and Carolyn W. Sherif. *Social Psychology.* New York: Harper, 1969.

West, Cornell. *Race Matters.* New York: Vintage Books, 1993.

Wilson, William Julius. *The Truly Disadvantaged: The Inner City, the Underclass, and Public Policy.* Chicago: University of Chicago Press, 1987.

CHAPTER 6

Theories of the Minority-Group Process

We have examined the ways in which minority groups have been treated as people apart. The documentation of an inequitable distribution of power, property, and prestige, the description and categorization of organizations to which minorities belong and/or in which they must react, and the variety of social psychological inputs and effects of prejudice and discrimination are all of interest to the student of minority-group relations. However, the sociologist must do more than document, describe, and categorize. The sociologist is also interested in explanation and prediction, to which ends models must be constructed. These models, or theories, consider the entire phenomenon of minority-majority relationships and attempt to make some generalizing statements about the process of these relationships: from contact and cause through to resolution. There are many such models in the field of minority-group relations. Some are more complete than others; some are more heuristic than others; and some have more explanatory power than others. Basically they can be categorized into two types, depending upon the kind of resolution they predict. The two models assume distinct outcomes for minority-group relations. The first and more traditional model assumes assimilation of the minority group into the majority. The second and more radical approach assumes continued separation of the minority group. The separation may be forced upon the minority or initiated by the minority. Examples range from exclusion and ultimate extermination, through reservation status, to establishment of a new nation-state.

Regardless of the model proposed, a necessary condition for minority-group status and its resolution is intergroup contact. It is difficult to conceive of minorities and majorities who are members of the same society and have not been in contact with one another. Identifiability implies a subject observing and interacting with an object. Likewise, differential power is meaningless unless it is power over some one or some group with whom one interacts. Further, differential treatment cannot occur in isolation, but requires contact. Moreover, group awareness implies an acknowledgment of "us" separate from "them."

The nature of the initial contact has been a dimension explored by many writers. That contact may shape the future course of the minority-majority relationship, determine who will play the minority role and who will play the majority, establish how great the differentials between them will be, and foreshadow the likely resolution. In some instances the initial contact between groups has been historically documented. Exploration, conquest, colonization, enslavement, or immigration represents the diversity of initial contacts. For some groups the initial contact may have occurred so far in the past that there is no record, so records may be fabricated in the form of a folk history. In the case of male-female relationships, where documentation of initial contact is an absurdity, a mythology or a religio-folk history has been created. Most of the world's religions, however simple or complex, have a story comparable to the Adam and Eve explanation of the initial contact between males and females.

A second necessary condition upon which all the theories agree is that the contact must be prolonged such that the differentials in power and treatment become apparent and entrenched at the distributive, organizational, and social psychological levels.

The divergences that develop as a function of the prolonged contact, the nature of the assumptions about the goals of the actors involved in the contact, and the course of actions that ensue after the initial contact provide the essential distinctions among the diverse theories of the resolution of minority-group status.

ASSIMILATION AS AN OUTCOME

Essential Concepts

Assimilation is a process by which minority and majority groups are merged into some total societal unit. There have been many divergent interpretations of the concept of assimilation, and perhaps its utility as a scientific concept can be challenged. It certainly cannot be thought of as unitary. In some instances it means that the minority group merges into the majority and loses its own distinct identity. In other instances it means that the minority and the majority form a new hybrid. In still other applications it means that the minority retains much of its identity and distinctiveness, but shares an equal status in the society with the majority, without prejudice and discrimination. Each of these definitions of assimilation have acquired different names. The first is called *Anglo conformity;* the second is the melting pot; and the third is called *cultural pluralism.* We shall comment on each of these shortly, for they are distinct goals within the theme of assimilation.

Assimilation also involves other processes, which have attained distinct labels. These include *acculturation* and *amalgamation.* Acculturation refers to cultural assimilation of the minority group, in which the minority adopts the culture, including the language, customs, and beliefs, of the majority. Amalgamation refers to the biological blending of the minority with the majority through intermarriage (as well as less formalized sexual relationships). We shall delineate additional aspects of assimilation shortly when we discuss the conceptualization by Milton Gordon.

Gordon[1] has developed an excellent assessment of the goals of the assimilative process (the three models cited previously). He suggests that the most common form imposed upon minorities is Anglo conformity. Here the majority attempts to "Americanize" the minority, socializing it to reject all aspects of its native (usually immigrant) culture and to seek to be a carbon copy of the majority society prototype. The Coles[2] first coined the concept of Anglo conformity in 1954. Gordon indicates that "the 'Anglo Conformity' theory demanded the complete renunciation of the immigrant's ancestral culture in favor of the behavior and values of the Anglo-Saxon core group."[3] The model has had a diversity of manifestations, and has not been enforced uniformly for all groups. In fact, groups that are identifiably closer to the majority than other minorities tend to be subjected to less rigorous and brutal "Americanization." The experiences of English-speaking groups, for example, have been less restrictive than the experiences of eastern European, southern European, or Spanish-speaking groups. Because the members of the majority are unable to understand the non-English speakers, they are less able to monitor their attitudes, beliefs, and conversations, and hence must expend greater effort in order to control them.

The melting pot theory, according to Gordon, "envisaged a biological merger of the Anglo-Saxon peoples with other immigrant groups and a blending of their respective cultures into a new indigenous American type."[4] The melting pot thus consisted of a hybrid culture and an amalgamation of peoples. It is problematic whether the melting pot phenomenon actually characterized the American scene. It may have had limited currency when there was not much diversity among the groups blending together (there is greater evidence for the melting pot among the northern European groups in the United States). However, Glazer and Moynihan[5] contend the phenomenon really did not exist in the United States. Ethnic minorities have retained much of their distinct cultural heritages, albeit with an American flavor, such that Little

Italy was not exactly like its European counterpart. The melting pot idea was a romantic view and probably could not have developed in a society in which the majority had enough resources to maintain its dominance over the various minorities. That is, a melting pot requires that the minority be able to exert enough influence over the majority to effect a merger of groups. Lacking that, the melting pot would require a friendlier and more benevolent majority willing to acknowledge that minorities may have some superior cultural elements. The melting pot concept accurately describes the nation of Mexico. There, the Spaniards crushed the Indian society, but did not replace it with their own. Rather, they intermarried and blended the Indian and Spanish heritage into a *mestizo* culture.

The experience in the United States was different. What has happened, as Gordon observes, is that American society has evolved a *transmuting pot.*[6] In the transmuting pot the majority selectively samples aspects of the minority group's culture and remakes them in an Americanized mold. Thus pizza is topped with hamburger and cheddar cheese; a manufacturer of Chinese food advertises that its product "swings American"; drive-in Mexican restaurants offer tacos and tamales American-style (without hot sauce); caftans and dashikis are made from colorfast and permanent press fabrics; and strawberry incense is burned before a plastic Buddha to rid the house of stale odors.

The third form of assimilation implies the least homogeneity for the populace. Gordon suggests that cultural pluralism "postulated the preservation of the communal life and significant positions of the culture of the later immigrant groups within the context of American citizenship and political and economic integration into American society."[7] Thus cultural pluralism implies equality of status of diverse groups, which retain their identity. If American society cannot be characterized as a melting pot, it is problematic that it could be described as pluralistic. Minorities retain their ethnic character, but inequality of status is still present. Several writers, including Gordon, have argued for the preferability of the cultural pluralist form as an American ideal. It certainly is the most democratic, except in its implementation. In order for cultural pluralism to succeed, the minority must impose restrictions within itself to discourage its members from blending into the majority. Although cultural pluralism has not been attained in American society, Gordon suggests that *structural pluralism* has. In the latter, there is a "structural merging . . . among the nationality groups within each of the three major religions, and in the occupational areas of the intellectual and art worlds."[8] Thus within religious organizations and in certain elite occupational groups, people of diverse backgrounds function together. American artists and scholars are artists or scholars regardless of their ethnicity; they are stratified only against nonartists and nonscholars. Likewise, Catholic organizations may be composed of Irish, Italian, German, and even Spanish American groups, all of whom identify themselves as Catholics.

Theories of Assimilation

Early in the present century sociologists proposed some models that they felt would account for the manner in which the patterns of minority-majority relations evolved and developed. Much of the debate on the issue of such patterns has concerned the universality and complexity of the models. Early models were assumed to be generalizable to all intergroup relation situations and often involved only one or a few variables. Frequently these early models were like some of the early attempts to define minority groups, based upon a limited set of traits observed in a particular society, subculture, or even region of the country. Nonetheless, attempts were made to generalize to the whole of mankind these models based upon limited observation.

Among the earliest theories advanced was Park's in 1926.[9] According to Park, new immigrant groups to a society move through four phases in a cycle from contact, to competition and conflict, to accommodation, to assimilation. Initially two groups, usually an indigenous group and an immigrant group, come into contact with one another and compete for some scarce resource such as wealth, property, or status. Because the resources are scarce and successful gain for one means loss to the other, competition results in open conflict between the two groups. However, because one group (usually the indigenous group) has more resources to mobilize, it maintains control over the market situation. The immigrant group accommodates or withdraws hostilities until some future time when they can have an advantage. As the two groups interact, the subordinate immigrant group copies or emulates the dominant indigenous group. Over time the two groups become more alike, with the immigrant or minority group accepting more of the culture of the dominant group. Eventually the differences are erased and, as holders of common values, the two groups merge into a single dominant group. Park considered the cycle to be unidirectional; that is, groups progressed through the four phases in order and only in the direction hypothesized. Once begun, the process is irreversible, and is repeated in turn with new minority groups. In this sense the process is cyclical.

Basing his race relations cycle upon the West Coast, Bogardus[10] proposed that there were seven distinct stages in the process of assimilation. Initial contact between the majority and the minority sparks the "curiosity" of the majority. Because the numbers of the minority are extremely small, they are not seen as a threat but are often viewed with sympathy. Curiosity yields to "economic welcome" when the minority becomes recognized as a source of cheap labor. As more members of the minority enter the labor market, members of the dominant society organize to protest the takeover by the minority, a stage Bogardus described as "industrial and social antagonism." (This antagonism is an essential component in Bonacich's split labor market theory described in Chapter 5.) Pressure is put upon political and governmental officials to pass laws limiting immigration and the rights and opportunities of the minority.

This is the stage of "legislative antagonism." In time, some citizens react against the laws. Friendship and a sense of injustice may spark this stage of "fair-play tendencies." But as Berry[11] notes, it is rather short-lived because of lack of organization, lack of finances, and extremism within the movement. An accommodation is reached after the full force of the restrictive legislation is felt. In the stage of "quiescence" attitudes become ameliorated and efforts to extend social and political rights emerge. At this point, attempts develop to resocialize (Americanize) the minority, to assimilate the group into the dominant group by making them culturally identical to the majority. In the final stage crises of identity arise between the first and second generations of the minority group. The stage of "second-generation difficulties" emerges because the children become more assimilated than their parent. In some respect the children are true cultural marginals[12] in that they are of both the minority and the majority culture, but fully integrated into neither.

A model by Brown[13] also assumed assimilation as the ultimate end product. It is unlike the others in recognizing that the assimilation process may be extremely slow and that other, albeit less likely, outcomes may occur in between. These alternative outcomes include total isolation of the minority or subordination of the minority into a caste. The former is impractical in a geographically mobile society like the United States, and the latter is unlikely because of espoused societal norms of equality, constitutional guarantees, and observable social mobility.

Still other cyclical theories of assimilation have been advanced.[14] However, they are basically similar to the three discussed here. The characteristic weakness of the early theories was that they were not universally applicable because they were based upon limited samplings of minority experiences. Lieberson synthesized and expanded the models of Park and his followers, noting that "many earlier race and ethnic cycles were, in fact, narrowly confined to a rather specific set of groups or contact situations . . . . "[15] Lieberson begins by postulating that intergroup contact initially involves "each population's maintenance and development of a social order compatible with its way of life prior to contact."[16] Thus developing conflicts center around institutions. Lieberson cited two basic forms of contact: subordination of an indigenous[17] group by a migrant group (e.g., Western European contact with American Indian groups) and subordination of a migrant group by an indigenous group (e.g., Anglo American contact with new migrant Western Europeans in the late nineteenth century or with the Chinese building the railroad in the mid-nineteenth century).

Lieberson makes problematic whether the indigenous or the immigrant group will be dominant. Thus unlike Park and those he influenced, Lieberson's model is applicable not only to a situation of minority-group entry into existing, well-developed societies (e.g., European and Oriental immigration to the United States). The model is also applicable to the conquest of native populations by colonial powers throughout history. It can account for the outcomes of power majorities who were numerically large as well as power majorities who were numerically small.

Although Lieberson's model accounts for greater diversity than the earlier models, it nonetheless rests upon a single variable—differential power. Power is a necessary condition, but it is not a sufficient condition, and certainly power alone cannot distinguish among the diversity of minority experiences. Berry[18] suggests that other variables must include: (1) the nature of the initial contact; (2) the extent of "tribal" solidarity of the minority group; (3) the effect of the dominant group upon the natural resources in the society; (4) values of the minority group; (5) attitudes of the majority group; and (6) existing norms with regard to intermarriage and sexual contact.

Lieberson's model could be further strengthened by application of Blalock's[19] conceptualization of power. By defining power in terms of its application rather than its potential, Blalock provides for a wider range of minority-majority relationships hinging not only upon differentials in the amount of resources available to each group, but also whether those resources are mobilized by the majority against the minority.

Lieberson's model depends upon a specific, historic point of initial contact between two groups of differing cultures. Hence the model cannot be applied to gender groups, which have always coexisted and which share a common (or complementary) culture.

Gordon[20] has delineated a complex seven-stage model of assimilation. His model was created to be applicable to the conditions of Anglo conformity, melting pot, or cultural pluralism, but is predisposed toward the Anglo conformity format. The first stage is identified as "cultural or behavioral assimilation" and involves the acculturation of the minority group, during which the dominant society's cultural patterns are adopted by the minority. Sequentially, the group the passes through a state of "structural assimilation," when there is large-scale entry by the minority into the majority's voluntary associations, cliques, and clubs. Gordon maintains that it is not sufficient for a select few members of the minority to be so accepted on an interpersonal level; there must be wholesale acceptance. It is on the structural level that the final outcome depends. Once a group is accepted structurally, all other forms of assimilation will proceed with relatively little difficulty.

Gordon's third stage is identified as "marital assimilation," or amalgamation. Here there is large-scale intermarriage between members of the minority and the majority. It is now clearly evident that structural assimilation is a necessary precondition, as large-scale intermarriage cannot occur without large-scale interpersonal acceptance.

After widespread intermarriage, the minority and the offspring from the intermarriages come to see themselves as members of the same group as the majority. Gordon describes this stage as "identificational assimilation." It is not the final stage, because there may still be little reciprocity in the identification. That is, the minority might see themselves as part of the majority, but the majority may not accept them as such. They may be defined only as the spouses of majority-group members.

Sometime after identificational assimilation, however, there is an abandonment of prejudice and discrimination against the group. Gordon calls the stage of cessation of prejudice, "attitude receptional assimilation," and the stage of cessation of discrimination, "behavioral receptional assimilation." Full and total assimilation occurs when the minority has passed into the stage of "civic assimilation." At this last stage there are no value or power conflicts between the groups. In fact, even on specific issues the group boundaries have vanished for both sides, and we can no longer speak of majorities and minorities.

Gordon's model is perhaps more heuristic than it is empirical. It suggests many intriguing hypotheses, including the role of structural assimilation and the multidimensionality of the assimilation process. However, the particular order has not been universal for all groups, and some groups have attained later stages of assimilation without earlier ones.[21] Further, minority groups are not homogeneous enough, as Gordon acknowledges, to permit the model's applicability to a group carte blanche. Thus Gordon observes that class differentiates the degree of assimilation of some religious groups, such as Catholics. Kitano,[22] in his application of the model to the Japanese American case, suggests that age and number of generations in the host society affect the stage of assimilation and the amount of assimilation within each stage.

Banton[23] provides six orders of intersocietal relations, and these models, when combined, provide three possible routes for minority-majority relations resolutions. The six orders include peripheral contact, institutionalized contact, acculturation, domination, paternalism (or colonialism), and integration. Peripheral contact involves exchanges between groups that do not influence the internal makeup or structure of the groups involved and do not affect their attitudes, beliefs, behaviors, or values. The so-called "silent trade" between the hunting and gathering Pygmies of the Ituri forest in the Congo and the Negro settlements of the neighboring agriculturalists is the example provided by Banton. Items to be traded are left separately at a designated location by each group. Each returns to examine the items left by the other and, if they are acceptable, completes the exchange. The parties never see one another. So long as the same kinds of items are exchanged (agricultural products for game and forest products) the relationship remains unchanged, and the impact of one upon the other is minimal.

Should the interaction be continuous and face-to-face, then Banton suggests that two other forms of relations will develop. The first is institutionalized contact, in which the two societies remain essentially intact, except that individuals at the geographical boundary between the two adopt relationships and special roles in both societies—sometimes as liaisons between the two. Banton argues that such a model is possible only if: "(1) one of the two groups has a strong centralized political structure such that a few leaders control the actions of other members, and these leaders use their power to try to dominate the other group; and (2) when two such societies enter into contact through some of the outlying members, there is no strong competition for resources. . . ."[24] Should the societies be small in size, the power structure more diffused, competition between groups minimal, and contact between them gradual, then Banton argues that acculturation, or cultural assimilation, will evolve. Here the two groups will tend to merge culturally, including linguistically, with the minority culture making more concessions than the majority. Historically, when racial groups or relationships between nationalities are involved, the pattern is more likely one of domination, in which one group imposes its will upon the other. In such situations slavery or near-slavery conditions may prevail for the dominated. There soon evolves a castelike system to rationalize the social order normatively and to ensure that members of the minority group do not intermarry, or become mobile into the majority group.

When the two groups are nations geographically apart, then the nature of domination will involve a home government (the colonial power) determining the internal policies of the dominated society (colony). Such a situation is what Banton has termed paternalism, and involves the same form of intergroup relations described by van den Berghe[25] under the same name.

Having delineated these orders of relationships, Banton arranges them into three sequences representing processes of resolution (see Figure 6-1). The first sequence begins with contact, but because of independent political power resources, the majority enforces a domination over the other group. If the economic base changes domination and becomes more difficult, a shift toward pluralism occurs. In the second sequence contact results in paternalism. Over time, the paternalistic power becomes weakened and a shift occurs toward integration. The third sequence also begins with contact, which leads to acculturation and then easily and quickly to integration.

FIGURE 6-1
Sequences of Minority Resolutions

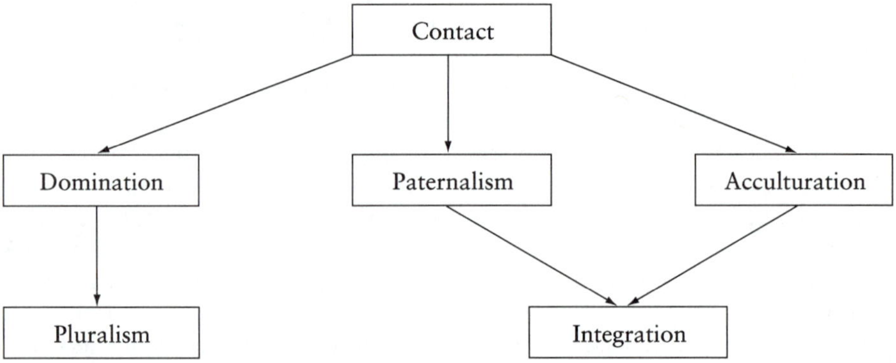

Source: Modified from Michael Banton, *Race Relations* (New York: Basic Books, 1967), p. 75.

Banton's model assumes an outside force impinging upon some indigenous population. His examples are most often drawn from British and American colonial histories. However, the model is less appropriate to minority-majority relationships that develop from within a given social structure. Likewise, a process evolving awakening minorities—women, homosexuals, new religious sects, and so on—cannot be fitted into this model.

Like Banton, Kinloch[26] emphasizes the role of colonialism in the determination of minority-majority relations. Kinloch constructs six conceptual steps for his model. The initial step is that of population growth (1), which will increase economic needs. This is followed by economic differentiation (2) and colonialism (3), either by means of migration, importation, or subordination. For Kinloch, colonialism is not a simple concept. Colonialism may be internal or external, direct or indirect. Whatever the type, the colonialism will create racial and/or ethnic minorities. Colonialism by elites will affect both group and individual levels of society in terms of politics, competition, identity, and stereotyping. The more colonial the economic system, the more rigid and racist the society will be.[27] With the creation of these minorities, the system will experience greater economic specialization (4), which can create gender and age minorities. The complexity of the minority hierarchies (5) will generate intergroup competition. This competition and hierarchical structure will eventually result in social change (6) in the direction of economic assimilation, diminished discrimination, and renewed population growth. The latter will begin the process anew.

The strength of Kinloch's model lies in its ability to account for the emergence of several different types of minorities (racial, ethnic, age, gender, and behavioral). In addition, through a series of interrelated propositions, Kinloch specifies under what conditions a society will move from step to step.

Utilizing the orientations of the distributive, organizational, and social psychological levels of analysis, van den Berghe[28] has advanced a multidimensional typology of majority-minority group relations. He has developed two polar or extreme types. No society is thought of as being purely one or another form of the dichotomy, but rather societies can be compared with one another in terms of the type. For van den Berghe the types are the *paternalistic* and the *competitive* systems. The paternalistic relationship is one resembling the "master-servant model."[29] In such a model "the dominant group, often a small minority of less than 10 percent of the total population, rationalizes its rule in an ideology of benevolent despotism and regards members of the subordinate group as . . . inferior, but lovable as long as they stay 'in their place.'"[30] There is little need for physical segregation because contact between the two groups follows set patterns prescribed by the dominant group and never implies equality of interaction (e.g., black-white relationships until recently in the American South, and male-female relationships societywide).

In the paternalistic system the division of labor is low, such that there are few status-role distinctions among members within each caste. Members of the dominant society tend to do relatively similar tasks, usually overseeing the activities of members of the minority group. Members of the minority group likewise tend to have little task differentiation, all generally engaging in menial, unskilled, and service activities. Race relations in such situations, because of the security of the dominant group's position, rarely are accompanied by deep, psychologically based prejudices. Van den Berghe contends that the paternalistic model is characteristic of the preindustrial, agricultural societies typical of colonialism. An ideology of racial superiority rationalizes the social system, and the caste lines are impenetrable. Although miscegenation is common, almost totally involving sexual relations between majority men and minority women, this is not assumed to imply equality.[31] Stereotypes in the paternalistic system stress the perception of the minority as "childlike, fun-loving, lazy, and good-natured."[32]

In a complex, industrialized, and urbanized society the pattern is of a competitive type of system. Van den Berghe indicates that the "dominant group is frequently a majority or a large minority (more than 20 or 25 percent)."[33] Although there still remains an ascription in terms of race, "class differences . . . become more salient relative to caste."[34]

Without clear race-bounded distinctions in terms of status, rank, and opportunities, threat to the dominant group is more intense. The dominant group must mobilize more of its resources to maintain its higher status. Under such instability, prejudice is a prevalent psychological need of the dominant group. Segregation emerges in order to ensure that equal status interaction does not occur. Miscegenation, which was common and did not imply equal status in the paternalistic system, ceases to be open, since it threatens the social order.

Parallel social institutions emerge in the competitive society, and these tend to be counterproductive for the whole society, putting strains on the relationship to eliminate all segregation and distinctions. As the minority gains in the educational, economic, and political prerequisites for equal status, it will demand a greater role in the society and in turn often drive the dominant group to attempt oppressive tactics. Stereotypes in the competitive system stress the perception of the minority as "aggressive, cunning, untidy, and dangerous."[35] The economic competition between the majority and Japanese Americans or Jewish Americans typifies this form of relationship.

Van den Berghe suggests that pluralism is not necessarily a democratic ideal. Rather, he sees pluralism (cultural pluralism involving the amount of cultural variation within a society, and social or structural pluralism involving the institutional segmentation of the social structure) as a concept which can describe conditions in both the paternalistic and the competitive format. Pluralism for van den Berghe indicates the degree of commonality of cultures and institutions in the society, and the extent to which there exist parallel structures for the majority and the minorities. Van den Berghe develops a typology of pluralism conditions operating at four levels of analysis: (1) the group level, indicating the number of groups and the rigidity of their boundaries; (2) the institutional level, indicating the number of parallel institutions and their compatibility with one another; (3) the value level, including the degree of consensus and compatibility of the value systems of the pluralistic groups; and (4) the individual level, including the extent to which "passing" by group members is possible. For Van den Berghe:

> The safest conclusion is that there is no necessary or universal association of pluralism with either democracy or tyranny. There are a few cases of moderately pluralistic politics that have also been fairly democratic, such as Switzerland or Belgium. . . . But many highly homogeneous societies, for example, a number of stateless and classless African societies like the Nuer, have also been quite democratic. . . . It is equally true, however, that most of the world's highly pluralistic societies have been quite undemocratic, albeit in a very different way from modern totalitarianism.[36]

Van den Berghe's usage of pluralism as a concept is unique. Depending upon the mix of the four levels of analysis, pluralism is not a resolution per se, but has potential outcomes of assimilation or separatism.

Contrary to most assimilation models, some minority groups do not occupy the lowest status in the society, nor are they likely to experience upward mobility. Blalock,[37] building upon the theories of marginality, advanced the concept of the "middleman minorities." In most instances, the middleman minority exists in societies that are peasant-feudal or colonial, in which there are few elites, a very small middle class, and an enormous peasant mass. The middlemen are separate, identifiable groups, which perform unique mediating functions. For example, they may form an economic link between the elites and the masses by collecting taxes, marketing goods, and lending small amounts of money. Such has been the case with Jews and the Chinese, both of whom have served as middleman minorities in several different societies at various points in time. The middleman groups tend to be relatively stable,[38] having high in-group solidarity and a "sojourner" self-definition. These groups are truly in the middle, subject to hostility and conflict from both the top and the bottom strata.

There have been numerous other criticism lodged against the assimilation models, and the early models in particular. The majority of such criticisms have focused upon the explanatory power of the models when applied to racial groups. Warner and Srole[39] suggest that groups that differ significantly from the majority in skin color and culture are likely to take more time to assimilate than groups which do not so differ. Lyman[40] argues that imposing such a condition makes the models tautological. That is, assimilation involves acculturation and amalgamation, but to contend that because of culture and biology some groups will take longer to assimilate is to engage in a certain degree of circularity.

Similarly, some assimilationist theories tend to be teleological. They posit an end product of a unilineal evolution which is planned either by social forces or social policy. Unfortunately, they never predict deadlines. Finally, the models tend to commit what Barber[41] has called the "the and also fallacy," "which in effect makes an abstract analysis immune to criticism or disproof, by simply attributing all discrepancies between hypothetical scheme and actual observation to 'other factors' in the situation."[42] Brown and others after Park suggested that assimilation might not be the immediate outcome, and other outcomes might intervene. But regardless of the amount of time it takes, assimilation will ultimately triumph. Thus if after several hundred years a group has not assimilated, but has progressed through a series of stages not specified in the model, the model is not challenged. The theorists tell us that we have not given the group and the majority enough time. Since "enough time" is not defined, millennia, even eons, may pass, and the model is still unchallenged. In short, the models are vague enough and possess an "escape clause" to prevent their being tested. They may be supported by a conceptual mechanism, similar to the one we mentioned in Chapter 5, which permits stereotypes to endure testing. If a negative case arises, it is defined as unsuitable because enough time has not elapsed and the group is in some indeterminate intermediate phase; if the group has assimilated, the model is validated.

Some writers, especially Park and several of his students, committed what has been called the fallacy of misplaced concreteness. They have defined reality as their theory, and in cases in which groups were not progressing through the stages in accordance with the theory, the groups rather than the theory were found to be at fault.[43]

Van den Berghe's conceptualization is not subject to these criticisms. His model was not designed to predict an ultimate outcome. Rather, it is a typology of relations between groups, the utility of which is to predict clusters of associations between variables within given societies. That is, its explanatory power is in linking a set of social, cultural, and historical conditions to the present development of given societies.

Assimilation models are not without their merits. They have been heuristic and they have been accurate in predicting the dynamics of some groups, particularly ethnic groups. But what may as yet be untested even with ethnic groups is the irreversibility of the models. One can imagine a time when a fully assimilated group may choose to reestablish its ethnic distinctiveness. This is happening in the United States today, partly as a response to the attempts by blacks to regain their African heritage. In reaction to the popularity of being a member of a minority group (provided one does not have to live in deprivation), many individuals whose parents and grandparents fought to become Americanized are today searching for their ethnic pasts.

SEPARATISM AS AN OUTCOME

Assimilation is only one possible resolution of the condition of minority status. There is an alternative resolution—separatism. Separatism is based upon the assumption that there can be no satisfactory coexistence between majority and minority groups within the context of a single society. Separatism thus means the formation of a geographically distinct nation-state for a minority group. This separatism might be thrust upon the minority group by the majority, or it might be initiated by the minority itself. The latter usually takes the form of a nationalist movement.

Imposed Separatism

Separation imposed by the majority is an extreme tactic. At least two basic forms of imposed separatism have been observable in the past century. The first type has occurred after the collapse of colonial empires. The indigenous people, newly powerful, expel the last remnants of colonialism, including the Europeans and the mixed-race peoples who were born of European and native parents. Under such circumstances Banton's model of domination does not lead to assimilation of the minority into the majority, but to imposed separatism by the new majority. There may also occur the expulsion of weaker minority groups who had lived in the colony. The emergence of new nations in the African continent has been followed by the departure of many Europeans and expulsion of numerous Asians. Independence for Guyana in South America was followed by a large-scale departure of mixed-race peoples known as the Guyanese Coloured, who had served the British as petty bureaucrats and as a buffer between the small white majority and the African and Asian minorities.[44]

A second form of imposed separatism involves either deportation of the minority to its former homeland or restriction of the minority to isolated, semiautonomous reservations encapsulated within the territory of the majority. The first form may arise in order to prevent warfare between minority and majority, whereas the latter may be a final outcome after warfare. When the latter type occurs it is often initiated by a desire to exterminate the minority, because the minority is either in the way of the majority or serves no function for it. This is done usually with a very small and/or weak minority. Of course, the two examples in American history are the white-imposed "Back to Africa" movements and the establishment of reservations for native Americans. In the period during slavery, many whites feared that unless blacks were deported back to Africa, every American city and town would experience slave revolts and black uprisings. Thus some "Back to Africa" movements were initiated and supported by whites.

Nationalism

When the minority group initiates separatism, it frequently takes the form of a nationalist movement. Essien-Udom offered a definition of such nationalism:

> The concept nationalism . . . may be thought of as a belief of a group that it possesses, or ought to possess, a country; that it shares, or ought to share, a

> common heritage, of language, culture, and religion; and that its heritage, way of life, and ethnic identity are distinct from those of other groups. Nationalists believe that they ought to rule themselves, and shape their own destinies, and that they therefore should be in control of their social, economic, and political institutions.[45]

Minorities have the potential of forming their own geographically distinct nation-states. These groups are usually large enough, with sufficient diversity of abilities and skills, to perform the variety of tasks needed to sustain a society. Further, once a strong sense of group awareness and solidarity is developed, the minority group has the potential to provide its members with all the social and psychological support necessary to establish and maintain a rewarding environment and culture. Three issues that are always problematic are: (1) developing a group awareness and then a consensus that nationalism is preferable to fighting for assimilation; (2) gaining freedom from the constraints imposed by the majority; and (3) securing a geographical territory in which to establish the new nation-state. All three are difficult, but the last poses innumerable problems. Land not presently claimed by one sovereignty or another is very scarce on this earth. Existing nation-states composed of people who were the racial or ethnic kinsmen of the minority group are often unwilling to accept a large influx of their "relatives" and are more likely to see them as an invasion of foreigners rather than returning kin. Finally, the majority is almost always unwilling to cede any of its own land to the minority group, even if the land was once owned by the minority or the minority presently represents the plurality of the population in that particular geographic area.

The migration of European Jews to Palestine after World War II to found the nation-state of Israel suggests that even in this century minorities can form new societies. However, such action also involves the displacement of numbers of people who had previously occupied the territory. Four wars in little more than a quarter of a century and the Palestine refugee question point to the fact that the formation of new nation-states with the displacement of existing groups creates new minorities and new hostility.

There have been several attempts at separatism in America. Black history is filled with "Back to Africa" movements and endeavors to establish black nations in the New World as well. Because white America was unwilling to accept black America, there was a growing pressure for Negro nationalism, which traced its roots back to the American Colonization Society of 1816 and the Negro Convention movements. The most effective leader of those who were convinced that equality was impossible in America was Marcus Garvey. After an initial failure in Jamaica, Garvey formed the Universal Negro Improvement Association (UNIA) in 1916. Estimates of his following range from two to six million by the early 1920s. Garvey solicited money to finance a steamship company, the Black Star Steam Ship Line, but pressure from the

NAACP and middle-class blacks, who did not want to see blacks leave the United States, eventually wrecked the movement. The UNIA and the Black Star Line collapsed in 1925. However, Garvey was successful in unifying a large proportion of black people, teaching self- and group pride. His work provided a legacy that fed other forms of nationalism, including the present Black Muslim organization.

The Black Muslims, under the leadership of Elija Muhammed, established an economic nationalism. Muslim-owned stores, farms, and schools have been established in various parts of the nation. Total separation from the "blue-eyed devils" (whites) has been the belief and practice of the organization. The Muslims have been effective in providing an identity for many blacks and have been successful in running drug rehabilitation programs based upon uplifting and dignifying the individual. Their separatism had taken the form of a continued demand that the "slave masters" (white America) give 25 states to the Black Muslims to establish a Nation of Islam for black people. In 1964, after his return from Mecca, Malcolm X broke with the main organization over his conviction that cooperation with whites was possible and rigid separatism was contrary to Allah's plan. A year later Malcolm X was assassinated while addressing a group of his followers. Since the death of Elija Muhammed, the Black Muslim organization has entertained the possibility of cooperation with some whites, especially under the leadership of Elija Muhammed's son Warif Deen Muhammed. Since 1985, the mosques have been operated independently and not under central control. Minister Louis Farrakhan came to the forefront after breaking with Warif Deen Muhammed in 1977, and now heads a group known as the Nation of Islam. Besides supporting the candidacy of the Rev. Jesse Jackson for the presidency of the United States in 1984 and 1988, Minister Farrakhan had been instrumental in organizing the Million Man March in 1995. Minister Farrakhan espoused a form of Afrocentrism. As Gerald Early has noted in his essay on "Understanding Afrocentrism,"

> Farrakhan has found three effective lines of entry among blacks that draw on the Afrocentric impulse: First, that Islam is the true religion of black people . . . Second, that black people need business enterprise in their own community in order to liberate themselves . . . and third, that Jews of European descent are not to be trusted.[46]

Afrocentrism itself was coined by Molefi K. Asante, Professor and Chair of African American Studies at Temple University.[47] It is an orientation intended to liberate African Americans from the Eurocentric views of Western society, supplanting it with the history, values, and cultural heritage of Africa. Given that white society so often devalues blackness, as we saw in studies reported in the previous chapter, Afrocentrism exalts a rich African heritage. Afrocentrism taken in the context of the American genre is a form of pluralism, posing an alternative view of what is to be valued. Afrocentrism also rages against a liberalism that "set free the individual, but did not encourage the development of a community within which the individual could flower."[48]

There have been numerous other attempts at separatism by minority groups in the United States. The Zionist movement was created to support the establishment of a Jewish state. Since the creation of Israel, however, American Jewish support has been in terms of financial contributions rather than massive immigration.

Reies Tijerina and his followers in *La Alianza* were convinced that Chicanos and Anglos could not live together in a common society. The Chicanos wanted to take back their land seized by Anglos in the nineteenth century and guaranteed to Mexican Americans at the time of Mexico's surrender to the United States in 1848. In 1967 the Chicanos of Tierra Amarilla (in northern New Mexico) elected their own local government and induced *La Alianza* to seize the land in the name of that government. *La Alianza* effectively controlled Tierra Amarilla for ninety minutes, after which the Anglo-dominated local government returned to power.

Although total separatism remains a philosophical goal of some segments of the minority population, it has received little minority support and met with little success. Only Liberia, established by a treaty between the United States and native princes in the region early in the nineteenth century, has been a successful attempt at minority nationalism. However, although Liberia was established to provide a homeland for black Americans, only a small portion of the black population ever sought refuge back in Africa.

Over the past two decades there has emerged and grown another alternative. It initially had some elements of separatism, but has become increasingly more pluralistic. The approach is sometimes termed *multiculturalism.* The thesis of multiculturalism involves open opposition to assimilation and especially its Eurocentric orientation and the recognition that the contributions of all racial and ethnic groups are to be valued. Marrett and her colleagues[49] have noted that multicultural education had two phases: one that focused upon the distinct cultural identities of the people of color for their own enlightenment and benefit, and a second that enlightened the consciousness of others, primarily of the majority group. As an educational tool in the schools and universities, multiculturalism has the potential of permitting us all to understand history and the elements of our society from diverse perspectives, recognizing that no group, including the dominant one, has a monopoly over comprehension of human events. The recognition that all peoples have a story to tell enlightens our perspective and reduces the likelihood of ethnocentrism. However, it cannot supplant one history with another, but should take the form that Banks noted: "If we are to remain a free and pluralistic society, we can neither do away with the Western canon nor exclude the contributions of people of color."[50] It is too easy to fall into political correctness and denounce any Western contribution because the Eurocentrism and Anglo Conformity models that relied upon the political and economic dominance of West had been used to justify racism and sexism.

CONCLUSION

It is not possible to make a generalization about the future of all minority groups. There is too much diversity in terms of their sizes, resources, histories, identifiability, differential power, differential treatment by the majority, and degree of self-awareness. Both models—assimilation and separatism—may operate in part for all minority groups. Within any society there are centrifugal and centripetal forces that pull apart a single group or combine parts of diverse groups. At any point in time one of these forces may predominate over the others. A society may first attempt to assimilate one or some of its minorities, and then follow with a period of dissolution of the unity and establishment of separatism. In addition, members of groups within complex societies possess varied and sometimes antithetical loyalties. In some instances members from diverse racial, ethnic, or gender groups may be united along the lines of other loyalties, including social class, careers, and even leisure-time activities. These could form additional dimensions of "structural pluralism" as Gordon described it.

Assimilation and separatism represent two polar types, which can be theoretically heuristic and even empirically plausible. However, they can never be seen as a final outcome. If by that phrase we mean a stable relationship that will never again change, we can assuredly say that this will never happen. Human society is dynamic. Final resolutions for one generation are only the starting point for new resolutions for the next generation. If, on the other hand, we wish to speak of the short run, we can assume that there will continue to be individual and personal mobility of racial, ethnic, and gender individuals. This has been the trend, accompanied by less significant gains, and in some instances losses, for the groups as a whole.

There are still other temporary resolutions. There can be continuation of colonial status for many minority groups; there can be coalitions among the poor and the minorities to seize power, prestige, and property, and to change the society and its ideology of racism; there can be limited pluralism in which the minorities retain some of their cultural or biological identities, but also share a common identity with the majority; there may be the splintering of the total nation-state into various minority enclaves; there can even be the wholesale extermination of some minority groups, which may then focus attention upon other minority groups; or there may be the unification of all groups against some new and as yet unrecognized out-group.

The United States is clearly a diverse society, made up of numerous peoples, all of whom have the right to their cultural heritage and all of whom can help to interpret reality. Pluralism, however, has another challenge, other than the constraints it places on the minority group, as noted earlier. The need to respect cultural differences without the establishment of group boundaries which classify people in "we" and "they." The glue that holds societies together is a commonality of culture and experience, even if that commonality is the recognition of diversity. Increasingly what binds American society together is their common goals for success and achievement. When pluralism is conjoined with ethnocentric in-group and out-group barriers, conflict is often the result. The recent histories of Lebanon and Bosnia testify to the fragile nature of a collective sense of "peoplehood" in the presence of both diversity and ethnocentrism. The challenge is daunting, but the cost of failure is extreme.

Summary

There are many models that attempt to predict the outcomes of minority-majority relationships. Most of these models have assumed assimilation as a goal, usually in one of the following forms: Anglo conformity, melting pot, or cultural pluralism. The constructs of Park, Bogardus, and Brown are examples of early attempts to develop a cyclical stage theory of intergroup relations. Lieberson expanded these earlier models into a more complex one which hinges on a single variable—differential power. Gordon delineated a complex model which includes seven stages of assimilation, beginning with cultural assimilation and culminating in civic assimilation. Banton provides yet another model of three sequences of racial orders, all of which are resolved in some type of assimilation—either pluralism or integration. Kinloch extends the concept of colonialism and in his theory accounts for the emergence of different types of minorities. Van den Berghe rejects a unidimensional view of pluralism in favor of a complex, multilevel typology, while emphasizing that pluralism is not intrinsically democratic. For van den Berghe, pluralism is not an outcome, but a condition of societies. Differing types of pluralism may develop into assimilation or separatism.

Assimilation models generally have had many criticisms lodged against them. They are sometimes tautological, teleological, and untestable. However, several of these models have been heuristic and have accurately predicted the dynamics of some groups.

Other models have posited an alternative resolution—separatism. Separatism may be imposed on a weak minority by a powerful majority, or it may be initiated by the minority in the form of nationalism. There have been several attempts at separatism in America. Garvey and the UNIA represent one of the strongest such movements for blacks in the past. Today the Black Muslims are among the larger separatist movements among the black minority. Zionism and *La Alianza* are separatist attempts within other minorities. However, we must conclude that although there may be short-run or temporary goals, one must approach the idea of final resolution with caution. Social life is dynamic and ever changing. The process of assimilation may be reversible. For any one minority group the forces of separation and the forces of integration may operate either simultaneously or consecutively.

NOTES

1. Milton M. Gordon, *Assimilation in American Life* (New York: Oxford University Press, 1964).
2. Stewart G. Cole and Mildred Wiese Cole, *Minorities and the American Promise* (New York: Harper, 1954).
3. Gordon, *Assimilation,* p. 85.
4. Ibid.
5. Nathan Glazer and Daniel Patrick Moynihan, *Beyond the Melting Pot* (Cambridge, MA: M.I.T. Press, 1963).
6. See Gordon, *Assimilation,* and George R. Stewart, *American Ways of Life* (Garden City, NY: Doubleday, 1954).
7. Gordon, *Assimilation.*
8. Ibid., p. 159.
9. Robert E. Park, *Race and Culture* (New York: Free Press, 1950).
10. Emory S. Bogardus, *Immigration and Race Attitudes* (Lexington, MA: Heath, 1928).
11. Brewton Berry, *Race and Ethnic Relations* (Boston: Houghton Mifflin, 1965).
12. See Robert E. Park, "Human Migration and the Marginal Man," *American Journal of Sociology* 33 (1928), pp. 881–93; Everett V. Stonequist, *The Marginal Man: A Study in Personality and Culture Conflict* (New York: Scribner, 1937); and Noel P. Gist and Anthony Gary Dworkin, eds., *The Blending of Races* (New York: Wiley-Interscience, 1972).
13. W. O. Brown, "Culture Contact and Race Conflict," in *Race and Culture Contacts,* ed. E. B. Reuter (New York: McGraw-Hill, 1934).
14. Others include E. Franklin Frazier, "The Impact of Urban Civilization Upon Negro Family Life," *American Sociological Review* 2 (1937), pp. 609–18; Louis Wirth, "The Problem of Minority Groups," in *The Science of Man in the World Crisis.,* ed. Ralph Linton (New York: Columbia University Press, 1945); Clarence E. Glick, "Social Roles and Types of Race Relations," in *Race Relations in World Perspective,* ed. A. W. Lind (Honolulu: University of Hawaii Press, 1955); Rose Hum Lee, *The Chinese in the United States of America* (Hong Kong: Hong Kong University Press, 1960); and Peter I. Rose, *They and We* (New York: Random House, 1964). See Stanford M. Lyman, *The Black American in Sociological Thought* (New York: Capricorn, 1973), chap. 2, for a discussion of these theories.
15. Stanley Lieberson, "A Societal Theory of Race and Ethnic Relations," *American Sociological Review* 26 (1961), p. 902.
16. Ibid.

17. For Lieberson, "indigenous" is any established group, not necessarily the original or aboriginal group.
18. Berry, *Race and Ethnic Relations.*
19. See Hubert M. Blalock, Jr., "A Power Analysis of Racial Discrimination," *Social Forces* 39 (1960), pp. 53–59, and *Toward a Theory of Minority-Group Relations* (New York: Wiley, 1967), chap. 4.
20. Gordon, *Assimilation.*
21. Gordon has come to acknowledge that the steps of assimilation do not necessarily occur in a set pattern for all groups. See Milton M. Gordon, *Human Nature, Class, and Ethnicity* (New York: Oxford University Press, 1978), pp. 173–76. Earlier this argument was raised by Harry H. L. Kitano, *Japanese Americans,* 2nd ed. (Englewood Cliffs, NJ: Prentice-Hall, 1976.)
22. Kitano, *Japanese Americans.*
23. Michael Banton, *Race Relations* (New York: Basic Books, 1967), chap. 4.
24. Ibid., p. 69.
25. Pierre van den Berghe, *Race and Racism: A Comparative Perspective* (New York: Wiley, 1967).
26. Graham C. Kinloch, *The Sociology of Minority Group Relations* (Englewood Cliffs, NJ: Prentice-Hall, 1979).
27. Graham C. Kinloch, *The Dynamics of Race Relations: A Sociological Analysis* (New York: McGraw-Hill, 1974).
28. Van den Berghe, *Race and Racism.*
29. Ibid., p. 27.
30. Ibid.
31. The mixed-race individuals who issue from such sexual unions often occupy positions intermediate to that of the two parents, or they assimilate with the lower caste. Gist and Dworkin (*Blending of Races*) have observed that if the mixed-race individuals occupy intermediate positions between the majority and the minority station, they may come to serve as those who do the dirty work for the majority in its control over the minority. If the society is one that later gains independence, then the suppressed native population (or minority) may seek retribution against the intermediate group. In many respects the products of the mixed-race unions come to be very marginal persons.
32. Van den Berghe, *Race and Racism.*
33. Ibid., p. 29.
34. Ibid.
35. Ibid.
36. Van den Berghe, *Race and Racism,* p. 147.
37. Hubert M. Blalock, Jr., *Toward a Theory of Minority Group Relations* (New York: Wiley, 1967).
38. Edna Bonacich, "A Theory of Middleman Minorities," *American Sociological Review* 38 (1973), pp. 583–94.

39. W. Lloyd Warner and Leo Srole, *The Social Systems of American Ethnic Groups,* Yankee City Series, vol. 3 (New Haven: Yale University Press, 1945). See also Lyman, *Black American.*
40. Lyman, *Black American,* pp. 49–51.
41. Bernard Barber, "Structural-Functional Analysis: Some Problems and Misunderstandings," *American Sociological Review* 21 (1956), pp. 129–35.
42. Ibid.
43. Lyman, *Black American.* For a presentation of the "fallacy of misplaced concreteness," see Alfred North Whitehead, *Science and the Modern World* (New York: Macmillan, 1925).
44. Dennis H. Gouveia, "The Coloreds of Guyana," in *Blending of Races,* ed. Gist and Dworkin, pp. 103–19.
45. E. U. Essien-Udom, *Black Nationalism: A Search for an Identity in America* (Chicago: University of Chicago Press, 1962).
46. Gerald Early, "Understanding Afrocentrism: Why Blacks Dream of World Without Whites," *Civilization* (1995), pp. 31–39 (Reprinted in John Kromkowski [ed.], *Race and Ethnic Relations 98/99,* Annual Editions, Sluice Dock, Guilford, CT: 1998, p. 120).
47. Molefi Kete Asante, "Afrocentric Curriculum," *Educational Leadership* 49 (1991/92), pp. 28–31.
48. Gerald Early, op. cit., p. 125.
49. Cora Bagley Marrett, Yuko Mizuno, and Gena Collins, "Schools and Opportunities for Mulitcultural Contact," in Carl A. Grant, ed., *Research and Multicultural Education: From the Margins to the Mainstream,* London: The Falmer Press, 1992.
50. James A. Banks, "Multicultural Education: For Freedom's Sake," *Educational Leadership* 49 (1991/92), pp. 32–36.

SUGGESTED READINGS

Banks, James A. "Multicultural Education: For Freedom's Sake," *Educational Leadership* 49 (1991/92), pp. 32–36.

Banton, Michael. *Race Relations.* New York: Basic Books, 1967.

Essien-Udom, E.U. *Black Nationalism: A Search for an Identity in America.* Chicago: University of Chicago Press, 1962.

Bonacich, Edna. "The Theory of Middleman Minorities," *American Sociological Review* 38 (1973), pp. 583–94.

Early, Gerald. "Understanding Afrocentrism: Why Blacks Dream of World Without Whites," *Civilization* (1995), pp. 31–39 (Reprinted in John Kromkowski [ed.], *Race and Ethnic Relations 98/99,* Annual Editions, Sluice Dock, (Guilford, CT: 1998), pp.1118–25).

Glazer, Nathan, and Daniel Patrick Moynihan. *Beyond the Melting Pot,* 2nd ed. Cambridge, MA: Massachusetts Institute of Technology Press, 1970.

Gordon, Milton M. *Human Nature, Class and Ethnicity.* New York: Oxford University Press, 1978.

Grant, Carl A. (ed.), *Research and Multicultural Education: From the Margins to the Mainstream.* London: The Falmer Press, 1992.

Kinloch, Graham C. *The Sociology of Minority Group Relations.* (Englewood Cliffs, NJ: Prentice-Hall, 1979).

Lieberson, Stanley. "A Societal Theory of Race and Ethnic Relations," *American Sociological Review* 26 (1961), pp. 902–10.

Lyman, Stanford. *The Black American in Sociological Thought: A Failure of Perspective.* New York: Capricorn, 1973.

Park, Robert E. *Race and Culture.* Glencoe, IL: The Free Press, 1950.

Van den Berghe, Pierre. *Race and Racism: A Comparative Perspective.* New York: Wiley, 1967.

CHAPTER 7

NEW DIRECTIONS

The changes that occurred in our society in terms of minority-majority relations during the 1950s and 1960s were dramatic. Those decades saw the outlawing of de jure discrimination, the declaration of a war on poverty, and racial upheavals in the cities across the nation. By contrast, the 1970s, especially the post-Vietnam and post-Watergate eras, seemed quiescent. However, the 1980s and 1990s have seen a reaction against the gains that minorities made during the Civil Rights era. Under the Reagan and Bush administrations and the Republican majority in Congress since the 1994 election there has been a retrenchment in intergroup progress. Affirmative action is under a full-blown attack as a result in part of a white backlash and there have been a disturbing number of high-profile racial incidents throughout the country. The incidents include the burning of some 70 black churches, the emergence of skinhead activism (worldwide) and white militias, the high-profile beating of Rodney King by Los Angeles police officers, the near-election as governor of Louisiana of Ku Klux Klan leader David Duke, the migration of jobs from the inner city to the suburbs and to the Third World. Despite the backlash, there have been substantial gains made by members of minority groups that have altered the fabric of intergroup relations and will continue to have profound effects beyond the year 2000.

Since the 1970s and 1980s the significance of race has changed, while the role of class has become even more profound. Changes in the national origin of immigrants that began in the 1960s and 1970s have meant that over 80 percent of immigrants to the United States come from Asia and Latin America. It has also led to considerable debate on the issue of undocumented or illegal immigration. Minority group members now make up the majority of the residents in several major American cities and often make up the overwhelming majority of students in large urban school districts. Minority group children in central-city public schools are often in poverty, and poverty is a major contributor to low academic performance. The result is that since the 1980s the U.S. Department of Education, the public, and U.S. corporations have asked whether the United States is "a nation at risk"[1] of economically falling behind much of the developed world.

The new directions of minority-majority relations are varied. They incorporate questions of the continued significance of the role of race. They address concerns about immigration and "ownership" of the society. The new directions involve the growing significance of multiple minority statuses and the rediscovery of ethnicity, or "ethnogenesis," that grew in the 1970s and continues among all groups but particularly among majority group members. Finally, the future of affirmative action as a tool to facilitate minority access to equal opportunities and equal statuses in the society has increasingly been under attack.

Is the Role of Race Declining?

In the discussion of the distributive dimension (see Chapter 3) we presented Milton Gordon's model of "ethclass"[2] to analyze values and beliefs of groups. We also discussed Wright and Perrone's[3] emphasis upon the predictive power of social class origin in explaining economic returns on educational investments. In the ethclass model it was shown that people of the same social class held common values and expectations regardless of their race or ethnicity. Likewise, in the neo-Marxian perspective, data indicated that individuals of managerial class origins were more likely to convert their educational opportunities into higher incomes regardless of their race, ethnicity, or gender than were individuals of working class backgrounds. Both of these orientations suggest that race, ethnicity, or gender alone will not accurately predict outcomes for individuals.

Twenty years ago, sociologist William J. Wilson[4] proposed that in modern America the significance of race has declined, but the importance of class has increased. Since World War II there has been an expanding African American middle class, with increased opportunities created by advances in industrial technology. Race has increasingly become a poor indicator of economic opportunity and occupational mobility. Instead, social class origins have become a better predictor. Those who received quality education, regardless of their race, experience upward mobility, moving away from an increasingly diverse multiethnic "underclass" (i.e., those at or below the poverty line). Many African Americans who remain in the underclass are remnants of the historical stages of the "plantation economy" and "industrial expansion." Both of these stages were characterized by interracial competition and oppression. Because the economic and industrial factors have dislocated the unskilled, regardless of their race, Wilson contended that future governmental policies should focus upon the problems of the unskilled underclass, rather than upon race and ethnicity alone. That is, public policy should not address social issues as if they were solely racial in nature, but should address the more difficult problems of class inequality.

Wilson cited substantial evidence to support his position and an inspection of national data provides additional support. Between 1959 and 1980, the percentage of African Americans below the poverty level dropped from 55 percent to 28 percent.[5] The percentage of African Americans having completed four or more years of college grew from 3.1 in 1960 to 7.2 in 1980 (and 11.8 percent among the cohort between the ages of 25 and 29).[6] The percentage of African Americans who held occupations as professionals, managers, or officials (high status occupations) grew from about three percent in 1940 to about 6.5 percent in 1960 to 16 percent in 1980.[7] Likewise, Sampson and Milam[8] demonstrated the growing black middle class had a strong sense of group solidarity.

Wilson's thesis was not without criticism. The Association of Black Sociologists[9] vigorously attacked Wilson's work. They pointed to the fact that in all social classes, blacks still experienced discrimination especially in the areas of housing, health care, education, and even employment. Hurst[10] found that race was very important (more so than class) in determining attitudes and subjective perceptions of exploitation and discrimination. Van Valey, Roof, and Wilcox[11] examined census data from 1960 and 1970 and found that residential segregation of blacks had not declined significantly. Thus, in the area of housing, race continues to be important. Similarly, the National Institute of Education[12] reported that urban public schools had become more racially segregated since 1970. Much of this increased segregation is due to white flight.[13]

Twenty years after the publication of *The Declining Significance of Race* 30.6 percent of African Americans are living below the poverty level (up from 1980, but down from the high of 33.1 percent in 1993); 12.4 percent of African American men and 14.6 percent of African American women have completed four or more years of college; and 15.5 percent of African American men and 22.2 percent of African American women hold occupations as professionals, managers, or officials.[14] The underclass is not declining and, relative to their numbers in the population, is still disproportionately composed of African Americans, as well as other racial and ethnic minorities. Thus, there is evidence drawn from economic and occupational data that the role of race has declined in our society. This is not to conclude that race is declining in all areas of social life. Nor should one assume that in those areas in which the role race has declined, its importance has totally disappeared. Nevertheless, what is true is that we have moved from a color caste society in which one's race nearly completely specified one's destiny and position in the social structure and where roles, statuses, and opportunities were rigidly defined by race to one where social class is more salient.

De jure discrimination, that which is prescribed by law and statute, no longer accounts for minority disadvantages, but there remain residuals due to de facto discrimination based upon individual preferences and practices and due to past-in-present discrimination.[15] Past-in-present discrimination involves benign practices that have the effect of discriminating because of a past history of discrimination that has disadvantaged the minority group. The key U.S. Supreme Court case of past-in-present discrimination is *Griggs* v. *Duke Power* in 1971.[16] Duke Power was departmentalized, with five operating departments, one of which, labor, paid much lower wages and was historically the only one open to African Americans. At the time of the enforcement of the 1964 Civil Rights Act in 1965, Duke Power required employees seeking to transfer to a department outside of labor to have a high school diploma. When African Americans applied for transfers out of labor, Duke Power added the passage of two written aptitude tests to the requirement for transfers. In the past, when transfers into departments other than labor were restricted only to whites, Duke Power had not mandated either a high school diploma or the tests. Past discrimination existed in the form of segregated and unequal schooling that resulted in a lower percentage of African Americans graduating from high school, a reduced chance that African Americans could pass the test, and the lack of a high school requirement for transfers when transfers were open only to whites. The present practice of tests and a high school diploma might have seemed reasonable, but constituted discrimination in light of past history. As Feagin and Eckberg note:

> The Court argued that institutionalized practices that are fair in form but negative in effect constitute illegal discrimination in certain situations (e.g., when the discriminatory device has not been proven to be a valid predictor of job performance).[17]

The Court reversed itself and permitted tests in the 1976 *Washington* v. *Davis* case involving written qualifying tests given to applicants for positions in the Washington, D.C., police department. African American candidates were four times more likely to fail the test than were whites. The Court ruled, however, that such tests were reasonable because they were race neutral and served the purpose of selecting people on the basis of abilities appropriate to the job.[18]

Immigration and New Minority Groups

The major sources for the creation of minority populations in America's past has been through various forms of immigration and colonization and conquest. Colonial expansion and conquest created the minority status of Native

Americans, Mexican Americans, while war with Spain made Puerto Ricans one of America's minority groups. African Americans became a minority through enforced immigration, slavery, and its aftermath. Other minority groups became minorities as a result of their voluntary migration to the United States. Up until the Immigration Acts of the 1920s the United States experienced successive waves of immigrants from Europe and, to a much lesser extent, from Asia. The assimilation of these groups are now in various stages.

A combination of political revolution and economic crises in the Third World nations, changes in the U.S. Immigration laws in 1965 and again in 1986, and the advanced level of technology in U.S. society have created conditions that encouraged new waves of immigration. These new waves do not exclusively contain peasant populations, as did the waves of immigrants at the beginning of the twentieth century. Some of the new immigrants have been highly skilled industrial workers and members of the well-educated middle class. The outcomes of civil wars have often resulted in the immigration of educational elites to the United States. The new waves of immigrants are coming from substantially different national groups than did earlier waves.

Table 7-1 depicts dramatically the changing shape of immigration to the United States since the beginning of the twentieth century. The percentage of immigrants coming from Europe has decline nearly every decade since the 1901–1910 era, with only a small jump following the World War II. At one time more than nine out of every ten immigrants came from Europe, while during the decade of the 1960s merely one-third were of European origin, and between 1981 and 1990, merely one in ten were from Europe. The slight upturn since 1991 has been principally due to the breakup of the Soviet Union and its former republics (between 1971 and 1980, 43 million people emigrated from what was then the Soviet Union, while between 1981 and 1990, 84 million people emigrated, and during the five years between 1991 and 1995, more than 277 million people emigrated).[19] By contrast with European immigration, there has been a monumental increase in the migration to the United States of people from Latin America and Asia.

Between 1901 and 1960, no more than three to six percent of the immigrants came from Asia, but the figure doubled between 1961 and 1970. Since 1971 migration from Asia has accounted for more than one-third of all immigrants coming to the United States Most are political refugees or family members of earlier waves of political refugees, as noted by Yen Li Espiritu in Chapter 15. The waves of migration primarily from Vietnam, Cambodia, and Laos following the end of the Vietnam War and the collapse of U.S.-backed governments in Southeast Asia accounted for most of the migration during the 1970s and 1980s. Since 1991, however, immigration from Asia has been principally from China, India, the Philippines, and Vietnam. This immigration is a product of political and economic upheavals in those nations.

Latin American migration to the United States grew from a trickle in the beginning of the twentieth century to less than 20 percent between 1941 and

TABLE 7-1
National Origins of Immigrants, 1901–1995

	1901–10	1911–20	1921–30	1931–40	1941–50	1951–60	1961–70	1971–80	1981–90	1991–95
Europe	92.5	76.3	60.3	65.9	60.1	59.3	33.8	17.8	9.6	13.9
Asia	2.8	3.4	2.4	2.9	3.1	6.2	12.9	36.4	38.4	31.2
Canada	2.0	12.9	22.5	20.5	16.6	11.0	12.4	2.6	1.6	1.4
Latin America	2.1	7.0	14.4	9.7	17.7	22.5	39.2	40.4	47.2	49.9
Africa	0.1	0.1	0.2	0.3	0.7	0.7	0.8	2.0	2.6	3.1
Other	0.4	0.3	0.1	0.6	1.7	0.3	1.0	0.8	0.5	0.5

1950, a significant portion of which was a result of the *bracero* labor program beginning in World War II. Since World War II Mexico has accounted for well over one-half of the immigration from Latin America. That percentage has risen steadily since the 1950s to the point that nearly one-half of all immigrants to the United States now come from Latin America. Beginning with the Fidel Castro's 1959 revolution in Cuba, many middle- and upper-class Cubans have left the country for the United States; their immigration was followed in the 1970s and 1980s by lower income populations. The number of Cubans entering the United States has varied with changes in Cuban government emigration policies. Many Cubans are concentrated in Miami, Florida, generating antagonism from the African American community, which sees them as competitors for employment. Another major source of immigration from Latin America has been due to political instability, civil war, and economic crises in Central America, especially since 1980. Chapter 12 by Rodriguez and Hagan documents the Central American immigration, Chapter 9 by Saenz discusses the immigration from Mexico.

Table 7-1 refers to documented immigration, or what has been termed legal immigration. There also is a substantial number of people who enter the United States illegally each year. By its very nature, undocumented or illegal immigration is difficult to determine; there are no immigration papers associated with such immigration. Only the numbers seeking amnesty and "green cards" (work visas) under the 1986 Immigration Reform and Control Act (IRCA), numbers caught by agents of the Immigration and Naturalization Service, and demographic estimates can arrive at an approximate number. Of course, the number of undocumented who are caught and returned to their home countries does not represent the population never caught and also reflects populations who are repeated border crossers. The Immigration and Naturalization Service estimated that in 1994 there were somewhere between 3.5 and 4 million people in the United States without documentation, although other estimates have been both higher and lower.[20] Fix and Passel of the Urban Institute reported in 1994 that, "The best current estimate of the size of the undocumented population was 3.2 million in October 1992, with growth estimated at 200,000 to 300,000 each year."[21]

Latin American immigration, particularly from Mexico and Central America created a need for the public schools to provide increased minority language instruction, either in the form of bilingual education or English as a second language. Migration from Southeast Asia has also necessitated such instruction, but to relatively fewer students. In Chapter 4 we discussed the growing opposition to bilingual education generally by the dominant population. There is another level of concern in the African American population regarding the new immigrants. Because many African Americans continue to work in lower-paying jobs, they are more often in economic competition with lower-skilled immigrants. Furthermore, many African Americans who occupy higher-paying, white-collar jobs do not have the comparative seniority on those jobs that whites have and may also be in competition with the more middle-class immigrants. The National Opinion Research Center's General Social Survey enumerated attitudes about competition with immigrants for jobs. One question asked, "What do you think are the chances that you or anyone in your family won't get a job or promotion while an equally or less qualified immigrant employee receives one instead?"[22] While 27.4 percent of white respondents felt that it was likely or very likely to happen, 64.7 percent of African Americans felt that it would happen to them. Thus, the new immigration is viewed as having negative consequences to American-born populations, especially among those who are likely to have to compete with the new immigrants.

Multiple Minority Statuses

Many members of minority groups belong to not one minority, but to two or even three simultaneously. Hence it is not always adequate to indicate that a person is African American, Mexican American, female, or elderly. In reality, many within those categories share multiple minority statuses. Thus, we could speak of elderly African American women, or Jews from India. With intermarriage among some groups it is possible for a person to share multiple ethnic or racial statues. Census data suggest that multiple minority membership tends to compound discrimination and disadvantage. Belonging to multiple minority groups makes one subject to cross pressures. These groups may exert different demands upon the individual-demands that may not only compete for time and resources but may be actually antithetical. Consider the case of elderly Mexican Americans or elderly Puerto Ricans. The U.S. Bureau of the Census[23] reveals that in 1996 the median age of the U.S. Hispanic population was 26.4 years, while the median age of the non-Hispanic white (Anglos) population was 37.0 years. Furthermore, 12.4 percent of all Hispanics were between the ages of 18–24, while 8.6 percent of all Anglos were between those ages. The reverse is true for the population between the ages of 50 and 64, where 8.8 percent of Hispanics fit into that older age group, 14.5 percent of all Anglos fit into that group. As such, both Mexican Americans and Puerto Ricans are a young population (see the chapters by Saenz [Chapter 9] and Torrecilha and his co-authors [Chapter 10]).

Older Mexican Americans or Puerto Ricans, nearing a retirement age, have personal interests in raising the retirement age to prolong their period of employability. However, as members of the Mexican American or Puerto Rican communities, they have an interest in the increased employment of their ethnic group, the majority of whom are young. To the extent that economic pressures place limits on the number of workers in the labor force, employers could retire older workers to make room for the young. A move for greater opportunities for the Hispanics by elderly individuals could lead to their own job termination. The individual must therefore balance roles; should he or she campaign for the rights of Hispanics or for the rights of the elderly? Although it does not need to be an either/or dilemma, in reality, it is seen as such by many minority individuals. The pervasiveness of one of the minority labels may simplify the choice of which minority role to emphasize. For example, during the early days of the women's liberation movement, many African American women chose not to join feminist groups because they felt that the discrimination they received as women was less pernicious than the discrimination they received as African Americans.[24] They therefore elected to fight racism rather than sexism.

There are consequences of multiple minority status for persons other than the multiple minority status individual. Employers under the constraints of affirmative action often seek out such people. If a businessman must hire both African Americans and women, getting a "two-for" (i.e., two for the price of one) in the shape of one African American female who is counted twice can satisfy affirmative action guidelines while changing actual hiring practices only minimally. And so hiring an elderly, handicapped, Puerto Rican female makes an employer appear four times as liberal as he really is.

THE REDISCOVERY OF ETHNICITY

Throughout this century there has been a discrepancy in American values. While lip service has been paid to the virtue of cultural pluralism, the dominant society has nonetheless demanded Anglo conformity in varying degrees. In prior centuries, black slaves and to a lesser extent Native Americans were stripped of their cultural heritages and made to conform to a simplified adaptation of white European customs. In the nineteenth and early twentieth centuries white Europeans were likewise subjected to majority pressures to surrender their cultural heritage in the promise of upward mobility. The Civil Rights Movement, the Black Liberation Movement, and the emerging focus on Afrocentrism has encouraged the rediscovery of African heritages. The concept of ethnogenesis described by Singer[25] is a name frequently applied to the creation or discovery of a group's ethnicity. Multiculturalism acknowledges this diversity of ethnic heritages and the legitimacy of different ethnic interpretations of reality, as do the many ethnic studies programs that exist on university campuses. During the late 1960s and the 1970s, Americans of European ancestry also began to rediscover their heritage.[26] Greeley termed this rediscovery as a new tribalism.[27] Four manifestations of the new tribalism can be cited. There is an increased interest in the "high culture" of the ethnic heritage, including art and literature that was not salient to parents or grandparents when they were peasants in the "old country." Americans who can afford it plan vacations back to the village, town, or at least the country from which their ancestors emigrated. Further, there is an increased tendency to name their children with ethnic names. The decades of the 1970s saw the use of names such as Marek, Sean, Anton, Kellie, and others by parents whose names were Mark, Fred, John, and Susan. Finally, Greeley observes that the new tribals may attempt to learn the language of their ancestors. This last step is considered the central element in the survival of ethnicity in our society. One might add that another indicator of the rediscovery of ethnicity is the popularity of ethnic studies courses, including those dealing with white ethnicity in some universities. The gender equivalent has been the development of women's studies courses and the emergence of men's studies.

There are many reasons for the rediscovery of white ethnicity. Some authors such as Gordon[28] view this quest for "peoplehood" as satisfying a deep psychological need to belong to some group less impersonal than the category "Americans." It is seen as the search for community among individuals in a mass society. After acculturation and assimilation of a group has reached an advanced stage, ethnic identification may only be nostalgic. There is often a discrepancy between the individual's claim to ethnicity and especially the claim to minority status and the recognition of such a claim by other. Pettigrew[29] proposed the concept of "affective ethnicity" to describe the condition under which the emotional identification diverges from the social and cultural aspects of identity. Pettigrew suggested that there is a psychological need to retain a modicum of identity with one's cultural heritage long after one has ceased to practice that culture. Blackwell[30] proposed that the rediscovery of ethnicity by whites is an attempt to dilute some of the gains that African Americans and Hispanics have made by use of their white ethnic status. That is, African Americans became successful in gaining some of their economic and political demands, and so ethnic groups who are white and who are in direct economic competition with African Americans felt a need to make competing demands for recognition. The competition for resources and the belief by some white ethnics that African Americans, Native Americans, Asian Americans, and Hispanics were "getting something for nothing" has led to considerable resentment. Current attitudes about affirmative action by whites reflect this resentment. There is, however, a less cynical view of the rediscovery of white ethnicity.[31] After surrendering their cultural heritage, many whites found that the promise of upward social mobility would not be realized for them. The African American experience taught these individuals that by the retaining of ethnic identifiability successful group claims could be made. Hence, white ethnogenesis represents a recognition that abandonment of ethnicity is no longer a prerequisite for mobility, but quite the opposite. In this view, white ethnogenesis is neither a nostalgic viewpoint nor a symbol of white resentment.

Affirmative Action and Its Challenges

Both advantage and disadvantage are often reproduced from generation to generation. The result is that there is a continuity and circularity to the distribution of property, prestige, and power. Groups with privilge tend to pass that privilege on to the next generation, and groups facing adversity pass that adversity on to their children, too. Under the aegis of affirmative action, the United States government has sought to break through the cycle of minority group disadvantage. This was done through a variety of court decisions, direct legislation, and agency regulations. Federal mandates, including *Brown* v. *Board of Education of Topeka, Kansas,* in 1954, the Voting Rights Act of 1965, the Immigration Act of 1965, and much of the 1964 Civil Rights Act, were designed to provide for equal opportunities for minorities.

When it became apparent that simply creating minority opportunities would not offset many decades of discrimination, statistical rules, specific goals, and time tables were created by the Equal Employment Opportunities Commission (EEOC), the Economic Development Administration (EDA), the Department of Housing and Urban Development (HUD), the Department of Health and Human Services (formerly HEW) the Office of Civil Rights (OCR), and a variety of other agencies in the federal government.[32] These were to ensure that minority groups were often overincluded in the provision of opportunities. Quotas were established allocating a certain number or percentage of jobs, places in college admission, financial assistance, and the like to members of minority groups. Federal funding was to be denied to uncooperative agencies, contractors, schools, and so on.

The actual term "affirmative action" arose out of the 1935 National Labor Relations Act, but referred at the time to labor organizing.[33] In the 1950s, as Reskin notes, President Eisenhower asked then Vice President Richard Nixon to investigate the causes of racial discrimination in defense industry hiring. Nixon reported that the cause was the latent effects of the way in which employees were recruited and hired. The Eisenhower administration did not act on the report. However, in 1961, President Kennedy issued Executive Order 10925, which established the Committee on Equal Employment Opportunity and required employers with federal contracts to take the necessary steps needed to provide equal treatment of employment candidates and current employees.[34]

Schuman and his colleagues have identified the three stages of affirmative action policy in the United States beginning in the 1960s. The first phase was a concerted effort to mitigate the institutionalized racism that occurred from traditional hiring practices that reduced the pool of minority applicants, "...such as advertising jobs via individuals or media having ties to a white community." In essence, this was an implementation of policies that arose from the findings of the study during the Eisenhower administration. The second phase directed federal funds to minorities by "...providing additional money to inner cities caught up in the consequences of poverty." The final phase was even more proactive by giving preference to minorities in employment, educational admissions, and educational financial assistance, "...as a way of both making up for past discrimination and accelerating the move toward equality of outcomes."[35]

Through the 1970s and the Carter administration the affirmative action policies were expanded and enforcement was vigorous. However, during the tenure of Presidents Reagan and Bush during the 1980s and early 1990s, there was considerable retrenchment. In fact, it was under the administrations of these two presidents that affirmative action and quotas became intertwined in the public's mind. Those majority group members who oppose affirmative action see quotas as undesirable because they are assumed to specify a *minimum* number of racial, ethnic, and gender minorities to be hired, promoted, or admitted to colleges and programs. As a minimum number they are thought to require employers and universities to lower standards in order to find enough poeple to fill the quotas. Sometimes, however, minorities also see quotas negatively because they argue that quotas set *maximum* numbers, thereby denying opportunities to larger percentages of qualified minority individuals. The common assumption that affirmative action requires every employer and all colleges and universities to select unqualified minority individuals over qualified majority individuals is incorrect. Citing the Office of Federal Contract Compliance regulations, Reskin notes that agency "... regulations expressly forbid quotas or giving less qualified workers preference based on their race or sex."[36] It is also true that "private firms that do not hold large federal contracts and have not been sued for violating Federal anti-discrimination laws have no obligation to practice affirmative action."[37] Under the Clinton administration the Justice Department has returned to enforcement of affirmative action. The executive branch fostered a Glass Ceiling Commission under the chairship of the Secretary of Labor. The Commission was initiated in 1991 in the Bush administration, but has been active in the Clinton administration locating practices that serve as barriers to promotion and equal pay for racial and gender minorities such as job segregation by race and gender and the underrepresentation of minorities in management positions.[38]

Affirmative Action and the Supreme Court. In 1978, the U.S. Supreme Court rendered two important judgments involving Allen Bakke's suit of reverse discrimination by the University of California Davis Medical School.[39] Bakke charged that the university's quota system, which set aside 16 out of 100 openings to medical school for disadvantaged minorities, discriminated against him because he was white. By a 5–4 decision, the Supreme Court ruled that the university had discriminated against Bakke by passing over him in favor of some minority students with poorer test scores and poorer academic records. The Court, in a series of six different opinions by the justices, held that the University of California, by using a fixed racial quota and rigid racial goal, had discriminated against Allen Bakke. The Court ordered the university to admit him. The Court also ruled that under the 1964 Civil Rights Act, institutions and agencies receiving federal monies may consider criteria other than test scores and academic records in admitting students and can adopt race-conscious criteria designed to redress past wrongs or to accomplish goals of student diversity (the Harvard model). Within the spectrum of the justices' opinions were those that supported race-conscious goals only if they redressed past discriminations against groups committed by the specific agency (Justice Powell's opinion) and those that supported such goals if they redressed past wrongs by the society historically (Justice Brennan's opinion). The crux of this issue is whether institutions are responsible for correcting wrongs committed by themselves in the recent past, or whether they must also consider past wrongs committed decades, generations, or centuries ago against people no longer living. That is, to what extent are minorities today true representatives of their ancestors? It should be apparent that the Bakke decision was not a definitive answer to the issues of affirmative action and reverse discrimination.

In 1979 the Supreme Court ruled in the area of employment discrimination as to whether companies without prior determination of past discrimination could establish voluntary affirmative action programs.[40] Kaiser Aluminum's plant in Gramercy, Louisiana, had created a training program leading to job advancement. Fifty percent of the openings in the program were reserved for black employees. Brian Weber, a white employee, argued that he was bypassed for the program despite his seniority over several of the black employees admitted to the program. The Court ruled that affirmative action programs are permissible even if there has been no demonstration of past discrimination by that company. (This is further support of Brennan's opinion on Bakke.) The Court also ruled that while the Kaiser plan did not obey the letter of the law because it had discriminated on the basis of race, it did keep within the spirit of the law by encouraging racial balance in occupations where balance had not existed before. The Court thus ruled against Weber and in favor of affirmative action.

As the 1970s ended, it became apparent from the conflicting Bakke and Weber decisions, as well as two indecisive district court rulings (*Detroit Police Officers Association* v. *Young,* 1979 and *Detroit Police Lieutenants and Sergeants Association* v. *Young,* 1979), that the dilemma between the rights of individuals to be judged on individuals merits and the need to redress wrongs committed against minorities would not easily be resolved. Decisions in the 1980s would be no more conclusive, but the court began to acquire a more conservative slant. Two decisions help to define the inconclusive nature of the issue. In 1984, the Court disallowed the promoting of minorities over more senior whites in the *Firefighters Local Union 1784 of Memphis, Tennessee* v. *Stotts*. However, such a promotion was permitted in the *International Association of Firefighters* v. *City of Cleveland* in 1986. But then, in 1989, the court moved to permit white males to sue on the grounds of reverse discrimination even if the affirmative action plan was approved by the courts (*Martin* v. *Wilks*). The decision overturned a set aside program for minority contractors in Richmond, Virginia. By the 1990s, the courts had ruled that affirmative action plans that are not "narrowly tailored to remedy past discrimination" may be invalidated (*Quirin* v. *City of Pittsburgh* [1992], *Maryland Troopers Association* v. *Evans* [1993], and *Black Firefighters Association* v. *City of Dallas* [1995]).[41] Thus, retirements and appointments of more conservative justices during the Reagan and Bush administrations have moved the Supreme Court to the right and facilitated attacks on affirmative action.

Affirmative Action and Public Opinion. The National Opinion research Center of the University of Chicago posed a series of questions regarding the issues associated with affirmative action to a national sample of Americans between 1988 and 1994. Presented in Table 7-2 are the responses of white and African American individuals to each of the questions. Results of the surveys are pooled across times in instances where the questions were asked during repeated samplings. The percentages are for the "favor" or "strongly favor" responses.

It is clear from Table 7-2 that African American and white respondents do not share a common perspective on affirmative action. It is also clear that there is not agreement within either group on the need for affirmative action, as it is expressed by the issues covered in the survey. Statistically significant differences between the two racial groups exist on all statements except the one that opposes quota. There the majority of whites and African Americans oppose quotas, and the difference between the groups is not statistically significant. However, it is likely that they are in agreement on quotas for different reasons (the difference between a quota as a minimum number and a quota as a maximum number). On the other questions there are substantial differences between African American and white opinions. Whites overwhelmingly oppose preferential hiring and promotion of blacks to compensate for past discrimination and also disagree that the government has an obligation to raise the standard of living of blacks. Most African Americans endorse both statements. The majority of whites feel, however, that black people will be chosen over whites in employment, job promotion, and admission to a college or university. But, whites are less likely than African Americans to believe that they or members of their own families will lose out due to the hiring or promotion of a member of the other race. African Americans overwhelmingly feel that equal or less qualified whites will get the job or promotion that they personally will be denied. Thus, in the abstract, whites expect affirmative action to work against their own group, but not specifically against them. What we may be seeing here is a substantially different perception of the social system. Whites feel that racial equality has already occurred and that blacks are not longer deserving of redress; they also feel that affirmative action has tended to imbalance the scales too far in the direction of minorities, while it has not actually affected them personally. African Americans see the system as unchanged and still supporting white privilege. They see a continued need for affirmative action given continued inequalities, but suspect

TABLE 7-2
Attitudes about Affirmative Action Issues Held by African American and White Americans

	Percentages of Endorsement by	
	White Americans	African Americans
Some people say that because of past discrimination, blacks should be given preference in hiring and promotion. Are you for or against the preferential hiring and promotion of blacks?	10.9	52.7
Irish, Italians, Jewish, and many minorities overcame prejudice and worked their way up. Blacks can do the same without special favors.	77.5	55.1
Some people think that blacks have been discriminated against for so long that the government has a special obligation to help improve their standard of living.	13.9	55.0
Should the government in Washington forbid racial quotas?	60.4	72.4
Does the place where you work have an affirmative action program or make any special effort to hire and promote minorities? (percent yes)	51.2	56.6
What do you think the chances are these days that a white person won't get a job or promotion while an equally or less qualified black person gets one instead? (percent somewhat likely or very likely)	73.9	36.9
What do you think the chances are these days that a white person won't get admitted to a college or university program while an equally or less qualified black person gets one instead? (percent somewhat likely or very likely)	78.5	24.5
What do you think are the chances that you or anyone in your family won't get a job or promotion while an equally or less qualified (member of the opposite race—black or white) employee receives one instead? (percent likely or very likely)	44.3	79.4

Source: *General Social Surveys, 1972–1996: Cumulative Codebook* (Chicago: National Opinion Research Center, 1997).

that whites will still benefit at the African American respondents' own expense given the way in which the social structure continues to operate.

Despite doubts about the decline of white privilege, nearly one-half of the African American respondents did not endorse preferential hiring and promotion; more than half felt that blacks could work their way up without special favors; and nearly one half did not feel that the government has a special obligation to blacks to improve their standard of living. Some portion of this opposition to affirmative action by African Americans is a response to white beliefs that most minorities who gained employment, job promotions, or admission to colleges and universities were actually unqualified and could not have openly competed with whites if ability and achievements were the only criteria considered. While affirmative action in employment, promotion, and college admissions has created opportunities for minorities, minority individuals still had to perform effectively to retain their jobs and to graduate from school. Whites will generally cite a personal anecdote or a story they heard from someone else of an unqualified minority group member gaining undeserved success. Many of these stories are stereotypes, but as we noted in Chapter 5, stereotypes are resistant to facts. While stereotypes that all or most all minorities who gained entry into a job or higher education because of affirmative action are really unqualified and took opportunities away from qualified whites has the effect of devaluing minority gains. Many African Americans (and other minority group members, as well) fear that the presence of affirmative action cheapens their hard-won personal achievements.

Concern about whites devaluing minority achievements ostensibly is the reason that some prominent, politically conservative African Americans such as U.S. Supreme Court Associate Justice Clarence Thomas and University of California regent Ward Connerly oppose affirmative action. Connerly has actively campaigned to ban affirmative action in admissions to the University of California and later headed the Proposition 209 initiate that banned affirmative action statewide. They argue that it is reverse discrimination and that it is an announcement that minorities cannot succeed on their own. A similar argument has been raised by the conservative economist Thomas Sowell[42] and Shelby Steele in his *The Content of Our Character.*[43]

The statistical guidelines established under affirmative action create, according to Jerome H. Skolnick,[44] a moral dilemma between "the individual claim of merit" and the "claim of minority group membership." That is, individuals, regardless of their minority-majority status, have the right to be judged on the basis of their individual merit. However, because minorities have been judged on their status rather than upon their individual merit for so many generations, they have the right to be compensated for past discriminations. As Skolnick observes, this is a "contemporary American dilemma." Nathan Glazer,[45] describing affirmative action as "affirmative discrimination, points to two "misunderstandings" of the federal government. First by establishing statistical quotas for minorities, the government is suggesting homogeneity among group members. By saying that *x* percent of the jobs or college openings should reserved for a specific minority group, it is assumed that no members of the majority are as disadvantaged as the designated minority group. In addition, Glazer argues, the government has assumed that segregation patterns are maintained only by majority will, never by minority choice. When quotas were established in public schools to ensure that every campus would have the same racial distribution of faculty, teacher turnover rates, even among minority teachers, increased.[46]

These responses are denials that discrimination still exists. Feagin and his co-authors cogently document the extent to which discrimination against African Americans remains virulent and still plagues even economically successful African Americans.[47] As Barbara Reskin concluded in her recent work on affirmative action for the American Sociological Association:

> The erosion in the relative economic standing of African Americans during the 1980 stemmed in part from the hiatus in affirmative action enforcement. Without government pressure for affirmative action, cronyism will reign supreme, and those protected by affirmative action will lose. Eliminating affirmative action will increase job discrimination based on sex and race and the wage gap between white men and other groups.[48]

Perhaps the most encouraging result of affirmative action has been documented by Bowen and Bok in their longitudinal study of the long-term consequences of race-conscious, affirmative action admissions policy in elite institutions of higher education, *The Shape of the River.*[49] Using the "College and Beyond Data Base," which consisted of admissions and transcript files of nearly 94,000 students who attended elite colleges and universities, three cohorts were selected consisting of the entering classes of 1951, 1976, and 1989 from 28 schools. The final database consisted of " . . . detailed 'life histories' of 45,184 individuals, including information on educational and occupational histories, restrospective views of college, personal and household income, civic participation, and satisfaction with life."[50] The study revealed that while African Americans who enter elite universities enter with lower test scores and grades, perform less well academically in college, and have lower graduation rates, those who graduate are as likely or more likely than their white classmates to earn advanced degrees or professional degrees, and are more active in their communities than their white peers. In short, African Americans who gained access to elite colleges due to race conscious admissions (affirmative action) became what Bowen and Bok refer to as "the backbone of the black middle class" and on average have made a larger civic contribution to the society than their white counterparts.

Summary

It is clear that the nature of minority-majority relations has been changing. It is no longer merely the ineraction between a few racial/ethnic minorities and an unidentified majority. Rather, social class and the partitioning of the majority are becoming issues. The society has abandoned the historical color caste system and replaced it with a more complex mosaic in which race, per se, does not completely define privilege or disadvantage. The past decades have seen the emergence of a multiracial underclass. Furthermore, new minority groups are emerging, including new immigrants from around the world. Their entry into the society has stimulated debates about the restriction of immigrantion and the curtailment of welfare benefits to immigrants. Other new minorities include groups that have been here since the nation's beginning, but have only recently awakened to their minority status. The elderly, those who are physically challenged, children, and gay and lesbian populations are included in these groups. As such, intergroup relations must necessarily include the concept of multiple minority group statuses.

White ethnic identities have been a salient issue for the past two decades, as many white Americans are rediscovering the cultural heritages that their parents and grandparents abandoned in exchange for the promise of assimilation and upward mobility. For many such individuals the promises were not fulfilled. Learning from the experiences of African Americans, Hispanics, and Native Americans, they are making new claims upon the resources of the society.

As the de jure practices of discrimination against racial, ethnic, and gender minorities have been abolished by civil rights laws, de facto practices based upon preferences and stereotypes have continued to flourish. Affirmative action laws emerged first to prevent both practices and to redress past discriminations. In recent years there has been substantial white opposition to affirmative action based upon the belief that equality among groups has been achieved. Some African Americans and other minorities also have questionned affirmative action in fear that whites will devalue the achievements of the minorities. Nevertheless, there is substantial evidence that there remains a need for affirmative action policies and that debate in government, the courts, and the society will not diminish as we enter the new millenium.

Notes

1. National Commission on Excellence in Education, *A Nation at Risk: The Imperative for Educational Reform* (Washington, D.C.: U.S. Government Printing Office, 1983).
2. Milton M. Gordon, *Assimilation in American Life: The Role of Race, Religion and National Origins* (New York: Oxford University Press, 1964).
3. Erik Olin Wright and Luca Perrone, "Marxist Class Categories and Income In Equality," *American Sociological Review* 42 (1977), pp. 32–55.
4. William Julius Wilson, *The Declining Significance of Race,* 2nd ed. (Chicago: University of Chicago Press, 1980).
5. Ibid., and *Statistical Abstracts of the United States,* 1979 (Washington, D.C.: Government Printing Office, 1980), p. 462.
6. Ibid.

7. Ibid.
8. William A. Sampson and Vera Milam, "The Intraracial Attitudes of the Black Middle Class: Have They Changed?" *Social Problems* 23 (1975), pp. 153–65.
9. "A.B.S. Statement Assails Book by Wilson," American Sociological Association *Footnotes* 6 (1978), p. 4. See also Charles V. Willie, *Caste and Class Controversy* (Bayside, NY: 1979).
10. Charles E. Hurst, "Race, Class, and Consciousness," *American Sociological Review* 37 (1972), pp. 658–70.
11. Thomas L. Van Valey, Wade Clark Roof, and Jerome E. Wilcox, "Trends in Residential Segregation: 1960–1970," *American Journal of Sociology* 82 (1977), pp. 826–44.
12. Center for National Policy Review (Catholic University Law School), *Trends in Black School Segregation, Volume 1* (Washington, D.C.: National Institute of Education, 1977).
13. David J. Armor, "White Flight, Demographic Transition, and the Future of School Desegregation," paper presented at the American Sociological Association Meetings, San Francisco, 1978. See also U.S. Commission on Civil Rights, *Twenty Years After Brown* (Washington, D.C.: Government Printing Office, 1977).
14. *Statistical Abstracts of the United States,* 1997, pp. 24–25.
15. Joe R. Feagin and Douglas Lee Eckberg, "Discrimination: Motivation, Action, and Context," *Annual Review of Sociology* 6 (1980), pp. 1–20.
16. Derrick A. Bell, Jr., *Civil Rights: Leading Case.* (Boston: Little Brown, 1980), pp. 253–60.
17. Feagin and Eckberg, p. 8.
18. Bell, pp. 356–66.
19. *Statistical Abstracts of the United States, 1996,* p. 12, and *Statistical Abstracts of the United States, 1997,* p. 11.
20. U. S. Bureau of the Census, "Illustrative Ranges of the Distribution of Undocumented Immigrants by State," Edward W. Fernandez and J. Gregory Robinson, Teachnical Working Paper No. 8, October 1994.
21. Michael Fix and Jeffery S. Passell, *Immigration and Immigrants: Setting the Record Straight* (Washington, D.C.: The Urban Institute, May 1994), p. 24.
22. National Opinion Research Center, University of Chicago, *General Social Survey Codebook,* 1997.
23. *Statistical Abstracts of the United States, 1997,* pp. 24–25.
24. See Nathan Hare and Julia Hare, "Black Women, 1970," *Transaction* 8 (1970), pp. 65–68, and Linda J. M. LaRue, "Black Liberation and Women's Lib," *Transaction* 8 (1970), pp. 50–58.
25. L. Singer, "Ethnogenesis and Negro Americans Today," *Social Research* 29 (1962), pp. 419–32.
26. Michael Novak, The Rise of the Unmeltable Ethnics (New York: Macmillan, 1971), and Andrew M. Greeley. *Why Can't They Be Like Us?: America's White Ethnic Groups* (New York: Dutton, 1971).

27. Greeley, *Why Can't They Be Like Us?*
28. Milton M. Gordon, *Assimilation in American Life,* and Milton M. Gordon, *Human Nature, Class and Ethnicity* (New York: Oxford University Press, 1978).
29. Thomas F. Pettigrew, "Three Issues in Ethnicity: Boundaries, Deprivations, and Perceptions," in J. Milton Yinger and Stephen J. Cutler, ed., *Major Social Issues: A Multidisciplinary View* (New York: Free Press, 1978), pp. 25–49.
30. James E. Blackwell, "The Power Basis of Ethnic Conflict in American Society," in Lewis A. Coser and Otto N. Larsen, ed., *The Uses of Controversy in Sociology* (New York: Free Press 1978), pp. 179–96.
31. Greeley, *Ethnicity.*
32. U.S. Commission on Civil Rights, *The State of Civil Rights: 1979* (Washington, D.C.: Government Printing Office, 1980).
33. Howard Schuman, Charlotte Steeh, Lawrence Bobo, and Maria Krysan, *Racial Attitudes in America: Trends and Interpretations, rev. ed.* (Cambridge, MA: Harvard University Press, p. 348).
34. Barbara F. Reskin, *The Realities of Affirmative Action in Employment* (Washington, D.C.: The American Sociological Association, 1998), p. 8.
35. Schuman et al., p. 101.
36. Reskin, p. 10.
37. Reskin, pp. 17–18.
38. Ibid.
39. See Allan P. Sindler, *Bakke, DeFunis, and Minority Admissions* (New York: Longmans, 1978) and Matthew W. Finkin, "Some Thoughts on the Powell Opinion in *Bakke,*" *Academe: Bulletin of the AAUP 65* (1979), pp. 192–96.
40. U.S. Commission on Civil Rights, *Civil Rights: 1979,* op. cit.
41. Reskin, p. 16.
42. Thomas Sowell, *Preferential Policies* (New York: Morrow, 1991).
43. Shelby Steele, *The Content of Our Character: A New Vision of Race in America* (New York: St. Martin's Press, 1990).
44. Jerome H. Skolnick, "Changing Civil Rights through Law: Can It Be Done?" in *Major Social Issues: A Multidisciplinary View,* J. Milton Yinger and Stephen J. Cutler, eds. (New York: Free Press, 1978).
45. Nathan Galzer, *Affirmative Discrimination: Ethnic Inequality and Public Policy* (New York: Basic Books, 1978).
46. Ibid.
47. See especially Joe R. Feagin and Hernan Vera, *White Racism: The Basics* (New York: Routledge, 1995), and Joe R. Feagin and Melvin P. Sikes, *Living with Racism: The Black Middle-Class Experience* (Boston: Beacon Press, 1994).
48. Reskin, p. 92.
49. William G. Bowen and Derek Bok, *The Shape of the River: Long-Term Consequences of Considering Race in College and University Admissions.* (Princeton, NJ: Princeton University Press, 1998).
50. Ibid, p.

Suggested Readings

Bowen, William G. and Derek Bok. *The Shape of the River: Long-Term Consequences of Considering Race in College and University Admissions.* Princeton, NJ: Princeton University Press, 1998.

Blackwell, James E. "The Power Basis of Ethnic Conflict in American Society." In Lewis A. Coser and Otto N. Larsen, eds., *The Uses of Controversy in Sociology.* New York: Free Press, 1976.

Feagin, Joe R. and Douglas Lee Eckberg. "Discrimination: Motivation, Action, and Context," *Annual Review of Sociology* 6 (1980), pp. 1–20.

Fix, Michael and Jeffery S. Passell, *Immigration and Immigrants: Setting the Record Straight,* Washington, D.C.: The Urban Institute, May 1994, p. 24.

Greeley, Andrew M., and William C. McCready. *Ethnicity in the United States: A Preliminary Reconnaissance.* New York: Wiley-Interscience, 1974.

Reskin, Barbara F. *The Realities of Affirmative Action in Employment.* Washington, D.C.: The American Sociological Association, 1998.

Schuman, Howard, Charlotte Steeh, Lawrence Bobo, and Maria Krysan. *Racial Attitudes in America: Trends and Interpretations, rev. ed.* Cambridge, MA: Harvard University Press.

Wilson, William Julius. *The Declining Significance of Race,* 2nd ed. Chicago: University of Chicago Press, 1980.

PART 2

THE REPORTS

Part Two of *The Minority Report* presents the individual reports by members of twelve minority groups. Some of the groups are readily recognized as minorities; some are increasingly seen as minorities; some used to be minorities but are rarely considered so anymore; and two have been emerging minorities, although their claims by those who would reserve minority status only to racial and ethnic groups might be challenged. When many people think of minority groups in American society, they most frequently cite African Americans, Chicanos or Mexican Americans, perhaps Puerto Ricans, and Native Americans. With some prodding Japanese Americans, Chinese Americans, and groups for Southeast Asia may be mentioned. If Hispanics as a group are cited then Central Americans will be considered by people, too. If we searched through one of the earliest minorities texts such as *Old World Traits Transplanted,*[1] written by Robert E. Park and Herbert A. Miller in 1921, we would also find the Jews and the Irish identified as minorities. Increasingly, women and to a lesser degree gays and lesbians are seen as recognizable minorities.

The twelve groups we have chosen do not form an exhaustive list of minority groups, past, present, or emerging, but they are representative of the multitude of groups that could be classified as minorities. Further, because there are gender and sexual preference minorities, the groups are not always mutually exclusive (one can be a member of a racial or ethnic minority and also be a member of either a gender minority or a sexual preference minority, or both). The groups differ in the extent to which they may present full claims to minority status. Further, there are differences among the groups in terms of the dimensions of minority status, as well as in power, prestige, and property. Some groups are more identifiable than others; some have greater power than others and have had diverse experiences of differential and pejorative treatment by the majority. Some have attained a group awareness; others have as yet to gain fully such an awareness. Some groups are clearly colonial peoples. Some seek separatism; others seek to or have assimilated into the mainstream, especially of the cultural pluralist variety.

African Americans; Hispanics such as Mexican Americans, Puerto Ricans, and Central Americans; Asian Americans such as Japanese Americans, Chinese Americans, and Southeast Asian groups; and Native Americans each belong to populations identified as racial minorities, although in another sense they are also ethnic minorities. That is, some of the distinctions among the groups are clearly cultural. For example, African Americans differ from black Puerto Ricans in terms of culture, although black Puerto Ricans differ from white Puerto Ricans in terms of race. White Puerto Ricans (often mestizos) differ from Mexican Americans principally in terms of culture, although there are some racial factors as well. Using the classic racial groupings, Mexican Americans are a mixture of Caucasians and Mongoloids, and culturally are a mixture of Indian, Spanish, and Anglo (North American white) heritages. They can also trace some of their heritage to Native Americans, as can Central American groups, especially Mayas. The Anglo part of their heritage is similar to that of the Irish Catholics. Native Americans have had considerable intermarriage with whites and in some instances with African Americans. In fact, some groups legally defined Native Americans as triracial.[2] The Japanese and Chinese differ from one another in terms of culture and some genetic factors due to centuries of isolation and endogamy. However, many Southeast Asian peoples, especially those from what was once French Indochina, differ from the Japanese and Chinese not only in terms of culture, but to some extent in terms of race because of miscegenation with the French. French colonialism also led a significant number of Southeast Asians to be Roman Catholics, which makes them share some cultural traits with the Irish Catholics. Most Jewish Americans are white and thus racially similar to the Irish and the Caucasian ancestry of the various mixed-race groups. To turn full circle, we should note that all African Americans, due to widespread miscegenation during the two and one-half centuries of slavery, have some white ancestors. African American culture, furthermore, is not disconnected from white American culture. Women, needless to say, represent a numerical plurality of each of the groups. And gay and lesbians may be drawn from any group.

Thus, although each of the groups in *The Minority Report* has, as a group, experienced a different history and a different relationship with the majority and with other minorities, all have some elements in common. After all, as we suggested in Chapter 1, minority status is a social definition, involving distinctions selected from the totality of reality. In a very real sense, we are all of mixed races and mixed cultures.[3]

Table II-2 presents a typology of the twelve groups, their varied experiences, and their relative status as minorities. In all instances the table presents the current status of the group relative to the majority. It must be recognized that the exact identification of the majority may change slightly with the groups. For all racial and ethnic groups the majority is the white population; but for women it is males, and white males in particular; for Jewish Americans it is Christians, or Protestants to be exact; for the Irish Catholics it is Protestants; and finally for gays and lesbians it is the straight community. The universal majority for the groups would then be white, Protestant, straight males. Within the table identifiability may be either cultural or phenotypic and varies from "none" to "very much." Power is the extent to which the minority group can influence the majority (get its way in the presence of opposition), and it varies by social class for each group. The range of variation in power is from "very little" to "very much." Treatment is an expression of the amount of discrimination currently experienced, and varies from "very little" to "very much." Group awareness is the final component of minority-group status, involving a consciousness of kind. There are static and dynamic aspects to group awareness. The static reflects the current level, the dynamic the direction of that

TABLE II-2
Typology of Minority Groups in Relation to the Majority

Group	Identifiability	Power	Treatment (Discrimination)	Group Awareness
African Americans	Phenotypic: Very Much Cultural: Some	Some (Increasing)	Very Much	Very Much (Still Growing)
Mexican Americans	Phenotypic: Variable Cultural: Much	Some (Increasing)	Much to Very Much	Much (Growing)
Puerto Ricans	Phenotypic: Variable Cultural: Much	Little (Increasing)	Much, but Varies by Race	Some to Much (Growing)
Native Americans	Phenotypic: Variable Cultural: Variable	Very Little (Increasing)	Very Much	Some (Growing)
Central Americans	Phenotypic: Variable Cultural: Much	Very Little	Very Much	Much
Japanese Americans	Phenotypic: Much Cultural: Some to Much	Some	Some	Much
Chinese Americans	Phenotypic: Much Cultural: Some to Much	Little to Some	Moderate	Much
Southeast Asian Americans	Phenotypic: Much Cultural: Some to Much	Little	Moderate	Much
Jewish Americans	Phenotypic: None Cultural: Some	Much	Little	Some (Diminishing)
Irish Catholic Americans	Phenotypic: None Cultural: Very Little	Very Much	Very Little to None	Very Little
American Women	Phenotypic: Very Much Cultural: Some	Some (Increasing)	Some to Much	Some to Much
Gays and Lesbians	Phenotypic: None Cultural: Some	Some	Much	Much (Growing)

level. The ranges are from "very little" to "very much" (static) and from "emerging" to "diminishing" (dynamic).

The table is intended to serve as a very loose skeletal framework to enable the reader to place each of the twelve groups in relation to one another. It in no way can communicate the intricacy and the individual flavor of each group. One must also recognize that there is considerable variation by social class, generation, and geographic region within each group. For the complexity of each group, for the manner in which each groups has experienced the minority situation in America, we must ask each to its Minority Report.

Notes

1. Robert E. Park and Herbert A, Miller, *Old World Traits Transplanted* (New York: Harper, 1921).

2. Brewton Berry, *Almost White* (New York: Macmillan, 1963), and idem, "America's Mestizos," in *The Blending of Races,* Noel P. Gist and Anthony Gary Dworkin, eds. (New York: Wiley Interscience, 1972), pp. 191-212.
3. Gist, Noel P., and Anthony Gary Dworkin, eds. *The Blending of Races: Marginality and Identity in World Perspective.* (New York: Wiley Interscience, 1972).

CHAPTER 8

African Americans in Contemporary America: Progress and Retrenchment

Cedric Herring

Introduction

African Americans are perhaps the most studied but least understood racial minority group in the United States. Thousands of pages of statistics about African Americans have been collected, tabulated, and published (e.g., Myrdal, 1944; National Advisory Commission on Civil Disorders, 1968; Jaynes and Williams, 1989; and U.S. Census Bureau, 1992). We have been measured, surveyed, and sorted into several different categories such as the "Black underclass" (Wilson, 1987), the "Black bourgeoisie" (Frazier, 1957), and the "new Black middle class" (Landry, 1987). Yet, despite all the research, many of the complexities of the Black community are often missed.

This chapter presents a profile of African Americans in the contemporary United States. In doing so, it presents basic information about the historical background of African Americans in the United States. It then presents data from the 1940s through the 1990s based on U.S. Census Bureau reports and surveys, the 1990 and 1991 General Social Surveys, and the 1992 National Survey of Black Americans. These data sources are used to provide information about African Americans' historical and current living conditions, sociodemographic characteristics, attitudes toward and patterns of interactions with various racial and ethnic groups, and assessments of race relations. The chapter concludes with an assessment of the general status of African Americans at the brink of the 21st Century.

A Brief Historical Overview

The experiences of Black people in America provide a significant challenge to the notion that the United States is a land of equality of opportunity. The bitter truth of racial domination has constantly reminded Africans in America that we have never been fully accepted as equals to others in America. The democratic rights guaranteed by such documents as the Declaration of Independence and the U.S. Constitution simply did not apply to Blacks.

While whites and most other immigrants came to the United States voluntarily, most Blacks first coming to America were forcibly transported in chains as chattel. The institution of slavery lasted well over 200 years after it was first legally recognized in 1661 in Virginia law (Pinkney, 1993). These laws regulated virtually every aspect of a slave's life. But ultimately because slaves were the property of slaveholders, slave owners maintained absolute power over slaves and did not have to recognize any civil or property rights of the slaves. Slave owners could freely sell, trade, or give away African Americans as gifts, irrespective of what consequences such transactions had on the slave or his or her family. Thus, men, women, and children of African descent could be separated at the discretion of the slaveholder.

The particular work performed by slaves depended on whether the slave was male or female, on a large plantation or on a small farm, in a rural setting or in an urban location, whether the slave owner specialized in cotton or some other product, etc. The hours of work were completely at the discretion of the owner. Nevertheless, because Blacks were forced to work without pay, the United States was able to become economically great. But for those centuries during slavery, the United States presented itself to the world as a hollow democracy which did not come close to living up to its creed of liberty and equality.

Slavery in the United States formally ended when President Lincoln signed the Emancipation Proclamation in 1862. However, the institution of slavery was not ended until the Union forces defeated the Confedaracy during the American Civil War in 1865. At that historical moment, America had the opportunity to extend full democratic rights to all of its people. During Reconstruction—the period of approximately a decade following the Civil War—it appeared that Black people would be allowed to exercise their citizenship and other rights associated with democracy such as freedom of movement in public facilities and equal access to employment. But by the turn of the century, it was clear that the system of privilege based on skin color was to triumph once again in America.

By the early 1900s, a formal system of racial segregation, known as Jim Crow Laws, was instituted in the South of the United States. This system required that Black and white people be segregated in public transportation, hospitals, jails, schools, churches, cemeteries, and so on, on the basis of race. This system of racial segregation allowed white supremacy to triumph over the democratic rights of African Americans. Thus, as recently as the 1960s, millions of American citizens were oppressed on the basis of skin color. The overwhelming majority of Blacks throughout the South were disenfranchised. As a result, Blacks held no significant political offices in the South and exercised little power nationally.

During the first half of the 20th Century, some major transformations altered race relations in America (Jaynes and Williams, 1989). First, massive South-to-North and rural-to-urban migration by the Black population produced conditions leading to profound changes in Blacks' social status. Second, World War II and the sustained economic growth which accompanied it permitted government efforts to improve Blacks' status in American society. And third, the modern Civil Rights Movement began to advance Blacks toward full citizenship rights by prompting important changes in the nation's political and educational institutions.

In the 1950s, the Civil Rights Movement emerged in the South where Black oppression was most intense and where the system of racial segregation was firmly entrenched. This movement utilized the strategy of nonviolent direct action. The goal of this strategy was to create widespread social protest to force America to face the issue of racial oppression. For such a strategy to succeed, the leaders and organizers of the movement had to persuade thousands of African Americans to become directly involved in dangerous social protest.

In battling to bring about social change, movement participants used innovative tactics such as sit-ins, economic boycotts, and mass marches. The goal of this massive protest activity was to overthrow the entire system of legal racial segregation and to empower African Americans in the South by seizing the franchise for them.

Race relations and racial attitudes in the United States have changed dramatically over the past three decades (e.g., Smith, 1981; Pettigrew, 1985; Schuman, Steeh, and Bobo, 1985; and Allen and Farley, 1986). Through its several important victories, the Civil Rights Movement affected this situation in some fundamental ways. Clearly, the social, political, economic, and legal status of African Americans was advanced by the modern Civil Rights Movement. For example, between 1940 and 1970 Blacks made gains relative to whites in per capita incomes, family incomes, educational resources, educational attainment, life expectancy, health status, rates of voter participation, etc. (Jaynes and Williams, 1989).

By the late 1970s, however, several societal forces were in place to question the very logic of the Civil Rights Movement and to initiate measures aimed at reversing the gains of that groundbreaking struggle. These forces were able to move rapidly and without effective opposition because no counterforce with anything near the power and passion of the Civil Rights Movement existed. Thus, by the 1980s, the Reagan administration promoted a major reversal in race-relevant public policies under the guise of attacks on "big government" and eliminating waste (Hudson and Broadnax, 1982).

Anti-equal opportunity policies were pursued even more vigorously during the Bush administration. President Bush vetoed a new version of the Civil Rights Act on the grounds that it would require employers to establish quotas. Proponents of the legislation argued that it would have broken no new ground and imposed no new burdens on employers, and that it simply restored the legal framework of the workplace to what it had been prior to a series of Supreme Court decisions in the late 1980s (Wilson, Lewis, and Herring, 1991). Also during the Bush era came more symbolic racism: political advertisements using the images of Black criminals, critiques of equal opportunity and civil rights legislation as "reverse discrimination" and confrontations over affirmative action as "quotas" (Herring, 1992).

Under the Clinton administration, many of these disputes continued but were fought under the banner of such issues as anticrime legislation, welfare reform, workfare proposals, and labor force policy.

These are a few of the historical conditions that have led to the unique circumstances of African Americans of today. As of 1992, there were 31.4 million Blacks living in the United States. This constituted 12.5 percent of the total U.S. population (U.S. Census Bureau, 1992). Nearly 6 out of 10 (57 percent of) African Americans are female. More than half (54 percent) of the Black population lives in the South, and more than 85 percent of African Americans live in metropolitan areas. Compared with whites, Black Americans tend to be younger. In 1992, their median age was 28.2 years, compared with 34.3 years for whites; the percentage younger than age 18 was larger for Blacks than for whites (33 percent versus 25 percent), and the percentage over age 65 was smaller than for whites (8 percent versus 13 percent).

Below, I present information about the current political, social, and economic situation of Blacks in America. In part, disputes about the "progress" made by African Americans continue because there are data which suggest that the socioeconomic position of African Americans relative to whites and other racial groups has improved (e.g., Glazer, 1976; Wilson, 1978; Farley, 1984; Allen and Farley, 1986; and Jaynes and Williams, 1989) as well as data which suggest that conditions for Blacks have deteriorated in recent decades (e.g., Hill, 1981; Farley, 1984; Murray, 1984; Allen and Farley, 1986; and Jaynes and Williams, 1989). Because of a history of progress and retrenchment, it is debatable whether African Americans are any better off socially, politically, and economically now than we were during the Civil Rights Movement.

HAS RACE DECLINED IN ITS SIGNIFICANCE?: A LOOK AT SOME TRENDS

Political Changes

The Civil Rights Movement was successful in its effort to seize the franchise for millions of southern Blacks and to create favorable political conditions for the exercise of the franchise by Blacks outside of the South. As Figure 8-1 shows, the number of Black elected officials skyrocketed from 103 in 1964 (before the 1965 Voting Rights Act) to over 7,335 by 1990. As Bobo and Gilliam (1990) point out, Black elected officials are to be found in the U.S. Congress, state legislatures, and city councils; on school boards; and as mayors of major cities. Without a doubt, the Civil Rights Movement ushered in a small-scale revolution in electoral politics, making it possible for significant numbers of African Americans to hold office for the first time since Reconstruction.

Some view the rise in the number of Black elected officials as an indication of the declining significance of race in American politics. But office holding and real empowerment can be two different realities altogether (Morris, 1992). The election of Black politicians has not automatically empowered the African American community, nor has it necessarily translated into social and economic equality. For example, while the number of Black elected officials topped 7,300, by 1994 African Americans made up 1 percent of U.S. senators, 2 percent of the nation's governors, and 5 percent of the U.S. House of Representatives. Similarly, at the same time that Blacks have become more

FIGURE 8-1
Changes in the Number of Black Elected Representatives, 1964–1990

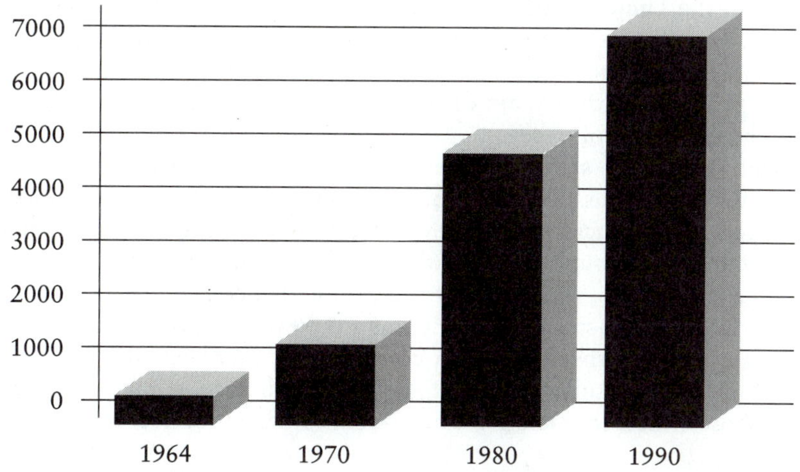

active in the electoral process, race has *increased* in its significance and surpassed class and all other characteristics as the primary organizing frame of American electoral politics (Huckfeldt and Kohfeld, 1989). As the proportion of whites who identify themselves as Democrats declined, the proportion of Black voters who identified themselves as Democrats increased from 57 percent in 1952 to more than 80 percent in 1988 (Herring, 1989; and Tate, 1992). Relatedly, the difference in the proportion of African Americans and whites voting for Democratic presidential candidates has increased from about 12 percentage points in 1948 to over 50 percentage points in the 1980s (Huckfeldt and Kohfeld, 1989:3). And one in five white voters report that they would *refuse* to vote for a qualified Black from their own political party for president of the United States (Williams, 1990). Thus, many of "the racial divisions that have affected the vote ever since the 1960s are persisting features of party and electoral politics" (Gurin, Hatchett, and Jackson, 1989).

Social and Economic Changes

In examining the patterns of change in the social and economic status of African Americans, there are some areas of dramatic and steady improvement. A notable example of this is in the area of educational attainment. African Americans steadily increased their levels of educational attainment, from an average of 5.8 years of education in 1940 to an average of 12.4 years in 1990. Accordingly, the educational attainment gap between Blacks and whites had dwindled to less than half a year by 1990.

Still, in 1990, Blacks had personal earnings that were less than two-thirds (62 percent) as much as those of whites. Earnings differences persist even after one takes educational attainment into consideration, as earnings gaps occur for each educational attainment level.

Still, education is often viewed as one of the primary means of upward mobility in the United States. Its impact on incomes is well established and powerful. Households whose adult occupants had eight or fewer years of education had median incomes of less than $13,000 compared with more than $28,000 for those with 4 years of high school and nearly $50,000 for those with 4 or more years of college.

Ideally, education should be the vehicle, equally accessible to all citizens, through which various occupational goals and levels of earnings can be attained. Yet, what educational achievement actually represents is debated by various schools of thought. Several theories have been offered to explain disadvantage in earnings. For the most part, these theories can be categorized as (1) those which characterize education as a "great equalizer" because it sorts people according to their ability to compete in a merit-based system that is free and open to all indviduals irrespective of their race, ethnicity, or gender; and (2) those which characterize education as a proxy for access to resources.

Is education the great equalizer, or do linkages between personal earnings and education merely reflect aspects of the structural arrangements of American society? Figure 8-2 shows mean years of educational attainment by race and gender. This diagram indicates that whites, on average, have the highest levels of educational attainment with 12.9 years. They are followed closely by Asians, who on average have 12.8 years of education. Blacks average just over 12 years, followed by Native Americans and others at 11.6 years and Latinos at 10.9 years of education. These patterns change somewhat when race by gender subgroups are examined, however. In particular, Asian men are the most highly educated subgroup with 13.5 years of education on average. They are followed by white men (with 13.1 years), white women (with 12.9 years), Asian women (with 12.2), Black women (with 12.1), and Black men (with 11.9).

Figure 8-3 presents average personal earnings by race, gender, and level of educational attainment. This figure shows that personal earnings generally increase for each race by gender subgroup with additional years of education. The increments to earnings vary dramatically by subgroup, however. For example, while a college degree versus a high school diploma is worth more than $20,000 per year more for a white man, it translates into about half that much per year for white women and Black women. It should also be noted that for each level of educational attainment, women earn less than men of the same racial group. Also, for each level of educational attainment, white men earn more than their Black counterparts. In other words, there are both

FIGURE 8-2
Mean Years of Educational Attainment by Race and Gender

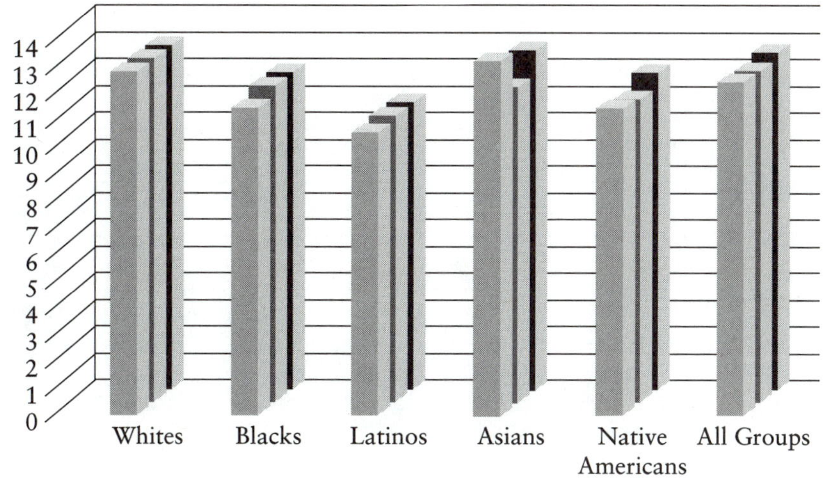

FIGURE 8-3
Mean Yearly Earnings by Race and Gender

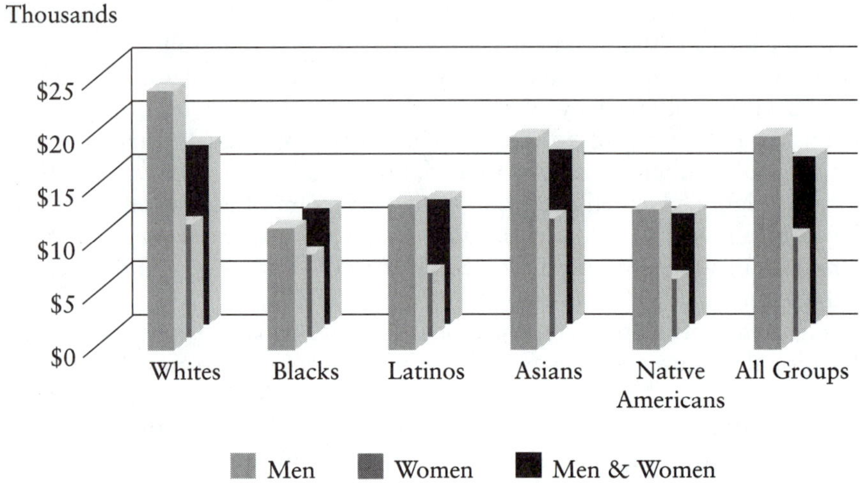

racial and gender differences in earnings even after levels of educational attainment are taken into account.

Trends in family income reveal even more grim news for African Americans. As Figure 8-4 shows, in 1947 African American families earned about

FIGURE 8-4
Changes in Median Family Income by Race, 1947–1989

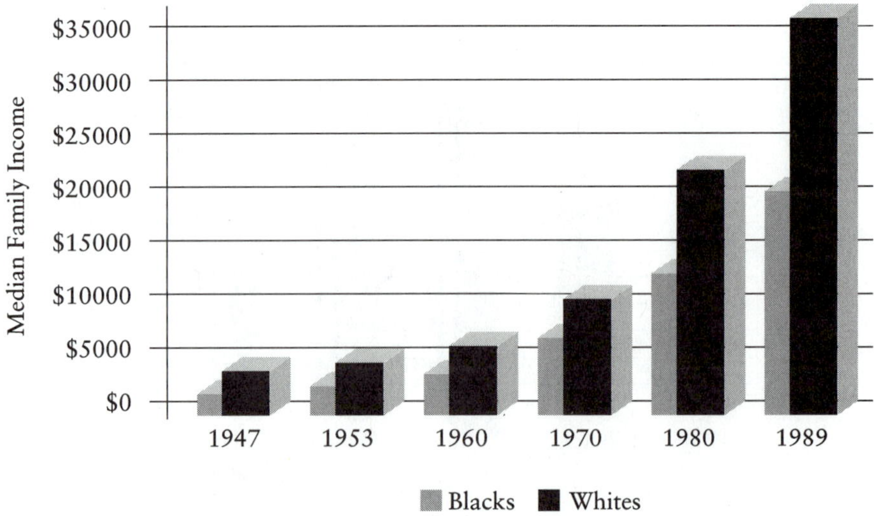

51 percent as much as white families. By 1989, African American families still earned only 56 percent as much as white families. Even more telling is the fact that since the years immediately following the height of the modern Civil Rights Movement, Black income as a percentage of white income has fallen from 61 percent in 1970. This trend clearly reflects a pattern of modest progress and subsequent retrenchment.

Changes in the occupational structure of the African American community suggest that Blacks have made progress in upgrading the kinds of jobs in which they are employed. As Figure 8-5 shows, however, this general improvement in occupation does not mean that the gap between Blacks and whites has closed, as whites have also substantially enhanced their occupational standing since 1940. Certainly, it is clear that much of this "upgrading" is due to the shift from goods production to knowledge production and the growing use of technology, which displaced a large number of farm and manual laborers. In particular, the percentage of African Americans working in professional, managerial, technical, and administrative occupations increased from 4 percent in 1940 to 18 percent in 1989. There were, however, parallel changes among whites in this upper echelon of jobs, as the percentage of whites in professional, managerial, technical, and administrative occupations increased from 15 percent in 1940 to 31 percent in 1989. Therefore, the percentage gap

FIGURE 8-5
Percentage of Black and White Males in Selected Occupational Types, 1940–1990

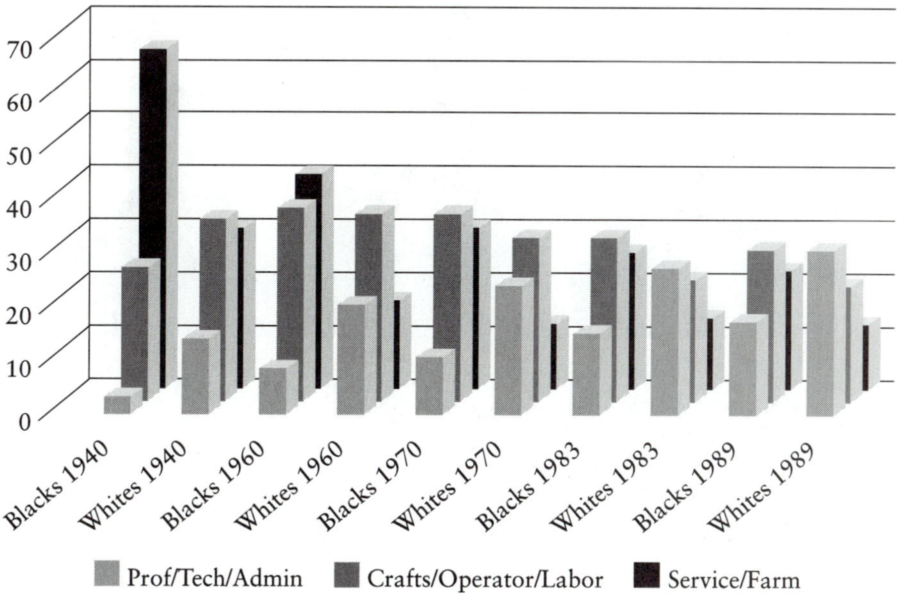

between Blacks and whites remained virtually constant over half a century. It is noteworthy that the largest relative gains for African Americans occurred in those middle, "transitional" occupations such as sales and clerical positions and as craft workers, operatives, and laborers.

The change from goods production to knowledge production and the increased use of technology also has had consequences for rates of Black unemployment and labor force participation. In the 1940s, "Black men were slightly more likely to be employed than white men, and Black women were significantly more likely to be employed than were white women" (Jaynes, 1990:10). Since 1960, however, the Black unemployment rate typically has been at least twice that of whites. A slight exception occurred in the early 1970s. Since that time, however, the ratio has approached 2.5 to 1.

Figure 8-6 shows that educational differences cannot account for the racial gap in unemployment rates. In all cases since 1975, the unemployment rates of African Americans exceed those of whites with comparable levels of

FIGURE 8-6
% Unemployed by Race by Education by Year

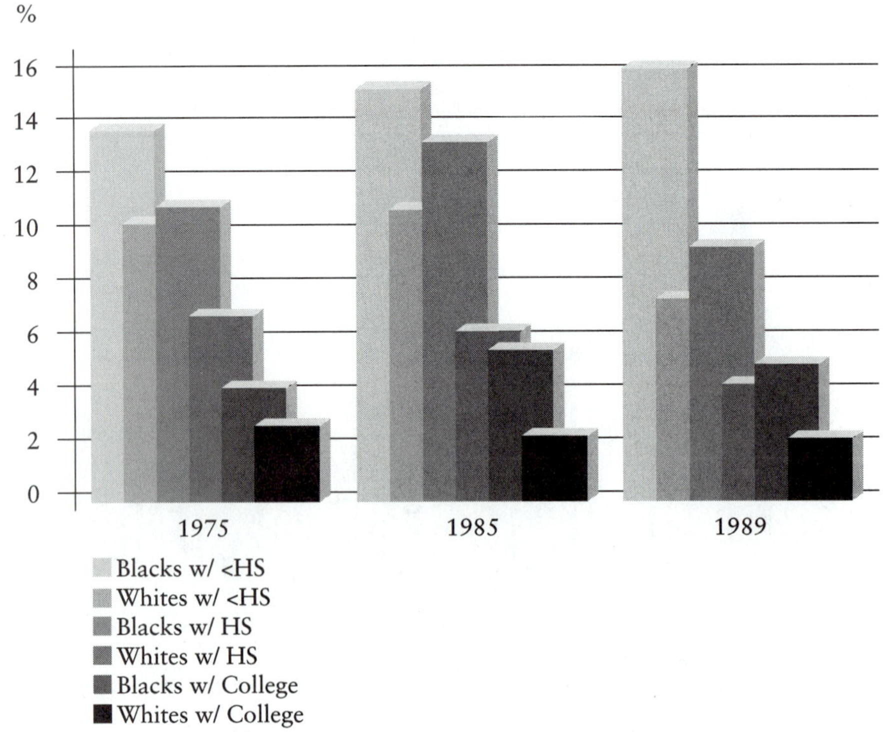

educational attainment. In 1989, Blacks with college degrees had levels of unemployment that even exceeded those of whites with high school diplomas.

A final indicator of the social and economic status of African Americans is the poverty rate. On this measure, there was dramatic improvement since 1960 when more than 55 percent of African Americans compared with 18 percent of whites lived below the poverty line. By 1970, these rates had fallen to 34 percent and 10 percent, respectively. Unfortunately, the pace of change did not continue after the 1970s, and during the 1980s the poverty rate actually increased for both Blacks and whites.

Again, education cannot account for the racial differences in poverty. As Figure 8-7 shows that African American at all levels of education are more likely than their white counterparts to be impoverished. For each of the periods examined, Blacks with college degrees were almost as likely to live in poverty as are whites *without* high school diplomas.

FIGURE 8-7
% Poverty by Race by Education and Year

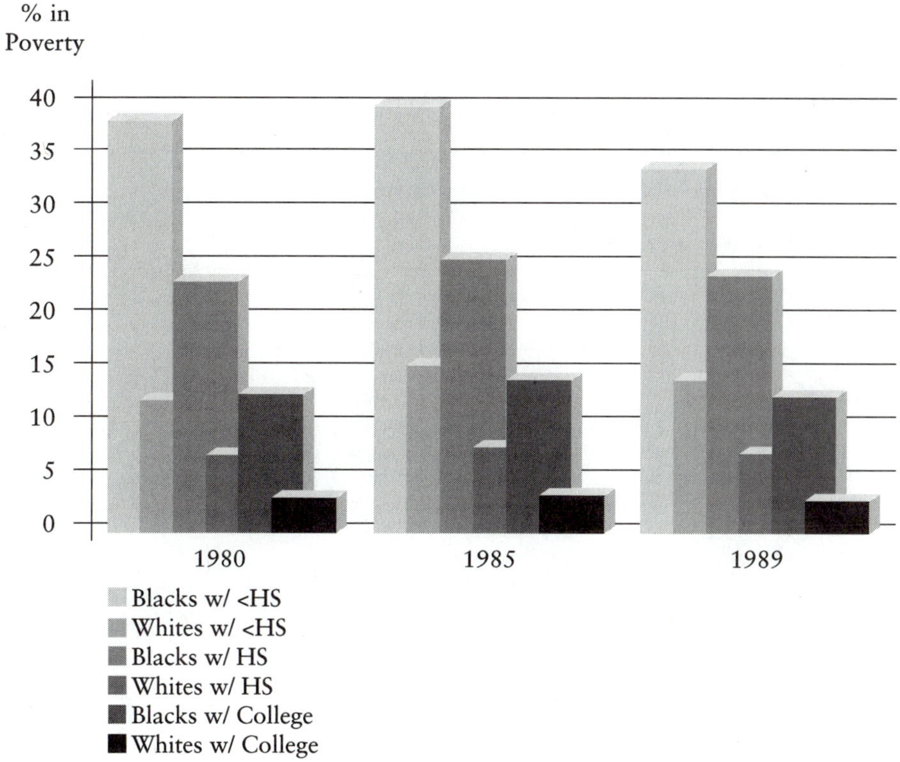

COMMUNITY, FAMILY TYPES, AND FAMILY INCOME

Arguments about poverty among African Americans often point to aspects of family structure differences between Blacks and whites. Additionally, they suggest that poverty among Blacks is largely an urban phenomenon. But do such family structure differences really account for Black-white differences in poverty rates? Do rural-urban differences make a big difference? Do rural African Americans differ from urban African Americans in their family characteristics? Do they differ from rural whites? Are differences between rural Blacks and urban Blacks any greater than those between rural whites and urban whites? Are any such differences consequential in terms of prospects for members of these different groups living below the poverty line? Is being "urban" or "Black" more consequential for one's propsects of living in poverty? Figures 8-8 through 8-10 present some preliminary answers to these questions.

Figure 8-8 presents the percentage distribution of family types for African Americans living in rural communities, African Americans living in nonrural settings, whites living in rural communities, and whites living in nonrural areas. This figure shows that while there are substantial differences in family types by racial group, few such dissimilarities occur between African Americans living in rural communities and African Americans living outside such

FIGURE 8-8
Percentage Distribution of Family Type and Marital Status by Race and Community Type

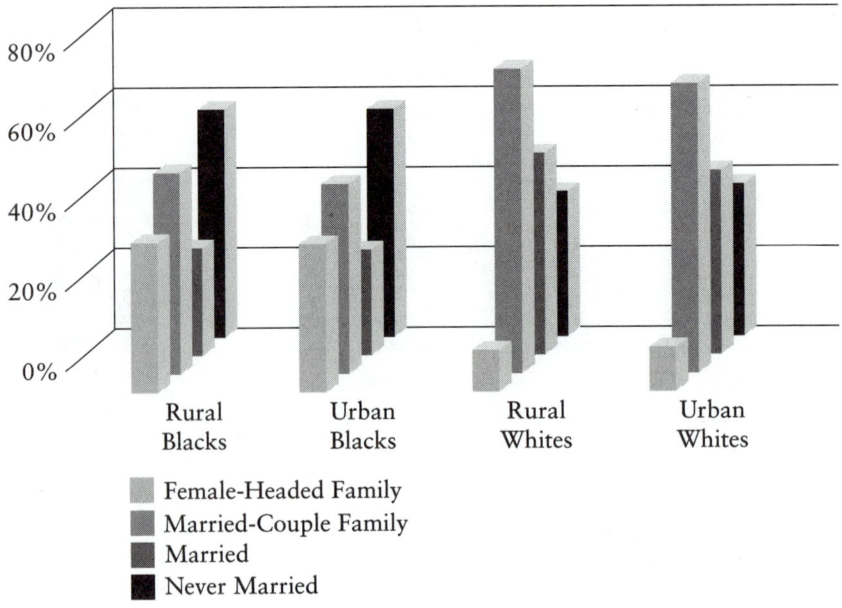

FIGURE 8-9
Mean Family Income by Race and Community Type

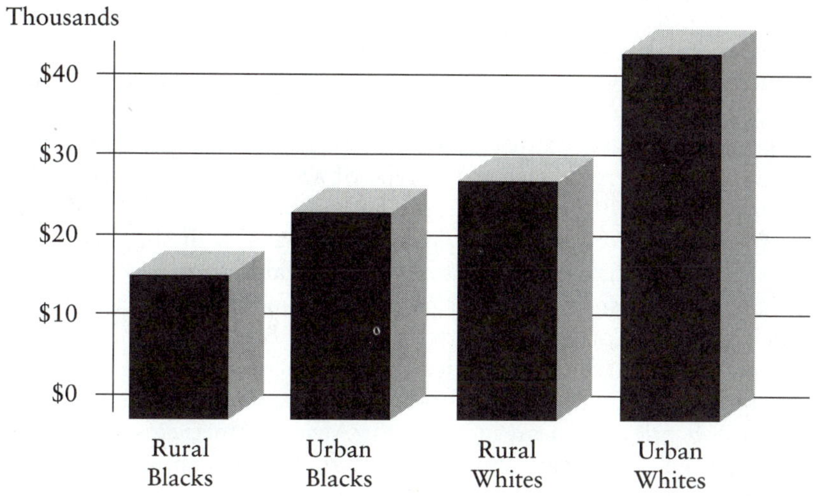

FIGURE 8-10
Percentage of Subpopulation Below the Poverty Line by Race and Community Type

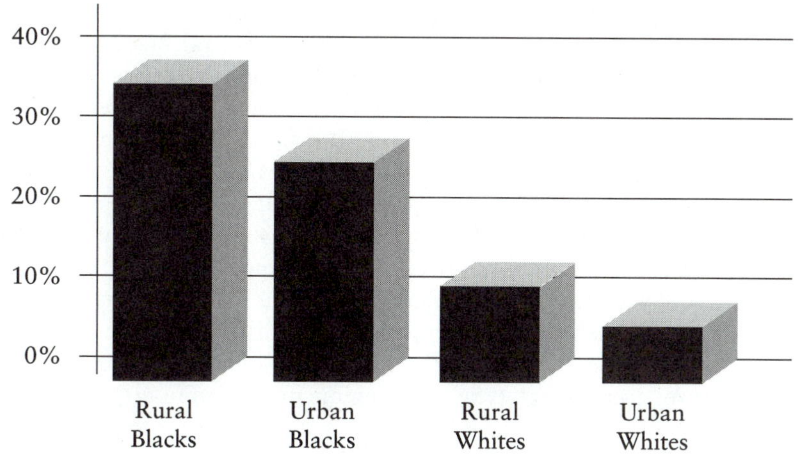

settings. In particular, half of Blacks living in rural places (50 percent) and nearly half of Blacks living in urban areas (48 percent) are members of families headed by married couples. In contrast, 77 percent of whites in rural communities and 72 percent of whites in urban areas are members of families headed by married couples. About one third of Blacks in rural settings (31 percent) and in urban locales (35 percent) are members of female-headed households. For whites, the proportion is closer to one in ten for those in rural communities (9 percent) and those in urban locations (10 percent). These patterns suggest that race accounts for much more of the tendencies in family types than does type of community setting.

Figure 8-8 also presents the relationship between marital status and community type for Blacks and whites. Again, while type of community appears to tell little about marital status, there are substantial dissimilarities between Blacks and whites, irrespective of the type of area in which they live. Slightly more than a quarter of Blacks in rural communities (27 percent) and in urban areas (27 percent) are currently married and living with their spouses. For whites, slightly less than half of those living in rural locations (49 percent) and those living outside such areas (46 percent) are married and currently living with their spouses. Conversely, more than half of Blacks in rural communities (56 percent) and urban communities (57 percent) have never been married. This compares with 38 percent of rural whites and 40 percent of urban whites.

Figure 8-9 presents mean incomes for African Americans and whites by community type. This chart shows that there are substantial family income differences by both race and community type. The overall mean family income is $39,404. For Blacks from rural communities, however, the mean family income is $19,070. For Blacks from urban areas, the mean family income is $27,911. For rural whites the mean family income is $31,392. And for urban whites, the mean family income is $44,936.

These group differences in family income also show up as differences in poverty rates. Figure 8-10 shows that 38 percent of rural Blacks and 29 percent of urban Blacks live below the poverty threshold. In contrast, 13 percent of rural whites and 9 percent of urban whites live below the poverty line.

These patterns suggest that there are real diferences between urban and rural populations in terms of family characteristics and poverty status. These differences occur for both African Americans and whites. These differences are not, however, what one might suspect when listening to arguments about the "urban underclass." Indeed, rural African Americans face even greater disadvantages. These results raise questions about whether it is accurate to characterize the problems of African American families as "urban" problems. Moreover, these patterns suggest that the effects of race supersede those of family structure, community type, and region in determining poverty status.

Employment, Underemployment, and Economic Hardship

Historically, African Americans have made important contributions to the American economy. In the 1990s, however, many people view the labor power of Black workers as redundant and superfluous. African Americans experience extreme underutilization of their skills and abilities, and they continue to lag behind whites and other groups in terms of their standing in the labor market.

Underemployment is a labor force concept that refers broadly to inadequacies in employment or employment-related hardships (e.g., Sullivan, 1978; Jones-Johnson, 1989; and Herring and Jones-Johnson, 1990). For example, as the labor force participation rates of racial minorities have increased, more attention has been focused on the tendencies of these groups to be impoverished. In part, this can be explained by the fact that most jobs created during the 1980s and the early 1990s and held by these groups have been characterized by wages insufficient to lift a family of four out of poverty, less than full-time work, or skill underutilization. Ironically, the underutilization of African Americans' skills and abilities has come at a time when the racial gap in skills has begun to close.

This section of the chapter focuses on the economic and material hardships faced by people with different underemployment statuses. It examines the linkage between underemployment types and bankruptcy and property loss, housing problems, material deprivation, and other types of personal financial devastation. It also uses data from the 1991 General Social Survey to underscore differences in the distribution of the consequences of underemployment by race.

Figure 8-11 presents the relationship between underemployment type and race. This graph shows that while less than half (48 percent) of African Americans have employment that is adequate, more than six out of ten (61 percent of) whites hold such employment. Conversely, whites have lower (or comparable) levels of underemployment than Blacks for each of the types of underemployment.

Figure 8-12 presents the relationship between underemployment type and experience with bankruptcies or property repossession by race. This graph shows that, for both Blacks and whites, the most severe forms of underemployment yielded the greatest likelihoods of suffering from bankruptcy or property loss. More than one out of five of the jobless, and more than one out of ten of involuntary part-timers reported bankruptcies or property repossessions. This compares with 4 percent of poverty-wage workers, 5 percent of those with skill mismatch, and 2 percent of those with adequate skill utilization who reported experiences with bankruptcies or property repossessions. There were, however, some substantial racial differences in the relationship between underemployment status and these kinds of economic hardships: More than half (57 percent) of jobless Blacks reported bankruptcies or property losses compared with 13 percent of jobless whites, and 13 percent of poverty-wage Blacks disclosed bankruptcies or property losses compared with 4 percent of poverty-wage whites.

Figure 8-13 presents the relationship between underemployment status and experiences with housing problems or homelessness by race. This chart

FIGURE 8-11
Distribution of Underemployment Status by Race

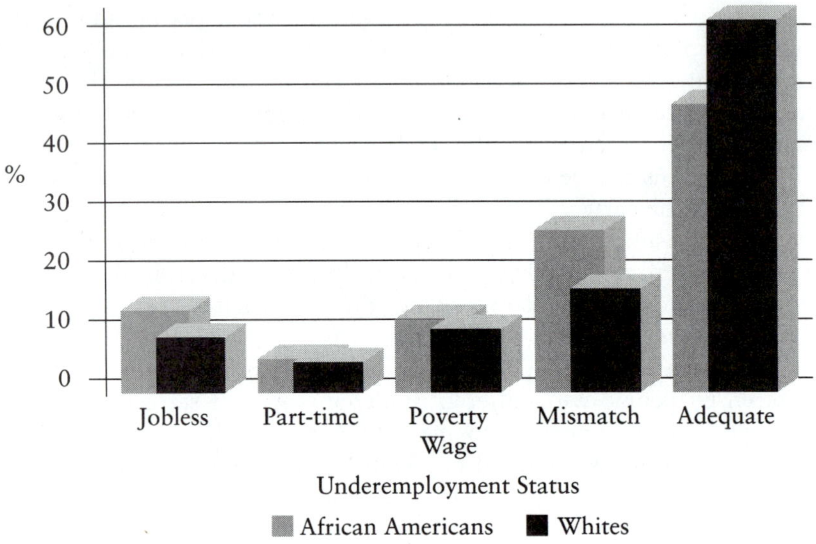

FIGURE 8-12
Percentage Experiencing Bankruptcy or Property Repossession by Underemployment Status and Race

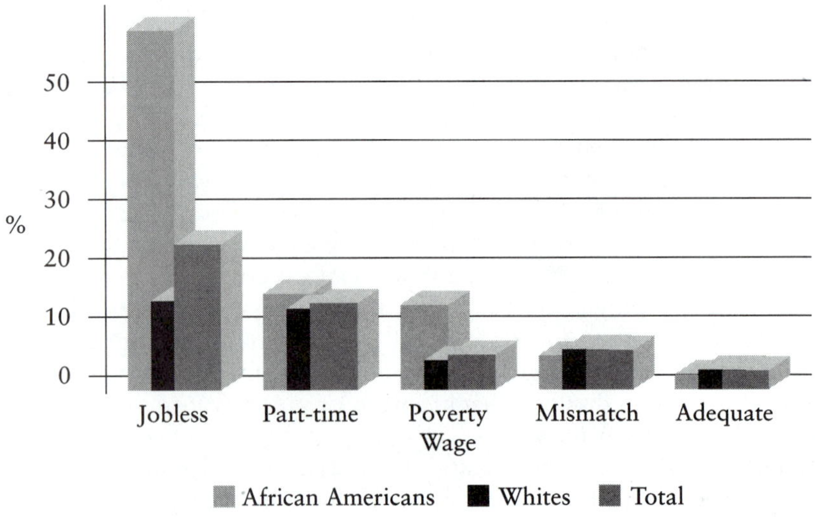

FIGURE 8-13
Percentage Experiencing Housing Problems or Homelessness by Underemployment Status and Race

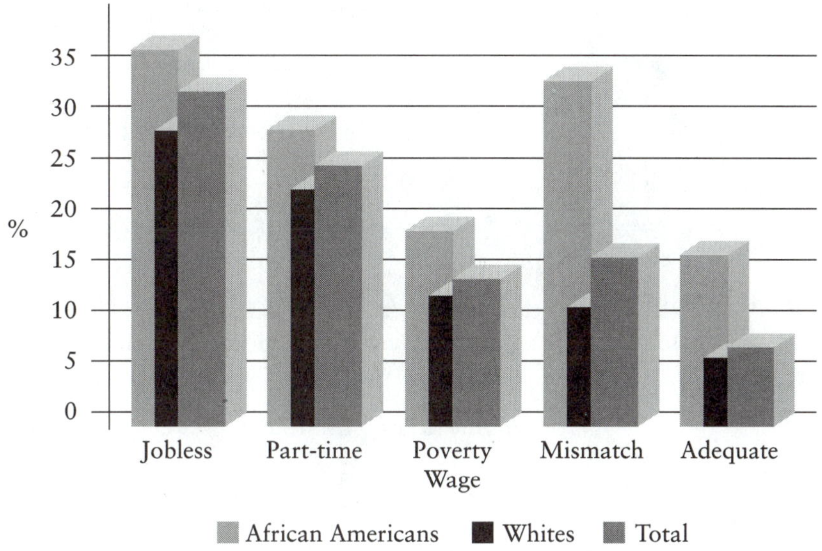

illustrates patterns similar to those found in Figure 8-13, as the most severe types of underemployment were generally associated with higher percentages of people enduring housing problems. Nearly a third (31 percent) of the jobless, 25 percent of involuntary part-timers, 14 percent of poverty-wage workers, 16 percent of those with skill mismatch, and 5 percent of those with adequate skill utilization reported housing problems. Again there were racial differences in the patterns. With each underemployment status, Blacks were more likely than their white counterparts to report housing difficulties.

Figure 8-14 illustrates the relationship between underemployment status and the inability to purchase food, medicine, or other necessities by race. Again the figure suggests that there was a general pattern in which the most severe types of underemployment were associated with higher percentages of people being unable to afford needed food and medicine. There again appeared to be racial differences, with Blacks generally faring worse than their white counterparts. An apparent exception to this pattern occurred among involuntary part-time workers: 23 percent of whites and 14 percent of Blacks reported that they had been unable to buy needed food or medicine.

Figure 8-15 presents the relationship between underemployment status and major worsening of financial status. As with the other graphs, this one shows that there was a tendency for the most severe types of underemployment to be

FIGURE 8-14
Percentage Unable to Buy Food, Medicine, or Other Necessities by Underemployment Status and Race

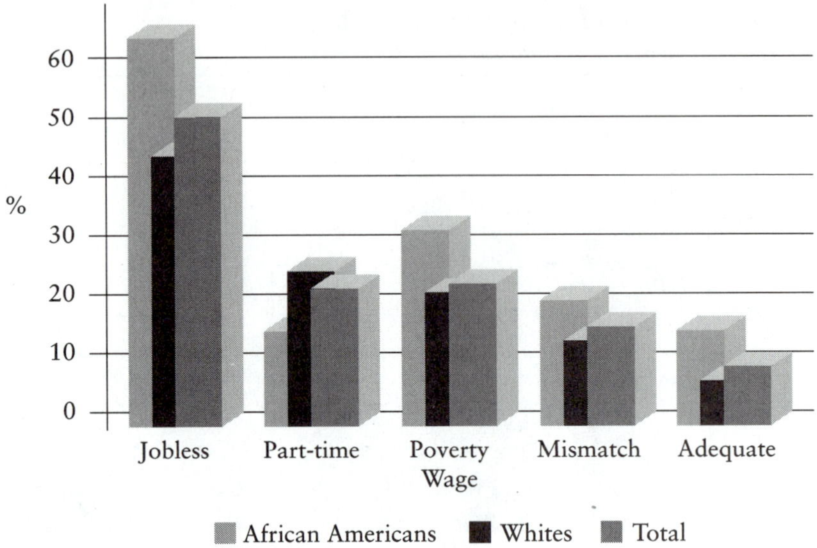

FIGURE 8-15
Percentage Experiencing a Major Worsening of Their Financial Status by Underemployment Status and Race

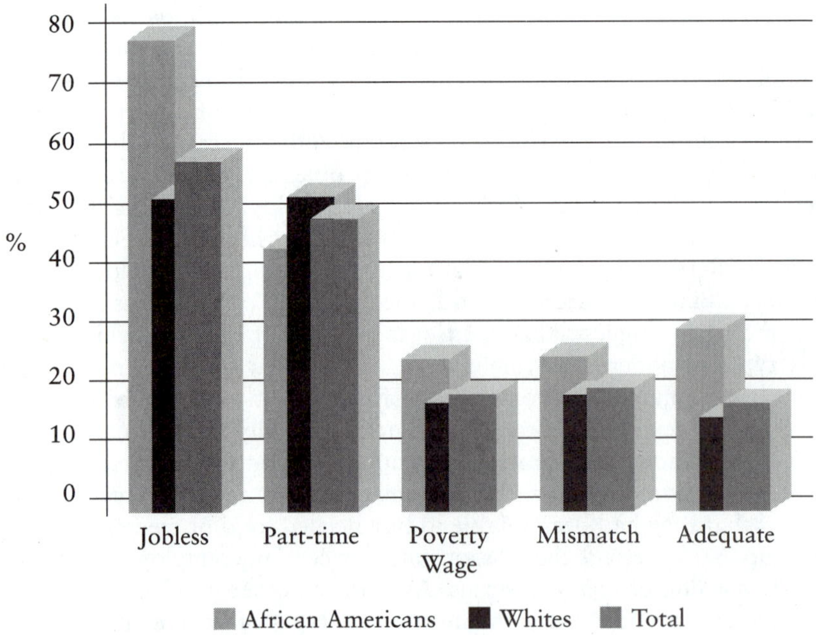

associated with higher probabilities of undergoing worsening financial conditions. Racial differences again suggest that greater proportions of Blacks than whites reported deterioration in their financial circumstances. Again the exception to this general pattern appeared to be those who involuntarily worked part-time.

SOCIAL DISTANCE AND RACE RELATIONS

"Social distance" refers to the level of unwillingness among members of a group to accept or approve of interactions with members of an outgroup. In racial and ethnic relations, it reflects the degree to which members of racial and ethnic groups are disinclined to accept members of other racial and ethnic out-groups in varying social contexts. This notion of social distance has become closely associated with theories of interethnic relations and prejudice.

In the United States, the dominant explanation of interethnic relations has been the "assimilation" perspective. This perspective, associated with Robert E. Park, one of the first major American theorists of ethnic relations, suggests that intergroup contacts and relations regularly go through stages of a race relations cycle. This progressive and irreversible cycle consists of "contacts," "competition," "accommodation," and eventual "assimilation." Migration and exploration bring peoples from different cultures into contact with each other. Contact in turn leads to new forms of social organization for both the natives and the newcomers. Also, with the new interactions come economic competition and subsequent conflict between the indigenous population and the foreigners. In the accommodation stage, both groups are compelled to make adjustments to their new social situations so that relations might be stabilized. Finally, in the assimilation stage, there will be an inevitable disappearance of cultural and ethnic differences that distinguish these once rivaling ethnic groups.

As mentioned in the historical overview, the social distance between Blacks and whites has historically been great, and legal devices have been used to reinforce such patterns. With the end of Jim Crow segregation, however, it is possible that the social distance between members of the dominant European-American society and African Americans has decreased. That is, it is possible that non-Black Americans are now more willing to accept and become involved in interactions with African Americans than has historically been the case. Indeed, there are theoretical perspectives that suggest reasons for believing that African Americans have become more assimilated into and accepted by white Americans than members of many other racial and ethnic groups.

Are some ethnic groups more likely to interact with African Americans than others? If differences on the magnitude of 20 percent are considered significant, and those of 10 percent are considered nontrivial, then Figures 8-16 through 8-20 show that there are nontrivial and significant differences in

FIGURE 8-16
Percentage Objecting to Having Their Children Attend Integrated Schools by Race and Ethnicity

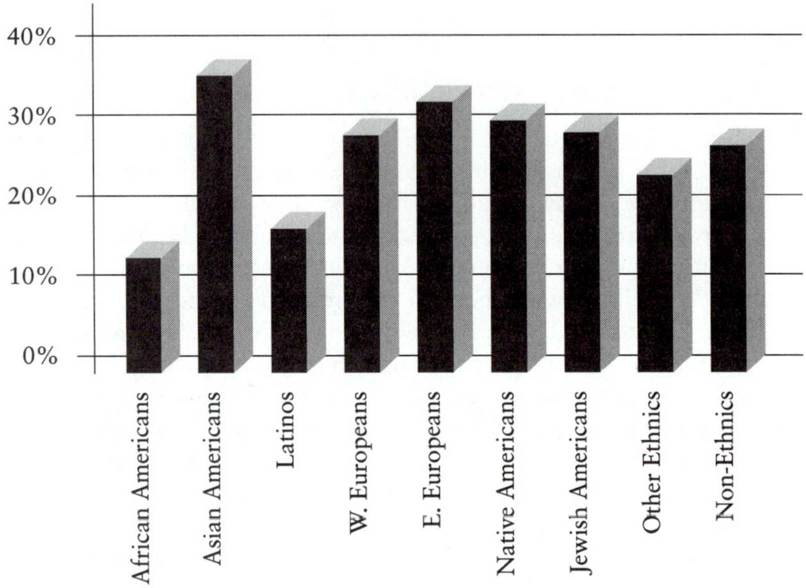

how likely various ethnic groups are to interact with African Americans in several contexts. Figure 8-16 presents the relationship between ethnicity and unwillingness to send one's children to schools where up to half the students are African Americans. This graph shows that while only one out of ten (10 percent) African Americans are unwilling to send their children to such schools, nearly four out of ten (37 percent) Asian Americans report that they would be unwilling to send their children to schools where half the students are Black. Other ethnic groups fall between these extremes, as 16 percent of Latinos, 25 percent of Western European Americans, 30 percent of Eastern European Americans, 24 percent of Native Americans, and 27 percent of Jewish Americans.

Figure 8-17 presents the relationship between ethnicity and support for laws banning interracial marriages. Support for such laws varies widely by ethnicity, ranging from a low of 6 percent of African Americans to a high of 35 percent of those who claim no ethnicity. Generally, support for such laws is much higher among European Americans, as 25 percent of those with Eastern European ancestry and 28 percent of those with Western European ancestry report support for such laws. In contrast, 6 percent of Asian Americans, 11 percent of Jewish Americans, and 12 percent of Latinos support such thinking.

FIGURE 8-17
Percentage Favoring Laws Banning Interracial Marriages by Race and Ethnicity

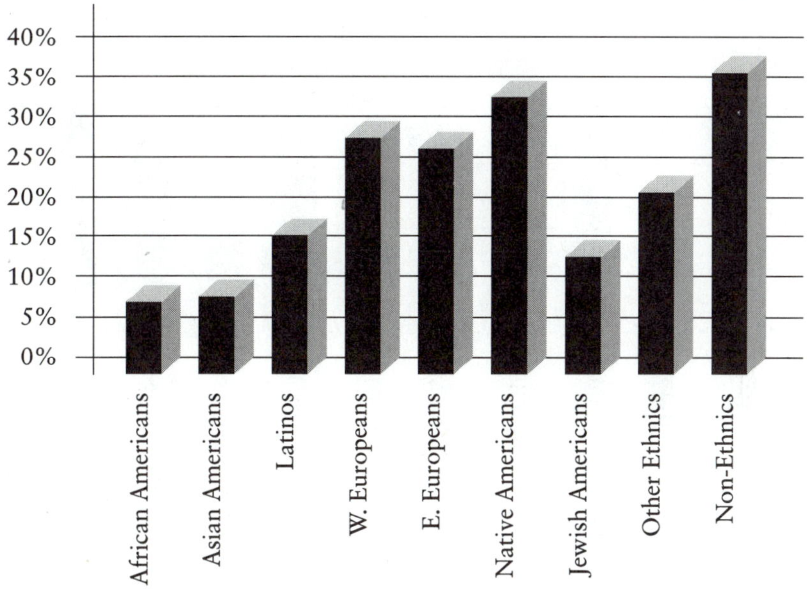

Figure 8-18 presents the unwillingness to vote for a Black presidential candidate by ethnicity. Again, there are nontrivial differences by ethnicity, with only 1 percent of African Americans saying they would be unwilling to vote for a Black presidential candidate, but 20 percent of Asian Americans reporting that they would be unwilling to vote for a Black presidential candidate.

Overall, the results in Figures 8-16 through 8-18 provide little endorsement of the idea that African Americans are accepted by other racial and ethnic groups. Figures 8-19 and 8-20 provide information about the relative social distance between African Americans and other ethnic groups versus the social distance between non-Blacks and other ethnic groups. Figure 8-19 shows the percentage of people from various racial and ethnic groups who are opposed to living in neighborhoods in which half the residents are white, Black, Jewish, Asian, or Hispanic. With only a couple of exceptions, this chart shows that higher proportions of the ethnic groups report opposition to living among Blacks than among any other racial or ethnic group. The only exceptions are African Americans and Jewish Americans. It is also interesting to note that, while there are some rank-order differences among the racial and ethnic groups, none of them are as likely to oppose living among whites as they are to disagree with living among other racial and ethnic groups. Also, European Americans show a great deal of opposition to living in neighborhoods with all racial ethnic groups.

FIGURE 8-18
Percentage Unwilling to Vote for a Black Presidential Candidate by Race and Ethnicity

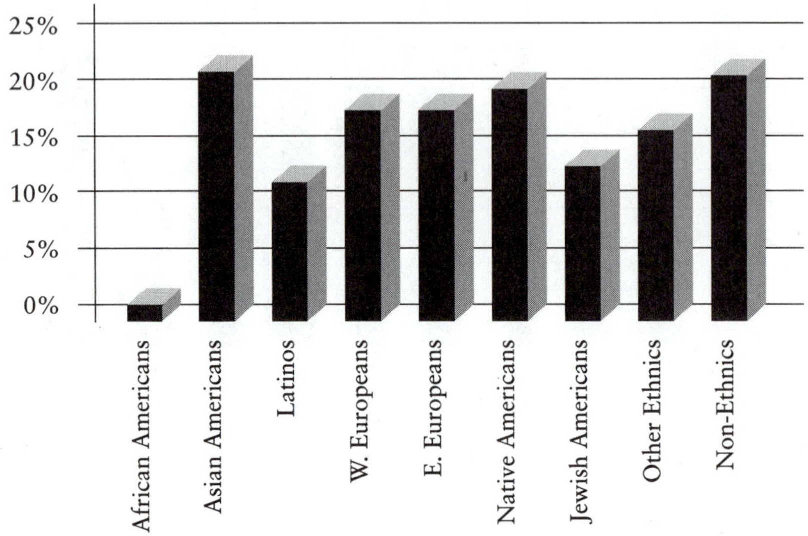

Figure 8-20 presents the percentage of people from various racial and ethnic groups who are opposed to a close relative marrying a person who is white, Black, Jewish, Asian, or Hispanic. This chart shows results that are very similar to those presented in Figure 8-19: With only one exception, Figure 8-20 shows that higher proportions of the ethnic groups report opposition to marriage with Blacks than with any other racial or ethnic group. The only exception is African Americans. Again, while there are some rank-order differences among the racial and ethnic groups, none of them are as likely to oppose marriage with whites as they are to oppose marriage with other racial and ethnic groups. Also, European Americans again show a great deal of opposition to marriage with all racial ethnic groups.

Unfortunately, these results tell us that despite the supposed declines in racial intolerance and prejudice and years of legislation and regulation, there are still sizable segments of the American population who do not want their children to go to school with Black children, who do not want to live in the same neighborhoods with Black people, who do not want to be led by Black leaders, and definitely do not want their relatives to be married to a Black person. The desire to get away from Blacks is greater than the desire to get away from virtually all other groups.

Finally, Figure 8-21 presents the percentage of various subgroups of African Americans who report that they are very satisfied with race relations.

FIGURE 8-19
Percentage Opposed to Living in a Neighborhood with Various Ethnic Groups by Ethnicity

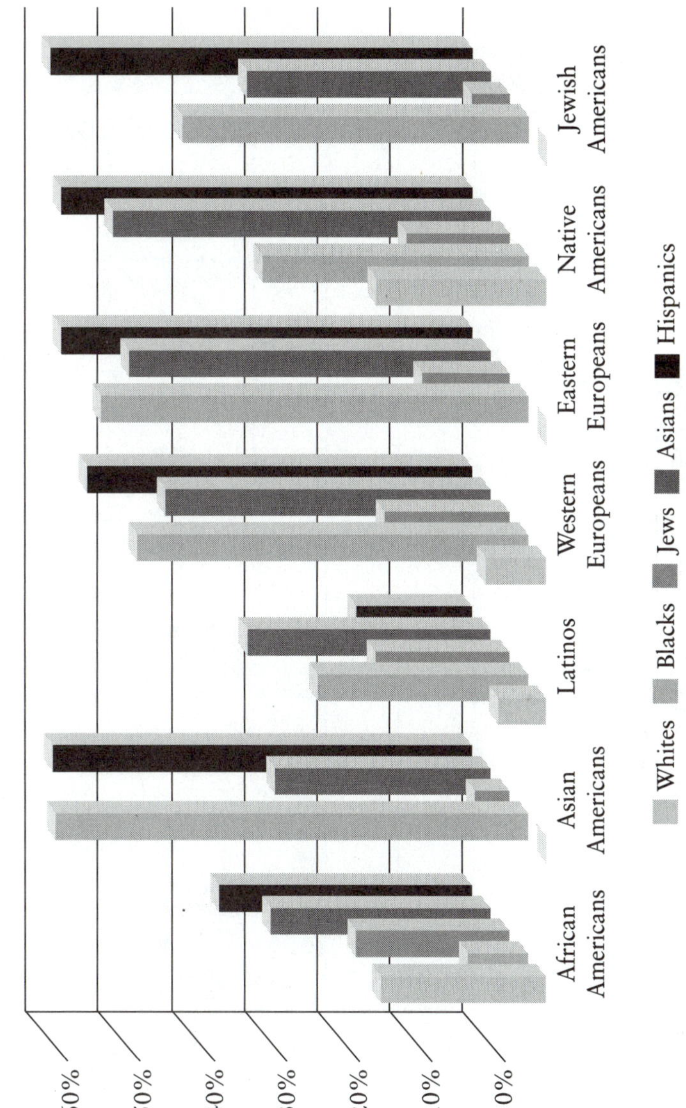

FIGURE 8-20
Percentage Opposed to Marriage with Various Ethnic Groups by Ethnicity

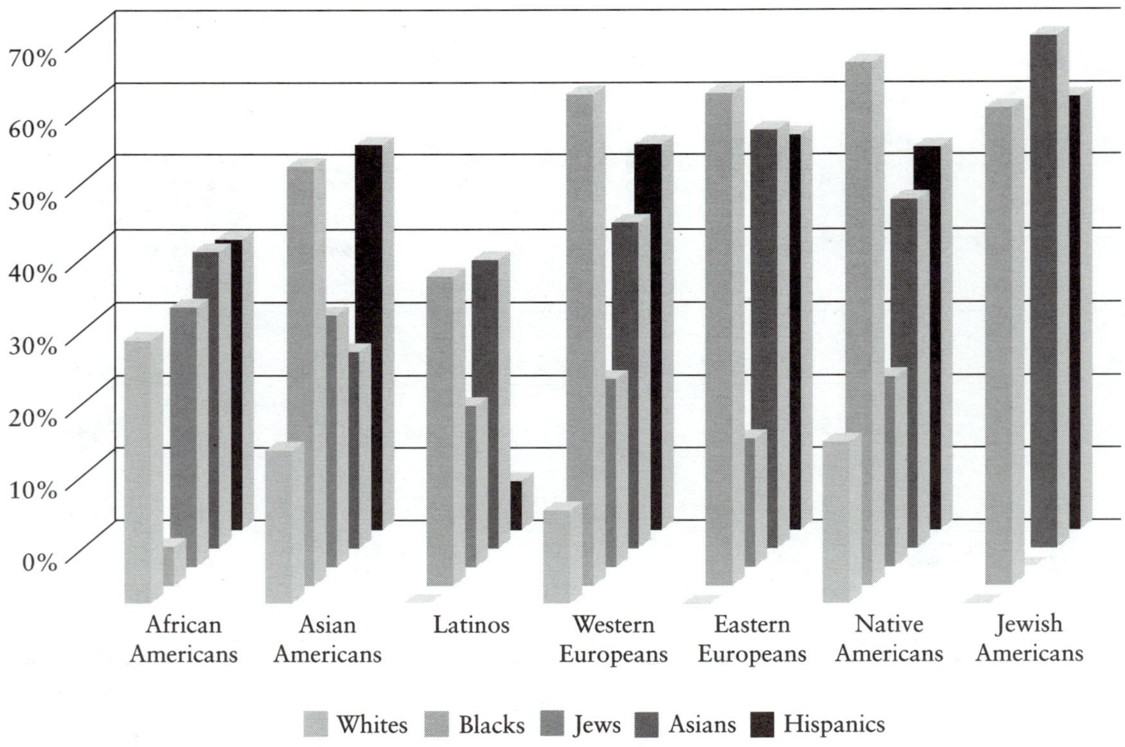

FIGURE 8-21
Percentage of African Americans Very Satisfied With Race Relations by Selected Characteristics

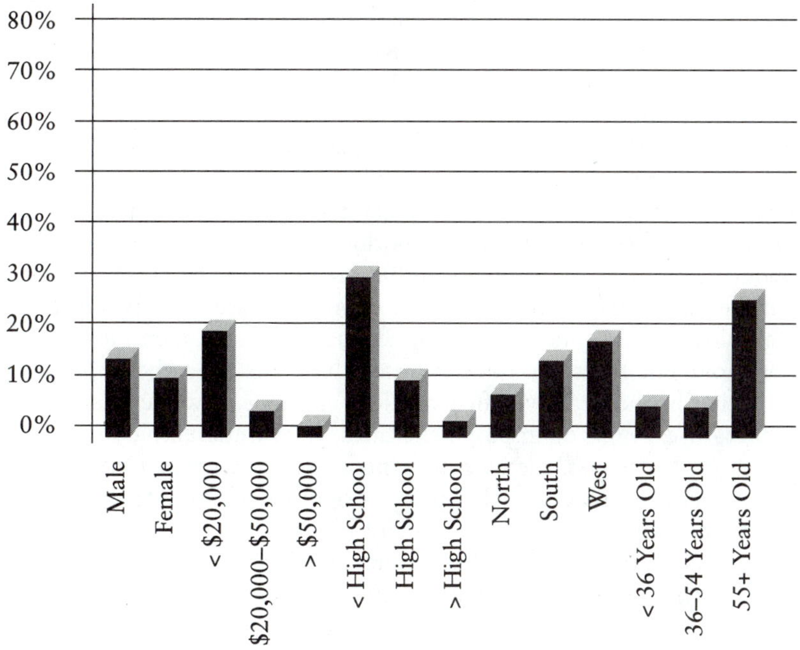

While less than one out of five (18 percent) African Americans reports being very satisfied with race relations as of 1992, these patterns do vary somewhat by subgroup. For example, while over a quarter (27 percent) of African Americans with incomes less than $20,000 per year report being very satisfied with race relations, less than one out of twenty (4 percent) of those with incomes higher than $50,000 report being very satisfied with race relations. Similarly, nearly four out of ten (39 percent) African Americans with less than a high school education report being very satisfied with race relations, but only 7 percent of Blacks with college educations are very satisfied with race relations. And while nearly a third of those age 55 and older report being very satisfied with race relations, only 10 percent of those who are age 35 or younger report being very satisfied.

African Americans and the Future

What does the future hold for Blacks in America? Not only will Blacks in America survive, we will multiply and grow. In 1992, the United States Census Bureau estimated that there were 31.4 million African Americans. This was an increase of about 5 million over the number of Blacks in America in 1980. Demographers project that by the year 2000 there will be more than 36 million Black Americans, more than 13.5 percent of the American population.

Politically, African Americans will also continue to grow, as demographic trends and voting patterns portend even greater numbers of Black elected officials. But the election of Black politicians has never automatically empowered the African American community, nor has it necessarily translated into social and economic equality.

Historically, African Americans have been disadvantaged in American society. It is clear that racial discrimination has played an important part in this disadvantage. African Americans have systematically been denied access to good jobs and other social rewards. As this chapter demonstrated, while levels of educational attainment between Blacks and other racial groups have become more equal, there have not been commensurate improvements in personal earnings, family incomes, occupational statuses, unemployment rates, underemployment rates, or poverty rates. Nor has there been proportional racial sharing in the negative effects of low earnings, low incomes, low occupational statuses, high unemployment rates, high underemployment, or high poverty rates. Moreover, the data presented in this chapter raises anew questions about whether race is declining in its significance for African Americans, and whether studies which optimistically point to gains made by more educated, typically younger Blacks are convincing. If history is any predictor, and if current patterns persist, presumed economic gains may in fact turn out to be illusory.

In terms of racial social distance and race relations, this chapter points out that while there have been reports of lower levels of racial intolerance and prejudice toward Black Americans, there are still substantial proportions of the American population who do not care to interact with African Americans in any meaningful way. Moreover, the overwhelming majority of African Americans are not very satisfied with the current state of race relations.

To the degree that public opinion has a bearing on the kinds of public policies government pursues, these results suggest that policies based on Blacks being socially accepted by whites or other racial groups in order to make material gains may not be very viable. So, if public leaders are sincere in their concerns about helping African Americans realize equal access and equitable outcomes, then perhaps they will again need to ruffle some feathers as historically has been the case in combatting racial bigotry against Black Americans.

References

Allen, Walter R. and Reynolds Farley. "The Shifting Social and Economic Tides of Black America, 1950–1980." *Annual Review of Sociology* 12 (1986), pp. 277–306.

Bobo, Lawrence and Franklin D. Gilliam, Jr. "Race, Sociopolitical Participation, and Black Empowerment." *American Political Science Review* 84 (1990), pp. 377–93.

Farley, Reynolds. *Blacks and Whites: Narrowing the Gap?* Cambridge: Harvard Univ. Press, 1984.

Frazier, E. Franklin. *The Black Bourgeoisie.* New York: Free Press, 1957.

Glazer, Nathan. *Affirmative Discrimination: Ethnic Inequality and Public Policy.* New York: Basic Books, 1975.

Gurin, Patricia, Shirley Hatchett, and James S. Jackson. *Hope and Independence: Blacks' Response to Electoral and Party Politics.* New York: Russell Sage Foundation, 1989.

Herring, Cedric. "Affirmative Action in America: A Provisional Assessment of Who Benefits and Who Sacrifices." Unpublished manuscript, 1992.

Herring, Cedric. "Convergence, Polarization, or What?: Racially Based Changes in Attitudes and Outlooks, 1964–1984." *Sociological Quarterly* 30 (1989), pp. 267–81.

Herring, Cedric and Gloria Jones-Johnson. 1990.

Huckfeldt, Robert and Carol Weitzel Kohfeld. *Race and the Decline of Class in American Politics.* Urbana and Chicago: Univ. of Illinois Press, 1989.

Hudson, William T. and Walter D. Broadnax. "Equal Employment Opportunity as Public Policy." *Public Personnel Management* 11 (1982), pp. 268–76.

Jaynes, Gerald David and Robin M. Williams, eds. *A Common Destiny.* Washington, D.C.: National Academy Press, 1989.

Jones-Johnson, Gloria. "Underemployment, Underpayment, and Psychosocial Stress Among Working Black Men." *Western Journal of Black Studies* 13 (1989), pp. 57–65.

Landry, Bart. *The New Black Middle Class.* Berkeley, CA: University of California Press, 1987.

Morris, Aldon. "The Future of Black Politics: Substance versus Process and Formality." *National Political Science Review* 3 (1992), pp. 168–74.

Myrdal, Gunnar. *An American Dilemma.* New York: Harper & Row, 1944.

National Advisory Commission on Civil Disorders. Report of the National Advisory Commission on Civil Disorders. New York: Bantam Books, 1968.

Pettigrew, Thomas F. "New Black-White Patterns: How Best to Conceptualize Them?" *Annual Review of Sociology* 11 (1985), pp. 329–46.

Pinkney, Alphonso. *Black Americans,* 4th ed. Englewood Cliffs, NJ: Prentice Hall, 1993.

Schuman, Howard, Charlotte Steeh, and Lawrence Bobo. *Racial Attitudes in America: Trends and Interpretations.* Cambridge, MA: Harvard University Press, 1985.

Smith, A. Wade. "Racial Tolerance as a Function of Group Position." *American Sociological Review* 46 (1981), pp. 558–73.

Sullivan, Teresa A. *Marginal Workers, Marginal Jobs: The Underutilization of American Workers.* Austin: University of Texas Press, 1987.

Tate, Katherine. "The Impact of Jesse Jackson's Presidential Bids on Blacks' Relationship with the Democratic Party." *National Political Science Review* 3 (1992), pp. 184–97.

U.S. Bureau of the Census. *Statistical Abstract of the United States: 1991.* Washington, D.C.: U.S. Government Printing Office, 1992.

Williams, Linda F. "White/Black Perceptions of the Electability of Black Political Candidates." *National Political Science Review* 2 (1990), pp. 45–64.

Wilson, Cynthia A., James H. Lewis, and Cedric Herring. *The 1991 Civil Rights Act: Restoring Basic Protections.* Chicago: Urban League, 1991.

Wilson, William Julius. *The Truly Disadvantaged: The Inner City, the Underclass, and Public Policy.* Chicago: University of Chicago Press, 1987.

Wilson, William Julius. *The Declining Significance of Race.* Chicago: University of Chicago Press, 1978.

CHAPTER 9

Mexican Americans

Rogelio Saenz

The Mexican American (or Chicano) population has the distinction of being of the earliest ethnic groups to inhabit the United States while at the same time representing one of the latest groups to enter the country. Segments of the Mexican American population can trace their ancestry in U.S. lands to periods predating the arrival of the ancestors of many European Americans. Yet, other portions of the group are members of the most recent waves that have emigrated to the United States on a legal or illegal basis. This unusual combination of deep historical roots and the continual flow of newcomers has served to create a unique situation in the case of ethnic relations involving Mexican Americans. Indeed, the large volume of immigration, U.S. proximity to Mexico, and historical conditions have resulted in the presence of a flourishing ethnic group equipped with a culture and language distinct from that of the mainstream population. Hence, one would be hard-pressed to find another ethnic group in the country that epitomizes a bilingual/bicultural group better than Mexican Americans.

However, despite their long presence in the United States, social scientists have only recently begun to "discover" the Mexican American population. Beginning in the late 1960s and 1970s, social scientists produced a string of books written about the group (Cabrera 1971; Galarza 1969; Gomez 1973; Grebler et al. 1970; Samora 1966; Servin 1970). The titles of some of these works aptly noted the social sciences' neglect of Mexican Americans, as exemplified by *Emerging Faces: The Mexican Americans* (Cabrera 1971); *Somos Chicanos: Strangers in Our Own Land* (Gomez 1973); *La Raza: Forgotten*

Americans (Samora 1966); and *The Mexican-Americans: An Awakening Minority* (Servin 1973). In the last decade, however, social scientists have devoted an increasing amount of attention to Mexican Americans. This expanding concern for Mexican Americans has been due primarily to the burgeoning presence of the group and to the increase of Mexican American social scientists.

In light of the unique experience of the Mexican American population and the large-scale growth in the group, this chapter provides an overview of the history, transformations, and demographic and socioeconomic trends of the Mexican American population in the United States It is intended as a reconnaissance of the past and present conditions of the Mexican American population, while at the same time providing glimpses of what the future may hold for this group.

Historical Overview

The Mexican American population has an extended history in the Americas.[1] During the prolonged presence of the group and its ancestors in the continent, the population has experienced dramatic transformations, many of which emerged through racial/ethnic and geopolitical conflicts. The earliest known ancestors of Mexican Americans occupied the southwestern portion of what is today the United States as well as large parts of Mexico centuries before the arrival of Europeans on the American continent. It is estimated that the Chichimecas ventured from the southwestern part of what is today the United States (a region called "Aztlan") to the Valley of Mexico (roughly the area where Mexico City stands today) in the tenth century (Rendon 1973; Vigil 1984). The migration flow of subgroups of Chichimecas continued over the next few centuries. One of these groups, the Aztec, would eventually become the dominant power in the Valley of Mexico, supplanting a host of competitors in about 1430 (Coe 1973; Vigil 1984). This period marks the indigenous stage in the transformation of the Mexican American population.

The Valley of Mexico and the ancestral line of Mexican Americans would be greatly altered by the arrival of Spaniards. Hernan Cortez set foot on Mexican territory in 1519. Upon reaching this land, the Spaniards were able to dominate the various indigenous groups through their technological and military might, the spread of European diseases which took a tremendous toll on the native population, and through the co-opting of the rival groups of the Aztec (Vigil 1984). Once arriving in Tenochtitlan, it became clear that the Spanish were not paying a social call. Rather, it became obvious that their intent was to obtain the riches of the area for themselves and for the mother country. The major avenue for accomplishing this task was through the conquest of the Aztec. Despite minor opposition, the Aztec Empire eventually fell to the Spaniards in 1521. New Spain became a colony to the mother country, with the riches and natural resources of the colony extracted to Spain and the native population providing the back-breaking labor. The indigenous population occupied the bottom rungs of the stratification system.

In many respects the situation arising in New Spain represented the classic colonization case in which a dominant group enters a country, conquers it, and exploits the human and natural resources of the colony (see Simpson 1973). Blea (1988) notes the advent of the *encomienda* system (estates granted by Spanish kings), which was characterized by the use of Indian labor allocated to Spanish landowners. However, the experience in New Spain differed somewhat in at least two respects. First, while Spaniards attempted vigorously to "save" the so-called "heathens" through Christianity, and Catholicism in particular, the indigenous population was able to resist to a significant extent. The religion emerging out of the colonial experience was far from identical to that of Spanish Catholicism. Rather, it represented a blending of Catholicism with the traditions, beliefs, and customs of the indigenous people, what Vigil (1984) refers to as "religious syncretism." Second, because of the absence of Spanish women in New Spain, Spanish men established sexual relations with indigenous women. The result of this tryst was the creation of the Mestizo, the offspring of the Spanish father and indigenous mother. The blending of the religious, cultural, and biological entities of the two groups over generations marked the transformation of the ancestors of Mexican Americans from indigenous people to Mestizos, who would become the majority in the region.

In New Spain the *gachupines,* those persons born in Spain, represented the group at the top of the stratification system, followed by the criollos (Spaniards born in the New World) and Mestizos, with Indians and Africans occupying the lowest levels (Vigil 1984). Vigil (1984) notes that internal strife, between criollos and gachupines, in the Spanish colony was spurred by Enlightenment ideas spreading across Europe as well as by desires to withdraw from Spanish dominance. Criollos, especially the more liberal wing of the group, attracted the support of Mestizos and Indians. In 1810, Father Miguel Hidalgo shouted his famous *Grito de Hidalgo* urging the masses to free themselves from Spain. The revolution would take an extended period of time, but New Spain would obtain its independence in 1821, a full three hundred years after its conquest at the hands of the Spaniards. This event marked yet another stage in the evolution of the Mexican American ancestry, as the Mestizo became the Mexican.

The celebration in Mexico did not last long, for its northern neighbor had already exhibited a strong interest in acquiring Mexican land. Acuna (1988) indicates that this desire extended back as far as 1776 when Benjamin Franklin identified Mexico and Cuba as targets for expansion. There was also conflict over Mexican land in the Louisiana Purchase of 1803, with the friction involving the U.S. government's claim that a portion of the region of Texas was included in the pact (Acuna 1988; McLemore 1994). Although the

United States ceded its claim with the Transcontinental Treaty of 1819, in which the country obtained Florida from Spain to settle the contention involving Texas land, Acuna (1988) points out that the claim was never surrendered.

The fledgling Mexican government, growing concerned about the encroachment of the United States in its Texas territory, made a move to open the settlement of the region to foreigners. Stephen Austin received settlement land to distribute to settlers, many of whom came from the southern United States and others coming from different countries (Acuna 1988). Initially, the settlers, including Mexicans living in the region, had cooperative relations (Alvarez 1973). However, the calm would fade as a result of demographic and political changes taking place in the region and in the country. The Texas region became predominantly of European origin, with Mexicans outnumbered five to one by 1835 (McLemore 1994). In addition, foreign settlers were not honoring their agreement to become Catholic and to pledge allegiance to Mexico (Acuna 1988). Two restrictions imposed by the Mexican government increased tensions. In 1829, the Mexican government put an end to slavery, a change which was not received well by U.S. settlers, many of whom were slave owners. In 1830, the Mexican government halted immigration, although undocumented immigration from the United States into Mexico took place.

Political turmoil within the nation's power structure also contributed to the increasing tensions in Texas. The Mexican government was amidst internal conflict between the federalist and centralist forms of government. The Texas settlers, including Mexicans in the area, favored the former, which pitted them against President Santa Ana (Alvarez 1973). As seditious activities took hold in Texas, Santa Ana sought to quell such stirring by leading his troops into Texas. After a relatively brief skirmish, Santa Ana's forces had won the battle of the Alamo. The victory was short-lived, however, as Santa Ana was caught by surprise in San Jacinto and forced to surrender, marking the independence of Texas in 1836 (Acuna 1988).

The independence of Texas paved the way for U.S. acquisition of the region. The severing of ties with Mexico resulted in the opening of the Texas border to immigrants from the United States, many of whom sought to make the region part of the United States. In 1845, the U.S. government granted statehood status to Texas, an event that heightened tensions between Mexico and the United States To complicate the situation, there was dispute over the southern boundary of Texas, with the U.S. government claiming the Rio Grande River as the boundary and the Mexican government pointing to the Nueces River located about 150 miles further north (Acuna 1988). The 150-mile region between the two rivers became a virtual "no-man's land." General Zachary Taylor, who was sent into the region at the orders of President Polk, provoked the Mexican army to attack (Acuna 1988; McLemore 1994). This skirmish was the final straw that brought about the Mexican-American War. The United States emerged as the victors, with the signing of the Treaty of

Guadalupe Hidalgo in 1848 marking the conclusion of the war. Among a variety of provisions, the treaty called for Mexico to surrender approximately half of its land to the United States in exchange for fifteen million dollars, and Mexicans who were on land that then belonged to the United States were given a year to decide whether to return to Mexico or become U.S. citizens with full rights as American citizens, including the protection of their land and language, law, and religious customs (Acuna 1988). Most Mexicans opted to remain on their land and became American citizens. This marked yet another transformation in the history of Mexican Americans, the change from Mexicans to Mexican Americans.

Thus began the experience of Mexican Americans in the United States. Alvarez (1973) notes that while they were "American" on paper, members of this group continued being Mexican by birth, by language, and by culture. In fact, Americans did not view them as real Americans. Essentially, Mexican Americans represented "baggage" that came with the acquisition of the southwestern portion of the United States. Once the United States acquired the Southwest, the door was opened widely to flows of Anglos from other parts of the country. In many parts of the region, Mexican Americans represented not only an ethnic minority but a numerical minority as well. The entrance of Anglos into the region brought about a rapid transformation of the industrial structure of the region from a ranching economy to a capitalist agriculture economy (Mirande 1985; Montejano 1987). The Anglo demand for land resulted in their use of a variety of legal and extralegal procedures to acquire land from Mexican Americans (Acuna 1988; Alvarez 1973; Barrera 1979; Montejano 1987). Through these means as well as the changing industrial structure of the region, Mexican Americans became largely a landless proletariat group (Barrera 1979, 1988; Mirande 1985; Montejano 1987). The majority of Mexican American workers were drawn to agricultural, mining, and railroad jobs (Barrera 1979; Moore 1976). It has been pointed out that at the time, Mexican Americans, by and large, represented a "caste" in the Southwest (Alvarez 1973).

Social scientists have observed that Mexican Americans shed their caste status during the World War II period. Mexican Americans participated heavily in the war effort, with men going off to war and older men and women finding employment in war-related industries (Alvarez 1973). Indeed, even Mexicans contributed to the U.S. war effort through their participation in the Bracero Program, an arrangement in which Mexico supplied workers to the United States for the country to deal with its war-induced labor shortage. Through their participation in the war, Mexican American soldiers, many of whom had only limited contact with people outside of their own barrios, witnessed the world that existed beyond the confines of their home communities. This provided a wider panorama of the position of Mexican Americans in the United States stratification system as soldiers came into contact with people from across the country as well as those in other parts of the world. Mexican

American soldiers performed valiantly, so much so that they were disproportionately represented among those receiving medals of honor.

Yet upon their return to their homes, life continued as usual, with Mexican Americans occupying the lower rungs of the stratification system. Mexican Americans were still treated as "second-class" citizens. Armed with their growing consciousness regarding the position of Mexican Americans, along with their demonstrated patriotism to the United States, Mexican American veterans became instrumental in pushing efforts to improve the conditions of Mexican Americans. Perhaps no other event solidified the group more than that taking place in Three Rivers, Texas, in which Felix Longoria, a Mexican American soldier killed in the war, was denied burial in the Anglo cemetery (see Green 1991; Pena 1982). This incident sparked the development of the G.I. Forum, founded in 1948 by Dr. Hector Garcia in Corpus Christi, Texas (Acuna 1988). Eventually, Mexican American protest received the attention of Senator Lyndon Johnson, who pushed to bury Longoria in Arlington Cemetery (Pena 1982). The G.I. Forum, along with an assortment of other organizations, became more actively involved in improving the standing of Mexican Americans through a variety of activities, including voter registration drives and community organization. The activities of these groups contrasted with those of the League of United Latin American Citizens (LULAC), formed in the late 1920s, which emphasized more conservative and accomodationist activities (Marquez 1993). While Alvarez (1973) views the generation of Mexican Americans coming of age in the mid 1940s to early 1960s as seeking assimilation, this group was quite active in forging new territory related to the demand for better living conditions for Mexican Americans. This initial form of activism would be dwarfed by the coming generation, however.

The 1960s marked a period of radical change in the national political and social landscape. A variety of social movements including the Black Movement, the American Indian Movement, the Women's Movement, and the Antiwar Movement came to the fore during the period. The Chicano Movement (*El Movimiento*) was born in this environment. The bellwether of the Chicano Movement was perhaps the takeover of political power by Chicanos in the early 1960s in Crystal City, Texas, a small rural community in south Texas. The Political Association of Spanish-Speaking Organizations (PASSO) and the Teamsters Union cooperatively mounted an impressive poll tax drive in the local Mexican American community (Shockley 1974). Five Chicano candidates, known as *los Cinco Mejicanos,* swept the local elections. The victory of *los Cinco Mejicanos* resulted in the complete transference of power from Anglo to Mexican American hands (Shockley 1974). While the victory was short-lived due to a variety of problems including internal strife, lack of political experience, and countering organization among Anglos and middle-class Mexican Americans, the triumph politicized the Mexican American community. Toward the end of the decade, Chicanos would retake political power in the community, spawning the development of *La Raza Unida Party* (see Shockley 1974), which gained political power in several south Texas communities and fielded a slate of candidates including a gubernatorial candidate in the 1970s.

The Chicano Movement came out of the working-class barrios of the Southwest (Murguia 1975). The younger segment of the population, including high-school and college students, were quite instrumental in the development of the Movement (Cuellar 1973). The predominant leaders of the Movement included such persons as Cesar Chavez, Corky Gonzalez, Jose Angel Gutierrez, and Reies Tijerina (Blea 1988). As in the case of the Black Movement, the Chicano Movement represented a decolonization movement. Decolonization movements mount efforts to repair the historical structural and psychic damage that has been leveled against a people (see Blea 1988; Murguia 1975). Thus, the Black Movement emphasized that "Black is Beautiful," in attempts to overturn the long-term efforts which had tried to make Blacks ashamed of being black. In the case of the Chicano, the movement protested and demanded change to the long historical discrimination of Chicanos, who represented a colonized people. Accordingly, mainstream societal institutions played a strong role in keeping Chicanos "in their place" in the stratification system, with Chicanos internalizing a view that they were "second-class citizens" who should be ashamed of having Mexican and Indian roots, of speaking Spanish, of having a Mexican or Mexican American culture, and so forth.

The Chicano Movement emphasized pride in the group's culture and Indian and Mexican roots (Lux and Vigil 1979). People in the movement became quite conscious about the history of Chicanos and about events taking place in the movement (Murguia 1975). The term Chicano, which had long had a negative, pejorative connotation, was hailed as an emblem of activism and pride. People boasted about their indigenous roots and their brown skin. Being *moreno* (dark skin) was seen more favorably than being *guero* (light skin) (Murguia 1975). Mexican and Chicano revolutionaries, including Pancho Villa, Benito Juarez, Emiliano Zapata, Juan Cortina, Gregorio Cortez, and Jacinto Trevino, were resurrected as icons and heroes in the movement. The Chicano Movement also sought to bring about the upward mobility of the entire group through self-determination (Murguia 1975). Thus, efforts were launched to improve the social and economic lives of Chicanos by empowering the community. Chicano schools and colleges were established. In addition, ventures were undertaken to develop ethnic enclaves containing all the institutions necessary for daily living in the barrio. It should be pointed out that Chicanismo was not embraced by the entire community, but rather by a segment disproportionately represented by younger and working-class members. For this segment of the population, as well as indirectly for others in the ethnic group, the Mexican American was transformed into the Chicano.

As was the case in other movements which took hold during the 1960s, the late 1970s saw the waning of these movements in a more conservative political climate (Garcia 1996). Chicanismo became less prevalent, as evidenced by relatively fewer people using the term Chicano to define themselves ethnically. For example, in the National Chicano Survey conducted in 1979, only 7 percent of persons of Mexican origin indicated that "Chicano" was the ethnic identity term they preferred (Saenz and Aguirre 1991; for similar results, see Garcia 1981). In the late 1970s, government agencies used the pan-ethnic term "Hispanic" to refer to people of "Spanish origin," including Mexicans, Puerto Ricans, Cubans, and other groups emerging from Latin America or Spain. Significant portions of the Mexican American group used the Hispanic term to define their ethnicity. In fact, following Alvarez's (1973) delineation of various generations of persons of Mexican origin in the United States, Garcia (1996) has referred to the current generation as the "Hispanic generation." With the use of "Hispanic," Mexicanness is downplayed in favor of the larger, overarching, umbrella term.

By the mid-1980s, however, people began reacting against the pan-ethnic Hispanic term arguing that it was a term that governmental bureaucrats (e.g., Office of Management and Budget) had imposed on the different "Hispanic" groups (Garcia 1996). Ethnic leaders, serving as spokespeople, have replaced the Hispanic identity with yet another pan-ethnic identity—"Latino." It appears that this term has taken root in certain areas of the country more than in others, however. A personal observation is that the "Latino" identity is most common in states that have a variety of Latino groups as opposed to only a few large Latino populations. Thus, the term appears to be the most popular in areas such as California, Illinois, New York, and Florida. While the jury is still out on the extent to which pan-ethnic identities will pervade in the Chicano community, the stage represents yet another transformation of the Mexican American population.

This section of the chapter has provided a historical overview of the experience of Mexican Americans and their ancestors in the Americas. As has been demonstrated, the population has experienced quite dramatic changes over time, with the movement from indigenous people, to mestizos, to Mexicans, to Mexican Americans. As has been suggested, there have been other changes of Mexican Americans since the 1960s that have affected significant portions of the community, in which the Mexican American has become the Chicano, who, in turn, has become the pan-ethnic Hispanic or Latino. This historical overview provides a useful context from which to examine the changes that Mexican Americans have experienced in the world of politics.

Transformations in Mexican American Politics

Taking a historical perspective, the political world of Mexican Americans has evolved significantly over time. For much of the nineteenth century, following the incorporation of Mexican Americans into the United States through the signing of the Treaty of Guadalupe Hidalgo, the political participation of Mexican Americans was limited to resistance against Anglo political, economic, and physical forces. The subordinate position of Mexican Americans and the violence leveled against them during the period led to the rise of Mexican American counterforces (see McWilliams 1990). Mexican Americans such as Gregorio Cortez, Juan Cortina, Joaquin Murieta, as well as *Las Gorras Blancas* in New Mexico, used violence against the Anglo power structure (Barrera 1988; Cuellar 1973; de la Garza 1979). In the early part of the twentieth century, however, the political experience of Mexican Americans involved their participation in *mutualistas* (mutual-aid societies) (Barrera 1988; Hernandez 1983; Moore 1976) and their involvement in political machines (Montejano 1987; Sierra 1984). Yet, this form of political participation was far from mainstream politics. In the *mutualistas,* most of which were immigrant-based associations, Mexican Americans developed leadership and organizing skills. Sierra (1984) has pointed out that the experience of Mexican Americans with political machines represented a stark contrast from that of European ethnic groups (e.g., Irish) with the political machines of northern cities (e.g., Boston, Chicago, New York). In the case of Mexican Americans, political bosses herded their Mexican American workforce to the polls, a situation that differed from the more symbiotic relationship between political bosses and ethnic communities in other parts of the country.

The earliest form of mainstream political experience for Mexican Americans came through the development of the League of United Latin American Citizens (LULAC) in 1929. LULAC emerged as the combination of *Orden de Hijos de America* and the League of Latin American Citizens. The leadership and membership of LULAC was almost exclusively limited to the middle-class, upwardly mobile segment of the Mexican American community (Marquez 1993). LULAC emphasized the Americanization of Mexican Americans through the development of Mexican Americans into good American citizens. At the risk of being a LULAC apologist, the emphases and goals of LULAC reflected the political environment of the time. Indeed, nativist forces reemerging during the World War I period sought to place restrictions on immigrants and questioned the loyalty of various ethnic groups to the United States (McLemore 1994). Despite its politically conservative agenda, LULAC brought about concern in the Anglo community, which saw LULAC fomenting conflict. In the coming years, LULAC would take a leadership role in efforts toward the school desegregation of Mexican Americans.

The World War II period resulted in the early formation of protest politics in the Mexican American community (Garcia 1984). As noted earlier, Mexican American soldiers who fought valiantly in WWII returned to the United States with a greater awareness of the conditions of Mexican Americans and elevated expectations regarding the treatment of the ethnic groups. While their views and expectations had been altered, the position of Mexican Americans had not. Several political organizations emerged in the 1940s and

1950s in efforts to better the plight of the Mexican American community (see Cuellar 1973; de la Garza 1979; Villarreal 1988). Among the most prominent organizations of the period were the American G.I. Forum in Texas and the Community Service Organization (CSO) in California. Toward the end of the 1950s, two political organizations [Mexican American Political Association (MAPA) and the Political Association of Spanish-Speaking Organizations (PASSO)] developed in efforts to create a base of Mexican American political candidates and political appointments.

As noted earlier, the 1960s and the advent of the Chicano Movement saw Mexican Americans place greater and more vocal demands on the American mainstream society and its institutions. This period has been associated with the "politics of protest" in the political evolution of Mexican Americans (Villarreal 1988). Some of the more prominent groups and organizations emerging during the period included the United Farm Workers (UFW) union, the *Alianza Federal de Mercedes,* the *La Raza Unida Party,* the Crusade for Justice, the Citizens Organized for Public Service (COPS), the Brown Berets, the Mexican American Student Confederation (MASC), Mexican American Youth Organization (MAYO), *Movimiento Estudiantil Chicano de Aztlan* (MECHA), United Mexican American Students (UMAS), the Southwest Voter Registration and Educational Project, the National Council of La Raza (NCLR), and the Mexican American Legal Defense and Educational Fund (MALDEF). These groups, as well as a host of others surfacing during the period, were quite instrumental in fighting for better treatment of Mexican Americans, voicing the concerns of the community, and in developing indigenous, grass-roots leaders, many with an ideological commitment to *La Raza.*

The political environment beginning in the late 1970s contrasted drastically with the "protest" milieu of the earlier decade (Garcia 1996). The series of protest movements that emerged in the 1960s waned in prominence. The advent of the "Reagan revolution," with the election of Ronald Reagan as president in 1980 signalled a swing to the right in the nation's political pendulum. Yet, largely because of the increasing Mexican American numbers, the period has witnessed the increasing presence of Mexican Americans in political leadership positions (Garcia 1996). The most prominent and nationally visible leaders have included Henry Cisneros and Federico Pena, who served as mayors of San Antonio and Denver, respectively, and then in the Clinton cabinet as Secretary of Housing and Urban Development and Secretary of Transportation, respectively. Yet, these politicians, as well as numerous others who emerged during the 1980s and 1990s, are drastically different—being much more mainstream—than the political leaders who arose during the 1960s (Garcia 1996; Villarreal 1988). In this vein, political observers have viewed the period as the "politics of moderation and recognition" (Villarreal 1988). In essence, the political world of Mexican Americans has become increasingly visible and more moderate and mainstream compared to the "politics of protest" of the 1960s. Still, the leaders emerging out of the protest organizations of the 1960s played a role in the development of contemporary Mexican American politicians, for they gave American society a glimpse of an alternative scenario, which made politicians such as Cisneros and Pena much more palatable to mainstream voters (Murguia, Personal communication). The leaders of the 1960s also served to inspire a certain segment of contemporary political leaders to fight on behalf of the Mexican American community.

Limited data are available to provide a general overview of the presence of Mexican American elected officials. The U.S. Bureau of the Census (1995) publication entitled *1992 Census of Governments: Popularly Elected Officials* contains information on the number of Hispanic popularly elected officials. Before presenting data from this source, it should be recognized that the data are based on: 1) all popularly elected officials of local governments regardless of the level of power associated with the office; and 2) all Hispanics regardless of subgroup membership. At the national level, there were 5,859 popularly elected officials of local governments, accounting for 1.4 percent of all elected officials whose ethnicity and gender could be determined. However, because of the large presence of Mexican Americans in the Southwest, we get a more accurate portrait of the presence of Mexican American elected officials in the five states in the region. New Mexico is the Southwest state where Hispanics have the greatest political representation, with nearly 36 percent of all elected officials being Hispanics. The remaining four states lag significantly behind New Mexico—Arizona (10.4 percent), Texas (8 percent), California (5 percent), and Colorado (3.5 percent).

This section has described the transformations that have taken place in the political world of Mexican Americans over their history in the United States. As noted above, to a significant extent, the increase in Mexican American officeholders has come about through the significant growth of the population. We now turn to an examination of the demographic and socioeconomic standing of Mexican Americans. The analysis will involve comparisons of Mexican Americans to the two other largest ethnic groups (Anglos and African Americans), as well as regional and generational analyses of Mexican Americans.

THE DEMOGRAPHY OF THE MEXICAN AMERICAN POPULATION

The Mexican American population represents one of the fastest growing populations in the country. For example, the nation's Mexican American population increased at a pace 5.5 times faster (55.4 percent) than the total population (9.8 percent) between 1980 and 1990 (Saenz and Greenlees 1996). The Mexican American population had an absolute growth of nearly 4.8 million people, increasing from 8.7 million in 1980 to almost 13.5 million in 1990. Thus, of the nearly 22.2 million people that were added to the U.S. population between

1980 and 1990, 21.5 percent were Mexican American. This share of the national growth is impressive given that Mexican Americans only constituted 5.4 percent of the total population in the country in 1990 (see Table 9-1).

The Mexican American population is not evenly distributed across the country. Rather, it is disproportionately located in the Southwest (Arizona, California, Colorado, New Mexico, and Texas), with about 83 percent living in this region. The group is well represented in the total population of this region, with one in five (20.3 percent) inhabitants of the Southwest being Mexican American in 1990. As can be seen in Table 9-1, the percentages of the nation's Anglos (17.7 percent) and Blacks (14.8 percent) living in this region are much smaller. In fact, nearly three of every four (74.2 percent) Mexican Americans in the United States make their home in two states (California and Texas). Outside of the Southwest, Mexican Americans are most likely to be

TABLE 9-1
Demographic and Socioeconomic Characteristics of Mexican Americans, Anglos, and African Americans in the U.S., 1990.

Demographic and Socioeconomic Characteristics	Mexican Americans	Anglos	African Americans
Total Population[a]	13,495,938	188,128,296	29,216,293
Pct. of Total U.S. Population[a]	5.4%	75.6%	11.7%
Regional Distribution:[a]			
Pct. in Southwest	83.3%	17.7%	14.8%
Pct. in Midwest	8.5%	27.2%	19.4%
Pct. in Northeast	1.3%	21.5%	17.8%
Pct. in South	3.4%	27.1%	46.8%
Pct. in West	3.5%	6.5%	1.2%
Pct. Less than 15 Years of Age	32.0%	19.6%	26.8%
Pct. 65 Years of Age of Older	4.2%	14.4%	8.5%
Pct. in Metropolitan Areas	88.0%	74.7%	83.8%
Pct. Foreign-Born	33.3%	3.3%	4.1%
Pct. Persons 25 and Older High-School Graduates	44.2%	79.1%	63.3%
Pct. Civilian Labor Force Unemployed	10.7%	5.0%	12.9%
Pct. of Workers in Managerial and Professional Occupations	12.4%	29.4%	19.4%
Median Family Income	$24,119	$37,628	$22,466
Pct. Families in Poverty	23.4%	6.4%	26.2%

[a] These data represent complete-count data obtained from the following source: U.S. Bureau of the Census. 1991. *1990 Summary Tape File 1C* [Machine-readable data files]. Washington, DC: U.S. Bureau of the Census. The remainder of the data presented in the table are from the following source: U.S. Bureau of the Census. 1993. *1990 Summary Tape File 4C* [Machine-readable data files]. Washington, DC: U.S. Bureau of the Census.

found in the Midwest (8.5 percent) and least likely to be located in the Northeast (1.3 percent). Eight states outside of the Southwest contained more than 75,000 Mexican Americans in 1990: Illinois, 623,688; Florida, 161,499; Washington, 155,864; Michigan, 138,312; New York, 93,244; Oregon, 85,632; Nevada, 85,287; and Kansas, 75,798.

Other distinguishing features of the Mexican American population include its youthfulness, its concentration in metropolitan areas, and the strong presence of immigrants. For instance, close to one-third of Mexican Americans were less than fifteen years of age in 1990, compared to nearly one-fifth of Anglos and slightly more than one-fourth of African Americans. In contrast, only 4 percent of Mexican Americans were sixty-five or older in 1990 versus 14.4 percent of Anglos and 8.5 percent of African Americans. Nearly 90 percent of Mexican Americans are located in metropolitan areas compared to 75 percent of Anglos and 84 percent of African Americans. Furthermore, fully one-third of Mexican Americans are foreign-born, a far greater proportion than for Anglos (3.3 percent) and African Americans (4.1 percent). While Mexican immigration to the United States has predominantly occurred in the twentieth century, the most significant waves have occurred in the period surrounding the Mexican Revolution and in the post-1965 period (Saenz and Greenlees 1996).

The Socioeconomic Standing of the Mexican American Population

Table 9-1 provides a comparison of the socioeconomic position of Mexican Americans compared to Anglos and African Americans. Regardless of socioeconomic indictor, Anglos have the most favorable socioeconomic position. Mexican Americans, however, fare the worst in the educational and occupational domains. Indeed, only 44 percent of Mexican Americans twenty-five years of age and older had a high-school diploma in 1990, compared to far greater proportions of Anglos (79.1 percent) and African Americans (63.3 percent). Similarly, Mexican Americans (12.4 percent) are the least likely to be employed in managerial and professional occupations—jobs with greater prestige and pay—compared to Anglos (29.4 percent) and African Americans (19.4 percent). In contrast, Mexican Americans fare somewhat better than African Americans in employment, family income, and poverty. Yet, still, compared to Anglos, Mexican Americans are twice as likely to be unemployed and four times as likely to be poor, while having a median family income that is only two-thirds as great as that of Anglos. Overall, then, Mexican Americans continue to lag significantly behind Anglos on most socioeconomic indicators, with the standing of the group being mixed relative to African Americans.

INTERNAL DIVERSITY OF THE MEXICAN AMERICAN POPULATION

Thus far, we have considered Mexican Americans as a homogenous group. Yet, the group is likely to be quite diverse socioeconomically on a number of dimensions, one of which is regional distribution. Table 9-2 compares Mexican Americans in five regions (Southwest, Midwest, Northeast, South, and West) on five socioeconomic characteristics.[2] In a broad sense, Mexican Americans in the Northeast tend to be the most favorably endowed socioeconomically, while their counterparts living in the West and especially the Southwest fare the worst. Those in the Northeast and South have the highest percentages of high-school graduates and employment in managerial and professional occupations and the lowest incidence of unemployment. Mexican Americans in the Northeast and Midwest, however, have the highest median family incomes and lowest poverty rates. By way of contrast, Mexican Americans of the Southwest, the region containing 83 percent of all Mexican Americans in the nation, have the lowest educational level and the highest levels of unemployment and poverty.

Generational status is yet another dimension on which Mexican Americans are likely to vary widely with respect to socioeconomic standing and related dimensions. Unfortunately, census data do not allow us to determine the

TABLE 9-2
Demographic and Socioeconomic Characteristics of Mexican Americans by Region, 1990.

Demographic and Socioeconomic Characteristics	Southwest	Midwest	Northeast	South	West
Total Population[a]	11,197,358	1,128,563	165,607	432,431	469,249
Pct. of Total Region Pop.[a]	20.3%	1.9%	0.3%	0.6%	3.2%
Pct. Foreign-Born	33.5%	32.1%	45.5%	31.1%	29.3%
Pct. Persons 25 and Older High-School Graduates	43.2%	47.9%	56.9%	51.6%	49.4%
Pct. Civilian Labor Force Unemployed	10.9%	10.4%	8.2%	7.4%	10.4%
Pct. of Workers in Managerial and Professional Occupations	12.4%	11.1%	17.5%	13.8%	11.2%
Median Family Income	$23,898	$28,551	$28,998	$24,222	$23,224
Pct. Families in Poverty	24.2%	17.4%	17.7%	21.0%	22.8%

[a]These data represent complete-count data obtained from the following source: U. S. Bureau of the Census. 1991. *1990 Summary Tape File 1C* [Machine-readable data files]. Washington, DC: U.S. Bureau of the Census. The remainder of the data presented in the table are from the following source: U.S. Bureau of the Census. 1993. *1990 Summary Tape File 4C* [Machine-readable data files]. Washington, DC: U.S. Bureau of the Census.

generational status of individuals. Information is only available to distinguish native- and foreign-born persons. However, census data allow us to identify different cohorts of foreign-born individuals on the basis of their year of immigration to the United States For example, the data permit us to compare native-born Mexican Americans to Mexican-born immigrants who entered the United States at different time periods (e.g., prior to 1970, 1970s, and 1980s). Because of variations in the demographic, particularly age, structure of the different categories, one needs to exercise caution in analyzing and interpreting the data. For instance, the native-born category is likely to contain a much younger population than the immigrant group that has been in the United States since the 1960s. Thus, variations in the socioeconomic patterns of these two groups are confounded by differences in the age structure of the groups. To compensate for this problem, we limit this part of the analysis to the group that is between the ages of twenty-five and thirty-four, an analytical strategy that allows us to control for variations in age structures across the groups of interest. The data for this analysis are taken from the 1990 U.S. Bureau of the Census' Public Use Microdata Samples (PUMS), a 5 percent sample of the population.

Table 9-3 compares native-born Mexican Americans with three cohorts of their foreign-born peers who came to the United States prior to 1970,

TABLE 9-3
Selected Demographic and Socioeconomic Indicators of Mexican Americans 25 to 34 Years of Age by Nativity and Period of Immigrants, 1990.

Foreign-Born by Period of Immigration				
Selected Indicators	**Native-Born**	**Pre-1970**	**1970s**	**1980s**
Pct. Distribution	51.4%	10.1%	12.5%	26.0%
Language Patterns:				
Pct. Monolingual English	39.5%	7.1%	3.1%	3.9%
Pct. Bilingual	57.1%	82.8%	57.8%	33.7%
Pct. Monolingual Spanish	3.4%	10.1%	39.1%	62.4%
Pct. in Southwest	83.2%	87.0%	84.0%	81.5%
Index of Dissimilarity Compared to Anglos on State Distribution	66.5	71.2	70.3	66.3
Educational Level:				
Pct. High-School Graduates	72.4%	61.9%	25.8%	27.9%
Pct. College Graduates	9.4%	8.2%	2.1%	4.3%
Pct. of Workers in Managerial and Professional Occupations	15.7%	13.7%	4.8%	3.9%
Mdn. Hourly Wage of Workers	$8.01	$8.38	$6.87	$5.63
Pct. of Families in Poverty	17.4%	17.0%	23.9%	31.5%

Source: U.S. Bureau of the Census. 1993. *1990 Public-Use Microdata Samples* [Machine-readable data files]. Washington, DC: U.S. Bureau of the Census.

during the 1970s, and during the 1980s. Because the three immigrant groups contain persons of similar ages, the three groups vary in the length of time that persons have been in this country. Thus, we can use these categories to obtain a rough portrait of the degree of acculturation and assimilation of Mexican Americans (see Gordon 1964). Overall, the majority (51.4 percent) of Mexican Americans twenty-five to thirty-four years of age are native-born. However, more than one-fourth (26.0 percent) emigrated to the United States in the 1980s.

The language pattern variable serves as a proxy for level of acculturation. We construct three language categories: 1) monolingual English (person speaks English at home); 2) bilingual (person speaks Spanish at home and speaks English "well" or "very well"); and 3) monolingual Spanish (person speaks Spanish at home and speaks English "not well" or "not at all"). The data reveal both an increasing proficiency in English and, concomitantly, a tenacious retention of Spanish. Indeed, for each group, aside from the most recent cohort of immigrants, the majority of members exhibit a bilingual language pattern. Approximately 83 percent of immigrants who arrived in the United States prior to 1970 are bilingual. While nearly three-fifths of native-born Mexican Americans are bilingual, two-fifths speak English at home. The prevalence of the monolingual Spanish pattern shows a continuous decline from a high of 62.4 percent among the recent immigrants to 3.4 percent among the native-born group. These results challenge the notion that Mexican Americans, particularly foreign-born ones, are not learning English. At the same time, however, the findings indicate that the group is not jettisoning its native language.

Table 9-3 also shows that Mexican Americans, across the different subgroups, continue to live in the Southwest. Over four-fifths of each subgroup was located in this region in 1990. In fact, the most recent immigrants have the lowest concentration (81.5 percent) in the five Southwest states, while the earliest cohort of immigrants has the highest (87.0 percent). The table shows indexes of dissimilarity based on comparisons of the state distribution of Mexican Americans in each subgroup to the distribution of Anglos. The index can be interpreted as the percentage of the group of interest (e.g., native-born Mexican Americans) that would have to move to other categories (e.g., states) in order to achieve the same distribution as the comparison group (e.g., Anglos). The index has a possible range of 0 to 100, with a value of "0" indicating that Anglos and the given Mexican American subgroup have the same distribution across the different states, and a score of "100" signifying that Anglos and the Mexican American subgroup are found in completely different states. The indexes demonstrate high levels of differences between Mexican Americans and Anglos on the basis of their state distributions. The earliest cohort of immigrants are the most dissimilar to Anglos on geographic distribution (index score of 71.2). The native-born (66.5) and most recent cohort of immigrants (66.3) have the most similar distributions to Anglos, although two-thirds of persons in each of the subgroups would need to relocate to other states in order to have the same distribution as that of Anglos.

We now turn our attention to the traditional measures of socioeconomic status—education, occupation, and income. More than seven in ten native-born Mexican Americans are high-school graduates. By way of contrast, the cohorts of immigrants arriving in the United States in the 1970s (25.8 percent) and 1980s (27.9 percent) have far lower educational levels. Still, however, relatively few Mexican Americans, regardless of subgroup, are college graduates. A similar pattern emerges in the case of the percentage of Mexican American workers employed in managerial and professional occupations, with native-born persons (15.7 percent) being the most likely to be working in such jobs.

The income dimension is indicated by two measures—the median hourly wage of workers and the percentage of families with incomes below the poverty level. There is a direct increase on the median hourly wage of Mexican American workers from a low of $5.63 among the most recent immigrants to a high of $8.01 among native-born persons. The poverty pattern shows a continual decline across cohorts from a high family poverty rate of 31.5 percent among the latest cohort of immigrants to a low of 17.4 percent among the native-born subgroup.

Overall, the data examining the different subgroups of the twenty-five to thirty-four age group provide support for the straight-line pattern associated with the assimilationist model (Gordon 1964). However, it is important to emphasize that these data illustrate the internal diversity of the group. Indeed, the socioeconomic patterns of the U.S.-born Mexican Americans twenty-five to thirty-four years of age lag significantly behind those of the total Anglo population (see Table 9-1) and those of their Anglo counterparts in the 25-34 age category (data not shown here). This suggests that Mexican Americans, even native-born ones, are far from being integrated completely into U.S. mainstream society. In fact, the trends from the language data suggest that cultural pluralism appears to best describe the condition of Mexican Americans.

CONCLUSION

This chapter has provided an overview of the Mexican American population. In many respects, it has taken a historical perspective to demonstrate the evolution of Mexican Americans, not only in the United States but in Mexico as well. Our journey back in time allowed us a glance at the group's indigenous roots, the influence of the Spanish, and the making of the Mexican American in the United States. The demographic and socioeconomic census data permitted us to view the diverse nature of Mexican Americans as well as to gauge the socioeconomic standing and demographic uniqueness of the group compared to other ethnic groups. The portrait of Mexican Americans materializing from this analysis does not support the views of some Mexican Americans or those outside of the community who see the group as a monolithic and static one. Rather, there is not one Mexican American group but a series of groups, each with its particular set of characteristics that are associated with different ways of looking at the world. At the same time, however, the analysis suggests that two parameters—language and regional patterns—give Mexican Americans commonalities in addition to their common national background. Despite the presence of Mexican Americans in this country for an extended period of time, the group, even those who were born in the United States, continue to hold onto their native Spanish language and to inhabit the Southwest.

The Mexican American population represents one of the most unique ethnic groups in the country. This is due to the combination of the long history of Mexican Americans in the United States and the continual flows of Mexican immigrants arriving in this country. The enduring immigration legacy, along with the unique history of Mexican Americans, the proximity to Mexico, and the concentration of Mexican Americans in the Southwest, have all played a role in the establishment of Mexican Americans as a bilingual/bicultural group. As the evidence indicates, although Mexican Americans—native-born and immigrant alike—are increasing their English proficiency, they have not abandoned their Spanish language. As such, cultural pluralism appears to describe the case of Mexican Americans.

The unique history of Mexican Americans and the ongoing large-scale Mexican immigration to the United States have produced great debate about the future outcome of Mexican Americans in this country. The debate has pitted those who view Mexican Americans as a colonized group versus those who see Mexican Americans as an immigrant group (see McLemore 1994). Those in the former camp emphasize the aggressive manner (i.e., warfare) in which Mexican Americans were incorporated into the United States Those in the latter camp stress that for the majority of Mexican Americans, their ancestors first immigrated in the twentieth century. In the debate, the question has become: Are Mexican Americans more like African Americans (the colonized view) or more like Europeans (the immigrant view)? In this vein, then, one can ask whether the subordinate socioeconomic position of Mexican Americans represents a "short-term" phenomenon that will be erased with the passage of time or whether it is a permanent fixture.

The conservative political environment taking hold in the late 1970s has intensified in the 1990s. In this milieu, minorities, immigrants, and welfare mothers have become scapegoats for the troubling economic times of the nation. Various events have taken place in the political scene which provide the substance to carry out programs and policies to limit services available to these groups. For instance, the Republican "sweep" in the congressional elections of 1994 signified a major shift in the direction of social programs and policies designed to help minorities and other disadvantaged groups. The "Contract With America" being pushed through Congress made many groups—including minorities, the disenfranchised, the poor, the powerless, and the voiceless—vulnerable in efforts to reduce the national debt. The passage of Proposition 187, whose future is still being debated in the courts, would cut undocumented immigrants from social services. At the national level, policies are being discussed which would extend such restrictions to legal immigrants. In California, efforts are well underway to end Affirmative Action and the state's voters will soon be voting on the California Civil Rights Initiative. In this environment, then, Mexican Americans as well as other minority groups, and groups with limited resources for that matter, would face severe limitations in various arenas of social life including politics, education, health, and employment. Obviously, these transformations could well affect the upward mobility of the group.

Yet, Mexican Americans and Latinos are in a favorable position to exert their demographic power on local, state, and national elections. Recall that nearly three-fourths of Mexican Americans in the country reside in California and Texas, the two largest states in the country. As a group, Latinos are disproportionately located in the largest and/or fastest growing states in the nation, including California, Texas, New York, Illinois, and Florida. These five states account for 36.3 percent of all U.S. representatives. Thus, Latinos have the numbers to "make or break" political candidates. Presidential candidates seeking the White House need to court the Latino population. In the coming century, demographic projections indicate that the Latino population will become the nation's largest minority population. At the same time, we need to emphasize that this represents potential political strength. Potential, instead of actual, strength since the Latino subgroups are quite diverse with respect to their histories, cultures, political views, and geographic patterns (see Aguirre and Saenz 1991; Bean and Tienda 1987). In addition, the fact that Chicanos and Latinos are a youthful population suggests that a significant portion are not eligible to vote. Further, the presence of persons who are not U.S. citizens in the Latino population also subtracts from actual political strength in the community. Finally, as is well known, there is a negative association between educational level and voting. The fact that Chicanos represent the least educated ethnic group in the country further detracts from the group's potential political strength.

NOTES

1. Due to space limitations, this section provides a general historical overview of Mexican Americans without going into great detail. Readers interested in greater details are advised to see Acuna (1988), Barrera (1979), Montejano (1987), and Vigil (1984).
2. The following is the list of states comprising each region: Southwest (AZ, CA, CO, NM, TX); Midwest (IL, IN, IA, KS, MI, MN, MO, NE, ND, OH, SD, WI); Northeast (CT, ME, MA, NH, NJ, NY, PN, RI, VT); South (AL, AR, DE, DC, FL,

GA, KN, LA, MD, MS, NC, OK, SC, TN, VA, WV); West (AK, HI, ID, MT, NV, OR, UT, WA, WY).

REFERENCES

Acuna, Rodolfo. *Occupied America: A History of Chicanos.* 3rd ed. New York: Harper Collins Publishers, 1988.

Aguirre, B.E., and Rogelio Saenz. "A Futuristic Assessment of Latino Ethnic Identity." *Latino Studies Journal* 2 (1991), pp. 8–18.

Alvarez, Rodolfo. "The Psycho-historical and Socioeconomic Development of the Chicano Community in the United States." *Social Science Quarterly* 53 (1973), pp. 920–42.

Barrera, Mario. *Race and Class in the Southwest.* South Bend, IN: University of Notre Dame Press, 1979.

Barrera, Mario. *Beyond Aztlan: Ethnic Autonomy in Comparative Perspective.* New York: Praeger, 1988.

Bean, Frank D., and Marta Tienda. *The Hispanic Population of the United States.* New York: Russell Sage, 1987.

Blea, Irene I. *Toward a Chicano Social Science.* New York: Praeger, 1988.

Cabrera, Y. Arturo. *Emerging Faces: The Mexican Americans.* Dubuque, IA: W.C. Brown Co., 1971.

Coe, Michael. "The Post-Classic Period: the Aztec Empire," in *Introduction to Chicano Studies: A Reader,* L.I. Duran and H. R. Bernard, eds. New York: Macmillan, 1973, pp. 59–77.

Cuellar, Alfredo. "Perspectives on Politics," in *Introduction to Chicano Studies: A Reader,* L.I. Duran and H. R. Bernard, eds. New York: Macmillan, 1973, pp. 558–75.

Galarza, Ernesto. *Mexican-Americans in the Southwest.* Santa Barbara, CA: McNally and Loftin, 1969.

Garcia, Ignacio M. "Backwards from Aztlan: Politics in the Age of Hispanics," in *Chicanas and Chicanos in Contemporary Society,* R.M. De Anda, ed. Boston: Allyn and Bacon, 1996, pp. 191–204.

Garcia, John A. "Yo so Mexicano . . . : Self Identity and Socio-demographic Correlates." *Social Science Quarterly* 62 (1981), pp. 88–98.

Garcia, Mario T. "Americans All: The Mexican American Generation and the Politics of Wartime Los Angeles, 1941–1945." *Social Science Quarterly* 65 (1984), pp. 278–89.

de la Garza, Rudolpho. "The Politics of Mexican Americans," in *The Chicanos: As We See Ourselves,* A. D. Trejo, ed. Tucson, AZ: The University of Arizona Press 1979, p. 101.

Gomez, David F. *Somos Chicanos: Strangers in Our Own Land.* Boston: Beacon Press, 1973.

Gordon, Milton M. *Assimilation in American Life.* New York: Oxford University Press, 1964.

Grebler, Leo, Joan W. Moore, and Ralph C. Guzman. *The Mexican-American People.* New York: Free Press, 1970.

Green, George N. "The Felix Longoria Affair." *The Journal of Ethnic Studies* 19 (1991), pp. 23–49.

Hernandez, Jose Amaro. *Mutual Aid for Survival: The Case of the Mexican American.* Malabar, FL: Krieger, 1983.

Lux, Guillermo, and Maurilio E. Vigil. "Return to Aztlan: the Chicano Rediscovers His Indian Past," in *The Chicanos: As We See Ourselves,* A. D. Trejo, ed. Tucson, AZ: The University of Arizona Press, 1979, pp. 1–17.

McLemore, S. Dale. *Racial and Ethnic Relations in America.* 4th ed. Boston: Allyn and Bacon, 1994.

McWilliams, Carey. *North From Mexico: The Spanish-Speaking People of the United States.* New ed., updated by M.S. Meier. New York: Praeger, 1990.

Marquez, Benjamin. *LULAC: The Evolution of a Mexican American Political Organization.* Austin: University of Texas Press, 1993.

Mirande, Alfredo. *The Chicano Experience: An Alternative Perspective.* South Bend, IN: University of Notre Dame Press, 1985.

Montejano, David. *Anglos and Mexicans in the Making of Texas, 1836–1986.* Austin: University of Texas Press, 1987.

Moore, Joan W. *Mexican Americans.* 2nd ed. Englewood Cliffs, NJ: Prentice-Hall, Inc., 1976.

Murguia, Edward. *Assimilation, Colonialism and the Mexican American People.* Austin: Center for Mexican American Studies, University of Texas at Austin, 1975.

Murguia, Edward. Personal communication.

Pena, Manuel. "Folksong and Social Change: Two Corridos as Interpretive Sources." *Aztlan* 13 (1982), pp. 13–42.

Rendon, Armando. "The People of Aztlan," in *Introduction to Chicano Studies: A Reader,* L.I. Duran and H.R. Bernard, eds. New York: Macmillan, 1973, pp. 23–34.

Saenz, Rogelio, and Benigno E. Aguirre. "The Dynamics of Mexican Ethnic Identity." *Ethnic Groups* 9 (1991), pp. 17–32.

Saenz, Rogelio, and Clyde S. Greenlees. "The Demography of Chicanos," *Chicanas and Chicanos in Contemporary Society,* R.M. De Anda, ed. Boston: Allyn and Bacon, 1996, pp. 9–23.

Samora, Julian, ed. *La Raza: Forgotten Americans.* South Bend, IN: University of Notre Dame Press, 1966.

Servin, Manuel P. *The Mexican-Americans: An Awakening Minority.* Beverly Hills, CA: Glencoe Press, 1970.

Shockley, John Staples. *Chicano Revolt in a Texas Town.* South Bend, IN: University of Notre Dame Press, 1974.

Sierra, Christine M. "Chicano Political Development: Historical Considerations," in *Chicano Studies: A Multidisciplinary Approach,* E.E. Garcia, F.A. Lomeli, and I.D. Ortiz, ed. New York: Teachers College Press, 1984, pp. 79–97.

Simpson, Lesley Byrd. "Work in Utopia." *Introduction to Chicano Studies: A Reader,* L.I. Duran and H.R. Bernard, eds. New York: Macmillan, 1973, pp. 125–42.

Vigil, James Diego. *From Indians to Chicanos: The Dynamics of Mexican American Culture.* Prospect Heights, IL: Waveland Press, Inc, 1984.

Villarreal, Roberto E. "The Politics of Mexican-American Empowerment," in *Latino Empowerment: Progress, Problems, and Prospects,* R.E. Villarreal, N.G. Hernandez, and H.D. Neighbor, eds. New York: Greenwood Press, 1988, pp. 1–9.

CHAPTER 10

PUERTO RICANS IN THE UNITED STATES

Ramon S. Torrecilha,
Lionel Cantú,
and Quan Nguyen

INTRODUCTION

Among the most important and immediately visible of the trends reflected in both the 1980 and the 1990 decennial censuses has been the increasing racial and ethnic diversity of the nation's population. Due in part to younger age structures and higher fertility rates, but most strikingly also to increased immigration, America's minority population has grown more rapidly than the population as a whole.

The minority population has also become more diverse. While African Americans are still the dominant minority group, Latinos are the fastest growing segment of the minority population. Heavy immigration from Latin America and relatively high birth rates have contributed to the rapid growth. Asians represent approximately ten percent of all U.S. minorities, but their numbers are expected to grow.

The groups identified as racial and ethnic minorities in the United States are in fact those that have historically experienced sustained, active, institutionalized and state-sanctioned efforts to prevent their full and equal participation in American society and its institutions. Among the most trenchant questions raised by our growing minority populations essentially concern: 1) where we have and have not progressed in reducing discriminatory barriers and providing genuine equality of opportunity, 2) how changing social and economic conditions, personal, family, and residential characteristics—acting independently of, or in interaction with discriminatory practices—are contributing to or impeding the full and equal participation of various sectors of minority populations, and 3) whether "inclusion" implies or requires an assimilation or convergence in which minority groups become indistinguishable from the majority, or instead permit the creation of a more inclusive society. This chapter addresses these issues by focusing on the experiences of Puerto Ricans in the United States.

Puerto Ricans as Ethnic Minorities in the United States

Situated in the central West Indies, Puerto Rico is a Caribbean island that has long been valued for its beauty and strategic location. Since its "discovery" by Columbus in 1493, Puerto Rico has felt the effects of a legacy of colonization and imperialism. The island was first colonized by the Spanish, who brought African slaves to the island after the near total destruction of its indigenous inhabitants. Four centuries later, in 1898, the island was seized by the United States in the Spanish-American War. Puerto Ricans today continue to be affected by the colonial experience in which the unequal relations of U.S. economic, political, and social ascendancy over Puerto Rico are reproduced and maintained at various levels of interaction (Bonilla 1989, Rodriguez 1991, Schaefer 1993).

Although citizenship status was extended to Puerto Ricans by the Jones Act of 1917[1] the island has remained a commonwealth of the United States despite the long debate over statehood or independence. At the center of this debate are Puerto Rico's two predominant political parties, the *Partido Popular Democratico* (PPD) or Popular Democratic Party and the *Partido Nuevo Progresista* (PNP) or New Progressive Party, and a militant nationalist group called the *Fuerzas Armadas de Liberación Nacional* (FALN) or Armed Forces of National Liberation. While the PPD dominates the Puerto Rican political scene and favors maintenance of the island's commonwealth status, the opposing PNP's goals include the admission of Puerto Rico to the United States as the fifty-first state. FALN, on the other hand, rejects any form of U.S. incorporation, and since 1974 has pushed for independence through political demonstrations and acts of violence. At the heart of each of these visions for the future status of Puerto Rico is how the Puerto Rican people define and maintain a distinct cultural identity unique from that of other U.S. Latino groups (Schaefer 1993).

In 1990, people of "Hispanic" origin[2] (as defined by the U.S. Bureau of the Census) represented approximately 9 percent (22.3 million) of the total U.S. population. Persons of Puerto Rican origin formed the second largest

"Hispanic" group (10.6 percent of Hispanics) in the United States with approximately 2.7 million people.[3] The aggregate Hispanic category as used in the census and social research distorts socioeconomic differences that exist among Latino groups. For example, in 1992, the poverty rate for Hispanics was 29.3 percent. An analysis of the poverty rate for specific Latino groups, however, reveals wide variations: 36.5 percent for Puerto Ricans, 30.1 percent for Mexican-Americans, and 18.1 percent for Cuban-Americans. The variations among Latino subgroups are not surprising given that these groups differ with respect to the time, political climate, and conditions under which they entered the country (whether they came as citizens or noncitizens, as political or economic immigrants, legally or illegally) and the regions where they settle (Northeast or Southwest, central city or rural), which together determine the types of jobs and other economic opportunities available to them. Further, Latino groups also differ in the resources they bring with them to this country—resources such as educational background and material assets, which have important implications for their standard of living. Hence, any analysis of the Latino population must pay careful attention to the ways in which its subgroups differ (Aponte 1991, Bureau of the Census 1994).

U.S. Puerto Ricans are distinct from other Latinos in at least three ways that are important to the framework of this chapter. First, unlike other U.S. Latinos, Puerto Ricans are native U.S. citizens whether born within the fifty United States or in Puerto Rico. Second, "Puerto Ricans are both the only colonial group to arrive en masse and the first racially heterogeneous group to migrate to the United States on a large scale" (Rodriguez 1991: xiv). And third, since the 1970s the Puerto Rican population has suffered from an acute economic decline marked by disproportionately high levels of poverty, low educational attainment, unemployment, female-headed households, and spatial segregation. By 1980, in fact, the economic status of Puerto Ricans had deteriorated to that of the poorest of American groups. Attempts to explain the causes of these conditions have generally taken two different theoretical approaches—a *human capital approach* and a *structural approach* (Rodriguez and Melendez 1992).

The human capital approach focuses on individual traits and resources, such as education and skills, as the main determinants of socioeconomic status. Poverty, for example, is explained by a lack of such "human capital" (e.g., a lack of formal education or job training results in poverty). A structural approach is centered on structural or institutional factors, rather than the individual, as the determinants of social reality. In this frame, poverty is a result of structural barriers (e.g., discrimination in institutions of education and in the work place). In light of these two approaches, we will examine social and economic variables from census data, recent scholarly research, and the voices of Puerto Rican Americans themselves to survey the socioeconomic standing of U.S. Puerto Ricans in the 1990s.

DEMOGRAPHIC CHANGES

The past two decades have been a period of substantial growth for the U.S. Puerto Rican population. Between 1970 and 1980 the U.S. Puerto Rican population grew by 41 percent and by 35 percent between 1980 and 1990, a rate four times faster than the national average. Factors which are in part responsible for this increase are birth and fertility rates and the age/sex distribution of the population. In 1989, the aggregate U.S. birth rate[4] was 16.3 with a fertility rate of 69.2 compared to 23.7 and 86.6 respectively for Puerto Ricans. In addition to these higher natality rates, in 1990 the median age of Puerto Ricans (24.7) was younger than that of the nation as a whole (31.7). The Puerto Rican age-sex pyramid (Figure 10-1) helps to demonstrate not only the composition of the population but also why, with its sizable youth base, growth is predicted to continue for at least the next few decades. Thus even if the birth rate for Puerto Ricans decreases, there will be so many women of reproductive age in the coming decades that their fertility will

FIGURE 10-1
Puerto Rican Age-Sex Pyramid

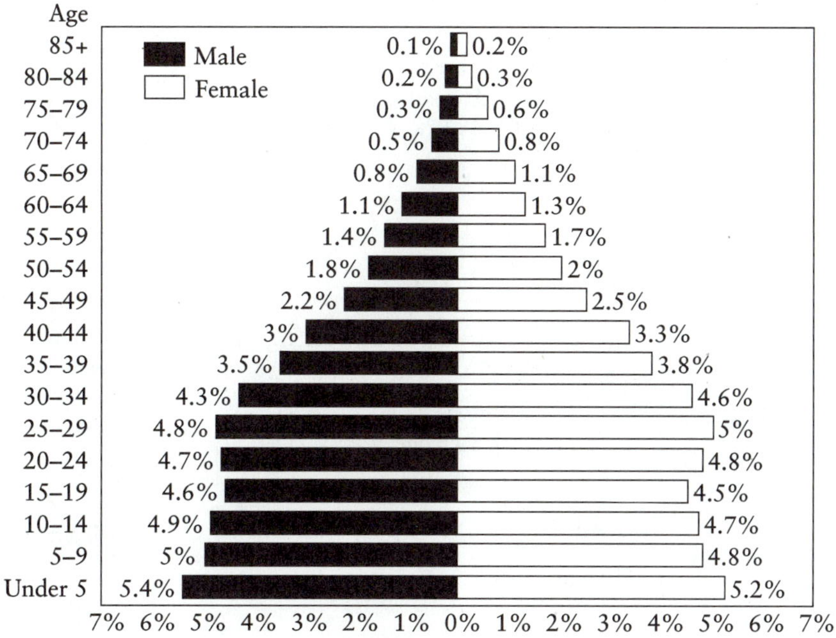

Source: U.S. Bureau of the Census. 1992. 1990 Census of Population: *General Population Characteristics,* United States, 1990 CP-1-1, Table 24.

increase the number of annual births for quite some time (U.S. Bureau of the Census 1992, U.S. Dept. of Health and Human Services 1993).

Another component of U.S. Puerto Rican population growth is immigration. The magnitude of Puerto Rican migration is not a new phenomenon. Puerto Ricans have a long history of Island to mainland (im)migration and return migration. Though some Puerto Ricans emigrated to the United States before the Spanish American War, the majority arrived after the 1898 U.S. annexation of the Island. The first wave of migrants arrived prior to WWII as agricultural labor recruits,[5] and during WWII a second wave was recruited for wartime labor. Both of these waves were relatively small, however, compared to post-WWII migration, the height of which was reached in the 1950s. Today, Puerto Rican (im)migrants comprise a substantial portion of the U.S. Puerto Rican population. In 1990, approximately 45 percent of the U.S. Puerto Rican population was born abroad (see Figure 10-2) (Fitzpatrick 1987, Schaefer 1993).

FIGURE 10-2
Place of Birth: U.S. Puerto Rican Population, 1980 & 1990

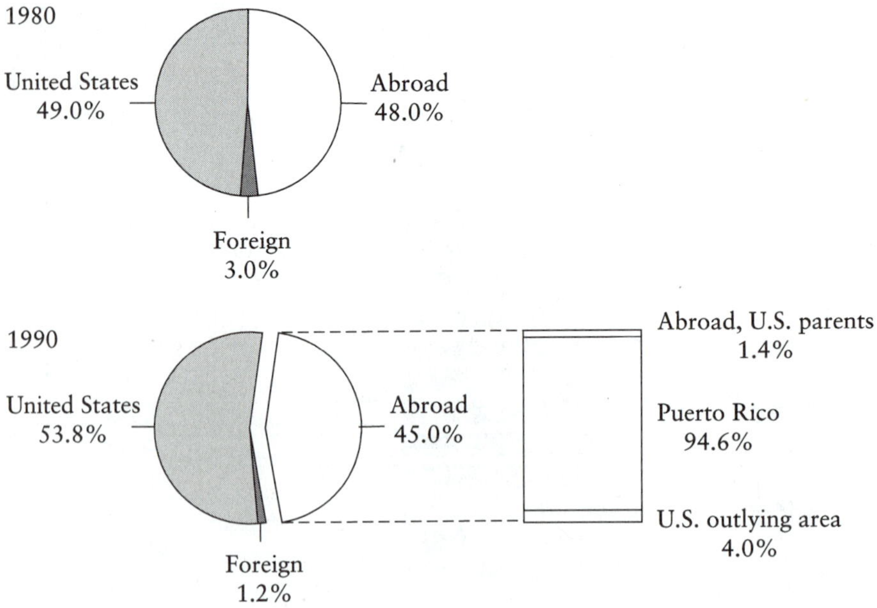

Source: U.S. Bureau of the Census. 1993. 1990 Census of Population: *Social and Economic Characteristics,* United States, 1990 CP-1-1, Table 116; and from 1983, 1980 Census of the Population: *Characteristics of the Population,* Vol. I, *General Social and Economic Characteristics,* Part I, United States Summary, PC80-1-C1, Table 167.

Numerous reasons for Puerto Rican migration, referred to as *push-pull factors,* have been asserted by researchers at both macro and micro levels of analysis. These include the "push" factors of population increase, poverty, and the effects of economic restructuring in Puerto Rico; and the "pull" factors of citizenship status, labor recruitment and the ties of established social networks in the United States. Other factors which contribute to Puerto Rican migration to the mainland over the past few decades are increased and cheaper air transportation, the lack of travel restrictions (as compared to international travel), and the vast improvement of communications technology (with which social networks are more easily maintained). However, not all Puerto Rican migrants to the United States stay permanently (Fitzpatrick 1987, Rodriguez 1991).

Return migration of Puerto Ricans to the Island occurs in significant numbers. The importance of this community is evident in the nickname of *Neorican* (or *nuyorican*), which traditionally refers to Puerto Ricans who return to the Island after living in the United States but is also used generally to refer to a U.S. born Puerto Rican. Because of the ease with which U.S. citizens can travel between the mainland and the Puerto Rican island, calculating the number of return migrants depends upon using census reports of where individuals resided five years prior to the census survey. In general, research has found that Neoricans return with more "human capital" such as formal education and job skills, as well as money, and that this population fares better than the nonmigrant population.

While the return migration flow is an important part of the Puerto Rican experience, the percentage of people moving from the Island exceeds that of those returning to it. If we consider the U.S. mainland and Puerto Rican island populations[6] as one group, then nearly 44 percent of the total "Puerto Rican" population was located in the United States by 1990. Indeed, for the first time, over half of the U.S. Puerto Rican population was born in the states; many of whom are caught in precarious economic circumstances (Fitzpatrick 1987, Schaefer 1993, U.S. Bureau of the Census 1992 & 1993a).

Historically, the geographic distribution of U.S. Latinos was influenced by the proximity of the "mother" country. For example, in the past, Mexican Americans have generally resided in the Southwest (near the Mexican border) while Cuban Americans and Puerto Ricans have resided on the East Coast. A majority of U.S. Puerto Ricans live in the Northeast[7] states and are concentrated in large urban areas. New York City retains the largest Puerto Rican community in the nation with approximately 33 percent of the total U.S. Puerto Rican population. In the past three decades, however, there has been an increased migration and decentralization among Mexican Americans and Puerto Ricans from these historical geographic centers. While a majority of Puerto Ricans continue to reside in urban areas, the percentage living in rural areas rose by 0.8 percent in the last decade, from 3.1 percent in 1980 to 3.9 percent in 1990. In addition, since 1960, there has been an increase in the

TABLE 10–1
Growth in U.S. Puerto Rican Population by Census Regions

Region	1980	1990	Percent Increase
Northeast	1,479,554	1,871,981	26.5
Midwest	208,076	257,594	23.8
South	181,641	405,941	123.5
West	135,690	192,238	41.7

Source: U.S. Bureau of the Census. 1983. 1980 Census of the Population: *Characteristics of the Population,* Vol. I, *General Social and Economic Characteristics,* Part I, United States Summary, PC80-1-C1, Table 233. And, 1992. 1990 Census of Population: *General Population Characteristics,* United States, 1990 CP-1-1, Tables 74, 124, 174 & 224.

Puerto Rican population living in smaller cities and in other regions of the country. Table 10-1 highlights changes in the geographic distribution of the Puerto Rican population by census regions (Bean & Tienda 1987, U.S. Bureau of the Census 1983 & 1992).

Notably, the populace in the South has increased dramatically over the past decade. The same pattern is evident in the West as well. In particular, migration patterns indicate a move from large cities like New York City and Chicago toward California, Colorado, Texas, Florida, and North Carolina. Although the causes for these transitions are debated, some scholars argue that these population shifts are linked to *global economic restructuring,* a complex term which, when simply defined, refers to shifts or changes in social, economic, and political structures manifested in a variety of ways on a global scale. The movement of industrial plants and factories from the Northeast and Midwest to the southern and western regions of the nation (as well as to Third World nations), an expansion of the service economy characterized by low-skill, low-wage work, and an accompanying urban renewal where working-class city dwellers find themselves pushed out of their neighborhoods are characteristic of such restructuring in the United States. These processes combine to necessitate the migration of Puerto Rican workers to the new sites of production in the South and the West as well as to exacerbate the economic conditions of those remaining in the urban cities (Lamphere, Robinson 1992, Stepick and Grenier 1994, Sassen-Koob 1982, Sassen 1988, Schaefer 1993).

The continuing growth of the U.S. Puerto Rican population has several implications for the future. First, as political influence depends in part on numerical size, Puerto Ricans, especially the second and third generation population, may play a more active role in political decisions in their local communities through political action groups and by virtue of their voting bloc. However, the very young population pyramid of Puerto Ricans suggests that, on the one hand, families will be burdened with the cost of caring for dependent children—hence, they will have less money to be put aside into savings for the future and further exacerbating their economic plight—and, on the other hand, there will be more competition for jobs due to the enlargement of the labor pool. In addition, continued growth of the Puerto Rican population, as well as the Hispanic population as a whole, will also force institutions such as health care providers and schools to become more sensitized to the needs (e.g., language, cultural) of Puerto Ricans.

ECONOMIC WELL-BEING

Although economic factors are often given as reasons for Puerto Rican migration from the Island to the United States (or for migration from New York to other parts of the country), past studies of the U.S. Puerto Rican population have found their economic standing to be extremely poor when compared to other American groups. Recently some scholars have argued, from a structural approach, that the socioeconomic reality of Puerto Ricans is becoming similar to that of African Americans. Applying William Julius Wilson's (1987) *underclass* model,[8] they argue that like African Americans, Puerto Ricans are an *underclass,* characterized in part by low levels of educational attainment and high levels of unemployment, female-headed households, poverty and spatial segregation. While there exists considerable debate about the underclass and its applicability to Latinos, scholars such as Joan Moore and Raquel Pinderhughes (1993) argue,

> To apply to Latino populations, it is clear that, at the very least, the underclass/deindustrialization framework must be expanded to take into account both the traditional and modern mixes of industry and of the informal economy in any given locale, along with immigration, the niches in urban space into which Latinos fall, and the extent of government investment. Even with such modifications, the perspective does not account for important cultural and historical differences in social organization between Latinos and others at the community and family levels (1993: xxxvii).

As previously discussed, the aggregate category of Hispanic or Latino is a problem in itself, but even as a group, the Latino experience in the United States is extremely different from that of African Americans. For example, Latino populations continue to be greatly influenced by (im)migration and reside in geographic areas that are differentially affected by economic restructuring. While there are similarities between the situations of African Americans and Puerto Ricans, research of Puerto Ricans has found that they do not neatly fit into the underclass model. Although many Puerto Rican neighborhoods have been negatively affected by economic restructuring they are, nonetheless, diverse and dynamic locations that do not fit the underclass profile. In the following sections, we will examine the social and economic conditions of Puerto Ricans, informed by both human capital and structural explanations (Darder 1992, Massey & Bitterman 1985, Massey & Denton 1989, Massey & Eggers 1989, Moore & Pinderhughes 1993, Rodriguez & Melendez 1992, Sullivan 1993).

Spatial Segregation

Various arguments have been made to explain spatial segregation. One explanation is that spatial segregation is the effect of economics or social mobility (i.e., as an ethnic group rises in social status there is increased spatial integration). Another explanation is that ethnic groups choose to remain spatially segregated to preserve ethnic bonds. These two explanations, however, fail to take into account structural barriers that prevent spatial integration. A third argument is that groups of similar "racial heritage" are less opposed to living near one another. In the case of Puerto Ricans, this explanation argues that because Puerto Ricans have in part a common ancestral African heritage with African Americans, these groups are less resistant to co-residence. While researchers have reported finding a high degree of spatial segregation in urban areas between Puerto Ricans and other groups, recent research by Santiago (1992) paints a more complex picture. She reports that although the level of segregation was high on average, segregation patterns "varied by region and size of place with Puerto Ricans experiencing the highest levels of segregation from Anglos in the Northeast and in smaller metropolitan areas" (Santiago 1992: 129). She found that on average Puerto Rican segregation from African Americans was only 3 percent lower than segregation from Anglos. Despite similar socioeconomic conditions for African Americans and Puerto Ricans, Santiago's findings do not support a "racial heritage hypothesis" (Bean & Tienda 1988, Santiago 1992, Tienda & Jensen 1988).

Educational Attainment

A significant contribution of the human capital approach is the recognition that educational attainment and English ability play a major role in the economic well-being of ethnic minorities. Those with more education, more job skills, and a better command of the English language have a substantial boost in the labor market, which is increasingly demanding a post-secondary degree as a prerequisite to a high-paying job. Those with low levels of education and those who have difficulty using English find themselves pushed into low-skill, low-wage jobs with little chance of advancement. The second scenario characterizes the experience of Hispanics in general and Puerto Ricans in particular. In November of 1989, high school dropout rates[9] for Hispanics, unlike their black and non-Hispanic white counterparts, remained perilously high at 31 percent, three times those of non-Hispanic whites (10.3 percent). For Puerto Ricans, the rates were higher still at 32.1 percent. These rates also vary by city: high school dropout rates for New York City's Puerto Ricans were estimated to be as high as 62 percent in 1987. Indeed, Hispanic dropouts on average complete fewer years of schooling than do non-Hispanic dropouts. While the total number of Hispanic college-aged youths[10] attending college have increased by 35.2 percent between 1980 and 1990, the enrollment of this cohort has actually declined from 20.4 percent in 1975 to 16.4 percent in 1990. While gains have been made in the educational attainment of Hispanics since the 1970s, the educational gap between Hispanics and non-Hispanic whites is substantial (see Figure 10-3) (Rodriguez 1991, U.S. Bureau of the Census 1991, 1993a , 1993b & 1994; U.S. Department of Education 1992).

Although nationally in 1993, a higher percentage of U.S. Puerto Ricans graduated from high school (59.8 percent) than Latinos in general (53.1 percent), a fewer percentage received bachelor's degrees (8 percent) than the Latino average (9 percent). When we couple these findings with the language barrier that Hispanics face, it is not surprising that they are concentrated in jobs that are labor intensive with menial pay. We should also recognize that more than just motivation and personal achievement, educational attainment, and the acquisition of such human capital have *structural* constraints, particularly for minorities. The practice of tracking pupils, the lack of a curriculum sensitive to the needs of non-English speaking students, the high student-teacher ratio, and the

FIGURE 10-3
Educational Attainment, by Type of Origin: United States, 1993

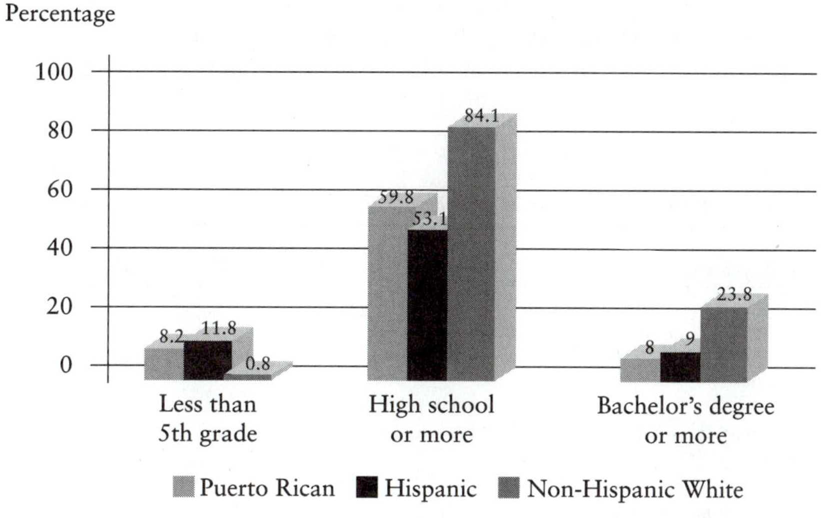

Note: Data applies to individuals 25 years and older. Hispanic category includes persons of Puerto Rican origin.
Source: U.S. Bureau of the Census. 1994. Current Population Reports, Series P20-475, *The Hispanic Population in the United States: March 1993*, Table 1.

economic constraints of school districts all conspire to increase the rates of high school dropout for Latinos, leaving them poorly equipped for the labor market. Thus, the polarization of the occupation structure (i.e., new job openings are concentrated in either in the highly paid, technical fields or the low-skilled, poorly paid stratum) and the continuing low levels of educational attainment for Latinos and Puerto Ricans result in a mismatch of qualifications, further decreasing their chances of economic stability and advancement (Bureau of the Census 1993a , 1993b & 1994).

Labor Force Status, Occupation, and Earnings

A comparison of the labor force status of U.S. Puerto Ricans, Hispanics, and non-Hispanic whites (ages sixteen and over) for 1993 (see Table 10–2) reveals both racial and gender differences. The unemployment rate for Puerto Ricans (age 16 and older) is consistently more than twice that of non-Hispanic whites and greater than that of the aggregate Hispanic category (with the exception of females unemployed). In addition, the civilian labor force participation is less than that of both Hispanics and non-Hispanic whites in all categories.

Figure 10-4 illustrates the industry distributions of the Puerto Rican, Hispanic, and non-Hispanic white male and female work force in 1993. Again we find racial and gender differences across categories. Women were more likely to be employed in the "technical, sales and administrative" category, while men were a majority of the work force in both the "precision production" and "operator" categories. Interestingly, Puerto Rican men represented a greater percentage of the work force in the top three categories than

TABLE 10–2
Labor Force Status: United States, March 1993

Persons 16 years & over	Puerto Rican	Hispanic†	Non-Hispanic White
Total			
% in civilian labor force	56.1	65.5	66.2
% unemployed	14.4	11.9	6.1
Males			
% in civilian labor force	68.6	79.2	75.2
% unemployed	17.2	12.4	7.1
Females			
% in civilian labor force	46.2	51.9	57.8
% unemployed	11.0	11.1	5.0

† Note: Hispanic category includes persons of Puerto Rican origin.
Source: U.S. Bureau of the Census. 1994. Current Population Reports. Series P20-475, *The Hispanic Population in the United States: March 1993*. Table 2.

FIGURE 10-4
Occupation, by Sex and Type of Origin: United States, March 1993

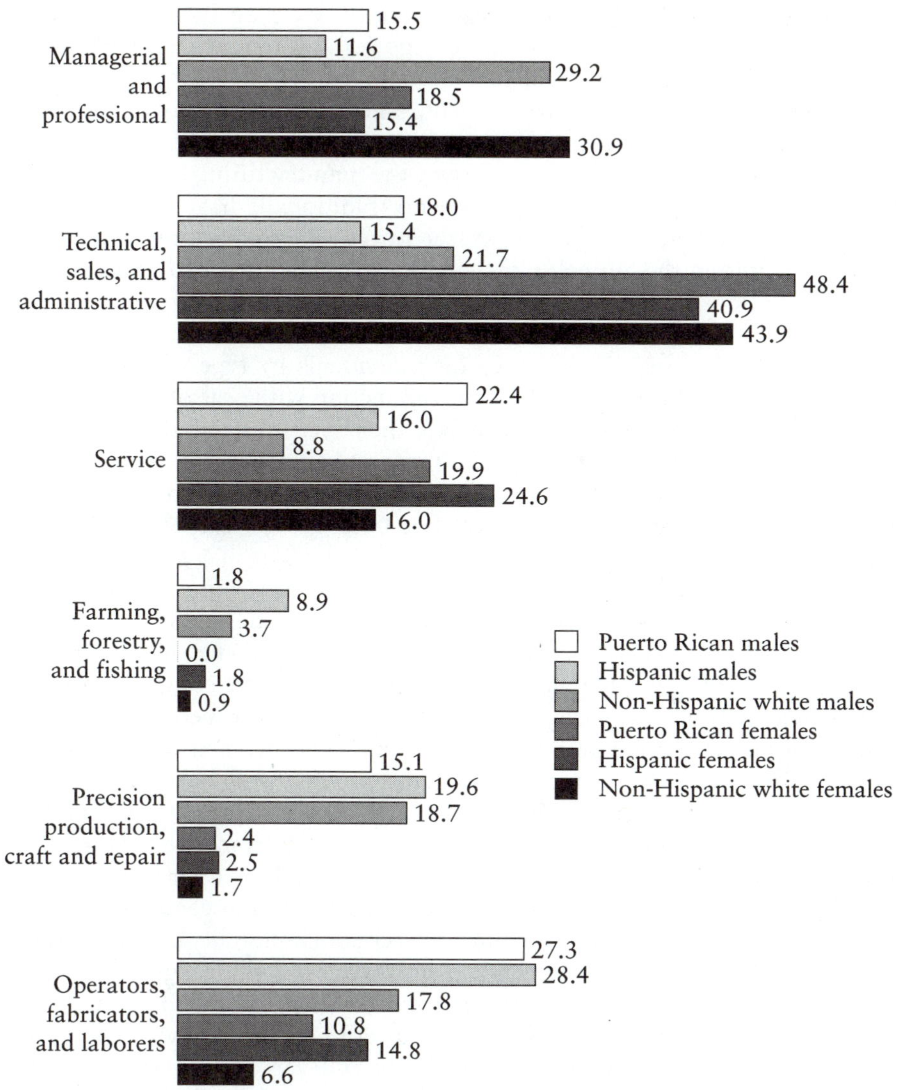

Note: Persons 16 years old and over. Data reflect characteristics for March 1993 and not adjusted for seasonal change.
Source: U.S. Bureau of the Census. 1994. Current Population Reports, Series P20-475, *The Hispanic Population in the United States: March 1993,* Table 2.

Hispanics in general and less so in the bottom three categories. These figures correspond with studies which report that approximately 20 percent of Puerto Rican emigrants had professional jobs waiting for them. Puerto Rican women were a greater percentage of the work force than Latinas as a whole in the "managerial" and "technical" categories and less so in all other categories. In general, Latinos tend to be employed in jobs with lower wages, which have little room for advancement, and have high turnover rates. Predictably, these factors influence their earnings as well. For the Latino poor the situation is a "catch-22": "The vitality of the manufacturing sector continues to be extremely important to Latinos, who traditionally have been employed as operatives and laborers. Ironically, the lower salary structures of manufacturing jobs within the Sunbelt may enhance the likelihood of Latino poverty, although Latinos are gainfully employed" (DeFreitas 1991, Fitzpatrick 1987, Santiago and Wilder 1991:505).

Figure 10-5 represents earnings for individuals by type of origin. When we consider the data of Figure 10-4 in conjunction with that of Figure 10-5, a logical pattern ensues: Women earn less then men in general with average earnings of $16,745.00 and $27,748.00 respectively; Hispanic and Puerto Rican women earn less than non-Hispanic white females; Puerto Ricans earn a bit more on average than Hispanics, but both groups earn less than non-Hispanic whites.

This pattern reflects the fact that Hispanic women suffer from what researchers have called the "triple oppression" of race, class, and gender. That is, while both Hispanic males and females earn less income than their white counterparts, Hispanic females are disadvantaged when compared to their own ethnic male counterparts, which suggests that gender inequity is at work. Further, even when compared to non-Hispanic white women—who also face gender discrimination at work—Hispanic women still earn less income, which indicates that race is also a factor in income inequality. In addition, Hispanic women's sex role socialization (e.g., the importance of staying in the home), the institutional barriers in education, as well as their low socioeconomic background, operate in conjunction with racial and gender discrimination in the workplace to severely limit the economic mobility of Puerto Rican women. It is important to remember, however, that these figures represent only those *individuals who received wages or salaries* and do not include *household* income distributions. Numerous studies have shown that household income is an important measure of poverty levels because the household is used as strategy for survival by pooling resources (DeFreitas 1991, Enchautegui 1992, U.S. Bureau of the Census 1994, Segura 1984, Tienda & Angel 1982, Krivo & Mutchler 1986).

INCOME DISTRIBUTION AND POVERTY RATES

A comparison of income distributions among U.S. Puerto Rican households in 1979 and 1989 (see Figure 10-6) reveals that there has been a significant in-

FIGURE 10-5
Earnings, by Sex and Type of Origin: United States, 1992

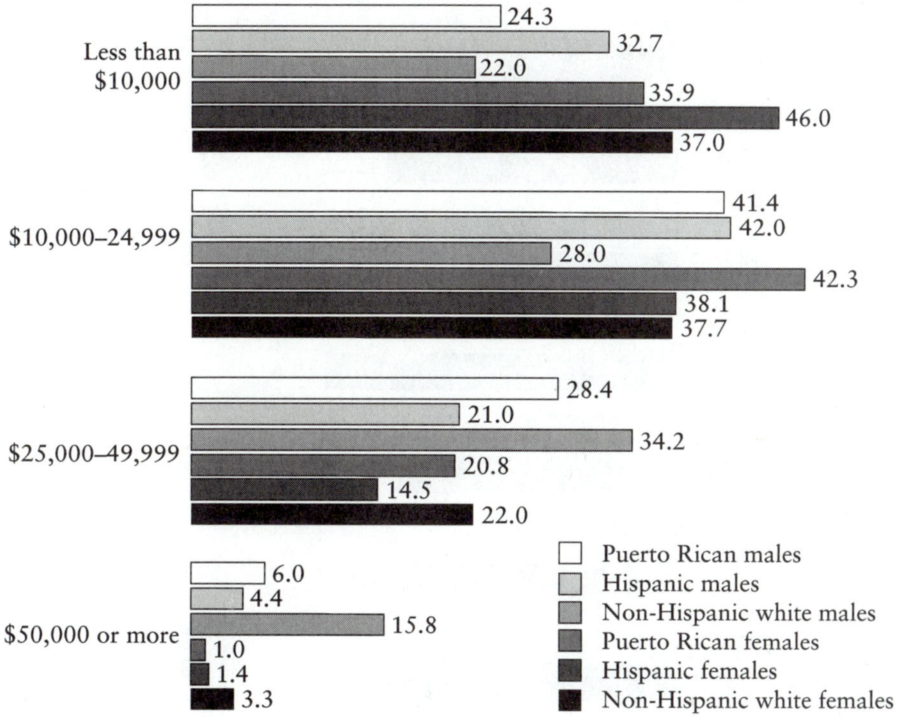

Note: Persons 15 years and over with earnings in 1992. Hispanic category includes persons of Puerto Rican origin.
Source: U.S. Bureau of the Census. 1994. Current Population Reports, Series P20-475, *The Hispanic Population in the United States: March 1993,* Table 2.

crease in overall household income. However, when taking the poverty rates for 1979 and 1992 (see Figure 10–7) into consideration, we find that the increased income levels have not been sufficient to remediate the economic deterioration which has affected Puerto Ricans in the United States since the 1970s.

Similarly, in a comparative study of American households, Jensen (1991) found that "Black and Hispanic-headed families were less likely than whites to rise above poverty due to secondary earnings. Puerto Ricans were particularly unlikely to do so, a result which squares with evidence of their declining labor market experiences" (Jensen 1991:130). Despite the fact that poverty levels for female-headed Puerto Rican families did decrease, poverty rates for the group remained more than double that of female-headed non-Hispanic white families. In addition the poverty levels for all other groups increased over the last decade.

FIGURE 10-6
Income Distribution of Puerto Rican Households: United States, 1979 & 1989

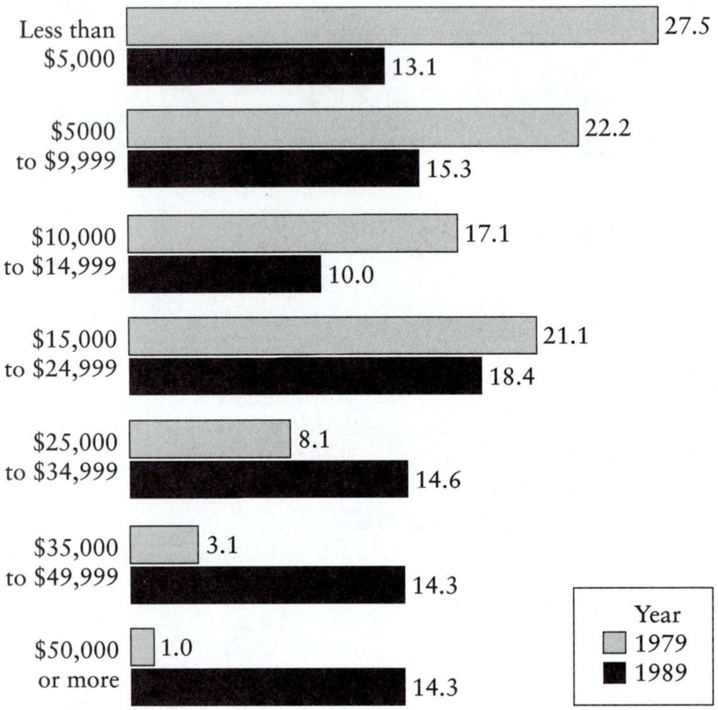

Source: U.S. Bureau of the Census. 1993. 1990 Census of Population: *Social and Economic Characteristics,* United States, 1990 CP-1-1, Table 120; and from 1983, 1980 Census of the Population: *Characteristics of the Population,* Vol. I, *General Social and Economic Characteristics,* Part I, United States Summary, PC80-1-C1, Table 166.

In examining poverty, the importance of social and economic transformations that have taken place since the 1970s cannot be stressed enough. While it is important, as human capital theorists have pointed out, to consider the personal achievements and assets that individuals bring into the labor market, even more crucial is the placement of poverty in the context of structural transitions and conditions which not only constrain the economic viability of individuals—even those with substantial human capital—but may also prevent the acquisition of such human capital itself.

While we should recognize the importance of structural constraints to the livelihood of Puerto Ricans, we should also consider the efforts by Puerto Ricans themselves to build a community that is responsive to their social conditions as well as their cultural identity and maintenance. A focus on economic

FIGURE 10-7
Poverty Rates, by Type of Origin: United States, 1979 & 1992

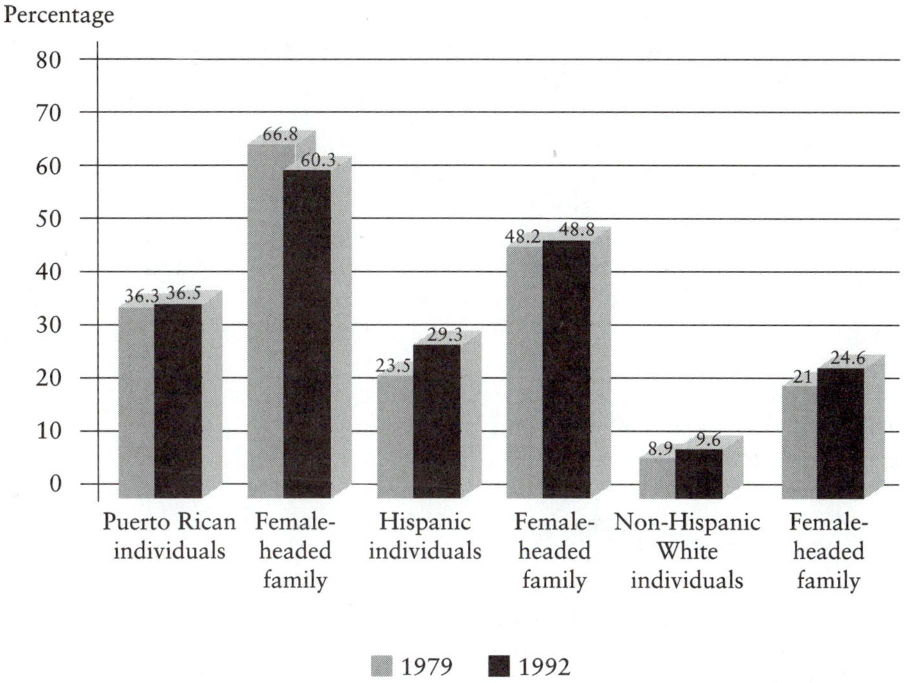

Note: Data for individuals exclude unrelated individuals less than 15 years of age.
Source: U.S. Bureau of the Census. 1994. Current Population Reports, Series P20-475, *The Hispanic Population in the United States: March 1993*, Table 2; and from 1983, 1980 Census of Population: *Characteristics of the Population,* Vol. I, *General Social and Economic Characteristics,* Part I, United States Summary, PC80-1-C1, Tables 167, 171.

factors of poverty—which tends to reduce individuals to puppets on a string—should not detract from an examination of individuals as active agents capable of changing their own situations. In the following sections, we survey some of the efforts that Puerto Ricans have made in maintaining their cultural identity and pride despite adversity.

ASSIMILATION AND DISSIMILATION

The American melting pot is a myth based on the idea that immigrants to the United States could, and should, give up their cultural differences to assimilate into "Americans" a unique blend of many cultures. As romantic as the notion may sound, in practice it maintained the segregation of certain groups, such as Latinos, through structural barriers meant to preserve the male, Christian, Anglo-Saxon cultural dominance. Theoretically, five structural variables, or characteristics, which are necessary for a minority group's assimilation are 1) the minority group's historical mode of entry into a society, 2) the size of the group, 3) the minority group's geographic distribution, 4) the racial characteristics of the group, and 5) cultural characteristics. In this framework Puerto Ricans (as well as most minority groups) are not assimilable because Puerto Ricans were incorporated by the United States involuntarily by conquest, they remain geographically concentrated though proportionately small in numbers, they are a racially mixed group, and culturally they are dissimilar from the dominant Anglo-Saxon group. A more recent model of incorporation, *cultural pluralism,* respects the diversity of Americans and regards the preservation of cultural differences as a strength that is in itself "American." As we shall discuss below, Puerto Ricans are the epitome of such cultural pluralism.

The Puerto Rican experience in the United States is marked by abundant evidence of both assimilation and dissimilation. These processes are influenced by historical, demographic, economic, cultural, and political factors. Included among these influences are the impact of access and frequency of travel to the island, language isolation, religious preference, and legal and political status. These influences are not of equal importance, nor is the list complete. Nevertheless, they are illustrative of major factors affecting assimilation and will be briefly touched upon here.

Because Puerto Ricans are citizens of the United States and travel to Puerto Rico is unrestricted, their movement between the mainland and the island is difficult to differentiate from that of non-Puerto Rican tourists. However, since Puerto Ricans are in effect "cultural" immigrants, their access to the Island plays an important role in their cultural maintenance. One way of measuring contact with the Island is the reported "residence of five years ago" recorded by the census. In 1990, approximately 8 percent of Puerto Ricans (age five and over) reported living on the island in 1985, an increase of 3 percent compared to that of 1980:1975. While contact with Puerto Rico serves an especially important function for island-born Puerto Ricans, for second and third generations, the Puerto Rican community of New York city serves as the wellhead of Neorican bicultural identity. Neoricans have created a distinct culture that bridges that of the island and the mainland. In New York the cultural duality finds new expression in music, dance, literature and poetry through the fusion of rhythm, style, and idiom (Fitzpatrick 1987, U.S. Census of the Bureau 1993b).

A perfect example of such fusion is the Puerto Rican music genre of *salsa.* Salsa is an increasingly popular blend of African, Latin, and U.S. rhythms that also crosses borders of class, language, and ethnicity. For U.S. Puerto Ricans, salsa is an important element of ethnic pride. Willie Colón, a popular salsa musician, explains his own personal connection to salsa this way:

> Now look at my case; I'm Puerto Rican and I consider myself Puerto Rican. But when I go to the island I'm something else to them. And in New York, when I had to get documents, I was always asked: "Where are you from?" "I'm American." "Yeah, but from where?" They led me to believe that I wasn't from America, even though I have an American birth certificate and citizenship . . . I live between both worlds but I also had to find my roots and that's why I got into salsa (quoted in Flores 1993:216).

Like other U.S. Latinos, the Puerto Rican does indeed live in two worlds. Like Colón, many U.S. Puerto Ricans feel that they are neither fully Puerto Rican nor "American." These worlds are separated by walls of class, race, culture, and language.

The Spanish language is also an important feature of cultural identity, pride, and maintenance. Figure 10-8, derived from results from the Latino National Political Survey (LNPS), gives some insight into the overall language ability of U.S. Puerto Ricans and how they compare to Latinos of Mexican

FIGURE 10-8
Overall Language Ability, by National Origin and Nativity

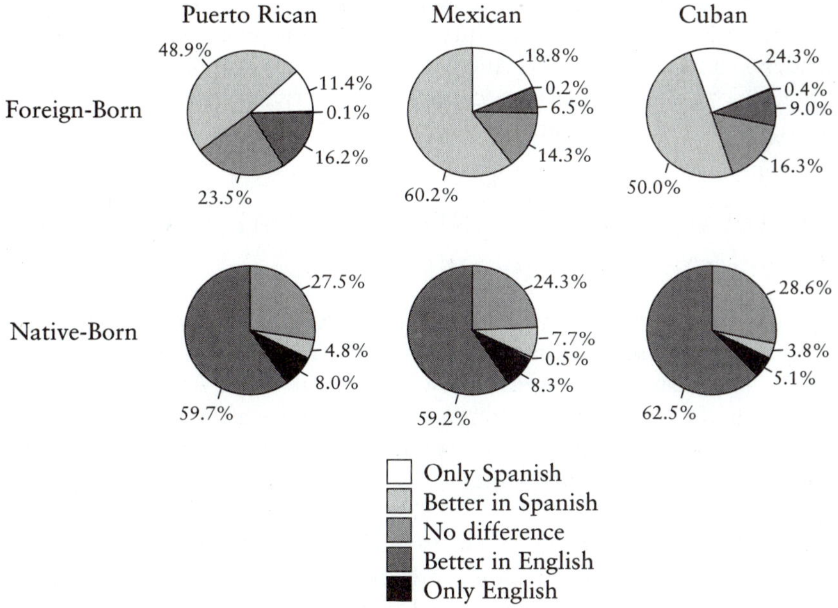

Note: Data from Latino National Political Survey.
Source: de la Garza et al. 1992. *Latino Voices: Mexican, Puerto Rican, & Cuban Perspectives on American Politics,* Table 2.29.

and Cuban descent. The pie charts reveal the overall language maintenance of all three Latino groups, all of which spoke some Spanish regardless of nativity. There are, nevertheless, some differences among foreign-born Puerto Ricans. Compared to Cuban and Mexican foreign-born ethnics, a significantly greater percentage of foreign-born Puerto Ricans speak either better in English or equally well in both languages. This difference may be an effect of the island's colonial history and bilingual education system.

Like the Spanish language, Catholicism is a common and salient characteristic of Latinos. While approximately 65 percent of Puerto Ricans identified as Catholic, responses to the LNPS regarding religion demonstrated a tendency for Puerto Ricans to be more similar to Anglos than either Cuban or Mexican ethnic respondents. More Puerto Ricans identified themselves as Protestant (22.3 percent) than Mexican (15.0 percent) or Cuban (14.4 percent) respondents did and, like Anglos, approximately a third of respondents reported a "born-again" experience (de la Garza et al. 1992:57).

Legally and politically, U.S. Puerto Ricans are in some respects situated in a kind of limbo. Due to their limited citizenship status, island-born Puerto Ricans do not have elected representation (although they are bound to selective service registration and military duty in time of war). Also, there is division over where Puerto Ricans want the future of the "Associated Free State" to go. In 1989, a majority of Puerto Rican Islanders voted in a referendum for the commonwealth to maintain its present status, but there are those who want Puerto Rico to become the fifty-first state and opponents who desire independence and complete self-rule. At a local level, Padilla (1987) has documented Chicago's Puerto Rican community's activism around issues of joblessness, education, and gentrification.

Cultural Duality and Personal Identity: The Voices of Experience

As the previous sections have demonstrated, Puerto Ricans are a diverse ethnic group in transformation. U.S. Puerto Ricans are the personification of "cultural pluralism"—living in many cultures at once. As the Puerto Rican poet Antonio Pedreira reflected, "[Puerto Ricans] are a border generation." In his book, *Divided Borders: Essays on Puerto Rican Identity* (1993), Juan Flores eloquently expresses this point:

> If the main design of the dominant culture is assimilation, the enforced melting-down of genuine cultural diversity, the most telling effect of the Puerto Rican cultural presence in the United States remains its emphasis on difference, and most notably on the distinction between cultures of colonial peoples and that of imperialist society. It is that core of resistance and self-affirmation that makes the Puerto Rican case so deeply revealing of the true

> content of newly furbished ideologies of pluralism for the colonized, whether at home or in the heart of the metropolis. In this sense, the Puerto Rican experience is indeed a link in spanning outward toward the cultures of the entire hemisphere and the colonial world. (1993:14).

The following case serves as one example of the Puerto Rican experience of cultural convergence.

Marta A.[11] is a 35-year-old Puerto Rican woman living in the Los Angeles area where she works as an electrician. Marta was born in Tampa, Florida, where her father was stationed while in the Air Force, but grew up in Brooklyn. Her mother, Blanca, was born in Maricao, Puerto Rico, in 1938 and moved to New York in 1954. After marrying her Puerto Rican–born husband, Antonio, the couple moved to Arizona in 1957. The couple moved numerous times across the country due mainly to Antonio's job, first with the Air Force and later with U.S. airline companies. Though Blanca feels that it is very important to maintain the Puerto Rican culture, English was the predominant language in the home where she and Antonio raised their three children. With regard to Puerto Rico, Blanca explains, "I will never forget my beautiful island. It is my home and I still have family remaining there but I don't visit often. I visit New York more often and I feel more at home with New York." When asked why she and her husband left New York, she says, "For a better environment. With all the crimes and the drugs, we wanted to look for a better life."

Though Marta says she has many relatives in Puerto Rico, she has only been there once, but she travels to New York about once every three years to visit family. Marta says, however, that fewer members of her family live in the New York area than before and that many have moved to other states like Minnesota and Florida. She says, "When I was growing up everyone was very poor. I mean welfare poor. In Spanish Harlem, both of my parents were dirt poor, especially my mom. She grew up in the country. She came here when she was sixteen; my Dad came when he was six. Now things have changed. No one's living there anymore. When I was growing up it was very family centered . . . very ethnic. Now it's nothing like it was. I miss all that."

Marta's story is a unique one. She did not grow up in a Puerto Rican neighborhood, but rather a white upper-class neighborhood where her father was the superintendent of the building they lived in. Marta says she struggled with her identity at that time and "tried to be white" by trying to keep up with the social activities of her more affluent classmates at the Catholic Parochial school which she attended. At age twelve she began the process of conversion to Judaism after a religious vision. At age eighteen she was formally converted to Judaism, though her family was opposed to it. Marta married a man of Polish descent at nineteen and lived in Israel for a while, where her two daughters were born. There she met other Jewish Puerto Ricans and Latinos with whom she made close ties. Her children, ages ten and thirteen, now live in New Jersey with their father. Her thirteen-year-old daughter is beginning to learn about her Puerto Rican heritage. She visits the Puerto Rico relatives in New York and is trying to learn Spanish. With regard to her ethnic identity Marta relates, "I'm real proud of my ethnic identity. I hate when people make stereotypes. I hate explaining things to people. Now that I'm an adult I can go back to it. With age I want it more and sometimes seek things that I miss like food and music and language—I love to salsa." There are, however, cultural aspects which trouble Marta. She says, "It's very patriarchal. I hate that part. I always hated how I was taught my view as a girl. Growing up, all my role models were in the kitchen and I knew that's not what I wanted." With regard to the political status of Puerto Rico, Marta thinks "Puerto Rico should be a state. I don't like it staying the way it is. I feel like it's being cheated and I can't see it ever being independent. It should be a state."

Conclusion

Puerto Ricans continue to feel the effects of the colonial experience. The political status of the island as a commonwealth is a marginalized one which affects the socioeconomic status of U.S. Puerto Ricans as well. The thesis that race has declined in significance in the post-civil rights era is primarily a statement on declining discrimination in labor markets based empirically on the convergence in the earnings of minorities and nonminorities. Yet while some gains have been made in the past several decades for some minority groups, the socioeconomic standing of Puerto Ricans became worse.

The experience of Puerto Ricans does not fit neatly to either the human capital or the structural approach. While the human capital approach highlights the importance of qualities such as educational attainment and job skills, it fails to consider the structural barriers to achieving them or succeeding even with those skills. And research has shown that Puerto Ricans who have moved from New York to other areas of the country fare better economically. Structural models such as Wilson's underclass hypothesis, on the other hand, neglect to consider immigration and cultural differences as important factors in explaining social inequality. A more useful model would need to integrate the important contributions from each perspective as well as paying attention to the differences that exist among Latino groups. For example, because of the growing number of Puerto Ricans living outside of the New York context, where much of the Puerto Rican research has been centered, it is important that regional differences receive greater attention in future research. Human capital such as educational attainment can then be measured pre- and post-migration to ascertain whether human capital determines the move or is increased by it, or both. Besides the human capital and structural approaches, we also need to consider Puerto Ricans as active agents of change instead of cogs in the machine—that is, we need to examine how Puerto Ricans are actively engaging in building a cultural and political community to better themselves instead of just being affected by impersonal processes. Finally, economic integration does not mean cultural assimilation; we need to recognize that cultural pluralism is an important part of the American experience.

NOTES

1. Island Puerto Ricans do not vote in U.S. congressional or presidential elections.
2. "According to the Census Bureau a person is of Hispanic origin or descent if the person identifies his or her ancestry as Mexican, Puerto Rican, Cuban, or other Spanish origin or culture, regardless of race. Origin or descent may be viewed as the nationality group, lineage or country in which the person or person's parents or ancestors were born" (U.S. Bureau of the Census, *Current Population Reports,* P23-183, *Hispanic Americans Today.* 1993:1). Throughout this chapter, the term "Hispanic" is used in reference to the census's category.
3. This number does not include Puerto Ricans residing in Puerto Rico (3,522,037). If this group is included then the percentage of Hispanics who are Puerto Ricans increases to approximately 12 percent (U.S. Bureau of the Census. 1993. *Current Population Reports,* P23-183, *Hispanic Americans Today*).
4. The estimated crude birth rate is that of live births per 1,000 total population. The estimated fertility rate is that of live births per 1,000 women aged 15–44 (U.S. Dept. of Health and Human Resources, *Vital Statistics of the United States—1989;* Volume I—*Natality.* 1993).
5. The Puerto Rican government passed laws in 1947 and 1948 to regulate the recruitment of farm laborers (many of whom worked in sugar cane) by maintaining a level of wage and workhours protection in labor contracts.
6. In 1990, Puerto Rico's population was approximately 3.5 million people (most of whom were Hispanic) (U.S. Bureau of the Census 1993a).
7. Census regions as designated by the Bureau of the Census include the following states and district: Northeast—CT, MA, ME, NH, NJ, NY, PA, RI, VT; South—AL, AR, DC, DE, FL, GA, KY, LA, MD, MS, NC, OK, SC, TN, TX, VA, WV; Midwest (designated as North Central prior to 1984)—IA, IL, IN, KS, MI, MN, MO, ND, NE, OH, SD, WI; West—AK, AZ, CA, CO, HI, ID, MT, NM, NV, OR, UT, WA, WY.
8. Based on his study of urban African Americans in the ghettos of America's Rust belt, Wilson argues that an "underclass" of the poor exists in the U.S. He argues that due to gains made by the Civil Rights movement, which ended housing segregation, middle-class blacks were able to leave the ghettos, which in turn broke the economic base of these neighborhoods. These effects were exacerbated by the movement of industry from the industrial Midwest and Northeast which further deteriorated neighborhood economies (Wilson 1987).
9. The dropout measure used here is the *status dropout rate,* which indicates the proportion of 16- to 24-year-olds in November of 1989 who were not enrolled in school and had not completed high school.

10. The college-aged cohort includes those between the ages of 18 and 24.
11. The following is from phone interviews conducted in October, 1994. Names given are pseudonymns.

References

Aponte, Robert. "Urban Hispanic Poverty: Disaggregations and Explanations." *Social Problems* Vol. 38, 4 (199), pp. 516–28.

Bean, Frank and Marta Tienda *The Hispanic Population of the United States.* New York: Russell Sage Foundation, 1987.

Bonilla, Frank. "Migrants, Citizenship and Social Pacts." *Radical America* 23, 1 (1989), pp. 81–89.

Darder, Antonia. 1992. "Problematizing the Notion of Puerto Ricans as 'Underclass': A Step Toward a Decolonizing Study of Poverty." *Hispanic Journal of Behavioral Sciences,* (February) 14, 1 (1992), pp. 144–56.

de La Garza, Rodolfo, L. DeSipio, F. C. Garcia, J. Garcia and A. Falcon. *Latino Voices: Mexican, Puerto Rican & Cuban Perspectives on American Politics.* Boulder, CO: Westview Press, Inc. 1992.

DeFreitas, Gregory. *Inequality at Work: Hispanics in the U.S. Labor Force.* New York: Oxford University Press, 1991.

Enchautegui, Maria E. "Geographical Differentials in the Socioeconomic Status of Puerto Ricans: Human Capital Variations and Labor Market Characteristics." *International Migration Review;* 26, 4(100) (Winter 1992), pp. 1267–90.

Fitzpatrick, Joseph P. *Puerto Rican Americans: The Meaning of Migration to the Mainland.* Englewood Cliffs, NJ: Prentice-Hall, 1987.

Flores, Juan. *Divided Borders: Essays on Puerto Rican Identity.* Houston: Arte Público Press, 1993.

Jensen, Leif. "Secondary Earner Strategies and Family Poverty: Immigrant-Native Differentials, 1960–1980." *International Migration Review* Vol. 25, 1(93) (1991), pp. 113–40.

Krivo, Laura J. and Jan E. Mutchler. "Housing Constraint and Household Complexity in Metropolitan America Black and Spanish Origin Minorities." *Urban Affairs Quarterly* Vol. 21, 3 (1986), pp. 389–409.

Lamphere, Louise, Alex Stepick, and Guillermo Grenier, eds. *Newcomers in the Workplace: Immigrants and the Restructuring of the U.S. Economy.* Philadelphia, PA: Temple University Press, 1994.

Melendez, Edwin, Clara Rodriguez, and Janis Barry Figueroa, eds. *Hispanics in the Labor Force: Issues and Policies.* New York: Plenum Press, 1991.

Moore, Joan. "Is There a Hispanic Underclass?" *Social Science Quarterly,* (June 1989) Vol. 70, 2, pp. 265–84.

_____ and Raquel Pinderhughes, eds. *In the Barrios: Latinos and the Underclass Debate.* New York: Russell Sage Foundation, 1993.

Murguía, Edward. *Assimilation, Colonialism, and the Mexican American People.* Austin: University of Texas Press, 1975.

Padilla, Felix M. *Latino Ethnic Consciousness: The Case of Mexican Americans and Puerto Ricans in Chicago.* Notre Dame, IN: University of Notre Dame Press, 1985.

Robinson, William I. "The Global Economy and the Latino Populations in the United States: A World Systems Approach." *Critical Sociology.* Vol. 19 no. 2. (1992) pp. 29–59.

Rodriguez, Clara. *Puerto Ricans: Born in the U.S.A.* Boulder, CO: Westview Press, 1991.

_____ and Edwin Meléndez. "Puerto Rican Poverty and Labor Markets: An Introduction." *Hispanic Journal of Behavioral Sciences* (February) 14, 1 (1992), pp. 4–15.

Santiago, Anne M. "Patterns of Puerto Rican Segregation and Mobility." *Hispanic Journal of Behavioral Sciences* (February) 14, 1 (1992), pp. 107–33.

_____ and Margaret Wilder. "Residential Segregation and Links to Minority Poverty: The Case of Latinos in the United States." *Social Problems* Vol. 38, 4 (Nov. 1991), pp. 492–515.

Sassen, Saskia. *The Mobility of Labor and Capital.* Cambridge: University Press, 1988.

Sassen-Koob, Saskia. "Recomposition and Peripheralization at the Core," in *The New Nomads.* Marlene Dixon and Susanne Jonas, eds. San Francisco: Synthesis, 1982, pp. 88–100.

Schaefer, Richard T. *Racial and Ethnic Groups.* New York: Harper Collins College Publishers, 1993.

Segura, Denise. "Labor Market Stratification: The Chicana Experience." *Berkeley Journal of Sociology* XXIX, (1984), pp. 57–80.

Sullivan, Mercer L. "Puerto Ricans in Sunset Park, Brooklyn: Poverty Amidst Ethnic and Economic Diversity," in *In the Barrios: Latinos and the Underclass Debate.* Joan Moore and Raquel Pinderhughes, eds. New York: Russell Sage Foundation, 1993.

Tienda, Marta and Ronald Angel. "Headship and Household Composition Among Blacks, Hispanics, and Other Whites." *Social Forces* Volume 61:2 (December 1982), pp. 508–31.

U.S. Bureau of the Census. (Dec.) 1980 Census of Population, *General Social and Economic Characteristics.* PC80-1-C1 Washington, D.C.: Government Printing Office, 1983.

_____. *The Hispanic Population in the United States: March 1991.* Current Population Reports, Series P20-455. Washington, D.C.: U.S. Government Printing Office, 1991.

_____. (Nov.) 1990 Census of Population, *General Population Characteristics.* 1990 CP-1-1. Washington, D.C.: U.S. Government Printing Office, 1992.

_____. 1993a. *Hispanic Americans Today.* Current Population Reports, P23-183. Washington, D.C.: U.S. Government Printing Office.

_____. (Nov.) 1993b. 1990 Census of Population, *Social and Economic Characteristics.* 1990 CP-2-1. Washington, D.C.: U.S. Government Printing Office.

_____. 1994. *The Hispanic Population in the United States: March 1993.* Current Population Reports, Series P20-475. Washington, D.C.: U.S. Government Printing Office, 1994.

U.S. Department of Education. *Digest of Education Statistics.* Washington, D.C.: National Center for Education Statistics, 1992.

_____. (Aug.) *Are Hispanic Dropout Rates Related to Migration? Issue Brief.* Washington, D.C.: National Center for Education Statistics, 1992.

U.S. Department of Health and Human Services. *Vital Statistics of the United States—1989*. Vol. I—Natality. Hyattsville, MD: CDC, 1993.
Wilson, William J. *The Truly Disadvantaged*. Chicago: University of Chicago Press, 1987.

CHAPTER 11

Native Americans

Donald E. Green

Historical Background

A discussion of the history of the native people of North America is problematic for several reasons. The longevity of the Indian experience in the geographical area that now constitutes the United States makes deciding with which temporal period to begin the discussion inherently difficult. In addition, oral history, as opposed to a written one, is the traditional method of recording the life experiences of these groups. As such, much of what is known about early American Indian societies is not based on the contemporary methods of sociological inquiry, but rather on anthropological accounts, inferential abstractions, and mere speculation (Snipp, 1989). Even more contemporary accounts of the native experience, which assume a greater degree of objectivity and scientific validity, are too often based on a monolithic view of American Indian societies (Belosi, 1989). As an American Indian sociologist, I have chosen to begin this discussion at that period of the Native American experience when extensive contact with the peoples of Europe began a series of fundamental changes in the social fabric of American Indian societies. Vine Deloria, an American Indian scholar who has written extensively on the indigenous people of North America, and his colleague Clifford Lytle, provide a useful framework to demarcate these periods of contact and change (1983). These two scholars identify an initial historical period as one of discovery, conquest, and treaty making (1532–1828). This era of Indian-white relations is significantly different from later ones for several reasons. As Deloria and Lytle point out, early European philosophy concerning notions of land rights and discovery asserted that Indians were the true owners of the continent and that, except for a just war, Indian consent would be required to gain title to their lands. As such, Europeans were socialized to acknowledge Indian tribes as sovereign entities and that European nations were morally and legally obligated to treat with them concerning issues of land rights, access to technology, and other trade goods.

During this period, Indian labor played a crucial role in the political economy of the fur trade (Kardulias, 1990). American Indian societies provided technical skills, capital investment (tools), and the human labor of procurement, processing, and transportation of beaver and other fur-bearing animals. And as Indian societies competed with non-Indian ones over the control of these highly valued resources, many Indian societies maintained considerable political and economic advantages over their European counterparts (Cornell, 1988). Unfortunately, this relatively equal playing field soon gave way to a different set of economic and political conditions. As Indian societies were increasing linked to the Euro-American mercantile economy, many became heavily dependent on European commodities (Kardulias, 1990). Intertribal warfare increased as indigenous societies completed for control of rapidly depleting hunting grounds, as well as access to European markets. By the late 1700s, Euro-Americans had begun to find alternative non-Indian labor for fur production, and the economic and political power of Indian societies was greatly reduced (Cornell, 1988).

Deloria and Lytle (1983) identify the next period of Indian-white relations as one of removal and relocation (1828–1887). As the United States continued to consolidate its military and economic power in North America, political conditions for American Indians changed for the worse. During this period it became increasingly apparent that Indian and non-Indian societies could not peacefully coexist in this country. Popular non-Indian opinion supported a policy of relocating Indian people as protection for both the tribes and the emerging American states. Andrew Jackson won the 1928 presidential election campaigning on a policy of voluntary removal (Deloria and Lytle, 1983). A fledgling U.S. Supreme Court also struggled with the political status of native people during this time, rendering a series of decisions between 1823 and 1832 that continue to serve as the framework for contemporary federal Indian policy. The first case, *Johnson* v. *MacIntosh,* established a new legal philosophy that discovery did give non-Indian parties legal title to Indian lands. Deloria and Lytle (1983) argue that Chief Justice Marshall's decision accomplished a transfer of a vested property right to a political one that recognized only quasi-sovereignty of Indian tribes over their internal affairs. In two subsequent cases, Marshall further outlined this new criteria for Indian-white relations. In the *Cherokee Nation* v. *Georgia* case, he characterized Indian people as wards of the federal government, and Indian tribes as "domestic dependent nations" in need of guardianship protection by the United States. In the last of these cases, *Worcester* v. *Georgia,* the idea of a limited internal sovereignty of Indian nations was introduced, which acknowledged the existence of Indian political institutions and the right of Indian tribes to engage in self-government. Ironically, on the legal merits, the Cherokee nation won this case, successfully arguing that the State of Georgia could not force them to dissolve their government and submit to state laws. Nevertheless, with Congressional passage of the Indian Removal Act of 1930, and President Andrew Jackson's refusal to carry out the U.S. Supreme Court decision, the lack of political power for both the court and Indian tribes was clearly evident (Deloria and Lytle, 1983).

What followed was a massive migration of Indian people from their native lands. The most notorious of these events was the Cherokee "Trail of Tears" in which sixteen thousand Cherokees walked "silently and resigned" from the state of Georgia to what is now eastern Oklahoma. The humiliating experience also was endured by many other tribes throughout the eastern and southern portion of the United States (Deloria and Lytle, 1983). The subsequent loss of the Indian land base was extensive. As late as 1800, more than 80 percent of what is now the contiguous forty-eight states was still considered Indian country. By 1900, however, fewer than eighty million acres remained in Indian control—less than 5 percent of the 1800 land holdings (Cornell, 1988).

Deloria and Lytle (1983) identify a third phase of Indian-white relations as that of allotment and assimilation (1887–1928). With the massive removal efforts virtually completed, federal Indian policy turned to a somewhat different method of resolving the "Indian problem." It was based primarily on a refinement of eighteenth-century agrarian theory, which argued that land ownership was an inherent right of individuals (Cornell, 1988). As Cornell suggests, American refinements of the theory included the notions that democracy and republicanism would be enhanced by all citizens having equal rights to land ownership. The policy was formalized in 1887 when the U.S. Congress, with the support of President Chester Arthur, passed the General Allotment Act, otherwise known as the Dawes Act. The legislation outlined the methods by which the remaining communal lands would be transferred to individual Indians. Many have documented this process and its devastating effect on Indian people (Jacobson, 1984). This social experiment was furthered by still other legislation to accomplish the goal of assimilation. These included the Major Crimes Act (1885), which removed Indian jurisdiction over most crimes in Indian country, and the Indian Citizenship Act (1924), which "granted" Indians citizenship in the United States.

Deloria and Lytle (1983) define a fourth period of Indian-white relations as that of reorganization and self-government (1928–1945). In the historical context of a decline in demand and profit for land, and mounting evidence of the failure of the allotment policies of the previous century to fully assimilate Indians into the dominant culture, United States political discourse on federal Indian policy focused increasingly on radical reform efforts (Cornell, 1988). In 1934, Congress passed perhaps one of the most important pieces of federal legislation directed toward American Indians, the Indian Reorganization Act (IRA). The IRA focused on both economic and political reforms to revitalize tribal governments. Economic reforms included efforts to stabilize and increase the land base of Indian country. Tribal economies were to be managed by newly created tribal business corporations and revitalized through access to revolving credit for new economic development activities. Political reforms focused on procedures to reconstruct tribal authority by adopting constitutional forms of government based on the American model of representative government, electoral districts, and centralized authority. Critics have argued that this legislation represented a continuing policy focus on assimilation and acculturation of Indian people (Clemmer, 1986). Those less critical of the IRA stress that it opened an avenue for tribal-level political participation that had not existed in the history of Indian-white relations (Cornell, 1988).

Deloria and Lytle (1983) identify a fifth phase of Indian-white relations as that of Termination (1945–1961). Defined by a 1953 U.S. House concurrent resolution supporting the goal of ending the unique political status of Indian people, the era was marked by a series of governmental activities that reflected both post-WWII budgetary concerns, as well as a renewed interest in "mainstreaming" American Indians into dominant political and economic institutions. For example, during this period, considerable efforts were devoted to encourage significant numbers of American Indians to voluntarily relocate to large urban areas. Beginning with a job placement service program for the Navajo in 1948, relocation programs sprang up across the United States providing transportation, placement, and economic support services for the newly arriving urban Indians (Sorkin, 1972). Unfortunately for those who chose to remain on their reservations, the dramatic increases in funding for these relocation programs coincided with an equally dramatic decline in support for reservation agriculture and industrial activities (Cornell, 1988). Not surprisingly then, by the middle 1970s, over one hundred thousand Indians had taken part in this program (Sorkin, 1972).

Additional legislative actions produced more direct assaults on tribal sovereignty. Perhaps not surprisingly, tribal groups selected for termination of their legal status as Indian people were those who had evidenced the most economic success and political stability. A number of the remaining tribes saw their ability to control their internal affairs reduced through Public Law 280. The legislation provided for the transfer of civil and criminal jurisdiction on Indian reservations to five state governments, and allowed all others to do the same if they so desired, without consent of tribal governments. Also during this period of termination, federal services for many Indian programs, including health and education, were transferred from BIA control to other federal agencies or state governments.

Deloria and Lytle identify the current period of Indian-white relations as that of self-determination (1961 to the present). This period is perhaps best defined by the 1970 presidential address to Congress by Richard Nixon in which he strongly attacked the policy of termination. Subsequent congressional activity embraced the policy of self-determination for Indian tribes through passage of the Indian Self-Determination and Educational Assistance Act (1975). However, given the existing political context, President Nixon's speech and subsequent congressional activity in many ways merely confirmed the inevitable. That is, numerous examples of collective action on the part of American Indians throughout the United States occurred prior to the introduction of self-determination policies. The 1969 occupation of Alcatraz Island, the 1972 Trail of Broken Treaties march and the subsequent takeover of the BIA headquarters in Washington, D.C., and the 1978 Longest Walk march are some of the more thoroughly documented events (Nagel, 1995). Moreover, both Indian and non-Indian groups had been criticizing the termination policies from the outset for their lack of Indian input and sweeping changes in Indian-white relations (Cornell, 1988).

The self-determination period has evidenced a more direct role for tribal governments in the lives of Indian people through a major transfer of decision-making authority from the BIA to tribal governments (Stuart, 1991). As a result of self-determination policies, tribal governments now have the ability to obtain direct control over federal funding for Indian services such as health, education, and infrastructure development (Deloria and Lytle, 1983). Federal policy also has encouraged increased economic development on Indian reservations, primarily in the form of increased access to natural resources such as oil and coal development (Snipp, 1986). In addition, there have been continuing efforts to increase U.S. labor force participation among Indian people (Sandefur, 1991). While many observers have welcomed the self-determination policies for the return of economic and political control to Indian tribal governments, others fear that the policy has an adverse effect on the visibility and influence of those groups whose goals and orientations remain either to the right or left of the status quo of Indian-white relations (Cornell, 1984).

SOCIODEMOGRAPHIC CHARACTERISTICS OF AMERICAN INDIANS

O'Hare (1992) has extensively examined the demographic profile of America's minority groups based on 1990 census data. Table 11-1 presents selected indicators of the sociodemographic characteristics of American Indians from his work. For comparative purposes, the sociodemographic indicators for other major racial groups in the United States also are included.

Educational Attainment

In general, American Indian educational achievement levels are among the lowest of all racial groups in the United States. The proportion of American

TABLE 11–1
Sociodemographic Characteristics of American Indians

	Race				
Category	American Indian	African	Hispanic	Asian	Non-Hispanic White
Educational Attainment (%)[a]					
College	11	14	10	47	28
Some College	30	26	20	20	27
High School	78	81	60	92	91
Labor Force Status (%)[b]					
Working	53	54	59	61	67
Unemployed	7	8	7	3	4
Not in Labor Force	40	39	34	36	34
Occupational Status (%)[c]					
White Collar					
M/P	17	17	13	30	28
T/A	26	29	26	33	32
Blue Collar					
Skilled	14	8	13	8	11
Semi- and Unskilled	20	22	24	12	14
Services	19	23	19	15	12
Farming, fishing and forestry	4	2	5	1	2
Median Household Income[d]					
1980	20,900	18,700	23,100	34,100	30,200
1990	20,000	19,800	24,200	36,800	31,400
Poverty/Welfare[e]					
% in poverty	32	33	29	14	9
% in deep poverty	14	16	10	7	3
% on welfare	51	47	44	19	13
% poor receiving welfare	87	85	79	62	61

Sources: a. O'Hare, American Minorities, Figure 9, p. 29; b. O'Hare, American Minorities, Figure 10, p. 32; c. O'Hare, American Minorities, Table 8, p. 33; d. O'Hare, American Minorities, Figure 11, p. 34; e. O'Hare, American Minorities, Table 11, p. 38.

Indian adults who have completed high school (78 percent) is second only to that of Hispanics. And while the proportion of young American Indians who have some college education is larger than all other groups, American Indian adults have the second lowest proportion of college graduates (11 percent). Again, only Hispanics have a lower proportion of their population who have completed a college degree (10 percent).

Labor Force Participation

As the second panel of Table 11-1 indicates, the percentage of American Indians in the workforce is the lowest of all groups examined (53 percent). Conversely, American Indians also have the highest proportion of individuals who are not currently seeking employment (40 percent). Moreover, the unemployment rate for American Indians (7 percent) is second only to African Americans. Collectively, these figures suggest that American Indians continue to be a significantly underutilized racial group in the United States labor force.

Occupational Status

Indicators of occupational status are presented in the third panel of Table 11-1. These data reveal that American Indian representation in white-collar jobs is similar to that of African Americans and Hispanics, but lower than that of Asian and non-Hispanic whites. Considering both categories of white-collar status, the proportion of American Indians in white-collar jobs (43 percent) is second lowest among the groups considered. Only Hispanics have fewer individuals in white-collar occupations (39 percent). These figures compare to 63 percent for Asian Americans and 60 percent for non-Hispanic whites. On the other hand, the latter groups have the lowest percentages of workers in blue collar occupations (20 and 25 percent respectively). Thirty-four percent of American Indians are employed in blue-collar occupations. African Americans and Hispanic workers make up 30 and 37 percent, respectively, of blue-collar workers. Similar differences are revealed in the service jobs category. American Indians and Hispanics represent 19 percent of the workforce in the service industry, compared to 23 percent for African Americans. Conversely, 15 percent of Asians and only 12 percent of non-Hispanic whites have service sector jobs.

Median Household Income

For comparison purposes, the median household income data for both 1980 and 1990 are presented. Data for 1990 reveal that American Indians have the second lowest levels of household income among the groups considered ($20,000), while Asian Americans have the highest levels ($36,800). More importantly, however, these figures indicate that American Indians were the only group that suffered a decline in household income between 1980 and 1990. Median household income figures for all other groups reveal increases that exceed the income decline noted for American Indians.

Poverty Indicators

Poverty indicators reveal racial patterns similar to those based on income levels. Thirty-two percent of all American Indians are considered at or below the poverty level, a figure second only to African Americans (33 percent). These figures compare to only 9 percent of the non-Hispanic white population at or below the poverty line. Fifty-one percent of the American Indian population is on welfare, the largest of any racial group considered. Only 13 percent of the non-Hispanic white population is receiving welfare payments.

In summary, these data reveal that American Indians continue to lag behind other racial groups in many indicators of socioeconomic well being. Labor force participation rates, poverty levels, and income inequality figures reveal a particularly disturbing picture of the overall quality of life for American Indians today.

CONTEMPORARY ISSUES FACING AMERICAN INDIAN POPULATIONS

In addition to the socioeconomic problems indicated above, American Indians face other crucial social and political issues that will affect the current population as well as future generations of Indian people. Among these include determinants of American Indian identity, increasing urban populations underserved by traditional tribal governance structures, lack of economic development in urban and reservation locations, and the struggle for Indian control of cultural artifacts and symbols.

American Indian Identity

Scholars addressing this issue have noted that traditional Indian perceptions of identity were intimately tied to the concepts of place and kinship (Cornell, 1988). In the contemporary American Indian experience, the importance of geographical location and extended family relationships remains for many a central feature of Indian identity. On the other hand, federal Indian policy has focused primarily on the concept of blood quantum as the sole criteria for identifying who are American Indians (Jaimes, 1992). And while federal court decisions have supported differential tribal government criteria for individual recognition as a member (Deloria and Lytle, 1982), federal government agencies have encouraged a one-fourth or greater degree of Indian blood as indicative of status as American Indian (Joe, 1991). Over the past several decades, however, census data have documented a demographic pattern that has raised important questions concerning the fluid nature of Indian identity.

Table 11–2 presents American Indian population totals based on United States Census data from 1960 to 1990. These past three decades have evidenced the largest increases in the American Indian population in the United States ever recorded by census enumerations. In 1960, the American Indian population was 523,591. By 1970, the population of American Indians grew by over 50 percent, evidencing a numerical increase of almost 200,000 people. The 1980 census figures reported the American Indian population of 1,364,033, an increase of over 70 percent. The American Indian population has continued to increase over the past decade, although the rate of increase has declined from the previous historical records. In 1990, census reports indicated that the American Indian population was 1,959,234, a 37.9 percent increase over the 1980 total. Demographers who have closely followed these

TABLE 11-2
American Indian Population Totals and Percent Changes for 1960, 1970, 1980 and 1990

Census Year	Total Population	% Change
1960	523,000	46
1970	792,730	51
1980	1,364,033	72
1990	1,878,285	38

Nagel, 1995; p. 951.

dramatic increases over the past three decades report corresponding data on birth and death rates over the same periods that suggest these increases cannot be attributed solely to natural increases in the American Indian population (Passel, 1976; Passel and Berman, 1986). Rather, they argue that a significant, albeit unknown, proportion of the increases are the result of individuals who previously did not identify as Indian for census purposes but have chosen to do so over the last three decades. This issue notwithstanding, still other demographers continue to stress that the census continually undercounts the American Indian population.[1]

Some scholars of the American Indian experience have noted that these increases correspond with a resurgence in the political, economic, and cultural activities of American Indians in the United States (Cornell, 1988; Snipp, 1989; Nagel, 1995). As mentioned previously, American Indian collective action began to increase dramatically in the late 1950s and early 1960s, primarily as a reaction to the disastrous federal Indian policies of the 1950s. The Indian protests to the unilateral policy of termination were followed by another period of political activism during the 1970s. These activities have been followed in the 1980s by more focused collective action involving the return to traditional hunting and fishing activities. Sanctioned by historical treaty rights gained through various land cessions during the late 1800s, and more recently reinforced by U.S. Supreme Court decisions, the reassertion of these rights has provoked considerable controversy in the states of Washington and Wisconsin (Josephy, 1982; Whaley and Bresette, 1994).

One interpretation of these events and the subsequent increases reported in census enumerations of American Indians focuses on the concept of ethnic renewal (Nagel, 1995). Beginning with the repudiation of the termination policies of the 1950s, and continuing with the increased political activities of American Indian people during the 1970s and 1980s, a historical context has emerged in which people of Indian decent, who previously identified as non-Indian, have engaged in "ethnic switching." That is, prior to 1960, many mixed-blood people and their descendants, as a result of past federal policies that encouraged assimilation and acculturation of Indian people into the dominant society, internalized dominant American society norms and values and chose to identify themselves racially as non-Indian. However, an increase in American Indian political activities during the last three decades, coupled with changes in the political culture as a result of these and other civil rights activities, has contributed to an increase in the numbers of individuals of Indian ancestry who now are willing to reclaim their status as American Indians. And while common wisdom has led some to believe that these individuals have engaged in "ethnic switching" primarily based on economic incentives, there are several reasons to suggest otherwise. First, tribal governments still maintain the sovereign rights to decide the official criteria for tribal membership and therefore determine who is eligible for the rights and benefits of membership in that tribal group. Second, the various public and private social institutions that provide economic, educational, and heath related services to Indian people typically require evidence of degree of Indian blood and/or tribal membership documents to qualify for them. In short, although self-identification through the census may be easy to accomplish, the ability to identify as Indian in order to benefit from long-term tribal, public, or private financial support is highly unlikely.

The changing identity patterns among people of Indian descent is also problematic for efforts to increase social cohesion within urban Indian communities. In the city of Milwaukee, for example, a recent effort by American Indians to mobilize for collection action suggests that the politics of Indianness has the potential to hinder efforts to address the needs of urban Indian constituencies. As a result of a year-long effort to secure federal funding to support a project to address the political and economic needs of Indians in the city, a grant was awarded to a local nonprofit Indian economic development agency to facilitate the creation of an urban governance structure that would identify and act on the needs of the Indian community. In numerous meetings held to secure community support and involvement in the project, American Indian identity or community membership criteria were debated. After the federal agency agreed to fund the project (with a substantially reduced budget and timeline), a number of meetings were held to increase awareness of the project and to facilitate the ambitious program. During the course of all of these meetings, however, the issue of just who was an Indian for the purposes of the project continued to sidetrack the mobilization effort. In many instances, individuals who had documented tribal memberships or were "papered Indians" argued for restricted blood quantum eligibility requirements, while others who lacked official documentation on their membership in a particular tribe, or had documented tribal memberships in tribes with more inclusive membership criteria, argued in favor of self-identification or community recognition.

Discussions also focused on differential perceptions of what the project represented to the community. For example, some perceived that the Indian community had been and would continue to be led by Indian "wannabes," who had little knowledge of what "real" Indians want and need. Others believed that only certain tribal groups were being represented in the effort. Still others perceived that the effort was being co-opted by a small group of insiders who would usurp the funding for their own economic benefit and not that of the larger Milwaukee Indian community. The agency board of directors administering the project became so disillusioned with its lack of progress that they seriously considered returning the remaining monies to the funding agency and discontinuing the project. The project, now under a new name and a separate organizational structure, has struggled to continue, primarily through the hard work of volunteers and in-kind support from various Indian and non-Indian institutions in the city. Nevertheless, the inability to reach a consensus on the issue of who is a member of the Indian community has been a major stumbling block for the project.

Urban American Indians

Over the past four decades, American Indians have increasingly become an urban population. Scholars attribute the urbanization of American Indians to several factors. Large numbers of American Indians migrated to urban areas in the 1940s to work in factory jobs left vacant by non-Indian workers who joined military forces during WWII (Cornell, 1988). Federal government relocation programs begun in the 1950s also contributed to the continuing migration of American Indians from rural reservations with few economic opportunities to large urban centers across the United States (Sorkin, 1972). Corresponding with these relocation efforts, federal government support for reservation economic development declined, which further contributed to a growing urban Indian population that is far removed from reservation communities, extended families, and clan relationships. As a result of the growing urban population, 1980 census data revealed that the majority of American Indians in the United States resided in urban areas.

According to 1990 U.S. Census data (O'Hare, 1992), however, only four of the country's largest cities have American Indian populations reaching 1 percent of the total population: Phoenix (2 percent); San Diego (1 percent); San Jose (1 percent), and Milwaukee (1 percent). Perhaps more importantly, urban Indians frequently lack access to those resources that tribal governments provide to reservations communities. For example, the Indian population in the greater Milwaukee metropolitan area has been estimated to be as large as eight thousand. This figure is larger than that for any single reservation population in the entire state, making American Indians in the city of Milwaukee the largest Indian population in the state of Wisconsin. However, as members of a number of different sovereign nations, American Indians who reside in the city have differential access to tribal resources, the right to participate in tribal political activity, and in some instances, an inability to legally claim their identity as members of a particular tribal group. Without the ability to use place and kinship as the source of one's Indian identity, many urban Indians must turn to the more contemporary identifiers of tribal voting rights, access to tribal resources, membership in supratribal organizations, and participation in community activities to foster their identity as native people.

The urban experience has facilitated a tremendous growth in the number of supratribal organizations and activities to meet the needs of an increasingly urbanized Indian population. In the city of Milwaukee, for example, there are over twenty different Indian organizations and agencies devoted to improving the economic condition, health, and social welfare of the Indian community. Unfortunately, in Milwaukee and other major cities, the total population of Indian people does not translate into a significant source of political power to advance Indian agendas, elect Indian public officials, or even have modest influences on local elections. Moreover, elected officials who make decisions concerning the allocation of federal, state, and local resources have not lost sight of this lack of political clout. Indian constituencies can be generally ignored by these public officials simply because there are virtually no political consequences for their lack of action.

Federal block grant programs provide a good example of this urban Indian social problem. Federal block grant monies have become an important source of revenue for many urban minority groups to enhance economic development and increase social services in their communities. Because decisions on the allocation of block grants are controlled by local political units, block grant monies are a primary means for public officials to reward constituents for their political support. However, in the case of urban Indians, the inability to significantly influence local elections results in an inequitable share of these federal dollars. In Milwaukee, for example, there is only one nonprofit Indian agency that receives funding through its federal block grant program. Its mission is to contribute to the economic development of the Indian population in the city through technical support services for Indian entrepreneurs, financial planning, and advocacy. Unfortunately, the amount of support for these efforts has been considerablely less than that for similar agencies that service other minority groups in the city with larger population bases than the Indian community.

Based on my experiences with individuals involved in the program, as well as my own observations having served on the board of directors for the agency over the past six years, often local public officials act on an erroneous assumption that Indian entrepreneurs either have direct access to tribal government resources or other federal support programs. Moreover, they are keenly aware of the lack of numbers (i.e., Indian voters) in their districts. One city council subcommittee meeting on economic development in which I gave testimony on the financial needs of the agency provides a telling example of this problem. In the meeting, local alderman raised questions concerning the actual numbers of Indians in the city, whether their residency was permanent or seasonal, and whether they are eligible to vote. Obviously, knowledge of the lack of significant numbers of Indian voters in the city is not lost to these officials when decisions are made concerning the allocations of these important federal dollars.[2]

Economic Development

As the previous discussion of the labor force participation indicates, the lack of economic opportunities for American Indians both on and off the reservation is another important contemporary issue. O'Hare (1992) examined minority business ownership between 1982 and 1987 and found that American Indian business ownership rates continue to be among the lowest in the United States. He reports that while Asian Americans own nearly 30 percent of all minority businesses, only 2 percent are owned by American Indians. A further examination of business ownership revealed an American Indian business ownership rate of fourteen per thousand persons compared to an African American rate of fifteen, a Hispanic rate of twenty-one, and an Asian rate of fifty-seven. Moreover, while American Indian business ownership improved between 1982 and 1987, the rate of growth was among the lowest of all minority groups examined. Only African Americans had a lower rate of growth in business ownership.

The lack of economic opportunities for urban Indians has been compounded more recently by efforts to exclude Indian people from affirmative action programs that reserve portions of government contracts for construction projects and procurement services for minority businesses. As a result of the U.S. Supreme Court decision in the *City of Richmond* v. *J. A. Croson Company* (1989), these programs have been scrambling to refine their funding protocols. The *Croson* decision has forbidden local, state, and federal governments from targeting contracts for construction and services based on mere population breakdowns. In other words, a finding that a minority group's proportion of a particular geographical area is greater than their representation in a particular industry is no longer enough evidence to prove discrimination, and therefore, not worthy of legal remedy. The decision has resulted in many governmental units freezing their minority programs pending studies that more explicitly document discrimination in various sectors of the economy. In the city of Milwaukee, the decision had its first major impact on the construction of a massive underground sewage system to prevent untreated water runoff from city sewers from pouring into the Milwaukee River and Lake Michigan. Per the *Croson* mandate, the city paid consultants to conduct a study to document specific cases of racial discrimination in the city construction industry. Perhaps not surprisingly, the study did document past discrimination for African-Americans, the largest minority population in the city, but ignored American Indians "due to their lack of sufficient numbers"

(MMSD, 1990). This created a new de facto categorization of minority status in the city which left American Indians out for the purposes of these minority programs.

And the effect of *Croson* has not been limited to the construction industry. Following this decision, the Milwaukee city council considered legislation that defined minority status in the city for the purposes of allocation of minority contracts for virtually all city government programs and services, as either being African American or a woman (Wysocky, 1989). After an initial backlash from a number of Indian individuals and agencies in the city, the legislation has been removed from consideration at this time. Nevertheless, the event does not bode well for American Indians. A similar situation has occurred in the city of Chicago as well (Murry-Ramos, 1994). Given that both cities have relatively large concentrations of American Indians, the prospects for other urban Indians in cities with even smaller Indian populations are not promising (*News from Indian Country* 1993).

Recent reservation economic development efforts have focused primarily on gaming operations. While initial federal legislation only allowed bingo halls, the 1988 Indian Gaming Regulatory Act authorizes tribes to negotiate with states for the operation of any games of chance that are legal in that state (Sokolow, 1990). The subsequent growth in Indian gaming operations has been phenomenal. In the state of Wisconsin, for example, there are now seventeen casinos operated by the state's eleven tribes. Nationwide, gross revenues for 1994 were estimated to exceed $1 billion dollars (Schultze, 1994).

One of the largest and most successful tribal casino operations in the United States is in the state of Connecticut. The Foxwoods High Stakes Bingo and Casino in Ledyard is operated by the Mashantucket Pequots. The gambling complex is reported to draw upwards of fifteen thousand people per day and employs over ten thousand people. Annual revenue from the resort is estimated to be over 600 million dollars (Boudreau and Peppard, 1994).

For some American Indian tribes, then, the gaming operations are creating employment and other economic development opportunities that far exceed any previous efforts. It is important to note, however, that gaming operations are not without both short- and long-term problems. In most instances, the operations are subject to compacts with non-Indian casino management companies who provide seed monies and business services (Cozzetto, 1995). Tribal governments must also negotiate gaming compacts with state governments which are increasingly including agreements to share revenues with the states (Boudreau and Peppard, 1994). And as these operations have become more numerous and increasingly profitable, the casinos are now receiving more scrutiny by public officials, the general population, and even tribal members themselves (Firkus and Parman, 1995). There are some indications from the public discourse on casino operations that when states have the opportunity to renegotiate these compacts, there could be even more restrictions on the operations, as well as more sharing of revenue. For example, in the state of Wisconsin, gaming compacts are scheduled for renewal over the next three years, and both the tribes and the state officials are taking hard stands on the issues of total revenues, profits, and state and local compensation (Rinard, 1997). Finally, common wisdom suggests that gaming revenues have the tendency to decline over the long term as the novelty of the activities wears off. In short, the long-term viability of these economic enterprises is certainly not guaranteed.

Controlling Cultural Artifacts and Other Symbols

Still another contemporary issue for American Indian people focuses on efforts to regain control over Indian cultural symbols and artifacts. The Native American Graves Protection and Repatriation Act (1990) has given tribal governments new authority to regain control over Indian artifacts that previously have been under the control of numerous museums and archives. Museums are now required to notify tribal groups of any artifacts that they have in their possession, and to allow groups to have access to them if they so desire (Echo-Hawk, 1992). The use of Indian caricatures as mascots and commercial symbols also is receiving considerable attention in recent years. A number of secondary schools, colleges, and universities have made decisions either to change their Indian mascots or enacted policies that limit their participation in sporting events with those institutions that continue to use Indian images as mascots. Of course, many other sports teams and educational and economic institutions continue to employ these images, arguing that doing so demonstrates honor and respect for the American Indian. The 1995 World Series of Baseball, for example, was played by two teams that use Indian symbols and caricatures, with very little attention devoted to the implications of this event for Indian people and their ability to control their images and symbols. Finally, it is important to note that there continues to be some disagreement among Indian people as to whether this issue is worthy of the attention it is now receiving. The members of the Cherokee Nation in the state of Georgia, for example, actually produce styrofoam tomahawks used by Atlanta Braves fans to show support for the team.

SOCIAL CHANGE AND AMERICAN INDIAN SOCIETIES

The sociological literature on social change has developed four distinct perspectives on change in American Indian societies: a world system approach; a variation on the concept of colonialism; a structural differentiation analysis; and a resource mobilization perspective. The world system approach focuses primarily on an economic analysis of change in American Indian societies. It employs the concepts of core, peripheral, and semiperipheral states to account for the economic marginalization of Indian societies for the benefit of non-Indian ones. The marginalization process has been described as one of incorporation of Indian societies into various world economic systems. One example of the world system approach to understanding change in American Indian societies is the work of scholars who have examined the incorporation of indigenous societies into the rapidly expanding world mercantile economy European between the seventeenth and nineteenth centuries (Kardulias, 1990). The world system approach emphasizes the overwhelming impact of the European fur trade on American Indian societies by documenting the changing patterns of procurement, migration, and social organization of indigenous groups as they competed for market positions in the fur trade (Kardulias, 1990). Utilizing world system terminology, the incorporation of native societies into the emerging world capitalistic economic system accounts for the current peripheral status of Indian nations in relation to core societies such as the United States.

Other world system scholars have focused more exclusively on the concept of incorporation, arguing that the traditional concept of incorporation is limiting, particularly in light of the American Indian experience in the United States. Hall (1987), for example, questions the extent to which native societies have been incorporated completely into the world economy. Cornell (1988) has acknowledged the importance of economic incorporation for explanations of social change in American Indian societies, but also has demonstrated the importance of political and cultural incorporation for a more complete understanding of contemporary American Indian societies. These scholars argue that it remains an empirical question what stage of political and cultural incorporation Indian societies are currently in, and suggest that more emphasis should be placed on accounts of the variation in the degree of incorporation among different tribal groups and individual tribal members. Another perspective on social change in American Indian societies expands on the concept of colonization. Snipp (1986), for example, has describe the Native American experience in the United States as a process of internal colonization. His analysis suggests that this process has resulted in two distinct historical periods. The first began with the transformation of American Indian societies into internal colonies. The second period completed the transformation process by creating depend nations. As the United States economic and military power enabled it to emerge as the dominant political entity in North America, the sovereignty of native societies changed from that of complete authority to control their political and economic affairs, to that of a more limited form that is continually subjugated to the United States. Through this process, then, Snipp argues that independent Native American societies became internal colonies, subject to increasing administrative control, as well as disastrous policies of assimilation, land dispossession, and culture loss. By the early 20th century, Snipp posits that Native American societies had become dependent nations. The dependency of native societies on the U.S. government has been accomplished by a persistent assault on native culture, the desolation of traditional governments, the establishment of the reservation system, and direct administrative control through the Department of Interior, and its Bureau of Indian Affairs (Snipp, 1986). And while contemporary Indian policy has become increasingly less restrictive by allowing tribal governments a larger degree of control over their affairs, the political and economic decisions of Indian people remain subject to administrative approval, and legal challenges to the tribal sovereignty continue, some with considerable success (O'Brien, 1991).

Other scholars of social change in native societies have focused on a resource mobilization model to understand change in Indian society. The resource mobilization perspective has developed generally in sociology in response to analyses of collective action in the United States during the last three decades (Jenkins, 1983). It focuses on concepts such as organization, leadership, money, and social cohesion, and examines the ability of groups to mobilize these resources to achieve social change. Of primary importance to this perspective is the argument that collective responses to historical conditions should not be viewed as irrational actions. Rather, collective action, if and when it does occur, can be viewed as rational activity on the part of rational actors who have examined the various rewards and costs for particular actions, albeit within particular historical contexts (Jenkins, 1983). This perspective challenges previous accounts of collective action and social change in native societies that have either viewed change as an overwhelming process in which native people have had no role or choice, or that when responses are made, they are primarily irrational. One example of the usefulness of this approach is the work by Thornton (1986). Focusing on the Ghost Dance movements of the late 1800s, Thornton argues that decisions by various tribal groups to participate in the two major Ghost Dance movements in 1860 and 1890 are rational responses to the dramatic depopulation of Indian people during the years immediately preceding the movements. Others have focused on the more contemporary Indian movements, particularly the American Indian Movement (AIM), or Red Power movements of the late 1960s and 1970s (Fortunate Eagel, 1992; Hauptman, 1986). For many scholars of federal Indian policy, the activities of the latter movements were catalysts for the return to a more bilateral relationship between the federal and tribal governments in the 1970s (Cornell, 1984).

Still another perspective on social change in American Indian societies is the structural differentiation analysis of Champagne (1989). He views social change as the institutionalization of increased specialization of relations among the various institutions and rules of order in societies. As such, his analysis focuses on the concept of institutional flexibility, or societal differentiation as a predictor of the degree to which indigenous societies will be able to accept and implement changes in their major macro-level political, cultural, economic, and normative orders. Champagne argues that permanent or institutionalized change will occur only if the preexisting social order evidences a level of societal differential and collective solidary that transcends more particularistic comments to village bands or kinship groups. A corollary hypothesis of structural differentiation theory, then, is that less differentiated societies have less capacity for change because of the segmented nature of their social order. Conversely, more differenentiated societies, those that evidence more specialization or differentiation among their various social orders, have a greater capacity for institutionalized change. Champagne's work in this area of social change has examined the institutional configurations of tribal groups in order to identify which forms of institutional differentiation are related to major social trends of change and continuity in American Indian societies.

All three perspectives offer several possible scenarios for the future. To the extent that political and economic incorporation of American Indian societies continues, a return to some version of a termination approach to federal Indian policy may be anticipated. For example, in the historical context of large federal government budget deficits and a lack of public support for tax increases, arguments favoring the end of the unique political status of Indian people could emerge. The treaty rights movements in the state of Wisconsin, of which the spearfishing controversy has gained the most public attention, is evidence of the potential for non-Indian backlash to increasing American Indian political and economic activities (Whaley and Bresette, 1994). Indian political activity, in the form of legal challenges to arrests for fishing practices in violation of state laws, is in itself an example of the degree of political incorporation of Indian people into the dominant culture legal institutions. And while supporters of assimilation policies should welcome this activity as evidence of the ability of Indian people to operate effectively in the U.S. legal institutions, federal court approval of Indian involvement in these traditional fishing activities were met with considerable protest activity by those who view this right as unconstitutional. Indians find themselves in a "catch-22" situation of exercising avenues for political and economic advancement encouraged by dominant cultural values, while such behavior is perceived by the dominant society as further evidence of the lack of need for federal protection through a unique political status.

The economic success of tribal gaming operations also creates the potential for a similar backlash. As still another example of the economic incorporation of Indian people into dominant American society, gaming revenues have resulted in a significant number of tribal governments now administrating multimillion dollar tribal budgets. These success stories in tribal economic development would appear to be welcomed by those who support a smaller role by the federal government in terms of financial support for tribal governments. For example, Boudreau and Peppard (1994) note that the Machantucket Pequots' Foxwoods Casino in Ledyard, Connecticut, employs over ten thousand, making it now the second largest employer in the region. However, these researchers examined the attitudes of local residents of the Machantucket Pequots' Foxwoods Casino and found that as annual revenues have increased, in general, public attitudes toward the tribe have become more negative. In addition, they report that an overwhelming majority feel that the tribe should share profits with the state of Connecticut.

In spite of these trends, however, the increasing economic power of tribal governments bodes well for Indian opportunities to mobilize for collection action. This is particularly relevant to efforts to resist non-Indian efforts to place restrictions on gaming enterprises. The economic success of the bingo and casino operations provides tribal governments and their constituencies an excellent opportunity structure to utilize direct and mobilization resources to increase the economic and political capacities of Indian people. The direct resource of money is the most obvious asset by which tribal governments can service their group interests, as well as both enhancing their position in the dominant political system and influencing other actors with that system. Gaming profits provide tribal governments with increasing revenue to meet the economic needs of tribal members through the development of the local infrastructure, diversify the economic base through nongaming economic development projects, and in a few instances, per capita monetary payments. Mobilization resources such as organizational networks and effective leadership also are enhanced by the success of the gaming operations. As individual tribal governments share experiences related to the gaming operations, new networks and mutual commitments are developed. These networks provide a vehicle by which tribal governments are able to share new ideas, solutions to problems, and other strategies to enhance economic and political goals. The gaming operations also provide a crucial pool of Indian leadership for the future. The skills and experience of running these large economic enterprises provide tribal governments with effective leaders who can put these resources to work in other arenas, both economic and political. The ability to engage in effective marketing and advertising campaigns that frame the gaming and other collective activities of tribal governments in contexts palatable to non-Indian interests are crucial to Indian efforts to sustain increases in economic and political power.

Unfortunately, still other possible scenarios of change in American Indian societies are not as optimistic. Increased economic development through gaming operations is not possible for all Indian people due to differential state laws and regulations. Approximately two-thirds of all native people are members of tribal groups that do not engage in high stakes gambling (Firkus and Parman, 1995). In addition, most of the economic gains from gaming revenue are restricted to those who reside on or near reservations where the gaming operations are located. This situation has the potential for an unequal distribution of the economic gains from bingo and casino operations, particularly for urban Indians who reside in cities far removed from their tribal homelands. The development of better education, health, and human service institutions on reservations is of little direct benefit to many urban Indians who live too far away to use these services. These situations create the potential for diminished social cohesion among a particular tribal group and have serious consequences for the ability of that group to mobilize against threats to these and other economic activities. In addition, the success of a particular gaming operation is subject to a variety of contextual factors, including geographical location, state and local politics, and market saturation. These situations create an unequal distribution of economic success from bingo and casino operations which can reduce the possibility for social cohesion across tribal groups (supratribalism). And as previously discussed, the lack of significant concentrations of Indians in virtually all political units of analysis (i.e., cities, counties, and states) in the United States already places American Indians in a difficult position to mobilize collectively against challenges to their economic and political situations at these levels of political activity. Any other conditions that threaten social cohesion across tribal groups (i.e., supratribal cohesion) even further exacerbates the potential for sustained collective action on the part of American Indians.

This latter situation is particularly problematic for the increasing urban Indian population. Given that the most significant changes in the economic situation of Indian people are the result of tribal gaming operations and the spinoff economic development on or near the reservations where these operations are located, urban Indians far removed from their traditional tribal areas find themselves increasingly dependent on non-Indian urban political and economic institutions that for the most part remain closed to them. As previously discussed, however, the social reality is that urban Indians from different tribal backgrounds and socioeconomic status are unlikely to achieve the level of social cohesion necessary to act collectively to effect change.

NOTES

1. In a related point, Snipp and Nagel (1987), compared census counts of American Indians with supplemental census information on the identification of specific tribal groups, as well as tribal membership roles, and found a high degree of correspondence between one's ability to identify with a specific tribal group and identifying as American Indian for census enumeration. Looking at 1980 census information, they found that over 73 percent of those individuals identifying as American Indian also identified with a particular tribal affiliation as well. Moreover, when comparing tribal enrollment information and census information for 113 tribal groups for which both sources of information were available, Snipp and Nagel found that in over 63 percent of cases, tribal enrollment figures were larger than corresponding census figures.
2. The agency filed an official complaint to the Department of Housing and Urban Development (HUD) citing the lack of funding over the years as evidence of racial discrimination. The official complaint was found to be unsubstantiated by HUD.

BIBLIOGRAPHY

Biolosi, T. "The American Indian and the Problem of Culture." *American Indian Quarterly* 12 (1989), pp. 261–69.

Boudreau, Frances A. and Donald M. Peppard, Jr. "New Game in Town." *Connecticut College Magazine* (1994), pp. 26–29.

Champagne, Duane. *American Indian Societies: Strategies and Conditions of Political and Cultural Survival.* Cambridge, MA: Cultural Survival, Inc., 1989.

Clemmer, Richard O. "Hopis, Western Shoshones, and Southern Utes: Three Different Responses to the Indian Reorganization Act of 1934." *American Indian Culture and Research Journal* 10 (1986), pp. 15–40.

Cornell, Stephen. "Crisis and Response in Indian White Relations: 1960–84." *Social Problems* 32 (1984), pp. 44–59.

______. *The Return of the Native: American Indian Political Resurgence.* New York: Oxford University Press, 1988.

Cozzetto, Don A. "The Economic and Social Implications of Indian Gaming: The Case of Minnesota." *American Indian Culture and Research Journal* 19 (1995), pp. 119–31.

Deloria, Vine, Jr. "The Rise of Indian Activism." in *The Social Reality of Ethnic America,* edited by R. Gomez, C. Collingham, R. Endo, and K. Jackson. Lexington, MA: D.C. Heath, 1974, pp. 179–87.

Deloria, Vine, Jr. and Clifford M. Lytle. *American Indians, American Justice.* Austin: University of Texas Press, 1983.

Echo-Hawk, Walter. "Preface. Special Edition: Repatriation of American Indian Remains." *American Indian Culture and Research Journal* 16 (1992), pp. 1–7.

Fortunate Eagle, Adam. *Alcatraz! Alcatraz! The Indian Occupation of 1969–71.* San Fransico: Heyday Books, 1992.

Firkus, Angela, and Donald L. Parman. *OAH Magazine of History* (Summer 1995).

Hall, Thomas D. "Native Americans and Incorporation: Patterns and Problems." *American Indian Culture and Research Journal* 11 (1987), pp. 1–30.

Hauptman, Laurence M. *The Iroquois Struggle for Survival: World War II to Red Power.* Syracuse, NY: Syracuse University Press, 1986.

Jacobson, Cardell K. "Internal Colonialism and Native Americans: Indian Labor in the United States from 1871 to World War II." *Social Science Quarterly* 65 (1984), pp. 58–71.

Jaimes, M. Annette. "Federal Indian Identification Policy: A Usurpation of Indigenous Sovereignty in North America," in *The State of Native America: Genocide, Colonization, and Resistance,* edited by M. A. Jaimes. Boston: South End Press, 1992, pp. 123–28.

Jenkins, J. Craig. "Resource Mobilization Theory and the Study of Social Movements." *Annual Review of Sociology* 9 (1983), pp. 527–53.

Joe, Jennie. "The Delivery of Health Care to American Indians: History, Policies and Prospects," in *American Indians: Social Justice and Public Policy,* edited by Donald E. Green and Thomas V. Tonnesen. Madison: The University of Wisconsin System, 1991, pp. 149–79.

Josephy, Alvin M. "The Great Northwest Fishing War: The Clashes over Native American Fishing and Hunting Claims," in *Now That the Buffalo's Gone: A Study of Today's American Indians.* New York: Knopf, 1982, pp. 177–211.

Kardulias, P. Nick. "Fur Production as Specialized Activity in a World System: Indians in the North American Fur Trade." *American Indian Culture and Research Journal* 14 (1990), pp. 25–60.

Murry-Ramos, Yvonne. "Urban Indian Agenda Ignored at All Levels of Government." *News From Indian Country,* (1993), p. 13.

———. "City of Chicago MBE/WBE Program: Smoke and Mirrors?" *Urban Visions,* March/April, 1994.

Nagel, Joane. "American Indian Ethnic Renewal: Politics and the Resurgence of Identity." *American Sociological Review* 60 (1995), pp. 947–65.

O'Brien, Sharon. "The Concept of Sovereignty: The Key to Social Justice," in *American Indians: Social Justice and Public Policy,* edited by Donald E. Green and Thomas V. Tonnesen. Madison: The University of Wisconsin System, 1991, pp. 44–108.

O'Hare, William P. "America's Minorities—The Demographics of Diversity." *Population Bulletin* Vol. 47, No. 4 (1992).

Passel, Jeffrey S. "Provisional Evaluation of the 1970 Census Count of American Indians." *Demography* 13 (1976), pp. 397–409.

Passel, Jeffrey S. and Patricia A. Berman. "Quality of 1980 Census Data for American Indians." *Social Biology* 33 (1986), pp. 163–82.

Rinard, Amy. "Gaming Compact Talks Stuck." *The Milwaukee Journal Sentinel,* June 13, 1997, p. 1A.

Schultze, Steve. "Wisconsin Economy: State's Gambling Growth May Have Spoiled the Odds." *The Milwaukee Journal,* March 17, 1994, p. 1B.

Snipp, C. Matthew. "American Indians and Natural Resource Development: Indigenous Land, Now Sought After, Has Produced New Indian-White Problems." *American Journal of Economics and Sociology* 45 (1986), pp. 457–74.

______. *American Indians: First of this Land.* New York: Russell Sage Foundation, 1989.

Sokolow, Gary. "The Future of Gambling in Indian Country." *American Indian Law Review,* 15 (1990), pp. 151–183.

Sorkin, Alan L. *American Indians and Federal Aid.* Washington, D.C.: Brookings Institution, 1972.

Stuart, Paul H. "Organizing for Self-Determination: Federal and Tribal Bureaucracies in an ERA of Social and Policy Changes," in *American Indians: Social Justice and Public Policy,* edited by Donald E. Green and Thomas V. Tonnesen. Madison: The University of Wisconsin System, 1991, pp. 93–108.

Thornton, Russell. *We Shall Live Again: The 1870 and 1890 Ghost Dance Movements as Demographic Revitalization.* Cambridge: Cambridge University Press, 1986.

Whaley, Rick with Walter Bresette. *Walleye Warriors: An Effective Alliance Against Racism and for the Earth.* Philadelphia: New Society Publishers, 1994.

Wysocky, Ken. "Minority Contract Law Unworkable." *The Milwaukee Sentinel,* 1989, p. 1A.

SUGGESTED READINGS

Bachman, Ronet. *Death And Violence on the Reservation: Homicide, Family Violence, and Suicide in American Indian Populations.* New York: Auburn House, 1992.

Cornell, Stephen. *The Return of the Native: American Indian Political Resurgence.* New York: Oxford University Press, 1988.

Champagne, Duane. *Social Order and Political Change: Constitutional Governments Among The Cherokee, The Choctaw, The Chickasaw, and The Creek.* Stanford, CA: Stanford University Press, 1992.

Deloria, Vine, Jr. *Red Earth, White Lies: Native Americans and the Myth of Scientific Fact.* New York: Scribner, 1995.

Fixico, Donald. *Urban Indians.* New York: Chelsea House, 1991.

Gedicks, Al. *The New Resource Wars: Native and Environmental Struggles Against Multinational Corporations.* Boston: South End Press, 1993.

Hall, Thomas D. *Social Change in the Southwest, 1350–1880.* Lawrence: University of Kansas Press, 1989.

Nagel, Joane. *Forthcoming. American Indian Ethnic Renewal: Red Power and the Resurgence of Identity and Culture.* New York: Oxford University Press.

Snipp, C. Matthew. *American Indians: First of this Land.* New York: Russell Sage Foundation, 1989.

Thornton, Russell. *American Indian Holocaust and Survival.* Norman: University of Oklahoma Press, 1987.

CHAPTER 12

Central Americans in the United States

Nestor P. Rodriguez and Jacqueline Hagan

Introduction

In the late 1970s, the seven countries constituting Central America entered into *la crisis,* a period of dramatic social instability. Displaced by the economic and political turmoil, large numbers of Central Americans fled their home communities to seek safety in other countries. Many of the region's displaced population migrated north to Mexico, the United States, and Canada. For tens of thousands of Guatemalans, the journey ended in refugee camps in southern Mexico.[1] For well over a million other Central Americans, the journey took them through Mexico and into the United States, where they settled and established communities in large metropolitan areas, including Los Angeles, Miami, New York, Washington, D.C., San Francisco, Houston, Chicago, Anaheim, New Orleans, and Dallas.[2]

Historically, Latin American migration to the United States has been dominated by Mexican migrants in search of agricultural or manufacturing employment and, more recently, in search of service jobs in U.S. cities. The massive influx of Central American legal and undocumented immigrants since 1980 has changed the composition of the Latin American immigrant and native-born population in the United States. Coming from different countries and ethnic origins, and varying dramatically in the social and financial capital they bring with them, Central American immigrants continue to reshape the social and cultural diversity of the Latin American population in the United States. This Latin American population now includes well educated and unskilled political refugees from El Salvador, wealthy landowners and peasants from Nicaragua, Garifuna (Black Caribs) from Honduras and Belize, and mestizo and Maya groups from Guatemala.

This chapter describes the growth and settlement experience of Central Americans in the United States. We begin the discussion with a brief historical overview of Central American migration to the United States. In this section, we trace the origins of Central American migratory streams to the United States, emphasizing the regional conditions that fueled the mass emigration of hundreds of thousands of Central Americans since the early 1980s. Drawing on historical flow data from the Immigration and Naturalization Service (INS) and recent census data, we describe the changing size, composition, and settlement patterns of Central Americans in the United States. The next three sections of the chapter are dedicated to a discussion of the background and settlement experiences of the four largest Central American populations in the United States: Salvadorans, Guatemalans, Hondurans, and Nicaraguans. In the subsequent section, we briefly profile the smaller Central American populations in the United States—Costa Ricans and Panamanians. We conclude the chapter with a discussion of the social and economic impacts and prospects of Central American communities in U.S. society.

BACKGROUND

Historically, Central American migration consisted largely of intraregional labor migration.[3] Generations of Central American migrant workers and settlers moved freely across the region's loosely defined borders. Receiving nations in the region paid little heed to these well-established migratory flows until the late 1970s, when the region erupted into an economic and political crisis. Civil war in El Salvador, revolution in Nicaragua, and widespread counterinsurgency operations in Guatemala contributed to the displacement and subsequent forced movement of individuals, families, and whole communities.

The massive post-1978 migratory flows forced the governments of some receiving nations (Costa Rica, Honduras, and Mexico) to take measures to limit the number of migrants allowed past their borders, forcing many of the displaced, mostly women and children, to seek temporary shelter in regional refugee camps sponsored by the United Nations High Commission for Refugees (UNHCR). Many of the region's displaced, however, also made their way north to the United States where they joined established communities of kin and friends from their own villages, towns, and communities.

It is difficult to document the historical origin of the Central American population in the United States because, until as recently as 1990, many arrivals were undocumented, having entered the country without papers. Official flow statistics on legal immigration data from INS, however, shows a steady increase in the number of Central Americans legally admitted to the

United States each decade since 1900, with the exception of a slight decline during the 1930 Depression period. From 1901 to 1910, fewer than one thousand Central Americans legally entered the United States. From 1911 to 1920, this figure increased to 17,159. In the following two decades the number declined to 15,769 and 5,861, respectively. During the forties, the number of legal arrivals from Central America increased to 21,831. During the fifties, decade, the total number admitted to the United States doubled, to 44,751. In the subsequent decade, 1961–1970, the figure more than doubled again, to 101,330. There was another large increase during the seventies, when more than 134,640 Central Americans legally entered the United States.

From 1980 on, we see an even more dramatic rise in the number of Central Americans admitted each year to the United States. The number of immigrating Central Americans averaged more than 24,000 in each of the first eight years of the eighties; reflecting the substantial growth in numbers of refugees and migrants fleeing political and economic turmoil in their home countries during this period. The numbers of Central Americans admitted to the United States skyrocketed from 1989 to 1991, when more than 350,000 were legally admitted to the United States.[4] The dramatic increase during this three-year period is somewhat misleading, as it includes several hundred thousand Central Americans who were living in the United States but adjusted their undocumented status to legal permanent status under the Immigration Reform and Control Act of 1986 (IRCA). The INS counts persons who legalized under IRCA in the yearly legal immigrant totals. Included in these figures are a smaller number of Salvadorans and Guatemalans who were also living in the United States in an undocumented status but were granted temporary protected status (TPS) under the 1990 Immigration Act.

The 1980 U.S. census, the first census to release initial figures on the number of Central Americans in the United States, counted 331,219 persons of Central American origin. Ten years later, this number had increased fourfold. As Table 12-1 shows, the 1990 census counted more than 1,323,830 persons of Central American origin, 85.6 percent of whom were born in Central America. These census figures, however, do not include the majority of the undocumented Central American population in the United States, estimated to be more than 500,000 in 1992.[5] In sum, from these figures we can estimate the current size of the Central American population in the United states to be close to two million.

The Central American population in the United States is concentrated in large metropolitan areas. In fact, more than 73 percent of the Central American origin population reside in ten metropolitan areas: Los Angeles, Houston, Chicago, Dallas, Anaheim, Washington, D.C., New York City, Miami, New Orleans, and San Francisco. Part of this residential settlement pattern can be explained by the labor market opportunities in these cities, but, more importantly, in the early 1980s many Central American migrants settled in areas where there was an established community of persons from their own country.

TABLE 12-1
Central Americans in the United States, 1990

Residence (PMSA)	Costa Rican	Guatemalan	Honduran	Nicaraguan	Panamanian	Salvadoran	Other	Total
Los Angeles	10,388	125,091	22,968	33,846	5,281	253,086	2,388	453,048
Houston	1,225	5,897	5,776	3,442	1,208	39,965	173	57,686
Dallas	722	2,242	1,656	1,096	696	10,466	62	16,940
Miami	4,743	8,242	18,102	74,244	6,729	7,339	135	119,534
Chicago	885	15,207	2,666	1,249	1,196	4,722	268	26,193
San Francisco	985	8,139	832	18,408	876	33,660	276	63,176
New York	6,953	18,089	23,487	9,953	23,266	27,169	733	109,650
Anaheim	1,249	7,650	1,259	2,409	707	12,122	52	25,438
New Orleans[1]	701	2,061	9,700	4,208	564	1,116	103	18,453
Washington DC[1]	1,682	9,396	3,525	8,000	3,779	51,893	252	78,527
Other[a]	27,690	66,765	41,105	45,803	47,771	123,543	2,568	355,185
United States	57,223	268,779	131,066	202,658	92,013	565,0811	7,010	1,323,830
Total Metropolitan	29,533	202,014	89,961	156,855	44,302	441,538	4,442	968,645

Notes: [1]These are not PMSAs but MSAs.
[a]Other includes other small rural areas
Source: Bureau of the Census, *1990 U.S. Census of Population and Housing*. Washington, D.C.: U.S. Government Printing Office, 1993.

During their initial period of settlement in the United States particular metropolitan areas tended to be associated with particular ethnic and national Central American groups. For example, in 1985, the large majority of Hondurans lived in one city—New Orleans. Similarly, Nicaraguans were heavily concentrated in Miami.[6] As Table 12-1 shows, however, the Central American population in the United States had grown so substantially that by 1990 all of the groups were increasingly well dispersed across all metropolitan areas.

Table 12-1 suggests an interesting relationship between the size of a Central American population and the proportion of the population that resides in metropolitan areas—the larger the size of the population the more likely its residents will reside in metropolitan areas. Among several factors, the clustering effect of social networks in settlement is likely affecting this relationship, and doing so in a circular manner. That is, larger populations produce a greater number of social networks, which in turn produce a greater concentration of the population, which in turn attracts a larger population.

The massive immigration of Central Americans in the 1980s created new issues of Latino community growth in the United States. One issue was that the arrival of Central American refugees helped stimulate opposition to U.S. foreign policy in Central America. Uprooted from their homelands, many Central Americans migrated to the United States against the background of intensive U.S. involvement in the political conflicts of the Central American isthmus. In El Salvador and Guatemala, the United States supported government forces against popular insurrections, and in Honduras U.S. agents organized and led an army of counter revolutionaries, contras, to topple the Sandinista government of Nicaragua.

For many critics of U.S. foreign policy in Central America, the massive influx of Central Americans literally brought home the human face of U.S. interventionist policy in Central America. In towns and cities across the country, U.S. citizens organized a sanctuary movement to support arriving Central American refugees. Many in the sanctuary movement, as well as fellow travelers, openly and actively criticized U.S. support of unpopular government regimes and contras in Central America. U.S. government agents conducted surveillance on sanctuary movement leaders and Central American activists in various U.S. areas and took action to restrict their activities.

A second issue created by Central American immigration in the 1980s concerned the diversification of the Latino population in the United States. Especially in the Southwest, the arrival of Central Americans created new national, and sometimes ethnic (Garifuna, Maya, etc.), components within the larger Latino population. The full consequences of this development are still unfolding, but some early effects are evident. In some cases, community leaders from Central America have provided political resources for advancing general Latino goals, such as bilingual education and improved work conditions for Latino workers. In other cases, Central American national and ethnic groups have increased the competition for community resources (jobs, public space, etc.) among the larger Latino population. No doubt among the greatest effects is the enlargement of the foreign-born segment of the Latino population, which in some localities is larger than the U.S.-born segment of Latinos. In several ways, U.S.-born Latinos contrast sharply with their foreign-born counterparts, for instance in language usage, customs, and national orientations. Yet this social and cultural orientation should not be overstated, as it is mainly a creation of first-generation immigrants during the earlier phases of immigrant settlement.

A third product of the large-scale arrival of Central American immigrants in the 1980s is the development of transnational communities between Latino settlements in the United States and sending communities in Central America. Similar to the transAtlantic community networks established by earlier European immigrants, Central Americans, like other Latino immigrants, have constructed sturdy transnational linkages to their communities of origin in Central America. In urban centers like Chicago, Houston, and Los Angeles, Central American immigrants maintain strong social, cultural, and economic ties to family members and friends in Central America through mail, telephone, and courier communication and through travel between the United States and Central America.

Earlier U.S. immigrants also stayed in contact with their communities of origin, but not with the facility afforded by today's advanced communication and travel technology. Many Central Americans can easily communicate with relatives in some of the most geographically remote Central American regions through long-distance telephone service and can fly back to their communities of origin within a matter of hours. Some Central Americans contact people in their home countries through the Internet. No European immigrant in the earlier part of the century could enjoy such close contact. It remains an empirical question, however, whether such transnational ties are reproducing among second generation Central Americans.

The arrival of political refugees and economic migrants from throughout Central America introduces significant new dimensions to the growth of this country's Latino population as well as to the growth of the U.S. population in general. As some segments of the U.S. Latino population prepared to ascend into higher institutional levels through assimilation and Civil Rights measures, the recent arrival of hundreds of thousands of Central Americans reinforced the Latino population's connection to its Latin American heritage.

SALVADORANS

Estimates indicate that by 1985 between 20 to 35 percent of the total population of Salvador (5.3 million in 1987) may have been displaced by civil war.[7] The 1990 U.S. census figures suggest that many of the internally displaced fled to the United States. As Table 12-1 shows, the 1990 census counted over 565,000 persons of Salvadoran origin, 82 percent of whom were foreign born. This figure does not include the lion's share of the undocumented Salvadoran population, estimated to be close to 300,000 in 1992.[8] Salvadorans are by far the largest of the five Central American immigrant groups in the United States. They represent close to half of all persons of Central American origin in the United States. The large majority of Salvadorans in the United States reside in urban areas with an established Latino population. About one half of all Salvadorans in the United States reside in California cities, especially in the Los Angeles area. Washington D.C. and Houston rank second and third in urban residence for Salvadorans in the country.

Table 12-2 provides a demographic profile of the five Central American groups in terms of age, sex, fertility behavior, household characteristics, and education. The fact that the majority of Salvadoran immigrants arrived in the 1980s is reflected in the group's young age structure. As the table shows, the median age of persons of Salvadoran origin in 1990 was 26.3, slightly lower than that of other Central American groups. The small difference is probably due to the presence of U.S.-born children. The young age structure of the Sal-

TABLE 12-2
Selected Sociodemographic Individual Characteristics of Central Americans in the United States, 1990

		Educational Attainment[a]		Ability to Speak English[b]			
	Median Age	Some College	BA	Don't Speak English Well	Speak Other Language	% Female aged 15 and over	Fertility Children born to Women 35 to 44[c]
Costa Rican	29.5	31.1	10.4	37.3	83.9	54.4	2.1
Guatemalan	27.0	15.9	3.9	65.2	94.3	48.3	2.6
Honduran	27.5	21.3	5.6	54.9	88.8	55.9	2.5
Nicaraguan	27.1	24.0	9.3	59.5	92.2	52.6	2.5
Panamanian	30.7	35.7	13.1	24.1	74.4	59.7	2.0
Salvadoran	26.3	13.2	3.5	67.8	95.1	48.5	2.6
Other	27.9	20.5	6.1	40.6	80.0	51.4	2.7
Total (N)	27.1						

[a] Persons 18–24 have been grouped with those 25 and over for each category and then the number, data reported from table 115, 1990 U.S. Population Census.

[b] Persons 5 and over data reported from table 115 is the N for each group, 1990 U.S. Population Census.

[c] Persons in labor force 16 years and older, data reported from table 117, U.S. Population Census.

Source: Bureau of the Census, *1990 U.S. Census of Population: Social and Economic Characteristics: United States.* Washington D.C.: U.S. Government Printing Office, 1993. Tables 114–119.

vadoran population, coupled with birth rates (2.5) higher than those of native born groups (1.9), is indicative of a population that will continue to increase in size in the coming years, contributing to the growth of more Salvadoran ethnic communities throughout the country. Table 12-2 also shows the diversity of household size and composition among Central American groups. What is perhaps most interesting is the large percentage of Salvadorans (31 percent) who live in households consisting of related kin, other than spouse, children, parents and parents-in-law. Studies have shown that Latino immigrants (undocumented or legal), arriving with little or no money, rely on immigrant households already in the United States to ease their settlement process.[9] These immigrant households consisting of kin and friends provide a host of resources, to undocumented newcomers, such as food, a place to sleep, and information about jobs. Thus, as undocumented migration continues and family members join newly legalized Salvadorans in the country, the size and composition of Salvadoran households should continue to swell and diversify.

Table 12-3 provides information on the groups' differential human capital skills, labor force participation, English proficiency, and occupational characteristics. As the table shows, more than 32 percent of all Salvadorans in the country speak English well despite the fact that most Salvadorans arrived in the United states less than ten years ago. This finding suggests that Salvadoran

TABLE 12-3
Selected Sociodemographic Family Characteristics of Central Americans in the United States, 1990

	Families	Persons per household	Subhouseholds with other than kin	Fertility rate of women aged 35–44	Median Income in households[d]	Poverty status of families[e] (%)
Costa Rican	13,279	3.2	11.4	2.2	30,785	13.4
Guatemalan	56,978	4.1	26.3	2.6	24,569	21.1
Honduran	27,445	3.6	20.6	2.5	22,109	25.5
Nicaraguan	42,608	4.1	26.0	2.5	25,717	20.1
Panamanian	21,622	2.9	9.3	2.0	27,872	13.1
Salvadoran	121,115	4.2	31.0	2.6	23,729	22.3
Other	1,740	3.6	16.0	2.7	22,304	28.4

[d] Reported number is of those is families with 3 or more workers, data reported from table 118, 1990 U.S. Population Census.
[e] Families below the poverty level in 1989, data reported from table 121, 1990 U.S. Population Census.
Source: Bureau of the Census, *1990 U.S. Census of Population: Social and Economic Characteristics: United States.* Washington D.C.: U.S. Government Printing Office, 1993. Tables 118–121.

immigrants are not incorporated into ethnic enclaves where English acquisition is not necessary, as is the case, for example, among Cubans in Miami.

Table 12-2 and 12-3 also suggest a pattern of educational and occupational mobility for Salvadorans in the United States. While only 3.5 percent of the Salvadoran population in the United States had completed college in 1990, more than 13 percent were enrolled in post-secondary education, including colleges and universities. By 1993, the number of college graduates of Salvadoran origin had increased to 4.6 percent.[10]

Like many recent Latino immigrants in the United States, Central Americans have high rates of labor force participation. It is especially high for Salvadorans; more than 76 percent of all Salvadorans sixteen and older are in the labor force. This figure slightly exceeds the labor force participation rate of most Los Angeles immigrant groups and is far higher than the 64 percent foreign-born and 65 percent native-born working populations.[11] Despite their high labor force participation rates, Salvadorans are overwhelmingly concentrated in blue-collar craft and low-skilled service jobs. This employment track is typical of most newcomer Latino immigrant populations living in U.S. metropolitan areas and contrasts remarkably with the heavy manufacturing and agricultural work activities of earlier Latino (mostly Mexican) immigrants in the United States.

Being the largest of the Central American populations in the United States, the impact of Salvadoran newcomers in U.S. areas is more pronounced than that of other Central American groups. In the largest U.S. concentrations of Central Americans—Los Angeles, Washington, D.C., and Houston—the presence of Salvadoran newcomers is visible especially in ethnic business enterprises and in a host of voluntary organizations supporting the community life of these Central American newcomers and other Latino immigrants. Salvadoran businesses include restaurants, especially *pupuserias,* notary offices to help with immigration papers and other paperwork, and voluntary organizations including soccer teams, legal aid offices (e.g., CARECEN), and groups supporting the reconstruction of war-torn communities of origin in El Salvador.

In the 1980s the new and developing Salvadoran communities in the United States experienced dynamic growth as social turmoil uprooted thousands of families from rural and urban localities in El Salvador. While many Salvadoran newcomers shied away from political activities in the United States, others quickly organized political education programs to inform U.S. citizens about the destructive consequences of U.S. intervention on behalf of the Salvadoran government and its National Guard forces. Salvadoran organizers collaborating with U.S. citizens, such as through CARECEN, organized delegations to visit devastated areas and refugee camps in El Salvador. Some Salvadoran activists participated in forming community-based organizations to provide assistance to newcomers and to promote self-help support among Salvadoran immigrants. Groups involved in political education and community based organizing also associated with U.S. members of the sanctuary movement in support of the many Salvadoran and other Central American refugees who entered the United States as undocumented immigrants. Of course, not all Salvadoran newcomers identified with leftist causes; a segment of the Salvadoran population in the United States supported the Salvadoran government and its war against the popular insurrection, and in doing so attempted to counter the efforts of their leftist compatriots.

In the early 1990s, as civil war strife ended in El Salvador, many of the Salvadoran organizers continued their community efforts but shifted their goals to assisting the maintenance of Salvadoran immigrant communities in the United States. Efforts of these community-based organizations include building health clinics, providing legal assistance for Central Americans facing deportation by the INS, and promoting public school programs closer to the distinct cultural needs of Central Americans.

GUATEMALANS

Guatemalans are the second largest Central American population in the United States, although with only about half the number of Salvadorans. The 1990 U.S. census counted close to 300,000 Guatemalans residing in the country. This figure does not include the majority of the undocumented Guatemalan population in the United States, estimated to be more than 120,000 in 1992.[12] Like their Salvadoran counterparts, Guatemalans tend to live mainly in metropolitan areas. Seventy-five percent of Guatemalans counted by the 1990 census lived in U.S. metropolitan areas. Fifty-nine percent of the total Guatemalan population in the country in 1990 was concentrated in the three metropolitan areas of New York, Los Angeles, and Chicago. The Los Angeles metropolitan area alone contained almost half (46.5 percent) of all Guatemalans counted in the 1990 census.

Children are predominant among Guatemalans in the United States, keeping the median age of this population at 27.0 years. As Table 12-2 shows, over half (51.7 percent) of Guatemalan females are younger than 15 years of age. The young age structure of Guatemalan immigrants is indicative of their recent arrival in the United States. Among Guatemalan females age 35 to 44 years, the birth rate is 2.6, which is similar to the level of other Central American women in the United States, with the exception of lower fertility levels among Costa Rican and Panamanian women of similar age.

The 1990 census found 4.1 persons per Guatemalan household. Over one-fourth (26.3 percent) of the Guatemalan households had members that were not relatives of the heads of household. As mentioned earlier, the nonrelatives often include boarders in family households and members of households of unrelated individuals, such as young men or women who work together.[13] Less than one-fifth of the adult Guatemalan population in the United States has attended college or received a college degree. Low levels of education translate into unskilled labor market niches in the U.S. economy. As Table 12-3 shows, while more than 75 percent of all Guatemalans are working, less than a quarter hold white-collar jobs. Most are concentrated in the blue-collar sector or low-paying service jobs, such as private domestic and maintenance work.

Being predominantly a population of new immigrants, Guatemalans in the United States have several characteristics reflecting their recent arrival. For example, a majority of Guatemalans (65.2 percent) counted in the 1990 census reported not being able to speak English well, and a large majority (94.3 percent), reported being able to speak another language. No doubt "another language" refers mainly to Spanish, but for many of the Guatemalans of Maya origin the reference also could be to an indigenous language (e.g., Cachiquel, Kanjobal, Quiché) of the more than twenty existing in Guatemala today.

Overall, the sociodemographic characteristics of Guatemalan newcomers are similar to those of their Salvadoran counterparts in the United States. This, of course, is not surprising. The similarity comes from fairly similar settings of emigration, settings characterized by severe economic and political instability, and from the socioeconomic backgrounds of populations with the greatest propensity to emigrate in large numbers, such as poor urban workers and peasants. These workers and small farmers, and their leaders, often face the harshest conditions of the Central American maelstrom.

While sharing difficulties with other Central Americans, the Maya who emigrated from Guatemala in large numbers in the 1980s also represented a unique experience—the suffering of indigenous communities under government repression. To eliminate guerrilla movements in the early 1980s, the Guatemalan army launched a counterinsurgency campaign that laid waste to over 400 Maya villages in the country's highlands. While the Guatemalan generals' scorched-earth policy received scant attention abroad, it forced the relocation of a massive number of Maya from Guatemalan highland provinces. To escape political violence, many Maya relocated to refugee camps in nearby southern Mexico; others migrated to areas in the United States (e.g., Los Angeles, Chicago, Houston, and Indiantown in Florida). Some Maya in the United States eventually migrated to Canada when it became clear that the U.S. government would only rarely offer them political asylum.

Many Guatemalans who were not directly affected by the political violence were indirectly affected when war conditions restricted their economic activities. In the western highlands of Guatemala, for example, the fear of political violence reduced travel and trading by Maya artisans and peasants and thus severely stifled the operation of marketplaces, which constitute a central means of economic exchange for indigenous communities. The broad cyclical decline of Latin American economies in the late 1970s and 1980s kept the Guatemalan economy depressed and further added to the decision of many Guatemalans to seek survival in U.S. areas.

The U.S. film *El Norte,* which dramatized the undocumented migration to the United States of a brother and sister fleeing a Guatemalan death squad, portrays a fairly accurate account of the hardships faced by many Guatemalan immigrants who arrive in U.S. areas without support from relatives or close friends. Lacking official permission to enter the United States or authorization to work, these immigrants usually must survive in the lowest sectors of the labor market, finding work in low-paying, irregular jobs with little or no opportunity for advancement. For many undocumented Guatemalan male workers without family support, street-corner labor pools become the chief employment agencies.

In U.S. metropolitan areas where Guatemalans from the same communities of origin have settled, large social networks have evolved to provide assistance to recent arrivals. For example, in Los Angeles, Chicago, Houston, and other settings, the Maya from Guatemala have established substantial community structures from their social networks, and newcomers thus find strong support in locating initial housing and information about jobs. Maya in Houston from the Guatemalan departments of *Totonicapán* and *El Quiché,* for example, have developed numerous social networks among kin, friends, and co-workers. These networks generally provide temporary housing to recent arrivals and help male arrivals find cleaning jobs in retail stores and female arrivals find domestic jobs in family households.[14]

As is the case with Central American communities in the United States, settlement patterns among Guatemalans vary by immigrant legal status, social class, and by ethnicity in the case of Maya newcomers. It is mainly the undocumented and peasant and working-class Guatemalan immigrants who often depend heavily on social networks to survive in the initial settlement stages because of a lack of resources. This also characterizes the situation of many Maya newcomers, but their involvement in social networks seems also to result from strong traditional bonds formed in their communities of origin. Very affluent Guatemalan newcomers, however, seem to lack even the immigrant image and function quite well in mainstream institutions. This is not surprising, since these are usually wealthy families from Guatemala City experienced in several world areas where they vacation, send their children to school, and maintain extra residences.

Guatemalans in the United States have added to the diversity of the country's Latino population. Guatemalans not only increase the presence of the Central American population, but in several U.S. areas add a striking ethnic dimension to the Latino population, especially the presence of different Maya subcultures. Yet, it is not clear if this new cultural dimension will have a lasting effect, since many of the Maya youth converge with the adolescent social and cultural styles of the large Latino youth population.

Hondurans and Nicaraguans

The combined number of Hondurans and Nicaraguans constitute about one-fourth of the Central American immigrant population in the United States. As

Table 12-1 shows, Hondurans are concentrated in New York and Nicaraguans are concentrated in Miami. For Hondurans, the second and third largest settlements are the Los Angeles and Miami areas, respectively. Among Nicaraguans, the second and third largest settlements are the Los Angeles and San Francisco areas. Both Central American populations are predominantly located in metropolitan areas; however, Nicaraguans had a larger metropolitan residence rate (77.4 percent) than Hondurans (68.6 percent).

Hondurans and Nicaraguans have median ages of 27.5 and 24 years, respectively. These median ages fall within the age range of Central Americans in the United States in general. However, Table 12-2 shows that in contrast with Salvadorans and Guatemalans, Hondurans and Nicaraguans have larger percentages of females over the age of 15, 55.9 percent and 52.6 percent, respectively. Moreover, the completed fertility level among Honduran (2.5) and Nicaraguan (2.5) women is slightly lower when compared to Salvadoran (2.6) and Guatemalan women (2.6). Further, both Hondurans and Nicaraguans have a smaller proportion of households with nonrelated members than is found among Salvadorans and Guatemalans. Coming from one of the poorest and most densely populated countries in the Western Hemisphere, Hondurans have the lowest household median income, $22,109, of all Central American nationalities in the United States. Yet, over a fifth of Hondurans and Nicaraguans reported having at least some college education, suggesting some socioeconomic diversity among these immigrant groups.

Table 12-3 shows that the percentages of Hondurans and Nicaraguans who reported in the 1990 census that they did not speak English well was smaller than found among Guatemalans and Salvadorans, but larger than found among Costa Ricans and Panamanians. Relatively greater fluency in English and higher college experience no doubt influence the greater white-collar employment of Hondurans and Nicaraguans than Salvadorans and Guatemalans. Of course, white-collar employment can also be located within ethnic businesses operating in the Spanish-speaking neighborhoods of many Central Americans in the United States. The fact that Honduran workers have a relatively high rate of white-collar employment (43 percent), but that Honduran households have a low median income level ($22,109) suggests that white-collar Honduran employees are located mainly in the lower paid jobs of office work or in businesses with low incomes.

Large-scale immigration fueled the growth of the Honduran and Nicaraguan populations in the United States in the 1980s. Like Salvadorans and Guatemalans, Hondurans and Nicaraguans emigrated from regions heavily afflicted by economic and political instability. In the 1980s, areas in Honduras became the encampment and training places from which the large U.S.-supported contra army staged incursions against the Sandinista-led government of Nicaragua. Honduras also became a major center of U.S. operations against the insurrection movement in nearby El Salvador. To some observers, Honduras in the 1980s resembled the war setting of Southeast Asia

20 years earlier.[15] While the Honduran military prospered from the large-scale U.S. presence in the 1980s, *la crisis* severely restricted the Honduran economy; by 1986, Honduran workers faced an unemployment rate of 41 percent.[16]

To add to the economic pressures faced by large numbers of Honduran workers and their families, Honduran military leaders initiated a policy of repression against any person or group that questioned the U.S. military presence, the contra camps, or the growing number of human rights abuses. A 1982 law prohibited traditional forms of popular protest, and hundreds of leaders of "popular organizations" (unions, campesino groups and student and professional organizations) were killed.[17] For thousands of Hondurans, emigration became the only escape from political violence and economic collapse.

In the United States, the presence of Garifuna (Black Caribs) among Hondurans gives this Central American population a racial and cultural diversity similar to Maya/mestizo differences among Guatemalans. Migrating from Caribbean coastal areas of Honduras in the 1980s, Garifuna newcomers have established communities in Los Angeles, Houston, New Orleans, and New York (Bronx). In these areas Garifuna communities organize and celebrate social and cultural events commemorating their African Honduran heritage. In Houston, for example, these events include a Garifuna Day Festival in late November and occasional intercity soccer tournaments, which draw the participation of Garifuna from Belize and nonblack Hondurans as well as Latinos in general.

In some cases, the sizable Honduran populations in several U.S. cities (e.g., Los Angeles, New Orleans, and New York) are an outcome of U.S.-Honduran linkages that predate the large Honduran influx of the 1980s. For example, the origin of the Honduran population in New Orleans, which numbered about ten thousand in 1990, is related to that city's early involvement in U.S.-Honduran trade. It is an involvement that dates back to 1899, when the first boatload of bananas from Honduras reached New Orleans.[18] Honduran mestizos and Garifuna have developed a strong attachment to New Orleans, seeing the city as an important social and cultural center and occasionally traveling from there to participate in Honduran social events in Houston. Yet, preferred areas of destination may vary by different immigration cycles, and for new Honduran immigrants the preferred top three U.S. metropolitan destinations in the mid-1990s were New York, Miami, and Los Angeles.[19]

In Nicaragua, the social climate was even worse in the 1980s. The reorganization of the Nicaraguan economy to achieve agrarian reform, including state farms, under war conditions had little chance for success. Reorganizing the economy included revitalizing agricultural production after the devastation of the popular armed struggle against the *somocista* forces. This was done in the context of heated strifes between major landowners and contentious *campesino* groups, all in the larger context of the regional economic crisis and a counterrevolutionary war supported by the United States government. Worn down by long years of war, a U.S. trade embargo, and a rate of inflation that reached twenty thousand percent in 1988, Nicaraguans voted in a new national leadership in a 1988 election arranged by the Contadora Peace Accords adopted by Central American countries in 1987.[20] For thousands of Nicaraguans, the decision had been made earlier to change their living conditions by migrating to the United States and other countries.

For Nicaraguans, Miami emerged as the preferred metropolitan settlement area in the 1980s. The earliest flows of Nicaraguans to Miami included wealthy landowners and small town elite who emigrated following the 1979 Sandinista revolution. More recent flows from Nicaragua to the United States developed in the late 1980s and early 1990s, and include peasants, urban workers, and former government employees. Some of these migrants made their way to Texas, where they temporarily found shelter in makeshift camps in the Lower Rio Grande Valley in southern Texas before boarding buses for Miami when they were allowed to proceed farther into the United States. For some, initial settlement in Miami occurred in a baseball stadium converted into a makeshift reception center.[21] Miami's attraction for a large number of Nicaraguans is partly based on its geographical and cultural familiarity. It is the closest major U.S. city to Central American countries, and it has a substantial Caribbean atmosphere.[22] As a center of Latino anti-Communist organizing, Miami also served as a major coordinating point for the U.S. Central Intelligence Agency's operations against Nicaragua's Sandinista government in the 1980s.[23] The Nicaraguan presence in Miami continues to make a significant contribution to the city's Latino mosaic even after some Nicaraguans left the city to restart businesses in their home country in the relatively more stable interval of the 1990s.

For most of the 1980s, the U.S. government aided the settlement of Nicaraguans in the United States by granting them political asylum (from Sandinista rule) at a rate 10 times greater than Salvadorans and 14 times greater than Guatemalans. From 1984 to 1990, this amounted to 12,480 approved applications of political asylum for Nicaraguans, compared to 1,170 approved applications for Salvadorans and a mere 171 approved applications for Guatemalans.[24] Not surprisingly, after the Sandinistas left power in the late 1980s, the granting of political asylum to new Nicaraguan applicants declined.

OTHER CENTRAL AMERICANS

The 1990 census counted small numbers of persons of Costa Rican and Panamanian origin. As Table 12-1 shows, Panamanian and Costa Rican immigrants total less than 10 percent of the entire Central American population in the United States. In contrast to the urban settlement pattern of other Central American populations in the United States, Panamanians and Costa Ricans are dispersed across metropolitan and nonmetropolitan areas throughout the United States. Nonetheless Panamanians are concentrated in New York, while the favored urban destination for Costa Ricans is Los Angeles.

Table 12-2 shows that the educational and occupational attainments of Panamanian and Costa Ricans significantly exceed those of other Central American groups. As Table 12-3 shows, entering the United States with human capital skills translates into a greater likelihood of white-collar professional employment. In contrast to the other Central American groups that are concentrated in unskilled and blue-collar jobs, more than half of all Costa Ricans and Panamanians hold white-collar and professional occupations. The different incorporation of these two groups is also indicative of their predominantly legal entry into the United States, many of whom enter with student visas and work authorization. This is especially important because it creates labor market opportunities and facilitates mobility.

Central Americans in the United States: A Cold War Product

While Central Americans have been coming to the United States since the turn of the century, the large majority arrived in the 1980s. The context of this massive influx of more than one million immigrants and refugees was the Reagan-Bush era of aggressive U.S. militaristic policies, opposing what was perceived to be communist expansion in Central America, sometimes at great cost to Central American lives. A secular economic decline, *la crisis,* also contextualized the large-scale migration of Central Americans to the United States. As atrocious as U.S.-supported counterinsurgency policies were in Central America in the 1980s, and they were extremely atrocious as descriptions of Central American political violence indicate,[25] one cannot simply attribute the mass migrations of Central Americans to the United States on the causal factor of U.S. intervention. This intervention affected the hostile environment that spurred migration, but by itself it probably did not determine the migration. International migration is a complicated social process, and among peasant and working-class peoples often develops from human strategies for family survival.

In our view, U.S. foreign policy towards Central America, however, did affect the immigration and settlement prospects of many Central American newcomers and the conditions of their U.S. communities. As we mentioned above, the U.S. government approved applications for political asylum at a much higher rate for persons emigrating from the Sandinista-led country of Nicaragua than it did for refugees from Guatemala and El Salvador. In many U.S. Central American communities, therefore, newcomers attempted to build lives, families, and community institutions under the strain of undocumented status. The fear of INS raids among Salvadorans and Guatemalans in cities such as Los Angeles and Houston contrasted sharply with the friendlier atmosphere that Nicaraguans with political asylum had in Miami in the early to mid-1980s, a setting of Latinos described by President Reagan as his kind of Hispanics.

Yet, while the heavy political origins of many Central American communities in the United States affected the settlement expenses of initial immigrant cohorts, in the mid-1990s, the emerging second generation of Central Americans seems to be structuring their community growth in a post-political manner. For the most part, right and left political concerns and movements are distant to this generation, which is primarily concerned with issues of education, employment, and social and cultural survival in often unfriendly and alien urban environments.

Notes

1. Elizabeth G. Ferris, *The Central American Refugees* (New York: Praeger Publishers, 1987); Edelberto Torres-Rivas, *Report on the Conditions of Central American Refugees and Migrants.* Hemispheric Migration Project, Occasional Paper Series (Washington, D.C.: Center for Immigration Policy and Refugee Assistance, Georgetown University, 1985); Sergio Aguayo, *El Exodo Centroamericano: Consequencias de un Conflicto* (Mexico, D. F.: Secretaria de Educacion Publica (SEP), 1985); Sergio Aguayo and Patricia Weiss-Fagen, *Central Americans in Mexico and the United States* (Washington D.C.: Center for Immigration Policy and Refugee Assistance, Georgetown University, 1988); Jacqueline Hagan, "The Politics of Numbers: Central American Migration During a Period of Crisis, 1978–1985" (unpublished Master's thesis, University of Texas at Austin, 1986).
2. For example, see Allan Burns, *Maya in Exile: Guatemalans in Florida* (Philadelphia: Temple University Press, 1993); and James Loucky, "Rejection, Reaffirmation, or Redefinition: Changing Identity of Indigenous Guatemalans in Los Angeles" (paper presented at annual meeting of the American Anthropological Association, November 17, 1988); and Nestor P. Rodriguez, "Undocumented Central Americans in Houston: Diverse Populations" *International Migration Review* 21(1):1987: pp. 4–25; and Jacqueline Hagan, *Deciding to Be Legal: A Maya Community in* Houston (Philadelphia: Temple University Press, 1994); and Terry A. Repak, *Waiting on Washington: Central American Workers in the Nation's Capital* (Philadelphia: Temple University Press 1995); and Cecilia Menjivar, "Immigrant Kinship Networks: Vietnamese, Salvadorians, and Mexicans in Comparative Perspective" (Division of Social and Cultural Studies, Graduate School of Education, University of California, Berkeley, California, [Forthcoming]); and Norma Chinchilla and Nora Hamilton, "New Directions for Latino Public Policy Research," The Center for Mexican American Studies, The University of Texas at Austin, Austin, 1989.
3. Jacqueline Hagan, "The Politics of Numbers."
4. U.S. Immigration and Naturalization Service, *Statistical Yearbook* (Washington, D.C.: U.S. Government Printing Office, 1979, 1983, 1985, 1992, 1991).

5. Michael Fix and J. S. Passel. *Immigration and Immigrants: Setting the Record Straight* (Washington D.C.: The Urban Institute, 1994) p. 24, table 2.
6. Jacqueline M. Hagan, "The Politics of Numbers"; and Michael Fix and Patricia Ruggles, "Impact and Potential Impacts of Central American Migrant on HHS and Related Programs of Assistance" (Washington D.C.: The Urban Institute, 1985).
7. Linda Peterson, *Central American Migration: Past and Present* (Washington D.C.: U.S. Government Printing Office, 1986) U.S. Bureau of the Census, Center for International Research, November.
8. Michael Fix and J. S. Passel, *Immigration and Immigrants: Setting the Record Straight.*
9. For example, see Harley L. Browning and Nestor Rodriguez, "The Migration of Mexican Indocumentados as a Settlement Process: Implication for Work," in *Hispanics in the U.S. Economy,* George Borgas and Marta Tienda, eds. (Academic Press, 1985).
10. Ruben Rumbaut, "Origin and Destinies: Immigration, Race, and Ethnicity in Contemporary America" in *Origin and Destinies: Immigration, Race, and Ethnicity in America,* Silvia Pedraza and Ruben Rumbaut, eds. (Belmont: Wadsworth, 1996).
11. Ibid.
12. Michael Fix and J. S. Passel, *Immigration and Immigrants: Setting the Record Straight.*
13. Nestor Rodriguez and Jacqueline Hagan, "Apartment Restructuring and Latino Immigrant Tenants Struggles: A Case Study of Human Agency," in *Comparative Urban and Community Research,* 1992: Vol. 4.
14. Nestor Rodriguez, "Undocumented Central Americans in Houston: Diverse Populations" *International Migration Review,* 1987: Vol. 21, No. 1, pp. 4–25; and, Jacqueline Hagan, *Deciding to Be Legal: A Maya Community in Houston.*
15. Nestor Rodriguez and Ximena Urrutia-Rojas, "Impact of Recent Refugee Migration to Texas: A Comparison of Southeast Asian and Central American Newcomers," in *Mental Health of Immigrants and Refugees,* Wayne H. Holtzman and Thomas H. Bornemann, eds. (Austin, TX: Hogg Foundation, 1990).
16. Benjamin Medea, *Don't Be Afraid, Gringo: A Honduran Woman Speaks from the Heart* (San Francisco, CA: The Institute for Food and Development Policy, 1987), xviii.
17. Terry A. Repak, *Waiting on Washington: Central American Workers in the Nation's Capital,* p. 45.
18. J. Mark Ruhl, "The Economy," in *Honduras, A Country Study,* 2nd Ed., James D. Rudolph, ed. (Washington, D.C.: U.S. Government Headquarters, Department of the Army, DA Pam 550-551, 1984) p. 19.
19. U.S. Immigration and Naturalization Service, *Statistical Yearbook,* 1994, table 19.
20. Terry A. Repak, *Waiting on Washington: Central American Workers in the Nation's Capital.*

21. U.S. Immigration and Naturalization Service, *Statistical Yearbook,* 1994, table 19.
22. Ibid; and Guillermo J. Grenier and Lisandro Perez, "Miami Spice: The Ethnic Cauldron Simmers," in *Origins and Destinies: Immigration, Race, and Ethnicity in America,* pp. 360–72.
23. Sharon S. Russell,. "Migration Patterns of U.S. Foreign Policy Interest," in *Threatened Peoples, Threatened Borders: World Migration and U.S. Policy,* Michael S. Teitelbaum and Myron Weiner, eds. (New York: W.W. Norton & Company, 1995), p. 51.
24. Ibid.
25. For example, see Roger Burbach and Patrick Flynn, eds., *The Politics of Intervention: The United States in Central America* (New York: New York Monthly Review Press, 1984); and Douglas Valentine, *The Phoenix Program* (New York: Avon Books, 1990), epilogue, pp. 420–29; and Mark Danner, *The Massacre at El Mozote* (New York: Vintage Books, 1994); and Marilyn Anderson and Jonathan Garlook, *Daughters of Corn: Portraits of Guatemalan Women* (Willimantic: Curbstone Press, 1988). While atrocities against Central American communities have diminished after the implementation of the Contadora Peace Accords, a high level of human rights abuses by death squads and paramilitary groups continues in the 1990s.

CHAPTER 13

Japanese Americans: Stories about Race in America

Lynn H. Fujiwara and Dana Y. Takagi

The history of Japanese Americans provides a revealing glimpse at the broader contours of racism and race relations in American society. We note that virtually all contemporary narratives about Japanese Americans focus on either their status as a "model minority" or, alternatively, the legacy of the internment experience during WWII. If the former is a story of overcoming oppression through assimilation, the latter is an account of the heavy penalties of racism and oppression. These stories about Japanese Americans, while certainly not the only ones, reflect the fact that Japanese Americans have been the object of extraordinary racism and have also been praised as models of assimilation. Clearly, there is a good deal at stake in the telling of different stories about racial groups. In the case of Americans of Japanese ancestral heritage, the contrast between narratives of assimilation and oppression is part of a continuing debate about the significance of race (and racism) in American society. Depending on one's point of view, Japanese Americans represent the promise or failing of American society. Indeed, Japanese Americans and other Asian Americans have frequently been depicted as Horatio Alger–style subjects (though not necessarily as speakers) in racial and political debates.

We suggest here that such stories ought to be seen as part and parcel of a historiography of American race relations. Making sense of Japanese American experiences in the United States means that we must take the whole of the historical record as well as the stories that we tell about that record. In short, our understanding of Japanese Americans is, at least in part, a reflection of the state of race relations in the larger society. Too often the study of racial groups in the United States narrowly focuses on the experiences of this or that group—as if race as an object of study was not deeply woven into the fabric of American politics and cultural practices. Japanese American experiences offer an excellent example of how a small minority group—a group that is largely considered outside or excluded from the black-white models of race—reveals significant currents in the historiography of race in the United States. In what follows we offer an overview of some key prewar, wartime, and postwar issues for Japanese Americans—the period of labor immigration, internment and WWII, and postwar racial/ethnic identity. The dominant tale about this history is that Japanese Americans have overcome a history of racism and become a "model minority." Indeed, this story is so thoroughly embedded in discussions about Japanese Americans that it is taken for granted as fact. We argue here for a different story—less self-congratulatory about race in America than the assimilation story—in which Japanese Americans continually help to refigure nationalism and citizenship in American society.

Demography and Immigration

Japanese Americans are a small minority group. Especially when compared with the dramatic increases in other Asian American populations between 1970 and 1990, for example Filipinos and Koreans, Japanese Americans are a relatively static population. The main reason for the difference is that while increases in other Asian American populations are fueled by natural population increases and the arrival of new immigrants, increases in the Japanese American group are based mainly on new births. According to the 1990 census, there were 847,562 Japanese Americans in the United States, of whom some 95 percent live in the western states (including Hawaii). Table 13-1 illustrates that in the western states over half of all Japanese Americans live in California (312,989, or 52.3 percent), and an additional 30 percent in Hawaii (247,486 or 29.1 percent).

Table 13-1 also shows that, historically, the Japanese American population has always been a tiny fraction of the total U.S. population. Moreover, during the late nineteenth and early twentieth centuries, the number of European immigrants dwarfed the number of Japanese immigrants. However, Japanese Americans have been at the center of strong nativist reaction at several key moments during the first half of the twentieth century. Some of the demography of present-day Japanese Americans—in particular the concentration of Japanese Americans in California and Hawaii—was shaped by different economies of race, immigration, and reaction over a hundred years ago.

TABLE 13-1
Distribution of Japanese in the United States, 1900-1990

Year	U.S. Including Hawaii and Alaska	Continental U.S.	West Coast States	%	California	%	Hawaii	Alaska
1900	85,716	24,326	18,269	75.1	10,151	41.7	61,111	279
1910	152,745	72,157	57,703	80.0	41,356	57.3	79,675	913
1920	220,596	111,010	93,490	85.1	71,952	64.8	109,274	312
1930	278,743	138,834	120,251	86.6	97,456	70.2	139,631	278
1940	285,115	126,947	112,353	88.5	93,717	73.8	157,905	263
1950	326,384	141,773	98,310	69.3	84,956	59.5	184,611	N.A.
1960	464,368	260,195	178,985	68.6	157,317	60.5	203,355	818
1970	588,324	369,755	259,456	70.2	213,277	57.7	217,715	854
1980	700,974	459,631	323,351	70.4	261,822	57.0	239,748	1,595
1990	847,562	598,010	393,405	65.8	312,989	52.3	247,486	2,066

Source: Setsuko Matsunaga Nishi (1995, p. 109), adapted from Kitano (1969, pp. 162-164); Thomas (1952, p. 575); U.S. Bureau of the Census (1973, Table 1; 1983, Table 62; 1993, Table 253).

There are three different eras of Japanese immigration: first, the period of labor immigration, 1884–1924; second, the post-WWII war brides, 1945; and third, the post-1965 era. The first period is the most significant for our discussion here—in that the bulk of the contemporary Japanese American population traces their roots to the Issei (first generation) immigrants of the late nineteenth and early twentieth centuries. Immigration comes to a virtual standstill between 1924 and 1965 except for the arrival of Japanese brides of U.S. servicemen stationed in Japan. In the post-1965 era Japanese emigration to the United States is negligible. Hence, in what follows, we focus mainly on the pre-1924 era for our discussion.

PREWAR AND LABOR IMMIGRATION, 1884–1924

The history of Japanese immigration to the United States and Hawaii begins with the political economy of labor shortages and Western expansionism in the late nineteenth century. Very specific historical transitions in Japan, Hawaii, and California set the conditions in which a circuit of labor migration from Japan to Hawaii to California flourished. In Japan, the so called bloodless revolution of 1868, the Meiji Restoration, led to a series of economic reforms with uneven economic effects in different parts of Japan. Economic dislocation wrought by changes in the tax system, for example, prompted farmers and peasants in Southern Japan to seek better opportunities elsewhere. In Hawaii, the colonization of the islands, a transition motivated by the desire of American-based sugar cane entrepreneurs, dispossessed native Hawaiians of their land and eventually paved the way for Hawaii to become first a territory of the United States in 1900 and later, the fiftieth state of the Union (1959). In the United States, westward expansion—an economic transition built around railroad construction, large-scale, industrial-style agricultural production, and manufacturing—created a demand for a flexible and mobile labor force.

American owners of sugar plantations in the Kingdom of Hawaii took the initiative in 1884. Two years after the passage of federal exclusion of Chinese labor (1882) from the United States, and after three decades of the importation of Chinese labor to Hawaii's plantations, recruiters for the sugar planters turned to Japan for their next source of labor. The Japanese were the second installment in a long line of Asian immigrants who labored on the plantations that included the Chinese before them and Koreans and Filipinos after. Using a modified contract labor system, the initial wave of laborers was recruited through emigration companies on behalf of sugar planters in Hawaii. In this system, laborers were advanced passage to Hawaii (which was deducted from earned pay once in Hawaii), obligated for a three-year period of work, paid a typical wage of nine dollars a month, and subject to strict rules governing working conditions, with punishment meted out for relatively minor infractions. By the 1890s, however, a small fraction of Japanese laborers, those with enough capital to finance their own passage across the Pacific, came on their own.

Between 1884 and 1894, approximately 30,000 Japanese went to Hawaii and Chan (1991) reports that some 50 percent of the new workers stayed in the islands. In the period 1894 to 1908, another 125,000 Japanese laborers arrived in the islands. As Takaki (1983) reports, at first Japanese laborers were welcomed by planters because many brought wives and children. The presence of women and children—family units—created a civilizing atmosphere, one that planters felt was lacking in the case of Chinese labor. However, the presence of families may have also contributed to Japanese departures from the islands as soon as their contracts expired. Wages and working conditions in the plantation system, as Takaki reports, were repressive. Japanese workers' discontent with the plantation system quickly changed planters' views of Japanese labor. The sugar industry moved quickly at the turn of the century to recruit anew a different group of laborers—Koreans and later, Filipinos—to the islands.

Japanese immigration to the western states, as was the case with Hawaii, was stimulated by the demand for labor. But unlike the contract labor and plantation economy of Hawaii, the western states, especially California, offered a different niche for Japanese immigrant labor than Hawaii. One flow of Japanese emigration to the United States mainland came directly from

Japan, the other, from Hawaii. Ichihashi (1924?) reports that Japanese immigrants were engaged in agricultural pursuits—share and cash tenancy and migratory labor (for example in sugar beet harvesting). As Fugita and O'Brien (1991), following in the tracks laid by earlier writings of Bonacich (1973, 1980) and Modell (1977), point out, a significant portion of Japanese immigrants moved into petit bourgeois positions in the California economy.

The movement of a substantial number of Issei out of wage labor created a Japanese American ethnic economy. While some have hinted that the ethnic economy heralded Japanese entry into the "middle class," a kind of "pulling themselves up by the bootstraps," most of the scholarship has suggested otherwise. As growers, tenant farmers, and small business owners, Japanese immigrants had a limited number of occupational alternatives. The proportion of wage labor jobs, for example those that had been available to Chinese workers during the 1850s, 1860s, and 1870s, had diminished by the turn of the century. The Issei found themselves excluded from unions and all but barred from public service jobs. California agriculture offered both migratory labor jobs and, unlike in the previous thirty years, opportunities for share and cash tenancy. Small business enterprises—from specialty crops to fishing to city trades—provided the Issei with an economically viable alternative to a virtual apartheid against nonwhites in the California economy.

Not that Japanese Americans managed to escape outright racism and discrimination. A series of legislative acts that targeted the Japanese are emblematic of the key role that Asian immigration played in the race politics of early-twentieth-century America. Unlike in Hawaii, where Japanese were the largest ethnic group in the islands at the turn of the century, the Japanese in California were but a small fraction of the U.S. population. However, as Daniels (1971) has so clearly demonstrated, size of a minority group has little to do with nativist reaction.

Four key acts aimed at the Japanese indicate the level of nativist fury against granting rights—civil and property—for Japanese immigrants. Both the 1908 Gentleman's Agreement and the 1924 National Origins Act involved federal limitations on Japanese immigration. The Gentleman's Agreement was an agreement between Japan and the United States to respond to a localized act of discrimination in San Francisco. A year earlier, the school board in San Francisco, emboldened by a rising tide of local anti-Japanese sentiment, segregated Japanese students from white students. The event became a focus of political struggle between the city and the federal government. When the school board refused to back down, the federal government brokered an agreement whereby Japan would discontinue issuing passports to laborers, a move that ostensibly would mollify the complaints of the anti-Japanese movement in California. Japanese arrivals in the United States did not, however, come to a grinding halt. After 1908, a new wave of immigrants from Japan—not laborers, but Japanese wives (through arranged marriages, a practice common in Japan) arrived by the thousands.

The 1913 Webb-Haney bill (also known as the alien land law), named after the two state congressmen authors of the measure, forbade aliens ineligible for U.S. citizenship from buying or leasing land in California. Thomas reports that the amount of land bought by the Issei during the first decade of the twentieth century was small. Issei were more likely to be engaged in leasing arrangements. Again, however, although the provisions of the bill did not specify a particular racial group, the historical context of debate and passage of the law was clearly intended to target the Issei. That the Issei responded to this law by placing title in the name of their Nisei children—American citizens by virtue of being born in the United States—infuriated anti-Japanese forces. Subsequent state legislation moved to block such "loopholes" in the land laws.

The Webb-Haney law raised the question of citizenship rights for the Issei and Nisei, an issue that emerged again during internment. Japanese, along with other Asian subgroups, were considered ineligible for citizenship—a right that was tested in 1922 in the Supreme Court. In *Ozawa* v. *United States,* the plaintiff argued that he ought to be considered eligible for citizenship. He argued that although he had been born in Japan, he had been educated in the United States, worked in the United States, believed in the U.S. constitution, and had virtually staked his life and family in America, not Japan. The court did not agree, citing a 1790 naturalization law stipulating that only whites are eligible to become citizens. Citizenship requirements were not changed for Japanese until 1952, under the terms of the McCarran-Walter Act.

The 1924 National Origins Act stands out as one of the most repressive immigration laws in American history. This policy, in effect until 1965, established quotas or limits on the numbers of immigrants who could enter the United States from different parts of the world. Again, this act, though it did not name the Japanese, has been widely recognized as a piece of legislation aimed at curtailing Japanese immigration. The act distinguished between two categories of immigrants—quota and nonquota. The annual quota was set at 2 percent of foreign-born citizens residing in the United States at the time of the 1890 census. However, since the Supreme Court, in the 1922 *Ozawa* case, found Japanese ineligible for citizenship, Japanese were inadmissible as immigrants. Thus, the 1924 act hit its mark. Japanese immigration to the United States came to a virtual standstill. This act, together with previous efforts to restrict Japanese immigration, land ownership, and citizenship rights, suggests how Japanese experiences were shaped in significant ways by popular and state responses to them. The Japanese, though a tiny minority group, were subject to extraordinary racial discrimination.

Interestingly enough, some of the key pieces of anti-Japanese legislation might be seen, at least in part, as the lack of codified law about Asian Americans. In terms of racial politics, the primary division has been between whites and nonwhites. The category nonwhite, however, meant black, or possibly Native American. But it never referred directly to Asians—indeed Asians, including Japanese Americans, were historically a noncategory in race relations. And in fact, until 1970 Japanese Americans were lumped together with other nonwhites in the category "Other" by the U.S. census. But anti-Japanese sentiment was real, and hostility to Japanese Americans resulted in a series of regressive legal and political decisions—federal limitations on immigration, for example.

What are the legal and constitutional rights of an ethnic group located outside the black-white paradigm? At no time in American history is the lack of constitutional rights for such a group more clear than during the second World War.

WWII AND INTERNMENT

Understanding the impact of World War II on Japanese Americans has become a center point for sociologists and social scientists engaged in contemporary critical analysis of the Japanese American experience. Recognized as devastating to the emerging Japanese American community was the internment of 120,000 persons of Japanese ancestry into ten different concentration camps dispersed throughout the interior United States in desolate locations. Executive Order 9066, signed by President Franklin D. Roosevelt on February 19, 1942, ten weeks after the bombing of Pearl Harbor, was the official act that gave the Secretary of War authority to designate military areas "from which any and all persons may be excluded as deemed necessary or desirable"(Chan, 1991; 125). Shortly after, the Pacific Coast, including Washington, Oregon, California, and southern Arizona became restricted zones from which Japanese American residents would face mass evacuation and relocation. Approximately forty thousand first-generation (Issei) Japanese—ineligible for citizenship under the arcane Naturalization Law of 1790—were immediately branded "enemy aliens." Some Issei were classified as potentially dangerous by the FBI, rounded up, detained, and in some circumstances incarcerated in high-security institutions. These potentially dangerous enemy aliens were leaders of community organizations, Japanese language school teachers, Shinto and Buddhist priests and priestesses, and newspaper editors. They were arrested under a blanket presidential warrant which did not specify any grounds for the arrests (Chan, 1991; p. 123).

Under the direction of Lt. General John L. DeWitt, the "Civilian Exclusion Order" issued on March 24 began the execution by the U.S. Army of movement of evacuees outside of prohibited and restricted areas. By March 27, DeWitt organized the Wartime Civil Control Authority (WCCA), an agency to expedite evacuation and internment of Japanese Americans. Japanese Americans were relocated first in temporary detainment centers or assembly centers and then moved to internment camps.

The War Relocation Authority (WRA) gave evacuation districts a seven-day timetable from the point of posting the exclusion order throughout the area. All residents of Japanese ancestry in the designated exclusion area were then required to register within two days. Processing and preparation of the evacuees took place on the fourth and fifth days following the posting of the exclusion order, and the actual movement of evacuees took place on the sixth and seventh days (Daniels, 1988; 217). Evacuees were ordered to bring only possessions they could carry. Given the extremely short period of preparation time from the posting of the exclusion order, Japanese residents were forced to abandon their homes, businesses, and other more substantial household belongings. The evacuees were not told where they were going, and families were able to move as units when possible . Resistance to the evacuation order was punishable by criminal penalty mandated by Public Law 503, signed by Roosevelt on March 19.

One of the stories that rationalized the evacuation both during and after suggests that this was an extraordinary act in the midst of a crisis of national security and world war. Now widely recognized as a regrettable mistake, the internment of Japanese Americans stands as a kind of blot in constitutional history. Although Executive Order 9066 was the act that instituted the relocation and incarceration of 120,000 persons of Japanese ancestry, of which two-thirds were American-born citizens, most scholars recognize that the necessary tools for the swift removal had been in place for some time before the United States declared war with Japan. According to Daniels (1988: 201), "Although the stated reason for the evacuation was 'military necessity,' it is known that politicians and not generals were its prime movers."

The immediate fear of a "yellow peril" on the mainland, and the widespread suspicion that Japanese Americans were guilty of espionage were not only falsehoods constructed through war hysteria and panic but also intentionally manipulative propaganda to gain mass support for the evacuation of West Coast Japanese Americans. Daniels (1988:202) notes, "Our military leaders knew that a full-scale invasion of North America was beyond the capabilities of Japanese forces, although hit-and-run naval raids were a possibility. Quite properly, however, our society is subject to political and not military decision-making. What is particularly disturbing about the Japanese American situation is that the civilians used a false doctrine of "military necessity" as a rationale for their political decision, and, in a mood of wartime blindness, the Supreme Court of the United States accepted the claim without requiring even a scintilla of evidence."

By mid-January 1942, politicians and nativist groups launched a political campaign to incarcerate persons of Japanese ancestry. Led by California congressman Leland Ford, as well as the entire congressional delegation from Washington, Oregon, California, and the Native Sons of the Golden West, the California Joint Immigration Committee, and other anti-Japanese groups asked Roosevelt to remove "all persons of Japanese lineage . . . aliens and citizens alike" from the West Coast (Chan, 1991; p.124). The political motivations for evacuation and incarceration, held by West Coast politicians and nativist groups, were primarily extensions from the preceding decades of racist anti-Japanese sentiment and exclusionist policy. According to Fugita and O'Brien (1991), "long-standing racism and particularly resentment over the economic success of the Japanese in agriculture on the West Coast played a major role in precipitating the evacuation" (p. 46). Okihiro and Drummond (1991) argue that particular pressure groups in California's agricultural industry were key players in support of evacuation and enabled the rapid transfer of farms from Japanese to non-Japanese operators, preserving the 1942 agricultural season without serious economic dislocation (pp. 170–174). The anti-Japanese sentiment held strongly by nativist California farm corporations is captured in this statement made by Austin Anson, managing secretary of the Grower-Shipper Vegetable Association:

> We're charged with wanting to get rid of the Japs for selfish reasons. We might as well be honest. We do. It's a question of whether the white man lives on the Pacific Coast or the brown men . . . If all the Japs were removed tomorrow, we'd never miss them in two weeks, because the white farmers can take over and produce everything the Jap grows. And we don't want them back when the war ends either." (Okihiro and Drummond, 1991; p. 170.)

Newspapers played a major role in fomenting hostility and fear toward Japanese Americans. On December 8, 1941, the day after the bombing of Pearl Harbor, the *Los Angeles Times* stated that California was a "danger zone" and civilians needed to be alert for spies, saboteurs, and fifth columnists.

Directed unquestioningly towards Japanese Americans without evidence, the *Los Angeles Times,* as well as the Hearst paper *The San Francisco Chronicle* warned Californians of enemy agents: "We have thousands of Japanese here . . . Some, perhaps many, are good Americans. What the rest may be we do not know, nor can we take a chance in the light of yesterday's demonstration that treachery and double-dealing are major Japanese weapons" (Daniels, 1988: 200).

Discussions on the role of racism, economic resentment, and political interests surrounding evacuation often refer to the contradictory logic of "military necessity." The contradictory logic is laid bare when one compares the different treatment of Japanese Americans on the West Coast and Japanese Americans in Hawaii. In 1942 the census showed over 125,000 persons of Japanese ancestry in the continental United States, while another 150,000 lived in the Territory of Hawaii (Daniels, 1991; 12). However with the exception of about one thousand individuals there was no wholesale evacuation of persons of Japanese ancestry in Hawaii. Fugita and O'Brien argue that if those of Japanese ancestry posed a threat to security, then obviously they would have been more dangerous in Hawaii, which was placed under martial law, and where Japanese Americans were much closer to the war zone (p. 48). The immediate response by the War Department was to transport all Japanese residents of the Hawaiian Islands to the United States mainland and incarcerate them there. However, there was little political and economic pressure for the removal of Japanese in Hawaii: they made up 37.3 percent of the population in the Islands, and their removal posed insurmountable logistic problems, not the least of which was the possible collapse of the local economy (Fugita and O'Brien; p. 48).

On the U.S. mainland, the Japanese American community, unprepared for evacuation, was in a state of shock and disbelief. Caught in an impossible dilemma, the Nisei (second generation) were U.S. citizens branded as "enemy aliens." Their parents, the Issei, had been denied citizenship rights though their futures were staked on American soil. Once in the camps the reality of injustice and frustration became ever more clear. Massive uprisings and demonstrations took place in internment centers such as Manzanar and Tule Lake, California; Heart Mountain, Wyoming; Topaz, Utah; and Poston, Arizona. To add to the deepening sense of injustice, the widely recognized and decorated Japanese American combat teams, the 442nd and 100th battalions fought for the United States in Europe, while their family members were back home incarcerated behind barbed wire under military occupation. While the 100th battalion consisted of Japanese soldiers from Hawaii, the 442nd included soldiers drafted right out of the camps.

The twin experiences of loyalty through military service and rebellion fueled by frustration were a logical response to the injustice of the evacuation. The complete suspension of rights guaranteed under the constitution for 80 percent of the Japanese American population (U.S. citizens) remains a stunning blot in American constitutional history. Three significant legal cases, *Hirabayashi* v. *United States, Yasui* v. *United States,* and *Korematsu* v. *United States,* challenged the constitutionality of the evacuation. Though each lost his case during WWII, these Supreme Court decisions would later become the center of the legal case for redress and reparations in the 1980s.

Gordon Hirabayashi, Minoru Yasui, and Fred Korematsu were U.S. citizens by birthright who intentionally violated the curfew and evacuation procedures to challenge the constitutionality of Executive Order 9066 and Public Law 503. They argued their loss of constitutional rights, such as "equal protection under the law," "the right for due process," as well as the lack of evidence for "military necessity," in each case, but the justices upheld the evacuation order, and each person was placed in forced incarceration.

The legacy of World War II permeates the Japanese American postwar experience in a multitude of ways. Loss of property and assets, most of which was not accounted for and therefore has never been reclaimed, was but one form of damage during the war. However, there were other types of damages—the loss of community organization and community institutions, the breakup of family organization, and untold psychological consequences of incarceration and trauma.

In August of 1945, America's concentration camps closed down, and the arduous work to reintegrate into the postwar victorious American society was to begin. Although free from forced incarceration, the victory against Japan with the atomic bombing of Hiroshima and Nagasaki placed Japanese Americans with the defeated enemy. Exhausted from the ordeal of camp living in usually harsh climate conditions, feeble and crowded barracks, the absence of loved ones, as well as the intensifying anger, resentment, and pain of their injustice, humiliation, and shame, Japanese Americans as dispossessed persons were forced to return to a hostile society and find ways to eke out a living, often with nothing more than train fare. With the total destruction of Japanese American ethnic communities, the internees had nothing to return to. The labor market was especially restrictive for the Issei. For older men, their options were limited to jobs as janitors and gardeners while women were confined to domestic work for white middle-class families. While two-thirds of internees returned to the Pacific Coast, many tried establishing themselves in areas like Chicago, Minneapolis, and Colorado, where Niseis looked for work in urban areas in need of secretarial and industrial laborers.

What is remarkable about the internment of Japanese Americans during the war is the deafening silence that surrounded the evacuation. In the decades following the war, the pain and humiliation of mass incarceration was so overwhelming, Issei and Nisei alike were reluctant to speak of it. Their silence was no doubt reinforced by popular suspicion and hatred of the Japanese, sentiments that were apparently not fully satisfied by nuclear attack on Japan. Perceived as "enemies," the majority of the Japanese American population could only hope to integrate into the social and economic realms, to rebuild their lives and strengthen the chances for the younger generation.

In the postwar period, racial politics shifted away from enemy aliens to "unruly" Blacks. After decades of increasing racial tensions across the nation, the visible inequalities of Black and Chicano subjugation and oppression, and the move towards civil rights, called into question the success of the status quo in America. The myths of racial inequality and middle class homogeneity were exposed first by beatnik culture, and later, by southern freedom rides, college student activism, and Timothy Leary–styled messages of "tune in and drop out." Japanese and other Asian Americans found themselves in a precarious situation. The intensifying attention towards poverty, institutionalized racism, and segregationist policy called into question the American racial opportunity structure. Was America an open or closed society? Was mobility possible for all classes and all racial groups? Mainstream social scientists and politicians took note of the "quiet," "hardworking," determination" of Japanese Americans, and decontextualizing their historical experiences branded them the "model minority." Thus in a matter of decades Japanese Americans had gone from "enemy Japs," to "model minorities." Politicians and social scientists seized the Japanese American experience to service a story of racial opportunity in America and to delegitimize complaints from Blacks about racial segregation, income inequality, unfair housing laws, discriminatory educational practices, and discriminatory welfare policy.

There is no doubt that the re-integration of Japanese Americans in the post-war era, especially in terms of educational achievement, was spectacular. But the educational prowess of the Nisei is partly based in the conjuncture of geographical and material conditions in the postwar era. The Nisei were in the right place at the right time: A booming postwar economy in the Pacific states, fueled by research and development funded by the federal government during the 1950s, greatly expanded educational opportunities as well as technical and professional job ladders. But it must be noted that educational achievement and so-called "acculturation" does not necessarily spell complacency.

By the late 1960s many forces had come into play that would ignite a redress and reparations movement agitating for compensation for the wrongs done to all persons of Japanese ancestry unjustly incarcerated during the war. Countering the misleading label of the "model minority," Japanese Americans, having made significant strides in education, began voicing their anger towards the injustice of wartime internment, and began demanding reparations from the U.S. government. According to Daniels (1988), during the late 1960s attitudes began to change within the Japanese American community toward the relocation and the advisability of publicly discussing it (p. 330). By the early 1970s a series of "pilgrimages" to Manzanar and Tule Lake and other internment camps reopened the wounds of injustice, while emphasizing the need for restitution. Successful campaigns were waged to declare the internment camps in California, Manzanar, and Tule Lake as historical landmarks. In 1970 the JACL passed the first resolutions calling for redress as an issue to be taken on by the JACL.

On February 19, 1976, the thirty-fourth anniversary of the signing of Executive Order 9066, Gerald R. Ford issued Presidential Proclamation 4417, which formally revoked the wartime document and apologized for the relocation (Daniels, 1988; p. 331). Unsatisfied with the lack of recognition for any wrongdoing in President Ford's proclamation, pressure for monetary compensation of $25,000 came from other redress organizations, such as the National Council for Japanese American Redress. Before Congress would consider any legislation to seek compensation, wrongdoing by the government needed to be determined to establish that an injustice did in fact occur. In 1980 the Commission on the Wartime Relocation and Internment of Civilians (CWRIC) held nationwide hearings resulting in the 1983 report Personal Justice Denied. The arguments and conclusions of the report helped to dispel skepticism over the injustice of the wartime evacuation and was crucial in gaining broader congressional support for redress. Most critically, the report denies the notion of "military necessity" and the justification for Executive Order 9066:

"The promulgation of Executive Order 9066 was not justified by military necessity, and the decisions which followed from it—detention, ending detention and ending exclusion—were not driven by analysis of military conditions. The broad historical causes which shaped these decisions were race prejudice, war hysteria, and a failure of political leadership. . . . A grave injustice was done to Americans and resident aliens of Japanese ancestry who, without individual review or any probative evidence against them, were excluded, removed and detained by the United States during World War II." (Daniels, 1988; p. 338.)

In 1984 and 1985, bills, with sponsors from Democrats and Republicans, were introduced in Congress to carry out the commission's recommendations, which set the amount to be paid to individual survivors at $20,000 each. Simultaneously, in 1983, Fred Korematsu, Minoru Yasui, and Gordon Hirabayashi, filed petitions for writ of error coram nobis, a device which allows a person convicted of a crime to challenge his conviction on certain grounds after his sentence has been served (Minami, 1991; p. 200). Coinciding with the redress movement, the petitioners were actually attacking the underlying legality of the exclusion and imprisonment. Once again challenging their convictions before the court forty years later, they were granted vacation of conviction, proving the legal basis for the exclusion and detention was totally discredited. According to Minami (1991) "There is, then, no longer any legal defense to the proposition that Japanese Americans are not entitled to redress for the horrible injustice committed against them during World War II" (p. 201). In 1988, President Ronald Reagan signed the Civil Liberties Act, appropriating fifty million dollars for redress payment in the 1990 fiscal year. In late 1989, President Bush signed into law an entitlement program to begin October 1, 1990, and end in 1993. To the oldest survivors first, along with a letter of apology, was a twenty thousand dollar payment of compensation.

POSTWAR PERIOD—JAPANESE AMERICAN IDENTITY AND CONTEMPORARY ISSUES

The most familiar dialogue surrounding the current social status of Japanese Americans has been about the story of "assimilation" and the persistence of ethnic identity as racial minorities. The debate is often framed or encompassed within discussions about specific relevant issues that remain most salient for Japanese Americans today. Questions concerning the continued presence of a Japanese American community, the emotional and structural damage from the internment camp experience, the increasing rates of outmarriage and mixed racial identity, common documentation of "glass ceiling" discrimination in upper management positions, and the contemporary phenomena of "Japan Bashing" due to economic and technological competition remain salient and primary issues that continue to face Japanese Americans approaching the twenty-first century.

However the oversimplified dichotomy between assimilationist arguments and narrow definitions of racial oppression leave our understanding of the Japanese American experience and we are unable to grasp the complex forces that have shaped contemporary issues of racial identity and social position. In order to approach a more comprehensive examination of the current status of Japanese Americans, any analysis must contextualize discussions about social positions and racial identities within the contemporary demographic and social location of Japanese Americans as it has emerged since World War II. We note five distinguishing and relevant conditions of postwar Japanese American experiences.

First, unlike other Asian groups, the Japanese American community does not have a continuous flow of Japanese immigrants in pursuit of settling and establishing lives in the United States. The most recent significant flow of immigrants from Japan consisted of war brides, married to American servicemen stationed in Japan, who were able to enter the United States as nonquota immigrants under the terms of the 1952 McCarrran-Walter Act. According to Chan (1991) the flow of Japanese women admitted as dependents of U.S. citizens was largest until the early 1970s. In the late 1950s the annual immigration of Japanese women ranged from 2,000 to 5,000 (comprising 80 percent of all Japanese immigrants); their number averaged 2,500 per year in the 1960s, declining to about 1,500 per year in the 1970s (p. 140).

While the Immigration Act of 1965 marks a notable shift in immigration policy and a growing political consciousness of racial fairness in immigration law, the conditions were not ripe for Japanese immigration. Japanese nationals did not look toward the United States with the same interest in economic opportunity or educational opportunity as did other Asian immigrants. As mentioned earlier, the increase in Japanese American population has remained relatively minuscule compared to other Asian groups, even though Japanese Americans were in an optimal position to petition for relatives under the 1965 amendment's kinship provisions under family reunification (Shinagawa, p. 106). According to Hing (1993), from 1965 to 1990 the Japanese American population increased by only 59 percent, from about 500,000 to a little over 847,500. During this period only 116,000 Japanese immigrated (p. 106). Japan's relative economic and political stability are notably the main reasons for recent declines in immigration, as well as trauma suffered during World War II, including both internment in the United States and the atomic bombings of Nagasaki and Hiroshima and the military occupation in Japan that was to follow.

Second, a slow-growing population has been compounded by ethnic identity questions, which we discuss in more depth below, especially concerning high out-marriage rates. With the current Japanese population of 847,562 (0.3 percent of the total U.S. population), the question and configuration of a sustainable Japanese American community has remained a prominent issue among Japanese Americans. Fugita and O'Brien report that while there is a good deal of variation by geographic area, out-marriage among Sansei males in their sample was 25 percent. National figures suggest an even higher out-marriage rate for males, and a 60-plus percent out-marriage rate for Sansei women.

Third, there is some difficulty in defining the "homeland" of Japanese America. Without an influx of working-class immigrants, Japanese ethnic enclaves and Japantowns have been deprived of the socioeconomic groups that generally sustain and need them (Hing, 1993, p.109). As a result the "Japantowns" of today tend to be more commercially oriented than residential, where businesses are primarily owned by Japanese Americans or Japanese companies. In areas like San Francisco's Japantown and Los Angeles's Little Tokyo, an increasing percentage of the commercial ventures are sponsored by Japan-based corporations. With Japanese Americans predominantly residing in suburban areas, social scientists have debated over the meaning and interpretation of these living patterns in relation to Japanese American identity and social position. For example, Montero (1980) argues that increases in socioeconomic status correlate with the movement away from Japanese communities, which in turn is positively related to assimilation (p. 87). However, when we examine movement "away" from the "Japanese community," we must recognize that a viable residential nexus constituting local employment does not exist for Japanese Americans in the same way as other Asian American groups. Others, such as Fugita and O'Brien (1991), argue that there is a persistence of community that forms beyond geographical and ecological barriers through voluntary associations and community based organizations that operate to meet exigencies of specific situations or needs faced by particular pockets within the Japanese American population. Likewise, given the age of telecommunications, no longer is it necessary for people to reside locally to community-based organizations in order to participate and identify with the community population and goals. Thus, although the function of ethnic communities may be to provide protection from racism, and Japanese Americans tend not to reside in densely populated ethnic enclaves, this does not mean that they have assimilated and do not experience racism.

Fourth, dogged by discussions of assimilation, Japanese Americans have often been perceived as nonvictims of discrimination—and hence, marginalized from discussions about contemporary racial inequality. In other words, while they might rightfully recall the legacy of the camps, current conditions suggest they are well on their way up the opportunity structure. Thus, discussions concerning the status of Japanese Americans as a racial minority group have consistently posed challenging questions for race relations theorists working to challenge assimilationist arguments as well as the construction of the "model minority" myth. On the one hand, Japanese Americans as racial minorities have obtained higher education levels than whites (see Table 13-1).

Their occupational distribution remains highly diverse with a higher percentage (28.5 percent) of professionals, managers, and executives than the white population (24 percent), fewer blue-collar workers (37.3 percent to 45 percent) and a little higher percentage of service workers (12.8 percent to 11.6 percent) (Shinagawa 1993, pp.109–110, also see Table 13-2).

Using income levels as indicators of structural assimilation must be cautioned, because although family income levels appear higher than whites, Japanese American income levels are drastically skewed by the high concentration of Japanese Americans residing in California and Hawaii, where the associated cost of living is also much higher. Japanese American family incomes are also skewed by the higher rates of multiple income families than the national average, since wives need to work in order to supplement insufficient incomes of their husbands necessary for their relative cost of living.
Yet given their relatively higher levels of education (see Table 13-3), occupational position, and family income, understanding Japanese Americans as a racial minority becomes complicated due to their lower levels of unemployment and poverty. Social scientists who have used education, occupation, and income as the determinant variables of assimilation or cultural accommodation may have insufficiently considered the complexity and pervasive impact of racial oppression. The argument that Japanese Americans have become a "model minority" that do not face the same effects of racism as other racial groups may not consider the multitude of ways Japanese Americans continue to face racism and racial discrimination.

Japanese Americans continue to experience low levels of advancement due to an invisible barrier, commonly referred to as the "glass ceiling," to upper managerial or executive positions. Exclusion of Asian Americans in general from the upper rungs of corporate and government hierarchies has been documented by the discrepancy between educational achievement and the proportion of those qualified people actually advanced to executive positions compared to whites. According to Henry Der (1993), citing the *Asian American Civil Rights Issues of the 1990s Report,* "the U.S. Commission on Civil Rights cites the 'glass ceiling' as one of five prevalent types of employment discrimination experienced by Asian Americans" (Der, p. 215). Research by Ong and Hee (1993) found that Asian Pacific American males are more likely to be in a professional occupation than non-Hispanic white males—23 percent versus 14 percent, a three-to-two ratio in favor of Asian Pacific American males. However, Asian Pacific American males lag behind in the executive and management positions—14 percent versus 17 percent for non-Hispanic males, a three-to-two advantage for white non-Hispanic males (Ong and Hee, p. 147). The 1988 Attorney General's Asian and Pacific Islander Advisory Committee's *Final Report* states that stereotypes of Asian Pacific Islanders as quiet, unassertive, and lacking leadership skills establish unconscious biases that create occupational barriers and limit employment opportunities for Asian Pacific Americans. Thus, while the predominantly native-born Japanese

TABLE 13-2
Occupational Distribution of Japanese Americans

	Total Count	Total Percent	Managerial	Professional	Technical and Sales	Administrative Support	Service	Farming, Forestry and Fishing	Precision Prod., Craft and Repair	Operative and Laborers
Total										
Japanese Americans	452,005	100.0	17.3	19.4	16.6	17.8	11.1	2.7	7.8	6.9
Asian Pacific Americans	3,411,586	100.0	12.6	18.1	17.9	15.4	14.8	1.2	8.0	12.1
General Population	115,681,202	100.0	12.3	14.1						
Female										
Japanese Americans	215,319	100.0	12.1	16.7	13.5	24.2	11.9	0.7	2.7	4.6
Asian Pacific Americans	1,590,897	100.0	10.0	14.9	15.6	19.8	14.4	0.5	3.6	9.6
General Population	52,976,623	100.0	10.1	14.8	14.4	24.6	15.1	0.8	2.1	7.6
Male										
Japanese Americans	236,686	100.0	24.2	22.8	20.3	10.0	10.2	5.1	14.2	9.8
Asian Pacific Americans	1,820,689	100.0	0.2	0.3	0.3	0.1	0.2	0.0	0.2	0.2
General Population	62,704,579	100.0	14.6	13.4	16.6	7.5	11.3	4.2	21.0	22.5

Adapted from Larry Hajime Shinagawa (1996, pp. 113-114) in *Reframing the Immigration Debate: A Public Policy Report.* Eds. Bill Ong Hing and Ronald Lee. LEAP Asian Pacific American Public Policy Institute and UCLA Asian American Studies Center.

TABLE 13-3
Educational Attainment of Japanese Americans (Persons 25 Years and Older)

	Total	Less Than Bachelor's	Bachelor's Degree	Master's Degree	Doctorate
Japanese Americans	623,511	65.6	24.4	8.8	3.5
Asian Pacific Americans	4,316,366	63.4	22.7	8.5	2.1
General Population	158,868,436	79.7	13.1	4.7	0.8

Adapted from Larry Hajime Shinagawa (1996, pp. 119-120) in Reframing the Immigration Debate: A Public Policy Report. Eds. Bill Ong Hing and Ronald Lee. LEAP Asian Pacific Public Policy Institute and UCLA Asian American Studies Center; U.S. Bureau of the Census (1990, Table 42).

Americans have statistically reached higher proportions of educational success and entry into white-collar occupations, this is not to say that as a group they do not experience continued forms of institutionalized racism.

Fifth, Japanese Americans, we think, are a unique and interesting example of internalized psychosocial response to the long-term effects of racial degradation. Internalization processes, for example, as outlined by Fanon, are characteristic of colonialism and slavery. However, with some extrapolation, Japanese American experiences are a good example of the subtlety of the culture of racism in America. The history of racist immigration policy, the nativist anti-Japanese movement, and the racial discrimination of internment during World War II clearly reveals the workings of oppression, dehumanization, and exploitation in U.S. racial politics. To this day, social scientists continue to work towards a more comprehensive understanding of the overall impact internment has had on the contemporary status of Japanese Americans. With the immediate silence that followed the aftermath of the camps and the quiet attempt to resettle and reintegrate into a victorious American populace while still associated with "the enemy," and commonly referred to as "Japs," the range and depth of effects from their injustice would not be dealt with until much later. Don Nakanishi (1993) frames the redress and reparations movement, referred to as the "resurrection of internment," as a latent collective response or reawakening to the racial injustice of the past through a highly visible contemporary struggle seeking reparations for the costs done to them by the racist actions of the state. Recognizing the perverse psychological trauma of the shame and guilt internees internalized silently for the first twenty years, Nakanishi argues that the redress reparations movement is a phenomena that challenges the model minority construction, while simultaneously underscoring the need for seeking greater convergence in race relations research (pp. 8–29). The latent collective response defies the notion of the model minority assumption that Japanese Americans have moved beyond racism, while simultaneously calling for a more multiracial framework to understand the way the process of oppression is experienced collectively beyond purely psychological forms but through cultural manifestations.

The psychological effects of internment have been most frequently noted among the Nisei (second generation): overwhelming feelings of shame and guilt, a desire to prove their "Americanness" at a time when they as citizens were labeled the "enemy." The effects of internment are also being noted among the offspring of internees, particularly in terms of their own ethnic identity and understandings of racism. Takezawa (1991) found that Sansei upbringing of Nisei internees is directly impacted by the typical patterns of guilt and shame. Because any association with Japan was met with discrimination and racism, Nisei parents did not enforce the teachings of Japanese language and cultural practices the way their Issei (first generation) parents prioritized. Likewise, while many Sansei children grew up knowing about their parents' incarceration during World War II, a great majority of Nisei internees could not openly discuss their experiences. Because it was Commonly understood as a sensitive issue, many Sansei reported feelings of anger and confusion, or more rarely, sensitivity detachment (Takezawa, 1991, p. 43–44). However, Takezawa argues that just as internment was identity-transforming for the Nisei, the redress movement, largely led by Sansei offspring, was transformative to their ethnic identity and sense of community. Looking for justice for their parents and relatives, the Sansei linked Nisei and Issei experiences to larger racial issues of inequality, institutionalized racism, and the danger of nativist movements.

The public government apology for internment and the redress movement could not have been more timely in an era of revitalized "Japan bashing." Technological competition between Japan and the United States, a contest whose stakes deepened with domestic recession and plant closings in the United States, reverberates on Japanese Americans in particular, and Asian Americans in general. Economic competition between first-world nations redounded as occasional acts of violent racism against Asian Americans. The Attorney General's *Final Report* concluded with the belief that the Japanese are engaging in unfair trade practices, and the growing hostility toward Japan and the Japanese has led to trade relations between Japan and the United States being described as a "trade war" (p. 26). Citing the U.S. Commission on Civil Rights 1986, Espiritu (1992) stresses the connection between anti-Japanese sentiment, scapegoating, and the increase of Asian violence. Anti-Japanese sentiment appeared on bumper stickers that read "Toyota - Datsun - Honda = Pearl Harbor" and "Unemployment Made in Japan" (Espiritu, p. 139). The most noted recent hate crime was the murder of 27-year-old Chinese American Vincent Chin in Detroit by two laid-off auto workers who yelled while crushing his skull with a baseball bat, "it's because of you ____ Japs that we're out of work" (Attorney General Report, 43). The reemergence of Yellow Peril took on greater momentum as media and politicians noted increasing rates of Japanese investment in U.S. real estate during the mid-eighties. Yet the foreigners who own the most American real estate are European, not Asian (Attorney General's Report, p. 26). Thus, the anti-Japanese narrative has not diminished within the American popular consciousness, and the prevalence of hate crimes continues to be an issue that Japanese Americans, as well as all racial minorities, cite as evidence of the need for more accurate recognition and treatment by the American criminal justice system.

Discussion

While the debate between the "model minority" and the persistence of ethnic identity seems to have dominated contemporary discussions concerning the status of Japanese Americans, the concern over interracial relationships, out-marriage, and multiracial identity have become the most pressing yet sensitive topics still to be understood more fully. Based upon earlier American sociological models of assimilationism (Park, 1950; Gordon, 1964), social scientists have continually looked at the phenomena of high out-marriage of Sansei Japanese Americans as an indicator of further assimilation, as well as the potential demise of a vibrant Japanese American community (Montero, 1980; Fugita and O'Brien, 1991). In this country, interracial marriage was deemed officially illegal by antimiscegenation laws that were not officially declared unconstitutional by the Supreme Court until 1967. California's antimiscegenation law was repealed in 1948 after Congress amended the War Bride's Act of 1945, which permitted the entry of Japanese brides married to Americans. Citing out-marriage rates in the 1980s of fifty percent by the Sansei generation, social scientists linked the increase of out-marriage to lessened social ties with Japanese American ethnic affiliations.

Some work outside the assimilationist paradigm has challenged the linear correlation between rates of outmarriage and levels of assimilation. Examining outmarriage from a more integrative approach, Hwang, Saenz, and Aguirre (1994) argue that assimilationist approaches alone do not adequately take into account community-level structural attributes (e.g. minority group size, and the ethnic heterogeneity of the community in which minority members reside) that create circumstances under which in-group preferences give way to structural necessity (pp. 397–399). In other words, factors such as minority group size, community configuration, and level of income congruency are seen as structural constraints that also work to shape the experiences and decisions to out-marry.

Researchers looking beyond the racial/white, oppressed/oppressor dichotomies have approached the phenomena of interracial relationships and outmarriage within the context of continual social change, significant social/political moments, and the increasing consciousness of diversity. Using 1980 and 1990 census data, Shinagawa and Young Pang (1996) look at outmarriage relationships within a pan-ethnic framework, and thus they compare the rates of ethnic—white, interracial—out-marriages as well as out-marriages to other Asian ethnic groups (interethnic marriages). In general, they found that for many Asian American groups, the out-marriage trend has increased towards interethnic marriages and exceeds interracial marriages. For Japanese Americans, there is a striking increase of interethnic marriages of Japanese Americans with spouses from other Asian groups, while the increase of interracial marriages has been very slow for men and actually decreased for Japanese American women. The authors argue that the factors leading to the increase of interethnic marriages have to do with the growing size and concentration of Asian Americans in the United States, the growth of social and personal networks, similarity in socioeconomic attainment among Asian Americans, common American cultural experiences, feelings of shared identity, and the growing racial consciousness and awareness by Asian Americans. Given the case that Japanese out-marriage rates to whites have remained relatively static over the decade while interethnic out-marriages have significantly increased, this poses challenging questions to arguments that see out-marriage as an indicator of assimilation, as well as out-marriage to the dominant group being a move towards status attainment. Possibly now the question begs the understanding of political consciousness and the impact of the sixties, as well as increasing levels of socioeconomic status, in order to fully engage in the complexities and multitude of contextual movements that affect out-marriage patterns. The offspring, often referred to as "hapa," of interracial relationships have had to negotiate the influences of and relationships to two different ethnic systems. In recent years there has been increasing insertion of perspectives, narratives, and academic work expressing a general marginalization they have experienced from both ethnic communities of their ancestral background. More in-depth research is needed to understand the multiple levels of marginalization and implications for Japanese Americans.

The continued persistence of racism within the social historical context of racial exclusion, discrimination, and injustice, as well as the desire for the preservation of culture, continue to be driving, unifying forces among Japanese Americans. In the last thirty years, the of the Japanese American experience has been "resurrected" through Day of Remembrance ceremonies that memorialize the internment and praise the redress movement. Organized pilgrimages to former camp sites such as Tule Lake, Manzanar, and Poston offer Issei and Nisei internees as well as Sansei an opportunity to revisit and resolve the past. Community-based, as well as nationally organized museums have also emerged as a way to preserve the history and culture of the immigrant generation, and also to narrate the experiences since their arrival. Holding on to both the themes of racial oppression and active resistance, Japanese American community organizations continue to work on issues facing their elderly population, the youth, civil rights in the work place, education, and hate crimes.

However, given the slow level of population growth, the lack of an incoming immigrant population, the further distance of the Yonsei (fourth generation)

TABLE 13-4
Timeline of Important Laws and Acts Impacting Japanese Americans

1790	Naturalization Act of 1790, stipulated that only "free white persons" were eligible for naturalization after maintaining a required period of residency.
1884–85	Japan permits laborers to work in Hawaii and passes first modern emigration law, as recruitment of Japanese workers increases.
1894	Addition Treaty with Japan, reaffirming its commitment to open travel.
1906	San Francisco Public Schools segregate Japanese students.
1907	"Gentlemen's Agreement," where Japan stops issuing passports to laborers desiring to emigrate to the United States; President Theodore Roosevelt signs Executive Order 589 prohibiting Japanese with passports for Hawaii, Mexico, or Canada to reemigrate to the United States.
1913	California enacts Alien Land Law prohibiting "aliens ineligible to citizenship" from buying land or leasing it for longer than three years.
1917	The Immigration Act of 1917 delineates an Asiatic Barred Zone from where no immigrants can come to the U.S.
1922	*Ozawa* v. *U.S.* declares Japanese ineligible for citizenship based upon the Naturalization Act of 1790.
1924	The Immigration Act of 1924 (National Origins Quota Act) denies entry to virtually all Asians.
1942	Executive Order 9066 authorized the Seccretary of War to designate military areas "from which any and all persons may be excluded as deemed necessary or desirable"; Congress passes Public Law 503 to impose penal sanctions on anyone disobeying orders to carry out Executive Order 9066. Internment of 120,000 West Coast Japanese Americans begins.
1944	Exclusion orders are revoked.
1945	World War II ends.
1952	McCarren Walter Act abolishes barred zone, but limits immigration to 2,000 within Asia-Pacific triangle; One clause of this Act grants the right of naturalization and a small immigration quota to Japanese.
1956	California repeals its alien land laws.
1965	The Immigration Act of 1965 abolishes "national origins" as basis for allocating immigration quotas.
1976	President Gerald Ford rescinds Executive Order 9066.
1981	Commission on Wartime Relocation and Internment of Civilians (set up by Congress) holds hearings across the country and concludes the internment was a "grave injustice" and that Executive Order 9066 resulted from "race prejudice, war hysteria, and a failure of political leadership.
1983	Fred Korematsu, Min Yasui, and Gordon Hirabayashi file petitions to overturn their World War II convictions for violating the curfew and evacutation orders. They were granted vacation of conviction, discrediting the legal basis for the exclusion and detention of Japanese Americans during the war.
1988	The U.S. Senate votes 69 to 27 to support redress for Japanese Americans.
1989	President George Bush signs into law an entitlement program to pay each surviving Japanese American internee twenty-thousand dollars along with an official letter of apology, beginning on October 1, 1990.

Sources: Sucheng Chan, *Asian Americans: An Interpretive History.* Boston: Twayne Publishers. 1994. pp. 192–99; Bill Ong Hing, *Making and Remaking Asian America through Immigration Policy, 1850–1990.* Stanford: Stanford University Press. pp. 195-97; *Asian Americans and Congress: A Documentary History.* Edited by Hyung-Chan Kim. Westport, CT: Greenwood. 1995.

from their cultural history, and the increasing rates of out-marriage by Sansei Japanese Americans, many question with concern the viability and longevity of a Japanese American community as well as ethnic identity. Possibly a revisualization of what a Japanese American community could be in a multicultural, Pan-Asian America will lead us to an even more viable, sustainable, and persistent community collective. These concerns will unfold in the coming decades as fourth-generation Japanese Americans reach their marital years.

CONCLUSION

We remain hopeful that a new generation of sociologists will move quickly beyond the simple dichotomies and stories that characterize race relations work: assimilation versus the resurgence of ethnic identity and community; discrimination versus achievement; class versus race; multiculturalism versus cultural pluralism. Table 13-4 provides a comprehensive list of key moments in Japanese American history. Dichtomies capture only parts of these experiences.

To move beyond these dichotomies will require critical analysis and bold thinking—and most of all, the recognition that the stories we tell about racial minorities are as much about them as they are about the fundamental ways that race is deeply woven into American politics and culture.

SUGGESTED READINGS

Bonacich, Edna. "A Theory of Middleman Minorities." *American Sociological Review* 38 (1973), pp. 583–94.

———. "Middleman Minorities and Advanced Capitalism." *Ethnic Groups* 2 (1980), pp. 211–19.

California Attorney General, Asian and Pacific Islander Advisory Committee. *Final Report.* Sacramento, CA, 1988.

Chan, Sucheng. *Asian Americans: An Interpretive History.* Boston: Twayne Publishers, 1991.

Daniels, Roger. *The Politics of Prejudice.* Los Angeles, CA: University of California Press, 1962.

———. *Asian America: Chinese and Japanese in the United States Since 1850.* Seattle: University of Washington Press, 1988.

Der, Henry. "Affirmative Action Policy," in *The State of Asian Pacific America.* Los Angeles, CA: LEAP Asian Pacific American Public Policy Institute and the UCLA Asian American Studies Center, 1993, pp. 215–31.

Espiritu, Yen. 1992. *Asian-American Panethnicity: Bridging Institutions and Identities.* Philadelphia: Temple University Press, 1992.

Fanon, Frantz. *Black Skin/White Masks.* Grove Press, 1991.

Fugita, Stephen S. and David J. O'Brien. *Japanese American Ethnicity: The Persistence of Community.* Seattle: University of Washington Press, 1991.

Gordon, Milton. *Assimilation in American Life.* New York: Oxford University Press, 1964.

Hing, Bill Ong. *Making and Remaking Asian America through Immigration Policy, 1850–1990.* Stanford, CA: Stanford University Press, 1993.

Hing, Bill Ong and Ronald Lee., eds. *Reframing the Immigration Debate.* Los Angeles, CA: LEAP Asian Pacific American Public Policy Institute and the UCLA Asian American Studies Center, 1996.

Hwang, Sean-Shong, Rogelio Saenz, and Benigno E. Aguirre. "Structural and Individual Determinants of Outmarriage Among Chinese-, Filipino-, and Japanese-Americans in California." *Sociological Inquiry* 64(4) (1994), pp. 396–414.

Ichihashi, Yamato. *Japanese in the United States.* Stanford, CA: Stanford University Press, 1932.

McClain, Charles. *Asian Americans and the Law: Japanese Immigrants and American Law.* New York: Garland Publishing, Inc., 1994.

Minami, Dale. "*Coram Nobis* and Redress," in *Japanese Americans From Relocation to Redress,* Roger Daniels, Sandra C. Taylor, and Harry H.L. Kitano, eds. Seattle: University of Washington Press, 1991, pp. 200–202.

Modell, John. *The Economics and Politics of Racial Accommodation: The Japanese of Los Angeles, 1900–1942.* Urbana: University of Illinois Press, 1977.

Montero, Darrel. *Japanese Americans: Changing Patterns of Ethnic Affiliation Over Three Generations.* Boulder: Westview Press, 1980.

Park, Robert E. *Race and Culture.* New York: The Free Press, 1950.

Nakanishi, Don T. "Surviving Democracy's 'Mistake': Japanese Americans and the Enduring Legacy of Executive Order 9066," *Amerasia* 19(1) (1993), pp. 7–35.

Okihiro, Gary Y. and David Drummond. "The Concentration Camps and Japanese Economic Losses in California Agriculture, 1900–1942," in *Japanese Americans From Relocation to Redress,* Roger Daniels, Sandra C. Taylor, and Harry H.L. Kitano, eds. Seattle: University of Washington Press, 1991, pp. 168–75.

Ong, Paul, and Suzanne J. Hee. "Twenty Million in 2020," in *The State of Asian Pacific America.* (Los Angeles, CA: LEAP Asian Pacific American Public Policy Institute and the UCLA Asian American Studies Center, 1993), pp. 11–23.

Shinagawa, Larry Hajime. "The Impact of Immigration on the Demography of Asian Pacific Americans," in *Reframing the Immigration Debate* edited by Bill Ong Hing and Ronald Lee. Los Angeles: LEAP Asian Pacific American Public Policy Institute and UCLA Asian American Studies Center, 1996, pp. 59–126.

Shinagawa, Larry Hajime, and Gin Yong Pang. "Asian American Panethnicity and Intermarriage." *Amerasia.* 22(2) (1996), pp. 127–152.

Takaki, Ronald. *Pau Hana: Plantation Life and Labor in Hawaii.* Honolulu, HI: University of Hawaii Press, 1983.

Takezawa, Yasuko I. "Children of Inmates: The Effects of the Redress Movement Among Third Generation Japanese Americans." *Qualitative Sociology* 14(1) (1991), pp. 39–55.

Yanagisako, Sylvia. *Transforming the Past: Tradition and Kinship among Japanese Americans.* Stanford, CA: Stanford University Press, 1985.

CHAPTER 14

CHINESE AMERICANS: FROM EXCLUSION TO PROSPERITY?

Jan Lin

The images and experiences of Chinese Americans have evolved dramatically in the last 150 years, since the first miners and railroad workers entered the United States through San Francisco (the "Mountain of Gold"). Public perceptions since the decades of immigrant exclusion and xenophobic agitations against the "inscrutable clannish Chinamen" have given way to a new image of the Chinese as a prosperous, upwardly mobile "model minority" with increasing political and economic clout. Changing images have been occasioned by real internal transformations in the social structure of Chinatowns, from insular, isolated "bachelor societies" to diverse and dynamic ethnic enclaves. These internal shifts are the outgrowth of wider political and economic variables, including the changing context of U.S. immigration policy, as well as improvements in the status of the home countries of China, Taiwan, and Hong Kong within the global economy.

The myth of success, however, masks a new underlying polarity in the socioeconomic profile of Chinese immigrants to the United States, who range from affluent Hong Kong tycoons and Taiwanese professionals to undocumented "boat people" brought by transnational smuggling rackets emanating from China's Fujian province. Beyond class differentiation, there is a growing home country and linguistic diversity among Chinese Americans, which hampers group awareness. Group solidarity is further hindered by the growth of new political and economic factions within Chinese American communities. Activist community organizers, second-generation professionals, and overseas Chinese investors have emerged as new, often competing actors in Chinatowns, as the power of the traditional exclusion-era merchant elite diminishes.

A social change perspective is thus of considerable utility in comprehending the experience of contemporary Chinese Americans. Established Anglo residents, local communities and governments have been alternately friendly and distrustful towards these new factions, which configure and align themselves in different alliances and conflicts from one locale to another. Anglo Americans are sometimes perplexed and ignorant of the subtle cultural nuances and socioeconomic complexities which characterize the contemporary Chinese American "community." Emblematic of these kinds of misunderstandings is the 1982 murder of Vincent Chin by unemployed Detroit autoworkers who mistook him for a Japanese man. This chapter will, hopefully, move us toward clarifications for the Anglo public and the Chinese American "community" itself.

Immigration History

The first wave of Chinese immigrants to arrive on American shores were primarily rural peasants from Guangdong province on the southeast coast of China near Canton (Guangzhou) and Hong Kong. The districts surrounding the Pearl River delta comprised the "fountainhead" (Sung, 1977: 10) from which almost all migrants came, with 60 percent originating from the county of Toishan. Toishan (which translates as "Mountain Plateau") was a rocky and barren region 800 to 1,000 miles above sea level that yielded a scant agricultural output capable of sustaining its peasants only four months of the year. To survive, the working population spent much of the year as itinerant peddlers, laborers, and merchants among the neighboring provinces of the Guangzhou/Hong Kong area (Chen: 18).

These migrants began arriving in the United States in the 1850s during the last decades of the Qing Dynasty. The Opium Wars (fought with the Western powers, 1839–1842) had disrupted the political and economic life of this area of China. The resolution of these conflicts in favor of the Western nations led to the designation of coastal cities such as Hong Kong, Canton, and Macao as "treaty ports" open to Western trade and influence. The result was to open the southeastern China region not only to trade in commodities, but also to manpower export, through the form of "contract laborers." Push factors motivating out-migration included war, famine, flood, and internal social unrest in the form of the Taiping Rebellion, a widescale peasant protest movement throughout the southeast China region.

Some laborers were more forceably transported to work in mines and guano pits in Mexico, Cuba, and Peru. These migrants were sometimes "shanghaied" via trickery or were prisoners of war taken as slave "coolies." The "coolie trade" to the Americas essentially replaced the Atlantic slave trade, which the British had abolished by the 1840s. In North America and Australia, transportation of Chinese labor more commonly involved a "contract" or "credit ticket" system, which enabled migrants to pay the considerable costs of transPacific passage via a period of debenture to a sponsoring ocean transport company or employer in the receiving nation. Frequently, a migrant arranged his "credit ticket" through the auspices of his clan or district association. Word of the discovery of gold in California in the 1840s spread to the Chinese provinces via Western treaty ports, and Chinese were packed into clipper ships by the thousands to mines in America, which they called "Gum Shan" (Mountain of Gold). Many also traveled to Hawaii to work as agricultural laborers and to British Columbia to work in fisheries and canneries. Australia was also a popular destination for gold miners.

During their first decades after arrival, Chinese migrants to the United States were geographically concentrated in the Pacific and western states. With the end of the gold rush in northern California, Chinese immigrants scattered throughout the surrounding states in the following decades to work on the railroads, in land reclamation projects, seasonal agriculture, fishing, canning, urban factory work, and as domestic and laundry workers. Railroad work drew the most immigrants. Thousands of Chinese laborers employed by Charles Crocker of the Central Pacific Company plowed eastward through rugged mountainous terrain in a race with Irish workers working westward for the Union Pacific, eventually meeting to complete the first transcontinental track at Promontory Point, Utah, on May 10, 1869.

The completion of the transcontinental railroad signified the end of the frontier, as new labor from the East Coast poured into western states. Labor market competition was the result, and anti-Chinese rioting and lynchings took place in many western states in the 1870s and 1880s. Nativist agitators fanned the xenophobic violence and gained political position in the western states on platforms urging repatriation or immigrant restriction. Endorsed by U.S. labor unions, restrictionist legislation was eventually passed in these western states and eventually on a federal level.

The Chinese Exclusion Act of 1882 was the first federal legislation ever passed (aside from an 1875 act which restricted prostitutes, convicts, and the mentally unstable) to bar any immigrants based on national origin. The act was renewed every ten years until 1943. The exclusion of new arrivals after 1882 led to the dropping off of Chinese population from a high of nearly 110,000 to less than 70,000 in the following decades. Exclusion also forestalled the development of more settled communities, effectively freezing Chinese settlements in the status of "bachelor societies." These exclusion-era "sojourners" mainly viewed their stay in the United States as temporary and remitted their earnings to families in China. Wives, who generally remained in the home village by Chinese custom and because the trans-Pacific journey was prohibitive in cost and considered extremely arduous, were even less inclined to emigrate to the United States with the onset of exclusion.

The exclusion laws mainly applied to unskilled Chinese laborers, since exceptions were made for government officials, ministers, professors, students, and "treaty traders" (merchants). A number of illegal entrants must also be added, such as "jump-ship" seamen and sailors who stayed in port after their ships departed, and visitors who overstayed their visas. Some were able to enter as the born-in-China children of immigrants already in America. Children's "slots" were sometimes given or sold to members of extended family or to other villagers. Slots were sometimes sold through brokers. A number of younger Chinese immigrants arrived during the decades of Oriental exclusion in such manner as "paper sons."

Since they remitted most of their earnings, bachelor "sojourners" lived an austere life in frontier towns and encampments or crowded into tenement rooming houses in urban Chinatowns, parsimoniously saving any nonremitted earnings to make periodic visits to China. These home visits were accompanied by great pomp and circumstance. Whole villages turned out to greet the visiting sojourner. The sojourner who had saved substantial money was able to buy improved housing and more land for his extended family. Other kin and friends expected gifts and loans. As a measure of his growing status in the home village, he was expected to contribute towards projects such as the building of schools and hospitals.

Legally arrived women in the initial decades of first-stage Chinatowns were generally merchants' wives. They were never seen and were kept in seclusion apart from the bachelor men who generally lived in rooming houses, sometimes ten or twelve to a room. Thousands of prostitutes and slave girls were smuggled in, however, to service the sexual desires of the laboring men. The brothels, gambling parlors and opium parlors of early Chinatowns were an outgrowth of the bachelor society, and unfortunately formed the popular perception of Chinatowns at the time. United States–Chinese cooperation against Japan during World War II created a favorable diplomatic climate for reforming the law excluding Chinese immigration to the United States. Congress rescinded the Chinese Exclusion Act in 1943. For the first time since 1882, a quota was set allowing 105 Chinese a year to enter the United States. Additionally, the War Brides Act of 1946 allowed thousands of wives and children of Chinese-American veterans of World War II to immediately join their husbands as special nonquota entries. From 1947 to 1953, almost 90 percent percent of the Chinese immigrants admitted to the United States were women (Sung, 1987: 22), primarily of the lower and middle classes. There were other special nonquota entries in the postwar period. After the 1949 Communist revolution in China, a series of Displaced Persons and Refugee

Acts in the 1950s enabled several thousand students, trainees, professionals, and government workers stranded in the United States to become American citizens. Many of these students and professionals had entered the United States during the war, when government training programs were established at many U.S. universities for Chinese students as a cooperative gesture of wartime alliance between the two countries (Tsai: 121).

It was the Hart-Cellar immigration act of 1965, however, that really changed the situation. National origin quotas (imposed in 1924), which gave preference to northern and western European immigrants, were lifted, and a new top quota of 20,000 for any one country was set, with an overall limitation of 170,000 from the Eastern Hemisphere. Members of immediate family of U.S. Chinese, including parents, spouses, and children, were allowed to enter as nonquota immigrants. The Communist government in China was not issuing exit visas, however, so most new Chinese immigrants had to come via Hong Kong and Taiwan. In 1979, improving diplomatic relations between the People's Republic of China (PRC) and the United States led to a relaxation of the Chinese bans on exit visas. The 1965 law established seven quota-enforced preference categories based on family reunification and special manpower requirements. Family reunification brought immigrants from all socioeconomic classes, but the manpower provisions of the Hart-Cellar Act brought mainly middle-class professionals and skilled workers to the United States.

After the end of the Vietnam War in 1975, many ethnic Chinese from Vietnam also began to settle in the United States, as diplomatic relations soured between the People's Republic of China (PRC) and Vietnam. The PRC invaded Vietnam in February 1979, prompting Vietnam to expel all ethnic Chinese living in its borders. Like the hundreds of thousands of refugees who fled the fall of Saigon, many settled in the United States. Heavily weighted towards a younger population, these arrivals were not only rural and working-class "boat people," but included many middle-class professionals and South Vietnamese government workers (Sung, 1987: 27–28).

The Chinese American population in the 1990s is thus much more diverse than that of the exclusion era. This diversity is reflected both in the geographic range of their home nations and accompanying linguistic differences. There is also a much greater socioeconomic range of immigrants, with the post-exclusion era including more middle-class and affluent Chinese. The growing economic strength of these immigrants is a reflection of rising prosperity in their home countries. Political factors have also been significant; Taiwanese immigrants have been strongly motivated by fear of PRC takeover, as well as Hong Kong Chinese, who must contend with Hong Kong's passing from British to PRC rule.

Many of the professional and middle-class Chinese immigrants of the post-1965 period have bypassed the dense, traditional central-city Chinatowns to settle in the suburbs. In some cases, they formed the nucleus of "satellite" or new "suburban Chinatowns," but a great many have assimilated into the

American middle class. These strongly upwardly mobile Chinese Americans and their second-generation offspring are the "model minority" hailed by the American press.

Linked with the most affluent migration stream is a flow of overseas Chinese capital, particularly from Hong Kong and Taiwan. This investment flow is manifested in Chinatowns in the form of real estate purchases and new construction (in hotels, condominiums, office towers, and shopping malls) and the opening of overseas bank offices. Overseas Chinese capital flow is not necessarily linked with the stream of professional Chinese Americans who seek to assimilate into the American middle class. Overseas investment furthermore has dramatically transformed the economic structure and urban geography of existing Chinatowns.

This new appearance of affluence to some extent masks an underlying polarity in the socioeconomic profile of Chinese Americans, a polarity which is considered in the next section. A stream of low-income Chinese continues to flow into the United States, and indeed what is most striking about the Chinese American class structure is the relative absence of a "middle," compared to the overall U.S. class structure.

The Current Geographic and Socioeconomic Profile

Chinese Americans have historically been, and are still currently, the largest subgroup among the Asian and Pacific Islander population in the United States. The 1990 census counted 1,645,472 Chinese in the United States, a 22.6 percent proportion of the total Asian and Pacific Islander population of 7,273,662.

There is a considerable diversity in home-country origin among Chinese immigrants to the United States. Among those Chinese Americans not born in the United States (921,070 in number), 57.5 percent were from the People's Republic of China (PRC), 16.0 percent from Hong Kong, and 26.5 percent were from Taiwan. Mandarin is the *lingua franca* among educated Chinese immigrants, but many immigrants (particularly the unschooled) speak only their regional dialects, of which there are a great variety (such as Taiwanese, Cantonese, Taishanese, Shanghai dialect, etc.).

Geographically, Chinese Americans are heavily concentrated in the western region. As Table 14-1 reports, more than half (52.8 percent) of the population resides in the western states, whereas less than a quarter (21.2 percent) of the general U.S. population resides in this same region. Chinese Americans are also overrepresented in the Northeast, with a 26.9 percent share as compared with 20.4 percent among the general population. The Midwest and South are regions of marked underrepresentation among Chinese Americans.

Turning to the geographical profile by metropolitan area, Table 14-2 shows that New York, Los Angeles, and San Francisco are the primary areas

TABLE 14-1
Chinese Population Compared with General U.S. Population, By Region, 1990

Region	Chinese Population	General Population
Northeast	26.9	20.4
Midwest	7.8	24.0
South	12.5	34.4
West	52.8	21.2
	N = 1,648,696	N = 248,709,873

Source: U.S. Census of Population and Housing, 1990, Social and Economic Characteristics, U.S. Summary.

TABLE 14-2
Metropolitan Areas with Greatest Chinese Population

New York PMSA	246,817
Los Angeles-Long Beach PMSA	245,033
San Francisco PMSA	162,636
Oakland PMSA	90,691
San Jose PMSA	65,027
Honolulu MSA	63,265
Boston PMSA	44,155
Anaheim-Santa Ana PMSA	41,403
Chicago PMSA	40,189
Washington, D.C. MSA	39,034
Sacramento	29,558
Houston PMSA	29,345

Source: U.S. Census of Population and Housing, 1990, Metropolitan Statistical Areas.

of residence among Chinese Americans. If the populations of Oakland and San Jose are counted as part of the broader "consolidated metropolitan area" surrounding San Francisco Bay, then the urban complexes of New York City, Los Angeles, and the San Francisco bay area account for 810,204 Chinese Americans, *nearly half* (49 percent) of the total Chinese American population.

Table 14-3 reports on income and poverty status. The high median annual household income of Chinese Americans ($36,259 as compared to $30,056 for the general U.S. population) fuels the popular perception of Chinese Americans as a prosperous minority. A closer look at the income profile, however, is highly revealing. Where the general population is more heavily concentrated in the lower-to-middle income levels (69.3 percent earn between $5,000 and $50,000 per year) than Chinese American households (57.1 percent earn between $5,000 and $50,000 per year), Chinese American

TABLE 14-3
Income and Poverty Status of U.S. Households, Compared with Chinese and Taiwanese Households, 1989

	U.S. Households	Chinese	Taiwanese*
	N = 91,993,582	N = 509,395	N = 20,990
Median household income	$30,056	$36,259	$42,316
Household income			
<$5,000	6.2%	7.5%	9.5%
$5,000–24,999	35.6%	27.9%	21.5%
$25,000–49,999	33.7%	29.2%	26.2%
$50,000–74,999	15.0%	18.3%	18.8%
$75,000≥	9.5%	17.0%	24.0%
Households on public assistance	7.5%	8.2%	5.1%
Persons below poverty level	13.1%	14.0%	13.7%

* Taiwanese data presented are a subset of the total Chinese population in the preceding column.
Source: U.S. Census of Population and Housing, Asian and Pacific Islander Databook, United States Summary, Table 5.

household incomes have a more *polarized* profile, with concentrations at the extremes, among the extremely poor and the more affluent. In 1989, 7.5 percent of Chinese American households earned less than $5000 a year, as opposed to 6.2 percent of all U.S. households. Meanwhile, affluent households earning $50,000 a year or more constituted 35.5 percent of Chinese American households, as compared with 24.5 percent of U.S. households in general. Taiwanese (a subset of Chinese) are even more polarized, with 9.5 percent of these households earning less than $5000 a year, and 42.8 percent earning $50,000 a year or more. Evidence of poverty in the midst of plenty is apparent when looking at poverty status. Households on public assistance comprise 8.2 percent of Chinese American households, as compared with 7.5 percent among the general U.S. population. Fourteen percent of the Chinese American population is below the poverty level, as opposed to 13.1 percent among the general U.S. population.

Table 14-4, which presents data on educational attainment, reinforces the picture of polarity demonstrated in Table 14-3. When compared with the general U.S. population, Chinese Americans are more highly concentrated at the extremes, among the very poorly educated and among the highly educated. Among Chinese Americans, 9.6 percent of those persons 25 and over received less than a fifth-grade education, as compared with 2.7 percent among the general U.S. population. Looking at the more highly educated, 40.7 percent of Chinese Americans received a bachelor's degree or higher, as opposed to 20.3 percent among the U.S. general public. Taiwanese are not highly represented in the poorly educated categories; 59.7 percent of this group received a bachelor's degree or higher.

TABLE 14-4
Educational Attainment of General U.S. Population Compared with Chinese and Taiwanese Americans (Persons 25 and over)

	General Pop.	Chinese	Taiwanese
Less than 5th grade	2.7%	9.4%	2.6%
5th to 12th grade, no diploma	22.1%	17.0%	7.4%
High school graduate, or equivalency	30.0%	14.5%	12.6%
Some college, or associates degree	24.9%	18.3%	17.6%
Bachelor's degree	13.1%	21.6%	25.2%
Post-graduate degree	7.2%	19.1%	34.5%

Source: U.S. Census of Population and Housing, 1990, Asian and Pacific Islander Databook, U.S. Summary.

TABLE 14-5
Occupation and Industry of General U.S. Population Compared with Chinese and Taiwanese Americans, 1990

	U.S. Population	Chinese	Taiwanese
Occupation			
Mgr/Prof	26.4%	35.8%	48.3%
Tech/Sales/Clerical	31.7%	31.2%	34.1%
Service	13.2%	16.5%	9.2%
Farm/For/Fish	2.5%	0.4%	0.2%
Prod/Craft/Repair	11.3%	5.6%	3.3%
Oper/Fabric/Labor	14.9%	10.6%	3.5%
Industry			
Agr/For/Fish	2.7%	0.4%	0.3%
Mining	0.6%	0.2%	0.3%
Construction	6.3%	2.4%	2.6%
Manufacturing	17.7%	18.6%	17.1%
Transp/Comm	7.1%	5.7%	4.7%
Trade	21.2%	29.1%	25.4%
FIRE	6.9%	8.5%	9.8%
Non-prof Services	9.4%	8.6%	8.5%
Prof Services	23.3%	23.0%	28.4%
Government	4.8%	3.4%	2.8%

Source: U.S. Census of Population and Housing, 1990, Asian and Pacific Islander Databooks, U.S. Summary, Table 4.

Table 14-5 presents data on the labor force status of Chinese Americans. Chinese Americans are overrepresented, relative to the general U.S. population, in the managerial/professional category (35.8 percent versus 26.4 percent of the general population) and service category (16.5 percent versus 13.2 percent), but underrepresented in farming/forestry/fishing, production/craft/repair, and operator/fabricator/laborer categories. Taiwanese are heavily concentrated in the professional/managerial (48.3 percent) and technical/sales/clerical (34.1 percent) occupations. Turning to the industry profile, Chinese Americans are over-represented, relative to the general U.S. populations, in the manufacturing (18.6 percent to 17.7 percent), trade (29.1 percent to 21.2 percent) and finance/insurance/real estate (FIRE) categories, but underrepresented in transportation/communications, construction, and agriculture.

LITERATURE REVIEW

The classic sociological literature on Chinese Americans may be usefully divided into four major categories: a) historical literature focusing on Chinese immigration and labor; b) seminal theoretical articles featured in major sociological journals which essentially investigate different aspects of Chinese American "assimilation"; c) ethnographic monographs in the "case study" or "community studies" tradition; and d) recent studies on social, political, and economic change in post-1965 "new Chinatowns."

Historical studies invariably focus on the anti-Chinese agitation and exclusionary legislation of the nineteenth century. The legislation in question is the Chinese Exclusion Act of 1882, which was the first U.S. immigration law ever to discriminate specifically against a particular ethnic or racial group. Major studies include Coolidge (1909), Sandmeyer (1939), Barth (1964), Saxton (1971), and Miller (1969). Barth takes somewhat of a "blame the victim" approach, to an extent conceptualizing exclusionary legislation as an American reaction to the clannishness of Chinese immigrants and their failure to adequately assimilate into American society. Coolidge, Sandmeyer, and Saxton on the other hand, consider more carefully how U.S. labor unions and nativist politicians in the western states had a common interest in scapegoating Chinese immigrants in a situation of regional economic decline. The regional debate was propelled into the federal arena, eventually leading to restrictionist immigration legislation. Miller relates how journalistic and literary images of the time helped to create an environment of nativist anti-Chinese xenophobia.

The seminal theoretical studies on the question of Chinese American assimilation, featured in influential sociological journals, have examined the "human ecology" of Chinatowns (Lee, 1949), the social psychology of the Chinese immigrant "sojourner" (Siu, 1952), and the socioeconomic utility of the Chinese "ethnic enclave" (Sanders and Nee, 1987; Zhou and Logan, 1989). The first two articles were heavily influenced by the writings of the Chicago School of Sociology, particularly as espoused by Robert E. Park. The second two articles take a "structural sociology" perspective which ultimately examines the question of social mobility through a use of a quantitative "returns on human capital" approach.

Rose Hum Lee's 1949 article in the American Journal of Sociology observed the deteriorated state of American Chinatowns and predicted their eventual demise. Exclusionary immigration policy had not only led to the decline of Chinese communities, but their eventual "withering away" was predicted through the continued upward mobility and sociocultural assimilation of the Chinese into American society. In a 1952 article also published in the *American Journal of Sociology,* Paul Siu joined the writings of Park on the "marginal man" with Georg Simmel's concept of the "stranger;" he felt the continued social isolation of the Chinese in laundry and restaurant work and their residential self-segregation in Chinatowns acted as a barrier to successful assimilation.

Whereas the aforementioned exclusion-era studies suggested the persistence of Chinese enclaves would block successful integration into U.S. society, post-exclusion research has turned to the new dynamism in American Chinatowns and examined what positive effects might be derived from ethnic residential and economic solidarity. Two recent articles (Sanders and Nee, 1987; Zhou and Logan, 1989) both published in the American Sociological Review have considered the role of "ethnic enclave economies" in incorporating Chinese Americans into the American socioeconomic structure. They utilized a "returns to human capital" methodology promulgated by Wilson and Portes (1980), who found significant positive socio-economic effects for immigrants working in Cuban enterprises, as compared with black workers working in comparable "peripheral sectors" of the Miami regional economy. Extending the analysis to Chinese workers in San Francisco, Sanders and Nee (1987) found an absence of positive effects, attributing this finding to the low-waged character of the restaurant and garment manufacturing work which Chinese immigrants were largely engaged in, work which offered little occupational mobility. Examining New York's Chinatown, Zhou and Logan (1989) generally found positive effects for male workers, accompanied by some negative effects for women, leading them to ponder "to what degree the positive functions of the enclave for men are derived from the subordinate position of women" (p. 818).

Of theoretical importance also is the contribution of Wong (1980), who closely examined the changing socioeconomic status of Chinese American men between 1960 and 1970. Hirschman and Wong (1986) utilized 1920–1960 census data on Chinese and Japanese Americans in examining their remarkable educational attainment. They employed a "middleman minority" theory to suggest that occupational advance by previous generations set a stage for educational attainment among latter generations.

The ethnographic "case study" research category includes two prominent studies on southern rural Chinese Americans. James Loewen's research on the "Mississippi Chinese" found that these immigrants fulfilled a "middleman minority" role in the South from Reconstruction to the modern era by selling retail goods and advancing credit to the African American community. Many Chinese Americans also took on black spouses. Robert Seto Quan's *Lotus Among the Magnolias* also examined the "Delta Chinese," in describing their customs and social structure.

San Francisco's Chinatown was the subject of Victor and Brett de Bary Nee's *Longtime Californ': A Documentary Study of an American Chinatown* (1972), an oral-history-type ethnography which highlighted intergenerational conflict. Chalsa Loo's more recent case study of the same community takes a social work perspective in examining mental health, attitudinal and identity issues.

New York's Chinatown has attracted perhaps the most ethnographic fieldwork attention. Bernard Wong is a major contributor. His first study (1982), a straightforward anthropological ethnography, gave a general introduction to the history and socioeconomic structure of the community, whereas his second book (1988) examined more closely the issue of social change, wherein the political structure of Chinatown had made a transition from a system of elite patronage to a system of organizational brokerage by a range of community organizations.

The last category of research on Chinese Americans also generally takes a community studies or ethnographic approach, situated within a background of social and political change, particularly emphasizing the global context. New York City continues to be a main focus of research, and the "suburban Chinatown" of Monterey Park, California, has also emerged as an important case study.

Peter Kwong's *The New Chinatown* (1987) is the seminal study in this regard. He examines the major new political issues confronting U.S. Chinatowns of the late twentieth century, including the issue of socioeconomic polarization, labor and community politics, overseas capital investment, the growing importance of Chinese immigrants in the garment industry, and the issue of organized crime. To some extent, his consideration of social change in New York City's Chinatown was predicated by Kuo's study of a decade earlier, which examined the fall of the "old guard" elite and rise of new activist community organizations. Hsiang-shui Chen's ethnography of a "satellite Chinatown" in the New York City borough of Queens highlights social and political changes within the global context; the Flushing-Elmhurst area of Queens is seen to be somewhat of a booming "world town," as Chinese Americans mix with other Asians, as well as recent immigrants from other world regions.

Fong's 1994 case study of Monterey Park, American's "first suburban Chinatown," examines community conflict and political realignment in the 1980s as established Anglo residents and politicians reacted to rapid Chinese newcomer settlement and overseas investment with a nativist "Official English" movement and a "slow-growth" antidevelopment movement. A host of articles have also been published on the same subject, including Wong (1989), Horton (1992), and Saito and Horton (1994).

The Perspective of Social Change

The "social change" perspective offers a highly useful analytic window through which to comprehend and interpret the great demographic, economic, and political shifts taking place in Chinatowns of the 1990s. Chinatowns are no longer the isolated, clannish, or "vestigial" enclaves depicted by exclusion-era writers such as Lee (1949) and Siu (1952), but dynamic enclaves thoroughly permeated by developmental change, community activism, and political conflict. Some of these conflicts are internal, but most involve relationships with actors and groups external to Chinatown. A new generation of Chinese activists is deeply involved with civil rights issues regarding racial violence, educational policy, political representation, and U.S. language policy. The workforce, community leadership, and business elites of American Chinatowns are closely involved in local developmental and planning issues. The internal changes have been well depicted by Bernard Wong as involving a shift from "patronage to brokerage." Chinatowns of the exclusion era were politically dominated by the Consolidated Chinese Benevolent Association (CCBA), an informal power structure largely drawn from leaders of the most powerful clan and district organizations in the community. Membership in these organizations depended on the family surname (clan) or regional district to which an immigrant traced his ancestral roots. These associations had originally assisted the first immigrants with credit arrangements, official paperwork, accounting, and transportation connected with passage to America, but continued to play a role throughout the exclusion period with judical matters, job search, housing, social welfare needs, cultural life, and funeral affairs. In essence, they functioned somewhat as "mutual aid associations," but in a strongly patriarchal fashion, as assistance was granted by the leadership in the form of patronage for which enduring loyalty was expected. Leaders were also generally appointed rather than democratically elected.

In the post-1965, post-exclusion era, new voluntary and activist organizations have grown to provide similar functions and services in American Chinatowns. The civil rights movement was a strong incubator of this new trend, and the strength and power of the new organizations depends on the extent to which they can broker political power, monetary resources, and services from external institutions such as local, state, or federal governments, as well as foundations, churches, and other charitable organizations. These new activist organizations are greatly at odds with the old informal political structure, which is often portrayed as a "feudal elite" which kept exclusion-era Chinatowns insular and clannish. The new organizations are staffed generally by latter-generation Chinese Americans who are more literate in English, and include many professionals, community activists, intellectuals, and students.

This shift in internal political structure has not been a "clean" one, however, as the CCBA and the new voluntary and activist organizations compete in the political field of post-exclusion Chinatowns for constituency and power. Added to this schism is a growing factionalization *within* the new "brokerage" style organizations. In New York City's Chinatown, the Chinatown Planning Council (a liberal organization of professionals which grew through substantial government and charitable funding) vied in the 1980s with Asian Americans for Equality (a more militant organization with Marxist roots that grew through legal and political activism, and eventually augmented its power through the local democratic party machinery) for power and resources. In Houston, the Council of Asian American Organizations has contended with the Asian American Coalition in the 1980s and 1990s for constituency, funding, and local political recognition.

In addition to this political factionalization, there is a growing economic factionalization in Chinese American communities between local businesspeople and the representatives of overseas capital. This division has been marked in New York City's Chinatown, the Los Angeles suburban Chinatown of Monterey Park, and the San Francisco Bay Area Chinatowns. Overseas capital has utterly transformed the landscape of U.S. (as well as Canadian) Chinatowns in the 1980s, provoking many political and planning conflicts.

The fact of internal factions in contemporary Chinatowns impinges significantly on the manner in which Chinese Americans interact with the external society. The interactions of Chinese Americans with established Anglo residents, communities, and local governments can be examined in the civil rights arena, in the political arena, and in urban planning.

Civil Rights and Political Redistricting

There has been more unity than factionalization in the civil rights arena, particularly in the areas of legal defense against racial violence, and in educational policy. The "Vincent Chin incident" is a cogent example of an issue that galvanized Chinese Americans nationwide for unified purpose.

In June 1982, Vincent Chin, a 27-year-old Detroit draftsman, was out for an evening with friends some nights before his scheduled wedding. Two white men, Ronald Ebens and his stepson, Michael Nitz, taunted the group, and a fistfight and chase ensued. Ebens and Nitz eventually clubbed Chin with a baseball bat, and Chin died four days later. Both men were laid-off autoworkers and apparently mistook Chin for Japanese (according to one eyewitness, Ebens made the remark before the altercation that it was people like Chin who were causing the loss of jobs in Detroit). The two assailants eventually received three years' probation and fines of some $4,000 each on manslaughter and second-degree murder charges. An outraged Asian American community lobbied nationwide with Congress and the Justice Department, which eventually ordered a civil rights investigation under the FBI. A federal grand jury indicted them on two civil rights counts, and Ebens was eventually sentenced to twenty-five years in jail. An appeal of the conviction ended in a retrial in 1986, however, which subsequently resulted in the complete acquittal of Ebens (Chan, 1991).

Another prominent case similar to the Vincent Chin incident ended differently. Jim Loo, also Chinese American, was killed in July 1989 in Raleigh, North Carolina, by two whites who mistook Loo for Vietnamese (the two assailants were brothers who had lost a third sibling in Vietnam). A successful legal campaign by a quickly organized Jim Loo American Justice Coalition (made more vigilante by the memory of Vincent Chin) this time witnessed the sentencing of one brother to thirty-seven years imprisonment in 1990 (Chan: 178–79).

The incidence of hate crimes such as the Vincent Chin and Jim Loo cases will not likely diminish in the future as domestic economic uncertainty and an increasingly competitive global economy may lead some U.S. whites to displace their frustrations on Asian Americans. Interestingly enough, perpetrators of pejorative violence against Asian Americans are confused by their own inability to properly identify national differences, since the two Chinese Americans killed in the above-mentioned cases were both misidentified. Only vigilance in the Asian American community in drawing the attention of state attorneys and federal officials to prosecuting will be a means of deterring future crimes.

Another civil rights issue affecting Chinese Americans is the issue of political redistricting and minority political representation. Asian American activists, along with African American, Latino, and gay activists, have questioned the traditional boundaries of political voting districts, which have historically been "gerrymandered" by entrenched white politicians with strong political machines and strong campaign war chests. The Voting Rights Act of 1965, along with amendments added in 1982, enables minority plaintiffs to challenge election results if they do not support minority candidates where there is a statistically strong proportion of minority population. In 1986, the *Thornburgh* v. *Gingles* decision of the Supreme Court further supported this position, ruling that it was "illegal for a state or locality with racial bloc voting not to create a district in which minorities are in the majority if such a district can be created" (Wei: 266). Challenges to political district apportionment and redistricting were common in minority areas throughout the United States following the release of 1990 census population data; in the Chinese American community, controversy was centered on New York City and Los Angeles. I will consider the New York City case.

In New York City, reapportionment hearings in 1991 were occasioned by the planned expansion of the city council from 35 to 51 seats. In Chinatown, redistricting proceedings were marked by severe political factionalization within the Chinese American community as rival organizations pushed different agendas. Since the population of Chinatown by itself was insufficient to support a 140,000-voter district on its own, adjoining districts had to be linked in coalition. A fierce fight among Chinatown advocacy organizations ensued. Asian Americans for Equality (AAFE) favored linking Chinatown with the affluent voters of the Wall Street financial district. Chinatown Staff and Workers Association and It's Time, however, felt that Chinatown's low-income population would be better served through being tied with the Latino population of the Lower East Side in a "multiracial district." The AAFE district won, but the AAFE candidate, Margaret Chin, eventually lost after a bitter contest in which many Chinatown voters were urged to defect to the Anglo candidate, who was promoted as a better advocate of the low-income community.

In Houston, by contrast, a Chinese American, Martha Wong, successfully captured a district seat in the 1993 city council election. An effort by Glenda Kay Joe to win an at-large seat, however, was unsuccessful.

Capital Factions, Political Conflict, and Planning

There has been factionalism in the Chinese American economic community in ways that do not necessarily parallel the political factionalism. The central schism has been a conflict between the interests of overseas investment capital and local Chinese American business and community interests. The overseas faction is a flow of grand capital which appears in Chinese American communities chiefly in the form of transnational Chinese banks and real estate projects (of an office, residential, commercial or mixed-use nature). Overseas Chinese capital flow into the United States is motivated both by political uncertainty and capital surplus in Hong Kong and Taiwan.

Local Chinese American enterprises, businesspeople, and residents have generally been at odds with the overseas capital faction, which has a displacing effect on local Chinese businesses. Local governments and the Anglo American community, however, have been equivocal about overseas Chinese capital. In New York City's Chinatown, city planners sought to encourage overseas investment. In Southern California's Monterey Park, however, city officials felt threatened by overseas Chinese capital.

In New York City's Chinatown city planners began encouraging overseas capital investment through the creation of a "Special Manhattan Bridge District" in 1981, which facilitated high-rise development in what had traditional been a low-rise tenement district. Two high-rise condominium projects involving overseas Chinese capital were announced shortly after the district was designated. Vociferous community opposition developed when it was learned that low-income residents had been harassed and displaced from the sites. Legal challenges eventually overturned both projects. In this environment of community opposition, city planners also retracted a proposed high-rise commercial tower, replacing this project with a new city jail. A few scaled-back high-rise projects (including a two banks, a condominium tower, and a hotel) have also been erected on less controversial sites (Lin, forthcoming).

A local sentiment against affluent overseas Chinese still pervades New York City's Chinatown. Since the bulk of Chinatown's population is still a low-income proletariat, there is also somewhat of a suspicion of middle-class professional and suburban Chinese Americans. Peter Kwong (1987) has defined this as a rift between the "uptown" and "downtown" Chinese Americans. The downtown constellation of community and political advocacy interests is furthermore highly factionalized, since the many organizations compete for funding and constituents, presenting a united front only when a common enemy is identified, such as overseas capital or the city bureaucracy.

I encountered this volatile political environment while doing research in New York City's Chinatown for my doctoral dissertation at the New School for Social Research from 1988 to 1991. Although I was a suburban Chinese American from Washington, D.C., I was accepted into the community through my work/study affiliation with the Chinatown History Project, a politically neutral organization which was generally held in high regard by community organizations for its interest in local historical documentation and cultural preservation. I was able to gain many contacts for interviews through the History Project's board of directors. When conducting my research and data-gathering on overseas investment in Chinatown, I emphasized instead my academic qualifications, which were well-regarded by the realtors, banking representatives, and city officials that I interviewed.

In Monterey Park, city officials were much less friendly to the encroachments of overseas Chinese capital, which began to be called the "Chinese Beverly Hills" and "Little Taipei" in the 1980s, as investors transformed the community with banks, restaurants, high-rise condominium and strip mall developments. The established Anglo community responded with a populist growth-control movement as they feared invasive "highland" high-density real estate development would disrupt their prosperity as "lowland" single-family property owners. A moratorium on new construction was installed by city council in 1987. The slow-growth movement also had a nativist tinge through association with the "official English" movement (a nationwide phenomenon in the 1980s) which sought to remove Chinese signage. A boisterous mayoral campaign in 1988 witnessed the emergence and victory of Judy Chu, a local Chinese American who positioned herself against uncontrolled foreign investment and promoted a platform of both "managed growth" and racial harmony (Fong: 174–5; Horton: 215–6; Wong: 117–9).

A new approach to Chinatown planning is emerging among city planners in both New York City and Houston that may promote the kind of growth that city officials desire while preserving community identity. The strategy of "urban tourism" seeks to promote Chinatowns as districts for eating, shopping, and cultural entertainment which appeals to out-of-town tourists, lunch-time employees, and conventioneers. Local "mom-and-pop" style restaurants, groceries, and curio shops are important elements to retain, as well as historically significant buildings.

The Houston Chinatown Coalition, led by businessman Dan Nip, has been promoting the economic development of Houston's Chinatown with an eye to capturing business from the Brown Convention Center, with adjoins the district. The plan is also promoted as a long-term strategy to revitalize the declining east-side of the central business district. As of summer 1994, city approval was very close on a tax-increment-financing district which would authorize a bond issue necessary to finance the infrastructural upgrading necessary for the plan to proceed. Nip plans restaurants, a cultural museum, and a large stone gate with benevolent lions (to be provided through a sister-city project with the Chinese city of Shenzhen).

In New York City's Chinatown, a tourism council (composed of local businesspeople and community representatives) was assembled in 1991 by the Manhattan borough president's office in an effort to promote artistic/cultural affairs and commercial activity. The tourism council helped to develop the Chinatown segment of the Gray Line trolley tour, which takes out-of-town tourists through selected districts of lower Manhattan. A competition for small grants to further develop the Chinatown arts and business community for tourism was being conducted by the Borough President's Office in 1995.

CHINESE AMERICAN CULTURE: CHANGING IMAGES AND IDENTITIES

The new interest among city managers in the tourist potential of Chinatowns is emblematic of a rise in the general recognition of Chinese culture in American life. The image of the insular enclave of the exclusion era gives way to one of a prosperous, dynamic neighborhood which is now a major stop on any sightseer's city tour. The days of chop suey and chow mein have faded as a more discerning American public is now more sensitive to the finer and sometimes subtle differences among Chinese regional cuisines such as Hunan, Sichuan, Cantonese, and Taiwanese. Beyond culinary appreciation, the American public is also consuming an increasing repertoire of Chinese American arts and entertainment.

An ebullient crop of emerging Chinese American film directors have also drawn the interest of the American public. Peter Wang's *A Great Wall* (1985) drew a theme of cultural distance and difference in humorously depicting a Chinese American family's visit to the PRC. Wayne Wang's *Dim Sum* (1987) treated with poignancy and sensitivity a mother-daughter relationship with regard to their different expectations about marriage, family and the community. In *Joy Luck Club* (1993), Wayne Wang further examines generational and cultural conflict and reconciliation among four sets of mothers and daughters. In *Eat a Bowl of Tea* (1989) Wayne Wang depicts patriarchy in the bachelor society of the 1940s in New York City's Chinatown. The young male protagonist suffers identity confusion and temporary sexual impotence so long as he is in the physical and social confines of Chinatown. In *The Wedding Banquet* (1993), Ang Lee revisits the subject of the "nonmasculine" Asian male with his alternately hilarious and sensitive treatment of a gay Taiwanese American professional's abortive attempt to hide his homosexuality from his parents through a wildly orchestrated wedding to an undocumented Chinese immigrant woman artist.

In literature, Maxine Hong Kingston's *The Woman Warrior* (1975) portrays an almost masculine strength and resilience in her woman protagonist, who suffers intergenerational conflict and emotional abuse. In *China Men* (1980), Hong Kingston transgresses time and space through a dream-space of mythological characters who reside in the minds and memories of the immigrant bachelor laborers she documents. Amy Tan's *Joy Luck Club* (1989), arguably the best known piece of recent Chinese American fiction, was adapted to film in 1993 (description above).

In the performing arts, iconoclastic playwright Frank Chin's *Chickencoop Chinaman* (1972) features a restless young man who seeks to escape the constraining poverty and clannishness of San Francisco's Chinatown. Chin's protagonist exudes an exaggerated machismo in a self-conscious effort to confront the societal myth of the emasculated, docile Chinese American male. Avant-garde jazz musician Fred Ho (formerly Houn) similarly projects an explosive manly presence with his commanding baritone saxophone as leader of the Afro-American Jazz Ensemble. Asian American resistance to a history of discrimination and oppression are central messages in his works, such as in his extended multimedia production, *Bamboo That Snaps Back*.

The themes of cultural duality, intergenerational conflict, identity confusion, and sexual tension that are explicit in the many literary and performing art works of contemporary Chinese Americans are sometimes resolved through familial reconciliation. These interpersonal and cultural conflicts and psychological tensions often go unresolved, however, implying that a social change perspective on Chinese American culture is highly relevant and will likely remain pertinent for some years to come. The sentiments of disquiet, restlessness, and paradox that confront the individual in the midst of a community undergoing social and cultural change is also a vital source of their artistic creativity.

THE OTHER SIDE OF PROSPERITY: THE NEW BOAT PEOPLE

Despite a general facade of prosperity, the question mark in the title to this article bids the reader to regard the "other side." The income profile of Chinese Americans as compared with the general U.S. population indicated that the heavy Chinese American representation in affluent strata was counterposed by a noticeable existence of a stratum in poverty. This "polarization" in the socioeconomic structure of the Chinese American population was also of noticeable import when examining political and planning conflicts in contemporary Chinatowns. Returning to the issue of recent Chinese American immigration, the persistence of poverty in the midst of dynamic change is thrown in dramatic light by turning to the issue of the "new boat people," a flow of undocumented immigrants smuggled onto U.S. shores by transnational syndicates.

The banner year in media attention to the issue of Chinese immigrant smuggling was 1993, when thousands of prospective undocumented immigrants were interdicted by the U.S. Coast Guard in unregistered ships attempting landfall, especially off the Pacific Coast from San Francisco to Baja California, but even in the frigid waters off New York City (Hood, 1993). Reports had surfaced in the late 1980s of a Canadian route through Buffalo, New York. In January 1989, a party was drowned when an overloaded raft capsized in the frigid waters of the Niagara River thirty feet away from the Canadian shore (Chan, et al, 1990).

Emanating mainly out of Fujian province, especially through the port of Fuzhou, these prospective immigrants pay up to $30,000 for fake passports and transpacific passage on rusting freighters, braving high seas on meager rations for months in appalling unsanitary conditions. Rather than economic motives, political asylum has been their main rationale for seeking U.S. shores, identifying especially recent political repression in China, and the restrictive one-child family planning policy. Many were repatriated immediately back to China before landfall, but those that managed to reach U.S. soil became eligible applicants for political asylum. The 288 passengers of the Golden Venture, which grounded just offshore of Long Island (enabling most of them to swim to the beach) in the borough of Queens, New York, in June 1993 fall into such a category.

A year after their apprehension by the Coast Guard, most of this group remained housed in detention centers and prisons in New York City and Philadelphia, awaiting the processing of their political asylum claims. The unresolved uncertainty of their detention has become a human rights issue. Many also reported severe treatment en route to the United States, and ongoing threats for recovery of their full passage fee by the criminal syndicates that arranged their voyage (Dunn, 1994).

The resolution of the plight of the Fujianese "boat people" is complicated by a growing anti-immigrant sentiment among the U.S. public. Anti-immigrant xenophobia crested in the 1992 election year, with conservative commentator Patrick Buchanan's "America First" campaign for the Republican presidential nomination, and former Ku Klux Klansman David Duke of Louisiana's similar bid (Muller: 226). These feelings have been further stoked by "radical conservative" media commentators, such as Rush Limbaugh and Howard Stern. A less vehement, but still penetrating nativism is growing among middle-class Republicans and independent voters, especially in states such as California and Florida. The neoliberal Democratic Clinton administration has endorsed the continuing value of immigration in general, but sought to clamp down on undocumented arrivals. With thousands of Haitian and Cuban "boat people" still detained at Guantanamo Bay, however, the problem of political refugees persists.

Newcomer Chinese "boat people" thus seem to have more in common with undocumented immigrants from other race and ethnic groups than established Chinese Americans. Although established Chinese American professionals may not interact with the newcomer immigrant poor, the images these arrivals provoke in the American public, and the policies which the U.S. government may implement, will affect all Chinese Americans at-large.

REFERENCES

Bressi, Todd. "Chinatowns Stand Their Ground," *Planning* (American Planners Association) 53, 12, 6 (November 1987), pp. 12–16.

Chan, Yuen Ying, and James Dao. "Merchants of Misery." *New York Daily News*. September 24, 1990.

Chan, Sucheng. *This Bittersweet Soil: The Chinese in California Agriculture*. 1860–1910. Berkeley, CA: University of California Press, 1986.

———. *Asian Americans: An Interpretive History*. Boston: Twayne Publishers, 1991.

Dunn, Ashley. "Golden Venture's Tarnished Hopes." *New York Times* June 5, 1994, pp. 39+.

Fong, Timothy P. *The First Suburban Chinatown*. Philadelphia: Temple University Press, 1994.

Hood, Marlowe. "Riding the Snake." *Los Angeles Times Magazine,* June 13, 1993, pp. 12–16+.

Horton, John. "The Politics of Diversity in Monterey Park, California," in *Structuring Diversity: Ethnographic Perspectives on the New Immigration,* L. Lamphere, ed. Chicago: University of Chicago Press, 1992, pp. 215–45.

Kuo, Chia-ling. *Social and Political Change in New York's Chinatown: The Role of Voluntary Organizations*. New York: Praeger Publishers. 1977.

Kwong, Peter. *Chinatown, New York: Labor and Politics, 1930–1950*. New York: Monthly Review Press, 1979.

———. *The New Chinatown*. New York: Noonday Press, 1987.

Lin, Jan. "Polarized Development and Urban Planning in New York's Chinatown," *Urban Affairs Review* 30, 3 (January 1995), pp. 332–54.

Loewen, James W. *The Mississippi Chinese: Between Black and White*. Cambridge, MA: Harvard University Press, 1971.

Loo, Chalsa M. *Chinatown: Most Time, Hard Time*. New York: Praeger, 1991.

Miller, Stuart C. *The Unwelcome Immigrant: The American Image of the Chinese, 1785–1882*. Berkeley: University of California Press, 1969.

Muller, Thomas. *Immigrants and the American City*. New York: New York University Press, 1993.

Nee, Victor G. and Brett de Bary Nee. *Longtime Californ': A Documentary Study of an American Chinatown*. New York: Pantheon 1972.

Okihiro, Gary Y. 1989. "Fallow Field: The Rural Dimension of Asian American Studies," in *Frontiers of Asian American Studies,* G.M. Nomura, R. Endo, S.H. Sumida, and R.C. Long, eds. Pullman, WA: Washington State University Press, 1989, pp. 6–13.

Saito, Leland T. and John Horton. "The New Chinese Immigration and the Rise of Asian American Politics in Monterey Park, California," in *The New Asian Immigration in Los Angeles and Global Restructuring*. Philadelphia: Temple University Press, 1994, pp. 233–63.

Sanders, Jimy M. and Victor Nee. "Limits of Ethnic Solidarity in the Enclave Economy," *American Sociological Review* 52 (1987), pp. 745–73.

Saxton, Alexander. *The Indispensable Enemy: Labor and the Anti-Chinese Movement in California*. Berkeley: University of California Press, 1971.

Siu, Paul C.P. "The Sojourner," *American Journal of Sociology* 58, 1 (July 1952), pp. 34–44.

Sung, Betty L. "Polarity in the Makeup of Chinese Immigrants," in *Sourcebook on the New Immigration:Implications for the United States and the International Community,* Roy Simon Bryce-Laporte, ed. New Brunswick, NJ: Transaction Books, 1980.

U.S. Bureau of the Census. 1993a. *1990 Census of Population and Housing, Asian and Pacific Islander,* CP-3-5. Washington, D.C.: Government Printing Office.

———. 1993b. *1990 Census of Population and Housing, Metropolitan Statistical Areas,* CP-1-1B. Washington, D.C.: Government Printing Office.

———. 1993c. *1990 Census of Population and Housing, Social and Economic Characteristics, U.S. Summary.* CP-2-1. Washington, D.C.: Government Printing Office.

———. 1993d. *1990 Census of Population and Housing, The Foreign-Born Population in the United States.* CP-3-1. Washington, D.C.: Government Printing Office.

U.S. Department of Commerce. *We the American . . . Asians.* Washington, D.C.: U.S. Department of Commerce, 1993.

Wei, William. *The Asian American Movement.* Philadelphia: Temple University Press, 1993.

Wilson, Kenneth and Alejandro Portes. "Immigrant Enclaves: An Analysis of the Labor Market Experiences of Cubans in Miami," *American Journal of Sociology* 80 (1980), pp. 295–319.

Wong, Bernard. *Chinatown: Economic Adaptation and Ethnic Identity of the Chinese.* New York: Holt, Rinehart and Winston, 1982.

———. *Patronage, Brokerage and the Chinese Community of New York City.* New York: AMS Press. 1988.

Wong, Charles C. "Monterey Park: A Community in Transition," in *Frontiers of Asian American Studies,* G.M. Nomura, R. Endo, S.H. Sumida, and R.C. Long, eds. Pullman, WA: Washington State University Press, 1989, pp. 113–26.

Woo, Deborah. "The 'Overrepresentation' of Asian Americans: Red Herrings and Yellow Perils," in *Race and Ethnic Conflict,* F.L. Pincus and H.J. Ehrlich, eds. Boulder, CO: Westview Press, 1994, pp. 314–25.

Zhou, Min. *Chinatown: The Socioeconomic Potential of an Urban Enclave.* (Philadelphia: Temple University Press, 1992), and John R. Logan. "Returns on Human Capital in Ethnic Enclaves: New York City's Chinatown," *American Sociological Review* 54 (October 1989), pp. 809–20.

CHAPTER 15

THE REFUGEES AND THE REFUGE: SOUTHEAST ASIANS IN THE UNITED STATES

Yen Le Espiritu

IMMIGRANTS AND REFUGEES

Social scientists and government officials have generally regarded immigrants and refugees as fundamentally different social groups. Immigrants are defined as persons who choose to emigrate in search of economic opportunities, while refugees are those who are forced to flee—often for their lives (Reimers 1985). While useful for the purpose of analysis, the terms *immigrants* and *refugees* mask the diverse motives and events which contribute to people's decisions to migrate. Since the motivations for migration often involve a complex mixture of interrelated economic, political, and personal factors, the difference between immigrants and refugees is a matter of continuum rather than simple categorization (Gold 1992).

While the immigrant/refugees distinction is a question of degree rather than type, political and legal definitions clearly separate the two categories. In the United States, the Refugee Act of 1980 officially eliminated the former practice of granting refuge—and government assistance—only to escapees from Communist-dominated countries. Adopting the United Nations guideline, the 1980 act defines as a refugee any person with a well-founded fear of political, religious, or other forms of persecution, regardless of the political bent of his or her country's regime (Keely 1984). In practice, however, the United States continued to favor escapees from communism above all others. Since 1980, this country has granted refugee status to escapees from Southeast Asia and Eastern Europe, while denying asylum to others fleeing non-Communist regimes such as Guatemala, Haiti, and El Salvador (Chan 1991: 164). In 1987, for example, of the 91,474 refugees admitted for legal residence in the United States, less than 10 percent came from the noncommunist world (U.S. Immigration and Naturalization Service 1987). Most often, political expediency underpins U.S. policy on refugees: depending on the relationship between the United States and the country of origin and the international context of the time, a particular flow of people may be classified as a political exodus or as a group of economically motivated immigrants (Portes and Rumbaut 1990: 23). Given these complexities, refugees should be viewed as a type of immigrant rather than as a group that is completely divorced from the concerns and experiences of the larger immigrant population (Kibria 1993: 12).

Contexts of Exit: The Southeast Asian Exodus

Unlike other Asian groups, there was no history of Vietnamese, Laotian, or Cambodian immigration into the United States prior to the mid-1970s (Skinner 1980).[1] With the collapse of U.S.-backed governments in South Vietnam, Laos, and Cambodia in 1975, over one million escapees from these countries have resettled in the United States. Data from the U.S. State Department indicate that by September 1991, Southeast Asians constituted the largest group of refugees worldwide admitted to the United States since 1975 (Le 1993). To understand why more than half of the refugees who have poured out of Vietnam, Laos, and Cambodia have landed in the United States, it is important to review briefly the history of U.S. military intervention in the wars that ravaged those countries.

Formerly known as French Indochina, Vietnam, Laos, and Cambodia were under French colonial rule from the nineteenth century until the beginning of World War II. In July 1941 the collaborationist Vichy French government permitted Japanese troops to operate in Indochina without interference. When the Japanese surrendered to Allied Forces, the French—with the support of the British and later the Americans—attempted to retake its former colonies. Having declared their independence from France in 1945, left-wing nationalist forces in Vietnam, Cambodia, and Laos fought to prevent French reoccupation. Unable to fight on several fronts simultaneously, France granted independence to both Laos and Cambodia in 1953. One year later, when the Viet Minh (the coalition of communists and nationalists formed by Ho Chi Minh in 1944) decisively defeated the French at the battle of Dien Bien Phu, the Geneva Agreement, which ended hostilities, partitioned Vietnam at the seventeenth parallel and reestablished the nation-states of Cambodia and Laos (Viviani 1984: 10; Chan 1991: 152–53; Welaratna 1993: 16–19).

Throughout the period from 1945 to 1975, a bloody civil war went on between North and South Vietnam. With each side receiving significant foreign assistance, what started out as a civil war became a war of foreign intervention (Viviani 1984: 11). As the Communist Viet Minh (supported by China and the Soviet Union) consolidated their power in the North, the United States pledged military and political support to the anti-Communist regime in South Vietnam. With the Communist victory in China in 1949 and the outbreak of war in Korea in 1950, Vietnam became vital to the United States mission of containing the spread of communism. When the National Liberation Front, commonly called the Viet Cong (South Vietnamese Communists), increased its military activity, U.S. involvement in Vietnam escalated into a ferocious ground and air war. In 1965, the United States (and their allies) committed large numbers of combat troops to Vietnam; the North Vietnamese retaliated by sending troops to the South to assist the Viet Cong. By the end of 1967 there were half a million U.S. troops in Vietnam and the United States was pouring two billion dollars of aid per month into the war (Chan 1991: 154). Between 1971 and 1973 Vietnam was almost completely dependent on U.S. financial and material assistance for the military, for administration, and for the economy (Viviani 1984: 13).

Neighboring Cambodia and Laos were pulled into the Vietnam War primarily because of their strategic locations. With the outbreak of fighting in Vietnam, the United States and South Vietnam pressured Cambodia's neutralist leader Norodom Sihanouk for support. Because of his fears of the power of Hanoi, Sihanouk, a staunch anticommunist, terminated relations with the United States and permitted the North Vietnamese and the Viet Cong to build temporary base camps in and to move supplies through Cambodia. In 1967, in order to deny sanctuary to the Vietnamese Communists, the United States started secretly bombing the Cambodian countryside, dropping more than one hundred thousand tons of bombs over a fifteen-month period. In April 1970 American-backed prime minister Lon Nol led a coup and deposed Sihanouk. During Lon Nol's rule, the American invasions and the aggressive acts of the Lon Nol army against peasants drove large numbers of Cambodians to join the Communist Khmer Rouge (Welaratna 1993: 22–23).

The Vietnam War also extended into Laos; the country was used as a major supply route for North Vietnam (the Ho Chi Minh Trail ran the length of eastern Laos). Begun in 1954, the civil war between the Pathet Lao (Laotian Communists) and the Royal Lao merged with developments in Vietnam: North Vietnam supported the Pathet Lao in order to protect the Ho Chi Minh trail while the United States backed the Royal Lao in an attempt to destroy this supply route (Takaki 1989: 460). Between 1965 and 1973 the United States dropped more than 2 million tons of bombs on Laos in order to halt the movement of troops and armaments to South Vietnam. By 1970, two-thirds of Laos had been bombed, creating more than six hundred thousand refugees (Chan 1991: 154; Kitano and Daniels 1994: 154). The U.S. Central Intelligence Agency recruited Hmong hill tribesmen to conduct American military operations in Laos; their missions included collecting intelligence on North Vietnamese movements, harassing Pathet Lao forces, and rescuing U.S. personnel. Numbering forty thousand in the late 1960s, the Hmong army was the main force holding back the Pathet Lao and their North Vietnamese allies in the latter's attempt to conquer all of Laos (Chan 1994).

In 1973, the United States signed a cease-fire agreement with North Vietnam and began withdrawing combat troops from the country. Without U.S. assistance, the civil war between North and South Vietnam ended on April 30, 1975, when North Vietnamese forces captured Saigon. Communists also came to power in Cambodia and Laos in April and December of 1975, respectively. Influenced by the pervasive American presence in their countries in the decade before 1975, some 135,000 Southeast Asian refugees—95 percent of whom were Vietnamese—fled to the United states that year (see Table 15-1). The number of refugees dropped to 15,000 in 1976 and 7,000 in 1977. Starting in 1978, a more heterogeneous second wave of refugees—the "boat people" from Vietnam and the "land people" from Cambodia and Laos—started streaming into the United States. Annual arrivals jumped from 20,574

TABLE 15-1
National Origin of Refugees by Year of Arrival (Fiscal Years 1975–1987)

		Percentage of Resettled		
	Total No. SE Asians Resettled	Cambodians	Laotians	Vietnamese
1975	135,000	3.5	0.6	95.0
1976	15,000	7.6	70.3	22.1
1977	7,000	11.5	15.4	73.1
1978	20,574	6.4	39.2	54.4
1979	76,521	7.4	37.4	55.1
1980	163,799	9.6	33.3	57.1
1981	131,139	20.5	14.6	65.0
1982	73,522	27.8	13.0	59.1
1983	39,408	33.8	7.4	58.8
1984	51,960	38.2	13.8	47.9
1985	59,970	38.5	10.6	50.9
1986	45,450	22.2	28.4	49.3
1987	40,112	4.83	8.9	56.3

Source: Le (1993: 170).

in 1978 to 76,521 in 1979 to 163,799 in 1980. Since 1981, when 131,139 refugees arrived from Vietnam, Laos, and Cambodia, the number entering the United States has slowly fallen to about 50,000 a year (Chan 1991: 162–63; Kitano and Daniels 1994: 150).

By 1990, the total number of Americans who trace their ancestry to Vietnam, Laos, and Cambodia was 1,1001,054. Accounting for 13 percent of the total Asian American population, the Southeast Asian refugee population—with 614,546 Vietnamese, 147,411 Cambodians, 149,014 lowland Laotians, and 90,082 Hmong—ranks third only after Chinese Americans (1,645,472) and Filipinos (1,406,770).

THE TWO WAVES OF SOUTHEAST ASIAN REFUGEES

Refugee departure is caused generally by a major change in government. The fact that some leave while most stay indicates that a change in government affects the political, economic, and social interests of some groups more than others (Viviani 1984: 5). In most refugee flows, the first group of refugees are usually the leaders of the last regime—military personnel, government officials, the well-to-do, and the educated—who have the most to lose from the new government (North 1984). The subsequent cohorts consist of individuals and families of more modest backgrounds who leave because of the economic hardships and political repression imposed by the new regime (Portes and Rumbaut 1990: 25). The Southeast Asian refugee migration began in April 1975 and proceeded in various phases. The first major wave consisted primarily of South Vietnamese urban residents who left before and immediately after the establishment of communist control of Saigon. Evacuated by U.S. forces, the majority were U.S. employees and members of the South Vietnamese military and government who feared reprisals from the Northern Communists. On the whole, these early arrivals were not representative of the old society but were strongly biased toward higher skills, education, and occupation (Liu 1979; Stein 1979).

In contrast, the second-wave refugees were poorer, less educated, less urbanized, and less westernized than the 1975 arrivals. They were also more ethnically diverse, consisting of ethnic Chinese from Vietnam, Cambodians, lowland Lao, highland Hmong, and smaller numbers of other ethnic groups (Chan 1991: 157). Their exodus was triggered by continued conflict, natural disasters, and deteriorating economic conditions in Vietnam, Cambodia, and Laos, and also by the legacy of thirty years of warfare which "demolished cities, destroyed farmland, denuded forests, poisoned water sources, and left countless unexploded mines" (Chan 1991: 157).

After their victory, the new Communist government in Vietnam began the reconstruction of society: they incarcerated former government officials and military personnel in reeducation camps, ordered urban business and professional elites to labor in remote "New Economic Zones," and closed down all private retail business. These harsh policies led to an unprecedented outflow of refugees, many of whom were ethnic Chinese. The government's decision in March 1978 to nationalize the economy affected the Chinese in Vietnam the most since they controlled about 80 percent of the country's retail trade. Furthermore, as relations between Vietnam and China worsened, the ethnic Chinese were viewed as China loyalists and targeted for discrimination. Caught in the political crossfire, some 250,000 Sino Vietnamese fled into the Guangxi province of China from March 1978 to July 1978, when the Chinese government closed the border. Another estimated half million joined other Vietnamese on crowded, leaky small fishing boats in a hazardous attempt to get to Thailand or Malaysia by sea. The horrors of their flight captured the attention of the world: An estimated 10 to 50 percent died en route, victims of starvation, drowning, rape, and robbery. Pirate attacks on boat people were frequent and brutal: In 1981, 77 percent of the boats which left Vietnam and eventually landed in Thailand were attacked; in 1982, 65 percent; and in 1983, 56 percent. During the spring of 1984, over 100 refugees died during a two-month period alone, victims of pirate attacks on the Gulf of Thailand (Winter and Cerquone 1984). Though tragic, the stories of the "boat people" represent a chapter in human history of great stoicism, courage, and self-sacrifice on the part of many Vietnamese (Viviani 1984: 38; Freeman 1989).

The people of Cambodia (renamed Kampuchea after 1975) faced an even greater calamity. Pol Pot's victory was followed by a reign of terror which ended with the death of some 1.5 million Cambodians—about a third of the country's entire population—and the forced relocations of many others. Under Khmer Rouge rule, relatively few Cambodians escaped because their movement was greatly restricted. When Vietnamese troops invaded Cambodia in 1979, hundreds of thousands of survivors of the genocidal Pol Pot years fled on foot to Thailand. By the end of 1979 more than six hundred thousand Cambodians—about 15 percent of Cambodia's remaining population—lived in makeshift camps along the Thai border, waiting either for resettlement or for peace in Cambodia so they could return to their homes. Although the United States contributed significantly to the destruction of Cambodia, the U.S. government was initially reluctant to resettle Cambodians, preferring instead to "focus resources on aiding the politically more important Vietnamese" (Tollefson 1989: 4-7). To date, there are some 150,000 Cambodian refugees in the United States, who were admitted only after intense lobbying by the Citizens' Commission on Indochinese Refugees in 1978 (Welaratna 1993: 167).

In Laos, the new Communist rulers instituted a bloody campaign of repression against the Hmong for the pro-American role they played during the war. An unknown number of them died; many others sought sanctuary in neighboring countries. In late 1979, 3,000 Hmong refugees were still trying to cross the Mekong River into Thailand. Lowland Lao have also fled their country in order to escape incarceration in reeducation camps (Chan 1994).

As late as 1983, more than 76,000 Laotians languished in Thai refugee camps awaiting resettlement; more than 75 percent of these were mountain people (Kitano and Daniels 1994: 154).

In sum, while the first wave of Southeast Asian refugees avoided many of the most traumatic elements of flight, the refugees who have arrived since 1978—the Vietnamese and ethnic Chinese "boat people," the survivors of the Pol Pot regime in Cambodia, and the Hmong and lowland Lao—have suffered terrible tragedies under the new Communist regimes, survived brutal journeys to neighboring countries, and endured prolonged stays in refugee camps prior to their resettlement in the United States.[2] The diversity of the refugees' origins and contexts of exit helps to explain their varying adaptation experiences in the United States.

ADAPTATION TO U.S. SOCIETY

"Structure of Refuge"

As the largest refugee group ever to so rapidly enter the United States, Southeast Asians posed a distinctive resettlement problem. Responding in part to this influx, the United States created a "structure of refuge"—a federal aid and resettlement system—to deal with refugees (Rumbaut 1989). While immigrants as a rule have received no special aid from the federal government, refugees are eligible for cash assistance and medical benefits after their arrival. Federal financial assistance to refugees has dwindled over the years. In 1982, federal reimbursement to the states for refugee expenditures declined from a period of thirty-six months to eighteen months; in 1988 the period was further reduced to twelve months (Office of Refugee Resettlement 1989: 36). Unfortunately, these changes occurred during the entry of the poorer, less-educated, and more devastated second-wave refugees, most of whom were unable to acquire the skills that would qualify them for decent jobs in twelve months (Hing 1993: 137).

The primary goal of the federal resettlement programs is to transform refugees into financially self-sufficient individuals as quickly as possible. For the most part, government agencies and sponsoring groups believe that in order to achieve self-sufficiency, refugees need to conform to mainstream American values (Liu 1979: 173; Skinner 1980: 108). Efforts to Americanize the refugees began soon after their arrival in the United States. In the processing camps,[3] for example, language classes and camp newspapers presented American customs and norms as patterns to emulate (Kelly 1977). Some refugees resented the emphasis on assimilation, fearing that they were being forced to replace their cultural traditions and languages with American ones (Wright 1980: 510). Contracted by the U.S. Department of State, the volags, or voluntary social service agencies, played a leading role in the resettlement of Southeast Asian refugees. These private agencies, which received a grant of

$500 for each refugee they aided, were responsible for ensuring that the refugees receive such needed services as English language classes, legal help, job counseling and placement, health assessments, and income support (Office of Refugee Resettlement 1983). However, Wilson and Garrick (1983) have shown that between 50 percent and 70 percent of refugees did not know how to obtain the services that were available to them. Oftentimes those refugees who needed a service most could not obtain it because their interactions with resettlement staff were marred by cultural and linguistic barriers (Gold 1992: 164). In a summary of the cultural interaction between Americans and the refugees, Robert Proudfoot (1990) lists twenty-six areas of frustration for both sides; these include cultural and value differences, unrealistically high expectations of success, unprepared sponsors, the lumping together of all refugees, and enormous language barriers. Along the same line, Welaratna (1993: 271–72) observes that resettlement officials and their Cambodian clientele had different concepts of success and failure. From the perspective of refugee resettlement officials, Cambodians have not established self-sufficiency because of their "welfare mentality." But from the Cambodian worldview, success is not measured by the American standards of economic wealth and individual freedom but by success in personal and family interactions. Welaratna's observation challenges many of the negative stereotypes about Cambodians that are perpetuated by mainstream Americans and calls attention to the need to incorporate the Cambodian worldview into public policies.

The refugees were required to have a sponsor—individuals or organizations willing to assist the refugees in adjusting to their new surroundings—before they could leave the refugee processing camps. Since few sponsors could house the large extended families of Southeast Asians, the families often ended up separated and divided. Thus not surprisingly, few Vietnamese stayed in their adopted communities; by 1978, about half had moved from their original locations to be closer to friends and relatives or to have access to better job opportunities and higher levels of public assistance (Social Security Administration 1978). Sponsors and refugees often had dissimilar views about how the refugees should act. For example, while sponsors assumed that refugees should accept any job offers, many refugees refused to take menial jobs because of the tensions involved in downward economic and social mobility (Skinner 1980: 112).

Reception by the U.S. Public

The majority of Americans did not welcome the Southeast Asians. A Harris poll taken in May 1975 indicated that more than 50 percent of the American public felt that Southeast Asian refugees should be excluded; only 26 percent favored their entry. Many seemed to share Congressman Burt Talcott's conclusion that, "Damn it, we have too many Orientals" (cited in Rose 1985:

205). Five years later, public opinion toward the refugees had not changed. A 1980 poll of American attitudes in nine cities revealed that nearly half of those surveyed believed that the Southeast Asian refugees should have settled in other Asian countries (Starr and Roberts 1981). This poll also found that over 77 percent of the respondents would disapprove of the marriage of a Southeast Asian refugee into their family and 65 percent would not be willing to have a refugee as a guest in their home (Roberts 1988: 81). Anti–Southeast Asian sentiment also took violent turns. Refugees from Vietnam, Laos, and Kampuchea in many parts of the United States have been attacked or even killed; and their properties have been vandalized, firebombed, or burned (United States Commission on Civil Rights 1992: 22–48).

Resource competition theory posits that self-interest explains public animosity toward immigrants. Especially during economic downturns, the native-born blame immigrants for the nation's problems and regard them as unwanted competitors (Bonacich 1972; Light 1983: ch. 13). Historically, Asians in the United States have borne most of the blame for economic woes (Saxton 1971; Kitano 1980; Wong 1985). Anti–Southeast Asian sentiment seemed to reflect the economic downturns of the late 1970s and early 1980s. The major economic dislocations of the period—and a perceived decline of U.S. global power—fueled a resurgence of racism, nativism, and xenophobia (Rumbaut and Rumbaut 1984; Omi and Winant 1986). In a context of high unemployment, climbing inflation, skyrocketing interest rates, and Federal cutbacks in programs for the poor, many Americans regarded the Southeast Asians as unwelcome competitors for scarce jobs and dwindling public resources. A 1980 poll conducted in nine cities indicated that 47 percent of the respondents believed that "Indochinese refugees take jobs away from others in my area" (Starr and Roberts 1982). In Orange County, California (the home of the largest concentration of Vietnamese in the United States), refugees were accused of receiving government assistance at the expense of American taxpayers, exacerbating the county's housing shortage, of draining community social support systems, of threatening the county's health standards, and of straining a tightening employment market (Desbarats and Holland 1983: 26). In Texas and California, competition between Vietnamese and white fishermen has erupted in violent confrontations (U.S. Commission on Civil Rights 1992: 40–41).

Southeast Asians have also competed with other U.S. racial and ethnic minorities for low-cost housing, jobs, and government assistance. African Americans and Chicanos have complained of a double standard in funding priorities. In a number of universities, for example, these two groups have charged that the Southeast Asian refugees were receiving a disproportionate amount of financial aid, thereby decreasing resources available to "indigenous" minority students (Skinner and Hendricks 1977). In the context of declining economic opportunities and increasing competition for economic subsistence in urban America, the potential for conflict among people of color is ever increasing. Because of their ethnic and cultural differences, the Southeast Asian refugees are perfect targets for the displaced hostility of the traditional inhabitants of urban areas.

Creating Their Own Refuge: The Southeast Asian Community

Ignoring the possible social and psychological consequences of separation, the government dispersed the Southeast Asian refugees as widely as possible in order to minimize the financial burden on any single locality, force a more rapid assimilation, and defuse the potential for ethnic organization (Hing 1993: 129). In 1975, more than 50 percent of the Vietnamese were resettled in states where the total number of Southeast Asians was under three thousand. But the refugees did not remain in their assigned locations; instead, the majority have remigrated to the Sunbelt states and reunited with family members and friends. California, with its sizable Asian population, warm climate, and generous public assistance programs, has the most Southeast Asian refugees, followed by Texas and Washington (See Table 15-2). In 1980, the California Department of Social Services estimated that one out of four refugees initially resettled elsewhere had moved to California (Desbarats and Holland 1983: 23–24). Although the influx of Southeast Asians to California has fallen to half its levels in the early 1980s, their annual immigration rate is still high, in the neighborhood of fifteen thousand persons (Ong 1990: 3). By 1990, California had over 45 percent of the country's Southeast Asian population (453,363) (*Asian Week* 1991). Within California, close to 40 percent of Southeast Asian refugees live in the Southern California counties of Los Angeles and Orange. Southeast

TABLE 15-2
Distribution of Southeast Asians in the United States, 1990

State	Total Number	Percent of Total
California	453,363	45.3%
Texas	85,029	8.5%
Washington	36,724	3.7%
Minnesota	36,459	3.6%
Massachusetts	33,732	3.4%
Virginia	27,178	2.7%
Pennsylvania	23,788	2.4%
Wisconsin	23,010	2.3%
New York	22,619	2.3%
Florida	20,379	2.0%

Source: U.S. Bureau of the Census, 1990 Census Report.

Asian ethnic groups are also clustered within metropolitan areas. In Los Angeles County, for example, Vietnamese are located in the San Gabriel Valley on the east side of Los Angeles, while Cambodians have largely settled in the city of Long Beach to the South (Ong and Blumenburg 1994: 118). Given their extraordinary growth rate, California's Southeast Asian population is projected to reach 613,000 by the year 2000 (Ong 1990, 4).

Reflecting the concerns of the United States with assimilation, most studies of Southeast Asians have focused on their relations with the larger society rather than on relations among Southeast Asians themselves. Thus we have very little information on the institutions, leaders, and collective goals of these emerging communities. The existing data suggest that through secondary migration, the Southeast Asian refugees have established new ethnic enclaves and created their own structure of refuge, providing social activities, financial assistance, and psychological support for compatriots (Gold 1992; Kibria 1993). By the early 1980s, over five hundred mutual assistance associations (MAAs) had been created within the refugee communities (Baldwin 1984). In Vietnamese communities, for example, negative experiences with resettlement officials have prompted some refugees to create their own networks, culturally informed organizations, and grass-roots movements as alternatives to mainstream resettlement agencies (Gold 1992: 165). In larger Hmong communities, the Lao Family Community—an organization linking Hmong families all over the United States—provides English classes, vocational training, and interpreter services for their members. As the mutual assistance associations become more established, they are also becoming more politically active, lobbying for refugee rights both in Southeast Asia and in the United States (Rutledge 1992: 57). These ethnic-based associations and enclaves have not been conflict free; most have had to manage internal strifes stemming from differing political ideologies, status distinctions, and competition for followers, leadership position, and funding (Kitano and Daniels 1994: 161).

Southeast Asians in the U.S. Economy: Diversity in Adaptation

Asian Americans are often celebrated as America's "model minority"—minorities who succeed through sheer hard work and whose examples should be emulated by others. Since their arrival in the mid-1970s, Southeast Asian refugees, particularly the Vietnamese, have gradually become incorporated into the myth of the Asian American success, particularly in the popular media. This glowing assessment tells only half-truths, masking the plight of disadvantaged subgroups and glossing over the problems of underemployment, misemployment, and unemployment. In reality, Southeast Asian entry into the U.S. labor market has been heterogenous. They are found today at the higher end of the labor market, but also in low-paid menial work and in business and self-employment.

Available evidence indicates that by the mid-1980s, those Vietnamese who had arrived in 1975 had achieved parity in their household income levels with the general U.S. population (Office of Refugee Resettlement 1988). Although the 1975 arrivals have made impressive strides in their economic adaptation, their high levels of household income may be an artifact created by the larger average number of workers in many Vietnamese American families. According to the 1990 census, the proportion of Vietnamese families with three or more workers was 21 percent compared with the national proportion of 13 percent (U.S. Bureau of the Census 1993). Thus their household incomes indicate the presence of more workers in each family, and not necessarily higher incomes. Moreover, there had been much downward mobility. According to a 1978 study of Vietnamese refugees, 30 percent had been professionals in Vietnam but only 7 percent were professionals in the United States (Stein 1979: 29). Similarly, a 1983 study found that 19 percent had been professionals in Vietnam but that here they represented only 6 percent (Haines 1986: 73).

While the majority of the 1975 arrivals have the skills and education which permitted their entry into the U.S. middle class, succeeding waves of less privileged refugees have had less economic success (Office of Refugee Resettlement 1990). The post-1978 refugees overall resemble a working poor population: their economic status is characterized by unstable, minimum-wage employment, welfare dependency, and participation in the informal economy. As Gold and Kibria (1993) reported, many second-wave Vietnamese refugees are employed in sectors of the economy that offer little chance for upward mobility. Faced with limited, low-quality job options, some refugees have withdrawn from the labor force: the labor force participation rates for Southeast Asian refugees declined from 55 percent in 1983 to 39 percent in 1987 (Office of Refugee Resettlement 1987: 131; 1988: 141). In 1985, ten years after Southeast Asian refugees first entered the United States, 50 percent of California's four hundred thousand refugees were fully reliant on welfare (Arax 1987: 1). At the national level, 1991 data indicate that the welfare-dependency rate of Southeast Asians in the first twelve months of their resettlement in the United States was about 45 percent for Vietnamese, 44 percent for Laotians (including Hmong), and close to 100 percent for Cambodians (Le 1993: 177).

According to the 1990 census, the economic situation of the Southeast Asian population, particularly of the Hmong, remains bleak (See Table 15-3). In 1989, the national per capita income was $14,143, compared to $9,032 for Vietnamese, $5,597 for Laotian, $5,120 for Cambodian, and only $2,692 for Hmong. The Hmong also had the highest poverty rate (63.6 percent) and lowest labor force participation rate (29.3 percent). Southeast Asians also had sharply lower socioeconomic status than the "average" Asian American. Table 15-3 shows that, whereas almost 38 percent of all Asian Americans were college graduates in 1989, the proportion of college graduates among

TABLE 15-3
Selected Social and Economic Characteristics for the Southeast Asian Population, 1990

Characteristics	United States	Total Asian	Vietnamese	Cambodian	Laotian	Hmong
Total persons	248,709,873	5,167,530	614,547	147,547	149,014	90,082
% high school grads[a]	75.2	77.6	61.2	34.9	40.0	31.1
% college grads[b]	20.3	37.7	17.4	5.7	5.4	4.9
% do not speak English "very well"	54.1	56.0	65.0	73.2	70.2	78.1
% in labor force[c]	65.3	67.4	64.5	46.5	58.0	29.3
Unemployment rate[d]	6.3	5.2	8.4	10.3	9.3	17.9
% managers or professionals[e]	26.4	31.2	17.6	9.8	5.0	12.8
Per capita income in 1989	14,143	13,806	9,032	5,120	5,597	2,692
Poverty rate in 1989[f]	13.1	14.0	25.7	42.6	34.7	63.6

[a] Percentage of all persons 25 years and over who have completed high school or higher.
[b] Percentage of all persons 25 years and over who have completed 4 or more years of college.
[c] Labor force rate for persons age 16 and over.
[d] Unemployment rate for persons age 16 and over.
[e] Percentage of employed persons 16 years and over whose occupation is in a managerial or professional specialty.
[f] Percentage of persons with income below the poverty level.
Source: U.S. Bureau of the Census 1993, pp. 9–10.

Southeast Asians ranged from 17 percent for the Vietnamese to 5 percent for the Hmong. Similarly, Southeast Asian unemployment rates and poverty rates were substantially higher than those of Asian Americans as a group. These statistics call attention to the danger of lumping all Asian groups together, since Southeast Asians do not share in the relatively favorable socioeconomic outcomes attributed to the "average" Asian American. Moreover, racial lumping is fundamental to racism because it permits outsiders "to order a universe of unfamiliar peoples without confronting their diversity and individuality" (Blauner 1972: 113).

Preliminary studies indicate that the mobility patterns of refugees may differ from those of other immigrants. In a study of the economic progress of eleven different immigrant groups, Chiswick (1979) concluded that refugees face the steepest barriers in achieving economic success. This is so because refugees are less likely to be a self-selected labor force than economic migrants. Instead, their numbers include many unemployable: young children, the elderly, religious and political leaders, and people in poor mental and physical condition (Portes and Rumbaut 1990). They are also less likely to have acquired readily transferable skills and are more likely to have made investments (in training and education) specific to the country of origin (Chiswick 1979; Montero 1980). For example, there are significant numbers of Southeast Asian military personnel with skills for which there is no longer a market in the United States. Coming from a preliterate and agricultural culture, the Hmong's economic prospect seems most dismal: In 1990, a large proportion lacked proficiency in English, urban job experience, and adequate education (See Table 15-3). A 1987 California study showed that many of the long-term welfare families have been Hmong (Nhu 1988).

While internal group characteristics—English proficiency, job skills, work experience, and education—are key determinants of economic success, differences in economic achievements are often the product of different economic opportunities (Morawska 1990: 196). For example, when European immigrants were arriving in large numbers in the late nineteenth century, the United States was becoming an urban industrial society. The growth of modern industry in northeastern and north central cities absorbed the millions of South and East European immigrants to the United States. In contrast, the Southeast Asians arrived in the United States during a period when opportunities for unskilled labor had declined drastically (Gold and Kibria 1993). Since the 1970s, the overall economic restructuring has generated, on the one hand, an increase in elite, highly-paid managerial, banking, and administrative jobs, and, on the other hand, a much larger growth in low-paying service and retail jobs. Meanwhile, higher paying, unionized manufacturing jobs have all but disappeared as firms moved production facilities to countries and regions where wages and levels of unionization are lower (Sassan 1988; Light and Bonacich 1988). Lacking the skills and education to catapult them into the primary sector of the economy, most Southeast Asians are employed in the secondary sector in which wages are low, working conditions unattractive or even dangerous, and mobility opportunities limited (Bach 1984; Caplan, Whitmore, and Bui 1985).

Southeast Asians have also created their own solution to labor market barriers through small business development. Historically, self-employment was the only alternative to joblessness for Asian immigrants. Business ownership is appealing because it offers the prospect of financial security, independence, and the opportunity to employ family members (Gold 1988). Of the three Southeast Asian groups, the Vietnamese have been the most active entrepreneurs and the Laotians the least (Portes and Rumbaut 1990: 92). Between 1982 to 1987, the number of Vietnamese-owned businesses increased 414 percent, from 4,989 businesses in 1982 to 25,671 businesses in 1987 with the reported receipts of $532,200,000 in 1982 to $1,361,000,000 in 1987. This increase is more remarkable when compared to the 87 percent increase for all Asian American populations, and 14 percent for all U.S. firms during the same period (United States Department of Commerce 1991). It is noteworthy that many of the more successful refugee entrepreneurs are of Chinese ethnicity; community activists estimate that up to 40 percent of entrepreneurs in Orange County's Little Saigon (the largest Vietnamese community outside of Vietnam) are Chinese Vietnamese. Using overseas Chinese capital, Chinese Vietnamese built most of the area's strip and enclosed malls that house retail stores, restaurants, and offices (Gold 1994: 199, 202). Cambodian refugees, on the other hand, have found a niche in the doughnut business—an ideal economic opportunity because it requires little business know-how and almost no English. Today, well over half of the small mom-and-pop stores and even Winchell's franchises are owned or managed by Cambodian families (Akast 1993).

Refugee entrepreneurs have played an important role in transforming urban neighborhoods. In some cases, they have revitalized declining inner-city neighborhoods; in others, they have created new ethnic commercial and cultural centers in suburban areas where Asians were once invisible. Their businesses also employ marginal workers such as refugees and Latino immigrants, and provide relatively cheap and available goods and services to low-income populations (Le 1993; Gold 1994). Ethnic entrepreneurship is often seen as proof of the benefits of the enterprise system: If people are ambitious and willing to work hard, they can "make it" in the United States. In reality, few immigrants and refugees manage to achieve upward mobility through entrepreneurship. Most ethnic-owned businesses have very low gross earnings and run a high risk of failure. The chances for business failure appear particularly high for Southeast Asian refugees; for every 20 businesses started by them each month, 18 failed during the first year (May 1987). Many businesses could not survive if it were not for the unpaid labor of spouses, children, relatives, and other oppressed workers. Consequently, wages and working conditions of many refugee businesses are dismal. As an example, in Southern California, many Cambodian-owned doughnut shops are open twenty-four hours a day, with the husbands typically baking all night, while wives and teenage children work the counter by day. Their profits come directly from their family labor and from staying open long hours (Akst 1993; Gold 1994). In addition to long working hours, and physical and financial risks, entrepreneurs also bear such "social costs" as domestic violence, child neglect, divorce, and family breakdown (Bonacich 1988). Thus it is critical to recognize that the ethnic economy is both a thriving center and a source of hardship and exploitation. In sum, Southeast Asian refugees are extraordinarily diverse. Although there is a tendency to lump them together as "refugees from Southeast Asia," these communities consist of multiple subgroups defined by ethnicities, socioeconomic backgrounds, different experiences before and after arrival in the United States, and different potentials for development (Le 1993: 184).

CULTURE, FAMILY, AND IDENTITIES

Migration to the United states has, in significant ways, challenged the balance of power in Southeast Asian families. These challenges arise from the greater relative equality in the nature and scope of resources that men, women, and children bring to their family life. Because of their new economic and social resources, women and children have an opportunity to contest the traditional hierarchies of family life. As a result, some Southeast Asian families find their traditional ties severely strained. As a Vietnamese elder lamented, "In America, there is nothing to hold our family together . . . . [H]ere in America, my wife and I will die a lonely death, abandoned by our children." (Cited in Freeman 1989: 368.) Charles Irby and Ernest Pon (1988) reported that loss of status and power leads to depression and anxieties in Hmong males. In particular, the Hmong women's ability to earn money for households "has undermined severely male omnipotence." (Irby and Pon 1988: 112.)

On the other hand, ethnographic evidence suggests that Southeast Asian women and children do not use their new resources to forge a radical restructuring of the old family system. One Cambodian wife explained her view on changing gender roles, "If we lived in Cambodia I would have behaved differently toward my husband. Over there we have to always try to be nice to the husband. Wives don't talk back, but sometimes I do that here a little bit, because I have more freedom to say what I think here. However, I am careful not to speak too disrespectfully to him, and in that way, I think I am different from the Americans." (Cited in Welaratna 1993: 233.) In an ethnographic study of Vietnamese American families, Kibria (1993) suggests that Vietnamese American women and children walk an "ideological tightrope"—struggling both to preserve the traditional Vietnamese family system and to enhance their power within the context of this system. According to Kibria, Vietnamese Americans, both old and young, attempt to create this ideological balance because they perceive the distinctive features of Vietnamese family life—the close, cooperative, and caring relations between kin—to be a source of cultural pride and a defining ingredient of Vietnamese American ethnic identity. For Vietnamese American women, the traditional family system is also valuable because it offers them economic protection and gives them authority, as mothers, over the younger generation. However, as men's, women's, and children's comparative access to and control over resources in the dominant society shifts, their ability to restructure the traditional patriarchal family system will also change.

Looking toward the Future

Devastated by war, traumatized by their flight, and overwhelmed by their resettlement experience, Southeast Asian refugees embrace the United States as a place of refuge—a place to build new lives, to work, and to raise their family. At the same time, many continue to mourn the loss of home and of country and to regard themselves as sojourners—ever hopeful that they can return to their country someday. The anguish, the longing for the way life used to be, the nostalgia—these remain central in the lives of the first-generation refugees, especially among those who have been victims of personal and institutional racism. According to a 1989 Los Angeles Times poll of Orange County's Vietnamese community, 83 percent of the households spoke Vietnamese as the main language; 76 percent of the population still had contact with friends and relatives in Vietnam; and 61 percent spent their money mainly in Vietnamese restaurants and stores (Emmons and Reyes 1989). However, as they watch their children—the one-and-a-half generation and the second generation—immerse themselves in the United States's social, economic, and political landscapes, many of the first generation are beginning to realize that they cannot live in a country—eat its food, listen to its music, learn its language, read its literature, share in its pain, join in its laughter—without also becoming a part of it. As Vietnamese American journalist Andrew Lam writes, "America quietly steps in one night and takes hold of one's mind and body and the Vietnamese soul of sorrows slowly fades away." But Southeast Asians do not leave their ethnic selves behind in order to become American. Some have expanded the mainstream definition of Americanness to include them; others have become politically active so that they can better assist their communities; still others lead transnational lives,[4] developing and maintaining multiple relations that link the United States and their country of origin. These diverse adaptation strategies remind us, once again, of the artificiality of the "Southeast Asian" category.

NOTES

1. Prior to 1975, there were approximately 20,000 Vietnamese in the United States, and the number of Cambodians and Laotians were too small to be counted. Most of the Vietnamese were wives of U.S. servicemen or international students (Skinner 1980; Wright 1980).
2. Approximately half a million persons, many of whom are children, continue to languish in crowded, unsanitary, crime-ridden refugee camps in the countries of first asylum in Southeast Asia and in Hong Kong, waiting for resettlement They face an uncertain and bleak future: The media have largely ignored their plight, international funds have dwindled, and offers from Western countries to resettle them have dropped considerably (Lam 1990; Chan 1994).
3. The U.S. government erected four receiving centers to process the refugees who arrived in 1975: Camp Pendleton in southern California; Fort Chaffee in Arkansas; Fort Indiantown Gap in Pennsylvania; and Eglin Air Force Base in Florida.
4. For a discussion of transnationalism, see Basch, Glick Schiller, and Blanc (1994).

REFERENCES

Akast, Daniel. "Cruller Fates: Cambodians Find Slim Profit in Doughnuts." *Los Angeles Times* March 9, 1993, pp. D1, D6.

Arax, Mark. “Many Refugees Work while Getting Welfare.” *Los Angeles Times,* February 9, 1987, p. 1+.

Asian Week. 1991. Asians in America: 1990 Census. San Francisco.

Bach, Robert L. “Labor Force Participation and Employment of Southeast Asian Workers in the United States.” Prepared for the U.S. Department of Health and Human Services, Office of Refugee Resettlement, August 1984.

Baldwin, Beth C. *Patterns of Adjustment.* Orange, CA: Immigrant and Refugee Planning Center, 1984.

Basch, Linda, Nina Glick Schiller, and Cristina Szanton Blanc. *Nations Unbound.* Langhorne, PA: Gordon and Breach, 1994.

Blauner, Robert. *Racial Oppression in America.* New York: Harper & Row, 1972.

Bonacich, Edna. “A Theory of Ethnic Antagonism: The Split Labor Market.” *American Sociological Review* 37 (1972), pp. 547–59.

_____. “The Social Costs of Immigrant Entrepreneurship.” *Amerasia Journal* 14 (1) (1988), pp. 119–28.

Caplan, Nathan, John Whitmore, and Quang L. Bui. “Southeast Asian Refugee Self-Sufficiency Study.” Report prepared for Office of Refugee Resettlement by The Institute for Social Research, University of Michigan, 1985.

Chan, Sucheng. *Asian Americans: An Interpretive History.* Boston: Twayne, 1991.

_____, ed. *Hmong Means Free: Life in Laos and in America.* Philadelphia: Temple University Press, 1994.

Chiswick, Barry. “The Economic Progress of Immigrants: Some Apparently Universal Patterns,” in *Contemporary Economic Problems,* W. Fellner, ed. Washington, D.C.: American Enterprise Institute, 1979, pp. 357–99.

Desbarats, Jacqueline, and Linda Holland. “Indochinese Settlement Patterns in Orange County.” *Amerasia Journal* 10 (1) (1983), pp. 23–46.

Emmons, Steve, and David Reyes. “Gangs, Crime Top Fears of Vietnamese in Orange County,” *Los Angeles Times* Feb. 5, 1989, p. 3.

Gold, Steven J. “Refugees and Small Business: The Case of Soviet Jews and Vietnamese.” *Ethnic and Racial Studies,* 11 (4) (1988), pp. 411–38.

_____. *Refugee Communities: A Comparative Field Study.* Newbury Park, CA: Sage, 1992.

_____. “Chinese-Vietnamese Entrepreneurs in California,” in *The New Asian Immigration in Los Angeles and Global Restructuring,* Paul Ong, Edna Bonacich, and Lucie Cheng, eds. Philadelphia: Temple University Press, 1994, pp. 198–226.

Gold, Steven, and Nazli Kibria. “Vietnamese Refugees and Blocked Mobility.” *Asian and Pacific Migration Review* 2 (1) (1993), pp. 27–56.

Haines, David. “Vietnamese Refugee Women in the U.S. Labor Force: Continuity or Change?” In *International Migration: The Female Experience,* Rita James Simon and Caroline Brettell, eds. Towata, NJ, 1986.

Hing, Bill Ong. *Making and Remaking Asian America Through Immigration Policy, 1850–1990.* Stanford, CA: Stanford University Press, 1993.

Irby, Charles, and Ernest M. Pon. “Confronting New Mountains: Mental Health Problems among Male Hmong and Mien Refugees.” *Amerasia Journal* 14 (1) (1988), pp. 109–18.

Keely, Charles B. 1984. "Current Status of U.S. Immigration and Refugee Policy," in *U.S. Immigration and Refugee Policy,* Mary M. Kritz, ed. Massachusetts: D.C. Heath and Company, 1984.

Kelly, Gail Paradise. *From Vietnam to America.* Boulder, CO: Westview, 1977.

Kibria, Nazli. *Family Tightrope: The Changing Lives of Vietnamese Americans.* Princeton: Princeton University Press, 1993.

Kitano, Harry H.L. *Race Relations.* Englewood Cliffs, NJ: Prentice-Hall, 1980.

Kitano, Harry H.L., and Roger Daniels. *Asian Americans: Emerging Minorities.* Englewood Cliffs, NJ: Prentice Hall, 1994.

Le, Ngoan. "The Case of the Southeast Asian Refugees: Policy for a Community 'At-Risk,'" in *The State of Asian Pacific America: A Public Policy Report.* Los Angeles: LEAP Asian Pacific American Public Policy Institute and UCLA Asian American Studies Center, 1993, pp. 167–88.

Lam, Andrew. "Ebbing Sympathy Strands Boat People." *San Jose Mercury News,* November 18, 1990.

Light, Ivan. *Cities in World Perspective.* New York: Macmillan, 1983.

Light, Ivan, and Edna Bonacich. *Immigrant Entrepreneurs.* Berkeley: University of California Press, 1988.

Liu, William. *Transition to Nowhere: Vietnamese Refugees in America.* (Nashville: Charter House Publishers, 1979.

Montero, D. *Vietnamese Americans: Patterns of Resettlement and Socioeconomic Adaptation in the United States.* Boulder, CO: Westview. 1980.

May, Lee. "Asians Looking to Broaden Horizons: Immigrants Prosper but Hope to Venture Outside the 'Business Ghetto.'" *Los Angeles Times,* Feb 2, 1987.

Morawska, E. "The Sociology and Historiography of Immigration," in *Immigration Reconsidered: History, Sociology, and Politics,* V. Yans-McLaughlin, ed. New York: Oxford University Press, 1990, pp. 187–238.

Nhu, T.T. "Work Ethic and Need Motivate Welfare Cheaters," *San Jose Mercury News,* April 7, 1988.

North, David S. "Refugee Earnings and Utilization of Financial Assistance Programs." Paper presented at the Refugee Policy Forum at Wingspread Conference Center in Racine, WI, Feb. 6–8, 1984.

Office of Refugee Resettlement. "A Short-Term Evaluation of the Changes in Federal Refugee Assistance Policy on State and Local Governments and on Refugees." Prepared by Urban Systems Research and Engineering, 1983.

_____. *Report to the Congress: Refugee Resettlement Programs.* Washington, D.C., 1987.

_____. *Report to the Congress: Refugee Resettlement Programs.* Washington D.C., 1988.

_____. *Report to the Congress: Refugee Resettlement Programs.* Washington, D.C., 1989.

_____. *Report to the Congress: Refugee Resettlement Programs.* Washington, D.C., 1990.

Omi, Michael, and Howard Winant. *Racial Formation in the United States: From the 1960s to the 1980s.* New York: Routledge and Kegan Paul, 1986.

Ong, Paul M. "California's Asian Population," in *California's Asian Population: Looking toward the Year 2000,* presented by Lucie Cheng and Paul Ong. Los Angeles: UCLA Center for Pacific Rim Studies, 1990, pp. 3–9.

Ong, Paul, and Evelyn Blumenberg."Welfare and Work among Southeast Asians," in *The State of Asian Pacific America: Economic Diversity, Issues & Policies,* Paul Ong, ed. Los Angeles: LEAP Asian Pacific American Public Policy Institute and UCLA Asian American Studies Center, 1994, pp. 113–38.

Portes, Alejandro, and Ruben G. Rumbaut. *Immigrant America: A Portrait.* Berkeley: University of California Press, 1990.

Proudfoot, Robert. *Even the Birds Don't Sound the Same Here.* New York: Peter Lang, 1990.

Reimers, David M. *Still the Golden Door: The Third World Comes to America.* New York: Columbia University Press, 1985.

Roberts, Alden E. "Racism Sent and Received: Americans and Vietnamese View One Another." *Research in Race and Ethnic Relations* 5 (1988), pp. 75–97.

Rose, Peter. "Asian Americans: From Pariahs to Paragons," in *Clamor at the Gates: The New Immigration,* Nathan Glazer, ed. San Francisco: Institute of Contemporary Studies, 1985, pp. 131–212.

Rumbaut, Ruben G. "The Structure of Refuge: Southeast Asian Refugees in the U.S., 1975–85." *International Review of Comparative Public Policy* 1 (1989), pp. 97–129.

Rumbaut, Ruben D., and Ruben G. Rumbaut. "The Refugee: A Piece of the American Mosaic." Paper presented at the Annual Meeting of the American Psychiatric Association, Los Angeles, 1984.

Sassan, Saskia. "New York's Informal Economy." Chapter 3 in *The Informal Economy,* Alejandro Portes, Manuel Castells and Lauren A. Benton, eds. Baltimore: Johns Hopkins, 1988.

Saxton, Alexander. *The Indispensable Enemy: Labor and the Anti-Chinese Movement in California.* Berkeley: University of California Press, 1971.

Skinner, Kenneth A. "Vietnamese in America: Diversity in Adaptation." *California Sociologist* 3 (2) (1980), pp. 103–24.

Skinner, Kenneth and G.L. Hendricks. "A New Minority: Indochinese Refugees in Higher Education." *Office for Student Affairs Research Bulletin* 18 (4): University of Minnesota. ERIC Reproduction Services No. ED 148274, 1977.

Social Security Administration. *Report to the Congress: Indochinese Refugee Assistance Program.* Washington D.C., 1978.

Starr, Paul D., and Alden Roberts. "Attitudes toward Indochinese Refugees: An Empirical Study." *Journal of Refugee Resettlement* 1 (4) (1981), pp. 51–61.

_____. "Attitudes toward New Americans: Perceptions of Indochinese in Nine Cities." *Research in Race and Ethnic Relations* 3 (1982), pp. 165–186.

Stein, Barry. "Occupational Adjustment of Refugees: TheVietnamese in the United States." *International Migration Review* 13 (1) (1979), pp. 25–45.

Takaki, Ronald. *Strangers from a Different Shore: A History of Asian Americans.* Boston: Little, Brown, 1989.

Tollefson, James W. *Alien Winds: The Reeducation of America's Indochinese Refugees.* New York: Praeger, 1989.

U.S. Bureau of the Census. *We the American Asians.* Washington, D.C.: U.S. Government Printing Office, 1993.

United States Commission on Civil Rights. *Civil Rights Issues Facing Asian Americans in the 1990s.* Washington, D.C.: U.S. Government Printing Office, 1992.

United States Department of Commerce, Bureau of the Census, Economics and Statistics Administrations. "Business Firms Owned by Asian Americans, Pacific Islanders, American Indians and Alaska Natives Increased 87 Percent Over Five Years, Census Shows," Washington, D.C., August 2, 1991.

Viviani, Nancy. *The Long Journey: Vietnamese Migration and Settlement in Australia.* Carlton, Victoria: Melbourne University Press, 1984.

Wilson, Wendell L. and Michael A. Garrick. "Refugee Assistance Termination Study." Washington State Department of Social and Health Services, 1983.

Winter, Roger and Joseph Cerquone. "Pirate Attacks Against Vietnamese Boat People Continue." *World Refugee Survey 1984* Washington, D.C.: U.S. Committee for Refugees, 1984, pp. 8–9.

Wong, Kent. "Statement of Kent Wong, Esq., Staff Attorney, Asian Pacifc American Legal Center." in U.S. House, Committee on Post Office and Civil Service, *Demographic Impact of Immigration on the U.S. Hearings,* 99th Congress, 1st session, 19 July 19, 1985, pp. 172–75.

Wright, Mary Brown. "Indochinese," in *Harvard Encyclopedia of American Ethnic Groups,* edited by Stephan Thernstrom, Ann Orlov, and Oscar Handlin. Cambridge: Harvard University Press, 1980.

SUGGESTED READINGS

Chan, Sucheng, ed. *Hmong Means Free: Life in Laos and in America.* Philadelphia: Temple University Press, 1994.

Freeman, James. *Hearts of Sorrow: Vietnamese-American Lives.* Stanford, CA: Stanford University Press, 1989.

Kibria, Nazli. *Family Tightrope: The Changing Lives of Vietnamese Americans.* Princeton: Princeton University Press, 1993.

Strand, Paul J., and Woodrow Jones, Jr. *Indochinese Refugees in America: Problems of Adaptation and Assimilation.* Durham, NC: Duke University Press, 1985.

Tehula, John. *Voices from Southeast Asia: The Refugee Experience in the United States.* New York: Holmes & Meier, 1991.

Welaratna, Usha. *Beyond the Killing Fields: Voices of Nine Cambodian Survivors in America.* Stanford, CA: Stanford University Press, 1993.

CHAPTER 16

Jewish Americans: A Religio-Ethnic Community

Eugen Schoenfeld

Some time ago I asked a college professor who was a friend of mine, "Do you believe in God?" Though somewhat startled by the question, he responded with out hesitation: "No!" I probed further by asking: "What do you consider yourself to be?" Since the topic of conversation was religion, he responded with some hesitation, "I am a Jew." His hesitation expressed this apparent paradox: How can anyone be a Jew and not believe in God? Is not belief in God a necessary prerequisite for a religious identity? Yet this professor's dilemma is not an isolated case. Many individuals who call themselves Jews reject religious rituals and confess to being agnostics if not atheists.

The paradox dissolves once we realize that being Jewish encompasses a multiplicity of identities. One may, for instance, place primacy on religious identity, or see oneself as a member of an ethnic group, or as a member of a national political group (as in the case of the Israelis). Contrary to popular misconception, Jews do not constitute a race, if by "race" we mean a category of people who possess biologically inheritable traits. What, then, is the common feature of the people who are called Jews? The answer is that there is no one common feature. Religion is one of several, as are a common history and culture, a common way of life, and finally a collective concern with the state of Israel.

Variations within identity are as old as Judaism itself. Such differences already existed, for instance, in the times of the prophets: Some Jews, who followed the prophets rather than the priest, opposed the strict ritual emphasis of religion, and endeavored to substitute plain moral requirements for elaborate ceremony and formal creed. Since the destruction of the Second Temple in A.D. 70, and the Jewish exile from the homeland, Jewish identity has remained primarily within the domain of religion and ritualism. Only since the nineteenth century have Jews begun again to emphasize other aspects of Judaism, such as a philosophical and moral concern and a national-political identity known as Zionism. Similarly, in the United States, being Jewish has a different essence to different people. Some perceive themselves as adherents of a particular religion, while others see them selves primarily as an ethnic group. In this regard Gans writes:

> I must . . . distinguish between two aspects of Jewish life, Judaism and Jewishness. By Judaism, I mean the Jewish culture (using that word, again, in its anthropological sense). But the term Judaism itself has two applications; we speak of traditional or of a symbolic Judaism. Traditional Judaism embraces a great complex of sacred and secular, ceremonial and everyday codes of behavior patterns. . . . Jewishness, on the other hand, refers to one's sense of identity as a Jew, and the concomitant sense of identification with other members of the Jewish community. Primarily a feeling of belongingness, Jewishness has been an effect rather than a cause of cohesion of that community.[1]

The present trend, Gans feels, is toward "Judaization," a trend manifested by the lessening importance of Judaism as a religion and the substitution of an "objects culture" based on such terms as Jewish candy, Jewish bacon, Jewish jokes, and stars of David.

Glazer is more explicit in his analysis of the source of Jewish identity. Viewing American Jewry from an historical perspective, he identifies the existence of what he calls "religious" and "secular" Judaism. Glazer claims these two aspects of Judaism are not only separate, but on occasion have been antagonistic. Glazer writes that in the 1920s and 1930s:

> The synagogue and religion offered but one center of life and interest among many on the American Jewish scene. Other specifically Jewish centers of activity, of equal or greater importance were constituted by philanthropic work by Jewish politics and by Jewish culture. The leading figures in these fields were often indifferent when actually not hostile to religion. And so one had a split between what one may call Judaism, the historic religion, and Jewishness; namely all the activities which Jews came to carry on without the auspices of religion.[2]

Melvin Tumin is another sociologist who has dealt with the question of Jewish identity in America, though in a peripheral manner. He observes that "Jews are concerned with the problem of their identity and consciously seek to come to terms with that problem at its most serious level."[3] This quest for identity, Tumin says, brings about a paradoxical situation. On the one hand there is an organizational reinvigoration; synagogues and day schools are everincreasing in numbers, a fact that would lead one to believe that there is a tendency toward increased Jewish identification. On the other hand, "Jews have been vocal and effective in their insistence . . . not to be identified as Jewish."[4] Thus, there are simultaneously "two opposing moves in Jewish life[one] toward a Jewish center and [another] I away from it. . . ."[5] What Tumin seems to observe is that there exists a duality in Jewish identification resulting from the divergence of religious and cultural aspects. Because of American values, the Jew seems constrained to return to his religious institutions. It is in regard to this point that Tumin writes:

> The return to the Jewish community and its center and its synagogue represents, as yet, nothing more . . . than a smooth fitting in of Jews into American life at its worst and on precisely the same terms as the Presbyterians, Baptists, and all others.[6]

This constraint toward a religious identification is further evidenced by the Jew's quest for status and a desire to be a hundred percent American. Tumin writes:

> In duplicating this 100 percent [sic] community-cum-church posture of the non Jewish American, the Jew vouchsafes himself as an allrightnik in the American host community operating with the morally dubious notion that one's neighbors will respect one more if one is religious, the Jew seeks to insure that acceptance. . . .[7]

Other scholars who have examined the nature of Jewish identity have found it to contain many component parts. A closer examination of the various subidentities, however, will show this multiplicity constitutes only two major dimensions: Judaism and Jewishness. Lazerwitz,[8] for instance, identified nine components of Jewish identity, but a subsequent factor analysis of his data showed that these components are not independent identities but form two identity clusters, which he designated as "religiopietistic" and "Jewish organizational." Although we are stressing the duality of Jewish identity, we must hasten to add that these identities are not completely independent. A commitment to Jewish ethnic culture does not preclude one's commitment to religion, nor does commitment to religion preclude commitment to ethnic culture. Lazerwitz[9] notes that Jews who are highly involved in the Jewish community are strikingly more religiously observant than those having a low involvement. Of what importance is this difference in the content of personal identity? Is it not sufficient that one should perceive oneself a Jew and thereby align oneself with the Jewish community? The answer is no. Differences in the content of one's identity entail a different reference group and consequently different values, norms, and outlook.

JEWS IN AMERICA: A HISTORICAL PERSPECTIVE

A historical approach to the understanding of Jewish Americans, their identity, religion, and life is imperative, for Jews are products of different countries and varied historical conditions, which have affected them in different ways. As a result, Jewish identity, world view, and attitude toward the Gentile community is by no means unilateral.

American Jews consist of an admixture of three groups of immigrants who came to this country at three different periods of its history from three different geographical areas. The oldest residents are the Spanish-speaking Jews (Sephardim), whose roots in this country are almost as old as the pilgrims. In 1654, in an attempt to escape Portuguese persecution, twenty-three Jewish families left the occupied Dutch colony of Racife in eastern Brazil and came to New Amsterdam, the present New York, another Dutch colony. The hospitality and freedom that the Jews enjoyed in the Dutch colonies in South America was not extended to them by Peter Stuyvesant, governor of New Amsterdam, who would have preferred to expel the new emigrants. However, the Dutch East India Company, proprietor of the colony, overruled the governor and permitted the new settlers to remain.

Although these Jews came from South America, their original home was the Iberian peninsula. After the Roman destruction of the Jewish homeland in Judea, Jewish cultural life shifted to Babylon, where a great Jewish civilization flourished for approximately seven centuries. But as the great Jewish schools in Babylon began to be closed, Jewish cultural life in Spain, which was now under Arab rule, was growing. In 1492, the year that marked the discovery of the American continents, Jews were being expelled from their homes in Spain. They carried with them into their new homes their old heritage of a love for learning and grace. Soon after the first twenty-three Sephardic families arrived in New Amsterdam, others of similar background came to join them, and Jewish communities were established in Newport, Rhode Island; Savannah, Georgia; Philadelphia, Pennsylvania; and Richmond, Virginia.

From 1840 until imposition of the quota system in 1924, Jewish emigration, primarily from Germany, Russia, Poland, and Hungary, was relatively heavy. Social conditions in the countries from which these Jews emigrated differed appreciably, and hence their attitudes toward religion and politics and their perception of the non-Jewish world also differed.

Let us now turn to the earlier emigrants—the German Jews. Jewish life in Germany until the nineteenth century was marked by the dominance of the yellow star, the badge of shame, and above all by the high walls of the ghetto. Jewish association with the "outside world" was very limited, and as a result life within the walls of the ghetto was governed by age-old traditions and the strict letter of religious law. Sachar writes:

> Limited intellectually, ground down economically, despised socially, disinherited politically, the Jews were also decried and persecuted for race and religion. It was not astonishing that, with no hope for participation in the life of the country, Jews swaddled themselves in their own traditions. . . . [10]

The rise of the enlightenment, with its idealism, and the subsequent revolutions of the eighteenth century also affected the freedom of the Jews, for the concepts of liberty and equality applied in some measure to the Jewish population of Western Europe. The walls of the ghettos, like those of Jericho, were falling, and with their destruction new trends in assimilation and acculturation gathered force.[11]

The authority of the Talmud, which for centuries had been the foundation of the Jewish religion, was now challenged; proponents of this challenge pointed out that the ancient doctrines and practices had too long resisted the natural process of change and evolution. Perhaps more significant than the changes in religious ritual was rejection of the nationalistic element in Judaism; the universal aspect, rather than restoration of Zion and return to the homeland, was emphasized. Religious acculturation accompanied general assimilation. The prayers were shortened and recited for the most part in the native language, new hymns in the vernacular were introduced, and the sermon, as in Protestant religious groups, became the most important part of the worship service. In short, the Western Jews started to shed their national and cultural identity and to assume the identity of their host. They now began to think of themselves as Germans, Frenchmen, or Englishmen who practiced a Jewish (Mosaic) religion, rather than as Jews bearing a separate ethnic or national identity.[12]

As Western Jews began to identify themselves culturally with Europe while maintaining their Jewish religion (although greatly reformed), Eastern Jews took an exactly opposite course—they began to minimize their religious affiliation, while simultaneously stressing the national and cultural elements of Judaism. This difference in the evolutions of the Western and Eastern Jew was directly related to the differences in their political and social situations. In the West, Jews found themselves becoming politically free and possessing increased educational and economic opportunities; in the East, the Jews' situation was just the opposite. Not only were they subjected to the confinement of the ghetto and to the restrictions of anti-Jewish laws, but they also had to endure the cruelties of the pogroms.

In 1791, at the order of Catherine the Great, Jews in Russia were confined to a small district in the Ukraine known as the "pale of settlement."

While their ghettos in Western Europe were being opened and the Jews were being granted greater freedom, in Russia the Jewish lot was worsening steadily, aggravated still further by the conscription law of Nicholas I.[13] The spring of 1881 saw the beginning of an outburst of hostilities against Russian Jews; these violent outbreaks were not random occurrences, but seemed rather to have been well planned and directed. In addition to this series of attacks, which the government seemed unable to control, the Jews also had to contend with the infamous "May laws" of 1882, which restricted their travel, business, and education. Needless to say, this hostile attitude of the host did not encourage Jewish assimilation, but instead turned them away from the path of integration. The budding "Haskalah," the movement of enlightenment, "changed its orientation; instead of worshipping the Shrine of European culture, it placed itself at the service of the national regeneration of the Jewish people."[14] This trend to nationalism, later known as Zionism, was political rather than religious, for the religious belief that suffering is the natural lot of Jews and a prerequisite for the coming of the Messiah became unacceptable to the leaders of the Haskalah. The doctrines of the Messiah—that is, the patient wait, submission to temporary difficulties, and postponement of retribution lost ground to the desire for an immediate solution of the Jewish difficulties. If religion taught that the Messiah was the only legitimate leader who might return the "exiles" to their national land, then this new movement was nonreligious, and in fact sometimes antireligious. Its imminent goal became self-determination and not God-determination.[15]

When we turn our attention to the Jewish Americans of today we discover that their identity is rooted in the orientations brought over by the Jewish migrants from both West and East. They are products of the cultural heritage of the German as well as the Russian Jews. It therefore becomes imperative that we now consider, even though briefly, how these influences were transmitted.[16]

The first wave of German Jewish migration into the United States began in the 1840s. Of the two million Germans who entered this country between 1850 and 1860, about 5 percent were Jews.[17] The social climate they found in America, together with their liberal tendencies, facilitated their acceptance of the American culture. The German Jews became an integral part of the "westward ho" movement, and with other American pioneers they crossed the great mountains and rivers, conquering the prairies and the forests of the new American frontier. Since there was as yet no concentration in urban areas, the German Jews did not form the voluntary ghettos characteristic of Russian Jews; American social conditions encouraged integration, and the German Jews responded. "The German Jews," writes Glazer, "were not only peddlers and merchants, but also manufacturers, intellectuals, politicians, and even workers, active in every sphere of American life."[18] This tendency to acculturate lessened the specialization of areas of interest, and consequently there was little to mark the German Jews apart from the rest of the population. Unlike the background of the German Jews, which emphasized assimilation, the Russian Jews' background was one of national and religious separatism. Whereas the German Jews came mostly from urban centers, the Russian Jews came from the isolated *shtetl.*[19] Whereas the German Jews looked upon America as their country, the Russian Jews saw it as just another *galuth,*[20] where, God willing, they might make a better income. Unlike the Western Jews, who settled in America at the time of frontier expansion and thus spread westward themselves, the Eastern Jews came at the time of urban expansion. Their future lay in the cities, where they rapidly formed a proletariat.[21] Whereas the German Jews in America maintained their religious identity, though changing the form and content of their ancient religion, the Russian Jewry was divided between those who continued the orthodox religion in the same manner as they had in Russia and those who became irreligious or antireligious.

When the Russian Jews began their migration into the United States, their voluntary mode of settlement was the ghetto. This self-isolation, together with the isolationist ideology that provided the mainstay of the *shtetl* existence, acted as a forceful prophylactic against changes in the orthodox religion. The ghetto synagogues came to possess a geographical identity, some bearing the name of the country from which the members had migrated, others the name of the province or town in which they were located.

The consequence of ghetto existence upon Jewish religion in America had been paradoxical. On the one hand, the ghetto, in its isolation from the rest of the population, made possible a continual religious orthodoxy by providing the physical means, such as synagogues, kosher food, and proper garments,[22] as well as the moral atmosphere. On the other hand, the ghetto also provided an opportunity for generating "nonreligious" Jews, that is, those who accepted and maintained the Jewish cultural heritage without following Jewish religious precepts. Regarding this point Glazer remarks:

> The relationship to Judaism of these almost totally Jewish residential districts was an ambiguous one. While they made it possible for every variant of Judaism to find a minimal number of adherents, they also made possible a varied social life that was utterly indifferent in many cases even hostile to Judaism. There were organizations that carried some kind of Jewish activity, but were formally anti- or areligious like Zionism and the Yiddishist groups.[23]

The antireligious Jewish movements in America are also associated with the rise of Jewish social organization and the development of the Zionist and socialist movements. Jewish social organizations such as the Jewish centers and the B'nai B'rith provided Jews with means for nonreligious identification. Glazer notes that:

> In the twenties and thirties, the center suggested to a number of people that it might be the nucleus for a new type of Jewish community. Its focus would not be religion but something we may call "Jewishness."[24]

The Zionist movement, begun in Russia and brought from there to America, proved a further means to nonreligious Jewish identification. More often than not, Orthodox rabbis opposed this movement; their opposition stemmed from a disagreement regarding the settlement of the Land of Israel. While the Zionists advocated immediate reestablishment of a homeland in Palestine, the rabbis contended that the only legitimate return to the "Holy Land" would come through the leadership of the Messiah, at a time to be decided by the Providence.[25] Nor were the Orthodox rabbis the only opponents of Zionism: The antinational and antitraditional position of the Reform rabbis was also in diametric opposition to Zionist aims. Prinz writes:

> The liberal branch of the rabbinate was openly hostile and attacked the new [Zionist] movement violently. The German rabbis prevented the holding of the first Zionist Congress in Munich. The American Reform Rabbis adopted resolutions which rejected Zionism with unmitigated violence.[26]

Finally, the Jewish socialist movement, brought to the United States by Russian Jewish migrants, presented another mode for nonreligious Jewish identification. It represented a movement in Russia the primary aim of which was political change, as one response to totalitarian government. Many Jewish youths, as members of an oppressed minority, joined left-wing organizations and selected socialist parties and their aims as a means by which they hoped to shed their minority status. Through such association with socialist political parties, Jews became involved with economic as well as political issues. They became concerned not only with the lack of political freedom and with czarist totalitarianism, but also with the economic position of labor.[27] When they migrated to America the Jewish socialists of Russia brought along their views concerning labor and politics, but political freedom, which once had been perhaps their main concern, lost its great significance to them. Instead, they found in America a new phenomenon to which they could transfer their socialist interests, namely, the Jewish proletariat.

In 1900 the majority of the Russian Jewish migrants were engaged in clothing manufacturing, and most of them were laborers.[28] Youths who in Russia had been members of the socialist organizations transferred their area of activity from the political sphere to the economic sphere of socialism and began to organize the Jewish proletariat into unions. The Bund, the Jewish socialist movement that followed the Jews from Russia to America, became the central point around which the Jewish proletariat rallied. Because of its progressive nature, the Bund broke away from religion and from religious organizations that stressed conservatism, orthodoxy, and an antiprogressive orientation, for change was interpreted as a departure from the ancient ideals, and the religious standpoint was thus viewed with suspicion.

With the help of the news media, the socialist ideologies of the Bund spread and became prevalent among the Jewish proletariat. During the first part of the twentieth century it was not uncommon for Jewish workers to read antireligious Yiddish newspapers, to vote socialist, and to join socialist-oriented unions. One such popular paper was the Jewish *Daily Forward,* whose editor was Abraham Cahan.[29]

In addition to organizing unions, the socialist groups also organized Yiddish schools which reflected the irreligious orientation of the socialist movement. Glazer describes these schools as follows:

> Many of the schools that Jewish children attended after public school were not only neutral toward religion but were in principle atheistic and antireligious. This was the case with a good part of the very active Yiddish school movement. Just as the passage of time, the arrival of new immigrants, and growing competence in adapting to the American scene had strengthened the institutions of Judaism, so had it strengthened the institutions of Jewish socialism, which were particularly attached to Yiddish, the language of the Jewish masses.[30]

The socialists were not the only Jews who wanted to minimize religion while maintaining the Jewish culture; there were also nonpolitical groups that wanted to minimize, even eliminate, the religious facet of Judaism, while maintaining its values and ideologies in order to maintain a culture that was Jewish in content. These groups established the Sholom Aleichem Yiddish schools, parochial schools whose purpose was to teach nonreligious Judaism.[31] The importance of this nonreligious cultural school is made clear by the fact that during the mid 1930s, seven thousand Jewish children in New York City alone attended them.[32]

The attitudes the first-generation Jews brought to the United States can be briefly summarized as follows: The German Jews stressed religious reforms while accepting the American cultural ethos and the Russian Jews brought both religious orthodoxy and nonreligiosity, but in both cases there was a strong inclination to maintain the Jewish culture. At this point it becomes necessary to view the impact that the aforementioned heritages have had on second-generation Jews in America.

Hansen points out that second-generation ethnic groups, in their desire to acculturate, tend deliberately to slough off behavioral characteristics and values associated with their immigrant background. In its briefest form Hansen's law states: "What the son wishes to forget the grandson wishes to remember."[33] This process of forgetting among the Jewish Americans was not an omnipresent phenomenon. It occurred only among the Russian Jews; the second-generation German Jew had fewer such characteristics to slough off, since his or her parents had already accomplished this back in Germany.

The second-generation Russian Jews, "Desperately anxious to become unequivocally American, were resentful of the immigrant culture to which the older generation seemed so eager to submit."[34] But, for the most part, Jewish religion and the Jewish culture were almost inextricably fused and seemed so inseparable to second-generation Eastern Jews that in their desire to dissociate themselves from Jewish culture, they also dissociated themselves from the Jewish religion. Warner and Srole vividly depict the second generation's dissociation from the synagogue in Yankee City; there was such a drop in the synagogue attendance, they point out, that an elder Jew in Yankee City declared, "Sometimes we haven't even got enough men for a minyon [quorum of ten men needed for a religious service]. . . ."[35]

In addition to dissociation from the synagogue, the second generation's process of Americanization included a breaking away from the self-imposed ghetto of their parents and settling in the suburbs instead. They left the area in which identification as a Jew could have continued even without observation of the Jewish religion. In the ghetto one heard and spoke Yiddish; there one could eat a kosher meal and partake of all the varieties of Jewish dishes, take part in the Jewish social movements, and read the Yiddish newspaper and novels.[36]

It was precisely the second generation's sloughing off of Jewishness and Judaism that paved the way for the third generation's desire to reenter Jewish life. Their parents having moved out of the ghetto into "better neighborhoods" and suburban areas, the children of second-generation Jews now "played with Gentile ones on a level of middle-class respectability that does not generally countenance the simple name calling and fistfighting of the old slum. . . . "[37] Through their association with Gentile children and the lack of symbols of their identity around them, the third generation posed the question, "Why am I a Jew?" as a central theme of self-inquiry, and made the question of identity a central problem of their intellectual life.[38]

Gans,[39] like Glazer, points out an increased consciousness of and concern with Judaism in America, and attributes it to the fact that since society was labeling Jews anyway, most parents of third-generation children decided to train their children in Judaism. This new concern with Judaism was but a manifestation of a new symbolic Judaism, which consisted in the possession and the display of Jewish "objects of culture."[40]

Jewish "objects of culture" are artifacts of Jewish significance used as religious symbols; their purpose is to tie Jews to their religious past. The rise of symbolic Judaism, argues Gans, was stimulated by the third generation children's need for religion, but this need does not explain why these "objects of culture" have become the means of Jewish religious expression. If the third generation does have a need for religious experience, one would expect that attendance at religious services and worship rituals would have increased; yet this has not occurred. Attendance at religious services in the United States is now just as poor as it was in Yankee City,[41] and many synagogues with a large membership still have difficulties forming a minyon.[42] But if the third-generation Jews do not need religion personally as a "psychological cushion" to help avert their fears, whence the use of the religious symbols?

Herberg says that one explanation for the return to religion is the fact that religious association satisfies one's needs for identity. "The third generation began to remember the religion of its ancestors to the degree at least of affirming itself Jewish in a religious sense. . . ."[43] The religious objects can thus be interpreted as symbols around which the Jews in America center their religious identity; these "objects of culture" have become their flags. Another explanation for the mushrooming of these "objects of culture" is the desire to display one's religious associations. This need among Jews to exhibit their relationship with their religion has been noted by other investigators. Warner and Srole, for instance, discovered this phenomenon among Yankee City Jews:

> It is noteworthy that the movement of the P2 Jews, who had been so markedly dissociated from the orthodox synagogue, into the synagogue structure was justified by their relations to the American social system. For example, a P2 upper-middle-class Jew, a leader in the campaign, after discussing how the younger Jews had thrown over their Jewishness, said: "The young men have found out that even to have the Christians like us, we should go to the synagogue. A Jew who is an honest Jew and takes an interest in his synagogue, that is, in his community, is really liked better by the Gentiles. A Christian who is a customer of mine told me that he would have more faith in one who was an "observing Jew" than in one who denied his religion.[44]

Jewish Americans today find themselves in a dilemma: how to maintain a religious identity while not practicing the ritualistic aspects of religion. How can they forgo the traditional religious behavior, such as synagogue attendance, keeping holidays and the Sabbath as days of rest, and keeping the Khasruth,[45] and identify themselves as Jews without the inconvenience of ritual laws? In what way can they symbolize their attachment to a religion without using the traditional means, which demand self-denial? This is where the religious "objects of culture" have a significant function. Instead of religious practice, present-day Jewish Americans publicly proclaim their Jewishness by wearing *mezuzahs* and "stars of David," displaying *menorahs* and *kiddish cups,* placing upon the table doilies and tablecloths with Jewish symbols, and displaying pictures and books on Jewish topics; this mode of identification seems to agree with the American ideal of properly displayed property.

The constraint toward a Jewish religious identification in the United States was observed long ago by Weber; its importance increased tremendously with the anticommunist concerns of the McCarthy era. To be a nonbeliever then was tantamount to a profession of communism, and one's display of "faith in a deity" was essential to one's "Americanism." In addition to this pressure to be "religious," increased commitment to one's Jewish identity was also facilitated by two factors: the aftermath of the Nazi atrocities and the rise of the state of Israel. In 1933 Hitler came to power in Germany during a period of social and economic disorganization; by blaming the Jews for the postwar economic chaos Hitler attempted to integrate German society as a first step to world supremacy. Not only did he legislate anti-Semitic regulations, but he also developed concentration camps as a means to solve the "Jewish question." The holocaust began in 1938 with a purge lasting several days and nights: Jews were killed, synagogues burned, millions of dollars worth of property was destroyed. In addition, German Jews were ordered to pay $400 million, the sum of fines assessed on Jews who possessed more than $2,000. During World War II both German Jews and Jews from countries occupied by the Germans were herded into concentration camps, where they were systematically killed either by gas or through overwork and starvation. By the end of the war in 1945 over 6 million Jews, or about one-third of the Jewish population of the world, had been killed. Such extinction was to have been, as Eichmann declared, the solution to the Jewish question.

Obviously, this threat to Jewish existence heightened Jewish consciousness and helped to develop stronger ties among Jews on both the social and political levels. With the defeat of Germany, some half-million Jews were left homeless, living in displaced persons' camps. Some of these emigrated to the United States with the help of organizations like the American Joint Distribution Committee (AJDC), Hebrew Immigrant Aid Society (HIAS), and the Organization for Rehabilitation through Training (ORT). Unlike the time of the mass immigration of East European Jews during the previous century, the Jewish communities in America were far better organized and hence able to help these new immigrants to settle, provide them with occupational opportunities, and integrate them into the mainstream of American life.

The second major event that heightened Jewish consciousness in the United States was the development of the state of Israel. In the light of the tragic events that befell the Jewish people during World War II, the United Nations voted to establish the State of Israel in the ancient homeland of the Jews. This realization of a 2,000 year-old dream has since electrified the imaginations of Jews and non-Jews throughout the world. However, the costs of developing the land, absorbing of immigrants from Europe and North Africa, and providing the defense for its survival have been enormous. The Jewish people in America have contributed both financial and moral support, resulting in a heightened Jewish identity among Jewish Americans. Moreover, the establishment of Israel has not only created a center for perpetuation of Jewish culture, but has also served as a symbol of security. No longer will Jews in any country be faced, as they were in Germany, with the problem of having to flee one country and yet having no other willing to accept them. The doors of Israel are open to any Jew, and when anti-Semitism becomes rampant in his or her home country, there is now a place open for emigration.

THE JEWISH RELIGION

Textbooks dealing with Jewish religion often begin by describing the three sects of Orthodox, Conservative, and Reformed Judaism. Differences among these three sects lie primarily in the degree of their acceptance of traditional rituals. However, the underlying moral conceptions and religious philosophy of all three divisions are remarkably similar, and therefore we shall treat the Jewish religion as a single entity.

The Jewish religion is based on the Torah—that is, the first five books of the Bible (the Pentateuch). Depending on the degree of one's orthodoxy, Jewish religious life is also influenced and determined by the Talmud—the rabbinic literature that developed during the first century B.C. and second century A.D. Although faith is an essential component of all religions, the primary emphasis of Jewish religion is placed not on faith but on the performance of commandments (Mitzvoth), and on rationalism rather than on emotionalism. (This is not to say that emotional involvement is totally absent.) Such emphasis on the obedience to Jewish law produced a "religious system [which] is in reality nothing but a contract between Jehovah and His . . . people, a contract with all its consequences and all its duties.[46]

The Synagogue and the Temple

The structure of Jewish communal worship is congregationalist; each place of worship determines its own existence. The rabbi is hired by the congregation and his future is determined by it. Although the primary function of the synagogue is to be a place of worship, it has many other purposes as well, some of which are traditional and historical while others are of more recent origin. The Hebrew words for the synagogue are: (1) house of worship (Beth T'filoh); (2) house of study (Beth Hamidrosh); and (3) house of gathering (Beth Haknesseth). Hence the synagogue has traditionally been a place of worship as well as a place where rabbinical students and lay people came to study, and a community center for various activities such as charitable work. Many of its activities have today been taken over by special community organizations, yet the synagogues and temples have not completely abrogated their functions. In addition to religious services, a synagogue today also provides for instruction of religion and Jewish history. Most synagogues and temples have Sunday schools where Jewish history is taught, as well as afternoon classes for the instruction of the Hebrew language, which is both the language spoken in Israel and the language of the prayers.

In the past, when Jews settled in a new community, the first communal activities were the erection of a synagogue and a cemetery. Today cemeteries are still part of the synagogue organization, and in many instances membership in a synagogue also assures burial in a Jewish cemetery. Obviously, the synagogue and the temple are centers for the rituals which are part of the Jew's life cycle (e.g., circumcision, Bar Mitzvah, weddings). In addition to these activities, present-day synagogues have also become social centers sponsoring various types of youth organizations, men's clubs, and women's auxiliaries.

The Rabbi. The word "rabbi" means teacher, which indicates that the rabbi's earlier function was not primarily religious (that is, his activity was not necessary for the attainment of salvation, as is the case with a priest or minister), nor was he essential to the performance of religious ritual from birth to death.[47] However, since most Jews lack the proper knowledge, this function has been taken over by a specially trained individual—the rabbi.

Among the Orthodox the rabbi serves the additional function of judge and ritual arbiter. In many Jewish communities there are Jewish civil courts, which have no legal standing but which are available to those Jews who wish to present cases of tort for arbitration to a rabbinical court. Such cases are decided on the bases of the religious-civil laws found in the Talmud. Obviously the rabbinical court's decisions have no legal authority and hence cannot be legally enforced, but are binding to the extent that the parties to the tort have accepted them to be binding.

Orthodox Jewish life is very complex. Daily life is guided by a great many rituals that define what a person may or may not wear, do, eat, and so on. When an Orthodox Jew has questions about the specifics of a given ritual, the permissibility of foods, or behavior during religious holidays, such questions are directed to the rabbi for interpretation and decision. Traditionally, the rabbi has had two main functions—to learn and to teach; today, however, he has become a quasi-minister whose role is similar to that of the Christian minister. Hence he is also expected to perform public relations and to help create a good Jewish image in the community. Moreover, he is the leader of a religious service in which the sermon has become central. Finally, similar to the minister, the rabbi is expected to counsel his flock, visit the sick, and provide for the general welfare of his congregation.

Rituals. Although we most often think of rituals in a purely religious context, they often have important communal consequences. Rituals in the Jewish religion, in addition to defining appropriate behavior vis-à-vis the deity, also serve as a vehicle for identity formation and hence for perpetuation of the ethnic group. To be a Jew one not only must perceive oneself as a Jew, but also perform acts motivated by the desire to be perceived as a Jew by others. In other words, rituals serve as means of integrating the Jewish community.

Jewish life in general, then, is governed by many rituals, and the extent to which those rituals are observed provides the major criterion for differentiation among Orthodox, Conservative, and Reform Judaism. For Orthodox Jews, all ritual laws are binding; Reform Jews, on the other hand, have eliminated many of the traditional rituals. It would be impossible to examine all the various proscribed rituals in the space of this report, but we shall examine a few of the major ones.

Dietary ritual (Kashruth). Almost everyone has encountered the term "kosher." It refers to dietary laws which determine what animals may be eaten and in what manner the meats of such animals should be prepared. For instance, only those mammals that chew the cud and have cloven hoofs may be used as meat. In addition, these animals must be slaughtered ritually; the meat must be voided of blood; and the mixing of meat and dairy products must be avoided. Finally, only the meat of the front half of the animal is usable, unless the hind quarters are specially cleaned and certain veins and tendons removed.

Holidays. Jewish holidays are considered days of rest, and as such forbid work. Restrictions on activity vary with religious orientation: Orthodox Jews may not work or cook, and are further restricted with regard to the distance they may walk and the transportation of objects in public areas, while Reform Jews limit these restrictions primarily to the pursuit of economically gainful employment. Most important, however, is the function of holidays as family days. The Sabbath, for instance, was traditionally the day in which the father examined his son about his studies, the family took leisurely walks, and kinsmen visited each other.

Judaism in America

Although most Eastern European Jews who settled in America were Orthodox Jews, this religious division soon gave way to the Conservative and Reform branches of Judaism. This change may be attributed to economic conditions and social mobility.

The constraints which orthodoxy imposed on Jewish life were difficult to observe. In the Eastern European small town (often known as the *shtetl*) Jews were primarily tailors and keepers of small shops, and these activities were subservient to religious demands. In the United States Jewish immigrants settled primarily in the large cities of the Northeast, where they became the proletariat of the garment business. The twelve-hour, six-day work week did not permit for the observance of the Sabbath and holidays, the latter of which often fell on week days.

Although Jewish religion stresses intellectualism in preference to emotionalism, Jewish life in Russian villages was not particularly conducive to the pursuit of knowledge. Life was difficult at best, most hours were spent in making a living, and there was hardly time for the leisure required for study. Prayer, emotion, and communal associations became a main feature of synagogue activities and were accompanied by increased emotionalism and conversation features often associated in the United States with the behavioral patterns of the lower class. As the Eastern European Jewish immigrants began to achieve financial success, they also sought middle-class respectability. To achieve the latter they needed not only to belong to a religion (which, according to Weber, is in itself a symbol of respectability), but to a religion in which decorum was central—a need fulfilled by the Conservative and Reformed branches of Judaism. The latter not only lowered ritual requirements, but also provided a worship service in which appropriate middle-class behavior was essential.

In addition to changes induced by mobility, synagogues and temples were also affected by the assimilating force of the majority religion. Instead of remaining a participatory religion in the tradition of Orthodox worship, Reformed Judaism became an audience religion. No longer do the worshipers in the Reformed temples surround the cantor in loud prayer; instead they face the performing rabbi quietly and with little participation. English, rather than Hebrew, has become the primary language of prayer, with the sermon as the dominant feature of the service. The meanings of holidays and their ritual observance have also acquired features of the dominant Christian religion. Chanukah, a minor holiday commemorating the Maccabean revolt against Rome, has now, because of its proximity to Christmas, assumed dominance. In fact, it is viewed by Christians as the Jewish Christmas, and with it Jews have incorporated the practices of giving gifts, sending cards, and occasionally decorating a "Chanukah bush."

SOCIAL VALUES

Of the many values that are part of the Jewish culture, the three most dominant are justice, charity, and communality. In contrast to Christianity, in which the dominant value is love, Judaism stresses above all the ideal of justice. This is not to say that love as a value is absent from Judaism nor justice from Christianity, but rather that if we examine the various components of the Christian and Jewish value systems, we will find that love supersedes all other values in Christianity as justice does in Judaism. Justice in Judaism is perceived as the foundation of life: "Justice, justice shall thou pursue that thou mayest live . . ."[48] As a value in Judaism, it seeks to prescribe equity in asymmetrical power relationships; its concern for the use and abuse of power and privilege is manifest in the Jewish practice of questioning and critically examining political systems. Perhaps this concern for justice may be related to the Jewish propensity to vote for liberal causes and to be predominantly associated with the Democratic party, a party most often associated with liberal causes.

Closely associated with the ideal of justice is that of charity. The Hebrew word for charity, *Tzedokoh,* is derived from the same root (*Tzadok*) as the Hebrew word for justice, *Tzedek*. In other words, charity as an activity is related to maintenance of justice, of equity between the weak and the powerful. As a result, an act of charity for Jews is a normative act and not an act of free will, a duty, not a choice; it is part of the Jewish legal structure and hence part of the communal structure. It is not surprising that the Jewish American community has created many organizations designed to provide various types of aid to those in need.

Finally, Jews place primacy on community orientation as opposed to self-orientation. Rejection of the community is tantamount to apostasy: it is the wicked son, parents are told, who removes himself from the collectivity. To Jews, life, as Zbarowski and Herzog wrote, is with people.[49]

The Jewish Community

Jews, like any other ethnic group in the United States, live within two communal organizations. First, they are part of the larger communities in which they reside, and second, they are part of their own ethnic subgroups, which provide emotional security and ethnic needs. In the larger communities they earn their living, participate in politics, receive the greater part of their education, and seek to achieve their social status; it is here that they are sanctioned if they violate the law or social norms. To this extent their membership and participation in the community is almost the same as that of any other member of the community in a similar socioeconomic position. Yet membership in an ethnicreligious group still presents constraints for social mobility, particularly in the status order. Faced with the need to stratify among themselves in terms of honor and prestige, Jews have in the past created status structures that parallel those of the majority group, by means of the same criteria prevalent in the status organization in the community at large. These status groups, moreover, represent distinct endogamous groups. The content of the status order of the Jewish community does not differ appreciably from that of the larger community with the exception of the importance of education as a determinant of status position. In the Jewish cultural system education is considered paramount and has great bearing in allocation of status honor. A college professor, though having a lower income than most professionals, will nevertheless be accorded greater honor than members of other occupations with greater incomes.

The "separate but equal" type of social organization, though representative of the first-generation-immigrant community, still exists in urban areas. This is because second- and third-generation descendants, having been socialized in America, began shedding the minority characteristics of their parents and attempted to enter the status organizations of the majority group. Their attempts have met with different degrees of success. Kramer and Leventman point out:

> Jews have been more successful in gaining entry into organizations based on the norm of inclusiveness than those based on exclusiveness. That is, more Jews belong to service organizations with civic functions (North State Centennial Committee or North City Aquacentennial Committee) than the more "social" organizations in which members are recruited by special invitation.[50]

An important difference between organizations based on inclusiveness and those based on exclusiveness is the degree of intimacy among the associating members. Association in inclusive groups is more often businesslike and confined to specific roles. (For instance, when an association is devoted to the promotion of a civic activity, each member of the group is assigned a task and interaction is most often associated with that member's task performance.)

This is not to say that members of an inclusive group will not develop informal ties, but simply that the primary reason for such a group's existence is not social. In such organizations as country clubs and athletic clubs, on the other hand, intimate association is more frequent; in the steam room and swimming pool the last vestige of formality is lost. Given these conditions, exclusiveness as a value for selecting members becomes most important. In other words, under conditions in which individuals do not have symbols (such as clothes) to define their social positions and to serve as a guard against intimacy, the right to select one's associates becomes imperative.

The need for a status hierarchy, however, is in itself not a sufficient reason for the development of a minority community. It is therefore important that we examine what other needs the subcommunity satisfies. Obviously, existence of the subcommunity can be attributed to the integrative nature of cultural similarity; it is understandable that people who share similar historical experiences, language, and so on, will seek each other's companionship. Although cultural similarity is an important explanation for association, development of the Jewish community and its continual existence is more attributable to the fact that it provides the means for fulfilling esoteric needs that cannot be satisfied by the larger community. These needs center around: (1) production-distribution-consumption; (2) socialization; (3) social control; (4) social participation; and (5) mutual support.[51]

Production-Distribution-Consumption

The economic life of American Jews is, as we said, centered in the general community. But it is the Jewish community that makes available to them the commodities necessary for their religious life. Observance of the dietary laws, for instance, would be impossible without the services of the subcommunity, and dietary needs are but one of many rituals that require special products. Other such products are prayer shawls, books, and so on.

Socialization

The Jewish religion, as we have indicated before, places emphasis on knowledge and study. In a section of the Bible that Jews have traditionally recited daily, Jews are instructed to "teach them [the laws] diligently unto thy children, and shalt talk of them when thou sittest in thine house, and when thou walkest by the way and when thou liest down, and when thou risest up."[52] Even before the birth of Christ, Jewish communities that had more than 25 children were instructed to provide public education. Although the injunction on learning is related to religious subjects, it was instrumental in developing a favorable attitude to learning in general[53] and a high esteem for the learned. Thus the rabbi, the learned teacher, is always seated at the head of the table, given the honorable seat in the synagogue, and generally treated with deference. This respect for the learned has become generalized to include secular as well as religious learning.

Another reason for the importance of education is to be found in the history of Jewish experience. Because of frequent persecutions, money and possessions were seldom a source of security; possessions were often taken away or left behind when Jews were forced to leave the country of their residence. Only education, knowledge, and skills were commodities that could never be taken away, and therefore they were seen as the foundation for security. A related consequence of the concern for education is that Jews generally seek to reside in parts of the cities and suburbs that have the best educational systems.

In addition to secular education, Jews also seek to provide their children with religious education, which is seen as the mechanism for the continuation of Jewish existence. Most Jewish children start their religious education at about the age of six and complete it at thirteen, when they become Bar or Bas Mitzvah, literally a son or daughter of the commandments, signifying their having gone through the rite of passage that marks entry into adulthood. These schools are most often part of a synagogue or temple, although there are several educational institutions directed and supported by the Jewish Board of Education. The latter aims to be nonsectarian by providing a curriculum acceptable to Orthodox, Conservative, and Reform Jews. The last ten years have seen a revival of religious parochial schools where, in addition to general subjects, Hebrew language is taught as a secondary language, and a concentration in religious and historical studies is offered. Next to the home, Jewish schools were and are the most important institutions for developing ethnic consciousness and identity; hence the Jewish community places primacy on the support and development of the educational system.[54]

Social Control

Social interaction founded upon a normative structure is essential to all communities. It is the nature of the norm that violations of norms will be sanctioned. In other words, in all social and patterned relationships there are elements of control, and to the extent that Jewish association is communal, it also includes mechanisms of control.

Social control can be either formal or informal. Formal control is constituted by the legal system and the sanctions imposed for violations of it. In the case of informal control, sanctions are imposed most often by breaking off associations and by withholding services and resources.

Formal social control is vested in the Beth Din (house of judgment), the Jewish court composed of three rabbis acting as judges. As we mentioned earlier, such a court has no legal status and is not legally empowered to implement its decisions. It serves only for those individuals who, out of their own volition, seek this court's arbitration, mostly in cases of torts and violation of contracts (which includes divorce as a process of contract dissolution). Judgment is rendered on the basis of Talmudic laws—a set of legal codes that includes the explanations of and amendments to the laws found in the first five books of the Bible. The most severe punishment this court can render is excommunication, which is reserved for those acts that undermine the continual existence of Jews as a people. One such act is intermarriage. Traditionally, the parents of an exogamous Jew have declared their son or daughter dead and have followed all laws and customs associated with mourning. However, with the continual increase in the rate of intermarriage, these severe sanctions have become less used, and generally persons who intermarry today are neither declared dead nor cut off from all communal relations.[55]

External pressures for conformity to ethnic and religious norms are becoming weaker. The Jewish community, the existence of which depends greatly on voluntary financial contributions, can no longer afford to isolate and sanction those whose conformity is marginal. Consequently, in the face of ever-increasing deviance, a reinterpretation and reevaluation of traditional norms has evolved. For example, the norm of "compulsory endogamy" has changed to "preferred endogamy," exemplified by the following statement: "I would prefer that my son marry a Jewish girl, but it is his choice, and as long as she is a good girl it will be all right." Social control based on the individual's fear of the subcommunity's retaliatory capability is declining. Similarly, fear of social isolation and ostracism is also declining. Being Jewish is no longer a necessary or sufficient, although often preferable, reason for friendship with another Jew. Without a sanctioning capability, then, what mechanism binds the Jew to this subcommunity? The primary reason is the individual's felt need for maintaining his or her identity. The individual adheres to Jewish values and norms because of a desire to be identified as a Jew and to derive both psychological and social benefit from such identification. Such an individual can maintain a sense of euphoria and, by self-identification as a religious person, also be identified as a respectable person.

Social Participation

Association among Jews is facilitated both by place of worship and by social and cultural centers. In addition to religious worship, synagogues have long served as centers for the development of personal associations. Presently, how ever, worship attendance among Jews is very low, perhaps lowest among all major religions in the United States. Lazerwitz[56] reports that only 28 percent of New York Jews attend services once a month or more frequently. Yet the synagogue or temple remains an important mechanism for initiating and maintaining social relationships among Jews. More importantly, ritual participation in such events as Bar or Bas Mitzvah, weddings, and other celebrations functions to reinforce Jewish identity, since such participation allows Jews to develop a sense of euphoria about being Jewish. Religion is not the only activity that brings Jews together. Horace M. Kallen, editor of the nonreligious

Jewish newspaper *Forward,* has often suggested that Jewish life in this country should be built on a variety of Jewish experiences political, social, and philosophical as well as religious. In Russia, for example, during the period of Jewish Enlightenment (1860–1900), a nonreligious expression of Jewish identity already existed: the Yiddish movement[57] encouraged the development of nonreligious literature based on the life experiences of Jews in the *shtetl* in Russia. Jewish centers in the United States became popular during the 1920s as places were Jews could not only learn English and prepare themselves for citizenship. These centers also furthered the development of Jewish literature and plays.[59]

Mutual Support

"All Jews are responsible for each other": so goes the Talmudic statement. This responsibility encompasses all facets of life which affect the welfare of Jews on both the individual and the community levels.

Since they have always comprised a community within a community, Jews have long been concerned with the image they project to the larger community, and particularly with its effect on anti-Semitism, a prejudice that is unfortunately still widely prevalent. Glock and Stark report that in a national sample one-third of the respondents scored in the highest category on the anti-Semitic Belief Index, while another 40 percent scored medium high. Thus 73 percent of the American public showed a considerable propensity for anti-Semitic beliefs.[59] Two national Jewish agencies, the Jewish Committee and the Anti-Defamation League of B'nai B'rith, have been concerned with organized intolerance to Jews in general, and particularly with the prevalence of anti-Semitism. Through the legal system these organizations have fought against discrimination in employment and residence, and have been successful in destroying restrictive covenants that specify that homes in certain areas will not be sold to minorities. The Jewish community also provides extensive support for individuals, primarily in the areas of health, the aged, youth services, immigration, and employment.

Concern with health dates back to the period of mass immigration in the 1890s, when living conditions in the crowded rooms in the lower east side of New York and other Jewish ghettos helped create a high incidence of tuberculosis. These conditions helped to bring about the creation of the first three Jewish hospitals and sanatoriums for tuberculosis victims, which became the forerunners of present-day Jewish hospitals. Later development of general hospitals has been related to Jewish dietary considerations; these hospitals, although nonsectarian, provided kosher meals as well as other ritual considerations for the practicing Jew. At the present time in the United States, fifteen of the sixteen cities with a Jewish population of more than forty thousand, and half of those cities with a Jewish population between sixteen thousand and forty thousand have a Jewish hospital.

Closely tied with health care facilities are the Jewish homes for the aged, which now care for nineteen thousand elderly persons. In addition to health care and social and personal services, these homes also provide for various religious considerations. (It is interesting that the Hebrew word for "home for the aged" is Beth Avoth, meaning literally "home of our fathers.")

Beginning in the 1880s, Jewish mass immigration from Eastern Europe included many Jews fleeing from Czarist persecution. These Jews left almost all their possessions behind and came to this country poor and often ill-equipped to survive the rigors of urban life. To help these people a number of agencies came into existence such as HIAS, ADJC, and ORT. A precedent for helping immigrants is found as early as 1828, with the foundation in New York of the Hebrew Benevolent Society. The B'nai B'rith (sons of the covenant) was organized in 1845, and it has concerned itself with philanthropic activities ever since. Immigration between the two world wars declined drastically, primarily because of the quota system, which limited the number of immigrants from each European country. Since World War II, however, Jewish immigration has again increased, and has consisted primarily of displaced persons from German concentration camps. The above-mentioned organizations, together with Jewish family services in particular communities, have provided financial, moral, and personal help in resettling the new immigrants.

Most Jewish communities, through the Jewish Federation or the community center, now provide various youth services. These include summer camps that, in addition to recreation, offer courses in Jewish history and language. Other services include employment counseling and placement and family counseling and adoption services.

JEWS AND ISRAEL

Israel has held a special place in the hearts and minds of Jews all over the world, and to understand it we must place it in some historical perspective.

Twice during their long national history Jews were forced to leave their homeland. First, Babylon defeated Judea and took most of its population captive further inland to Babylon and Persia. This period, known as the Babylonian exile, lasted seventy years. When Babylon was defeated by Cyrus, he permitted the Jewish captives to return to Judea under the leadership of Ezra and Nehemiah and to rebuild their homeland. This second period of Jewish existence in their homeland ended with the Roman defeat of the Jewish rebellion and struggle for independence. In 70 A.D. under the leadership of Titus Vespasian, the temple was destroyed and Jews again were taken captive, followed by a complete dispersal of Jews, most of whom went to live in Persia and Egypt and finally in Europe. Still, and in spite of their life in Diaspora, Jews continued to regard Israel as their homeland and retained in their prayer a statement of the hope of returning as free and independent people to their ancient homeland. This hope has intensified every time Jews were persecuted.

In the middle of the nineteenth century a new and more secular political (as opposed to religious) group was established, the main objective of which was to reestablish a Jewish homeland in the ancient land of Judea. This movement, known as Zionism, has spread particularly as a result of continued Jewish persecution in czarist Russia, form of persecution known as pogroms. In the West, Zionism has also gained momentum as a direct result of the Dreyfus affair.[60] As a result of these persecutions, Israel, as a safe haven for Jews, has been viewed by Jews as most essential for Jewish survival. The events that occurred during the Nazi regime in Europe when 6 million, or more than a third of the world's Jews, lost their lives, reinforced the Jewish belief of the essentiality of an independent Jewish country and led the United Nations to support an earlier plan for the partition of the British mandate known as Palestine, thus creating the Jewish State of Israel. American Jews have supported the establishment of this state for almost no Jewish family in this country has escaped experiencing some personal loss as a direct result of the Holocaust.

Although in this country Jews have always experienced political freedom, they nonetheless have also experienced a certain degree of anti-Semitism. Though not official and of questionable legality, a certain degree of social, economic, and professional exclusion has been practiced in the past and some of it remains in the present. In a recent study on American anti-Semitism, Quigley and Glock report:

> Anti-Semitic stereotypes were found to be common in contemporary America. Many Americans think of Jews as unethical, dishonest, aggressive, pushy, clannish, and conceited. On the basis of such beliefs, more than a third of the public were classified as anti-Semitic. Another third were found to hold moderately anti-Semitic beliefs, with the remaining third consistently rejecting all negative stereotypes of Jews.[61]

If, as it is reported, two-thirds of the American public manifests some to a high degree of anti-Semitic beliefs, these feelings and attitudes tend to manifest themselves in various ways and continue to reinforce the beliefs among Jews for the necessity of a safe haven. The importance of this safe entry to Jews in America takes on even more meaning when they are faced with Jewish conditions in Russia. The continual need for Jewish emigration in other countries (Russia and Iran for instance) serves as a continual reminder to American Jews of the importance of Israel to world Jewry.

Black-Jewish Conflict

Jews and African Americans have historically shared many interests. Both communities have shared a commitment to liberal political policies. These are evident in their similar voting practices. For instance, this similarity is evident in the 1992 election. Both Jews and African Americans have strongly supported Clinton. Blacks have cast 82 percent and Jews 78 percent for Clinton. Jews' political perspective has been committed to liberal issues which led to their support for civil rights movement. This commitment is founded in the ethical commitment to justice.[62] Jewish commitment to both to the rights of Blacks and human rights in general can be seen in the Jewish support of the NAACP. Joel and Arthus Spingarn were early leaders of this organization, and it was Kivie Kaplan who as the National President of the NAACP who in Roy Wilkins' view was instrumental of making the organization both important and financially viable. Arnold Aronson during the 1960s who was the executive secretary of the Leadership Conference on Civil Rights. Who can forget also Schwerner and Goodman, two Jews, and Chaney, an African American, who lost their lives in their quest for civil rights.[63]

However, in recent years the relationships between African Americans and Jews have become strained and which is evident in the rise of Black anti-Semitism. While the contributing factors to this phenomenon are complex we wish, in this chapter, to focus on the following factors: economics, quotas, the new left, and the Nation of Islam.

Quinley and Glock have observed that Black anti-Semitism, unlike white, has primarily an economic basis.[64] Urban Blacks frequently patronize local Jewish stores and frequently live in homes and/or apartments owned by Jewish landlords. Such relationships were found to increase levels of anti-Semitism due to Black perception of economic exploitation. On the other hand, findings also show that many Blacks identify with Jews and see them as fellow victims. Hence the overall level of Black anti-Semitism does not differ greatly from that of white anti-Semitism.

However, the most vociferous anti-Semitism in the Black community comes from the Nation of Islam. Both their vitriolic attack on Jews and its tone is similar to the Nazi propaganda in Germany. This is exemplified in the speeches given by Louis Farrahkan and his aide Khallid Abdul Muhammad to students in Kean College in New Jersey. Muhammad, for instance, blamed the holocaust on Jews themselves and attacked the Jews in America for "sucking our blood in the Black community." Black anti-Semitism is not new, and like anti-Semitism among whites a great part of it can be attributed to historical Christianity.[65] However, the anti-Semitism of the Nation of Islam may arise from a different source. Midge Decter's explanation of this phenomenon is quite apropos. She writes:

> Anti-Semitism . . . provide [sic] the Blacks with a simulacrum of toughness—of all the people they hit, the Jews are least likely to exact equal retribution.[66]

She concludes that Farrahkan seeks to redirect and reorganize Black servitude. Their message is: "Get off drugs, and get yourself a substitute dependency on hatred—it's a whole lot quicker as a therapy than learning how truly to stand on your own two feet. In other words, the Jews as a methadone."[67]

Two other factors should be mentioned as sources of Jewish and Black strain. These are the question of quotas and attitude toward Israel.

Briefly, one aspect of the affirmative action program was the proposal to establish a system of quotas for minorities as means to ensure adequate inclusion in occupations and education. Quotas, however, may and have served two different and diametrically opposed ends. Quotas not only can define the parameters of inclusion but at the same time can provide a systematic means for exclusion. It is the latter use of quotas that American Jews have experienced. Quotas were used in this country to limit Jewish enrollment in colleges, medical schools, and law schools as well as in housing. (For instance, unofficial "gentlemen's agreements" limited Jewish enrollment in medical schools, law schools, and so on to a specified percentage, which has varied from school to school.) To combat such practices, Jews have strongly supported the more democratic process based on meritocracy; that is, admission to and participation in any educational or occupational system should be primarily based on ability and performance. Many Jews believe that the use of quotas, regardless of the intention, reestablishes a particularistic form of decision making; that is, decisions are based not on what a person does but who he or she is. Because of these differences in views, each group sees the other as threatening their interests. This situation in turn helps to increase group conflict.

Another source of Jewish-Black conflict has arisen out of a Black shift away from supporting Israel. In the 1960s the New Left movement shifted its support to the Palestinian cause and away from Israel. Since the Black leaders identified the New Left as its strong ally, it followed that a realignment in the traditional coalition should occur. That is, the new Black militant leaders together with the New Left leaders began supporting the Palestinian cause, thus legitimizing the PLO, which is perceived by the Jewish community to be by its very nature anti-Israel. This threat to the existence of Israel, the symbol of continued Jewish future, has thus fostered a break in the traditional alliance between Jews and Blacks and has decreased the Jewish commitment to fight for Black rights.

PRESENT TRENDS AND FUTURE PROSPECTS

Recent studies of Jews in the United States show two important trends. First, Jews are becoming secularized and integrated into the American society. This integration is best indicated by the following. Even though Jews constitute a small percentage of the total U.S population, they are none the less not considered by the government as a minority. Second, the Jewish population in the United States is not increasing. This phenomenon, we shall argue, is due to the following two factors: low birth rate and high rate of intermarriage.

The 1990 Jewish population survey (Kosmin et al. 1991) shows that the core Jewish population is estimated to be 5.5 million persons and 6.6 million of all persons of Jewish descent. This accounts for an extremely small growth for the last twenty five years (since 1975) when all the people of Jewish descent was 6.1 million. In this chapter we will limit our analysis to the Jewish core population, that is, to 5.5 million born Jews, those who maintain their identity both in their religion and ethnicity (4.2 million), those born as Jews but perceive themselves as secular but also maintain their Jewish ethnicity (1.1 million), and to those who are Jews by choice, that is those who converted and those who have selected to be Jews, albeit without conversion (185,000). In contrast to the 185,000 proselytes, the number of Jews who exited their religion (635,000) greatly outnumbers those who have entered Judaism. Both, those who converted into and those who converted out of Judaism are primarily women which in both instances was the result of intermarriage.

The lack of Jewish population growth is also attributable to the very low birth rates among Jews. Regardless of age, cohort Jewish women have, on the average, fewer children than non-Jewish white women. For instance, Jewish women in childbearing ages such as 25–34 have on the average only .87 children compared with 1.29 to non-Jewish white women. The average number of children ever born to Jewish women who are 35–44 years old is 1.57 compared to 2.00 to non-Jewish women. This is due to two factors. First, Jewish women delay childbearing until their late twenties and early thirties. Second, and perhaps associated with the first, is that Jewish women postpone their childbearing because of their education. The 1990 population study shows that over thirty-seven percent of the younger Jewish women (ages 25–44) have post-graduate degrees.

Let us now turn to examine Jewish assimilation. Gordon considers intermarriage as the best index of assimilation. We may say that assimilation is associated with status mobility, that is, the acceptance of Jews into social circles. Status groups as Weber (1958:188) indicates tend to confine marriages to the same status circle. Thus we may get an estimate of the degree of Jewish assimilation into American culture by looking at their rates of intermarriage. Prior to 1965 9 percent of Jews married outside of their religion and ethnic group. By 1974 it was 25 percent, increased to 44 percent by 1985, and has been over 52 percent since 1985 (Kosmin et al. 1991). In short, religion which has served as a barrier to intermarriage has been considerably weakened to the extent that only 22 percent of the core Jews have indicated an opposition to the idea of intermarriage.

Increased rates of intermarriage is but one indication of Jewish secularization. Most Jews in the United States have left historical orthodoxy and have joined either the conservative synagogues (40.4 percent) or reform Judaism (41.4 percent). Only 6.8 percent of those constituting the core of American Jews remained orthodox. An additional 3.2 percent consider themselves and are members of traditional synagogues, that is, not orthodox but not conservative. In fact, the locus of Jewish identity has changed from religion to an ethnic and community based identity that has been referred to as Jewish Civil Religion (Breslauer 1989).

The decline of religiosity among Jews is evidenced in religious attachment and practices. While 41 percent of the core Jewish population are members of a synagogue only eleven percent attend synagogue weekly and 59 percent attend services during the High Holidays. Fasting on the Day of Atonement, which was considered to be the most significant of all Jewish rituals, is observed by only 61 percent of the total core Jewish population. This does not mean that Jews are rejecting their identity. Simply that there is a shift of identity from religion to ethnicity, to a cultural and historical foundation. Thus, while 70 percent of all Jews considered themselves to be a cultural group only 49 percent considered themselves to be also a religious group.

Secularization has been found to be related with education. Thus, because Jews as a group are highly educated it is therefore no wonder that Jews are one of most secularized religious or ethnic groups. Among the 25–44 age group of males only 12 percent had less than a grade school education but almost 35 percent have college degrees and 39 percent have post-graduate degrees. Education, as it has been indicated earlier is a most important and cherished value among Jews.

Still, in spite of the open mobility in America which is associated with increased intermarriage and the acceptance of Jews into status group, Jews, nonetheless, will to a great extent maintain their identity. The reason is anti-Semitism. Simmel in his study of social conflict tells us that one of the consequences of real or perceived conflict is increased heightening of one's identity. Throughout the history of Jews, anti-Semitism has always been a force of Jewish identity maintenance. This force still operates today. Eighty-three percent of Jews still feel that anti-Semitism is a serious problem. Recent events show the rise of the religious right and various militant organizations like the "militia" that espouse anti-Semitism thus reinforcing this perception. In addition to anti-Semitism the State of Israel with its accomplishment is an additional source of identity maintenance. The establishment of the State of Israel provided an important link for Jews to their historical past; to a great extent, the life and identity of world Jewry is tied to the cultural life of the people of Israel. The positive accomplishments of that state have helped to maintain pride in Jewishness as well as to change the image of the Jews from an acquiescent martyrlike people to that of a people who can actively determine their life fate. In other words, Israel has helped to strengthen the Jews' pride in being Jewish, and the constant threat to this state's continued existence acts as an additional force for heightened Jewish consciousness and identity.

Notes

1. Herbert J. Gans, "American Jewry: Present and Future," *Commentary* 21 (1956), pp. 424–25.
2. Nathan Glazer, "The Jewish Revival in America: I," *Commentary* 20 (1955), p. 493.

3. Melvin Tumin, "Conservative Trends in American Jewish Life," *Judaism: A Quarterly Journal of Jewish Life and Thought* 17 (1964), pp. 133.
4. Ibid., p. 135.
5. Ibid.
6. Ibid., p. 137.
7. Ibid.
8. Bernard Lazerwitz, "The Ethical Impact of Jewish Identification," *Judaism: A Quarterly Journal of Jewish Life and Thought* 18 (1969), pp. 421.
9. Ibid.
10. Abram L. Sacher, *A History of the Jews* (New York: Knopf, 1930), p. 260.
11. Cecil Roth, "The Jews of Western Europe," in *The Jews: Their History, Culture, and Religion,* ed. Louis Finkelstein (New York: Harper, 1949), pp. 250–83.
12. Sachar, *A History of the Jews,* pp. 273–98.
13. Under this law, Jews in a community were obliged, by fair means or foul, to fill a given quota for the Russian armed forces. In many communities bands of "Cathers" kidnapped Jewish children as one of the means to satisfy the ever-increasing demand for soldiers. Life in the *shtetls* of the pale are described in the works of Shalom Aleichem, J. L. Perez, Mendele Mocher S'forim, and J. Fichman.
14. Rufus Learsi, *The Jews in America: A History* (New York: World, 1954).
15. We will omit for our purposes the migration of the Spanish Jews, Sephardim, and will begin with the massive migration of the German Jews.
16. Excellent presentations of the Jew's struggle in Russia are Louis Greenberg, *The Jews in Russia: The Struggle for Emancipation* (New Haven: Yale University Press, 1944), and S. M. Dubnow, *The History of the Jews in Russia and Poland from the Earliest Times to the Present Day,* trans. I. Friedlander (Philadelphia: Jewish Publication Society of America, 1916).
17. Learsi, *Jews in America.*
18. Glazer, "Jewish Revival," p. 16.
19. M. Zabrowski and E. Herzog, *Life Is with People: The Culture of the Shtetl* (New York: Schocken Books, 1962), p. 12. *Shtetls* are "small towns and enclaves within the area stretching from the eastern borders of Germany to the western regions of . . . Russia (embracing Poland, Galicia, Lithuana, White Russia, the Ukraine, Berserubia, Slovakia, and northeastern regions of Hungary)."
20. Refers to a diaspora or all lands outside Israel.
21. Glazer, "Jewish Revival."
22. Garments that are *shatnez* free, that is, certified not to contain a mixture of wool and linen.
23. Glazer, "Jewish Revival," p. 494.
24. Nathan Glazer, *American Judaism* (Chicago: University of Chicago Press, 1957), p. 91.
25. In Mukacevo (the author's home town) in Czechoslovakia there were frequent fights between the Zionist and the Orthodox youth, and the chief rabbi of the

community excommunicated the faculty of the local Zionist Hebrew School because they rejected the messianic concept.

26. Joachim Prinz, *The Dilemma of the Modern Jew* (Boston: Little, Brown, 1962).
27. Howard M. Schaar, *The Course of Modern Jewish History* (New York: World, 1958), pp. 323–46.
28. C. Bezalel Sherman, *The Jew within American Society: A Study in Ethnic Individuality* (Detroit: Wayne State University Press, 1965), p. 87.
29. Sachar, *A History of the Jews,* pp. 327–28, notes that the Yiddish dailies represented definite political and economic views, and that those of the Daily Forward were socialist. "The Forward," he writes, "became the representative voice of American Jewish socialism. . . . The 'light' category . . . [the] so-called human interest happenings, [were] retold and interpreted from the 'Socialist-Jewish point of view.'" By 1902, this newspaper became very popular and achieved a circulation of 200,000.
30. Glazer, *American Judaism,* p. 87.
31. The roots of Yiddish orientation can be traced to the influences of such writers as Mendele, Sholem, and Peretz. For a more extensive discussion see Yudel Mark, "Yiddish Literature," in *The Jews,* ed. Finkelstein, p. 859.
32. Glazer, *American Judaism.*
33. Ibid.
34. Ibid.
35. W. Lloyd Warner and Leo Srole, "Assimilation or Survival: A Crisis in the Jewish Community of Yankee City," in *The Jews: Social Patterns of an American Group,* ed. Marshall Sklare (Glencoe, IL: Free Press, 1958).
36. Glazer, *American Judaism,* pp. 72–105.
37. Glazer, "Jewish Revival," p. 493.
38. Ibid.
39. Gans, "American Jewry," pp. 422–30.
40. Bernard Lazerwitz, "Jews In and Out of New York City, " *Jewish Journal of Sociology* 3 (1961), pp. 254–60.
41. Bernard Lazerwitz, "Religion and Social Structure in the United States," in *Religion, Culture, and Society,* ed. Louis Schneider (New York: Wiley, 1964), p. 641.
42. The author is acquainted with many synagogues in St. Louis and Memphis, and in the small towns of southern Illinois, where members are assigned dates so that a "minyon," the necessary ten men for public service, is assured.
43. Will Herberg, Protestant-Catholic-Jew (Garden City, NY: Doubleday, 1955), p. 190.
44. Warner and Srole, "Assimilation," p. 355.
45. The dietary laws, which specify what Jews may and may not eat.
46. Werner Sombart, *The Jews and Modern Capitalism,* trans. H. Epstein (Glencoe, IL: Free Press, 1951).

47. There is one ritual for which a Kohen (hereditary priest) is necessary: the "redemption of the first born." If a woman's first child is a male, he is ritually redeemed from the deity who proclaimed in the Bible, "Sanctify unto me all the firstborn . . . ." (Exod. 13:2).
48. Deut. 16:20.
49. Zbarowski and Herzog, *Life Is with People.*
50. Judith Kramer and Seymour Leventman, *Children of the Gilded Ghetto* (New Haven: Yale University Press, 1961), p. 98: "For reasons of service to the community, or humanitarian or democratic ideals, organizations based upon the norms of inclusiveness attempt to recruit as many members as possible, regardless of socioeconomic background. In contrast, organizations based upon the norm of exclusiveness represent status communities and select their members according to specific social and economic qualifications."
51. Roland Warren, *The Community in America* (Chicago: Rand McNally, 1963), p. 208.
52. Deut. 6:7.
53. The importance of education among Jews can be evidenced from the following statistics: In Province, R.I., for instance, in 1960, 8.2 percent of its total population 25 years and older (including Jews) have had graduate or postgraduate training, compared with 33.8 percent of its Jewish population. Similar differences were found in New York, where in 1964, 15.9 percent of its population held graduate or postgraduate degrees compared with 27.4 percent of its Jewish population (Marshall Sklare, *America's Jews* [New York: Random House, 1971], pp. 5160).
54. Of all the monies collected by the Jewish Federation, one-fourth is allocated to Jewish education (*The American Jewish Yearbook* [New York: American Jewish Committee, 1972]).
55. Of all marriages between 1966 and 1972, 31.7 percent were intermarriages (Fred Massarik, *Intermarriages: Facts for Planning* [New York: Council of Jewish Federation, n.d.]).
56. Lazerwitz, "Jews In and Out of New York City."
57. Yiddish is jargon based on the German language, with an admixture of Hebrew and the language of the country.
58. For further discussion, see Glazer, *American Judaism.*
59. It is interesting to note that anti-Semitic attitudes are related to belief systems. Members of conservative religions are more likely to be anti-Semitic than members of liberal religions. For instance, it is lowest among Unitarians (11 percent) and highest among Baptists (40 percent). See Charles Y. Glock and Rodney Stark, *Christian Beliefs and Anti-Semitism* (New York: Harper Torchbooks, 1966).
60. Captain Dreyfus was found guilty of espionage against France and sentenced on fabricated evidence to Devil's Island. His innocence was evident, but the prosecution was greatly influenced by anti-Semitic factors.
61. Harold E. Quigley and Charles Y. Glock. *Anti-Semitism in America* (New York: Free Press, 1979), p. 19.

62. Schoenfeld, "Justice an Illusive Concept in Christianity," *Review of Religious Research* 30 (1989), pp. 236–45.
63. James Farmer, "Foreword," in *Bridges and Boundaries: African Americans and American Jews,* Jack Salzman, Adina Black and G.S. Sorin, eds., (New York, George Braziller, Inc., 1992.
64. Ibid., p. 67.
65. Ibid.
66. On the other hand, Quigley and Glock found white anti-Semitism to be rooted in religious beliefs.
67. Midge Decter, "Why Did Blacks Turn on Jews?" in *Time,* February 28, 1994.

Suggested Readings

Breslauer, S. Daniel. *Covenant and Commitment in Modern Judaism.* New York: Greenwood Press, 1989.

Glazer, Nathan. *American Judaism.* Chicago: University of Chicago Press, 1957.

Glock, Charles Y., and Rodney Stark. *Christian Beliefs and Anti-Semitism.* New York: Harper Torchbooks, 1966.

Goldstein, Sidney, and Calvin Goldscheuder. *Jewish Americans.* Englewood Cliffs, NJ: PrenticeHall, 1968.

Gordon, Milton. *Assimilation in American Life: The Role of Race, Religion, and National Origins.* New York, Oxford University Press, 1964.

Kosmin, Barry A., S. Goldstein, J. Waksberg, N. Lerer, A. Keysar, J. Scheckner, *Highlights of the CJF 1990 National Jewish Population Survey.* New York: The Council of Jewish Federations.

Kramer, Judith, and Seymour Leventman. *Children of the Gilded Ghetto.* New Haven: Yale University Press, 1961.

Quigley, Harold E., and Charles Y. Glock. *Anti-Semitism in America.* New York: Free Press, 1979.

Schaar, Howard M. *The Course of Modern Jewish History.* New York: World, 1958.

Sherman, C. Bezalel. *The Jew within American Society: A Study in Ethnic Individuality.* Detroit: Wayne State University Press, 1965.

Simmel, Georg. *Conflict.* Trans. K.H. Wolf. Glencoe, IL: The Free Press, 1955.

Sklare, Marshall. *America's Jews.* New York: Random House, 1971.

Weber, Max. *From Max Weber.* Trans. H.H. Gerth and C.W. Mills. New York: Oxford University Press, 1946.

Wirth, Louis. *The Ghetto.* Chicago: University of Chicago Press, 1928; Phoenix Books, 1958.

CHAPTER 17

Irish Catholic Americans: A Successful Case of Pluralism*

Robert E. Kennedy, Jr.

Is knowledge about the historical experience of European immigrants in the United States helpful in understanding contemporary American minority-group relations? Are social organizations used today by racial or linguistic minorities similar to those created by some European immigrant groups to aid their members? The immigration history of one group is particularly relevant in answering these questions—that of the Roman Catholic Irish.

The Catholic Irish were the first large, non-Protestant immigrant group in American cities. They established social institutions and ways of dealing with the majority population that for decades influenced the lives of later-arriving ethnic and racial groups. The Protestant Irish immigrants were much smaller in number, and were not as subject as the Catholic Irish to severe social and economic discrimination. Because religion was not asked in the census, however, we cannot distinguish between Protestants and Catholics in government reports on Irish immigrants. Thus, although we shall present statistical information about "Irish immigrants" that includes some Protestants, the focus of this paper will be upon the Irish Catholics.

By the mid-nineteenth century, the Irish were the largest single immigrant group in the United States and accounted for more than 40 percent of all

*Except for an inserted editorial note (an update by the editors), this is a reprint of the chapter from the second edition.

TABLE 17-1
Percent Distribution by Country of Birth of the Foreign-Born Population of the United States, 1850–1920

Country of Birth	1850*	1860	1880	1900	1920
Ireland	42.8	38.9	27.8	15.6	7.5
Germany	26.0	30.8	29.4	25.8	12.1
England, Scotland, and Wales	16.8	14.2	13.6	11.3	8.5
Sweden, Norway, and Denmark	0.9	1.8	6.6	10.4	8.5
Italy	0.2	0.3	0.7	4.7	11.6
Russia, Lithuania, and Finland	0.1	0.1	0.5	4.7	12.2
Poland	0.0	0.2	0.7	3.7	8.2
Other	13.2	13.7	20.7	23.8	31.4
Percentage totals	100.0	100.0	100.0	100.0	100.0
Total foreign-born population in thousands	2,245	4,139	6,680	10,341	13,921

Source: Nils Carpenter, *Immigrants and Their Children, 1920*. Washington, D.C.: Government Printing Office, 1927, pp. 78-79, Table 43.
*Figures for each census year relate to countries as constituted in that year.

foreign-born persons (Table 17–1). If assimilation had been their goal, then today, over 130 years later, it would seem that the Irish and their descendants have succeeded. Persons of Irish birth and ancestry are found in almost all aspects of American life, and many have become Irish in name only. But some Irish originally did not come to this country to give up their ethnic heritage; they came to create a life based on their own culture, which they felt had been denied them in their homeland. They valued the constitutional freedoms guaranteed by their adopted nation as the means for establishing separate control over their own political, educational, and religious affairs.

Many Irish immigrants in the United States also brought with them intense anti-English sentiments, which in some ways became anti-Anglo-Saxon attitudes in this country. Far from desiring to emulate the ways of the native-born "Yank," some Irish Catholic immigrants scorned elements of the then-prevailing American lifestyle. In an overwhelmingly rural nation the Irish concentrated in the larger cities. While many Protestants believed religion was a matter of individual responsibility and a personal salvation, Irish Catholics assumed the ultimate authority in spiritual matters rested not with the individual but with a religious hierarchy. In opposition to the Jeffersonian belief in creating an informed electorate through the ideal of universal public education Irish Catholics insisted on operating their own private schools where they could educate their children as they saw fit.

Contrary to the American emphasis on monetary success as the main criterion for individual achievement, many Irish Catholic American children were brought up to value pursuits which helped others in their family or their ethnic community. In a guide to potential Irish emigrants published in 1873, the Irish author expounded on the American virtues of hard work, moderate living, and a lifelong savings plan as the means to success, and then he defensively added:

> Be it understood that the object of the writer is not to destroy or warp any of the grand and beautiful traits of character in our race for which they are distinguished all over the world. Filial devotion, love of friends, and readiness to relieve their wants, are characteristics of our race that deserve all honor.[1]

Minority-group membership was a social reality for the Irish that often determined individual behavior. Elsewhere, for example, I have described the independent effect of minority-group status on the family size of Catholics in Northern Ireland.[2] Although several other aspects of life in Ireland have changed over the past century, the current troubles in Northern Ireland illustrate the enduring reality of Ireland's history of intergroup conflict—a history that had a direct impact on why so many Irish left Ireland for the United States. The behavior of the Irish in America is more understandable with knowledge of conditions in Ireland a century or more ago, when the forebears of most Irish Americans began arriving in this country.

Conditions in Nineteenth-Century Ireland

The hostility of many Irish immigrants to things Anglo-Saxon, their strong identity with Roman Catholicism, their rejection of rural living, and their intense concern with political power all have historical roots in their reasons for leaving Ireland. Emigration from Ireland was linked to four major topics, the first of which was the relationship between the major religious denominations.

Protestants and Roman Catholics

Even though the majority of the Irish population was Roman Catholic, laws once existed that discriminated against them because of their religion. The issue was one of power rather than numerical minority or minority status, with the Protestant minority being dominant. Irish Catholics lost much of their status with the passage by the English between 1695 and 1746 of what became known as the Penal Laws. As J.C. Beckett has commented: "The essential purpose of the Penal Laws was not to destroy Roman Catholicism, but to make sure that its adherents were kept in a position of social, economic, and political inferiority."[3]

By the beginning of the nineteenth century the Penal Laws were gradually lifted, but social discrimination against Catholics maintained the power and privileges of Protestants over Catholics. As late as 1926 the disproportionate representation of Protestants in the better jobs was still apparent. Even though Protestants accounted for only 7 percent of the male labor force in the Republic of Ireland at that time, half of the bank officers were Protestants, as were 41 percent of the heads of commercial businesses, 40 percent of accountants, and 36 percent of lawyers.[4]

Under such circumstances a movement of Catholics from Ireland to the United States would hardly have been surprising. Given the discrimination suffered by Catholics in Ireland, however, it was difficult for them to pay their own passage across the Atlantic. This need was met in large part by the loyalty of the Irish in the United States to family and friends left behind. During the second half of the nineteenth century, Irish immigrants in the United States sent back to Ireland $260 million.[5] This money paid for at least three-quarters of all Irish emigration to the United States between 1848 and 1900, and without it Irish Catholic mass emigration to America would not have happened.[6]

Land Ownership, Eviction, and Famine

Because of the Penal Laws, by the early nineteenth century most of the land in what is today the Republic of Ireland was owned by Protestants. They leased their land to tenant farmers who were predominantly Catholic (as was the landless laboring class). As is sometimes the case with slum landlords today, many early nineteenth-century Irish landlords tried to get as much rent from as many tenants as possible. Tenant holdings were fragmented and living standards declined, until a large segment of the rural population became dependent on a single crop for their staple food—the potato. Following a poor potato harvest, the nutritional level worsened and epidemics accompanied by starvation became increasingly common.

Why didn't the Irish eat their other crops or even their livestock to avoid starvation during failures of the potato harvest? They needed to pay the rent to avoid eviction, and they had nothing to pay the rent with except their cash crops. As Irish historian George O'Brien put it:

> The extraordinary spectacle of Irishmen starving by thousands in the midst of rich cornfields was thus witnessed. One case, typical of many others, is recorded of a man's dying of starvation in the house of his daughter, who had in her haggard a substantial stack of barley, which she was afraid to touch, as it was marked by the landlord for his rent.[7]

Tenants were able to resist eviction to some degree by murders, burnings, cattle mutilation, and other forms of agrarian terrorism directed against the landlord, his agents, and persons who might move into an evicted tenant's holding. Evictions were more prevalent during famine times. But contrary to what one might expect, persons officially reported as evicted made up only a small minority of all reported emigrants between 1849 and 1882.[8] The great majority of emigrants from rural Ireland did not wait for eviction before deciding to leave the country. For these individuals, the act of emigration was also a decision to give up farming as a way of life.

Between 1800 and 1979 there were eight extensive famines in Ireland, the worst one occurring between 1845 and 1848.[9] Because the 1845–1848 famine was one of the most severe in Irish history, and because at least 3 million persons emigrated from Ireland between 1845 and 1870 (compared with a total national population of about 8 million in 1841), it is often assumed that this famine initiated mass emigration from Ireland. Actually, the famine accelerated a mass movement out of the country that was well under way by the 1820s.[10] And that mass out-migration continued for decades after adjustments to the 1845–1848 famine were over: by 1891, 39 percent of all Irish-born persons in the world were living outside of Ireland.[11]

Irish Agricultural Technology

Irish Catholics may have rejected agriculture in Ireland given the land tenure system there (as late as 1895 only 12 percent of all farmers owned their own holdings) and the destitution that periodic crop failures had brought them. But this does not explain why so few took up farming after their arrival in the United States. A major reason for their urban preferences lies in the contrast between Irish and American agricultural techniques.

Due to the fragmentation of farms that had taken place in the early nineteenth century, by 1841 four out of five Irish holdings were smaller than fifteen acres. These small farms were worked by manual methods using the spade, scythe, and wooden rake and pitchfork. The farmers did not need, and could not afford to support, a horse and the relatively expensive capital investment in horse-drawn implements.

In the United States, on the other hand, farmers were not limited by the availability of farmland. In 1862, for example, Congress passed the Homestead Act, which promised ownership of a 160-acre tract of public land to family heads who cleared the land and lived on it for five years. Horses and horse-drawn implements were essential to exploit even part of such a large acreage, and by the mid-nineteenth century horse-drawn techniques had become the dominant method of commercial agriculture in the United States.

The Irish immigrant to America during the nineteenth century may have been a farmer or a farm laborer back in Ireland, but in most cases he would have had little, if any, firsthand experience with the horse-drawn methods required to make the most of agricultural opportunities in his new nation. His lack of interest in clearing and settling previously uncultivated land on the frontier is understandable in large part on such technical grounds alone.

Many Irish immigrants also had no interest in homesteading opportunities because they were more concerned with earning a cash income as soon as possible after arrival. Often their passage across the Atlantic have been paid by a relative or friend, and some felt obligated to do the same favor for potential emigrants still in Ireland. Urban jobs, even the most menial, provided such an income, while the capital investment required to establish a homestead would have consumed any cash earnings for a period of years.

Relative Social Status of the Sexes

The fourth major topic was linked to the decisions of thousands of females to emigrate: their relatively low status in Ireland. Although the situation of females had improved by the late 1950s, an Irish sociologist was still able to describe the status of teenage girls in rural Limerick in the following way:

> When a daughter reaches sixteen, if she remains on the farm, she must do a full day's work, and too often her life is one of unrelieved drudgery . . . [Girls] are favoured neither by father nor mother and accepted only on sufferance. This is, perhaps, too strong a conclusion, and it would be better to say they are loved but not thought of any great importance.[12]

In contrast to daughters, sons in the Irish family system were given preferential treatment, second only to their father. Women and children did not eat until after the men and the older boys had had their fill, a practice that systematically made the more nutritious food and larger helpings available to the favored sex. In rural areas the division of labor also gave preference to males: Women were expected to help with the men's work, but men would be ridiculed for helping with women's work. Women were usually called out into the fields to cut turf, to plant, cultivate, and harvest potatoes, and to assist at haymaking time.[13]

Elsewhere I have argued that the dominance of Irish males over females was sufficiently extreme to result in relatively higher female mortality; several comparisons of mortality by sex, nationality, rural-urban residence, age, and cause of death all indicate that the subordinate status of Irish females did indeed increase their mortality levels from what they otherwise might have been.[14]

Because the opportunities for improving one's social status were relatively much greater for females than for males away from their families, and in urban than in rural areas, migration to urban areas appealed more strongly to Irish females than males.[15] The movement to the United States of Irish females not only made the Irish immigration stream larger than it otherwise would have been, the preference of the Irish females for cities also contributed to the urban concentrations of the Irish in their adopted country.

NINETEENTH-CENTURY IRISH IMMIGRANTS

Most Irish immigrants in the United States were satisfied to remain in the Eastern Seaboard states throughout the second half of the nineteenth century. Almost two-thirds of all Irish-born persons in the United States in 1850 lived in just three states; New York, Pennsylvania, and Massachusetts (Table 17-2). Forty years later over half of the Irish-born still resided in those three states, and the relative increase in other states took place primarily among only four: New Jersey, Illinois, Connecticut, and California. The limited geographic dispersal of the Irish is understandable, given their reasons for coming to the United States. Most were rural-urban migrants not interested in settling the interior of the nation. They persisted in living in the East in spite of having been encouraged by some Irish writers of the time to take advantage of the cheap land available.

The Irish preference for urban living is understated by the statewide figures. In 1870, for example, of all the Irish-born persons in the United States, about 16 percent were living in the New York City area alone (New York City, Brooklyn, and Jersey City, New Jersey). Besides New York, the Irish concentrated in Boston and Philadelphia in the East, Chicago in the Midwest, and San Francisco in the West (after the gold rush days). The Irish were so

TABLE 17-2
Geographic Dispersal of the Irish: Percent Distribution of Irish-Born Persons by State and Territory, United States, 1850, 1870, 1890

State	1850	1870	1890
New York	35.7	28.5	25.8
Pennsylvania	15.8	12.7	13.0
Massachusetts	12.0	11.6	13.9
Ohio	5.4	4.5	3.7
New Jersey	3.2	4.7	5.4
Illinois	2.9	6.5	6.7
Connecticut	2.8	3.8	4.2
California	0.3	2.9	3.4
Subtotals	78.1	75.2	76.1
Other states and territories	21.9	24.8	23.9
Percentage totals	100.0	100.0	100.0
Total Irish-born persons in the United States	961,719	1,855,827	1,871,509

Source: U.S. Bureau of Statistics, *Arrivals of Alien Passengers and Immigrants in the United States from 1820 to 1892*. Washington, D.C.: Government Printing Office, 1893, 90-121, Table 14.

prevalent in these cities, in fact, that in 1870 about one in five persons living in Boston, New York City, and Brooklyn actually had been born in Ireland, as had about one in six or seven persons in the populations of San Francisco, Philadelphia, and Chicago (Table 17-3). The sizes of the Irish ethnic communities in these cities were even larger, since the figures refer only to the Irish-born immigrants and do not include children born in the United States to Irish parents.

The relative lack of other foreign-born groups in these cities increased the visibility of the Irish. By the 1870s Germans were arriving in large numbers, but they dispersed themselves more widely than the Irish, many bypassing the eastern cities for the towns and farmlands of the Mississippi River valley. Almost by default, the Irish continued to compose almost two-thirds of all foreign-born persons in Boston by 1870, and about half or more of all the immigrants living in New York City, Brooklyn, and Philadelphia (Table 17-3). The extensive historical research on how the Irish fared in New York City, Boston, and Philadelphia has been summarized concisely by Marjorie Fallows in her recent book.[16] At this time the Irish also made up the majority of foreign-born persons in several smaller cities and towns, such as Jersey City, Albany, and Providence. In such cities being a "foreigner" most often meant being Irish, and the relatively large numbers of the Irish and their children made their "non-American" ways conspicuous to the native-born Americans.

TABLE 17-3
Urban Concentrations of the Irish: Irish-Born Persons as a Percentage of the Foreign-Born and the Total Populations of Selected Cities, United States, 1870

	Irish Born as a Percentage of		
City	Total City Population	Total City Population	All Foreign-Born in City
Boston, Mass.	250,526	22.7	64.7
New York, N.Y.	942,292	21.4	48.3
Jersey City, N.J.	82,546	21.4	55.5
Albany, N.Y.	69,422	19.1	59.8
Brooklyn, N.Y.	396,099	18.7	51.1
Providence, R.I.	68,904	17.5	70.4
San Francisco, Calif.	149,473	17.3	35.1
Pittsburgh, Penn.	86,076	15.2	47.2
Philadelphia, Penn.	674,022	14.3	49.9
Chicago, Ill.	298,977	13.4	27.7

Source: U.S. Bureau of Statistics, *Arrivals of Alien Passengers and Immigrants in the United States from 1820 to 1892*. Washington, D.C.: Government Printing Office, 1893, pp. 122-33, Table 15.

Prejudice, Hostilities, and Discrimination against the Irish

Today the Irish are not considered to be a biologically distinct race, but such was the case in nineteenth-century America. Irish persons were believed by many Americans to have certain inferior traits which were intrinsic to the "Irish race." Because this American attitude explains much of how the Irish were received, it is worth quoting at length from at least one contemporary expression of the belief. In 1852 a Massachusetts clergyman wrote a letter to a Boston newspaper urging his fellow Americans to accept the Irish because they would be useful but not competitive:

> How much use are the Irish to us in America? The Native American answer is, "none at all." And the Native American policy is to keep them away. A profound mistake, I believe, for the precise reason that, in the pure blood they are so inefficient as compared with the Saxon and other Germanic races which receive them. I am willing to adopt the Native American point of view, and to speak with an *esprit du corps* [*sic,*] as one of the race invaded. Now if we Americans were inferior in ability to the Celts, we might complain. But this is not true. We are here, well organized, and well trained, masters of the soil, the very race before which they [the Irish] have yielded everywhere besides. It must be, that when they come in among us, they come to lift us up. As sure as water and oil each finds its level they will find theirs. So far as they are mere hand-workers they must sustain the head-workers, or those who have any element of intellectual ability. Their inferiority as a race compels them to go to the bottom; and the consequence is that we are, all of us, the higher lifted because they are here.[17]

Some Americans were not content to let the Irish settle to the bottom on their own; they used physical coercion against the Irish and against Irish institutions. As early as the 1830s organized resistance against Irish Catholics had begun in New York and in Massachusetts, with ethnic and religious tensions often centering around the Catholic convent schools. As Hofstadter and Wallace comment: "The unfamiliar nature of convent schools in particular gave rise to all sorts of speculation about immoral behavior and to sensational rumors about secret passageways from priests' homes to nunneries, the sexual abuse of female students by confessors, and the burial of illegitimate babies in convent crypts."[18] On the night of August 11, 1834, without warning, a mob attacked the Ursuline Convent in Charlestown, Massachusetts, drove out the ten adults and sixty children, and ransacked and burned the main building and the surrounding structures. News of the incident spread quickly and reinforced many Irish in their belief of the necessity to band together in defense of themselves, their families, and their community.

Quarrels and fights between Irish Catholics and American Protestants were common beginning as early as the 1820s, and an unusually large (and lengthy) riot occurred in Philadelphia in 1844, during which both sides armed themselves with cannon. By the end of the fighting, which erupted sporadically between May and July of that year, at least fifty persons had been killed or injured, and more than thirty homes and two churches had been burned down in the Irish section of the city. The riot had been sparked by Protestants incensed at a decision by the public school authorities to allow the use of the Catholic as well as the Protestant Bible in local schools.[19]

Paralleling open violence against the Irish was strong discrimination against their employment in any but the most menial jobs. The words, "No Irish need apply," appeared in newspaper notices beginning in the 1830s, and were only part of the problem many Irish experiences in seeking employment. There was what George Potter has called the silent conspiracy among employers not to hire Catholic Irish help: "An applicant's obvious Gaelic name or the sound of his brogue barred the door to employment, regardless of his personal qualities or qualifications, frequently on the justification that American or Protestant Irish help would not work by his side."[20]

It is an open question, however, whether more Irish were kept out of the American mainstream by discrimination or whether more kept themselves out in their drive to establish separate religious, social, and political institutions and organizations.

Irish American Social Institutions

The separatist element of the Irish immigrant population once, in 1818, went so far as to petition Congress for national aid and a piece of land on which to settle Irish charity cases at the exclusion of other groups. Congress turned down the request on the grounds that formal assignment of a national group to a particular territory could lead to similar requests by other nationalities and thereby fragment the nation. The noted historian of American immigration history, Marcus Hansen, remarked that "probably no decision in the history of American immigration policy possesses more profound significance," since it established the principle that ethnic communality would have to be achieved by the voluntary action of individuals with no help from the government (Indian Americans excepted).[21]

Facing open hostility from native Americans, and prevented from establishing exclusive Irish enclaves by the action of Congress, the Irish emphasized the establishment of their own social institutions in the large American cities where most of them lived. As Oscar Handlin said of the Boston Irish:

> The flourishing growth of Irish institutions was an accurate reflection of their consciousness of group identity. Unable to participate in the normal associational affairs of the community, the Irish felt obliged to erect a society within a society, to act together in their own way. In every contact therefore the group, acting apart from other sections of the community, became intensely aware of its peculiar and exclusive identity.[22]

Priority was given to establishment of schools, churchees, hospitals, and services, which together, in the eyes of the Irish, constituted their Roman Catholic religious institutions. The influx of Irish immigrants after 1840 placed great strains upon the existing Catholic facilities; nevertheless, native American Catholics welcomed Irish immigrants as the means for bringing about a revival of Catholicism in the United States. The Irish did not disappoint them.

The Irish enlarged or began Catholic parishes not only in the large cities but along the transportation routes into the interior that Irish laborers helped construct. Irish immigrants and their children entered into Catholic religious vocations in such large numbers that they soon predominated in the Roman Catholic hierarchy in the United States. A study of all American Catholic bishops revealed that between 1789 and 1935 some 58 percent either had been born in Ireland or had been the son of an Irish-born father.[23] By the 1970s the Irish still were disproportionately overrepresented among American Catholic clergy and the hierarchy.[24] Through their predominance in the American Catholic church, the Irish exercised considerable influence on American ethnic relations by playing a mediating role between the general society and the later arriving, Catholic, foreign-born groups.[25]

Irish ethnic sentiments were especially pervasive in the controversy over Catholic parochial schools and public taxes collected for educational support. Many native-born Americans considered public schools the most effective instruments for Americanizing recent immigrants from Europe. The Irish, on the other hand, fresh from the experience of English-controlled schools in Ireland, insisted that only the parent had the right to decide where and how his or her children were to be educated. Compulsory public school attendance laws were denounced by Irish Catholic newspapers, which contended that education must be the work of the church and not the state. The Irish also argued that school taxes collected by the state from Catholics who operate their own schools should be returned to them. The controversy continues to this day. The net result has been that the educational assimilation of Catholic immigrant groups into American life was less rapid than it otherwise might have been.

While the Catholic church was open in its political opposition to public school taxes, it was often accused of using its parishioners indirectly to achieve other political ends. The connection of Irish Catholicism with organized politics has been called "Irish Catholic power," with the assumption that the Catholic hierarchy directed the behavior of Irish politicians and the votes of Irish immigrants. From this viewpoint, the separatism of the Irish was not due to their own desires, but to the actions of their religious leaders:

> The Irish peasants were likable and eager to please; they deeply desired to adjust themselves to the new culture; but their priests and bishops stood for certain

> separatist and non-American practices which immediately inflamed the opposition and put the whole Irish Catholic community on the defensive.[26]

This American belief was similar to the opinion once popularly held in England that the Irish "electorate was entirely under the thumb of the priesthood."[27] Actually, the historical association between the church and Irish political leaders in both countries often was one of open disagreement. Throughout the nineteenth century most Irish nationalist leaders emphasized a clear separation between church and state. The conflict of interests became most extreme in Ireland after 1916, when the Catholic hierarchy denounced the popular Sinn Fein political party and excommunicated several of its leaders.[28]

Irish political and labor leaders in the United States, as in Ireland, maintained clear limits to the authority of the church. In 1870 a popular organization dedicated to the liberation of Ireland, the Fenian Brotherhood, was condemned by the Vatican and its members threatened with excommunication. In response several Irish American newspapers urged that the Vatican's action be ignored because "the jurisdiction of the Church could not be extended properly to purely temporal questions."[29] Many priests and bishops also denounced oath-bound labor societies such as the Knights of Labor, in which the Irish were prominent, and the Molly Maguires and Hibernians, whose members often were violent participants in labor troubles. One of the first seeping condemnations of secret societies by the church in America, in fact, was not against the anti-Catholic Masons but against "Corkonians and Connaught men," who were organizing Irish laborers on public works.

Far from being under the thumb of their priests, many Irish did not hesitate to ignore their religious leaders when they believed their secular goals were at stake. The agreement on many, perhaps most, political matters between the hierarchy and the Irish electorate sprang not from the dominance of one over the other but rather from the fact that for decades most members of the Catholic hierarchy in the large eastern cities were Irish; they were themselves part of the Irish community and reflected the same ethnic beliefs and values as their parishioners.

IRISH POLITICAL AND LABOR ORGANIZATIONS

The Irish supported the Catholic church, through which they received spiritual and moral guidance, educated their children, cared for their sick and infirm, and gave assistance to their destitute and poverty stricken. But some things the church could not provide, goals the Irish sought in the face of opposition from Americans who were anti-Irish. The Irish formed associations to give themselves political power needed to overcome the ethnic discrimination they faced. The intense Irish concern with power relationships grew from their goal of having the ability to direct their own lives and those of others:

> Nothing strikes the historian of the American Irish so forcibly as their desire to wield power. As churchmen, nationalists, and politicians, they were possessed by the need to bend others to their will. Perhaps this was to be expected of a people whose homeland was subject to the world's greatest empire, and whose national symbol was a weeping woman and a broken harp.[30]

Control over local city politics or a labor union was indeed the ladder scaled by many Irish immigrants and their children in their climb up out of poverty. But it should not be forgotten that for many persons in the Irish community, politics was their goal in life, and not merely the means to a better life. To some Irish political and labor leaders, power had intrinsic rewards independent of opportunities to gain material wealth. To these men power was built on giving and receiving loyalty, on strong organizations that could be depended on to deliver the votes, and on a pragmatism that avoided ideological extremes.

Although the emotional appeals of the ardent Irish nationalist would be given deference by Irish Americans of all walks of life, even this type of idealism was shunned by the successful Irish political boss. The conflict of interests between the Irish nationalists and the Democratic Irish political bosses in the United States led to an attempt in the 1880s by Irish nationalists to win the Irish American vote over to the Republican party. But the attempt failed as appeals to free Ireland from English rule did not carry as much weight with the Irish voter as did the patronage and political power on the local scene which was held by the Irish bosses.[31]

The Irish were successful in gaining political control in several cities not only because of their population concentrations but also because of the experience with Anglo-Saxon political institutions, processes, and laws that they brought with them from Ireland. In Ireland they had known this form of government primarily through the Penal Laws, and the subsequent dominance of Irish affairs by either Irish Protestants or the English themselves. They had been the oppressed struggling to win political control over their own homeland. In the United States they found themselves an alienated people within the larger society, a Catholic minority in a Protestant society that shared many of the anti-Irish prejudices of the English. Given their situation, they used their knowledge of Anglo-American political structures first to gain control over local governments, and then, through the Democratic party, to influence state, regional, and eventually national politics in the United States.[32]

Through their political power the Irish forced American politics to pay greater attention to the ethnic sensibilities of their constituents, thereby paving the way for the entry into American political life of subsequent immigrant groups.[33] The Irish not only innovated ethnic politics in the United States, they kept control over many key political positions in a way that exceeded their power on the basis of numbers alone. Their high level of political activity continued into the twentieth century,[34] and the ultimate political goal finally was won with the election of John F. Kennedy as the thirty-fifth president of the United States. Some Irish Americans consider Kennedy's election to have been the "supreme moment in the history of Irish America."[35]

The organization of labor provided another source of power and control over potentially a larger number of jobs. The labor movement, in addition to the church and the political machine, was the third important area in which the Irish created a mediating role for themselves in American society. They were dominant in the American Federation of Labor (AFL), and produced most of the second- and third-level leadership below the AFL president, Samuel Gompers (who was of Dutch Jewish extraction).[36] The "father of Labor Day," for example, was not Gompers but an Irish American, Peter J. McGuire, a cofounder of the AFL who in 1881 proposed the idea of a national holiday to honor labor.

Until the 1930s and the drastic changes in the labor movement under Roosevelt's New Deal, successful unionization of a trade generally followed its domination by the Irish. In trades with comparatively few members but with strategic locations in industry, such as plumbing and carpentry, the Irish were able to obtain numerical dominance and bring about unionization. In other occupations with a larger number of workers, such as the teamsters and longshoremen, the Irish were able to create Irish-controlled unionization through their organizational abilities and community cohesiveness. Where the Irish were not strong, as in the steel industry and in large-scale manufacturing, no other single nationality group was able to obtain a dominant position over the work force—the exception being the Eastern European Jews' development of strong unions in the garment industry. The heterogeneity of the work force in other industries weakened the labor movement. The success of the Irish in unionizing the building trades, the dockworkers, and the teamsters laid much of the foundation for the subsequent upsurge in the American labor movement during and after the New Deal.

TWENTIETH-CENTURY IRISH-AMERICANS

Irish immigrants left an impact on American society that has persisted to this day. But what of their descendants? Did they lose their ethnic identity and gradually assimilate into the general American culture, as one might expect from the melting pot theory of American minority relations? Or is there still such a thing as a distinct, viable Irish American ethnic group in the United States?

As Moynihan has pointed out, several factors operated to bring about a decline in Irish identity in America, including the reduction in Irish immigration, the fading of Irish nationalism after the partitioning of Ireland in 1921–1922, and the relative lack of contact of the majority of American Irish with the culture of Ireland.[37] Because of the custom of patrimonial descent, individuals with family names such as O'Toole, Maguire, and Flynn are continually reminded by others of their Irish background; they are less likely to forget than those whose mother, but not father, was Irish, or those who, while of Irish descent, have surnames such as Smith, Nagle, or Costello. Being Irish in name only, however, is only a pale reflection of the intensely felt sense of Irish identity held by the immigrants themselves.

The degree of marital assimilation of a minority group into American society can be indicated by rates of in-marriage within the group. If most newly arrived members of an ethnic group marry native-born American persons or immigrants from other ethnic groups, then their assimilation will be high. On the other hand, if most immigrants persist in marrying only persons born in their own country of origin, then their assimilation into the more general society will be low. In several immigrant groups the relative lack of women resulted in any women born in the home country being in great demand as marriage partners for their compatriots. For this reason the in-marriage rates for male immigrants are better indicators of assimilation than those of female immigrants.

According to this measure, by 1920 the assimilation of Irish-born men in the United States was still relatively low. Although the Irish had been among the first of the large European immigrant groups, their rate of in-marriage was closer to that of more recently arrived groups. From statistics of legitimate births registered in the United States in 1920, 71 percent of the Irish-born fathers had Irish-born wives compared with 83, 82, and 75 percent, respectively, of Italian-born, Polish-born, and Russian-born fathers whose wives had been born in their husbands' countries of origin. The figures for the earlier-arrived groups of Scandinavians, British, and Germans were 48, 34, and 30 percent, respectively.[38]

Another measure of marital assimilation is the durability of ethnic marriage patterns among children of the foreign-born immigrants. Ireland was, and continues to be, the most extreme case of the general Western European practices of late marriage and of high proportions of persons who never marry.[39] To what degree did the American-born children of Irish immigrants continue the Irish late-marriage conventions? Compared with 12 other ethnic groups in 1950, the Irish Americans were the most persistent in continuing their late marriage and non-marriage customs, and were quite distinct from the native while population. The proportion never married among persons aged forty-five and over, for example, was about 9 percent for both sexes in the total white population of the United States in 1950, compared with 23 percent for females, and 18 percent for males, among American-born whites of Irish parentage.[40] Distinctly different Irish Catholic marriage, divorce, and other family practices have persisted to the present day.[41]

If an ethnic group is occupationally well assimilated into American life, then the occupational status of its foreign-born members would be similar to that of native-born white Americans. Although individual Irish families have been found among the very rich in America since the nineteenth century,[42] our concern here is with the Irish American ethnic group as a whole. Judging by an index of general socioeconomic status, by 1950 assimilation was high among such early immigrant groups as the English and the Germans, but remained low among the Irish foreign-born, who had essentially the same status level as more recently arrived immigrants from Italy and Poland.[43] Among the children of immigrants, however, the status of those of Irish descent was much improved: about the same level of status as those of English, Welsh, or Scandinavian descent, and higher than those of German, native-born American, Italian, or Polish descent. The occupational indexes of status for Irish Americans, whether Irish-born or native-born of Irish descent, were not similar to that of the general American white population: the Irish immigrants were much lower, and their children were much higher. Upward social mobility among the second-generation Irish was higher than that of any other group—and greater than that expected by the melting pot thesis.

By the late 1960s and early 1970s Irish Catholics ranked above the United States average on years of education completed, occupational status, and average family income based on national surveys. In contrast, Irish Protestants ranked below the national averages on each of the three indicators of social status. A complete explanation of Irish Catholic upward social mobility awaits future research.[44] Nevertheless, at this time it seems reasonable to conclude that the important mediating role that the highly urbanized Catholic Irish had created for themselves in several American institutions facilitated the rise of the children of successive waves of immigrants from Ireland. Irish dominance in American Catholic educational institutions, for example, probably encouraged Irish American students to stay in school and further their formal education. In any case, a 1963 survey revealed that among white, Catholic, ethnic groups in the United States, the Irish had the highest proportion of high school graduates (77 percent).[45] In 1961 a young Irish American was about twice as likely to graduate from college as a typical American of any other national origin, and his choice of occupation was quite different from the average American college graduate: Irish Americans were three times as likely to be lawyers than the general populations of 1961 graduates, twice as likely to be medical doctors, but only half as likely to be engineers.[46]

Judging from the persistence of marriage practices, educational accomplishments, and occupational choices, a strong sense of ethnic identity persists among many Americans of Irish descent and influences their daily lives. They have not given up many aspects of their ethnic heritage even though they have moved up in occupational status, moved out of the central city poverty areas into the suburbs, and spread across the United States from their concentrations in a handful of large cities. Although they have become middle class, many of their members remain different from their white Anglo-Saxon Protestant neighbors. As Andrew M. Greeley commented about the present situation of Irish Catholics in America: "The Irish may be 'different,' but neither they nor the WASPs are inclined to mention the differences very often."[47]

Editorial note: The Irish and even Irish Catholics represent a population that has so sufficiently been assimilated into the core culture that they no longer can be considered an ethnic minority. Nevertheless, there is a recrudescence of interest in Ireland, but it tends to be shared with many Americans who cannot claim Irish ancestry. In a sense, this represents an expansion of the definition of the care culture. In fact, the 1990s have experienced a resurgence of interest in all cultural things Irish. In 1996, the "Riverdance" phenomenon and its offshoot, "The Lord of the Dance," became a widely pursued entertainment. Forms of Irish folk dance, colorfully and dramatically executed, were presented by groups touring U.S. cities, were featured on television, and sold hundreds of thousands of compact discs to an adoring public. Recently, Thomas Cahill published the popular work, *How the Irish Saved Civilization,*[48] a history of pre-medieval Irish monasteries and how they preserved learning during the period between the fall of the Roman empire and the rise of the medieval institutions on the European continent.

CONCLUSION

Is the history of the Irish American ethnic group a model for subsequent ethnic immigrant groups or for racial minorities in the United States? They were considered racially inferior at one time; they suffered extreme hostility and discrimination; they gradually established their own social and religious institutions; they gained political power and forced American society to recognize ethnic concerns; they secured control over certain occupations in some cities; and their children and grandchildren were able to make substantial achievements in upward social mobility.

If the Irish are a model, then they are an example of cultural pluralism rather than complete assimilation. Irish immigrants were able to establish control over several aspects of their daily lives which was separate from the Anglo-Saxon Protestant majority. And although many of the descendants of the Irish immigrants have structurally assimilated into the American mainstream, others retain a sense of ethnic identity and persist in keeping some distinctively different elements in their lifestyles, especially in regard to family life, political participation, religion, and occupational choice.

NOTES

1. Stephen Byrne, *Irish Emigration to the United States* (1873; reprinted ed., New York: Arno Press and the New York Times, 1969), p. 37.
2. Robert E. Kennedy, Jr., "Minority Group Status and Fertility: The Irish," *American Sociological Review* 38 (1973), pp. 85–96.

3. J. C. Beckett, *The Making of Modern Ireland: 1603–1923* (London: Faber & Faber, 1966), p. 159.
4. Ireland, *Census of Population, 1926, General Report,* vol. 3, pt. 1, pp. 114–29, Table 17.
5. George O'Brien, *The Economic History of Ireland from the Union to the Famine* (London: Longmans, 1921), p. 242.
6. Arnold Schrier, *Ireland and the American Emigration, 1850–1900* (Minneapolis: University of Minnesota Press, 1958), p. 111.
7. O'Brien, *Economic History,* p. 167.
8. Robert E. Kennedy, Jr., *The Irish: Emigration, Marriage, and Fertility* (Berkeley: University of California Press, 1973), pp. 31–31.
9. Cecil Woodham-Smith, *The Great Hunger* (London: Four Square Editions, 1965), pp. 32–33.
10. William Forbes Adams, *Ireland and Irish Emigration to the New World from 1815 to the Famine* (New Haven, Conn: Yale University Press), p. 111.
11. Ireland, *Censuses of Population, 1946 and 1951, General Report,* Table 21, p. 40.
12. Patrick McNabb, "Social Structure," in *The Limerick Rural Survey, 1958–1964,* ed. Rev. Jeremiah Newman (Tipperary: Muintir Na Tire Rural Publications, 1964).
13. Conrad M. Arensberg and Solon T. Kimball, *Family and Community in Ireland,* 2nd ed. (Cambridge, MA: Harvard University Press, 1968), pp. 35–50.
14. Kennedy, *Irish: Emigration,* pp. 51–65.
15. Ibid., pp. 66–85.
16. Marjorie R. Fallows, *Irish Americans: Identity and Assimilation* (Englewood Cliffs, NJ: Prentice-Hall, 1979), pp. 32–44.
17. Edward E. Hale, *Letters on Irish Emigration* (Boston: Phillips, Sampson, 1852), pp. 53–54.
18. Richard Hofstadter and Michael Wallace, eds., *American Violence: A Documentary History* (New York: Vintage, 1971), p. 298.
19. Ibid., pp. 304–305.
20. George Potter, *To The Golden Door: The Story of the Irish in Ireland and America* (Boston: Little, Brown, 1960), pp. 163–69.
21. See Milton M. Gordon, *Assimilation in American Life: The Role of Race, Religion, and National Origins* (New York: Oxford University Press, 1964), p. 133.
22. Oscar Handlin, *Boston's Immigrants: A Study in Acculturation,* rev. ed. (New York: Atheneum, 1970), p. 176.
23. Carl Wittke, *The Irish in America* (Baton Rouge: Louisiana State University Press, 1956), pp. 88–102.
24. Andrew M. Greeley, *The American Catholic: A Social Portrait* (New York: Basic Books, 1977), p. 26.
25. Gordon, *Assimilation in American Life,* pp. 216–17.

26. Paul Blanshard, *The Irish and Catholic Power: An American Interpretation* (Boston: Beacon, 1953), p. 254.

27. Brian Inglis, *The Story of Ireland,* 2nd ed. (London: Faber & Faber, 1965), p. 201.

28. Donald McCartney, "From Parnell to Pearse," in *The Course of Irish History,* ed. T. W. Moody and F. X. Martin (Cork: Mercier Press, 1967), pp. 307–12.

29. Wittke, *Irish in America,* p. 96.

30. Thomas N. Brown, *Irish-American Nationalism: 1870–1890* (Philadelphia: Lippincott, 1966), p. 133.

31. Ibid., pp. 134–51.

32. Edward M. Levine, *The Irish and Irish Politicians: A Study of Cultural and Social Alienation* (Notre Dame, IN: University of Notre Dame Press, 1966), pp. 6–7.

33. Lawrence J. McCaffrey, *The Irish Diaspora in America* (Bloomington: Indiana University Press, 1976), p. 150.

34. Andrew M. Greeley, Political Participation among Ethnic Groups in the United States: A Preliminary Reconnaissance," *American Journal of Sociology* 80 (1974), pp. 170–204.

35. John B. Duff, *The Irish in the United States* (Belmont, CA: Wadsworth, 1971), p. 85.

36. This discussion of the Irish in the labor movement is based primarily on William V. Shannon, *The American Irish* (New York: Macmillan, 1963), pp. 140–41.

37. Nathan Glazer and Daniel Patrick Moynihan, *Beyond the Melting Pot* (Cambridge, MA: MIT Press, 1963), pp. 250–51.

38. Nils Carpenter, *Immigrants and Their Children, 1920* (Washington, D.C.: Government Printing Office, 1927), pp. 234–35, Tables 106, 107.

39. Kennedy, *Irish: Emigration,* pp. 139–72.

40. David M. Heer, "The Marital Status of Second-Generation Americans," *American Sociological Review* 26 (1961), pp. 233–34.

41. Greeley, *The American Catholic,* pp. 188–89.

42. Stephen Birmingham, *Real Lace: America's Irish Rich* (New York: Harper, 1973).

43. Charles B. Nam, "Nationality Groups and Social Stratification in America," *Social Forces* 37 (1959), pp. 328–33.

44. Fallows, *Irish Americans,* pp. 65–80.

45. Andrew M. Greeley, *Why Can't They Be Like Us?: America's White Ethnic Groups* (New York; Dutton, 1971), pp. 66, 67.

46. Andrew M. Greeley, "Occupational Choice among the American Irish: A Research Note," *Erie-Ireland* 7 (1972), p. 4.

47. Andrew M. Greeley, *That Most Distressful Nation: The Taming of the American Irish* (Chicago: Quadrangle, 1972), p. 256.

48. Thomas Cahill, *How the Irish Saved Civilization: The Untold Story of Ireland's Heroic Role from the Fall of the Roman Empire to the Rise of Medieval Europe.* (New York: Doubleday, 1995).

SUGGESTED READINGS

Arensberg, Conrad, and Solon T. Kimball. *Family Community in Ireland,* 2nd ed. Cambridge, MA: Harvard University Press, 1967.

Fallows, Marjorie R. *Irish Americans: Identity and Assimilation.* Englewood Cliffs, NJ: Prentice-Hall, 1979.

Glazer, Nathan, and Daniel Patrick Moynihan. *Beyond the Melting Pot.* Cambridge, MA: MIT Press, 1963.

Greeley, Andrew M. *That Most Distressful Nation: The Taming of the American Irish.* Chicago: Quadrangle, 1972.

Handlin, Oscar. *Boston's Immigrants: A Study in Acculturation,* rev. ed. New York: Atheneum, 1970.

Kennedy, Robert E., Jr. *The Irish: Emigration, Marriage, and Fertility.* Berkeley: University of California Press, 1973.

Potter, George. *To the Golden Door: The Story of the Irish in Ireland and America.* Boston: Little, Brown, 1960.

CHAPTER 18

Women: The Fifty-One Percent Minority

Dana Dunn

My childhood memories include building model cars with my father, making rubber band guns from scrap wood, and mixing smelly, smoke-producing concoctions with my chemistry set. I possessed only a few dolls, given to me by relatives, and they were promptly retired to the attic. My bedroom was an imaginary jungle, where I communed with an array of stuffed animals, beasts of the most ferocious variety. In the summers, I climbed the big tree in my backyard, and there I read "Trixie Beldon" books. Trixie was a girl about my age whose adventures seem far more grand than any I had yet participated in. As is typical of most girls, I was excited about shopping for a new Easter Sunday outfit. But it was not the shiny, patent-leather, baby-doll shoes that captivated me; rather it was the small turtle being given away with each purchase. In brief, I was the quintessential tomboy. My parents boasted about their outgoing, adventurous, and somewhat mischevious daughter. They did not seem to mind that I deviated from the "sugar and spice and everything nice," frills, ruffles, and pastels ideal. At the time all this was occurring, I was your typical, self-centered child, oblivious to the gender messages contained in the unfolding drama of my life.

When I was eleven going on twelve, something happened that set me thinking about gender issues and specifically, gender inequality. It was Halloween and dusk was approaching. I was completing the finishing touches on my younger brother's surprise costume when my father returned home from work. He glanced into the room, observed my brother in a lavender dress, my mother's wig, and bright pink lipstick, and growled, "Just what do you think you are doing?" What followed was not pleasant. My brother and I were reprimanded by both parents for the costume. "Do you want people to think your brother is a sissy?" my father asked in a disgusted tone. The only way my brother was allowed to go trick or treating that Halloween was to reuse the previous year's werewolf costume.

Over pancakes the next morning, my parents attempted to reason with us so that we would better understand the error of our ways. A long discussion ensued which can be summarized with the following statement: boys should not emulate girls because doing so is equivalent to abandoning a privileged status in favor of an inferior one. It did not take me long to extend their line of reasoning and grasp why it was okay for me to be a tomboy.

What loving parents wouldn't understand their daughter's desire to occupy a privileged status? Once the implications of this newfound knowledge fully registered, I was angry. Looking back, this event may well have sparked my long term interest in gender inequality.

Michael Bailey, a professor of psychology at Northwestern University conducting research on tomboys, states, "Feminine behavior in young males is usually stifled and discouraged, but tomboy behavior is tolerated and sometimes encouraged." (DMN 1994). The terms *sissy* and *tomboy* are not considered parallel. *Tomboy* has a neutral to positive connotation, *sissy* a negative one. This pattern indicates that U.S. society views the sexes as unequal and provides the rationale for viewing women as a minority group.

Conceptualizing Women as a Minority Group

As a tall, red-haired sociologist with two chihuahuas, I am in the numerical minority. As a woman, I am a member of a group that constitutes about 51 percent of the world's population—a numerical majority. Yet as a woman I am also a member of a subordinate group with less power than members of the dominant group (men)—what sociologists term a minority group. Confused? In a now classic article, Hacker (1951) first explained why women should be thought of as a minority group. She demonstrated that women share several characteristics with racial and ethnic minorities: they are discriminated against; they are more likely than their male peers to perform menial, monotonous work for little reward both at home and in the workplace; they are stereotyped on the basis of ascribed attributes; and they occupy a marginal status in society. Since Hacker's early work it has become common to conceptualize women, along with the elderly, the disabled, and homosexuals, as a nontraditional or "new" minority group (Lindsey 1994).

While women do have much in common with racialethic minority groups, there is an important difference between the two groups that creates a problem in categorizing women as a minority. The fact that women marry men violates an important tenet of Wagley and Harris's (1958) model of characteristics of minority group. Wagley and Harris argue that members of minority groups typically marry within their own group, a pattern referred to as endogamy. Women are exogamous; they select marital partners from outside their own group. In fact, women marry members of the majority group.

A related, complicating factor in viewing women as a minority group is the sharing of economic resources between husbands and wives. This pooling of resources causes husbands and wives to have similar socioeconomic standing, and often results in women having higher socioeconomic standing than other minorities. Furthermore, the similarity of husbands and wives along socioeconomic dimensions makes it difficult to examine the status of married women separate from that of their husbands (Baxter 1994; Goldthorpe 1983).

It is possible, however, to view marriages of men and women in a different way—one that supports the conceptualization of women as a minority group. Marriages between men and women are the primary basis for the formation of household economic units in this and most societies. Women who do not conform to this model have a great deal more difficulty than men surviving as independent adults. For example, 12 percent of male householders without wives present lived in poverty in 1990, while over 33 percent of female householders without husbands present lived in poverty during the same year (Bureau of the Census 1991). Even higher rates of poverty among mother-only families and the more general phenomenon of the feminization of poverty provide further evidence of single women's relative economic disadvantage. Women are about 30 percent more likely to be poor than men (Caspar, McLanahan, and Garfinkel 1994). Inability to be self-supporting as an independent adult can be interpreted as a sign of women's marginal status and minority group membership.

The belief that women should be dependent upon men has long historical roots in the United States. Prior to the twentieth century, women were discouraged from remaining single as adults. They were expected to be continually dependent upon men—on fathers in childhood, on husbands as adults, and on sons in old age. Laws that prohibited single women from holding property in their name combined with social pressures to reinforce this dependence of women upon men. Along these lines, it is interesting to note that the first women's rights convention held in Seneca Falls, New York, in 1848 yielded a document modeled after the Declaration of Independence which declared that, among other things, women had the right to maintain an identity separate from their husbands (Deckard 1975). More recent social conventions such as referring to adult married women as Mrs. John Doe further reinforce the dependent, marginal status of women.

The Interaction of Racial, Ethnic, and Gender Disadvantage

If women are a minority group, then what can we say about women who are also members of racial and ethnic minority groups? The traditional view is that such women are "double minorities": that the disadvantages associated with the two minority statuses are cumulative. This cumulative disadvantage or "double jeopardy" approach results in a hierarchy of statuses wherein majority-group men are ranked above majority-group women, who are ranked above minority-group women. Views are divided as to the precise placement of minority-group men in the hierarchy—some argue that minority men are situated below majority group women; others argue that they are situated above majority group women.

Statistical profiles comparing racial and ethnic minority women to majority-group women often support the cumulative disadvantage perspective. For example, racial and ethnic minority women on average receive the lowest wages and hold the worst jobs (see Table 18-1). They are far more likely to live in poverty than their majority-group counterparts (Zinn and Dill 1994). Maternal and child mortality rates for racial and ethnic minorities are also much higher than those for the majority group (Bureau of the Census 1992).

Recent scholarship on race, ethnicity, and gender suggests that the cumulative disadvantage approach is inadequate for explaining the complex dynamics of racial, ethnic, and gender inequality. Proponents of this view argue that the disadvantages associated with the two different types of minority status are not merely additive; rather, they interact (Almquist 1989, 1995; Andersen 1993; King 1988; Wilkinson, Baca-Zinn, and Chow 1992). Most often this interaction results in extreme disadvantage for racial and ethnic minority women, but occasionally there are deviations from such a pattern. For example, at higher education levels, black women receive higher returns to education than white women (Sapiro 1986). The fact that black women are more likely than white women to reject gender stereotypes for women provides an-

TABLE 18-1
1990 Median Income of Full Time, Year Round Workers

	By Sex and Race	
	Women	Men
Black	$18,518	$21,540
Hispanic	$16,186	$19,134
White	$20,840	$30,186

Source: U.S. Bureau of the Census, 1991.

other example of how the interaction of two minority statuses can be associated with advantage. Further statistics will be interwoven in the following sections of this chapter to illustrate how racial and ethnic diversity patterns women's lives.

A PROFILE OF WOMEN'S STATUS IN THE CONTEMPORARY UNITED STATES

An examination of differences in the situation of women and men in various social institutions provides evidence of patterned inequalities between the sexes and illuminates women's minority-group status. The following sections of this chapter present gender comparison "snapshots" for several major social institutions.

Family and Household Arrangements

The domestic sphere has traditionally been considered the domain of women, yet sociological analysis of a number of family-related issues, including the household division of labor, marital power, marital satisfaction, and spouse abuse indicate that women are disadvantaged relative to their male counterparts in families. Regardless of how one defines or measures housework, it is quite clear that wives still do much more of it than husbands (Ferree 1991; Thompson and Walker 1991). The adage that "men work from sun to sun but women's work is never done" especially rings true today in dual-worker families where women work full time outside the home and then come home to perform what Hochschild (1989) calls a "second shift." In a study of fifty dual-worker couples, she found that the second shift results in employed women performing about an extra month of full-time work each year. Most studies show that the housework contribution of husbands does not change much when their wives begin working, and that husbands of working wives spend only about one-third as much time on housework as their wives (Baca-Zinn and Eitzen 1993). This gender imbalance in housework among dual-worker couples suggests that work-family conflict is a far more serious problem for women than men.

Child care and elder care tasks are also performed disproportionately by women in dual worker families, thus exacerbating the role overload experienced by women. La Rossa and La Rossa (1981) find that while new fathers are willing to assist with child care tasks, they view the primary responsibility for caring for the baby as the mother's. They suggest that this difference explains why mothers experience more stress in adapting to parenthood than do fathers. Women's care-provider responsibilities often do not diminish significantly when the children leave the nest because that is the point in time at which aging parents and parents-in-law are in need of care. In this society the bulk of the care of old people is provided informally by women relatives

(Aronson 1992; Brody 1985; Walker 1985). This gender division of caregiving serves to constrain women's employment opportunities, and thus their access to resources and independence (Finch 1984; Hooyman and Ryan 1987). Gender gaps in housework and caregiving (family work) contribute to a gender gap in marital satisfaction. Studies indicate that a fair division of family work between husbands and wives is associated with higher levels of marital satisfaction for women, and that overburdened wives are less satisfied with their marital relationships. In contrast, husbands are more satisfied with their marriages and less critical of their wives if their wives do more than their fair share of family work (Thompson and Walker 1991).

The burden of "family work" also falls disporportionately to single women. In 1990, 25 percent of all families with children under the age of eighteen were single-parent families, and 90 percent of these single parent families were headed by women. The incidence of mother-only families among Blacks and Hispanics is much higher than the average—49 percent for Blacks and 29 percent for Hispanics (U.S. Bureau of the Census, 1991). Women who head mother-only families must peform the work of two parents—breadwinning, housework, and child care. The resulting stress experienced by single mothers is great (Baca-Zinn and Eitzen 1993). Our society often attributes the serious problems of today's youth to the inability of single mothers to perform in an unreasonably demanding role. When single mothers are blamed for rising rates of juvenile crime and declining educational achievement among other things, seldom does attention turn to the responsibility of fathers.

The unequal distribution of power and decision making in marriages provides further evidence of women's minority-group standing. The control of economic resources is the most critical factor influencing the apportionment of power in families, and as later sections of this chapter will show, women are disadvantaged with respect to access to economic resources. Numerous studies show that as the comparative economic resources of husbands and wives becomes more equal, so does the distribution of power (Beckman and Hauser 1979; Blood and Wolfe 1960; Blumstein and Schwartz 1983; Lips 1991; Spitze 1988). Full-time homemakers who are financially dependent upon their husbands possess the least power in marriages. Women are the primary providers in only about 20 percent of marriages (Conant 1986), but even in these households societal norms of male dominance most often result in men possessing more power than women (Baca-Zinn and Eitzen 1993). Research also shows that partners in marriages exercise power in different ways. Men are more likely to use direct or authoritarian approaches, while women use a more subtle approach referred to as influence. Influence is a power style that is common to minority groups who believe that a direct approach will meet the powerful resistance of the dominant group (Colwill 1982).

The incidence of violent, coercive power in families is high, and this type of power is more frequently used by men than women (Dobash and Dobash

1979; Gelles and Straus 1988). Prior to this century, wife beating was viewed as a legitimate way for men to express their power over women. While wife abuse is no longer legally sanctioned, this historical legacy combines with male socialization for aggression to create a climate wherein women are still viewed as appropriate targets for violence (Dobash and Dobash 1979). Traditional gender arrangements that isolate financially dependent women in the home lead many battered women to perceive that they have no options. Murray Straus, an expert on family violence, suggests that this perception is often an unfortunate reality. He argues that "The sexual inequalities inherent in our family system, economic system, social services, and criminal justice system effectively leave many women locked into a brutal marriage." (Straus 1977–1978, p. 447)

Employment Patterns

The influx of women into the paid labor market is one of the most striking social changes of this century. By 1990, women constituted over 45 percent of the labor force (U.S. Department of Labor 1992). Table 18-2 provides historical data on men's and women's labor force participation rates, indicating that the gap between men's and women's labor force participation rates has narrowed steadily over the course of this century.

Women's labor-force participation rates vary little across racial and ethnic groups. Unemployment rates, however, are two times higher for racial and ethnic minority women (except Asians and Pacific Islanders) than white women. (See Table 18-3 below).

Despite the dramatic increases in women's labor-force participation, they continue to be employed in a far more narrow range of occupations than their male counterparts (Kemp 1994). One-third of all employed women in 1990 worked in just 10 of the 503 detailed occupations listed in the census (Reskin and Padavic 1994). The term *occupational segregation* is used to refer to the concentration of same-sex workers in an occupational category. In 1985, over two-thirds of the employed women in the United States worked in occupations that were at least 70 percent female (Jacobs, 1989). Women are most overrepresented in the broad census occupational categories "Administrative

TABLE 18-2
Labor Force Participation Rates for Men and Women

Year	1900	1910	1920	1930	1940	1950	1960	1970	1980	1990
Men	80.0	81.3	78.2	76.2	79.2	86.4	83.3	79.7	77.4	76.1
Women	18.8	23.4	21.0	22.0	25.4	33.9	37.7	43.3	51.5	57.5

Source: U.S. Department of Labor, 1992.

TABLE 18-3
Women's Labor Force and Employment Status by Race and Ethnicity

	Native American	African American	Asian/Pacific Islander	Hispanic Origin	White
% in Labor Force	56.3	55.1	59.5	60.1	55.9
% Unemployed	5.0	13.1	12.1	5.5	11.2

Source: U.S. Bureau of the Census, Census of the Population 1990.

support, including clerical" (79.8 percent female) and most underrepresented in the category "Precision production, craft and repair" (8.5 percent female) (U.S. Department of Labor 1991). Several factors contribute to the concentration of women in a narrow range of traditional occupations. They include gender role socialization, constraints resulting from work-family conflict, and a factor that women have in common with racial and ethnic minorities—hiring discrimination.

Occupations are also "vertically" segregated by sex such that higher-level positions are heavily male dominated. Only a few women reach the top of the corporate hierarchy. Women, in combination with racial and ethnic minorities, held less than 5 percent of senior management positions in 1990 (Fierman 1990). The extremely low representation of women in top-level positions has led many to argue that a "glass ceiling" blocks their on-the-job mobility.

The Earnings Gap

Sex segregation in the workplace is a key contributor to the pay gap between the sexes. The higher the proportion of women workers in an occupation, the less that all workers in that occupation earn (Reskin and Padavic 1994). Female-dominated occupations, on average, pay less than male dominated occupations, even when job inputs such as education, skill and experience are controlled (England 1992). This means that the work that women perform for pay is devalued—it is not remunerated on the basis of its worth to the employer. Research shows that over 35 percent of the male-female earnings gap is the result of the different occupational distributions of men and women (Treiman and Hartman 1981).

Just how much more do men earn than women? For the 30 years between 1950 and 1980, women who worked full time, year round earned about 60 cents for every dollar earned by men who worked full time, year round (Blau and Ferber 1986). After 1980 the gender gap in pay began to narrow, so that by 1990 women earned about 71 cents for every dollar men earned (Institute for Women's Policy Research 1993). About 30 years have passed since passage of the Equal Pay Act but the monetary cost of being female is still high.

Explanations for earnings differences between the sexes are numerous and extend beyond employment segregation. Some portion of the gap in pay between the sexes can be accounted for by sex differences in productivity, a seemingly legitimate explanation. For example, men work more hours per week than women, and this difference accounts for about 14 percent of the pay gap (Reskin and Padavic 1994). Men also have more workplace experience and senority than women (England and Farkas 1986). While these productivity-related factors appear nondiscriminatory on the surface, it is important to keep in mind the reasons women work fewer hours and have less experience. As was noted earler, women bear a disproportionate share of family responsibilities, which serves to constrain their ability to work outside the home. Overt discrimination also contributes to earnings differences between women and men, despite the existence of legislation prohibiting unequal pay for equal work.

Educational Attainment and Achievement

Education is an important tool for minority groups seeking to raise their status. Education provides information and skills essential for economic success and also confers prestige on its recipients. Education has been a priority for women seeking to improve their condition for centuries, and today women receive nearly the same overall level of education as men (Sapiro 1994). The U. S. government first supported equal education and forbade gender discrimination with Title IX of the Education Amendments Act of 1972, which stated "No person in the United States shall, on the basis of sex be excluded from participation in, be denied the benefits of, or be subjected to discrimination under any education program or activity receiving federal financial assistance." The same equality of opportunity issues that had been receiving attention for racial and ethnic minorities were finally being addressed for women.

To fully understand the extent of educational equity it is necessary to look beyond the average amount of education attained by each sex. An examination of educational attainment by sex *and by education level* reveals an interesting pattern. Focusing on higher education in 1990, women earned 53 percent of the bachelor's degrees and 53 percent of the master's degrees, but only 36 percent of the doctoral degrees, 34 percent of the medical degrees and 42 percent of the law degrees (U. S. Department of Education 1992). The rule for higher education appears similar to that for the workplace—the higher you go, the fewer women you find. Educational patterns are similar to workplace patterns in terms of the presence of sex segregation as well. There is probably no need to elaborate the patterns of segregation by academic discipline here; as a student you are likely to be quite familiar with them.

Staffing patterns by sex in educational institutions exemplify vertical employment segregation. Women's proportion of various education positions is presented in Table 18-4 below. As the pay and prestige associated with the position increases, the percent female decreases.

A micro-level examination of what goes on in schools, particularly at the lower levels, provides further insight into females' educational disadvantage. Results of a national study by the American Association of University Women (1992), "How America's Schools Short-change Girls," indicate that girls are systematically denied opportunities to develop in areas in which boys are encouraged to excel. Studies show that teachers treat girls differently than boys, with one of the most important differences being in the area of overall amount of contact. Boys receive more attention from the teacher than girls overall, particularly attention of the type that fosters confidence and self-esteem (AAUW 1992). The AAUW attribues the fact that 60 percent of girls in elementary school report that they are happy about themselves as compared to only 29 percent in high school in large part to these gender differences in teacher-student interaction.

Politics and the Law

Thomas Paine described women in the late eighteenth century as " . . . robbed of freedom and will by the laws . . . ." At roughly the same point in history Abigail Adams, the wife of the future president, wrote the following to her husband: "In the new code of laws . . . I desire you would remember the ladies . . . Do not put such unlimited power into the hands of the husbands. . . . If particular care and attention is not paid to the ladies, we are determined to foment a rebellion, and will not hold ourselves bound by any laws in which we have no voice or representation." (Flexner 1971, pp. 14–15.) Two centuries later, women's legal status is much improved. Basic rights not previously accorded to women, such as the right to hold property,

TABLE 18-4
Women as a Proportion of Educators by Education Level

Level	Percent Women
Kindergarten	99
Elementary	85
Secondary	52
Assistant Professor	38
Associate Professor	25
Professor	12

Source: U.S. Department of Education 1992; AAUW 1992.

to testify in court, and to establish credit in one's own name, have now been won. Despite these improvements, the law is not gender neutral; it systematically disadvantages women (Lindsey 1994).

Richardson (1988, p. 104) argues that the following gender-biased assumptions permeate the law and its interpretation:

1. Women are incompetent, childlike, and in need of protection.
2. Men are the protectors and financial caretakers of women.
3. Husband and wife are treated as "one" under the law. The "one" is husband.
4. Males and females are biologically different, which gives them differing capabilities and differing standards on which to judge their actions.

The existence of protective legislation provides some support for points one and two of Richardson's argument. Both women and racial and ethnic minorities are considered to be "protected groups" under the Constitution. Title VII of the Civil Rights Acts of 1964 prohibits employment discrimination on the basis of race, color, religion, national origin, and sex. Such protections are encoded in the law when it is believed that a group is systematically disadvantaged as a result of its minority-group standing. Protective legislation is a "double-edged sword": it benefits women by fostering movement toward equity, but at the same time it reinforces the notion that women are dependent and in need of protection. Further, the employment targets resulting from Title VII have led to accusations of reverse discrimination. This phenomenon can create the impression that women hired for nontraditional jobs are less qualified than their male counterparts and result in their not being taken seriously on the job.

Women are visibly absent from the positions charged with creating, modifying, interpreting and enforcing the law. They are underrepresented as politicians, judges, lawyers, and criminal justice officials (Sapiro 1994). For example, women hold only about 25 percent of all positions as lawyers and judges and 15 percent of all positions as police officers and detectives (Bureau of the Census 1992). The only avenue of input into the legal system that approaches gender equity is voting. Today women's voter turnout is similar to men's (Mandel 1995), and women do vote to support their rights (Klein 1984). Women's high level of participation in electoral politics is striking considering they were only granted the right to vote in 1920, long after men who were members of racial and ethnic minority groups.

Equal representation among the ranks of political elites is thought by Chafetz (1990) to be the most important change required to produce a system of gender equality. While 1992, a record-breaking year for women in elective office, was labeled by the media as "The Year of the Woman and Politics," women are still substantially underrepresented in political office (Center for the American Woman and Politics 1994). Table 18-5 shows the percentages of

TABLE 18-5
Percentages of Women in Elective Offices

Level of Office	1975	1985	1994
U.S. Congress	4	5	10
Statewide Elective	10	14	22
State Legislatures	8	15	21
County Governing Boards	3	8	NA
Mayors and Municipal Councils	4	14	NA

Source: Center for the American Woman and Politics 1994.

women in key elective offices for three time periods. Once again, the general rule is the higher the position, the fewer women. This underrepresentation of women in political office means that they do not have an equal voice in critical decisions that affect their lives. Carroll (1985) found that women politicians are more committed to representing women's interests than their male counterparts. Recent research on male and female state legislators finds that the women in office are more likely than their male colleagues to have established and worked for legislative priorities addressing women's interests (Carroll, Dodson and Mandel 1988).

Women face a number of obstacles to political office holding. Family roles detract from women's access to political office in a number of ways (Sapiro 1982; Lynn 1984; Whicker and Areson 1993). First, political career ladders are lengthy ones; thus, women who delay entry into politics to start a family are disadvantaged. Second, work-family conflict detracts from women's ability to compete for and participate in political office. And third, women are underrepresented in higher status occupational roles that enhance access to political office. Discrimination at various levels of the political process also impedes women's access to public office. It is important to note that a lack of political interest among women is not among the reaons listed for a scarcity of women in political office (Lips 1991; Merritt 1982).

Health and Health Care

Women in the United States and most other countries live longer than men, and female death rates are lower than male death rates for all age groups and major causes of death (Verbrugge and Wingard 1991). In the United States, a white male born in 1980 had an average life expectancy of 70 years compared to 77 for a white female; an African American male born that year could expect to live to 64 compared with 73 for an African American female (Sapiro 1994). It might be tempting to conclude from this data that women must be an advantaged rather than disadvantaged group, but this would be an oversimplification. Average life expectancy is determined by both lifestyle factors and biological factors. Men's lifestyles are somewhat more hazardous to their health than women's (Harrison and Ficarroto 1992). For example, men are more likely than women to work in hazardous work settings, and they have higher rates of substance abuse. Men are also disadvantaged biologically. A number of genetically based diseases such as hemophilia disproportionately strike men (Sapiro 1994). It would be inappropriate, therefore, to conclude that women's longevity results solely from an advantaged lifestyle.

Recent information on gender and medical research is suggestive of minority group status for women. The U. S. Public Health Service reported in 1985 that bias in the funding and conduct of medical research had resulted in a limited understanding of women's health needs. Women are commonly excluded from medical research because their menstrual cycles complicate the research design and out of fear that experimental treatments may damage their reproductive capability (Rothman and Caschetta 1995). The unfortunate consequence of excluding females from medical research is that medical recommendations based on research with male-only samples are commonly generalized to women (Cotton 1990). For example, the widely disseminated finding regarding the ability of aspirin to prevent heart attacks is based on research with male-only samples. This is despite the fact that the medical community is quite aware that there are significant differences in the arterial systems of men and women. Similarly, despite the fact that AIDS is a leading killer of women in many metropolitan areas, most of what we know about AIDS is obtained from research on men (Minkoff and DeHovitz 1991). Until this gender inequity in medical reearch is corrected it is difficult to know which is worse for women: the illness, or the prescribed cure based on research with male-only samples.

PERPETUATING WOMEN'S DISADVANTAGE

Women's disadvantaged, minority-group status is perpetuated in a number of ways. Male advantage is sometimes maintained through intentional, overt discrimination. Subtle means of perpetuating systems of gender inequity are even more common. Gender stereotypes, gender role socialization, and gender-biased language provide examples of less overt and perhaps even unintentional contributors to the maintenance of gender inequality and women's minority status.

Gender stereotyping involves making assumptions about what someone will be like on the basis of knowledge of their sex. Masculine and feminine stereotypes are common knowledge, and need not be presented here. Not only do these stereotypes shape expectations about what average women and men will be like, they are also used to allocate women and men to social roles. Feminine stereotypes of fragility, weakness, irrationality, and passivity result in the segregation of women into inferior, constraining, and/or less rewarding roles, while masculine stereotypes of strength and rationality have the opposite effect for men. It is interesting to note that gender stereotypes function for women in much the same way as they do for racial and ethnic minorities; because they involve traits that are negatively valued, they serve to constrain options and restrict social roles.

Traditional feminine stereotypes present a dilemma for many women today. Conformity creates a restricted and inferior role set while resistance to the stereotypes is viewed as a form of social deviance and often penalized. Many women today are reluctant to identify themselves as feminists because they fear loss of social approval. Students in my Women and Society class, often enthusiastic about the subject matter and interested in improvements in women's status, tell me that they cover the title of the assigned book for the course when walking in the halls with their friends from other classes. They are concerned that their peers who see them carrying *Women: A Feminist Perspective* (Freeman 1995) will ostracize them for challenging gender stereotypes. Such concerns can cause even those with strongly vested interests in gender role change and gender equity to conform to restricting and disadvantagous stereotypes.

Gender stereotypes are learned through the process of gender role socialization. This process begins at the moment of birth, when male and female children are handled differently by caretakers, and continues throughout the childhood years. Most parents actively teach their children to behave in accordance with traditional gender roles. This learning is reinforced with gender role socialization in the schools and peer group, by the media, and other sources. Research shows that gender-traditional child-rearing practices may not always reflect parents' or other socializing agents' beliefs. Instead, habit may compel parents and others to treat children gender-traditionally (Weitzman 1979). Most of what parents know about rearing children they learned from their own parents, who were gender-traditional. Similarly, teachers who unconsciously treat students in gender-biased ways probably learned to do so from their own gender-biased teachers and their earlier experiences in gender-traditional schools. Breaking these patterns will allow for gender-neutral socialization and contribute to the erosion of gender stereotypes that disadvantage women.

A key focus of early socialization is the acquisition of language. The language we learn is gender-biased and further influences our views about gender roles. The English language systematically ignores women, and by doing so implies that they are inferior. The use of masculine pronouns and occupational titles with the suffix *man* provide two examples. While some argue that these *-man* terms are generic—that they are understood to also include women—research does not bear this out. Numerous studies show that both children and adults are more likely to develop masculine imagery in response to the *-man* terms (Switzer 1990; Henley 1989; Harrigan and Lucic 1988; Hamilton 1988). Our constitution declares that all *men* are created equal.

Surely they presumed that *men* was a generic term and included women. Or could they have been making a statement about women's minority-group standing?

PROSPECTS FOR CHANGE: EMPOWERING THE FEMALE MINORITY

Women will continue to be a minority group until levels of gender inequality are significantly reduced. Chafetz (1990) argues that a societal reduction in gender inequality can be accomplished in two ways: intentionally and unintentionally. Intentional change involves activist and social movement activity oriented toward reducing levels of gender inequality. Unintentional change refers to structural changes in the larger society that result in improvement in women's status relative to men.

Women's Movements

Sociologists argue that social movements most often emerge as a result of perceptions of injustice and inequity and a desire to change such patterns (Turner and Killian 1972). The women's movement is no exception. Large-scale women's movement activity developed for the first time in the United States after the Civil War. The war sensitized the population to issues of inequality, and abolitionist activity afforded significant numbers of women their first activist experience. Following the war, the introduction of the Fourteenth Amendment to the Constitution restricted the right to vote to men, thus providing the spark that ignited the movement (Deckard 1975).

A central focus of much nineteenth century women's movement activity was women's suffrage. Many activists viewed the right to vote as a pivotal reform which would automatically lead to other improvements for women. Women won the right to vote in 1920, but the other anticipated reforms did not automatically follow suit. Women's movement activity dissipated for some decades and reemerged in the 1960s to address these remaining areas of inequity. The movement for civil rights for racial and ethnic minorities provided the perfect context for the resurgence of the women's movement. Contemporary women's movement activity has been quite influential, so influential that some argue it has recently produced a backlash (Faludi 1991). This backlash is argued to be an attempt to undermine the gains women have made as a result of movement activity.

The first phase of the contemporary women's movement involved agitating for equality for women in all arenas of life (e.g., family, workplace, politics). This theme often inspired a "women should emulate men to get ahead" agenda. The dress for success movement and the denigration of the homemaker role common in the 1970s and early 1980s provide examples. Many women, cognizant of negative female stereotypes, attempted to disassociate themselves from their gender by adopting and exhibiting male traits. According to Lips (1991), it is common for members of minority groups to attempt to avoid a negative social identity by rejecting identification with their own group. Emulation of majority group behaviors and characteristics makes the minority individual more acceptable to the majority group. In that sense, the strategy is effective. Women who behave like men are more likely to get ahead in the corporate world and the political arena. But blending in with the dominant group to get ahead is problematic in another sense. It reinforces the idea that feminine traits and behaviors are inferior and must be abandoned in order to achieve positions of influence.

A different agenda has emerged for many segments of the women's movement today. It involves challenging the negative social identity assigned to women and urges a reevaluation of women and their role in society (Buechler 1990). One example is the recognition that running a household and rearing children is important work requiring much skill and effort. Another example is provided by the issue of comparable worth and the suggestion that female-dominated occupations are underpaid given the importance of the work involved. This new phase of the women's movement advocates increased gender role flexibility and more options for women. It is also more sensitive to diversity among women and responsive to the differing concerns of women of color (Andersen 1993; Ferree and Hess 1985). As a result, it reaches out to more women and has the potential for greater impact.

The fact that the women's movement has met with some success could potentially jeopardize its future impact. This could occur for two reasons. First, backlash or counter-movement activity may develop as the gains resulting from the movement threaten the vested interests of the majority group (Chafetz and Dworkin 1987). Second, younger cohorts experiencing improved circumstances may be less willing to agitate for change. These young women may be less likely to subjectively realize their minority group status and view themselves as objects of collective discrimination (as required by definitions discussed in Chapter 1).

Structural Change

Structural changes at the societal level, including demographic, technological, and economic change, can also provide an unintentional impetus toward gender equality. For example, Chafetz (1990) argues that as societal changes enhance women's access to resource-generating work roles, women experience status gains. The last half of the twentieth century has seen a marked increase in the demand for female labor, due in part to technological change and resulting changes in the nature of work. In the new economy, job creation rates for female-typed jobs (e.g., clerical and personal service work) have outpaced job creation rates for male-typed jobs (e.g., manufacturing and other blue collar jobs). This structural change in the economy provides women an advantage, not only in terms of access to work but also as it "trickles down" to family and interpersonal relationships. When women are perceived to be more important producers of resources they are able to exhange their contributions for status gains in other social arenas (Blumberg 1978; Chafetz 1984). These status gains result in positive changes in women's self-definitions and have the potential to erode women's minority-group standing.

REFERENCES

Almquist, Elizabeth M. "The Experience of Minority Women in the United States: Intersections of Race, Gender and Class," in *Women: A Feminist Perspective,* 4th ed., Jo Freeman, ed. Mountain View, CA: Mayfield, 1989.

Almquist, Elizabeth M. "The Experiences of Minority Women in the Unites States: Intersections of Race, Gender and Class," in *Women: A Feminist Perspective,* Jo Freeman, ed. Mountainview, CA: Mayfield, 1995, pp. 573–606.

American Association of University Women (AAUW). *How Schools Shortchange Girls.* Washington, D.C.: AAUW Educational Foundation, 1982.

Andersen, Margaret L. *Thinking about Women: Sociological Perspectives on Sex and Gender.* New York: Macmillan Publishing, 1993.

Aronson, Jane. "Women's Sense of Responsibility for the Care of Old People: 'But Who Else Is Going to Do It?'" *Gender and Society* 6 (1992), p. 829.

Baca-Zinn, Maxine, and D. Stanley Eitzen. *Diversity in Families.* New York: Harper Collins, 1993.

Baca-Zinn, Maxine, and Bonnie Thornton Dill. "Difference and Domination," in *Women of Color in U. S. Society,* M. Baca-Zinn and B.T. Dill, eds. Philadelphia: Temple University Press, 1994, p. 312.

Baxter, Janeen. "Is Husband's Class Enough? Class Location and Class Identity." *American Sociological Review* 59 (1994), pp. 220–35.

Beckman, L.J., and B.B. Houser. "The More You Have the More You Do: The Relationship Between Wife's Employment, Sex Role Attitudes and Household Behavior." *Psychology of Women Quarterly* 4 (1979), pp. 160–74.

Blood, Robert O., and Donald M. Wolfe. *Husbands and Wives.* New York: Free Press, 1960.

Blumstein, Phillip, and Pepper Schwartz. *American Couples: Money, Work, Sex.* New York: William Morrow, 1983.

Brody, E. M. "Parent Care as a Normative Family Stress." *Gerontologist* 25 (1985), pp. 19–29.

Blau, Francine, and M. Ferber. *The Economics of Women, Men and Work.* Englewood Cliffs, NJ: PrenticeHall, 1986.

Blumberg, Rae Lesser. *Stratification: Socioeconomic and Sexual Inequality.* Dubuque, IA: William C. Brown, 1978.

Buechler, Steven M. *Women's Movements in the United States.* New Brunswick: Rutgers University Press, 1990.

Carroll, Susan. *Women as Candidates in American Politics.* Bloomington: Indiana University Press, 1985.

Carrol, Susan, Debra L. Dodson, and Ruth B. Mandel. *The Impact of Women in Public Office: An Overview.* New Brunswick, NJ: Center for the American Woman and Politics, 1988.

Caspar, Lynne M., Sara S. McLanahan, and Irwin Garfinkel. "The Gender Poverty Gap: What We Can Learn From Other Countries." *American Sociological Review* 59 (1994), pp. 594–605.

Center for the American Woman and Politics. *Fact Sheet.* New Brunswick, NJ: Center for the American Woman and Politics, 1994.

Chafetz, Janet Saltzman. *Sex and Advantage: A Comparative, MacroStructural Theory of Sex Stratification.* Totowa, NJ: Rowman and Allenheld, 1984.

Chafetz, Janet Saltzman. *Gender Equity: An Integrated Theory of Stability and Change.* Newbury Park, CA: Sage Publications, 1990.

Chafetz, Janet Saltzman, and Anthony Gary Dworkin. *Female Revolt.* Totowa, NJ: Rowman and Allenheld, 1986.

Colwill, Nina L. *The New Partnership: Women and Men in Organizations.* Palo Alto, CA: Mayfield, 1982.

Conant, Jennet. "The New Pocketbook Issue." *Newsweek,* December 1, 1986, p. 72.

Cotton, Paul. "Is There Still Too Much Extrapolation from Data on Middle-Aged White Men?" *Journal of the American Medical Association* 263 (1990), pp. 104–50.

Deckard, Barbara. *The Women's Movement: Political, Socioeconomic, and Psychological Issues.* New York: Harper and Row, 1975.

Dobash, R. Emerson, and Russell P. Dobash. *Violence against Wives.* New York: Free Press, 1979.

England, Paula. *Comparable Worth: Theories and Evidence.* New York: Aldine de Gruyter, 1992.

England, Paula, and George Farkas. *Employment Household, and Gender: A Social, Economic and Demographic View.* New York: Aldine Publishing Co., 1986.

Faludi, Susan. *Backlash: The Undeclared War against American Women.* New York: Crown, 1991.

Ferree, Myra Marx. "Feminism and Family Research." in *Contemporary Families: Looking Forward, Looking Back,* edited by Alan Booth. Minneapolis: National Council on Family Relations, 1991, pp. 103–21.

Ferree, Myra Marx, and Beth B. Hess. *Controversy and Coalition: The New Feminist Movement.* Boston: Twayne Publishers, 1985.

Fierman, Jacklyn. "Why Women Still Don't Hit the Top." *Fortune* July 30, 1990, pp. 40–62.

Finch, J. "Community Care: Developing Non-Sexist Alternatives." *Critical Social Policy* 9 (1984), p. 618.

Flexner, Eleanor. *Century of Struggle.* New York: Atheneum, 1971.

Freeman, Jo. *Women: A Feminist Perspective.* Mountain View, CA: Mayfield, 1995.

Gelles, Richard J., and Murray A. Straus. *Intimate Violence.* New York: Simon and Schuster, 1988.

Goldthorpe, John. "Women and Class Analysis: In Defence of the Conventional View." *Sociology* 17 (1983), pp. 465–88.

Hacker, Helen M. "Women as a Minority Group," *Social Forces* 30 (1951), pp. 60–69.

Hamilton, Mykol C. "Using Masculine Generics: Does Generic *He* Increase Male Bias in the User's Imagery?" *Sex Roles* 19 (1988), pp. 785–99.

Harrigan, Jinni A., and Karen S. Lucic. "Attitudes Toward Gender Bias in Language: A Reevaluation." *Sex Roles* 19 (1988), pp. 129–40.

Harrison, James, James Chin and Thomas Ficarrotto. "Warning: Masculinity May be Dangerous to Your Health," in *Men's Lives,* Michael Kimmel and Michael A. Messner, eds. New York: Macmillan, 1992.

Henley, Nancy M. "Molehill or Mountain: What We Know and Don't Know About Sex Bias in Language," in *Gender and Thought: Psychological Perspectives,* Mary Crawford and Margaret Gentry, eds. New York: Springer Verlag, 1989.

Hochschild, Arlie, with Anne Machung. *The Second Shift.* New York: Viking Press, 1989.

Hooyman, N. R. "Women as Caregivers of the Elderly: Catch-22 Dilemmas." In *The Trapped Woman,* J. Figueira McDonough and R. Sarri, eds. Newbury Park, CA: Sage, 1987.

Institute for Women's Policy Research. "The Wage Gap: Women's and Men's Earnings," *Research-in-Brief.* Washington, D. C.: Institute for Women's Policy Research, 1993.

Jacobs, Jerry A. *Revolving Doors: Sex Segregation and Women's Careers.* Stanford, CA: Stanford University Press, 1989.

Kemp, Alice Abel. *Women's Work: Degraded and Devalued.* Englewood Cliffs, NJ: Prentice Hall, 1994.

King, Deborah. "Multiple Jeopardy, Multiple Consciousness: The Context of a Black Feminist Ideology." *Signs: Journal of Women in Culture and Society* 14 (1988), pp. 42–72.

Klein, Ethel. *Gender Politics.* Cambridge, MA: Harvard University Press, 1984.

LaRossa, R., and L. LaRossa. *Transition to Parenthood.* Beverly Hills, CA: Sage, 1981.

Lindsey, Linda L. *Gender Roles: A Sociological Perspective.* Englewood Cliffs, NJ: Prentice Hall, 1994.

Lips, Hilary M. *Women, Men and Power.* Mountain View, CA: Mayfield, 1991.

Lynn, Naomi. "Women and Politics: The Real Majority," in *Women: A Feminist Perspective,* Jo Freeman, ed. Palo Alto, CA: Mayfield, 1984.

Mandell, Ruth B. "A Generation of Change for Women in Politics," in *Women—A Feminist Perspective,* Jo Freeman, ed. Mountain View, CA: Mayfield, 1994, pp. 405–29.

Merritt, Sharyne. "Sex Roles and Political Ambition." *Sex Roles* 8 (1982), pp. 102–136.

Minkoff, Howard, and Jack DeHovitz. "Care of Women Infected with the Human Immunodeficiency Virus." *Journal of the American Medical Association* 263 (1991), pp. 559–62.

O'Malley, Kathy. "Taking a Look at Tomboys." *Dallas Morning News.* August 2, 1994.

Reskin, Barbara and Irene Padavic. *Women and Men at Work.* Thousand Oaks, CA: Pine Forge Press, 1994.

Richardson, Laurel Walum. *The Dynamics of Sex and Gender: A Sociological Perspective.* New York: Harper and Row, 1988.
Roth, Barbara Katz, and Mary Beth Caschetta. "Treating Health: Women and Medicine," in *Women: A Feminist Perspective.* Mountain View, CA: Mayfield Publishing, 1994, pp. 65–78.
Sapiro, Virginia. "Public Costs of Private Committments of Private Costs of Public Committments: Family Roles versus Political Ambition." *American Journal of Political Science* 26 (1982), pp. 265–79.
Sapiro, Virginia. *Women in American Society.* Palo Alto, CA: Mayfield, 1986.
Sapiro, Virginia. *Women in American Society.* Palo Alto, CA: Mayfield, 1994.
Spitze, Glenna. "Women's Employment and Family Relations: A Review." *Journal of Marriage and the Family* 50 (1988), pp. 595–618.
Straus, Murray A. "Wife Beating: How Common and Why?" *Victimology* 2 (1977–1978), p. 34.
Switzer, Jo Young. "The Impact of Generic Word Choices: An Empirical Investigation of Age and Sex-related Differences." *Sex Roles* 22 (1990), pp. 69–82.
Thompson, Linda, and Alexis Walker. "Gender in Families," in *Contemporary Families: Looking Forward, Looking Back* Alan Booth, ed. Minneapolis: National Council on Family Relations, 1991, pp. 275–96.
Treiman, Donald J., and Heidi I. Hartmann. *Women, Work and Wages: Equal Pay for Jobs of Equal Value.* Washington, D.C.: National Academy Press, 1981.
Turner, Ralph, and Lewis Killian. *Collective Behavior.* Englewood Cliffs, NJ: PrenticeHall, 1972.
U.S. Bureau of the Census. *Census of the Population.* CPS1, Supplementary Reports, Detailed Occupation and Other Characteristics from the EEO File for the States, 1990.
U.S. Bureau of the Census. "Marital Status and Living Arrangements: March 1990." *Current Population Reports* Series P20, No. 450. Washington, D.C.: U.S. Government Printing Office, 1991.
U.S. Bureau of the Census. "Money Income and Poverty Status of Families and Persons in the U.S., 1990." *Current Population Reports* P60, No. 174. Washington, D.C.: U.S. Government Printing Office, 1991.
U.S. Bureau of the Census. *Statistical Abstract of the United States.* Washington, D.C.: U.S. Government Printing Office, 1992.
U.S. Department of Education, Office of Educational Research and Improvement. *Digest of Education Statistics.* Washington, D.C.: U.S. Government Printing Office, 1992.
U.S. Department of Labor, Bureau of Labor Statistics. *Employment and Earnings: 39.* Washington, D.C.: U.S. Government Printing Office, 1991.
U.S. Public Health Service. "Women's Health: Report of the U.S. Public Health Service Task Force on Women's Health Issues." Washington, D.C.: U.S. Department of Health and Human Services, 1985.
Verbrugge, Lois M., and Deborah L. Wingard. "Sex Differentials in Health and Mortality," in *The Sociology of Gender,* Laura Kramer, ed. New York: St. Martin's Press, 1991, pp. 447–58.
Wagley, C., and M. Harris. *Minorities in the New World.* New York: Columbia University Press, 1964.

Walker, A. "From Welfare State to Caring Society? The Promise of Informal Networks," in *Support Networks in a Caring Community,* J.A. Yoder, J.M.L. Jonker, and R.A.B. Leaper, eds. Dordrecht: Martinus Nijhoff, 1985.

Weitzman, Lenore J. *Sex Role Socialization: A Focus on Women.* Palo Alto, CA: Mayfield.

Whicker, Marcia Lynn, and Todd W. Areson. "The Maleness of the American Presidency," in *Women in Politics: Outsiders or Insiders?* Lois Lovelace Duke, ed. Englewood Cliffs, NJ: Prentice Hall, 1993.

Wilkinson, Doris, Maxine Baca-Zinn, and Esther NganLing Chow. "Guest Editors Introduction." *Gender and Society* 6 (1992), pp. 341–45.

SUGGESTED READINGS

Andersen, Margaret L. *Thinking about Women: Sociological Perspectives on Sex and Gender.* New York: Macmillan Publishing, 1993.

Baca-Zinn, Maxine, and Bonnie Thornton Dill. *Women of Color in U. S. Society.* Philadelphia: Temple University Press, 1994.

Chafetz, Janet Saltzman. *Gender Equity: An Integrated Theory of Stability and Change.* Newbury Park, CA: Sage, 1990.

Freeman, Jo. *Women: A Feminist Perspective.* Mountain View, CA: Mayfield, 1995.

Gender and Society. Official Publication of Sociologists for Women in Society. All Issues. Newbury Park, CA.

Kramer, Laura. *The Sociology of Gender.* New York: St. Martin's, 1991.

Lindsey, Linda L. *Gender Roles: A Sociological Perspective.* Englewood Cliffs, NJ: PrenticeHall, 1994.

Sapiro, Virginia. *Women in American Society.* Mountain View, CA: Mayfield, 1994.

CHAPTER 19

Lesbian and Gay Americans

Shelley J. Correll

Not surprisingly, the third edition of *The Minority Report* is the first to include a chapter on lesbians and gays. The reason for the current inclusion and past exclusion is that lesbians and gays have only in recent decades emerged as a minority group. This is not to suggest that homosexuality is a new phenomenon. To the contrary, homosexuals have existed in all cultures and all historical periods and have, at many points in time, experienced pejorative treatment if knowledge of their homosexuality was made public. However, only in recent history have lesbian and gays, as a group, possessed all four criteria used in this book to identify minority status. Thus, the historical experience of lesbian and gay Americans provides us with an example of a recent emerging minority group. Like other minority groups, as lesbian and gay Americans became more identifiable, they were increasingly subjected to differential power and pejorative treatment, which served to heighten group awareness. However, exactly how lesbians and gays came to be identifiable, the kinds of discrimination they faced and the unique experiences many have had with institutions, such as the family, serve to remind us that each minority group, while sharing minority status, has a unique experience in American society.

This chapter will proceed as follows. First, I will provide an overview of the history of lesbian and gay Americans. I will then use the criteria of identifiability, differential power, pejorative treatment, and group awareness to assess the current minority status of lesbian and gays. Finally, I will examine lesbians and gays as a minority group from the distributive, organizational, and attitudinal dimensions, and, in so doing, I will provide a few comments on the current issues in the lesbian and gay community.

The Historical Experience of Lesbian and Gay Americans

In the paragraphs to follow I will trace the emergence of gays and lesbians as a minority group from the 1920s to the present. In so doing, I will follow the experiences gays and lesbians have had with social institutions, such as the legal system, medical establishment, family, and workplace. I will also note for each period whether a distinct lesbian and gay culture exists and the extent to which gays and lesbians were organized as a group and were politically active.

The 1920s will serve as a historical starting point because prior to this decade it was not common for gays and lesbians to be identifiable as a separate kind of people (Adam 1995). The first gay and lesbian political group in the United States was founded by Henry Gerber in 1924, but the group was short-lived due to legal persecution of group members. The formation of this group, along with other changes discussed below, suggests that gays and lesbians first began to be identifiable the early 1920s. It is useful, however, to first ask why gays and lesbians did not begin to develop minority status prior to the 1920s.

Pre-Movement Years

Adam (1995) notes that homosexuals have not always been considered as a separate "people." Historical evidence from non-Western cultures shows that in many societies it has been common practice for many, and sometimes all, males to have homosexual relations, at least for periods of their lives. In many of these societies, sexual relations between older and younger males were considered part of the ritual acts associated with moving into manhood. Adam contends that where "sexuality between men is both obligatory or common to all, the idea of homosexual 'persons' makes little sense." (Adam 1995, p. 1).

In the United States, as well as other countries, "romantic friendships" were common among middle-class women as early as the eighteenth century (Faderman 1981). Letters written between romantic friends indicate that these relationships were usually intensely passionate. Romantic friendships were widely recognized and tolerated, if not encouraged, in the centuries prior to the twentieth. Part of the reason for the acceptance of romantic friendship between women was that women at the time were thought to be overly emotional and, therefore, in need of closer relationships than men could provide. Further, proper women were thought to have no sexual drive, meaning that sexual relationships between women were not recognized as such! Romantic friendships were allowed to persist without condemnation in the United States until the early 1920s. Until this time, *Ladies Home Journal* and *Harper's* carried passionate tales of love between women (Faderman 1981).

As with the case of obligatory male homosexuality in the non-Western cultures, the common experience of the romantic friendship illustrates that as long as homosexual sex was not considered abnormal or threatening to existing gender and family relations, homosexuality was not the basis for pejorative treatment and could not, therefore, be the locus for a group identity.

Thus, in the years prior to the 1920s, gay and lesbian relationships were embedded in larger social institutions, such as the family. Gay groups and a distinctive gay culture were virtually nonexistent. Therefore, lesbian and gay Americans could not be considered a minority group at this time. However, changes in the institution of the family, brought about by larger economic and social changes at the turn of the century, would offer more opportunities for gays and lesbians to establish relationships outside of the traditional family structure.

The 1920s through World WW II: The Emergence of the Homosexual Person

The industrial revolution brought about changes in the institution of the family that impacted all Americans, but for gay men and lesbians working outside of the family network afforded previously unknown opportunities to establish intimate same-sex relationships. As men increasingly moved to urban centers seeking employment, they had more contact with other men. For gay men, urban coffeehouses, parks, and pubs emerged as venues for meeting one another. Katz (1983) reports that most urban centers in the United States had a gay underground culture by the early 1900s. While these were gay men's establishments, small numbers of women were reported frequenting them (Katz 1983).

The impact of the industrial revolution was felt later by women since women continued to be tied to the family for economic security for a longer period. However, as more women entered the paid labor force, women increasingly gained financial independence. While this newfound financial independence provided all employed women with more options outside of the traditional role of wife and mother, economic self-sufficiency was crucial for lesbians who desired to have primary same-sex relationships outside of the family network. In addition to financial independence, the movement of work outside the family sphere also gave women more contact with members of their same sex.

The World Wars provided broader employment opportunities for men and women. Many women worked outside of the home for the first time during this period and women were employed in a wider range of better paying jobs. The men and women who left the farm to enter the military in large numbers during the wars made friendships in same-sex environments and were often exposed to the more developed gay cultures in the port cities of Europe (Berube 1990). Upon returning to the United States, many were unwilling to be confined to the traditional roles and small-town life that they had previously accepted without challenge.

In sum, the increasing contact men and women had with members of their same sex and the financial independence many experienced for the first time during the period of the 1920s through World War II facilitated the emergence of a distinct, albeit underground, gay culture. What distinguishes the homosexual relationships of this period from those of earlier times is that the relations in the more recent era occurred outside of the family network and at odds with existing societal norms.

The underground nature of the gay culture of this era prevented most gays and lesbians from being identifiable to heterosexual Americans and undoubtedly reduced the amount of persecution gays and lesbians as a whole experienced. So, while homosexuals emerged as a "separate kind of people" during this era, they still did not have the sense of group awareness necessary to be considered a minority group. Groups with political agendas formed in this era, but they were often small and short-lived.

As the gay culture continued to flourish, at least in small urban pockets, gays and lesbians gradually became more visible. The burgeoning presence of the medical profession brought further attention to gays and lesbians. As the medical profession expanded its jurisdiction, many new conditions and types of behaviors came to be defined as illnesses (Abott 1988). The newly powerful professional organization representing the medical profession began defining homosexuality as a pathology during this period, and homosexuals were often referred to by terms such as "sex perverts" (Adam 1995). These labels not only drew attention to gays and lesbians, they also provided legitimation for the arrest and institutionalization of gays and lesbians for several decades.

The end of World War II created a murky picture for lesbians and gays, as well as members of other minority groups. While the war had brought about unprecedented employment opportunities and resulting economic freedom, the end of the war ushered in an era that idealized the social order of prewar times. Gays and lesbians became more visible and enjoyed a flourishing culture, yet larger American society became less tolerant of "nontraditional" lifestyles. In this new, more conservative era, lesbians and gays would be subjected to increasing discrimination and persecution.

Post–World War II: The Conservative Fifties

During the conservative McCarthy era large numbers of lesbians and gays lost their jobs, were imprisoned for breaking laws that forbade homosexual relations, and were placed in mental hospitals. Indeed, the interactions gays and lesbians had with many social institutions actually worsened in this decade. As the medical establishment continued to consider homosexuality pathological, the family members of lesbians and gays often had them committed to mental institutions (Weiss and Schiller 1988). Those who were not institutionalized were often ostracized from their families. In response to the negative treatment by their families, lesbians and gays increasingly moved to large urban areas that had a supportive gay culture. Gay and lesbian communities expanded during the 1950s and often served as surrogate families.

The gay pubs or bars of the 1950s continued to be mostly underground establishments due to frequent raids by the police. Most developed elaborate plans for thwarting police. Adam (1995) describes the use of double sets of doors to screen patrons. When the police arrived at the door the lights would be turned up to signal patrons to act "straight." When police were successful in their raids, they would arrest the patrons and often provide local newspapers with the names of those arrested. Many lesbians and gays lost their jobs and were further alienated from their families when their names were published.

As increasing numbers of gays and lesbians experienced discrimination from their families, the police, the medical establishment and their employers, they began to form groups with the goal of improving their treatment in American society. The leaders of these early groups referred to their efforts as "homo*phile* movements," in order to deemphasize the sexual aspects of homosexual relationships. One of the earliest homophile groups, the Mattachine Society, emerged in the 1950s in Los Angeles with the goal of helping "our people who are victimized daily as a result of our oppression" (see Adam 1995, p. 68 and Katz 1976, p. 412). Homophile groups were not civil rights groups, but were more interested in assimilation. The strategy of the homophile movement, then, was to de-emphasize the differences between homosexual and heterosexual Americans. Homophiles believed that if they could appeal to the notion of a common humanity and leave sexuality as a private matter, then they would be less identifiable as unique and, therefore, subjected to less pejorative treatment. The Mattachine Society even went so far as to describe itself as being "interested in the *problems* of homosexuality (italics mine, Martin and Lyon 1972, p. 231). In summary, while gays and lesbians seemed to be more persecuted in the 1950s than in previous decades, the common experience of persecution provided a basis for an emerging group identity.

The 1960s: Gay and Lesbian Civil Rights

One of the main objectives of any group that adopts an assimilationist strategy is to decrease visibility, and thereby, reduce oppression. However, by the 1960s, gay and lesbian Americans were, like African Americans, Chicanos, women and others, beginning to realize that assimilationist strategies were not improving their situation in American society. Following the lead and adopting some of the tactics of the black civil rights movements in the 1960s, gay and lesbian individuals began operating more as a cohesive group to demand civil rights. The Mattachine Society moved away from talking about the "problems of homosexuality" to proclaiming "gay is good." No longer content to let the medical establishment and the legal system define who they were, the Mattachine Society and other newly emerging gay political groups began to demand "rights and equality as citizens" of the United States (Adam 1995).

The demands for civil rights brought increased visibility to gays and lesbians as a group. In the 1960s, magazines, including *Time* and *Life*, carried articles that attempted to introduce Americans to the gay and lesbian culture. Weiss and Schiller (1988) claim that this unprecedented interest of the straight world served to decrease the isolation felt by gay people, especially in the more rural parts of the United States.

The civil rights demands of lesbian and gay Americans were not met with automatic acceptance. Bar raids, jailing, and institutionalization continued and, in many places, increased. What had changed, however, was that gay and lesbian Americans increasingly saw their individual persecution and discrimination as part of a larger group experience. This realization led to increased feelings of frustration and anger. In June of 1969, this common frustration erupted into a collective event, commonly called the "Stonewall rebellion," which is often identified as the start of the gay and lesbian liberation movement.

Stonewall to the Present: Gays and Lesbians as a Minority Group

On June 27, 1969, police raided the Stonewall Inn, a gay bar in New York's Greenwich village. On the surface this raid seemed no different than the raids that regularly occurred in gay bars around the country. However, on this night bar patrons responded to the raid by fighting back. Hundreds of gay men hurled bricks and bottles at the police. Rioting continued for three days and reverberations were felt around the country. The gay bar, which had long been a focal point of gay culture, was transformed from a social gathering spot into a place for the organization of political activity. Schiller and Weiss (1988) contend that the rebellion at the Stonewall Inn started a process where "an isolated and stigmatized group of individuals transformed themselves into a vital influential political movement" (p. 6). In the year prior to the Stonewall riots, only a handful of gay and lesbian political organizations existed, but in the year following, there were hundreds.

An early political victory was won by the newly emergent political groups when they pressured the members of the American Psychological Association to remove homosexuality from its official diagnostic manual in 1973–74. For a century, the classification of homosexuality as a psychopathology had been used to legitimate the institutionalization and imprisonment of lesbians and gays.

Shortly after the Stonewall rebellion, gays and lesbians began winning political office. Elaine Nobel was elected to the Massachusetts House in 1974 to become the first openly gay candidate to win elected office. By 1992, there were over 75 openly gay and lesbian elected officials.

While many gains have been made in decriminalizing homosexuality and securing civil rights for gay and lesbian Americans, there is still considerable regional variation in the policies affecting gays and lesbians. Only nine states have civil rights laws that afford gays and lesbians the same kind of antidiscrimination protection that other minority groups enjoy. In thirty-nine states, employers can still fire workers solely because they are gay or lesbian. Twenty-one states still have laws on their books that outlaw consensual homosexual sex (called "sodomy" regardless of the nature of the sexual activity).

Due to the continued persecution of gays and lesbians, most who are openly gay or lesbian continue to live in urban areas and often concentrate in gay neighborhoods within the urban area (The Philip Lief Group 1996). These neighborhoods, often called "gay ghettos," are characterized by the large number of businesses and organizations run by and catering to the gay community. In addition to bars and cafes which had been around, even if underground, for decades, churches, community centers, bookstores, and other establishments have emerged. Gay- and lesbian-oriented businesses, such as travel companies, Internet providers, life insurance companies, just to name a few, have also flourished in recent years. In short, highly developed, distinct gay and lesbian cultures are present in all major American cities (see the travel book published by Fodor's in 1996, *Gay Guide to the USA,* for an example of the expanse of the gay community in American cities).

Finally, the impact of the AIDS epidemic on the gay and lesbian community cannot be overstated. In San Francisco alone, the Center for Disease Control estimates that over 22,000 men died from AIDS between the early years of this disease and 1995, and a disproportionate share of these men were gay. The pervasive tragedy of this disease has united gay and lesbian political groups in pushing for more federal money for AIDS research. Publicity about AIDS has also served to make gays and lesbians more visible to Americans in all regions of the country.

In summary, the history of lesbians and gays in America depicts an emerging minority group. While barely considered a "separate kind of people" at the beginning of the century, by the 1960s gays and lesbians became more identifiable. Higher visibility resulted in increased levels of pejorative treatment by the police, the medical establishment, and even their own families, which resulted in heightened group awareness. Today gays and lesbians can justifiably be considered a minority group. In the next section, we evaluate the current minority status of lesbian and gay Americans.

THE MINORITY STATUS OF LESBIANS AND GAYS IN AMERICA

Four characteristics are used in this book to identify minority status. Members of the group must be identifiable, subjected to differential power and pejorative treatment, and have a sense of group awareness. Different minority groups possess these four characteristics to varying degrees. In this section we evaluate the minority status of gay and lesbian Americans by comparing their unique experiences as a group to each of the four criteria in turn.

Identifiability

One of the reasons homosexual Americans could not be considered as a minority group in the early part of this century is that they were rarely identifiable. Since lesbians and gays do not share common physical traits that are usually used to distinguish minority from majority group members, such as a common skin color, it is easy for gays and lesbians to "pass" as heterosexual. Stereotypes often portray gay men as overly feminine men and lesbians as overly masculine women. While some gay men and lesbians may fit these descriptions, so do many heterosexual men and women. The physical appearances of lesbians and gays are as varied as their heterosexual counterparts.

When lesbians or gays want other people to be aware of their sexual orientation they often must "come out" to them. That is, they must clearly state, "I am a lesbian," or be assumed to be heterosexual. The ease of passing as straight, coupled with the negative consequences of being openly gay, have allowed many gays and lesbians to be "out" in some aspects of their lives, such as in interactions with their friends, and "in the closet" in other arenas, such as at work or in family interactions.

As gays and lesbians have become increasingly accepted in society, more gays and lesbians have been willing to take the risk of coming out. Thus, while it is unlikely that the proportion of people who are sexually attracted to members of their same sex has increased over time, it is true that more people are currently willing to identify themselves as gay or lesbian.

Since the census or other national polling organizations do not routinely ask Americans about their sexual orientation, it is difficult to gauge the size of the gay and lesbian population. The earliest well-known attempt to quantify the homosexual population was carried out by the Kinsey Institute in 1948. They determined that approximately 10 percent of men and 2–6 percent of women were exclusively homosexual. Further, they found that 50 percent of men and 28 percent of women responded erotically to persons of the same sex. However, some studies have concluded that percentages of men and women who *identify* themselves as gay, lesbian, or bisexual is smaller than that found by Kinsey. That is, a higher percentage of people appear to engage in homosexual behavior than self-identify as gay, lesbian, or bisexual (Philip Lief Group 1996).

Gay and lesbian political leaders are aware of the importance of having people be openly gay. The Human Rights Campaign (HRC), the largest gay and lesbian political organization, sponsors "National Coming Out Day" each October. The purpose of this event is to encourage gays and lesbians to come out to their neighbors, co-workers, and families. HRC contends that if more gays and lesbians would be open about their sexuality, Americans would become more supportive of gay and lesbian issues. There is some evidence to support this contention. A survey conducted by *U.S News & World Report* in 1993 found that 73 percent of those who knew someone gay or lesbian favored equal rights for gays and lesbians, compared to only 55 percent of those who say they do not know anyone who is gay or lesbian (Shapiro, Cook, and Krackov 1993).

The identifiability of gays and lesbians varies greatly by region. Overlooked Opinions, a marketing firm which collects demographic and attitudinal data on gay and lesbian Americans, reports that while people in the mountain states are very likely to say they know someone gay, those in the south and those in small towns often claim not to know anyone who is gay or lesbian (see Philip Lief Group 1996, pp. 104-06). Not surprisingly, it is the same areas where lesbians and gays are less visible that gays and lesbians have fewer civil rights, such as laws that prevent employment discrimination. Therefore, even though visibility might improve the plight of lesbians and gays in the long run, the immediate consequences for individual gays and lesbians who elect to come out in less tolerant areas are often substantial.

While the importance of being identifiable is recognized by most gay and lesbian political groups, the strategies employed for increasing visibility are hotly debated. The practice of "outing," or revealing the sexual orientation of famous gays and lesbians against their will, has been employed by some groups and individuals who believe that the benefit to lesbians and gays, as a group, outweighs the likely negative treatment to the individual outed. Other groups instead encourage individuals to come out voluntarily and work toward creating an environment where being openly lesbian or gay does not illicit negative consequences. For example, some groups have pushed companies to adopt domestic partnership policies, whereby the partners of gay and lesbian employees are entitled to the same benefits as the spouses of heterosexual employees.

Perhaps the single biggest reason gays and lesbians are more identifiable in American society today than in the past is due to the increased visibility that AIDS has brought to the community. The disproportionately high number of deaths of gay men resulting from this disease, in and of itself, focused attention on the gay community. The tragedy and pervasiveness of death inspired many gays and lesbians to become politically active for the first time. The group ACT UP developed the saying "silence=death" as a part of its effort to convince gays and lesbians to be open about their sexuality and to demand to be treated fairly. Gay and lesbian political groups rallied around the common cause of pressuring the federal government to commit more funding to AIDS research.

In recent years, gays and lesbians have become more identifiable in the entertainment media as well. Gay and lesbian characters have become common on television shows in the 1990s. When the TV character Ellen Morgan declared that she was a lesbian during prime time in April of 1997, it was the first time that a leading character was portrayed as openly gay on television. While the show has been attacked by conservative political leaders, there is no doubt that this show has contributed to the increased identifiability of gays and lesbians as a minority group.

In summary, the identifiability of gays and lesbians has increased greatly since the early 1900s and even more drastically since the late 1980s. In most regions of the country, most Americans now claim to personally know someone who is gay or lesbian (Philip Lief Group 1996).

Differential Power

Differential power is the result of one group controlling a disproportionate number of the valued resources, such as jobs, education, wealth, and political power. In considering the minority status of lesbians and gays it is useful, then, to ask whether gays and lesbians control fewer valued resources than the heterosexual majority. We will compare the number of education, income, and other resources in more detail in the section on the distributive dimension of analysis below, but for now I will merely mention that evidence suggests that gays and lesbians are at least as well educated as their heterosexual counterparts and have incomes and jobs that are roughly comparable to the dominant majority. Recall that different minority groups possess the four criteria used to establish minority status in varying degrees. Gays and lesbians, as a group, appear to experience less of a power differential from the dominant majority than some other minority groups, especially if power is defined by the attainment of good jobs and above-average incomes.

In fact, the educational and financial status of gays and lesbians might appear to indicate that gays and lesbians possess as many resources as heterosexual Americans. However, gays and lesbians do lack the power to make many life course decisions that other Americans routinely make. For example, gays and lesbians cannot legally marry and therefore cannot receive the sanctioned financial benefits of marriage, such as the right to file joint income tax returns. In 1997, the United States congress overwhelming passed the "Defense of Marriage Act," which denies federal recognition of gay marriage. In twenty-one states it is not even legal for gays and lesbians to have consensual sex. Homosexual couples are usually not allowed to adopt children and have, in many cases, had their biological children taken away from them. Thus, the heterosexual majority, by enacting or failing to enact laws, effectively controls the life course and life chances of gays and lesbians.

Pejorative Treatment

Since the earliest times when homosexuals were considered a separate kind of people, lesbians and gays whose sexual orientation was made public have experienced pejorative treatment, such as discrimination, physical attack, and stereotyping. While some improvements have been made in recent years (for example, homosexuality is no longer considered a pathology and gay bars are rarely raided), lesbians and gays continue to face discrimination, physical attacks and other negative treatment as a consequence of their sexual orientation.

The practice of "gay bashing" is still common in the United States. Gay bashing is the physical assault of lesbians and gays on account of sexual orientation (Philip Lief Group, 1996). A national report coordinated by the New York City Gay and Lesbian Anti-Violence Project indicates a slight increase in gay bashing in the United States in recent years. Some of these assaults have resulted in death and the perpetrators, who are often minors, commonly receive light sentences (for a city-by-city listing of numbers of gay bashings see Philip Lief 1996, pp. 107–11). In an interview with the gay and lesbian newsmagazine, *The Advocate,* United States Attorney General Janet Reno argued for including sexual orientation in federal hate crimes legislation. Hate crimes are violent assaults directed at an individual due to his or her perceived membership in a minority group. Reno cited FBI statistics that show that the number of hate crimes increased in 1996, during an era when other violent crimes had dropped. While sixty-five hundred hate crimes were racially motivated in 1996, more than twelve hundred were based on sexual orientation (Condon 1997). However, violent acts directed at members of sexual minorities are not covered in current federal hate crimes statutes protecting other minority group members.

In addition to physical attacks, gays and lesbians still routinely experience discrimination in American society, especially in employment. According to the Human Rights Campaign, in the eleven states that have laws against workplace discrimination due to sexual orientation, over two thousand discrimination complaints have been filed. (For up-to-date developments on this topic and other issues that effect the gay community, see the Human Rights Campaign's web page at http://www.hrc.org). Currently, there is no federal legislation that protects gays and lesbians from losing their jobs due to their sexual orientation. Additionally, the domestic partners of gay and lesbian employees are often not eligible for benefits to which heterosexual employees are entitled, such as health care coverage.

Finally, it is still common for openly lesbian and gay Americans to experience discrimination from their family members. Family conflict is one form of pejorative treatment that is unique to gays and lesbians as a minority group. For example, ethnic minorities usually grow up with the support of their families in dealing with racism. In fact, it is likely that they are educated about racism by their parents when they are children. Gays and lesbians, on the other hand, often become aware of their sexual orientation in isolation and must turn to groups and individuals outside of their immediate families for support. The feeling of isolation is commonly cited as one of the prime reasons gay and lesbian youth are more likely than their heterosexual peers to run away from home and attempt suicide. An African American lesbian acquaintance of the author's is fond of saying, " It is easier to be black than lesbian because you don't have to tell your mother you're black." This statement is not meant to diminish the pejorative treatment experienced by African Americans, but rather to show that while every minority group experiences pejorative treatment, each group's experiences are distinctive.

While some improvements have been made, gays and lesbians are still clearly subjected to physical attacks, discrimination, and other forms of pejorative treatment. In fact, the pejorative treatment criteria is perhaps the most salient in establishing the minority status of gays and lesbians of the four criteria used in *The Minority Report.*

Group Awareness

Group awareness is the process whereby individual minority group members come to see that the pejorative treatment to which they have been subjected as individuals is commonly experienced by members of their group and is the result of being identified as a minority. Even though openly gay and lesbian individuals were subjected to pejorative treatment and differential power for most of this century, it has only been since the Stonewall rebellion described earlier that substantial numbers of gays and lesbians began to identify as a group and work collectively to combat discrimination.

In the years immediately following the Stonewall rebellion, hundreds of gay political groups formed. At this time lesbians were more likely to identify with feminists than with gay men (Adam 1995). It was common for lesbians in the 1970s to perceive that the discrimination they experienced was the result of being female, rather than being a member of a sexual minority. Adam contends that women first had to address the fundamental problems facing all women, such as equal opportunity in employment, in order to have sufficient financial independence to become lesbian (Adam, 1995, p. 99). As the overall status of women in the United States improved, and as the political climate of the 1980s become more conservative, lesbians increasingly considered themselves a sexual minority. The tragedy of AIDS further aligned lesbians with gay men in the common cause of fighting for more funding for AIDS research.

The current group awareness of gays and lesbians is evidenced by the sheer number and diversity of gay and lesbian organizations, businesses, and newspapers and magazines. While the objectives and strategies of gay political groups are diverse, all are aware that the discrimination gays and lesbians experience is due to their sexual orientation. The Human Rights Campaign uses traditional political tactics, such as lobbying Congress and urging group members to write their representatives on issues that are important to the gay community. The Lambda Legal Defense and Education Fund is a nonprofit gay law firm dedicated to obtaining civil rights through the courts. Both of these organizations, along with hundreds of others, work within the existing political system.

Other groups, such as ACT UP, Queer Nation, and Lesbian Avengers, use more "in your face" direct action strategies. Direct action strategies often entail having participants become directly and physically involved in trying to disrupt or change the social and/or political order. The saying, "whatever means necessary," used by ACT UP in the late 1980s, made clear that ACT UP was willing to go beyond legal limits to have its demands for more AIDS funding heard. Direct action strategies often force heterosexuals to notice, even if unapprovingly, the presence of lesbians and gays. Queer Nation's slogan, "We're here, We're queer, Get Used to it," demonstrates both their "in your face" type of strategy and their demand for inclusion. While these groups differ in their tactics, and sometimes even in their goals, the sheer number of gay and lesbian groups existing today points to a developed a sense of group awareness.

In summary, gays and lesbians have emerged as a minority group based on the criteria of identifiability, differential power, pejorative treatment and group awareness. Lesbians and gays are increasingly "out," making themselves identifiable. Even though some progress has been made, lesbians and gays still experience differential power and pejorative treatment, which have served to heighten group awareness.

Minority groups differ in the quantities of each of the four criteria they possess. Gays and lesbians, while more identifiable now than in the past, are still probably less visible than a group that shares common physical features. Likewise, gays and lesbians have educational and occupational levels similar to that of the dominant majority. However, gays and lesbians experience more or different kinds of pejorative treatment than many other groups. For example, federal laws that protect women and ethnic minorities from workplace discrimination do not apply to lesbians and gays. Even laws which are meant to curb hate crimes directed at members of various religious and ethnic groups do not extend to gays and lesbians. The result is that gays and lesbians are fired from their jobs and are physically attacked due to their sexual orientation. These very visible forms of discrimination, along with all kinds of other pejorative treatment, serve to remind lesbians and gays of their status as minority group members. Not surprisingly, the level of group awareness is very high in the gay and lesbian community.

I now turn to examining the experiences of gays and lesbians from the three levels of analysis introduced in the first part of this book: the distributive, organizational, and attitudinal dimension.

The Distributive Dimension

The distributive level of analysis focuses on how a group differs from the dominant majority in the number of valued resources it possess, such as income, education, and access to political power. These comparisons are easily made for many minority groups since the government routinely collects information on race and ethnicity, amount of education, type of work, and other demographic characteristics of American citizens. However, the census and other national polling organizations rarely ask respondents about their sexual orientation, making demographic comparisons between homosexual and heterosexual persons difficult.

The demographic data that does exist on lesbians and gays is often obtained from volunteer surveys included in magazines or handed out at gay and lesbian events. The lesbians and gays who subscribe to gay publications or attend gay events are probably not representative of all lesbian and gay Americans. Certainly, those who subscribe to magazines and attend gay or lesbian events are more likely to be "out" than those who do not. It is also likely that those who subscribe to magazines and attend events, especially national events, are wealthier and more educated than the larger gay and lesbian population. This is to suggest that the statistics presented here probably paint a more inflated picture of the resources possessed by gays and lesbians than would be found if we had data on all, or a representative sample, of lesbian and gay Americans. Nonetheless, as they are some of the only data available, I present them and urge the reader to use caution in making comparisons.

Statistics reported in *The Advocate* and by Overlooked Opinions, suggest that gays and lesbians are more educated and have higher mean income levels than their heterosexual counterparts. While the median level of education for Americans in 1996 was approximately 13 years (General Social Survey 1996), lesbians and gays had 15.7 median years of schooling (Overlooked Opinions, as reported in Philip Lief Group 1996). Likewise, a higher percentage of gay and lesbian Americans, compared to the American population as a whole, report holding professional jobs. While the gay and lesbian figures are probably biased upward, they still suggest that gays and lesbians, unlike members of most other minority groups, have educational and occupational resources that are comparable to the dominant majority.

Perhaps, the resource most denied to gay and lesbian Americans is the political power necessary to achieve equal protection and equal opportunity under the law. While most minorities are protected by civil rights acts and workplace antidiscrimination laws at the national level, gays and lesbians have no such protection. Currently, gays and lesbians are not even included in federal hate crimes legislation, which protects religious and ethnic minorities. And, as previously mentioned, gays and lesbians are not protected at the national level from losing their jobs due to their sexual orientation.

There is some evidence that advances are being made in achieving civil rights for gays and lesbians. A few states, several local communities, and many businesses now include sexual orientation in their nondiscrimination clauses. The "gay vote" is also increasingly valued in elections. President Clinton was the first elected president in American history to have actively courted the gay and lesbian vote in his 1992 campaign.

The education and income levels of gays and lesbians paint the picture of a successful minority group. However, as long as gays and lesbians do not have the political resources necessary to achieve civil rights protection, they are being blatantly denied access to the paths of self-determination that are available to other Americans.

The Organizational Dimension

Since gays and lesbians have long been disproportionately concentrated in specific areas within large urban communities and have also been excluded from many of the organizations of larger society, it is not surprising that they have often formed their own religious, business, community, and political organizations. This section will first summarize the experiences that gays and lesbians have had with dominant social organizations such as the schools, police, and religious institutions. I will then describe some of the gay and lesbian organizations that exist in American society.

The Schools

As with other minority groups, gay and lesbian youth commonly have difficulty in school systems that are geared for the majority child. Forty-five percent of gay males and 20 percent of lesbians report being verbally harassed in high school (Philip Lief Group 1996). According to the National Gay and Lesbian Task Force, gay and lesbian youth are two to three times more likely than their heterosexual peers to attempt suicide. School events, such as proms and other dances, are tailored to the heterosexual teenagers. Teachers often assume students are heterosexual in discussing issues such as dating and health.

Gay and lesbian teenagers frequently lack role models in the school. Even though most schools probably have gay and lesbian teachers and counselors, many are afraid to be openly gay for fear of losing their jobs. National organizations, such as the Gay, Lesbian, and Straight Teachers' Network and the Gay and Lesbian Caucus of the National Federation of Teachers, fight for the rights of gay and lesbian teachers, but tolerance varies greatly by region.

Gay and lesbian community leaders have also begun to work with gay, lesbian, and bisexual students to set up support groups. As of 1993, over one hundred lesbian and gay support groups existed in high schools around the nation (Philip Lief Group 1996). However, these groups are regionally concentrated and, in some states and communities, lesbian and gay support groups are denied permission to meet in school buildings or hold school-sanctioned events. In 1996, one high school in Salt Lake City, Utah, banned all nonacademic clubs, including the 4H and Bible clubs, rather than allow the formation of a gay and lesbian club.

The pejorative treatment gays and lesbians experience in the public school led some gay and lesbian leaders in the New York area to work with the New

York public schools to establish an all-gay high school, called the Harvey Milk school. Others have recognized the need for gay and lesbian students to have separate social events. In the Oakland, California area, for example, businesses help fund a gay and lesbian prom.

The Police

Gays and lesbians, like members of other minority groups, have historically had conflicts with the police. In fact, the history of gays and lesbians in America is filled with stories of police raiding gay bars and harassing the clientele. In urban areas at least, this situation has improved. Most urban police departments now have liaisons to the gay and lesbian community and work with the community to provide security for gay and lesbian events and to reduce hate crimes directed at the gay and lesbian community.

Acting on the belief that a more representative police force increases effectiveness, large police departments, such as the Los Angeles Police Department, actively recruit gays and lesbians into their ranks by advertising in gay and lesbian publications, such as *The Advocate* (see for example, the November 11, 1997 issue).

Religious Organizations

Openly gay and lesbian persons have not historically been welcomed in churches and synagogues in American society. Fundamentalist churches, in particular, have often been vocal in their refusal to allow gays and lesbians to be members of their congregations and adamant in their denunciation of homosexuality. (For quotes from religious leaders see, Philip Lief Group 1996, p. 350). When gays and lesbians are excommunicated or shunned from the churches of their childhood, many lose a form of social support that most Americans take for granted. It is not surprising then that gays and lesbians have often formed their own churches.

The largest gay and lesbian religious organization, the Metropolitan Community Church, was founded in 1968 and now has approximately 230 congregations in the United States (Philip Lief Group 1996). One gay and lesbian synagogue in New York has over one thousand members, making it one of the largest synagogues in New York. Recently, some long-standing denominations, including the Methodists and Episcopalians, have begun welcoming, or at least allowing, gays and lesbians as members of their congregations. More controversial, some congregations now permit gays and lesbians to serve as clergy.

Other Gay and Lesbian Organizations

In addition to those organizations already described, many other gay and lesbian organizations exist today in major cities in the United States. Gay and lesbian support groups, bookstores, bars, coffee shops, and sports teams, just to name a few, serve as culture-maintaining organizations. Bars have an been an important cultural organization historically and, for many decades, served as the only safe gathering place for gays and lesbians. However, with increasing visibility and acceptance in larger American society, the diversity of culture-maintaining organizations has increased.

Like other minority groups, gays and lesbians were often not welcome in the businesses operated by the dominant majority and thus, found it necessary to establish their own businesses within their own communities. Adam (1995) claims that by the late 1970s every major city in North America and Europe had a remarkable network of bars, restaurants, travel agents, lawyers, life insurers, social services, and physicians which catered specifically to a gay clientele. He also notes that many women-owned and operated businesses, which were geared towards the lesbian community, emerged during this decade.

Today, it is less common for majority-run organizations to discriminate or refuse to do business with gays and lesbians. Some mainstream organizations have aggressively attempted to break into what they see as a lucrative gay market. The travel guide publisher, Fodor, for example has begun releasing a series of gay travel guides for cities that are common vacation destinations for gay and lesbian travelers.

Politically, the gay and lesbian community is fractionated into many diverse civil rights type organizations, suggesting a lack of consensus in the goals and strategies of social reform. Some issues that currently divide the community are gay marriage and gay service in the military. While many political groups believe that gays and lesbians should be able to marry their life partner in the same way that heterosexual Americans do, others argue that marriage is a patriarchal institution that gay and lesbian Americans should not desire to emulate. In a similar fashion, many gays and lesbians are active in the fight to end the policy of expelling individuals from the military based on sexual orientation. Others, however, argue that gays and lesbians should not want to serve in this organization.

These two issues, and many others, can be subsumed under a more general disagreement. That is, most of the more mainstream gay organizations usually support policies that would provide gays and lesbians with the same rights as heterosexual Americans. In this sense, their ultimate goal is full participation in the existing American society. Gays and lesbians, they argue, should be allowed to marry, to serve in the military, to not be fired from their jobs and not be subjected to violence because of their sexual orientation. More radical gay and lesbian groups, however, believe that gay liberation cannot occur within the existing system and gays and lesbians therefore should not attempt to emulate the practices of heterosexual Americans. As diverse as the ideologies and strategies might be, however, discrimination, violence, and tragedy often unite gay and lesbian groups towards common causes. The increased funding for AIDS research, for example, was the result of the efforts of many groups with diverse strategies all agreeing on a common goal.

Thus, from the organizational level of analysis, we can see that the lesbian and gay community is comprised of a panoply of political, business, and culture-maintaining organizations. The number of these organizations has increased in recent decades at the same time that the organizations of dominant American society have become more welcoming of gays and lesbians.

THE ATTITUDINAL DIMENSION

As with racism and sexism, heterosexism is an ideology that is undoubtedly maintained by a complex set of dynamics. Psychological studies have shown that having prejudiced attitudes towards gays and lesbians is correlated with racial prejudice and the endorsement of traditional gender roles (Henley and Pincus 1978). This means that individuals who express racist or sexist attitudes are more likely than those who do not to be prejudiced against homosexuals. While fully examining the process by which a heterosexist ideology is maintained or changed is beyond the scope of this chapter, we can examine the relative strength of heterosexist attitudes over time.

The General Social Survey, which is administered approximately every two years, measures the attitudes of a random sample of the United States population on a wide variety of topics. In each year the survey was administered, respondents were asked if they thought homosexual relations were wrong and if they thought homosexuals should be allowed to teach in college. Table 19-1 shows the percentage of respondents whose responses indicate a tolerance for homosexuality. That is, the percentage of individuals who think homosexual relations are *never wrong* and the percentage who think homosexuals *should* be allowed to teach college is listed for each year. The percentages are then graphed in Figure 19-1.

The percentage of individuals who believe homosexual relations are never wrong has gone up and down slightly from the early 1970s, but no clear change was seen until the 1990s. Since this time, as gays and lesbians have more clearly emerged as a minority group, attitudes towards homosexuality have become more tolerant. Thus, the 1996 figures show that approximately 28 percent of Americans surveyed believed that homosexual relations are never wrong, an increase of over 150 percent from the 1973 figure.

Even many of those who believe homosexual relations are morally wrong do not think gays and lesbians should be discriminated against in employment. Figure 19-1 illustrates that the percentage of Americans who think gays and lesbians should be allowed to teach college has increased over time, with a sharp increase occurring in the early 1990s. By 1996, 77 percent supported the rights of gays and lesbians to teach college, compared to 49 percent in 1973.

Other surveys have found similar patterns. For example, in 1996 *Newsweek* reported that 84 percent of Americans thought gays and lesbians should have equal access to job opportunities, and 80 percent said they should have equal access to housing. However, 56 percent were opposed to the concept of legally sanctioned, same-sex marriage (Kaplan and Klaidman 1996).

TABLE 19-1
Attitudes Towards Homosexuality, 1973-96

Year	Homosexual Relations (Percent Approving)	Teaching College (Percent Approving)
1973	11.2	49.4
1974	13.5	53.0
1976	15.9	53.9
1977	14.9	51.4
1980	14.6	56.8
1982	13.4	57.0
1984	14.3	61.3
1985	13.7	59.7
1987	11.9	58.4
1988	12.8	59.6
1989	15.7	66.6
1990	12.8	65.9
1991	16.0	65.8
1993	22.0	71.7
1994	23.3	73.0
1996	28.2	77.3

Source: General Social Survey, 1973–96.

FIGURE 19-1
Attitudes Towards Homosexuality

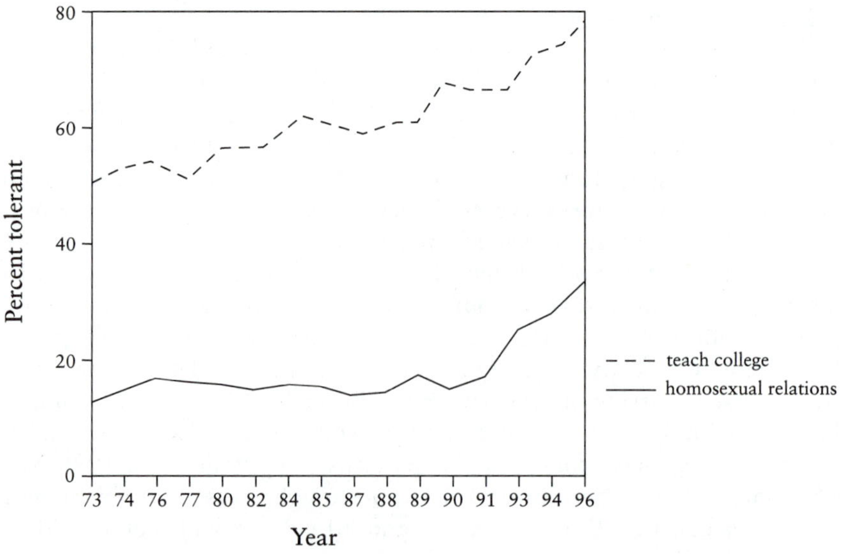

Source: General Social Survey, 1973–96.

Taken together, these surveys suggest that Americans have become more tolerant of homosexuality, but support for the rights of gays and lesbians is more complex than might be expected. That is, there seems to be broad support for the equal treatment of gays and lesbians in employment and housing. Many Americans, however, continue to see homosexuality as wrong and do not support the rights of gays and lesbians to establish families through marrying or adopting children.

CONCLUSION

Comparing the experiences of gays and lesbians to that of other minority groups, we can see many similarities. For example, when dominant organizations were unwelcoming to gays and lesbians, they, like other minority groups, responded by forming their own organizations. However, the experiences of gays and lesbians are in many ways unique. Most notably, gays and lesbians become aware of their sexual orientation in isolation from and often at odds with their families. The consequences of this isolation, as we have seen, can be dire for many homosexual teens, who are more prone to suicide than their heterosexual counterparts. While lesbians and gays share the common features used in this book to identify minority status, lesbians and gays, like all minority groups, have had a unique experience in American society.

REFERENCES

Adam, Barry D. *The Rise of a Gay and Lesbian Movement,* rev. ed. New York: Twayne Publishers, 1995.

Abbot, Andrew. *The System of Professions: An Essay on the Division of Expert Labor.* Chicago: University of Chicago Press, 1988.

Berurbe, Alan. *Coming Out under Fire: The History of Gay Men and Women in World War II.* New York: Free Press, 1990.

Collins, Andrew. *Fodor's Gay Guide to the U.S.A.* New York: Fodor's Travel Publications, Inc., 1996.

Condon, Lee. "Topic of the Day: Hate Crimes." *The Advocate,* Issue No. 747, November 25, 1997, pp. 45–47.

Faderman, Lillian. *Surpassing the Love of Men: Romantic Friendship and Love Between Women from the Renaissance to the Present.* New York: William Morrow and Company, Inc, 1981.

Henley, Nancy, and Fred Pincus. "Interrelationship of Sexist, Racist, and Antihomosexual Attitudes." *Psychological Reports* 42 (1978), p. 83.

Kaplan, David A., and Daniel Klaidman. "A Battle, Not the War." *Newsweek* Vol. CXXVII, No. 23 (June 30, 1996), pp. 24–30.

Katz, Jonathan. *The Gay/Lesbian Almanac,* 1st ed. New York: Harper and Row, 1983.

Katz, Jonathan. *Gay American History: Lesbian and Gay Men in the USA, a Documentary.* New York: Avon Books, 1976.

Martin, Del, and Phyllis Lyon. *Lesbian/Woman.* San Francisco: Glide Publications, 1972.

Philip Lief Group, Inc. *The Gay Almanac.* New York: Berkeley Books, 1996.
Shapiro, Joseph P., Cook, Gareth G., and Andrew Krackov. "Straight Talk about Gays." *U.S. News & World Report,* Vol. 115, No. 1 (July 5, 1993), pp. 42–48.
Weiss, Andrea, and Greta Schiller. *Before Stonewall: The Making of a Gay and Lesbian Community.* Tallahassee, FL: The Naiad Press, Inc., 1988.

SUGGESTED READINGS

Adam, Barry D. *The Rise of a Gay and Lesbian Movement,* rev. ed. New York: Twayne Publishers, 1995.
The Advocate: The National Gay and Lesbian Newsmagazine. 1967 to present. Los Angeles: Liberation Publications, Inc.
Berurbe, Alan. *Coming Out under Fire: The History of Gay Men and Women in World War II.* New York: Free Press, 1990.
Faderman, Lillian. *Surpassing the Love of Men: Romantic Friendship and Love Between Women from the Renaissance to the Present.* New York: William Morrow and Company, Inc, 1981.
Human Rights Campaign, Web Page: http://www.hrc.org.
Philip Lief Group, Inc. *The Gay Almanac.* New York: Berkeley Books, 1996.
Rosenberg, Robert; Scagliotti, John; and Greta Schiller. 1985. "Before Stonewall: The Making of a Gay and Lesbian Community." [videorecording] New York: Cinema Guild.
Weiss, Andrea, and Greta Schiller. *Before Stonewall: The Making of a Gay and Lesbian Community.* Tallahassee, FL: The Naiad Press, Inc., 1988.

Index of Names

Index of Subjects